WARSAW INDOLOGICAL STUDIES

VOLUME 5

Editor:
Piotr Balcerowicz

WARSAW 2012

World View and Theory in Indian Philosophy

Edited by

Piotr Balcerowicz

MANOHAR
2012

WARSAW INDOLOGICAL STUDIES SERIES
VOLUME 5

EDITOR:
Piotr Balcerowicz

Cover design: Piotr Balcerowicz
Layout design and fonts, typeset by: Piotr Balcerowicz

Publication co-financed by
the Faculty of Oriental Studies, University of Warsaw

First Edition: Delhi, Dec. 2012

ISBN 978-93-5098-012-5

Published by
Ajay Kumar Jain
for
Manohar Publishers & Distributors
4753/23 Ansari Road, Daryaganj
New Delhi 110 002

Printed at
Salasar Imaging Systems
New Delhi 110 035

TABLE OF CONTENTS

THEORY OF WORLD VIEW

Preface

How can we know that our brain (consisting apparently of cool and moist tissue) allegedly is neither an organ providing control over actions of our bodies nor responsible for our mental processes, including information processing, thinking and rationality, but an organ meant solely to cool hot blood heated up in our hearts? As Aristotle argues, 'Since everything needs its opposite [to counterbalance it], so that it preserves its moderation and the mean (for it is in the mean, not in either of the extremes, that true essence and rationality lies), nature has developed the brain to counterbalance the region of the heart alongside the heat contained in it...' (*On the Parts of Animals* 652b).[1] Such a conclusion was not merely driven by a lack of adequate understanding of physical structure and functions of living organisms in Ancient Greece and Aristotle's general presupposition that everything needs its opposite to counterbalance it, which provided a theoretical scheme for his endeavour to describe the workings of human body and its anatomy. In fact, his conclusion, which seems so counterintuitive from the viewpoint of modern science, which allocates the site of all mental processes precisely in the brain, was influenced by a dualistic world view which juxtaposed inert matter, e.g. bodies (including celestial bodies) and souls, as the singular conscious agents that trigger all motion in the universe, expressed by the Stagirite just a few lines before the above reasoning: 'Indeed, nutrition and causing motion of the body are the functions of the soul' (*On the Parts of Animals* 652b). Ergo they cannot belong to the body and its brain. Rationality and source of motion had therefore to lie outside of the body, composed of inanimate matter, and such a world view consequently left no room for even a faint possibility that the brain could perform any operations and tasks which are nowadays associated with it.

The above case can serve as an illustration of how our theories, including philosophical theories and whole philosophical systems, are effectively affected by preconceived beliefs and are construed within a conceptual framework imposed by a particular world view, to which we have been acculturated and which often proves much more rigid and inflexible then one would expect.

[1] Which could be expressed in India as: **hr̥dayôṣṇa-rakta-śītī-karaṇârtho mastiṣkaḥ hr̥dayôṣṇa-pratyudyamatvāt, anta-dvaye yad antam tad sāmyâvasthârthaṁ tad-vīparītântâkāṅkṣam*, or in a similar manner.

World View and Theory in Indian Philosophy
Warsaw Indological Studies 5 (2012) 7–9.

Philosophers are humans, flesh and blood and belief, in whom rationality and irrationality meet like in any other omnivorous or vegetarian human. Philosophical systems and theories are, in theory at least, constructed rationally and supposed to fulfil a requirement of consistency, whereas world views often are not. When dealing with, say, what is good, desirable, useful, pleasurable etc., ethics as a system is a theory, whereas morality understood as people's set of beliefs on how to live properly is not. In traditional societies world views, one of whose roles was to provide an explanation for things we objectively could not (or subjectively did not want to) investigate fully rationally and thoroughly, were often shaped by religious convictions. In addition, world views were equally an emanation of a particular social set-up (including power structure) and a position a particular individual or group occupied within it, and when it expresses the group's interests of social, economic and political nature, they become ideologies.

But a question arises whether we can at all speak of world views or ideologies in Indian philosophies or theoretical systems (scientific, legal etc.), or in classical Indian culture in general? Further, provided we could answer the above in the positive, what would be the way to draw a differentiating line between a philosophical theory and a world view in India so that it could be equally meaningful and useful in our cultural analysis of Indian cultural and intellectual context?

Clearly Indians were not exception, and we may justifiably expect that we can indeed speak of world views and ideologies also in India which had their palpable impact on how theoretical (philosophical, legal and other) systems were constructed and on how the understanding of certain ideas and notions was affected, and often restricted by the way one believed the world was or should be. Also in India such world views and ideologies which nurtured philosophical theories were frequently of religious nature, but not exclusively.

What was then the actual background of world views and ideologies which were at work while particular philosophical theories were being developed in India? How far was social, cultural, religious, linguistic and other factors influenced the way philosophical theories where moulded? And to what degree, if at all, the same factors informed world views and ideologies? Did language have any traceable impact on the formation of world views, ideologies or philosophical theories? Did philosophical ideas and legal theories reflect social structure, power set-up or political institutions? And *vice versa*, were theories and philosophical concepts of how the society and the state should function reflected in institutions in classical Indian society? What was the actual relationship between world views and theories in India? Were the relations between 'background' phenomena on the one hand and ideologies and theories on the other universal or specific to pre-modern India? Are conceivable findings to these questions merely India-specific or can one extrapolate results obtained from the study of Indian traditions and cultures to other regions of the world? Can these findings tell us anything universal about what it means to be human, to have a world view, to entertain a belief or to rationally develop an explanatory theory?

These are the considerations and reflections, mediating between research on the Indian tradition of thought and other branches of cultural studies, which informed a range of analyses compiled into the present volume. Some of these contributions, albeit not all, were presented in person by the authors during the International Conference 'World view and theory in Indian philosophy', which was held in Barcelona, Spain, between 26–30 April, 2009 (for a detailed programme of the Conference see below p. 11). This *Congreso Internacional 'Teoría e ideología en las filosofías de la India'* was at the same time the first conference on South-Asian Studies held in Spain, which attracted most (if not all) Spanish Indologists with an intention to boost South-Asian studies in the Iberian Peninsula.

The Organising Committee of the Conference comprised as organisers Piotr Balcerowicz (no academic affiliation), Johannes Bronkhorst (Université de Lausanne), Claus Oetke (Stockholm University), Martín Sevilla Rodríguez (Universidad de Oviedo) and José Virgilio García Trabazo (Universidade de Santiago de Compostela). The Co-organiser was Casa Asia (www.casaaisia.org) which provided the (absolutely marvellous!) venue for the conference. The advisory board of the Organising Committee included Juan Arnau (CSIC, Consejo Superior de Investigaciones Científicas) and Juan Luis Vermal (Illes Balears). The Conference was sponsored by the grant under the Antoni Montserrat Programme 2009, summoned yearly by Casa Asia, without which the conference could not have taken place.

CASA ASIA

I would like to avail myself of this opportunity to express, on behalf of the organisers of the conference and myself, most profound thanks to Casa Asia and its most friendly and efficient staff for the excellent co-operation and organisation as well as for the generous Antoni Montserrat grant. I personally fell most obliged to my dear colleagues who were conference organisers and advisers for their invaluable involvement in the conference as well as to Eva Borreguero, the director of Eucational Programmes of Casa Asia, Barcelona, for exemplary collaboration.

The present volume appears as Volume Five of the series *Warsaw Indological Studies* edited by the undersigned, and its publication is in part supported by the Faculty of Oriental Studies, the University of Warsaw.

Lahore, Autumn 2012

PIOTR BALCEROWICZ

SESSION PROGRAMME OF THE INTERNATIONAL CONFERENCE 'WORLD VIEW AND THEORY IN INDIAN PHILOSOPHY' 26–30 April, 2009, Barcelona, Spain

27 April, 2009

Session 1: Theory of Debate, Logic and Epistemology:

Juan Arnau: Philosophy at Stage: Theatricality, Ritual and Logic in Ancient India
Brendan Gillon: The Correspondence Principle: Its Versions and Its Uses
Stephen Phillips: Cannibalizing Nyāya Epistemology

Session 2: Theoretical Topics of Buddhist Philosophy:

Birgit Kellner: On the Relationship between *bāhyârtha-vāda* and *vijñāna-vāda* in Dharmakīrti's Thought
Helmut Tauscher: Empty or Shining Bright?

Session 3: Later Buddhism and Sāṁkhya:

Joerg Tuske: Śāntarakṣita on the Emotions
Emilio García Buendía: Parmenides and the *Sat-kārya-vāda* Doctrine of Sāṁkhya

28 April, 2009

Session 4: Hermeneutics, Mīmāṁsā and Law:

Larry J. McCrea: Rationalization and Sincerity in Mīmāṁsā Hermeneutics
Timothy Lubin: The Relation Between *Adhikāra* and *Pramāṇa* in Legal Contexts
Paolo Magnone: *Aho kauśalam apūrvam.* Hermeneutical Wrigglings about the *Īśôpaniṣad*

Session 5: Nyāya Philosophy:

Ernst Prets: Fragments of Early Nyāya
Hiroshi Marui: The meaning of a Diversity of Established World Views or Tenets (*siddhānta*) in Debate: What Does Jayanta's Explanation of *Nyāya-sūtra* 1.1.26–31 tell us?

29 April, 2009

Session 6: Jaina and Buddhist Thought:

Akihiko Akamatsu: 'Sky-flower' in Perspectivism
Peter Flügel: Epistemological Foundations of the Jaina Doctrine of Omniscience
Ferran Mestanza: Theoretical View (*dṛṣṭi*) and the Literary Genre of Philosophical Summa (*siddhānta-saṁgraha*) in Buddhist Indian Literature

Session 7: Sāṁkhya, Yoga and Nyāya-Vaiśeṣika:

Óscar Pujol: Physicalism and Consciousness in the *Yoga-sūtra*
Piotr Balcerowicz: The Nyāya-Vaśeṣika tradition and the *Artha-śāstra*

Session 8: General Topics in Indian Philosophy:

Johannes Bronkhorst: Buddhist Thought *Versus* Brahmanical Thought
Olivia Cattedra: *Sūkṣma* and *Bandhutā*, Subtle Visions of the World, Its Origins and Its Projections in the Actual Vision of the World
Claus Oetke: Tacit Assumptions in Indian Philosophies

Session 9: Indian Epics:

Ana Agud: The Relative Weight of the Different Ideologies in the *Bhagavad-gītā*
Shujun Motegi: On the Concept of Non-possession in the *Mokṣa-dharma*
José Virgilio García Trabazo: *Dharma* and Literature: On the World View of the Classical Indian Epics

30 April, 2009

Session 10: Religious Salvation:

Parimal G. Patil: Navya-Nyāya Theories of *mukti*
Takanori Suzuki: On the Theories of Emancipation among Vaiśeṣikas

Session 11: General Perspective of Indian Thought:

Vincent Eltschinger: Apocalypticism, Heresy and Philosophy
Andrew J. Nicholson: Unifying Hinduism: Philosophy and Boundary Formation in Late Medieval India
Sven Sellmer: Implicit and Scientific Psychology as Elements of Indian World Views

Contributors

Piotr Balcerowicz (www.orient.uw.edu.pl/balcerowicz), of no nationality (which he emphasises), professor of philosophy and Indian studies, currently based in Warsaw, Poland; specialises in Indian philosophical tradition, with emphasis on epistemological thought and Jainism. He teaches Indian philosophy and Indian religions as well as intercultural relations, theory of conflict and contemporary history of Asia, especially South Asia, Central Asia and the Middle East. He published extensively on Indian philosophy and religion, but also on the Middle East and Central Asia, and authored a number of books on Indian philosophy, Jainism and history of Afghanistan. His books include: *Jaina Epistemology in Historical and Comparative Perspective. Critical Edition and English Translation of Logical-Epistemological Treatises: Nyāyâvatāra, Nyāyâvatāra-vivṛti and Nyāyâvatāra-ṭippana with Introduction and Notes* (2001, [2]2009), *History of Classical Indian Philosophy. Part One: Beginnings, Analytical Trends and Philosophy of Nature* (in Polish, 2003). Since 2002, with his NGO Education for Peace, he has been involved in various development co-operation projects, especially in Afghanistan, Pakistan, Burkina Faso and Burma/Myanmar.

Johannes Bronkhorst. After initial studies of Mathematics and Physics with Astronomy at the Free University in Amsterdam (Kandidaats/B.Sc. in 1968), Johannes Bronkhorst took up the study of Sanskrit and Pali, first at the University of Rajasthan (Jaipur, India), then at the University of Pune (India). In Pune he obtained an M.A. in 1976 and a Ph.D. in 1979. After his return to the Netherlands he obtained a second doctorate from the University of Leiden in 1980 (with the highest distinction). Bronkhorst remained attached to the University of Leiden as a researcher until 1987, in which year he was appointed full professor of Sanskrit & Indian Studies at the University of Lausanne (Switzerland). He remained there until his (mandatory) retirement in 2011. Bronkhorst has published some hundred and seventy research papers, all in specialised journals, more than fifteen books, besides numerous reviews. His most recent books are: *Greater Magadha* (2007), *Aux origines de la philosophie indienne* (2008), *Buddhist Teaching in India* (2009), *Language and Reality* (2011), *Buddhism in the Shadow of Brahmanism* (2011), *Karma* (2011), *Absorption: Human Nature and Buddhist Liberation* (2012).

World View and Theory in Indian Philosophy
Warsaw Indological Studies 5 (2012) 13–18.

Emilio García Buendia studied law and philosophy at the Complutense University of Madrid. His doctorate studies were in the Institute of Religious Sciences of the same institution. He works at the Department of Logic and Philosophy of Science of the Complutense University. The field of his research is in philosophy of mind and in Indian philosophy, especially Yoga and the *Yoga-sūtra*s.

Lawrence McCrea is Associate Professor of Sanskrit Studies at Cornell University. He is the author of *The Teleology of Poetics in Medieval Kashmir* (2008), co-author (with Parimal Patil) of *Buddhist Philosophy of Language in India: Jñānaśrīmitra on Exclusion* (2010), and co-editor (with Yigal Bronner and Whitney Cox) of *South Asian Texts in History: Critical Engagements with Sheldon Pollock* (2011). He has published numerous articles on Sanskrit poetry, poetics, hermeneutics, language theory and epistemology.

Vincent Eltschinger received his PhD in Indology and Buddhist Studies from the University of Lausanne. Since 2003, he has been a research fellow at the Institute for the Cultural and Intellectual History of Asia of the Austrian Academy of Sciences. His research work focuses on the religious background, the apologetic dimensions and the intellectual genealogy of late Indian Buddhist philosophy. His publications include several books and numerous articles dedicated to various aspects of the Indian Buddhists' critical interaction with orthodox Brahmanism.

Jonardon Ganeri's work has focused primarily on a retrieval of the Sanskrit philosophical tradition in relation to contemporary Anglo-American analytical philosophy, and he has done work in this vein on theories of self, concepts of rationality, and the philosophy of language, as well as on the idea of philosophy as a practice and its relationship with literature. He has also worked extensively on the social and intellectual history of early modern South Asia and on the political idea of identity. He has affiliations with universities in the UK, Australia and Korea. His books include: *Semantic Powers: Meaning and the Means of Knowing in Classical Indian Philosophy* (1999), *Philosophy in Classical India: The Proper Work of Reason* (2001), *Artha: Meaning* (2006), *The Concealed Art of the Soul. Theories of Self and Practices of Truth in Indian Ethics and Epistemology* (2007), *The Lost Age of Reason: Philosophy in Early Modern India 1450–1700* CE (2011), *The Self. Naturalism, Consciousness, and the First-Person Stance* (2012).

Brendan S. Gillon has research interests in the history of logic and metaphysics in India, Sanskrit linguistics and natural language semantics. He has published extensively in all of these areas. He is editor of *Logic in Earliest*

Classical India (2010) and the co-editor of *Semantics: A Reader* (2004). In collaboration with Richard Hayes, he has translated the first 38 verses and their prose commentary of Dharmakīrti's *Svârthânumana* chapter of the *Pramāṇavārttika*. After teaching philosophy at the University of Alberta and the University of Toronto, he became a member of McGill University's Department of Linguistics. He is also an associate of McGill University's Department of Philosophy as well as of the University of Toronto's Institute for the History and Philosophy of Science and Technology.

Timothy Lubin (MTS, Harvard; PhD, Columbia) is Professor in the Department of Religion, and Lecturer in Religion and Law in the School of Law, Washington and Lee University, as well as Associated Researcher in the Department of Indology, French Institute of Pondicherry, in India; he taught earlier at Harvard University and the University of Virginia. His research spans Brahmanical normative and doctrinal texts as well as epigraphy. He is especially interested in ritual, ethical and legal traditions, the connections between them, and their reception in modern India.

Hiroshi Marui is Professor at the Department of Indian Philosophy and Buddhist Studies, the University of Tokyo, holding the degree of Doctor of Letters from the University of Tokyo. His major fields of research include Nyāya and Vaiśeṣika.

Paolo Magnone (www.jambudvipa.net) is an Italian scholar of Sanskrit literature and Indian philosophico-religious culture. After his undergraduate education in classical studies and besides linguistic and oriental studies at the IsMEO, he received his degree in Philosophy from the Catholic University of the Sacred Heart in Milan, where he was later appointed professor of Sanskrit Language and Literature, a position he has been holding since 1992. Starting in 2010 he has also been teaching Oriental Religions at the ISSR (Higher Institute for Religious Sciences) in Milan. His main research interests include thematic studies in the epico-purāṇic literature; mythological narratives with a text-critical, hermeneutical and comparative approach; the philosophy of the *Upaniṣad*s and Sāṁkhya–Yoga in the light of the commentators.

Shujun Motegi is Professor at the Department of Education, Shinshu University (Nagano, Japan), with M.A. from Kyoto University (1980). He is interested in early stage of Indian philosophical thought before systematisation. His publications include: *Yuktidīpikā, The Most Significant Commentary on the Sāṁkhyakārikā*, Vol. 1 (1998); '*Śābda* in the *Yuktidīpikā*' (2006); 'Early Concepts of Logic in Sāṁkhya' (2010); 'Translative Studies of the *Mokṣadharma* (XXX)' (in Japanese, 2012, continued).

Andrew J. Nicholson is Associate Professor of Hinduism and Indian Intellectual History at the State University of New York at Stony Brook, USA. He holds degrees in Religious Studies (M.A., University of Chicago), Philosophy (M.A., DePaul University), and South Asian Languages and Civilizations (Ph.D., University of Chicago). He is currently co-director of the American Academy of Religion's Yoga in Theory and Practice Consultation, an associate of the Columbia University Seminar on South Asia, a trustee of the American Institute of Indian Studies, and a senior fellow at the University of Chicago's Martin Marty Center for the Advanced Study of Religion. He has published work on the Vedānta, Sāṁkhya, Pātañjala, and Pāśupata philosophical traditions in India. His book *Unifying Hinduism: Philosophy and Identity in Indian Intellectual History* (2010) won the 2011 award for Best First Book in the History of Religions from the American Academy of Religion.

Claus Oetke. Born in Germany, he studied at the University of Hamburg (Germany) in Indology, Philosophy and Sinology. Doctorate in 1973. From 1973–1983 he was a lecturer (*wissenschaftlicher Assistent*) at the Institute for Culture and History of India and Tibet in Hamburg. Habilitation in 1983 and professorship at the same institute. Short-term teaching activities as a visiting professor in Vienna (Austria) and Kiel (Germany). 1987–1992 he held 'Heisenberg Professur' of the 'Deutsche Forschungsgemeinschaft' (DFG), which led to visiting professorships at the University of Pennsylvania (Philadelphia, USA), the Australian National University in Canberra (Australia) and the University of Texas at Austin (USA). Since 1993 Head of the Department of Indian and Tibetan Studies at the University of Stockholm. Main topics of research: Tibetan translations from Chinese Buddhist texts, problems of person and self in the Indian philosophical tradition, studies in early Madhyamaka-Buddhism, Indian theories of inference and proof ('Indian logic'), Theoretical issues of interpretation, linguistic semantics.

Stephen H. Phillips is professor of philosophy and Asian studies at the University of Texas at Austin and has been visiting professor of philosophy at the University of Hawaii, Manoa, and at Jadavpur University, Kolkata. He received a PhD from Harvard University after having attended Harvard College and for two years the Sri Aurobindo International Centre for Eduction in Pondicherry, South India. He is the author of seven books, including (with N.S. Ramanuja Tatacharya) a 750-page translation of the perception chapter of Gaṅgeśa's *Tattva-cintā-maṇi*, entitled *Epistemology of Perception* (2004), an overview of Yoga philosophy and defense of Yoga psychology and philosophy, *Yoga, Karma, and Rebirth: A Brief History and Philosophy* (2009), which was named by *Choice* an 'Oustanding Academic Title' for 2010, and most recently, *Epistemology in Classical India: The Knowledge Sources of the*

Nyaya School (2011). He is also editor or co-editor of several anthologies and has published more than fifty papers, including first-time translations of late classical Sanskrit philosophic texts.

Ernst Prets is Project Director at the Institute for the Cultural and Intellectual History of Asia (Institut für Kultur- und Geistesgeschichte Asiens), Austrian Academy of Sciences in Vienna, and Lecturer at the Institute for South Asian, Tibetan and Buddhist Studies, University of Vienna, currently working with other colleagues on the project: 'Fragments of Indian Philosophy' (nyaya.oeaw.ac.at). He holds a diploma in Hungarian (1975, University of Debrecen) and a diploma in Hindi (1996, University of Leipzig). He received a PhD from the University of Vienna in 1992 (Bhāsarvajña's system of proof). He worked for many years on a *Dictionary of Indian Epistemology, Logic and Methodology*. His research focuses on the tradition of Indian debate, epistemology and logic, including the tradition of *Caraka-saṁhitā* and the school of Nyāya. His publications include the *Terminologie der frühen philosophischen Scholastik in Indien. Ein Begriffswörterbuch zur altindischen Dialektik, Erkenntnislehre und Methodologie* in three volumes (1991, 1996, 2006; together with Gerhard Oberhammer and Joachim Prandstetter) and a number of publications on debate and argumentation in India, including the Indian medical tradition, as well as on the tradition of Nyāya and Vaiśeṣika.

Takanori Suzuki is a researcher of the Nyāya-Vaiśeṣika. While dealing with the historical development of the theory of inference in the Nyāya tradition from Uddyotakara to Udayana, Suzuki has also recently focused on the Vaiśeṣika history of the ninth to eleventh century, in which the Vaiśeṣika are thought to have finally merged the Nyāya into one tradition. His main research achievement has so far been published as 'On the Historical Development of the Concept of Inferential Upādhi' (*Asiatische Studien / Études Asiatiques*, 2011) and 'Text, Context, and Author's Intention: Two Frames of Reference in the Vaiśeṣika school' (in Toshihiro Wada (ed.): *Indian Philosophy and Text Science*, Delhi 2010). He presently teaches comparative studies of Indian and Western thought and contemporary cultural studies of India at Aichi Bunkyo University, Japan.

Joerg Tuske is Associate Professor of Philosophy at Salisbury University in Maryland. He has published several articles on Indian philosophy, especially in the areas of epistemology, logic and philosophy of mind. At Salisbury University he is also the Coordinator of the South Asian Studies minor and the Director of a Study Abroad program with Pune University and S.P. College, Pune.

Jean-Marie Verpoorten has been a teacher of classical languages (Greek and Latin) in two secondary schools in Belgium for a period of 35 years. His doctoral dissertation (1974) 'L'ordre des mots dans l'*Aitareya-brāhmaṇa*', being a study of the Vedic ritual literature and of the *Śabara-bhāṣya*, was published (1977) by the University of Liège. He published *Mīmāṁsā Literature* in *A History of Indian Literature* (fasc. VI.5) in 1987. He also carried out and inquiry into the debates on perception between Mīmāṁsakas and Buddhists as contained in the 6th chapter of the *Prakaraṇa-pañcikā*. In 1996 he was appointed lecturer of Buddhism at the University of Liège. In 2003 he was a visiting lecturer at the university of Louvain (Satsuma foundation) with the topic 'Acte retributif, renaissance et transmigration dans le bouddhisme des origines', subsequently published in 2012. At present he is working on a French translation and commentary of the 6th chapter of the *Prakaraṇa-pañcikā* on the *pramāṇa*s and *pratyakṣa*. He published a number of papers on a variety of topics in various journals and volumes (especially *Acta Orientalia Belgica*, Bruxelles), but also reviews, especially in *Bulletin d'études indiennes*, Paris.

World Views in Contention and Exchange

Buddhist Thought *Versus* Brahmanical Thought

JOHANNES BRONKHORST

Roughly until the middle of the first millennium CE, an important general distinction opposed Buddhist and Brahmanical philosophical thought in the South Asian subcontinent: Buddhist philosophers were of the opinion that our common sense world is not ultimately real, Brahmanical philosophers were convinced that it is. During a number of centuries, all Buddhist philosophers denied the reality of the world of our everyday experience, and all Brahmanical philosophers accepted it.

This striking distinction between Buddhist and Brahmanical philosophies raises an intriguing question. How is it to be explained? Nothing in the teaching of the Buddha as traditionally handed down suggests that ordinary reality does not exist. This idea was introduced later into the Buddhist tradition and subsequently preserved. Why? Was there perhaps a non-philosophical reason behind the Brahmanical attachment to ordinary reality, and for the Buddhist inclination to do away with it? Why were these Buddhists so determined to prove the illusory nature of ordinary experience?

The thesis I wish to explore in this paper is that indeed not only philosophical reasons are behind this great divide. Before exploring possible explanations of this divide, however, it will be necessary to establish that it existed. To do so, I have to recall very briefly some known facts about the early history of Indian philosophy.

To begin with Brahmanism, it is well-known that the first mention of Vedānta (or Vedāntism) as a philosophical school dates from the sixth century CE, when it is referred to by the Buddhist thinker Bhavya. Before that time, other philosophical schools debated with each other. Vedānta did not participate in these debates, nor was it criticised by others. The only sensible conclusion one can draw is that Vedānta did not exist as a philosophical school at that time.

Other Brahmanical philosophical schools did exist during that period. Two ontologies in particular were widely discussed: Vaiśeṣika and Sāṁkhya. Variants of these were used in the texts of Nyāya and Yoga. We cannot enter into details, but note that these two ontologies looked upon the world and the objects it contains as really existing entities.

World View and Theory in Indian Philosophy
Warsaw Indological Studies 5 (2012) 21–28.

In this respect these two ontologies were in striking contrast with Buddhist ontology. The earliest Buddhist ontology was developed in Northwest India, probably by the Sarvāstivādins. This ontology recognised the existence of constituent *dharma*s, but not that of things composed of *dharma*s. The objects of our everyday experience, such as houses and chariots, exist as little as human beings which, too, are thought of as an accumulation (and successions) of *dharma*s. Subsequent Buddhist thinkers—most notably Nāgārjuna—developed proofs to show that the world of our experience does not exist. These proofs had the further consequence of showing that no *dharma*s exist either. A further noteworthy development in Buddhism was the idealism which we associate with Vasubandhu and other thinkers of the Yogācāra school. Whatever the differences between the various Buddhist thinkers, all of them agreed that the world of our experience does not exist as such.

This shows that there was, roughly until the middle of the first millennium CE, a fundamental difference between Buddhist and Brahmanical thought. In spite of all the internal differences and disagreements, all Buddhist philosophers rejected the existence of the common sense world, and all Brahmanical philosophers accepted it. Why?

I announced that the answer to this question may not be philosophical, or not only philosophical. In order to investigate this possibility, let us first look somewhat more closely at what philosophy represents in Buddhism and in Brahmanism. It soon becomes clear that it played different roles in these two traditions.

Buddhist philosophy in its various manifestations *is* Buddhism, or at any rate Buddhism as learned debaters wished to depict it. Being defeated in a debate by a Buddhist opponent might therefore imply that one had to accept his position and therefore become a Buddhist oneself. The same cannot be said of Brahmanical philosophy in its various manifestations. No one could reasonably claim that Sāṁkhya and Vaiśeṣika *are* Brahmanism, that they (or one of them) constitute what Brahmanism really is about. Brahmanism is primarily about society and about the role of Brahmins in it. One can adhere to it without feeling in any way bound by Brahmanical philosophy. A Buddhist defeated in a debate with, say, a Sāṁkhya, might become convinced of the truth of the Sāṁkhya philosophy; he would not become a Brahmin for that matter, nor necessarily someone who accepted the Brahmanical vision of society.

In view of this difference, there is a fundamental asymmetry between Buddhist and Brahmanical philosophy, an asymmetry that would make itself felt in debate situations: Brahmins might become Buddhists, but Buddhists could not become Brahmins unless they were already Brahmins. In other words, Buddhists might hope to strengthen their ranks by convincing Brahmins of the superiority of their thought, but Brahmins could not entertain such hopes.

This asymmetry was not just theoretical. We know of Brahmins who converted to Buddhism. Some few examples must suffice. Udbhaṭasiddhasvāmin, the author of two works called *Viśeṣa-stava* and *Sarvajña-mahêśvara-stotra*, and his brother Śaṅkarasvāmin, author of the *Devatā-vimarśa-stuti*, both of uncertain date, appear to have been Brahmins who converted to Buddhism.[1] Legend claims the same with regard to Aśvaghoṣa and Mātṛceṭa, and modern research supports this at least in the case of the former of these two.[2] Bāṇa's *Harṣa-carita*, a classical Sanskrit literary work, tells of a hermitage (he does not use the term *āśrama*) in the Vindhya mountains headed by Divākara, a Brahmin of the Maitrāyaṇī branch who had converted to Buddhism; his hermitage was used for scholarly and peaceful debate between followers of all schools imaginable, from Jainas to Kṛṣṇa devotees, materialists, followers of Tantra and Vedic ritualists.[3] I know on the other hand of no examples of Buddhists who had converted to Brahmanism.

This takes us to another question. Buddhists could not convert to Brahmanism in the ordinary sense: they could not become Brahmins unless they were already Brahmins. One is a Brahmin by birth, not through conversion. So what happened to Brahmins who converted to Buddhism? Could they remain Brahmins? Remember that Brahmanism primarily stands for a social order. Could a Brahmanical convert to Buddhism keep his position in society as a Brahmin while at the same time accepting Buddhist ideas and soteriological ideals?

Some indications suggest that this was indeed possible. The Kashmirian author Śaṅkaranandana leaves no doubt about his Buddhist convictions in his works, yet is consistently referred to as a Brahmin in the Buddhist tradition.[4] Many of the leading scholars at Nālandā, the great monastery/university of the eastern Ganges valley, came from Brahmin families.[5] There are also several famous Brahmanical Buddhist authors. Hartmut SCHARFE (2002: 139) enumerates, beside Aśvaghoṣa, the philosophers Nāgārjuna and Vasubandhu, and the grammarian Candragomin. He further points out that Faxian, a Chinese Buddhist pilgrim, saw in the monastery at Pāṭaliputra two famous professors of Mahāyāna, Rādhāsvāmin and Mañjuśrī, whom he calls Brahmins; this suggests that they were both Brahmins and Buddhists. SCHARFE also refers to a story told by the Tibetan historian Tāranātha, which tells that the Brahmin Haribhadra was defeated in a debate by a Buddhist and, as a result, converted to Buddhism; however, he and his son, who worked as a Buddhist missionary, continued to be called Brahmins. All these cases suggest that a social position as a Brahmin was considered compatible with an intellectual choice for Buddhism.

This conclusion finds support in the fact that Jainism, too, came to have its Brahmins. Especially the Digambaras appear to have accepted this notion.

---

[1] SCHNEIDER (1993: 12) and (1995); HAHN (2000).

[2] JOHNSTON (1984, II: xviii). Cf. HARTMANN (1987: 216).

[3] SCHARFE (2002: 163).

[4] ELTSCHINGER (2006).

[5] SCHARFE (2002: 139, n. 45), with a reference to MISRA (1998: 282–302).

Jinasena's *Ādi-purāṇa*, for example, states in so many words that Bharata, the son of the Jina called Ṛṣabha, gave the title *dvija* ('twice-born') to a number of particularly virtuous devotees. He thus justifies and testifies to the existence of Brahmins among the Jainas.[6] Prabhācandra's *Nyāya-kumuda-candra*, too, does so.[7] It must further be noted that in modern India one can be Brahmin and Christian at the same time.[8]

Our reflections so far emphasise the asymmetry between Brahmanism and Buddhism during the period that concerns us. They do not yet explain why Buddhists should reject common sense experience as corresponding to reality while Brahmins did not. More clarity may be obtained by considering the social roles which the two played at that time.

Brahmins and Buddhists were in competition with each other. One of the ways in which this competition manifested itself was the debate, in which thinkers confronted each other. These debates were fundamental to the development of Indian philosophy, and were to a considerable extent responsible for the different positions elaborated.

The most important debates took place, at least ideally, at the royal court.[9] Debates were therefore more than just philosophical events; they were also political events in the sense that the winner of a debate and his school might profit greatly from the victory, while the loser might lose all, including his life.

The court, then, played a central role (whether real or imagined) in the development of Indian philosophy. What was the role of Brahmins and Buddhists at the royal court? Asking this question brings to light another asymmetry between these two groups.

---

[6] JAINI (1979: 289 f.).

[7] DUNDAS (1991: 172 f.)

[8] See, e.g., DAS (2005: 89): 'In einem 1892 publizierten Buch, das Aufsätze der Jahre 1887–1889 vereint, berichtet Bhudev Mukhopadhyay über seine Begegnung mit einem tamilischen Christen, der stolz darauf war, ein Brahmane zu sein. Obwohl bereits sein Urgrossvater Christ gewesen sei, habe die Familie nie andere als Brahmanen geheiratet. Gegenwärtig sei er zu einem Tempelfest in Tanjore unterwegs, wo die Familie ab und zu die dort üblichen Verehrungsrituale der Gottheiten (*pūjā*) ausführe, denn schliesslich habe man nur die Religion gewechselt, nicht aber die Kaste.' BAYLY (1999: 18): 'In south India it is common to encounter Christians who take pride in Brahman ancestry, and until recently many north Indian Muslims identified with the caste ideals of the lordly Rajput. Furthermore, as James Laidlaw has shown, most of the powerful north Indian traders who follow the austerely anti-Brahmanical Jain faith are as insistent as their Hindu neighbours on the importance of marrying within named Vaishya merchant jatis, while simultaneously claiming descent from converts of princely Rajput caste.' In 2004 the journalist Edward LUCE and his wife 'dropped in for tea at the home of a well-known Goan Catholic author. . . . I naïvely asked her whether there was any Portuguese blood in the family. "Oh no, that is out of the question", she said. "Our family is Brahmin."' (LUCE (2006: 311)).

[9] BRONKHORST (2007).

The Brahmins, to begin with, had a long tradition of offering services to kings. The services they offered took primarily two forms: ritual support and political advice. It is not necessary to enter into details. Vedic ritual offered the kind of magical protection that no king might wish to do without. And the political advice that we find in Brahmanical works like the *Artha-śāstra* and the *Manu-smṛti*—not to speak of numerous other texts, among them the *Mahābhārata* and the *Rāmāyaṇa*—was no doubt of the greatest utility for rulers faced with the political reality of their days.

The Buddhists had nothing comparable on offer. They had very little in terms of ritual, and even less in terms of useful political advice. The few Buddhist texts of political advice that have survived—ascribed to the likes of Mātṛceṭa and Nāgārjuna—are totally impractical, and do little beyond counselling the king to be good, and if that does not work, to become a monk.

The Buddhists of that time were obviously aware of their shortcomings in the realm of political counselling, for they left this job to Brahmins. Buddhists started depicting society and their own history in Brahmanical terms. This is clear from the fact that, from the time they started using Sanskrit (itself a major concession to Brahmanism), Buddhists started depicting the good kings of their own past—the father of the Buddha, the Buddha himself in earlier lives—as ideal Brahmanical kings.

Buddhists might henceforth still be heard at the royal courts, but hardly in order to solve problems connected with the daily running of a kingdom. Theirs was a different domain, the domain of spiritual well-being, rebirth and ultimately liberation, and they accepted this.

In this situation it would hardly have been appropriate for Brahmins to argue that the everyday world of the king, the world in which he had to stay in control, in which he might have to combat neighbouring kingdoms or survive revolts, did not really exist. Quite on the contrary, the Brahmins were there to advise him in the world of political reality, to keep him in power, and to allow him to extend his sovereignty. Their philosophy, if they had to engage in philosophical debate, was a philosophy that was solidly anchored in the reality of the ordinary world, because that was the world in which Brahmins made themselves useful. The Buddhists, on the other hand, played on the spiritual sentiments of the ruler, his fear of death, his concern about future lives. They defended positions in which the reality of the present world was denied, in which thinkers were led to abandon, at least in thought, this everyday world.

This, then, is the explanation I propose for the great philosophical divide between Brahmins and Buddhists until roughly the middle of the first millennium CE. It does not answer all questions, and indeed, it would be unrealistic to expect that it would explain more than some broad tendencies. Two major questions in particular demand our attention.

The first of these two questions is related to the suggestion that debates between Buddhists and Brahmins may not, or hardly, have taken place before the middle of the first millennium. This is the suggestion made, with much caution, by Vincent ELTSCHINGER (2012) in his thought-provoking contribution to this volume ('Apocalypticism, Heresy and Philosophy'). ELTSCHINGER is certainly right in observing that, with few exceptions, philosophical texts from before this date do not usually criticise thinkers across the line dividing Brahmanism and Buddhism. Really polemical literature starts later; ELTSCHINGER (2012) mentions the Mīmāṁsaka Kumārilabhaṭṭa in particular as an early, and fierce, critic of Buddhism. What is more, ELTSCHINGER (2012) argues convincingly that the period following the collapse of the Gupta empire saw increased animosity between Brahmins and Buddhists. Our claim to the extent that the competing positions of these two movements are responsible for at least some of their philosophical views might be considered to be threatened by these observations.

I do not think it is. The opposition between Brahmins and Buddhists may have been less fierce during the centuries preceding Kumārila, it is yet clear that the two did not develop in isolation. This can be shown in a variety of ways. Most striking, perhaps, is that the very ontology of Vaiśeṣika can be shown to be an inversion of Sarvāstivāda ontology, and therefore deeply indebted to the latter.[10] Equally important is the circumstance that all schools of Indian philosophy—including all the Brahmanical and Buddhist ones—had to come to terms, during the early centuries of the Common Era, with a set of problems that had hitherto played no role in any of them. These problems were linked to the conviction that words and things are closely related, and gave rise to a variety of different solutions: among them the *satkārya-vāda*, the *śūnya-vāda*, the *ajāti-vāda*, the *anekānta-vāda*, and much else.[11] It follows that Brahmanical and Buddhist thinkers were acquainted with each others' philosophies, and formed their own to at least some extent with those others in mind. This suggests that Buddhist and Brahmanical thinkers have confronted each other in debate from the beginning, even if these confrontations may have been less violent (and perhaps also less frequent) during the time preceding the middle of the first millennium. It could even be argued that Indian philosophy owes its very existence (and its beginning) to the availability of some form of public debate.

A new form of Brahmanical philosophy starts to participate in public debate roughly from the middle of the first millennium CE onward. This is the Vedānta philosophy, thus called because it claims to be based on the texts called *Upaniṣad*s, which constitute the end (*anta*) of the *Veda*.[12] One of its branches, Advaita Vedānta, became in course of time exceptionally popular.

---

[10] BRONKHORST (1992).

[11] BRONKHORST (2011).

[12] Though not strictly speaking a Vedāntin, we should include Bhartṛhari as an early representative of this new development.

Advaita Vedānta is remarkable in that it abandons the most important single feature that united the different Brahmanical philosophies until its time. Advaita Vedānta, unlike Vaiśeṣika and Sāṁkhya, and unlike other forms of Vedānta, accepts that the phenomenal world is an illusion. In other words, Advaita Vedānta claims for itself a position which had hitherto been the exclusive property of Buddhist philosophy.

The appearance of this totally different kind of Brahmanical philosophy is interesting from a philosophical point of view. It is also interesting from a general cultural point of view. If our reflections so far are correct, the 'realistic' bias of Brahmanical philosophy had to be understood in the light of the practical role which Brahmins played at and around the royal court. The tendency of Buddhist philosophers to deny the reality of the phenomenal world would then be linked to their incapacity to play a role, even an advisory role, in practical politics. The appearance and growing success of at least one Brahmanical philosophy that yet claimed that the phenomenal world is an illusion suggests that some important changes took place in South Asia roughly from the middle of the first millennium onward. These changes, one would think, concerned the relationship between religion and power. A detailed analysis of this issue must be left for another occasion.

BIBLIOGRAPHY

BAYLY 1999 = Bayly, Susan: *Caste, Society and Politics in India from the Eighteenth Century to the Modern Age*. The New Cambridge History of India IV.3, Cambridge University Press, Cambridge 1999.

BRONKHORST 1992 = Bronkhorst, Johannes: 'Quelques axiomes du Vaiśeṣika', *Les Cahiers de Philosophie* 14 ('L'orient de la pensée: philosophies en Inde') (1992) 95–110.

BRONKHORST 2011 = Bronkhorst, Johannes: *Language and Reality: On an episode in Indian thought*. Brill, Leiden–Boston 2011.

BRONKHORST 2007 = Bronkhorst, Johannes: 'Modes of debate and refutation of adversaries in classical and medieval India: a preliminary investigation', *Antiquorum Philosophia* 1 ('Forme di dibattito e di confutazione degli avversari nel pensiero antico') (2007) 269–280.

DAS 2005 = Das, Rahul Peter: 'Kaste', in: Ute Pietruschka (ed.): *Gemeinsame kulturelle Codes in koexistierenden Religionsgemeinschaften: Leucorea-Kolloquium 2003*. Hallesche Beiträge zur Orientwissenschaft 38, Halle (Saale) 2004: 75–116.

DUNDAS 1991 = Dundas, Paul: 'The Digambara Jain warrior', in Michael Carrithers; Caroline Humphrey (eds.): *The Assembly of the Listeners: Jains in Society*. Cambridge University Press, Cambridge 1991: 169–186.

ELTSCHINGER 2006 = Eltschinger, Vincent: 'Les œuvres de Śaṅkaranandana: Nouvelles ressources manuscrites, chronologie relative et identité confessionnelle', *AION* (*Annali dell'Istituto Universitario Orientale di Napoli*) 66 (2006) 83–122 [published 2010].

ELTSCHINGER 2012 = Eltschinger, Vincent: 'Apocalypticism, Heresy and Philosophy', in the present volume: 29–85.

HAHN 2000 = Hahn, Michael: 'Śaṅkarasvāmin's Devatāvimarśastuti', in: Christine Chojnacki; Jens-Uwe Hartmann; Volker M. Tschannerl (eds.): *Vividharatnakaraṇḍaka. Festgabe für Adelheid Mette.* Indica et Tibetica 37, Indica et Tibetica, Swisttal-Odendorf 2000: 313–329.

HARTMANN 1987 = Hartmann, Jens-Uwe: *Das Varṇārhavarṇastotra des Mātṛceṭa.* Herausgegeben und übersetzt. Abhandlungen der Akademie der Wissenschaften in Göttingen, philologisch-historische Klasse, Dritte Folge, Nr. 160; Sanskrittexte aus den Turfanfunden 12, Vandenhoeck & Ruprecht, Göttingen 1987.

JAINI 1979 = Jaini, Padmanabh S.: *The Jaina Path of Purification.* Motilal Banarsidass, Delhi 1979.

JOHNSTON 1984 = Johnston, E.H.: *The Buddhacarita or Acts of the Buddha.* Part I: *Sanskrit text of cantos I–XIV*; Part II: *Cantos I to XIV translated from the original Sanskrit supplemented by the Tibetan version, together with an introduction and notes.* 2 Vols., Motilal Banarsidass, Delhi 1984 [first edition: Panjab University Oriental Publications 31–32, Published for the University of the Panjab, Lahore, Baptist Mission Press, Calcutta 1935–1936].

LUCE 2006 = Luce, Edward: *In Spite of the Gods. The Strange Rise of Modern India.* Little, Brown, London 2006.

MISRA 1998 = Misra, B.N.: *Nālandā: Sources and Background.* Vol. 1. B.R. Publishing Corporation, Delhi 1998.

SCHARFE 2002 = Scharfe, Hartmut: *Education in Ancient India.* Handbook of Oriental Studies, Sect. II: India, 16, Brill, Leiden 2002.

SCHNEIDER 1993 = Schneider, Johannes: *Der Lobpreis der Vorzüglichkeit des Buddha. Udbhaṭasvāmins Viśeṣastava mit Prajñāvarmans Kommentar. Nach dem tibetischen Tanjur herausgegeben und übersetzt.* Indica et Tibetica 23, Indica et Tibetica, Bonn 1993.

SCHNEIDER 1995 = Schneider, Johannes: 'Der Buddha als der wahre Śiva: Udbhaṭasiddhasvāmins Sarvajñamaheśvarastotra', *Berliner Indologische Studien* 8 (1995) 153–187.

Apocalypticism, Heresy and Philosophy[1]

VINCENT ELTSCHINGER

0. Introduction.

The greater part of this paper deals with the evolution of the Brahmanical and Buddhist apocalyptic prophecies found in texts that date from the second to the sixth century CE. As I shall try to demonstrate in the first part of my essay, the Brahmanical prophecies provide an interesting and somewhat corroborative echo to Harry FALK's (2006) suggestive assumptions regarding the 'tidal waves in Indian history':[2] while the *Mārkaṇḍeya* section of the *Mahā-*

[1] This study has been made possible by the generous financial support of the Austrian Science Fund (FWF, project P21050–G15: 'Tradition und Wandel in der indischen buddhistischen Logik') and the Numata Foundation. I wish to express my most sincere thanks to Johannes Bronkhorst, Danielle Feller, Erika Forte, Gérard Fussman, Deborah Klimburg-Salter, Helmut Krasser, Marion Rastelli, Isabelle Ratié, Cristina Scherrer-Schaub, Ernst Steinkellner and François Voegeli for their careful reading of my text and their many suggestions. I also wish to extend my thanks to those who asked questions and/or raised (polite) criticism during my lectures in Barcelona (Peter Flügel), Tōkyō University (Hiroshi Marui, Jan Nattier, Peter Skilling, Kiyotaka Yoshimizu) and Ryūkoku University (Shoryū Katsura, Kyō Kanō, Yūko Yokochi). Special thanks are due to Yūko Yokochi, whose profound knowledge of the Purāṇic world(s) and materials has been beneficial to this paper in many ways, and to Alexis Sanderson, for sharing his exceptional erudition and feeling for Sanskrit with me. Cynthia Peck-Kubaczek deserves my heartfelt gratitude for revising my English. Giovanni VERARDI's important 2011 contribution appeared between the completion of this essay and its publication.

[2] Harry FALK has attracted the attention of scholars to the oscillating, 'tidal'-like changes in social order, economy, technology, political self-representation and religiosity that took place during the four phases of Indian political history between 320 BCE and the fifth century CE (Mauryas; Śuṅgas, Kaṇvas etc.; Śakas, Pahlavas and Kuṣāṇas; Guptas). According to FALK (2006: 146), the 'character of society changes twice … from an extroverted attitude, with thriving foreign contacts on an economic as well as scientific level to an introverted one, where traditional, or "brahmanical" values are preferred to inspiration gained from outside.' Whereas the Mauryas and the foreign dynasties ruling between 50 BCE and 250 CE show a 'positive attitude toward innovation', 'those who defeated or succeeded these innovative dynasties reverted to introspective self-containment'. While he admits that this dichotomy is a 'gross simplification' liable to occasional exceptions, FALK (2006: 164) concludes as follows: 'All cases have yielded similar results: the foreign or foreign-inspired dynasties display an extroverted attitude; they have contacts to foreign rulers, they deal in large scale with foreign economies; they present themselves as individuals; men look at

World View and Theory in Indian Philosophy
Warsaw Indological Studies 5 (2012) 29–85.

bhārata as well as the *Yuga-purāṇa*, both likely to have been composed or at least updated during the first two and a half centuries CE, consider foreign, *mleccha* rule[3] as the hallmark of the *kali-yuga* and/or of its final period (*yugânta*), Gupta *purāṇa*s such as the *Vāyu-*, the *Brahmâṇḍa-* and the *Viṣṇu-purāṇa* hold the increase in 'heresy' and 'heretics' (*pāṣaṇḍa, pāṣaṇḍin*)[4] to be the most distinctive feature of the *kali-yuga*. My aim here is to show that this new apocalyptic concern with Buddhism and Jainism can be seen as one part of the ideological and rhetorical background against which the Brahmanical philosopher Kumārilabhaṭṭa (sixth century[5]) turned the ritualistic Mīmāṁsā into the most uncompromising anti-Buddhist philosophical system ever created in ancient India. The second part of this paper deals with the Indian Buddhist counterparts to the Brahmanical views on the degeneration of Dharma. At the present stage of my research and reflections, the Indian Buddhist prophecies regarding the decline and final demise of the Sad-dharma do not seem to have had any discernible impact on the development of Buddhist philosophy during the sixth century. Nevertheless, they provide indicative evidence to the effect that by the turn of the sixth century, certain Indian Buddhists started paying attention to new threats and, in reaction, modified their apocalyptic schemes by taking up the hitherto purely Brahmanical pattern of four ages (*yuga*). On one hand, Brahmanical apocalyptic rhetoric testifies to an increasing concern with Buddhist and other anti-Vedic denominations as well as hostility towards

---

their male forefathers, women enjoy roles in public life. The kings want people to count their reign in dynastic years and they are polytheistic, with remarkable tolerance. The indigenous dynasties, however, are the very opposite. Their main attitude is introverted; they are modest in their titles and stress their descent from pure brahmin mothers, when at the same time women withdraw from public activities. The economy is rather local with no or little need for high-value currencies; their religion is basically henotheistic; their feeling for time is Vedic with no need for a starting point.'

[3] On *mleccha*s, see THAPAR (1971) and PARASHER (1991), especially pp. 222–261 on *mleccha*s as foreigners and foreign rulers whose behaviour opposes the *varṇâśrama-dharma*, as well as on the great flexibility apparent in this designation.

[4] For a conceptual discussion on the applicability of 'heresy' to things Indian, especially to the *pāṣaṇḍa*s/*pāṣaṇḍin*s, *nagna*s and *nāstika*s, see DONIGER O'FLAHERTY (1971: 272–287) and (1983: 109–117). In the following, 'heretic'/'heresy' is used, by convention more than by conviction, to translate *pāṣaṇḍin*/*pāṣaṇḍa*, the terms used most often by Brahmanical sources to designate non- or anti-Vedic (ascetic) groups. I render the functionally equivalent Buddhist term *tīrthika* as 'outsider' or sometimes simply as 'non-Buddhist', not as 'heretic', since 'heresy' usually designates, within one and the same denomination, an ethical and/or doctrinal and/or practical option (hence often a 'sub-denomination') considered deviant by self-appointed representatives of orthodoxy/orthopraxy. The only term I might otherwise conceive of as an equivalent of *tīrthika* is 'gentile', which came to designate non-Jews for Jews and pagans for Christians. However, at least originally, this word contains a strong ethnic or national component that is entirely missing in the Buddhist notion of *tīrthika*.

[5] On the chronology of Kumārila and Dharmakīrti, see KRASSER (2011).

the same; on the other hand, the Buddhist prophecies simultaneously bear witness to a growing awareness of e x t e r n a l causes of decline, such as political (Mihirakula) and socio-religious (Śaiva threats; Pūraṇa Kāśyapa paradigm) hostility. Considering that there is surprisingly little evidence for p h i l o s o p h i c a l polemics between Buddhists and non-Buddhists before the (end of the) fifth century,[6] one might see these roughly contemporaneous apocalyptic prophecies as providing interesting materials with which to formulate the social and ideological background of this sudden transposition of mutual rivalry to the philosophical level. But before I turn to these materials, let me add a few remarks on my use of the terms 'apocalypticism' and 'apocalyptic'.

Since Norman COHN's (1970) influential book *The Pursuit of the Millennium*, social scientists and theologians have paid increasing attention to messianism, millenarianism and apocalypticism. According to the American historian Bernard MCGINN (1998: 32), apocalypticism does not consist primarily in an interest in the 'End' as such, but in a concern with the structure and meaning of history, in the 'ability to locate current events within a scheme of universal meaning, to transcendentalize the present by viewing it from the aspect of the End'. In other words, apocalypticism is less concerned with the ἔσχᾶτον (already described in generally available prophecies) than with the social and political p r e s e n t ,[7] which is seen as in a crisis and needing a meaning that is related to the End. As such, apocalypticism is a 'way in which contemporary political and social events were given religious validation by incorporation into a transcendent scheme of meaning.'[8] Of particular relevance is the apocalyptic rhetoric's regular tendency to proceed *ex post facto* in a *vaticinium ex eventu*, i.e. as 'history disguised as prophecy'.[9] As MCGINN (2000: 88) has it, '[o]ne of the characteristics of apocalyptic eschatology is its drive to find meaning in current events by seeing them in light of the scenario of the End. Such *a posteriori*, or after-the-fact, uses of apocalypticism are often reactions to major historical changes … that do not fit into the received view of providential history. By making a place for such events in the story of the end, the final point that gives all history meaning, apocalyptic eschatology incorporates the unexpected into the divinely foreordained and gives it permanent significance.'[10] Developing a 'typology of the negative and positive functions of

---

[6] See below, n. 143.

[7] Note also MCGINN (1998: 31): '[T]heologians and students of the history of religions should … be prepared to admit how inextricably apocalypticism is intermingled with the "political" sphere at all times.'

[8] MCGINN (1998: 31). Note that contrary to COHN, MCGINN does not hold apocalypticism to originate in oppressed, poor and uneducated social milieux. Rather, '[t]he social type to which most medieval apocalyptic propagandists conform was … the well-educated and well-situated clerical intelligentsia' (MCGINN (1998: 31–32)).

[9] MCGINN (1998: 7).

[10] See also MCGINN (2000: 120–121).

apocalyptic beliefs', McGinn (1998: 30) distinguishes between a positive and a negative political use of apocalypticism, these in turn being divided into *a priori* and *a posteriori* positive uses on the one hand, and active and passive negative uses on the other hand.[11]

The present state of our knowledge forbids any clear-cut statement concerning the political purpose(s) and/or use(s) of ancient Indian apocalyptic prophecies. While it seems reasonable to view persons with political power as one intended (but not necessarily reached) audience of at least some Brahmanical texts, nothing similar can be said concerning Buddhist predictions, which are likely to have served the purely intra-monastic purpose of clerical repristination.[12] Similarly, our sources provide no hint of active negative apocalypticism. True, most documents point to a negative form of apocalypticism in that they unambiguously condemn what they regard as the dramatic signs of the End (e.g. *mleccha* rule, Adharma and heresy in Brahmanical sources; moral and disciplinary laxity, lack of knowledge and spiritual attainments in the Buddhist sources) and lay at least r e f o r m i s t demands for their eradication. What c a n be said, however, is that most of these documents testify to an *a posteriori* apocalyptic reading of current states of affairs and often reflect conscious attempts at updating pre-existing end-of-time scenarios and symbols.

1. *Mleccha* and *pāṣaṇḍa/pāṣaṇḍin* in Brahmanical apocalypticism.

1.1. Apart from the respective names of the four ages, which are borrowed from the Vedic game of dice and its four throws (from the winning throw, *kṛta*, to the losing throw, *kali*), nothing is known about the prehistory of the doctrine of the four *yuga*s.[13] A fairly developed form of the theory of the four ages is

[11] In positive political uses, the 'rhetoric of apocalypticism [is] used in support of the political and social order' (McGinn (1998: 33)); in its *a priori* form, it makes use of a pre-existing apocalyptic scenario in order to provide present events with a meaning and to prompt people to make decisions and to act; in its *a posteriori* form, it extends the scenario 'to include transcendentalized versions of recent events, thus giving final validation to the present by making a place for it at the End' (McGinn (1998: 33); *a posteriori* positive apocalypticism proved especially productive in connection with three decisive historical events: the conversion of the Roman Empire, the encounter with Islam, and the 'Great Reform' of the eleventh and twelfth centuries). In negative political uses, the 'rhetoric [is] directed against the present evil order' (McGinn (1998: 32)); whereas its active form comes 'very close to revolution' (McGinn (1988: 133); as in the case of the Hussite Taborites in fourteenth-century Bohemia), its passive form is by far the most frequent.

[12] As Alexis Sanderson has kindly informed me (personal communication, May 2010), the *Mañjuśriya-mūla-kalpa* might provide an exception to this. In verses 53.816–818 and in 427.6 ff., 'the end-time is used to explain … why the state must now rely on the services of the Mantranaya for the maintenance of sovereignty and to defend itself against the enemies of the faith.' The expression used in this connection is *paścime kāle paścime samaye śāsana-vipralope vartamāne*.

[13] Secondary literature about the four *yuga*s includes Huntington (1964), Church (1971), Dwivedi (1977), Yadava (1978–1979), Sharma (1982), von Stietencron (1986), Kane (1993: 885–968), Biardeau (1994), Koskikallio (1994), Michaels (1998: 330–335), Sharma

found in its two earliest extant sources, the *Mānava-dharma-śāstra* (MDhŚ) and the *Mahā-bhārata* (MBh).[14] Unfortunately, both the dates of these two texts and their mutual relations belong to one of the most intricate problems to be encountered in Indology.[15]

1.2. The *Mānava-dharma-śāstra* contains only very short account of the four *yugas*. It is to be emphasised that MDhŚ 1.81–86 is of no apocalyptic purport, but rather consists in a cosmological description of the gradual degeneration of Dharma and humankind through the ages. According to the *Mānava-dharma-śāstra*, Dharma is complete, 'four-footed' (*catuṣ-pad*), in the *kṛta-yuga*, but has one less 'foot', or portion (*pādaśas*), in every subsequent *yuga* due to the gradual appearance of thievery (*caurika*), lying (*anṛta*) and deceit (*māyā*). As for the religious duties (*dharma*) of human beings, they are different in each age, 'in proportion to the decrease of each age' (*yuga-hrāsânurūpatas*).[16] During the *kṛta-yuga*, humans are free of sickness (*aroga*), achieve all their goals (*sarva-siddhârtha*) and have a lifespan of four hundred years (*catur-varṣa-śatâyus*), but their life-spans (*āyus*), expectations (*āśis*) and powers (*prabhāva*) decrease from age to age (*anuyugam*). And whereas austerities (*tapas*) are paramount (*para*) in the *kṛta-yuga*, knowledge (*jñāna*) predominates in the *tretā-yuga*, sacrifice (*yajña*) in the *dvāpara-yuga*, and giving (*dāna*) is the only thing left in the *kali-yuga*. As one might expect given the non-

(2001: 45–76) (≈ SHARMA (1982)), GONZÁLEZ-REIMANN (2002). Unfortunately, the materials discussed in VERARDI (2011: 139–147) (and *passim*) could no longer be taken into consideration.

[14] On the Babylonian origin of the Kalpa theory and of the duration assigned to the *kali-yuga* (432,000 years), see PINGREE (1963: 238–239). Here the author simply asserts that 'the first text to describe the kalpa precisely … was a pre-second-century work which was the common source of a passage occurring in the twelfth book of the Mahābhārata and in the first book of the Manusmrti.'

[15] On this problem, see BRONKHORST (forthcoming). According to OLIVELLE (2005: 23), the MDhŚ is to be dated to the second–third centuries CE on account of its mentioning the minting of gold currency, and 'the author(s) of the epic knew of and drew upon material from the [MDhŚ]'. But as pointed out by BRONKHORST, this statement is problematic since leading scholars in the field of Epics (Biardeau, Hiltebeitel, Sutton, and Fitzgerald as far as the 'main *Mahā-bhārata*' is concerned) are inclined to date the *Mahā-bhārata* to the period between the third and first century BCE. A solution to this seems to be to consider the problem, as OLIVELLE himself seems to do, in the light of FITZGERALD's (2006: 269) opinion that 'the main MBh … was fashioned and promulgated sometime in the second or first centuries BCE', but that it 'grew in the four or five hundred years between the fixing of the main MBh and its recognition as a *śatasāhasrikī saṁhitā* during the Gupta era' (2006: 270). In other words, the MDhŚ might be "a text which was composed, in its earlier form, at a time when the 'main [*Mahā-bhārata*]" existed already, but the archetype underlying its Critical Edition not yet. In a certain way the [MDhŚ] is therefore contemporaneous with the [*Mahā-bhārata*], in the sense specified' (BRONKHORST (forthcoming: 9)).

[16] Translation DONIGER–SMITH (1991: [12/]79). On MDhŚ 1.85 and *dharmāḥ*, see LINGAT (1961), who discusses the problem (raised already in Medhātithi's *Manu-bhāṣya* (ManuBh 69.3–6) of an eternal Dharma being subject to change according to time/*yugas*.

apocalyptic nature of the text, MDhŚ 1.81–86 does not allude to any historical event or figure as characteristic of any of the four ages. To be more precise, the *Mānava-dharma-śāstra*, though it is aware of *mleccha*s (without any clear hint at *mleccha* rulers on the Āryāvarta, however),[17] heresies (*pāṣaṇḍa*) and heretics (*pāṣaṇḍin*), does not associate any of them with the *kali-yuga*, as the texts to be considered below variously do.

1.3.0. A few preliminary remarks are necessary before turning to the *Mahā-bhārata*'s depictions of the *kali-yuga*. Recent studies by SUTTON, BIARDEAU, FITZGERALD and HILTEBEITEL have shed new light on the old issue of Buddhism in/and the Sanskrit Epics. All four agree that 'Aśoka is the most high-impact historical figure on the [*Mahā-bhārata*]', although they 'differ over how and where to trace that impact'.[18] For instance, BIARDEAU poses, 'as [her] fundamental hypothesis, a causal rapport between the conversion of Aśoka and the composition of the [*Mahā-bhārata*]', the latter making up a 'brahmanical manifesto'.[19] And indeed, whatever their views on the way to trace the figure of Aśoka (and/or other kings) in the *Mahā-bhārata* and the chronology of the Epic, these scholars seem to agree that the *Mahā-bhārata* is part of a new Brahmanical self-assertive strategy made necessary, *inter alia*, by the growing impact of Buddhism and its religio-political power.[20] And in

[17] See PARASHER (1991: 246–247).

[18] HILTEBEITEL (2005: 114).

[19] BIARDEAU (2002, II: 749) as translated in HILTEBEITEL (2005: 109).

[20] Note, e.g. HILTEBEITEL (2005: 116): 'The [*Mahā-bhārata*] and the *Rāmāyaṇa* are both designed to sustain a subtle, patient, and emerging political theology that propounds a new *bhakti* framework in which royal patronage and Brahman prestige are provided with new places and meanings. ... The [*Mahā-bhārata*] in particular often reflects greater antipathy toward Buddhism than Biardeau indicates.' Or, in FITZGERALD's (2006: 276) words: 'If we step back and look at the whole of the MBh in the historical context which it most likely deliberately addressed—namely, post-Nandan, post-Mauryan, particularly post-Aśokan, north India sometime after 250 BCE, we can gain, I believe, some general insight into the development of the *Mahābhārata*'s arguments on *varṇadharma* and brahmins. Aśoka had preempted the brahmin monopoly on the teaching of Dharma (he launched a "Dharma-campaign" in his various edicts, presuming to teach "Dharma" on his own authority); and not only did he do an endrun around the brahmin magisterium, he, like his Mauryan predecessors, patronised the *nāstika* ("heathen") elites of Jains, Buddhists, and others and became a lay Buddhist himself. And within this relatively cosmopolitan empire Aśoka forbade brahmins to offer animal sacrifices and criticised various of their festivals. The Nandas, the Mauryas—Aśoka in particular—and their client kings were certainly kings fostering the kind of *saṅkara* the *Mahābhārata* finds abhorrent, the kind of *saṅkara* the *Mahābhārata* wishes to guarantee can never arise. The newly chartered kingship of the *Mahābhārata* is designed expressly to apply violence (the king's *daṇḍa*) within society to prevent *saṅkara* from arising, to maintain *varṇadharma*. According to the *Bhārata* this is the main purpose of the king and his instruments of force. ... These tales make unambiguous the epic's understanding of the basic political reality that there can be no *varṇadharma*, no hierarchy, without the king's violence.' See also FITZGERALD (2004: 120).

the *Mahā-bhārata*, this new self-assertion and its demands with regard to the 'Dharma king' are cast into an 'apocalyptic ... narrative', i.e. into a 'narrative of apocalyptic purge and its demand for *kṣatriya* kingship'.[21] My point in sketching current research on the *Mahā-bhārata* is the following: one can view the *Mahā-bhārata per se* as an apocalyptic narrative developed against the background of a 'long history of Brahman dissatisfactions ... with heterodoxies and heterodox rule'[22] and see its scattered explicit depictions of the *kali-yuga*, mainly in the form of apocalyptic prophecies, as not necessarily mirroring this original concern. In other words, the *Mahā-bhārata*, as a compilation, may well be cryptically concerned with Buddhism (*inter alia*), and yet the passages of relevance to us need not, as originally independent materials, reflect the Epic's overall purpose.

The *Mahā-bhārata* devotes several passages of noticeable length to the four *yuga*s. In the Epic, two kinds of texts should be distinguished: On the one hand, passages (such as 3.148) of a purely cosmological purport and close in intent to MDhŚ 1.81–86; on the other hand, passages (such as 3.186.24–55 and 3.188, in the so-called *Mārkaṇḍeya* section) which present themselves as apocalyptic prophecies (generally in the future tense) predicting the pitiable condition of society, kingship, morality and behaviour at the collapse of the *kali-yuga*. Whereas the first kind of sources remain entirely silent about heresy and the like, the second type provide, though surprisingly rarely, a few hints that heretics are heralding the last times.

1.3.1. As a purely cosmological account of the *yuga*s, MBh 3.148.5–37[23] is well in tune with the spirit (but certainly not with the doctrine) of the *Mānava-dharma-śāstra*. It provides Hanumat's answer to the following request by Bhīma: 'Enumerate the *yuga*s and [describe] the proper conduct in each *yuga*. Tell me about the modes of Dharma, desire (*kāma*), and profit (*artha*); about size, courage, and life and death.'[24] According to Hanumat, there was only one *Veda* (with one set of *mantra*s and injunctions, but without *sāman*, *yajus* and *ṛc*

[21] FITZGERALD (2004: 122). As BIARDEAU (2002, II: 747) as translated in HILTEBEITEL (2005: 109) points out, the *Mahā-bhārata* 'is a matter of an apocalyptic crisis of the world that leads a temporal cycle ... from its genesis to its end, while passing through a long war-sacrifice, or, better still, a long sacrificial session of apocalyptic magnitude—since it brings about the birth and disappearance of all the sovereigns of the Earth, all the while assuring the continuity of the future existence of the Earth purged for a while of the wicked.'

[22] HILTEBEITEL (2005: 122).

[23] See BIARDEAU's (2002, I: 538–539) short summary and GONZÁLEZ-REIMANN's (2002: 215–221) translation. My account of MBh 3.148.5–37 is largely indebted to GONZÁLEZ-REIMANN's translation.

[24] MBh 3.148.9:

yuga-saṅkhyāṁ samācakṣva ācāraṁ ca yuge yuge /
dharma-kāmârtha-bhāvāṁś ca varṣma vīryaṁ bhavâbhavau //

Translation GONZÁLEZ-REIMANN (2002: 215).

sounds!) and accordingly one Dharma (consisting in renunciation—*sannyāsa*—, i.e. the practice of *ātma-yoga*) in the *kṛta-yuga*.[25] The Dharma of the stages of life (*āśrama*, leading to the supreme goal) and social classes (*varṇa*, including Sva-dharma ('appointed duty')) was respected.[26] There were neither supernatural beings (gods etc.) nor *traiguṇya* ('the [set of] three constituents'), trade, human labour, tasks, diseases, suffering or bad dispositions (calumny, arrogance, slander, laziness, hatred, fear, envy, quarrelling, or selfishness).[27] In the *tretā-yuga*, Dharma is diminished by one quarter.[28] This age is characterised by the appearance of ritual (*sattra*, *kriyā*, *yajña*) and by people being truthful and devoted to charity.[29] Though this is not stated explicitly, we ought to understand that this second age is dominated by the *sattva*(*-guṇa*). In the *dvāpara-yuga*, Dharma is reduced by a half, while the hitherto unique *Veda* is divided into four parts (ritual, too, becomes differentiated).[30] In many respects, the *dvāpara-yuga* heralds the *kali-yuga*: people become *rājasa* and decline in their regard for truth despite their still being devoted to austerities and giving;[31] diseases and calamities gradually appear[32] so that, 'greatly afflicted by them, some people practice austerities [while o]thers perform sacrifices, wishing to obtain earthly goods or heaven.'[33] In the *kali-yuga*, the dark (*tāmasa*) age, only a fourth part of Dharma remains.[34] Vedic practices decline along with the performance of sacrifices.[35] Lazy and impassioned, people are beset with natural disasters, diseases,[36] calamities, and mental as well as physical suffer-

[25] MBh 3.148.13, 19, 21.

[26] MBh 3.148.17, 20.

[27] MBh 3.148.10, 12–15, 22.

[28] MBh 3.148.23.

[29] MBh 3.148.22–25.

[30] MBh 3.148.26, 28.

[31] MBh 3.148.28–29.

[32] MBh 3.148.30.

[33] According to MBh 3.148.31:

yair ardyamānāḥ subhṛśaṁ tapas tapyanti mānavāḥ /
kāma-kāmāḥ svarga-kāmā yajñāṁs tanvanti câpare // ,

and parts of GONZÁLEZ-REIMANN's translation (2002: 217).

[34] MBh 3.148.32–33.

[35] MBh 3.148.33.

[36] Note GONZÁLEZ-REIMANN (2002: 168–169): 'Even medical treatises blamed the existence of sickness on the *kaliyuga*. In a chapter devoted to the spread of epidemics, the *Caraka Saṁhitā* (3rd–5th centuries) … explains the origins of disease as the consequence of the gradually declining energy and well-being of people brought about by the passage of the *yuga*s. As rains, crops, and the quality of diet and life-style diminish, so does the body's resistance to disease, and this coincides with the shorter life-spans caused by the advance of the *yuga*s [CarS 3.3.24]. At the conclusion of this cosmic etiology of disease the treatise quotes the following: In each *yuga* a fourth of dharma is sequentially removed, as are the qualities of

ing.[37] And '[w]hen the world is in a state of decay, the conditions that allow for its advancement are destroyed. The religious practices (*dharma*) performed at the end of the *yuga* produce opposite results.'[38]

1.3.2. As apocalyptic prophecies focusing on the *kali-yuga* and especially its end (*yugânta*), our second and third *Mahā-bhārata* passages yield a decidedly different testimony. Both have been invoked as bearing explicit witness to Buddhism and heresy as a prominent feature of the Epic's description of the last times.[39] But are heresy and/ or Buddhism so prominent in these prophecies? The relevant passage of MBh 3.186 covers about 30 verses, with only a single short hint of *pāṣaṇḍa*s. As for MBh 3.188, it comprises 93 verses, of which verses 14–93 form the prophecy proper. The verses supposedly concerned with Buddhism are only two, representing approximately $^1/_{40}$ of the relevant text, and it is possible that they are a later addition.[40] Much more striking is this second passage's (MBh 3.188) strong, almost refrain-like emphasis on *mleccha*s or, better, the barbarisation of the world. Indeed, verses 29, 37, and 45 begin with the statement: *mleccha-bhūtaṁ jagat sarvaṁ bhaviṣyati* ('the entire world will become barbarised'); as for verse 70, it declares that 'the earth will be overthrown with *mleccha*s' (*mahī mleccha-samākīrṇā bhaviṣyati*).[41] And though MBh 3.186.24–55 lacks such a refrain-like insistence, it is even more precise regarding the *mleccha*s: '[At the collapse of the *yuga*,] O prince among humans, [there will be] on earth numerous *mleccha* kings, ill-governing, evil and entirely dedicated to lying. [These] sovereigns, O [you] best among humans, [will be] Āndhras, Śakas, Pulindas, Yavanas, Kāmbojas, Aurṇikas, Śūdras and Ābhīras.'[42] I shall turn back to this strong concern with *mleccha*s later on.

---

living beings. In this way, the world is [gradually] destroyed [CarS 3.3.25: *yuge yuge dharmapādaḥ krameṇānena hīyate / guṇapādaś ca bhūtānām evaṁ lokaḥ pralīyate //*].'

[37] MBh 3.148.34.

[38] MBh 3.148.36:

loke kṣīṇe kṣayaṁ yānti bhāvā loka-pravartakāḥ /
yuga-kṣaya-kṛtā dharmāḥ prārthanāni vikurvate //

Translation González-Reimann (2002: 218).

[39] See Biardeau's (2002, I: 588–612) summary of and commentary on MBh 3.188; see also Biardeau (2002, II: 759–762) and Hiltebeitel (2005: 124–129).

[40] See below, § 1.3.4.

[41] I can hardly resist the impression that the kernel of this text originally consisted in a depiction of the dark ages centred on the omnipresence of *mleccha*-(-rule) that was built upon this refrain (occurring every eight verses?).

[42] MBh 3.186.29–30:

bahavo mleccha-rājānaḥ pṛthivyāṁ manujâdhipa /
mithyânuśāsinaḥ pāpā mṛṣā-vāda-parāyaṇāḥ //
āndhrāḥ śakāḥ pulindāś ca yavanāś ca narâdhipāḥ /
kāmbojā aurṇikāḥ śūdrās tathâbhīrā narôttama //

1.3.3. In addition to statements concerning the general decline of Dharma and the paucity of righteous people (*dharmiṣṭha*),[43] MBh 3.186.24–55 gives considerable emphasis to lying and falsity, hypocrisy (especially religious hypocrisy and imposture), trickery (especially in business and trade matters, which it does not see positively), false accusation and adultery: these are unmistakable signs of the *yugânta*.[44] Religious duties—*svādhyāya* ('one's own recitation [of the *Veda*]'), *yajña* ('sacrifice'), *japa* ('muttering'), *vrata* ('[religious] observance'), *piṇḍa* ('funerary oblation')—sink into oblivion;[45] capital sins—such as *pānapa* ('one who drinks alcohol'), *guru-talpaga* ('one who violates his teacher's bed'), *brahma-vadhyā* ('one who murders a Brahmin'), various types of thievery—immorality, ill-behaviour, greed and violations of spoken etiquette corrupt social order;[46] transgressions regarding licit food, intercaste relationships and marriage bonds tend to increase dramatically.[47] Last but not least, the burden of taxes (*kara-bhāra*), the decline of human faculties—*āyus* ('health[/life]'), *bala* ('strength'), *tejas* ('ardour'), *parākrama* ('energy'), *deha* ('body'), *sāra* ('firmness'), *satya* ('truth(fulness)')—and various kinds of natural and physiological disturbances are considered as making life extremely precarious and dangerous.[48] *pāṣaṇḍa*s are but one element of this eloquent description: '[These formerly righteous persons are] confused by numerous *pāṣaṇḍa*s and praise the food [begged] from others(?).'[49] If generous, one might also interpret our text's allusion to the regions (*diś*) that are covered with the signs (*dhvaja*) of erroneous Dharma(s) as a hint of unspecified heterodoxies.[50] That's all, and it is not much.

1.3.4. In MBh 3.188, the longer of the two passages, the *ṛṣi* Mārkaṇḍeya's teaching on the evil times (*kaluṣaṁ kālam*) to come starts with a four-verse statement about the now familiar reduction of Dharma by one quarter in every *yuga*, and the parallel decline in human beings' lifespan (*āyus*), vigour (*vīrya*),

---

[43] MBh 3.186.45, 47–48.

[44] MBh 3.186.25, 33, 38, 40–42, 46, 49, 55.

[45] MBh 3.186.25, 27–28.

[46] MBh 3.186.33, 35, 38, 40, 42, 50.

[47] MBh 3.186.26–28, 31, 42, 55.

[48] MBh 3.186.32, 35, 37, 40, 44, 48, 51–54.

[49] MBh 3.186.43ab:

bahu-pāṣaṇḍa-saṅkīrṇāḥ parânna-guṇa-vādinaḥ /

[50] MBh 3.186.39:

lobha-moha-parītāś ca mithyā-dharma-dhvajâvṛtāḥ /
bhikṣârthaṁ pṛthivī-pāla cañcūryante dvijair diśaḥ // —

—'Twice-born, O protector of the earth, are [then] roaming about in order to beg [alms] in the regions seised by greed and error and covered with the signs of erroneous Dharma(s).'

Begging for alms does not necessarily refer to extra-Vedic denominations or individuals.

intelligence (*buddhi*), force (*bala*) and glory (*tejas*).[51] Among the characteristic features of the *kali-yuga* that recur in this prophecy, one might mention the following: macro- and microcosmic disturbances growing into cosmic disasters,[52] shortening of life-expectancy, lessening of strength and firmness,[53] restless wandering and living in towns and cities,[54] lack of truthfulness,[55] and the abandoning of behavioural observances, sacrifices, religious festivals and funerary rituals.[56] Also repeated in this passage is the increase of ignorance as well as its concomitant pseudo-erudition.[57] Worth mentioning in this connection is the extremely peripheral place allotted to the features traditionally ascribed to the groups challenging Vedic authority and *Veda*-based Dharma, such as being a denier (*nāstika*), being contemptuous (*nindaka*) of the *Veda*, or being led astray by *hetu-vāda* ('sophistry').[58] These traits, however, do not describe *pāṣaṇḍa*s (a term which only occurs at the beginning of MBh 3.189), but human beings, especially Brahmins. Similarly, religious hypocrisy is ascribed to all four caste-classes.[59] As for the *topos* of Śūdras teaching Brahmins, in spite of its later occasional connection with Buddhism, it also has nothing to do with heretics.[60]

The bulk of this passage is concerned with immorality, whose most recurrent aspects are violence, harshness and cruelty.[61] Of great frequency are also theft,[62] human passions (especially greed),[63] offences against marriage bonds and family relationships,[64] mixing of castes and transgressions of Svadharma,[65] the breaking of dietary rules and licit means of livelihood,[66] and, last but not least, violence to and taxes imposed on Brahmins.[67] The only passage likely alluding to heresy can therefore only be interpreted as of comparatively marginal importance:

---

[51] See MBh 3.188.10–13.

[52] MBh 3.188.68–69, 74–76, 79, 81.

[53] MBh 3.188.15–16, 31, 47–48, 62.

[54] MBh 3.188.58, 60, 83–84.

[55] MBh 3.188.15, 18, 38, 76.

[56] MBh 3.188.22, 26, 29, 45, 69.

[57] MBh 3.188.16, 32, 36, 38, 41, 46, 54, 72–73.

[58] MBh 3.188.22, 26.

[59] MBh 3.188.14.

[60] MBh 3.188.54.

[61] MBh 3.188.17, 22, 28, 32, 50, 52, 55–56, 59, 71, 77–78, 84.

[62] MBh 3.188.22, 30, 34, 36–37.

[63] MBh 3.188.16–17, 24, 31–33, 39, 50, 53, 55, 57, 82.

[64] MBh 3.188.35, 42, 44, 49, 77.

[65] MBh 3.188.18–19, 41, 57, 62–63, 69.

[66] MBh 3.188.21, 24–25, 27, 43, 52, 67, 71.

[67] MBh 3.188.57–58, 61, 70.

> ‘The world will be totally upside down: people will abandon the gods and will offer *pūjā* to *eḍūkas*; Śūdras will refuse to serve the twice-born at the collapse of the *yuga*. In the hermitages of the great R̥ṣis, in the settlements of Brahmans, at the gods’ temples (*deva-sthāna*), in the caitya sanctuaries, and in the abodes of the Nāgas, the Earth will be marked by *eḍūkas* and not adorned by houses of the gods. At the expiration of the *yuga*, that will be the mark of the *yuga*’s end.’[68]

These verses have been interpreted (BIARDEAU, HILTEBEITEL etc.) as referring to (proto)*stūpas* (the *eḍūkas*) and, as such, as presenting Buddhism as a sign of the last times. But as recent studies by FLÜGEL (2008) and BRONKHORST (2009) clearly show, *stūpas* were also erected by the Jainas (and maybe the old Magadhan culture as a whole). Moreover, the meaning of *eḍūka* is not at all unambiguous, and thus this term does not necessarily refer to *stūpas*.[69] One can also note, finally, that these verses contain the only occurrence of (*yugântasya*) *lakṣaṇam*, a wording reminiscent of later, Purāṇic formulations.

---

[68] MBh 3.188.64–66:

viparītaś ca loko ’yaṁ bhaviṣyaty adharôttaraḥ /
eḍūkān pūjayiṣyanti varjayiṣyanti devatāḥ /
śūdrāḥ paricariṣyanti na dvijān yuga-saṅkṣaye //
āśrameṣu maha-rṣīṇāṁ brāhmaṇâvasatheṣu ca /
deva-sthāneṣu caityeṣu nāgānām ālayeṣu ca //
eḍūka-cihnā pr̥thivī na deva-gr̥ha-bhūṣitā /
bhaviṣyati yuge kṣīṇe tad yugântasya lakṣaṇam //

Translation (slightly modified) HILTEBEITEL (2006: 126); see also BIARDEAU (2002, II: 759) and BAKKER (2007: 15).

[69] According to Amarasiṁha (AmK 2.2(*pura-varga*).4a$_2$b), an *eḍūka* is a walled structure in which bones are deposited (*eḍūkaṁ yad-antar-nyasta-kīkasam /*). The best discussion of the terms *eḍūka / aiḍūka* to date is BAKKER (2007); see also ALLCHIN (1957). Contrary to the *aiḍūka* (for which the locus classicus is *Viṣṇu-dharmôttara-purāṇa* 3.84.1–15, quoted and discussed in BAKKER (2007: 12, n. 4, and 12–13)), which did not contain any physical remnants of the dead, *eḍūkas* can be defined as ‘[b]urial mounds or sepulchral monuments that actually contain the ashes and / or bones of the deceased’ (2007: 19); for a physical description, see BAKKER (2007: 43). According to BAKKER (2007: 40), ‘we may take it for certain that the author of the VDhP calqued his Hindu *aiḍūka* on a Buddhist example [see already BAKKER (2007: 13–14)—V.E.], but by doing this he elaborated on what must have been a monumental tradition that was common to all Indian religions, most pronounced within Buddhism, less in Jainism and inconspicuous in the Hindu mainstream.’ Referring to the *Mahā-bhārata* passage under consideration, BAKKER (2007: 33, n. 76) quotes ALLCHIN (1957: 1) (‘Since Lassen it has been generally accepted that this description of the *Kali-yuga* refers to the spread of Buddhist practices and the popular desertion of Brahmanical temples.’), and adds: ‘This is not to say, however, that the composer of this passage was exclusively thinking of Buddhism. He might have lashed out at all pan-Indian practices frowned upon by the orthodox that involved the erection of monuments over mortuary remains. *Eḍūka* thus seems to be a wider term than, for instance, *stūpa*, and it clearly has here, if not in all cases where it occurs, a pejorative connotation.’

Here it might be suspected of placing emphasis on an element that was lacking in a more original version of the text.

1.3.5. The so-called *Mārkaṇḍeya* section provides what might be the first (and rather tenuous) occurrence of heresy in the apocalyptic scenario. Not only this, it also ends on the famous, properly messianic prophecy of the advent of Kalki(n)[70] that would eventually crystallise into Viṣṇu's tenth and final *avatāra*.[71] In other words, MBh 3.186 and 188 present a vivid socioreligious depiction of the *kali-yuga* and prophesise the imminent rise of a new *kṛta-yuga*: 'As the *kṛta* dawns, things return to their proper course. A Brāhmaṇa called Kalkin is born, and he becomes a universal ruler, a *cakra-vartin*. He destroys the foreigners, and re-establishes the rule of the twice-born by means of a Vedic horse sacrifice. Order is then restored and Dharma adhered to, the brahmanical social order prevails, and rituals are again practised. Each social class performs its appointed duty and the people prosper.'[72] Besides multiple allusions to the final destruction of all *mleccha*s and *dasyu*s, this prediction contains a brief mention of *pāṣaṇḍa*(s): at the time when the new *kṛta-yuga* dawns in the areas conquered by Kalki(n) and his fellow Brahmins, 'hermitages [now] bereft of heretics will be firm in truth.'[73]

1.4. What about the dates and provenance of these apocalyptic and messianic prophecies? Many scholars are ready to accept that major parts of the *Mahābhārata*'s books 3 and 12 represent later additions. As GONZÁLEZ-REIMANN (2002: 95) points out, 'Mārkaṇḍeya's entire teaching on the *yuga*s has no connection to the Epic story.' Moreover, *Mārkaṇḍeya* himself acknowledges external sources at the time of concluding his prophecy: 'I have told you everything about the past and the future as I remember it from the *purāṇa* recited by [the god] Vāyu, which is praised by the *ṛṣis*.'[74] Basing himself on close similarities between Mārkaṇḍeya's teachings and the extant *Vāyu-purāṇa*, GONZÁLEZ-REIMANN is inclined to postulate (in addition to an older version of the *Vāyu-purāṇa*) (a) common source(s) for both texts. According to MITCHINER and GONZÁLEZ-REIMANN, the so-called *Yuga-purāṇa* (YuP) is a very likely candidate for being a source of both the *Mārkaṇḍeya* section and

---

[70] See MBh 3.188.89–3.189.9 and HILTEBEITEL's (2006: 127) translation.

[71] See below, § 1.7.2 and n. 111.

[72] GONZÁLEZ-REIMANN (2002: 95).

[73] MBh 3.189.9cd$_1$: *āśramāḥ hata-pāṣaṇḍāḥ*[a] *sthitāḥ satye*. [[a] S MSS: *hata-pāṣaṇḍāḥ*; K4, D1 MSS: *hata-pākhaṇḍāḥ*; Ed.: *saha-pāṣaṇḍāḥ*.] Translation HILTEBEITEL (2006: 127) (modified).

[74] MBh 3.189.14:

> *etat te sarvam ākhyātam atītânāgataṁ mayā /*
> *vāyu-proktam anusmṛtya purāṇam ṛṣi-saṁstutam //*

Translation GONZÁLEZ-REIMANN (2002: 96).

(an older version of) the *Vāyu-* and *Brahmâṇḍa-purāṇa.*[75] This text, strictly speaking not a *purāṇa*, is nothing other than a 115–verse chapter of the *Gārgīya-jyotiṣa*, a work that is referred to in the *Mahā-bhārata* at least twice.[76] As GONZÁLEZ-REIMANN observes, the *Yuga-purāṇa* presents itself as Śaṅkara's (= Śiva's) answer to Skanda's question about the events supposed to take place at the *yugânta*, a question very similar to the one posed by Yudhiṣṭhira to Mārkaṇḍeya. And even more than Mārkaṇḍeya's teachings, the *Yuga-purāṇa* insists on foreign, *mleccha* rule as the hallmark of the *yugânta*.

After a short liminary dialogue between Skanda and Śaṅkara (verses 1–4), the *Yuga-purāṇa* goes into an original depiction of the *kṛta-yuga* (verses 6–13),[77] the *tretā-yuga* (verses 14–22)[78] and the *dvāpara-yuga* (verses 23–36, with an interesting allusion to the plot of the *Mahā-bhārata*). The apocalyptic prophecy regarding the *kali-yuga* is built on a lengthy succession of kings, wars, *coups d'état* and an ever-increasing state of desolation and ruin.[79] According to the *Yuga-purāṇa*, the first king of the *kali-yuga* was Janamejaya Pārīkṣit, who quarrelled with the twice-born. But the first blow to the ideal city of Puṣpapura (Pāṭaliputra?) came from a coalition between Pañcālas, Māthuras and (Indo-)Greeks (*yavana*), which brought political disorder in the different realms (verses 47–48) and was responsible for the appearance of Adharma.[80]

[75] On the *Vāyu-* and *Brahmâṇḍa-purāṇa*, see below, § 1.6.

[76] MBh 9.36.14–17 and 13.18.25–26.

[77] The *kṛta-yuga* is described as of supreme virtue (*brāhmaṇyam uttamam*), devoid of fear (*bhaya*), death (*mṛtyu*), thieves (*taskara*), greed (*lobha*), anger (*krodha*), passion (*roṣa*), deceit (*dambha*), calumny (*paiśunya*), meanness (*kṣudratā*), sexual union (*maithuna*), and full of (punitive) justice (*daṇḍa-pradhānatā*). Men were possessed of the strength of *tapas*. The *devas*, *gandharvas*, *kinnaras*, *dānavas*, *yakṣas*, *rākṣasas* and *uragas* were born during the *kṛta-yuga*, which ends in a great battle (*mahā-yuddha*)!

[78] During the *tretā-yuga*, the *kṣatra* was created by Svayambhū and feminine qualities (*straiṇā guṇāḥ*) as well as women (*nārī*) appeared; the four social classes were occupied with their own deeds (*sva-karman*). The *agni-hotra* was regularly performed and there were multitudes of *śāstras*, *mantras* and *japas*; the priests dwelt in forests (*araṇyâyatana*) and were learned in the *Vedas* (*veda-parāyaṇa*); human beings were not deceitful (*aśaṭha*), Kṣatriyas were skilful in protecting people (*prajā-pālana*), 'judicious and steadfast guardians of the Vipras' (*viprāṇāṁ viśeṣa-jñā rakṣitâraḥ samāhitāḥ*, MITCHINER (1986: 89)); *vaiśyas* delighted at their own deeds, and Śūdras at service (*śuśrūṣā*). The world was devoted to Dharma and absorbed in the practice of truth (*satya-vrata-samāhita*).

[79] For a summary, see PARASHER (1991: 239–241).

[80] YuP 50 and 52–55:

> *brāhmaṇāḥ kṣatriyā vaiśyāḥ śūdrāś câiva yuga-kṣaye /*
> *samaveṣāḥ samācārā bhaviṣyanti na saṁśayaḥ // 50 //*
> *cīra-valkala-saṁvītā*[a] *jaṭā-valkala-dhāriṇaḥ /*
> *bhikṣukā vṛṣalā loke hoṣyanti laghu-vikriyāḥ // 52 //*
> *tretâgniṁ vṛṣalā loke hoṣyanti laghu-vikriyāḥ /*
> *oṁ-kāra-prathitair mantrair yugânte samupasthite // 53 //*
> *agni-kārye ca japye câgnike ca dṛḍha-vratāḥ /*
> *śūdrāḥ kali-yugasyânte bhaviṣyanti na saṁśayaḥ // 54 //*

Let it be noted in passing that the only occurrence of *pāṣaṇḍa* in the *Yuga-purāṇa* appears along with this description of Adharma: 'At that end of the *yuga*, men will be allied with *pāṣaṇḍas*: they will make friends for the motive of [gaining] women.'[81] After the fall of the Yavanas and their disappearance from Madhyadeśa, seven kings will reign in Sāketa; a mighty king of the Śakas will follow their rule, but his kingdom will soon be destroyed. The *Yuga-purāṇa* then mentions the names of a series of rulers (the *mleccha* Āmrāṭa Lohitākṣa, who will destroy the four *varṇas*; Gopāla, a righteous king; Puṣpaka; Anaraṇya; the Brahmin Vikuyaśas; Agnimitra, who will quarrel with the Brahmins; Agniveśya, who will fight against the Śabaras). After their rule and the resultant shortage of men, women will become predominant (*strī-pradhāna*). The king Satuvara 'will afflict the earth with his rule' (*hatvā daṇḍena medinīm*, verse 87, MITCHINER (1986: 95)), before the last rulers, the 'terrible' (*ghora*) Śakas, 'will destroy a quarter of living beings by arms' (*caturbhāgaṁ ca śastreṇa nāśayiṣyanti prāṇinām*, verse 89ab, MITCHINER (1986: 95)) and 'take a quarter of the wealth to their own city' (*hariṣyanti śakāḥ kośa-catur-bhāgaṁ svakaṁ puram*, verse 89cd, MITCHINER (1986: 95)). Disasters and cataclysms herald the end of the *kali-yuga*.

Note that the *Yuga-purāṇa* does not mention the advent of the *kṛta-yuga* or Kalki(n), but 'explains that, as things get worse and the end of the *yuga* approaches, several geographical regions … will be safe havens … Although it does not explicitly say so, the text implies that at that time, and in those places, a new *kṛtayuga* will commence … According to Mitchiner, the author of the YuP was convinced that the *kaliyuga* had ended after the defeat of the Śakas

---

bho-vādinas tathā śūdrā brāhmaṇāś cārya-vādinaḥ /
dharma-bhītatamā vṛddhā janaṁ bhokṣyanti nirbhayāḥ // 55 // —

[[a] Emendation (Sanderson, May 2010): *-saṁvītā*; Ed.: *-sañcītā*.]

—'At the end of the Yuga, Brahmins, Kṣatriyas, Vaiśyas and Śūdras will be similar in dress, and of similar conduct—there is no doubt. … In the world, low-born Bhikṣukas (mendicants), quick to anger, clothed in bark-cloth [and] wearing matted hair and bark-garments, will offer oblations into the three Śrauta fires. In the world, once the end of the *yuga* has approached, low-born men—contemptible and loathsome—will offer oblations into the three Śrauta fires with *mantras* manifested by [i.e. opening with] the sacred syllable "*om*". Śūdras who practice with firm commitment the (daily? *agnike* to be read *āhnike*?) observance of the fire-sacrifice and the repetition [of *mantras*] will exist at the end of the *yuga*—there is no doubt. Śūdras will also be utterers of "*bho*", and Brahmins will be utterers of "*ārya*": [and] the elders, most fearful of the Dharma, will fearlessly exploit the people.'

Translation MITCHINER (1986: 92) (modified). For verse 51, see below, n. 81.

[81] YuP 51ad$_1$:

pāṣaṇḍaiś ca samāyuktā narās tasmin yuga-kṣaye /
strī-nimittaṁ ca mitrāṇi kariṣyanti …

Translation MITCHINER (1986: 92).

and a new *kṛtayuga* was beginning ….'[82] This, again, accords well with Mārkaṇḍeya's teachings, which clearly reflect the belief that a thousand-year *kali-yuga* would imminently come to its end. As suggested by GONZÁLEZ-REIMANN (2002: 97) and other scholars, '[a]t some point in the last centuries BCE and the early centuries CE, there must have been real expectations that *kali* would end in the foreseeable future, but later, as social conditions did not bear out these expectations, the figures were reinterpreted and the end of the *yuga* was pushed farther into the future.'[83] MITCHINER (1986: 13) dates the *Yuga-purāṇa* to the last quarter of the first century BCE,[84] and remarks that the mention of the Ābhīras as *mleccha* rulers in the *Mārkaṇḍeya* section makes it unlikely that it is earlier than 250 CE, a conclusion which 'coincides with those of Dwivedi, Yadava, and R.S. Sharma, who, on the basis of the social, political, religious and economic conditions described, attribute the *Mārkaṇḍeya* section on *yugânta* in the Epic to the third or fourth centuries CE.'[85] Taking 250 CE as the point in time when the *Mārkaṇḍeya* section may have been composed or, at least, updated, we might conclude that, by this time, apocalyptic prophecies were still interpreting *mleccha* rule and political chaos as end-time symbols which were incomparably more significant than *pāṣaṇḍa*/*pāṣaṇḍin*s.

1.5. The passages examined so far yield consistent results. Purely cosmological depictions of the *yuga*s such as MDhŚ 1.81–86 and MBh 3.148.5–37 do not allude to historical events, figures or threats when dealing with the *kali-yuga*. In contrast, passages dedicated to apocalyptic eschatology, i.e. prophecies such as MBh 3.186, 3.188 and the *Yuga-purāṇa*, do include lengthy *ex post facto* descriptions of their socio-historical environment. And contrary to what would be expected from later Purāṇic accounts or interpolated passages of the *Mahābhārata*,[86] *pāṣaṇḍa* and *pāṣaṇḍin*s play virtually no role in these early prophecies. From hundreds of verses, only five can be interpreted as hinting at (signs of) heterodoxies and/or heteropraxies heralding the End: MBh 3.186.43 (*bahu-pāṣaṇḍa-saṅkīrṇā āśramāḥ*), MBh 3.188.64 and 66 (*eḍūka*), MBh 3.189.9 (*āśramāḥ saha-pāṣaṇḍāḥ*), and YuP 51 (*pāṣaṇḍaiś ca samāyuktā narāḥ*). What does seem to matter in these apocalyptic and messianic foreseeings is the overwhelming presence of foreign, *mleccha* rulers alluded to in refrain-like manner and at times even mentioned by name. This, however, is hardly surprising on the hypothesis that the bulk of these texts were composed during the first 250 years of the first millennium CE, i.e. at a time when significant parts

[82] GONZÁLEZ-REIMANN (2002: 99).

[83] According to NATTIER (1991: 43), also the Buddhists regularly updated their reckoning of the *sad-dharma-vipralopa* (see below, § 2.1).

[84] See also PARASHER (1991: 239).

[85] GONZÁLEZ-REIMANN (2002: 99). See DWIVEDI (1979: 290), YADAVA (1978–1979: 32) and SHARMA (1982: 187–188).

[86] See below, § 1.7.3.

of north-western and northern India were under Śaka, Pahlava and especially Kushana (Kuṣāṇa) rule. In other words, these predictions mirror the Brahmanical orthodoxy's most dramatic concern of the day and are likely to be meant as incentives for the main addressee of the Epic, the Dharma king.

1.6. The *vāyu-proktaṁ purāṇam* referred to as an authoritative scripture at the close of the *Mārkaṇḍeya* section (MBh 3.189.14) underwent a process of reworking and lengthening that led to the composition, sometime during the fourth century CE (i.e. in the early Gupta era), of what VIELLE (2005) has proposed to call the '"classical" *vāyuprokta Brahmāṇḍapurāṇa*'.[87] As already recognised by scholars such as Kern and Kirfel, this text forms the nucleus of the extant *Vāyu-* and *Brahmâṇḍa-purāṇa* (VāP and BḍP).[88] In other words, the common parts of these two originally identical *purāṇa*s are likely to provide us with the most ancient layer of extant Purāṇic literature. Fortunately, these *purāṇa*s' accounts of the *yuga*s, especially of the *dvāpara-* and *kali-yuga*, belong to this early layer, providing an extremely important landmark in the history of apocalyptic prophecies and hence, anxieties. VāP 58 ≈ BḍP 1.2.31 can be analysed as follows: (1) a (gloomy, *kali-yuga*-like) description of the (second half of the) *dvāpara-yuga* (VāP 58.1–29 ≈ BḍP 1.2.31.1–29); (2) a description of the conditions and events characteristic of the *kali-yuga* (VāP 58.30–100 ≈ BḍP 1.2.31.30–100): (2a) a general depiction of the *kali-yuga* (VāP 58.30–72 ≈ BḍP 1.2.31.30–72); (2b) advent of Pramiti (VāP 58.73–88 ≈ BḍP 1.2.31.73–88); (2c) last events (VāP 58.89–100 ≈ BḍP 1.2.31.89–100); (3) rise of a new *kṛta-yuga* (VāP 58.101–126 ≈ BḍP 1.2.31.101–126).[89]

In the following, I shall focus briefly on the first part (= 2a) of these two *purāṇa*s' apocalyptic prophecy.[90] Something is extremely striking about this

[87] On MBh 3.189.14, see above, § 1.4 and n. 74.

[88] See VIELLE (2005: 537–543), and also ROCHER (1986: 33, 157 and 244–245).

[89] Contrary to the Epic Kalki(n), Pramiti is not a Brāhmaṇa (although he is surrounded by myriads of Brāhmaṇas) and not directly responsible for the advent of a new *kṛta-yuga*. After defeating thousands of *mleccha* kings (the famous list given in VāP 58.81–83 ≈ BḍP 1.2.31.81–83 includes, among others, *draviḍa*s, *siṁhala*s, *gāndhāra*s, *pahlava*s, *yavana*s, *tuṣāra*s, *barbara*s, and *cīna*s) and slaughtering innumerable *pāṣaṇḍa*s and *adhārmika*s, Pramiti dies. Only a few human beings survive the end of the *kali-yuga*, but in an increasingly miserable moral and material condition. According to VāP 58.99–101 ≈ BḍP 1.2.31.99–101, at one point, their condition is so pitiable that they become disgusted (*nirveda*), start pondering (*vicāraṇa*), attain equanimity (*sāmyāvasthā*), awakening (*sambodha*) and piousness (*dharma-śīlatā*), thus provoking the sudden rise of the new *kṛta-yuga* (*aho-rātraṁ tadā tāsāṁ yugaṁ tu parivartate*). In other words, Pramiti annihilates the moral and political conditions that were responsible for the prolongation of the *kali-yuga* and creates those that will eventually lead to the advent of the *kṛta-yuga*.

[90] Provided that the use of the future tense can be used as a stylistic criterion for apocalyptic discourse, only one part of this passage can properly be termed a 'prophecy', however. On phraseological and stylistic grounds, I am fairly convinced that VāP 58.30–72 ≈ BḍP 1.2.31.30–72 is composed of at least two distinct layers. In VāP 58.30–41 ≈ BḍP

prophecy: whereas the *mlecchas* are never mentioned in this account,[91] the *pāṣaṇḍas* are given much more importance than in the *Mahā-bhārata* and the *Yuga-purāṇa*, which testifies to a significant shift in emphasis having taken place. During the *kali-yuga*, 'kings, nearly all Śūdras, promote heretics (/heresies)'[92] and everything is 'filled with heretics of wrong morality and conduct.'[93] Interestingly, our texts provide several details concerning the identity of the *pāṣaṇḍas*. Without a doubt, the following verse alludes to the Buddhists: 'And when the end of the [*kali-*]*yuga* [will be] imminent, Śūdras with white teeth, having subdued their senses, [with] shaved [heads] and wearing reddish garments will practise religion.'[94] And in a subsequent passage, our sources even go to the trouble of classifying the *pāṣaṇḍas*: 'And when the Kali age [will have been] reached, there will appear in like manner [people] wearing reddish garments as well as Nirgranthas and [people] wearing [human] skulls, others who [will] sell the *Veda*(s), others who [will] sell the sacred places (/objects), and yet other heretics who [will] challenge [the system of] caste-classes and life stages.'[95] The Buddhists, the Jainas and the Kāpālikas start a long career as unmistakable signs of the (end of the) *kali-yuga*.

1.2.31.30–41, the future tense is missing entirely; *tiṣya* occurs four times instead of the more usual *kali*; the locatives *tiṣye* and *kalau* lack any fix syntactic position in the verses in which they occur. On the contrary, VāP 58.42–63 ≈ BḍP 1.2.31.42–63 is written in the future tense; *tiṣya* never occurs; the locative *yugânte pary- / praty-upasthite* (missing in VāP 58.30–41 ≈ BḍP 1.2.31.30–41, but strongly reminiscent of Epic formulations and thus likely to belong to the same source as that of the *Mārkaṇḍeya* section, possibly the original *vāyu-proktaṁ [brahmâṇḍa-]purāṇam*) occurs five times as *pāda* d, here again in refrain-like manner (almost all of the locatives, i.e. *yugânte, tasmin kalau yuge, yugânteṣu, yuga-kṣaye*, occur in the verse's last *pāda*). The last part of the passage, viz. VāP 58.64–72 ≈ BḍP 1.2.31.64–72, is of a more hybrid character. Note, however, that neither the future tense nor *yugânte pary- / pratyupasthite* occurs in VāP 58.64–70 ≈ BḍP 1.2.31.64–70, whereas both are found in the last two verses, viz. VāP 58.71–72 ≈ BḍP 1.2.31.71–72.

[91] Note that the *mlecchas* occur, most probably as a literary stereotype, in the prophecy concerning the exploits of Pramiti; see above, n. 89, and VāP 58.78, 84, 89 ≈ BḍP 1.2.31.78, 84, 89.

[92] VāP 58.40ab ≈ BḍP 1.2.31.40ab:

> *rājānaḥ śūdra-bhūyiṣṭhāḥ pāṣaṇḍānāṁ*[a] *pravartakāḥ* /

[[a] BḍP: *pākhaṇḍānāṁ*.]

[93] VāP 58.52ab ≈ BḍP 1.2.31.52cd:

> *kuśīla-caryā-pāṣaṇḍair vṛthā-rūpaiḥ*[a] *samāvṛtam*[b] /

[[a] BḍP: *vyādha-rūpaiḥ*; [b] Emendation (< BḍP): *samāvṛtam*. VāP: *samāvṛttam*.]

[94] VāP 58.59 ≈ BḍP 1.2.31.59cd–60ab:

> *śukla-dantā jitâkṣāś ca muṇḍāḥ kāṣāya-vāsasaḥ* /
> *śūdrā dharmaṁ cariṣyanti yugânte paryupasthite*[a] //

[[a] BḍP: *samupasthite*.]

[95] VāP 58.64cd–66ab ≈ BḍP 1.2.31.65–66:

> *kāṣāyiṇas*[a] *ca nirgranthās tathā kāpālinaś*[b] *ca ha* // 64 //
> *veda-vikrayiṇaś cânye tīrtha-vikrayiṇo 'pare* /

1.7.0. As we shall see in the following, the *Viṣṇu-purāṇa* (hereafter ViP) strengthens the tendency observed in the *Vāyu-purāṇa* and the *Brahmâṇḍa-purāṇa*. Although HAZRA (1937) and PATHAK (1997, I: 22–23) date it to the beginning of the fourth century (i.e. the dawn of the Gupta dynasty), scholars such as WINTERNITZ (1981: 521), RENOU (1985, I: 418/§ 834), HACKER (1960: 67), GAIL (1969: 921), DONIGER O'FLAHERTY (1983: 108)[96] and GONZÁLEZ-REIMANN (2002: 170–171)[97] are rather inclined to date the *Viṣṇu-purāṇa* to the fifth or the beginning of the sixth century, i.e. in the last part or the close of the Gupta rule over northern India.

1.7.1. The *Viṣṇu-purāṇa* (6.1) also contains an apocalyptic prophecy describing the miserable condition of mankind during the *kali-yuga*. Here, Parāśara answers Maitreya's question about the nature of the *kali-yuga* (*kaleḥ svarūpam*) 'in which the blessed four-footed Dharma gets ruined'.[98] This prophecy betrays a strong concern for the immorality and misbehaviour of women: self-willed, frivolous, speaking harsh and false words, women will marry wealthy men only, have numerous progeny but little fortune, stuff themselves and have unlimited power over their husbands.[99] The *kali-yuga* will also be characterised by various disorders in the stages of life,[100] members of the different *varṇa*s will attach themselves to prohibited activities,[101] kings will fail to protect people and despoil them by levying excessive taxes.[102] Starvation, mainly due to draught, will plague people and doom them to exile and the violation of dietary rules.[103] Life will not exceed twenty years and young girls of the age of five, six or seven will give birth to children.[104] Human understanding will decline, whereas vices, defilements and sin will increase.[105] Decisions and hierarchy will depend on wealth alone.[106] Rituals will be abandoned or left to humans' fancy or arbitrariness, since the *Veda*s will be neglected and religious authority will amount

varṇâśramāṇāṁ ye cânye pāṣaṇḍāḥ[c] *paripanthinaḥ // 65 //*
utpadyante tathā[d] *te vai samprāpte*[e] *tu kalau yuge /*

[[a] Emendation (< BḍP): *kāṣāyinaś*. VāP: *kaṣāyinaś*. [b] BḍP: *kāpālikāś*. [c] BḍP: *pākhaṇḍāḥ*. [d] BḍP: *tadā*. [e] Emendation (< BḍP): *samprāpte*. VāP: *saprāpte*.]

[96] Between 400 and 500 CE.

[97] Fifth century. For other tentative dates, see ROCHER (1986: 249).

[98] See ViP 6.1.8–9. ViP 6.1.8ab:

dharmaś catuṣ-pād bhagavān yasmin viplavam ṛcchati //

[99] ViP 6.1.16–18, 21, 28–31.

[100] ViP 6.1.10, 14, 32–33.

[101] ViP 6.1.10, 23, 36–37, 53.

[102] ViP 6.1.34–35, 40.

[103] ViP 6.1.24–26, 38, 52–54.

[104] ViP 6.1.39–43.

[105] ViP 6.1.43, 57–58.

[106] ViP 6.1.12, 16, 19–20, 22.

to free thinking.[107] Considering these and other features, the *Viṣṇu-purāṇa*'s prophecy may not seem to differ in any significant way from that of the *Mahā-bhārata*. But when it comes to foreign rule and heresy, the shifts are more obvious than those found in the *Vāyu-purāṇa* and the *Brahmâṇḍa-purāṇa*. First, ViP 6.1 does not allude to *mleccha*s at all (although ViP 4.24.98 still has Viṣṇu's *avatāra* Kalkin destroy the *mleccha*s and *dasyu*s and re-establish people in their Sva-dharmas). Second, and again in stark contrast to the *Mahā-bhārata*, heresy and heretics are now seen as one of the most prominent features of the *kali-yuga*. Consider first the following part of the prophecy:

> 'Given to the vow of living on alms and bearing the marks of homelessness, the vilest Śūdras, [duly] honoured, will betake themselves to a livelihood based on heresy. And the Vedic path having disappeared, people being beset with heresy, human beings will have a short life due to the increase of Adharma.'[108]

Most interesting are, however, verses 6.1.45 and 49–51, which are worth quoting in full:

> 'As soon as an increase in heresy comes to notice, O Maitreya, the high-minded should infer an increase of *kali*. … When there is no delight in Vedic teachings [but] fondness for heresies, the intelligent wise ones should infer an increase of *kali*. During the *kali*[*-yuga*], O Maitreya, people sullied by heresies will fail to honour Viṣṇu, the lord of the world, the god who is the creator of everything. People struck by heresies will speak thus: "Wherefore the gods, wherefore the Brahmins (*vipra*), wherefore the *Veda*s, wherefore the purity born of the ablutions (*ambu-janman*)?"'[109]

As we can see, the insistence on heresy and the total absence of foreign rulers betray a significant evolution from the *Mahā-bhārata* and the *Yuga-purāṇa*, as

[107] ViP 6.1.10, 11, 13–15, 27

[108] ViP 6.1.37 and 39:

bhaikṣa-vrata-parāḥ śūdrāḥ pravrajyā-liṅgino 'dhamāḥ /
pāṣaṇḍa-saṁśrayāṁ vṛttim āśrayiṣyanti sat-kṛtāḥ //
veda-mārge pralīne ca pāṣaṇḍâḍhye tato jane /
adharma-vṛddhyā lokānām alpam āyur bhaviṣyati //

[109] ViP 6.1.45 and 49–51:

yadā yadā hi pāṣaṇḍa-vṛddhir maitreya lakṣyate /
tadā tadā kaler vṛddhir anumeyā mahâtmabhiḥ // 45 //
na prītir veda-vādeṣu pāṣaṇḍeṣu yadā ratiḥ /
kaler vṛddhis tadā prājñair anumeyā vicakṣaṇaiḥ // 49 //
kalau jagat-patiṁ viṣṇuṁ sarva-sraṣṭāram īśvaram /
nârcayiṣyanti maitreya pāṣaṇḍopahatā janāḥ // 50 //
kiṁ devaiḥ kiṁ dvijair vedaiḥ kiṁ śaucenâmbu-janmanā /
ity evaṁ vipra vakṣyanti pāṣaṇḍôpahatā janāḥ // 51 //

well as a consolidation of the features observed in the *Vāyu-purāṇa* and the *Brahmâṇḍa-purāṇa*.

1.7.2. That this strong emphasis on heresy is not just peripheral or incidental to the *Viṣṇu-purāṇa* can be seen from many other passages in this early *purāṇa*. Most significant in this connection is a famous myth which likely finds its first occurrence in our text. It would soon provide the ideological background for the seventh-century integration of the Buddha into the list of Viṣṇu's *avatāras*. According to this myth, Viṣṇu produced a deluder or heresiarch called Māyāmoha (or, in other accounts, Māyāpuruṣa) out of his own body in order to vanquish the Asuras (or Daityas) who were invincible due to their pious Vedic observances.[110] The early date of the *Viṣṇu-purāṇa*'s version of the story can be established both by the fact that the heresiarch is not yet considered as an *avatāra* of Viṣṇu,[111] and by the fact that his bewildering preaching is not located at the beginning of the *kali-yuga*, as most later versions of the story have it. As we shall see, this myth sheds more light on the identity of the heretics alluded to in the prophecy discussed above.[112]

Maitreya asks Parāśara about the identity, the practice/behaviour (*samācāra*) and the nature of the *nagna*, i.e. the heretic (ViP 3.17.4). Parāśara's answer is as follows:

---

[110] On this and parallel myths, see CHOUDHARY (1956: 240–243), DONIGER O'FLAHERTY (1971: 306–333; especially 308–313), KLOSTERMAIER (1989: 54–55), DANDEKAR (1997: (especially 146–148), PATHAK (1997: 24) (who claims, on rather shaky arguments, this myth to be a later addition), SAINDON (2004: 24–41; especially 34–35). Note also GONZÁLEZ-REIMANN (2002: 191, n. 32): 'That heretic teachers who did not accept the existence of the *ātman* and criticized the *Vedas* and animal sacrifices were really gods who incarnated in order to confuse—and thus destroy—the demons, is an idea that had been stated earlier in the *Maitrāyaṇīya Upaniṣad* (7.8–10), but with no mention of the *yugas*.' That the *Maitrāyaṇīya-upaniṣad* is earlier than the ViP is far from certain.

[111] The Buddha is not yet regarded as Viṣṇu's *avatāra* in the *Viṣṇu-purāṇa* or the *Harivaṁśa*. According to HAZRA (1940: 41–42), 'it is highly probable that the Buddha began to be regarded as an incarnation of Viṣṇu from about 550 A.D.' (quoted in SAINDON (2004: 20)). According to HAZRA (1940: 41, 84, 88) and KANE (1997: 721), this incarnation became popular during the seventh century, as is testified by a Pallava inscription dated to the end of the seventh century (see KANE (1997: 721, n. 1725) and MAHALINGAM (1988: no. 250)). The doctrine of Viṣṇu's ten *avatāras* (with the Buddha as the ninth, taking place at the beginning of the *kali-yuga*, and Kalki[n] as the tenth and final one, at the end of the *kali-yuga*) is well established in the *Matsya-*, *Garuḍa-* and *Agni-purāṇa* (see CHOUDHARY (1956: 239, nn. 1 and 9) for references).

[112] That the Jaina *anekânta-vāda* and the Buddhist *madhyamaka* and *vijñāna-vāda* (see below) are meant here as heresies (*pāṣaṇḍa*) is made clear by ViP 3.18.23:

> *anyān apy anya-pāṣaṇḍa-prakārair bahubhir dvija /*
> *daiteyān mohayām āsa māyā-moha 'timoha-kṛt //* —
>
> —'By the numerous ways of [yet] other heresies, Māyāmoha, the absolute deluder (*atimoha-kṛt*) deluded all the other demons, O twice-born.'

> 'The triple [sacred science], called the *ṛc*, the *yajus* and the *sāman*, is the [protecting] cover (*āvṛti*) of the [social] classes, O twice-born; one who is "naked" (*nagna*) is any sinner who through delusion casts off that garment. Since, O twice-born, the triple [sacred science] is the garment of all the [social] classes, one is [said to be] *nagna* ("naked") when it has been abandoned, O twice-born, no doubt [about this].'[113]

Parāśara then sets about telling the story that his grandfather Vasiṣṭha had already recited to Bhīṣma. After a grandiose hundred-year battle, the gods were defeated by the demons (*asura*, *dait*[*e*]*ya*). They went to see Viṣṇu on the shore of the ocean of milk, praised him and asked him how to vanquish the demons:

> 'We have not been able to slay those enemies who, [because they are] intent upon the duties of their own [social] classes and follow the Vedic path, are protected (*āvṛta*) by [their] austerities. Be pleased to give us, O soul of all, the means which might enable us, O Bhagavat, to slay these demons.'[114]

As we can see, the Asuras owe their invulnerability to their strict adherence to the *Veda* and the rules laid down in it. As an answer, Viṣṇu produced a Māyāmoha out of his own body, handed it over to the gods and said:

> 'This Māyāmoha will bewilder all these demons; as a result [of this bewilderment], it will be possible to kill them [since they will be] excluded from the Vedic path.'[115]

Māyāmoha sets out and sees the demons practising austerities on the bank of the Narmadā River. Disguised first as a Jaina ascetic, i.e. naked (*digambara*), bald (*muṇḍa*) and carrying a peacock-feather fan, Māyāmoha asks them whether they expect this-worldly (*aihika*) or other-worldly (*pāratrya*) results from their austerities, and invites them to conform to his teaching (*vākya*, *dharma*) if

---

[113] ViP 3.17.5–6:

ṛg-yajuḥ-sāma-sañjñeyaṁ trayī varṇâvṛtir dvija /
etām ujjhati yo mohāt sa nagnaḥ pātakī dvija //
trayī samasta-varṇānāṁ dvija saṁvaraṇaṁ yataḥ /
nagno bhavaty ujjhitāyām atas tasyāṁ na saṁśayaḥ //

[114] ViP 3.17.39–40:

sva-varṇa-dharmâbhiratā veda-mārgânusāriṇaḥ /
na śakyās te 'rayo hantum asmābhis tapasâvṛtāḥ //
tam upāyam aśeṣâtmann asmākaṁ dātum arhasi /
yena tān asurān hantuṁ bhavema bhagavan kṣamāḥ //

[115] ViP 3.17.42:

māyā-moho 'yam akhilān daityāṁs tān mohayiṣyati /
tato vadhyā bhaviṣyanti veda-mārga-bahiṣ-kṛtāḥ //

they really long for liberation (*mukti*). Māyāmoha then teaches them the *anekânta-vāda* ('the doctrine of multiplexity of reality'),[116] and the demons are taken away from the Vedic path (*veda-mārgād apākṛtāḥ*) and made to give up their Sva-dharma. The demons spread this delusive teaching, and within a few days, 'the triple [sacred science] was generally abandoned by these demons.'[117] Māyāmoha then addresses other Asuras under the guise of a Buddhist monk, i.e. wearing red garments (*raktâmbara-dhṛt*):

> 'If you long for heaven (*svarga*) or for liberation (*nirvāṇa*), O Asuras, then away with the corrupted *dharma*s of animal slaughter (*paśu-ghāta*) etc., [and] listen (*nibodhata*) [to me]. Know that all this only consists in cognition (*vijñāna-maya*). Understand my speech, which has [already] been told in this way by perfect sages (*samyag-budha*) in the [world]. This world, being without a foundation (*anādhāra*), is addicted to the objects of a [purely] erroneous cognition (*bhrānti-jñāna*); corrupted by [defilements] such as desire, it is made to roam about incessantly (*atyartham*) in the narrow corridor/defile of existence.'[118]

As the author(s) of this passage insist, the Buddhist Māyāmoha seduces the demons mainly through reason(ing) (*yukti*) and argumented speech (*vacanaṁ yukti-yojitam*), urging them to renounce the *Veda*s in the following way:

> 'Trustworthy words do not fall on earth from the sky, O [you my sweet] Suras; I and others like you should [only] accept words possessed with reason(ing).'[119]

According to him, to consider ritual violence (*hiṁsā*) to be virtuous does not stand to reason(ing) (*na yukti-sahaṁ vākyam*), just as it is childish speech (*arbhakôdita*) to consider that offerings (*havis*) burnt in fire yield results. As a

---

[116] See ViP 3.18.9–10. Skt. *anekânta-vāda* occurs at 3.18.12a.

[117] ViP 3.18.15cd:

alpair ahobhiḥ santyaktā tair daityaiḥ prāyaśas trayī //

[118] ViP 3.18.17–19:

svargârthaṁ yadi vo vāñchā nirvāṇârtham athâsurāḥ /
tad alaṁ paśu-ghātâdi-duṣṭa-dharmair nibodhata //
vijñāna-mayam evâitad aśeṣam avagacchata /
budhyadhvaṁ me vacaḥ samyag-budhair evam ihôditam //
jagad etad anādhāraṁ bhrānti-jñānârtha-tatparam /
rāgâdi-duṣṭam atyarthaṁ bhrāmyate bhava-saṅkaṭe //

[119] ViP 3.18.31:

na hy āpta-vādā nabhaso nipatanti mahīṁ surāḥ /
yuktimad vacanaṁ grāhyaṁ mayânyaiś ca bhavad-vidhaiḥ //

surāḥ in place of the expected (but metrically impossible) *asurāḥ* is a rather clumsy formulation. As Alexis Sanderson (personal communication, May 2010) suggests to me, this might also be explained as coaxing flattery.

result of his bewildering teaching and the Asuras' spreading it further, the latter gave up their 'native/innate' (*nija*) Dharma, the Dharma of the triple sacred science (*trayī-dharma*; or: taught in the *Veda* and the Smṛtis—*veda-smṛty-udita*) and all instruction based on the Vedic path (*sarvāṁ trayī-mārgâśritāṁ kathām*). And while some of the demons started condemning (*vinindā*) the *Veda*s, others despised the gods and still others reviled the whole complex of sacrifices and ritual acts (*yajña-karma-kalāpa*). Here is the predictable conclusion of Parāśara's story:

> 'These demons having thus gone astray, the immortal [gods] undertook most excellent preparations and [made themselves] ready for fighting. Then, O twice-born, a battle between gods and demons again took place, and the demons, [now] enemies of the true [Vedic] path (*san-mārga*), were slain by the gods.'[120]

A few verses later, the author(s) draw(s) the moral of the story: 'This disadvantage was born of [the demons'] having conversed with heretics … Therefore, one should avoid conversation and contact with the sinful heretics (*pāṣaṇḍin*).'[121] In other words, the Māyāmoha myth serves as an aetiological foundation for the normative literature's recurrent prohibition of any kind of contact with *pāṣaṇḍin*s. According to the *Mānava-dharma-śāstra*, one 'should not give honour, even with mere words, to heretics',[122] nor should one 'live in a kingdom ruled by a servant … or overrun by gangs of heretics.'[123] It is hardly surprising, then, that the *Viṣṇu-purāṇa* prohibits conversation (*sambhāṣaṇa*, *ālāpa*), civility (*anupraśnā*), physical contact (*sparśana*), cohabitation or commensality with heretics. And whereas the mere sight of a heretic requires one to stare at the sun for purification, physical contact with him dooms one to ablutions.[124] The Māyāmoha section ends with the following conclusion:

> 'One should not give honour, even with mere words, to heretics, people who persist in wrong action, people who act like cats,

---

[120] ViP 3.18.33–34:

ittham unmārga-yāteṣu teṣu daityeṣu te 'marāḥ /
udyogaṁ paramaṁ kṛtvā yuddhāya samupasthitāḥ //
tato daivâsuraṁ yuddhaṁ punar evâbhavad dvija /
hatāś ca te 'surā devaiḥ san-mārga-paripanthinaḥ //

[121] ViP 3.18.79a and 96ab: *pāṣaṇḍâlāpa-jāto 'yaṁ doṣaḥ ... tasmāt pāṣaṇḍibhiḥ pāpair ālāpa-sparśanaṁ tyajet*. See also ViP 3.18.98 (where the sinful heretics are termed *veda-vāda-virodhin*) and 3.18.103.

[122] MDhŚ 4.30: *pāṣaṇḍinaḥ ... vāṅ-mātreṇâpi nārcayet //*. Translation DONIGER–SMITH (1991: 77). See also YDhŚ 1.130 and 271–272 (JOSHI (1987: 311–312)). YDhŚ 2.70 and NSmṛ 4.180 disqualify heretics and deniers as witnesses (DONIGER O'FLAHERTY (1983: 121)).

[123] MDhŚ 4.61: *na śūdra-rājye nivaset ... na pāṣaṇḍi-gaṇâkrānte ....* Translation DONIGER–SMITH (1991: 79).

[124] See ViP 3.18.43–50 and 95–96.

> hypocrites, rationalists, and people who live like herons. As for contact, even at a distance, with these extremely sinful, misbehaving heretics, it should be avoided. Therefore, may one shun them. These are the naked ones whom I have presented to you, who [upon being] seen ruin funerary rites, people conversation with whom destroys the merit of one day.'[125]

1.7.3. As the normative conclusions drawn by the author(s) already testified, the Māyāmoha myth, far from being a benign story, is expected to have a direct and compelling bearing upon those listening and adhering to the teachings of the *Viṣṇu-purāṇa*. This relevance for contemporary society did not escape the attention of those who, at an indeterminate point in time, adapted and interpolated the story into the *Mahā-bhārata*.[126] In doing so, these late editors filled what is likely to have been perceived as a lack in the great Epic, viz. its paying no or only marginal (explicit) attention to heretics as heralding the *kali-yuga*. The Buddha, now Viṣṇu's last *avatāra* before Kalki(n), is depicted as active at the beginning of the *kali-yuga*; the narrative framework of the *devâsura* struggle has been cut off in order to anchor the episode in human time:

> 'When the *kali-yuga* begins, I [Viṣṇu] will speak at the court of righteous kings in the language of Magadha after sitting under the *rāja-taru* tree. As Buddha, the son of Śuddhodana, wearing a reddish garment, [with my head] shaved and with white teeth, I will confuse mankind. When I become the Buddha, the Śūdras will enjoy [the benefits of] the ceremonies for the ancestors; all men will shave [their heads], and they will dress in red. The Brāhmaṇas will not study [the *Veda*s], and they will not keep the [ritual] fire … When the *kali-yuga* ends [I will be born as] Kalkin, a yellowish-brown Brāhmaṇa, son of Viṣṇuyaśas and having a Yājñavalkya chaplain. And with the help of all my Brāhmaṇa followers I will completely destroy the foreigners and the heretics.'[127]

---

[125] ViP 3.18.100–102:

pāṣaṇḍino vikarma-sthān vaiḍāla-vratikāñ chaṭhān /
haitukān baka-vṛttīṁś ca vāṅ-mātreṇâpi nârcayet // 100 //
dūratas tais tu samparkas tyajyaś câpy atipāpibhiḥ /
pāṣaṇḍibhir durācārais tasmāt tān parivrajayet // 101 //
ete nagnās tavâkhyātā dṛṣṭāḥ śrāddhôpaghātakāḥ /
yeṣāṁ sambhāṣaṇāt puṁsāṁ dina-puṇyaṁ pranaśyati // 102 //

ViP 3.18.100 = MDhŚ 4.30 (translation DONIGER–SMITH (1991: 77)). On the cats' and the herons' behaviour, see MDhŚ 4.195–196.

[126] MBh vol. 12.2 / XVI: 2104a–2105a, Appendix I.31.

[127] MBh vol. 12.2 / XVI: 2104ab, Appendix I.31, lines 1–7, 18–21:

tataḥ kali-yugasyâdau bhūtvā rāja-taruṁ śritaḥ /
bhāṣayā māgadhenâiva dharma-rāja-gṛhe vadan /

The son of Śuddhodana is reported to rely on the *bauddha-dharma* and to teach compassion (*dayā*) toward living beings; seeing the whole world as merely consisting of the *skandhas*, Śūdras will make donations to Śūdras, people will engage in actions that merit rebirth in hell (*narakârha*), the Brahmins will be devoid of purity and neglect their Sva-dharma, sons will pay no obeisance to their fathers, women to their husbands, servants to their masters, and the mixture of caste-classes (*varṇa-saṅkara*) will prevail.[128]

1.7.4. Here, as elsewhere, the meaning of the Māyāmoha myth (and of the concomitant adoption of the Buddha as an *avatāra* of Viṣṇu[129]) is perfectly clear: what occurred to the demons of old threatens contemporary society if it allows heretical indoctrination to undermine its Vedic foundations and the Brahmins' symbolic and ritual power. Decades or even centuries of indigenous Gupta rule have made the *mleccha* threat momentarily recede into the background of apocalyptic eschatology. Instead, the most conservative milieux now perceive heterodoxy, mainly Buddhism and Jainism, as the most threatening challenge to Brahmanism and accordingly update their prophecies and create new myths. Note, however, that references to *mleccha*s remain abundant in Purāṇic literature, especially in connection with Kalki(n) (or Pramiti/ Pramati) and the famous Purāṇic motif of the dynasties of the *kali-yuga*.[130] What I intend to stress here is that considered in themselves, the prophecies concerning the *kali-yuga* mirror significant shifts regarding the elements at work during the last age. According to DONIGER O'FLAHERTY (1983: 125), the Māyāmoha myth, a 'Gupta myth',[131] mirrors 'the Paurāṇikas' hope that the Gupta kings would exterminate

---

kāṣāya-vastra-saṁvīto muṇḍitaḥ śukla-dantavān /
śuddhodana-suto buddho mohayiṣyāmi mānavān /
śūdrāḥ śrāddheṣu bhojyante mayi buddhatvam āgate /
bhaviṣyanti narāḥ sarve muṇḍāḥ kāṣāya-saṁvṛtāḥ /
anadhyāyā bhaviṣyanti viprāś câgni-vivarjitāḥ / ...
tataḥ kali-yugasyânte brāhmaṇo hari-piṅgalaḥ /
kalkir viṣṇu-yaśaḥ-putro yājñavalkya-purohitaḥ /
sahāyā brāhmaṇāḥ sarve tair ahaṁ sahitaḥ punaḥ /
mlecchān utsādayiṣyāmi pāṣaṇḍāṁś câiva sarvaśaḥ //

Translation GONZÁLEZ-REIMANN (2002: 171) (slightly modified according to the interpretation [Alexis Sanderson, personal communication, May 2010] of *yājñavalkya-purohita* as a *bahu-vrīhi* compound).

[128] See SAINDON (2004: 29–30) for the Sanskrit text and a French translation of the passage.

[129] Note KLOSTERMAIER (1989: 54): 'Some authors seem to think that, among the *avatāras* of Viṣṇu, Buddha would have been received in a spirit of tolerance. But the way in which this Buddha-*avatāra* is described in the *Viṣṇupurāṇa* and the general Hindu attitude of considering both good and evil as coming from the same Supreme Being would suggest that we have here an early and unmistakably hostile Hindu text dealing with Buddhism.'

[130] See PARASHER (1991: 241–244).

[131] DONIGER O'FLAHERTY (1983: 117).

heretics.'[132] It has even been conjectured that these conservative segments of society transferred the messianic myth connected to the advent of Kalki(n) (or Pramiti/ Pramati) on historical rulers such as Candragupta II Vikramāditya (r. 375–415)[133] or Yaśodharman of Malvā, who defeated the Hūṇas around 530.[134]

As is testified to by the *vāyu-proktaṁ brahmâṇḍa-purāṇam*, heretics and heresy seem to enter apocalyptic discourse and anxieties in the early Gupta era and have clearly become their central concern as the Gupta empire starts to crumble. This is likely to reflect the Brahmanical confidence with Gupta, *bhāgavata* rule, i.e. with a partly restorative dynasty noted, e.g. for the repeated performance of the *aśva-medha*. But this may also betray Brahmanical exasperation with regard to its (alleged) policy of religious tolerance (at least as far as patronage and especially land grants were concerned). Thus, by the turn of the sixth century, the Brahmanical orthodoxy's hostility towards Buddhism and Jainism crystallises in a complex network of behavioural prescriptions, apocalyptic and messianic prophecies, aetiological myths and literary tropes deriding Buddhist monks and nuns.[135] It is easy to show that this complex network had a direct bearing on at least one decisive segment of Indian philosophy during the sixth century CE, Kumārilabhaṭṭa's Mīmāṁsā.

1.8. By the end of the fifth century CE, the bulk of the Mīmāṁsā still consists in a complex system of ritual exegesis introduced by an increasingly large but philosophically shaky section dedicated to Vedic apologetics. Sometime in the middle of the sixth century, however, Kumārilabhaṭṭa provides the system with a new shape and purport by turning it into a socially conservative and even restorative philosophical enterprise centred on the intrinsic and unconditioned validity of the *Veda*, as well as the normativity of all that can claim to be 'rooted' in the *Veda* (*veda-mūla*).[136] Kumārila's endeavour is not only apologetic (showing that the *Veda*, especially its positive and negative injunctions,

---

[132] A few pages earlier, DONIGER O'FLAHERTY (1983: 108) terms this story 'the most important of the anti-Buddhist myths of this period'. According to her, '[i]n the Purāṇic texts, the Buddha was depicted as deluded and destructive, for these texts of the Gupta period were weapons in a battle between the instigators of the Hindu revival and the still thriving establishments of Jainism and Buddhism' (1983: 108). As Yūko Yokochi has rightly pointed out to me, however, one should refrain from considering the Purāṇic milieux in their entirety (especially the Śaiva) as socially conservative and promoting Vedic restoration.

[133] On Pramiti and Candragupta Vikramāditya, see AGRAWALA (1963: 228–231) and DONIGER O'FLAHERTY (1983: 122–127).

[134] See JAYASWAL (1917).

[135] See BLOOMFIELD (1924) and KHER (1979).

[136] As Lawrence McCrea rightly insisted in his paper ('Rationalisation and Sincerity in Mīmāṁsā Hermeneutics') read at the conference 'World View and Theory in Indian Philosophy' (Barcelona, Casa Asia, 26–30 April, 2009), by no means does this imply that Kumārila's philosophy can be adequately characterised as orthodox in the primary, purely doctrinal sense of the word. Quite to the contrary, Kumārila's philosophy is of a decidedly innovative and thought-provoking character. See the paper in the present volume, pp. 119–135.

provides the only access to the supersensible Dharma), but also, perhaps even mainly, heresiological (refuting all extra-Vedic accounts of religious authority, reality, and epistemology). Since Buddhism radically challenges Vedic authority, the caste system, and Brahmanical prerogatives in symbolic and ritual matters, it becomes Kumārila's favourite target. In his *Śloka-vārttika* (MŚV), however, Kumārila rarely ventures beyond the limits of carefully argumented and well informed philosophical debate when criticising Buddhist doctrines. Things are quite different in the *Tantra-vārttika* (TV), Kumārila's commentary on *adhyāya*s 2 and 3, which, being only marginally concerned with philosophy proper, is very likely addressing a different, more ritually oriented audience. Here, Kumārila leaves the well-mannered ground of philosophical exchange to give free rein to his abhorrence and hostility towards Buddhism, allowing us to look deeper into the r e a l , non-philosophical motivations of Kumārila's radical anti-Buddhist stance. And Purāṇic apocalyptic eschatology is likely to bear a significant responsibility on Kumārila's heresiological attitude and rhetorical strategy.

Kumārila's familiarity with at least part of the apocalyptic prophecies considered above is clear from the following statement:

> 'It is recorded in the *purāṇa*s that in the *kali* [age, heretics] such as the Buddhists will cause the ruin of the Dharma. Who deigns to listen to their speech?'[137]

This important verse encapsulates all we already know about the Purāṇic emphasis on heterodoxy as a sign of the last age, on the prohibition of verbal and physical contact with the heretics, and on the latter's responsibility for the ruin of the Dharma. Consider now the following passage:

> 'By arguing and exhibiting that they contradict the Śruti, we show [in the present section] that the [treatises] that are not adopted by those who are familiar with the triple [Vedic science] cannot be relied upon [in order to cognise Dharma. These consist of] the treatises of [mixed] religion-cum-irreligion that are adopted by the Sāṅkhya, the Yoga, the Pāñcarātra, the Pāśupata, the Buddhists and the Jainas; they aim at nothing but proselytising people, acquiring [wealth and gaining public] veneration and renown; their composition is [entirely] based on reason(ing) [but such a reason(ing)] that is contrary to the triple [Vedic science], where the greed and other [vices of their authors] are manifest, and that resorts mainly to perception, inference, analogy and presumption; by exhibiting the occasional success of a few [magic] formulas

[137] TV ad MS 1.3.7/II: p. 123.24–25:
smaryante ca purāṇeṣu dharma-vipluti-hetavaḥ /
kalau śākyâdayas teṣāṁ ko vākyaṁ śrotum arhati //

> and decoctions capable of [things] such as curing poison, subjugating, ruining and maddening [other people], they teach various things that pertain mainly to [mere] livelihood [but] are perfumed by a few elements agreeing with the Śruti and the Smṛtis, such as non-violence, truthfulness, self-restraint, giving, compassion.'[138]

As Halbfass has repeatedly pointed out, Kumārila's endeavour must be understood as an attempt to neutralise ethical and religious relativism by demonstrating that only the *Veda* and the *Veda*-based Smṛtis can supply behavioural and practical maxims. In this passage, Kumārila identifies the pseudo-, heterodox Smṛtis challenging the Śruti and Smṛti by laying down norms that, for the most part, are found to contradict the *Veda*-based Dharma. And as we can see, Kumārila is far from attempting to federate all the denominations that post-classical India and Western scholarship have classified as 'hinduistic' or even 'orthodox'. According to him, Sāṁkhya, Yoga, Pāñcarātra and Pāśupata are no less heterodox than Buddhism and Jainism. Interestingly, Kumārila's emphasis on their vile and deceitful seduction echoes the *Viṣṇu-purāṇa*'s depiction of the heresiarch Māyāmoha. Moreover, most of the clichés that had long been associated with heretics recur in Kumārila's description, the most significant one being their resorting to autonomous, non-scripturally based reason(ing) and argumentation. As Kumārila says, these are the revilers of the *Veda* (*veda-nindaka*), the 'sophists' (*haituka*) and the deniers (*nāstika*) who according to Manu should be carefully avoided by righteous Brahmins.

In another passage of his *Tantra-vārttika*, Kumārila adduces three arguments in order to deny the Buddhist Dharma any Vedic foundation:

> 'With the exception of a few statements about [things] such as self-restraint and giving, all the statements of [heretics] such as the Buddhists contradict all the fourteen [authoritative] disciplines of knowledge and have been uttered by [people,] such as the Buddha, whose conduct was swerving from and contradictory to the path of the triple [Vedic science. And] since they have been delivered to deluded [people] who are external to the triple [Vedic

[138] TV ad MS 1.3.4 / II: p. 112.17–24: *yāny etāni trayī-vidbhir na parigṛhītāni ... lokôpasaṁgraha-lābha-pūjā-khyāti-prayojana-parāṇi trayī-viparītâsambaddha-dṛṣṭa-lobhâdi*[a]*-pratyakṣânumānôpamānârthāpatti-prāya-yukti-mūlôpanibaddhāni sāṅkhya-yoga-pāñca-rātra-pāśupata-śākya-*[*nir-*]*grantha-parigṛhīta-dharmâdharma-nibandhanāni viṣa-cikitsā-vaśī-karaṇôccāṭanônmādanâdi-samartha-katipaya-mantrâuṣadhi-kādācitka-siddhi-nidarśana-balenâhiṁsā-satya-vacana-dama-dāna-dayâdi-śruti-smṛti-saṁvādi-stokârtha-gandha-vāsita-jīvikā-prāyârthântarôpadeśīni ... teṣām evâitac-chruti-virodha-hetu-darśanābhyām anapekṣaṇīyatvaṁ pratipādyate.*

[[a] Emendation (Sanderson, May 2010): *-dṛṣṭa-lobhâdi-*; Ed.: *-dṛṣṭaśobhādi-*.] My translation of this passage is tentative (I owe the translation of *dharmâdharma* as 'religion-cum-irreligion' to Alexis Sanderson (personal communication, May 2010)).

science] and, for the most part, representatives of the fourth caste-class [i.e. Śūdras], they cannot be rooted in the *Veda*.'[139]

First, most of the Buddhist tenets contradict the *Veda*-based *vidyā-sthāna*s ('disciplines of knowledge'), a point he makes again elsewhere when spelling out the names of the authoritative disciplines:

> 'Indeed, the disciplines of knowledge accepted by the learned [ones] as authoritative regarding Dharma are strictly limited in number, fourteen or eighteen, and are called *Veda*, Upaveda ('secondary *Veda*'), Aṅga ('limb [of the *Veda*]'), Upāṅga ('secondary limb [of the *Veda*]'), *Aṣṭā-daśa-dharma-saṁhitā*, *purāṇa*s, Śākhā-śikṣā ('recensional phonetics') and Daṇḍa-nīti ('politics'). But the works of [heretics] such as the Buddhists or the Jainas are neither recorded nor accepted among them.'[140]

Second, the Buddha, considered a Kṣatriya, is found guilty of having transgressed his Sva-dharma through his teaching activities. And third, he preached his Dharma to Śūdras whom the Brahmanical orthodoxy denies any contact with the *Veda*. In short, the Buddhist Dharma cannot lay claim to *veda-mūlatva*.

The threat of ethical, doctrinal and ritual relativism is stressed in yet another interesting passage of the *Tantra-vārttika*. But here, Kumārila explains the decisive role that accrues to the orthodox literati and philosophers in the gloomy last age:

---

139 TV ad MS 1.3.4 / II: p. 113.22–114.1: *śākyâdi-vacanāni ... katipaya-dama-dānâdi-vacana-varjaṁ sarvāṇy eva samasta-catur-daśa-vidyā-sthāna-viruddhāni trayī-mārga-vyutthita-viruddhâcaraṇaiś ca buddhādibhiḥ praṇītāni. trayī-bāhyebhyaś caturtha-varṇa-niravasita-prāyebhyo vyāmūḍhebhyaḥ samarpitānîti na veda-mūlatvena sambhāvyante.*

140 TV ad MS 1.3.7 / II: p. 122.2–5: *parimitāny eva hi catur-daśāṣṭā-daśa vā vidyā-sthānāni dharma-pramāṇatvena śiṣṭaiḥ parigṛhītāni vedôpavedâṅgôpāṅgâṣṭā-daśa-dharma-saṁhitā-purāṇa-śākhā-śikṣā-daṇḍa-nīti-sañjñakāni. na ca teṣāṁ madhye bauddhârhatâdi-granthāḥ smṛtā gṛhītā vā.*

Note also TV ad MS 1.3.4 / II: p. 114.26–115.10:

eta eva ca te yeṣāṁ vāṅ-mātreṇâpi nârcanam /
pāṣaṇḍino vikarma-sthā haitukāś câita eva hi //
etadīyā granthā eva ca manvādibhiḥ parihāryatvenôktāḥ /
yā veda-bāhyāḥ smṛtayo yāś ca kāścit kudṛṣṭayaḥ /
sarvās tā niṣphalāḥ proktās tamo-niṣṭhā hi tāḥ smṛtāḥ //

tasmād dharmaṁ prati trayī-bāhyam evañ-jātīyakaṁ prāmāṇyenânapekṣyaṁ syād iti siddham.—'And these are the ones whom no [one should] honour even by mere words, for these are the heretics, the ones who persist in wrong action and the sophists [mentioned by Manu]. And [authoritative legislators] such as Manu have said that their works must be avoided. All the Smṛtis that are external to the *Veda* and those which exhibit wrong views have been declared useless, for they are recorded as resting on darkness. It is therefore established that something like that, external to the triple [Vedic science] as it is, cannot be relied upon as authoritative with regard to Dharma.' The first stanza is adapted from MDhŚ 4.30 = ViP 3.18.100.

> 'If we did not declare, without any respect [for them], these [treatises] as non-authoritative, other [people], thinking that [their non-authoritativeness] is impossible, would share their views. Or, due to the brilliant facility [manifested by them], their [constantly] stating reasons [for what they say] or the *kali-yuga* [which we are living in, these people] would fall into the error of renouncing, for instance, the violence [done] to animals [as it is] prescribed for the ritual. Or, basing themselves on the [idea] that, like those of Manu and others, [these treatises] are rooted in the Śruti, since there is no difference between being composed by a Brahmin and by a Kṣatriya, they would even *bona fide* (*sacetaso 'pi*) regard [what these treatises teach] as a mere alternative to [that which is] laid down in the Śruti. [But] even if one came across a certain contradictory Smṛti professed by [authoritative legislators] such as Manu, still this [possibility of following one or the other] only applies within the [Vedic corpus]. We shall [never re]gain the purity of the Dharma unless we refute all those [pseudo-paths] that totally contradict the [well-]established path of the triple [Vedic] science.'[141]

According to Kumārila and the *purāṇa*s he alludes to, heretics, especially the Buddhists, are responsible for the degeneration of Dharma during the *kali-yuga*. But as the *Yuga-purāṇa* and the messianic myth of Kalki(n) make clear, we should refrain from considering this eschatological degeneration as a purely mechanical, inescapable process. At least in certain places and under proper political circumstances (note Kumārila's insistence on the king in his discussion of the caste-classes, e.g. at MŚV 5.14.27–29), the repristination of the threatened Dharma (and even the rise of a new *kṛta-yuga*) is possible, and this is likely to be the meaning of Kumārila's philosophical endeavour to eradicate Buddhist heresy.

1.9. To be clear, my aim is certainly not to hold Gupta apocalyptic eschatology *itself* as responsible for the conspicuous heresiological turn of the Mīmāṁsā during the sixth century, and even less as responsible for the striking

[141] TV ad MS 1.3.4 / II: p. 113.1–10:

> *yadi anādareṇâiṣāṁ na kalpyetâpramāṇatā /*
> *aśakyâivêti matvânye bhaveyuḥ samadṛṣṭayaḥ //*
> *śobha-saukarya-hetûkti-kali-kāla-vaśena vā /*
> *yajñôkta-paśu-hiṁsâdi-tyāga-bhrāntim avāpnuyuḥ //*

brāhmaṇa-kṣatriya-praṇītatvâviśeṣeṇa vā māna-vādivad eva śruti-mūlatvam āśritya sacetaso 'pi śruti-vihitaiḥ saha vikalpam eva pratipadyeran.

> *tena yady api labhyeta smṛtiḥ kācid virodhinī /*
> *manv-ādy-uktā tathâpy asminn etad evôpayujyate //*
> *trayī-mārgasya siddhasya ye hy atyanta-virodhinaḥ /*
> *anirākṛtya tān sarvān dharma-śuddhir na labhyate //*

new directions taken by Indian philosophy from this century on.[142] Rather, my use of apocalyptic prophecies is aimed at showing the growth of a Brahmanical hostility that may, at least in part, explain why Brahmanical schools such as Nyāya and Mīmāṁsā turned their attention towards Buddhism, and why the Buddhist epistemologists changed their habits and the meaning of Buddhist philosophy radically during the sixth century. Brahmanical orthodoxy and Buddhism had been familiar with each other for many centuries, but in spite of the development of eristic-dialectical (*vāda*) traditions in both of them and the narratives of debates between their representatives, there are very few textual or otherwise documentable hints at there having been a sustained p h i l o - s o p h i c a l confrontation before the (end of the) fifth century.[143] The change

[142] As Kyō Kanō has pointed out to me, such a one-sided interpretation of the rise of sixth-century philosophy would certainly fail to explain intra-Brahmanical debate, e.g. between Nyāya and Mīmāṁsā.

[143] For an overview of narratives about debates in ancient and early medieval India, see BRONKHORST (2007) (with important epigraphic evidence) and CABEZÓN (2008) (mainly Chinese and Tibetan accounts); for an overview of extant eristic-dialectical literature, see KANG (2003) and (2006); for a paradigmatic account of debate, royal courts and academies and the rise of eristic-dialectical treatises, see FRAUWALLNER (1984). To sum up my views on this issue (for updated versions of these views and detailed analyses of the materials, see ELTSCHINGER (2012: §§ 2–4), and ELTSCHINGER (forthcoming: §§ 2.1.3–4, 2.2–3): With a few exceptions (Āryadeva's *Catuḥ-śataka*, the pseudo-Nāgārjuna's *Vaidalya-prakaraṇa*, discussions scattered throughout Vasubandhu's *Abhidharma-kośa-bhāṣya*), the Buddhists start criticising Brahmanical (and sporadically Jaina) philosophies systematically during the first half of the sixth century, or slightly earlier in the case of Dignāga (Dignāga, Dharmapāla, Dharmakīrti, Bhāviveka, Guṇamati, *Sagāthaka* of the *Laṅkâvatāra-sūtra* etc.). The same seems to hold true of the Brahmanical philosophers' critique of Buddhist doctrines (*Nyāya-bhāṣya* and *Nyāya-vārttika*, *Vṛtti-kāra-grantha* and especially MŚV, *Yukti-dīpikā*). More generally, sustained philosophical confrontation between Buddhists and non-Buddhists starts to be reflected in extant philosophical literature from the beginning of the sixth century onwards. It is certain, however, that certain Buddhists viewed debate, or, rather, the 'science of evidence' (*hetu-vidyā*, identified as debate in the *Hetu-vidyā* section' of the *Yogācāra-bhūmi*) as an heresiological, apologetical and proselytical device meant to defeat non-Buddhist opponents, protect the Sad-dharma, and strengthen the Buddhists' faith and number (*Bodhisattva-bhūmi*, *Mahāyāna-sūtrâlaṅkāra*, **Upāya-hṛdaya* / **Prayoga-sāra*). But it is noteworthy that although they are dedicated to the theory of debate, the Buddhist and non-Buddhist eristic-dialectical traditions (reflected in at least parts of works such as the *Caraka-saṁhitā*, *Nyāya-sūtra*, *Ṣaṣṭi-tantra*, *Yogācāra-bhūmi*, *Abhidharma-samuccaya*, *Vāda-vidhi* etc.) contain neither descriptions of actual debates nor materials testifying to their being intended for disputations between, say, Brahmins and Buddhists (the '*Hetu-vidyā* section' of the *Yogācāra-bhūmi* even testifies to the contrary, i.e. that disputations rather took place between Buddhist denominations themselves, as extant Madhyamaka, Yogācāra and Abhidharma works, but also 'doxographies' such as those of Vasumitra, Bhavya and Vinītadeva, so amply witness). This is certainly not to say that direct encounters between Brahmins and Buddhists of different persuasions never took place before the turn of the sixth century. What I mean is that the extant philosophical and eristic-dialectical literature, as well as narratives of debates, provides no conclusive evidence to this effect. As far as the narratives are concerned, however, we may look for alternative

occurring at this time can hardly be explained purely incrementally in terms of a *problemgeschichte*. In this case, such an explanation would be just as good as no explanation at all. To cite the transition from a 'systematic' period of Indian philosophy, in which all schools, gradually but separately, built their own doctrinal identities, to a 'post-systematic' period, in which these schools engaged in disputation, still requires an explanation as to why this transition occurred and why all these schools were simultaneously ready and eager to debate with one another. The factors responsible for this sudden outburst of philosophical confrontation cannot be seriously looked for within the competing traditions themselves, since here the reasons are most likely to be of a non-philosophical and socio-historical character. But by looking closer at the evolution of the Brahmanical apocalyptic eschatology, I hope I have been able to uncover one part of the ideological background against which these philosophical shifts and many other things make sense. What we need is a general explanation as to why so many innovations in Buddhist India took place slightly before or after 500 CE: the foundation of these *mahā-vihāra*s or *vihāra-maṇḍala*s 'mimicking feudally grounded fortresses',[144] the nearly contemporaneous rise of Buddhist Tantrism and epistemology, the strong decline of Abhidharmic creativity and controversy,[145] etc. Needless to say, the present paper does not provide an explanation of this type, but it highlights one *sine qua non* factor of this explanation, viz. a dramatic increase of hostility towards Buddhism as the Gupta dynasty, until then tolerant and maintaining the status quo, starts to crumble.

2. Indian Buddhist apocalypticism.

2.0. In spite of a few recent groundbreaking studies, research on Indian Buddhist apocalypticism is still in its infancy. Improving on the work of

interpretations. In this connection, CABEZÓN (2008) provides insightful remarks (but note that CABEZÓN (2008: 72) considers it 'foolish ... simply to lump all this material under the category of "legend" and to summarily dismiss it'). As CABEZÓN (2008: 90) rightly points out, '[g]iven the importance of debate/argument to Indian identity, it is not surprising to see the narratives of the great debates as central features of the lives of these individuals [Nāgārjuna, Āryadeva, Asaṅga, Vasubandhu, Dignāga, Dharmakīrti etc.].' In other words, these stories, or what CABEZÓN (2008: 91) aptly calls 'argumentational lives', have a 'powerful force in the construction of scholastic communal identity'. Whatever their value as witnesses of actual, historical debates, 'these stories create for elite Chinese and Tibetan monastic audiences—and to the extent that they were built on Indian fragments, perhaps for late Indian monastic audiences as well—a sense of identity through varied forms of affiliation to a relatively fixed group of eminent Indian monks who together form a kind of "fleshly canon," if you will' (CABEZÓN (2008: 90)). A similar 'fleshly canon' is recorded in the very interesting Jaina inscription (twelfth century, near Śravaṇabeḷagoḷa) discussed by BRONKHORST (2007: 269–272).

[144] DAVIDSON (2002: 167).

[145] On the latter two aspects, see ELTSCHINGER (forthcoming: especially §§ 2.3) concerning the decline of Abhidharmic creativity.

PRZYLUSKI and LAMOTTE, NATTIER has provided a detailed picture of the Buddhist 'timetables of decline' through her analysis of the 'Prophecy of Kauśāmbī' embedded in the *Candra-garbha-sūtra* and other sources. More recently, BOUCHER's in-depth investigation of the *Rāṣṭra-pāla-paripṛcchā-sūtra* (RPS) has drawn attention to the apocalyptic dimensions of the early Mahāyāna's vitriolic criticism of mainstream Buddhism in its concessions to secular society. However, assuming that apocalyptic rhetoric was nearly always associated with present-day events and/or situations of a social, political, economic or institutional nature, much research remains to be carried out regarding the historical background of at least some of the most significant prophecies of decline. There is indeed evidence to suggest that major political breaks in Indian history—the rise of Kushana rule, the Gupta empire and its gradual collapse, the alleged Hūṇa terror and the rise of Islamic domination—brought about an increase (if not always a complete reassessment) of Indian Buddhist apocalypticism. Whereas Indic sources are scarce in number and most often are difficult to interpret, the Chinese Buddhist canon and Dunhuang materials seem to provide valuable information in this regard. However, as LÉVI and especially ZÜRCHER have pointed out, most of the relevant materials are of an apocryphal character, or at least can be shown to have been reworked and/or interpolated in early medieval China (albeit through the agency of Indian translators like Narendrayaśas) under purely Chinese religio-political circumstances. One should, then, be extremely cautious with such materials when tackling Indian apocalypticism and its historical background.

2.1. Two things are striking about the Indian Buddhist accounts of time and history with regard to the duration of Buddhism itself. First, the surprisingly short life-span ascribed to Śākyamuni's dispensation. As already pointed out by NATTIER, the timetables of decline prophesising the demise of the Good Law (*sad-dharma-vipralopa*) range from 500 to 5,000 years after the Buddha's *parinirvāṇa*,[146] and seem to have been gradually updated according to the

[146] These figures may or may not be further subdivided into distinct phases that account for the gradual decline (see NATTIER (1991: 27–64)). Among the many interesting results of NATTIER's groundbreaking study, one may note that, contrary to what the standard rendering ('counterfeit Doctrine') might suggest, Skt. *sad-dharma-pratirūpaka* hardly ever seems to hint at a second, degenerate period of the Law (SN II: p. 224.5–6 being the only exception; see NATTIER (1991: 87)). The Indian Buddhist sources also do not seem to provide any textual foundation for the East Asian third period of Buddhism, the so-called *mofa* / *mappō* (末法). According to NATTIER, the most likely candidate as an equivalent of *mofa*, Skt. *paścima-kāla*, does not mean 'the final period', but 'the latter period'. This point has been challenged by BOUCHER (2008: 66) who contends that, at least in the context of the *Rāṣṭra-pāla-paripṛcchā-sūtra*, 'final' provides a more satisfactory rendering than 'latter'. Note, however, that BOUCHER does not contest NATTIER's results regarding the complete lack of an Indian Buddhist basis for the triple division of Dharma into [*sad-dharma* /] *zhengfa* / *shōbō* (正法), [*(sad-)dharma-pratirūpaka* /] *xiangfa* / *zōbō* (像法) and [*paścima-kāla* /] *mofa* / *mappō*. For a critique of NATTIER's view of *mofa* as a Chinese 'apocryphal word', see HUBBARD (1993: 141–142).

Buddhists' awareness of the time elapsed since the passing away of their founder. Second, the strong emphasis laid on purely internal causes of decline. According to NATTIER (1991: 120), the Pāli canon points to seven causes connected with the 'laxity within the *saṅgha*': '1. the admission of women into the monastic community;[147] 2. lack of respect toward various elements of the Buddhist tradition; 3. lack of diligence in meditation practice; 4. carelessness in the transmission of the teachings; 5. the emergence of divisions within the *saṅgha*; 6. the emergence of a false or "counterfeit" Dharma;[148] and 7. excessive association with secular society.'[149] Interestingly enough, the Pāli canon shows no awareness of any external cause of the decline and/or demise of the Good Law. Like the sources to be considered below, the Pāli canon does not hold outsiders (*tīrthika*) as instrumental in the final collapse of Buddhism.

Among these internal causes, factors 5 and 7 recur with considerable frequency in Mahāyānist as well as non-Mahāyānist sources. In the *Thera-gāthā*, for instance, the elder Pārāpariya complains that in earlier times, monks 'were not as eager for the necessities of life, for medicines and supplies, as they were for the annihilation of the outflows (*āsava*). In the forest, at the foot of trees, in caves and grottos, devoting themselves to seclusion, they lived making [the annihilation of the outflows] their aim. ... Now, these elders ... have all passed away.'[150] In his *Manoratha-pūraṇī*, Buddhaghosa declares that monks 'will enter into secular occupations and ordinary family life.'[151] The shorter *Parinirvāṇa-sūtra*,[152] which divides its thousand-year timetable into ten hundred-year periods, states that '[d]uring the first several periods believers are still devoted to the practice and preservation of the Dharma, but as time goes on they become more preoccupied with the externals of the Buddhist tradition rather than its essence. A turn for the worse begins during the seventh and

[147] As NATTIER (1991: 32–33) convincingly shows, the famous story according to which the admission of women into the regular community was responsible for the shortening of the Dharma's duration can be found only in Mahīśāsaka, Dharmaguptaka, Theravādin, Haimavata and Sarvāstivādin sources, i.e. in sources originally belonging to the Sthavira line. In other words, '[t]he date of emergence of this tradition should ... be placed during the period from 340–200 BCE'. On the *Mahā-vibhāṣā*'s exegetical accommodation of this tradition implying a 500-year timetable in contrast to the Sarvāstivādin 1,000-year timetable, see NATTIER (1991: 43–44) and LAMOTTE (1976: 212–213).

[148] See above, n. 146.

[149] NATTIER (1991: 120).

[150] *Thera-gāthā* verses 924–925 and 928 in NATTIER's (1991: 124) revised translation. According to NATTIER (1991: 125), Pārāpariya condemns 'the excessive involvement of monks with secular society'; in the following stanzas, he also vituperates 'the variety of tactics used by monks to acquire worldly goods and fame' (verses 936–944).

[151] NATTIER (1991: 57). Timetable: 5,000 years divided into 5 × 1,000 years (the basis of the Theravāda doctrine). Note that this statement concerns the end of the fourth 1,000-year period.

[152] *Folin niepanji fazhu jing* 佛臨涅槃記法住經 T 390. See NATTIER (1991: 43, n. 40) and LAMOTTE (1976: 213).

eighth centuries, and during the ninth and tenth periods Buddhist monks turn their attention almost exclusively to worldly activities.'[153] As for the Tibetan version of the *Candra-garbha-sūtra*,[154] it proclaims that 'during the second sub-period even monks will not practice the Dharma in accordance with the Buddha's teachings. They will engage in worldly pursuits, occupying themselves in a variety of secular trades.'[155] The issue of quarrels and dissension within the Buddhist *saṅgha* is no less recurrent. According to the *Aṅguttara-nikāya*, 'then [monks] revile one another, accuse one another, quarrel with one another, and repudiate one another; those of no faith do not find faith there and the faithful fall away.'[156] The *Prophecy of Kātyāyana*[157] predicts that 'there will be anger and fighting.'[158] The Chinese version of the *Candra-garbha-sūtra*[159] foresees that 'in the latter five hundred years, quarrelling and debate will be well-established.'[160]

2.2. The emphasis on internal divisions finds its paradigmatic expression in a story that would eventually transcend sectarian affiliations and geographical/cultural borders, the 'Prophecy of Kauśāmbī'. According to NATTIER (1991: 226), the 'Kauśāmbī decline prophecy appears to have emerged in northwest India sometime between the second century CE and the middle of the third', under Kushana rule. The archetype of the story[161] as reconstructed by NATTIER can be summarised as follows: 'Three foreign kings (the Greeks, Sakas, and Parthians) are named as the cause of disruption within the Indian Buddhist community.[162] A pious Buddhist king (unnamed), ruling at Kauśāmbī, invites all the monks of Jambudvīpa to a *mahā-dāna* feast at the suggestion of his

[153] NATTIER (1991: 45).

[154] For a critical edition and English translation of the Tibetan text, see NATTIER (1991: 228–277). Timetable: 2,000 years divided into 4 × 500 (with the last 500-year period divided into two further periods).

[155] NATTIER (1991: 53).

[156] AN III: p. 180 in Nattier's revised translation (1991: 123). According to NATTIER (1991: 123), '[m]ore specifically, the issue in this passage seems to be the hostility and argumentation that can emerge in sectarian rivalries.' On early Buddhist attitudes towards debate and argumentation, see COLLINS (1982: 127–131 and 139–141), and ELTSCHINGER (2012: § 1).

[157] *Foshi biqiu jiazhanyan shuo fa meijin jie baiershi zhang* 佛使比丘迦旃延說法沒盡偈百二十章 T 2029. Timetable: 1,000 years divided into 3 × 300 and 1 × 100 years.

[158] T 2029, 49.12b26–c1 in NATTIER's translation (1991: 45).

[159] I.e. section 15 (*Yuezangfen* 月藏分) of the *Mahā-sannipāta-sūtra* (*Dajijing* 大集經 T 397). Timetable: 2,000 years divided into 4 × 500 years.

[160] T 397[15], 13.370b8–11 in Nattier's translation (1991: 52).

[161] This archetype probably consisted only of verses. Of uncertain sectarian affinity, it may have been recorded in a northwest Prākṛt in the Kharoṣṭhī script.

[162] In later recensions of the story, these Yavana, Śaka and Pahlava kings are reported to have invaded northwest India and to have ruined Buddhist *stūpa*s and temples.

advisor, the monk Śiṣyaka.[163] A dispute then breaks out between an Arhat, Sūrata, who insists on strict observance of all monastic rules, and a group of more complacent monks;[164] Sūrata is killed by a disciple of Śiṣyaka, who in turn is killed by a *yakṣa*.'[165] This prophecy of decline might be the earliest among those ascribing external causes to the demise of the Dharma. But this story reveals more than that. As NATTIER (1991: 227) points out, 'it is not the invasions themselves that are portrayed as bringing an end to the Dharma ... but the munificence of a well intentioned Buddhist king. Moreover, it is the Buddhist community itself ... whose actions result in the death of an Arhat, and ultimately in the disappearance of the Dharma from the world.' According to her, this story 'makes good sense as the product of a Kushan environment', in a time where 'the Buddhist subjects of ... a cosmopolitan realm [were] presumably enjoying all the material and spiritual benefits afforded by the long-lasting *pax kushanica*.'[166]

2.3. If NATTIER's hypothesis is correct, one might extrapolate the following explanation: the 'Prophecy of Kauśāmbī' perhaps mirrors the worries aroused in a disciplinary conservative fraction of north-western Buddhist communities by the *saṅgha*'s laxity under Kushana rule. Indeed, the Kushan period coincides with major institutional and economic breaks within Buddhist communities (among them, the 'emergence in India of a new type of social institution with considerable clout: the fully institutionalised, permanently housed, landed monastery'[167]). Put in other words, the early centuries CE lay the foundations of what Gregory SCHOPEN has termed 'Mainstream Buddhism', and inaugurate the 'Middle period' of Indian Buddhism. But if the 'Prophecy of Kauśāmbī' *in statu nascendi* still gives voice to traditionalist claims within 'Nikāyic' communities (Dharmaguptaka, Sarvāstivādin?), it certainly did not take long for this new form of institutional Buddhism to arouse the criticism of yet another segment of its members, those who were eventually responsible for at least one of the trends of early Mahāyāna. Daniel BOUCHER provides the following summary of recent research and reflections on this issue:

---

[163] In later recensions of the story, the king is named Mahendrasena and is said to have crushed the three foreign invaders; the invitation to the feast (sometimes a *pañca-varṣa* feast) is sometimes accounted for as expressing the king's feelings of guilt with regard to the death of so many people in war.

[164] In various recensions of the story, the *tri-piṭaka* master Śiṣyaka himself decides to abridge the *prātimokṣa-sūtra* recitation on the grounds that the precepts are no longer respected by anybody. Sūrata protests this, arguing that the full text should be recited, which arouses the wrath of Sūrata's disciples.

[165] NATTIER (1991: 215 and 217). In later recensions of the story, this murder is followed by a struggle involving all the monks gathered in Kauśāmbī (i.e. all the monks of Jambudvīpa). This results in the death of all of them, which coincides with the final demise of the Dharma. At any rate, the story ends with the murder of both the last *tri-piṭaka* master and the last Arhat.

[166] NATTIER (1991: 227).

[167] SCHOPEN (2004/1994: 81/553).

> 'What Gregory Schopen has termed the Middle Period of Indian Buddhism, roughly the first half of the first millennium, can be characterised by a highly organised, sedentary Buddhism with a complex administration governed by an equally complex legal system. Monks living in these monasteries were bound in a tangled web of relationships to lay donors and their fellow monks, relationships that required the constant negotiation of property rights and ritual obligations. The monastic disciplinary codes give every indication that the monks governed by them were fully entrenched in the socioeconomic milieu of contemporary society and were "preoccupied—if not obsessed—with avoiding any hint to social criticism and with maintaining the status quo at almost every cost".'[168]

As scholars such as SCHOPEN, SILK, NATTIER and BOUCHER have strongly argued in recent years, it seems nearly certain that at least some of the promoters of early Mahāyāna reacted against Mainstream Buddhism by clamouring for a return to wilderness dwelling and the strict observance of the purificatory ascetic qualities (*dhuta-guṇa*). And this gave rise to new apocalyptic voices. BOUCHER's work on the *Rāṣṭra-pāla-paripṛcchā-sūtra* provides a unique opportunity to take a closer look into the development of this *locus classicus* of the Mahāyānist criticism of the Mainstream's deep interaction with secular society and upper-class donors. According to BOUCHER (2008: 78), the authors of the *Rāṣṭra-pāla-paripṛcchā-sūtra* 'reject accommodation with the socioeconomic milieu by insisting on a rigorist interpretation of monastic discipline'. The *Rāṣṭra-pāla-paripṛcchā-sūtra* is a 'sectarian product at the level of intramonastic tension and fractionalization'[169] where 'the status quo relationship between monks and laity, a relationship founded on the exchange of material and symbolic commodities ... had become disordered.'[170] As FINOT already noticed,[171] the *Rāṣṭra-pāla-paripṛcchā-sūtra*'s depiction of contemporary Buddhism is perhaps unique in its severity. Its authors bemoan fellow monastics for behaving like householders, roaming 'among upper-class patrons in towns' and performing 'services for people in the household.'[172] They have wives, sons and daughters, delight in visiting relatives, and think about them day and night.

[168] BOUCHER (2008: 67), quoting SCHOPEN (2004/1995: 96/478).

[169] BOUCHER (2008: 80).

[170] BOUCHER (2008: 83).

[171] See FINOT (1901: ix–xi). On p. ix: 'La prophétie est en réalité un tableau satirique des mœurs relâchées du clergé bouddhique. La vivacité et la précision de cette peinture, qui reflète sans doute des faits réels, en font un intéressant document d'histoire religieuse.'

[172] The following examples are borrowed from BOUCHER's translation (2008: 137–141) of RPS verses 177–216 (see also FINOT's French translation in FINOT (1901: ix–xi)). For similar Chinese (apocryphal) statements, see ZÜRCHER (1982: 17–18).

They give themselves up to agriculture, keep cows, horses and asses. Always preoccupied with profit, they practise trades, have stores and many goods, and mix up what belongs to the *stūpa*, to the *saṅgha* and to themselves. Engaged in the affairs of the monastery, they have male and female slaves and lots of attendants. As a predictable corollary to their intimate association with secular society, they have given up meditation, study and the virtues of the Buddha; deficient in the virtues of a monk, they are nothing but hypocrites and deceivers. These monks have no regard for the rules of training or for the *prātimokṣa* or for *vinaya*; given to immorality and devoid of prescriptions, they are undisciplined, arrogant, and consumed by jealousy and pride. Last but not least, they are surrounded by a coterie of students who venerate them, but who themselves are also undisciplined. The description given here is far from exhausting the depiction in the *Rāṣṭra-pāla-paripṛcchā-sūtra*, and provides a lively Buddhist counterpart to the Epic and Purāṇic accounts of the *kali-yuga*/*yugânta*.

No less interesting is the historical stratigraphy of the text. The *Rāṣṭra-pāla-paripṛcchā-sūtra* was first translated into Chinese in 270 by the Yuezhi monk Dharmarakṣa, and a second time around 585–592 by the Gandharian monk Jñānagupta.[173] As BOUCHER observes, '[t]he crucial period, then, for understanding significant developments in the history of the text can be placed roughly between 270 and 550 CE, corresponding approximately to the north India Gupta period.'[174] Interestingly enough, although the overall charge is basically the same in the two earliest Chinese versions, the text as translated by Dharmarakṣa seems to contain no hint of apocalyptic rhetoric. The references to the pitiable behaviour of contemporary monks as a sign of the imminent demise of the Good Law only appears in the broadly expanded text translated by Jñānagupta. These Gupta or slightly post-Gupta interpolations consistently link apocalypticism with the disruptive forces undermining the *saṅgha*: 'Hostile to one another, they are constantly engaged in seeking each other's faults … Monks, who are unrestrained during the final period [of the Dharma] are far removed from morality and virtue. They cause this Dharma to disappear as a result of their contentiousness, strife, and envy.'[175] Or, a few pages later: 'Always honoured but devoid of virtue, [such monks] will be divisive, treach-

---

[173] Respectively, *Deguang taizi jing* 德光太子經 T 170 and *Huguo pusa hui* 護國菩薩會 T 310[18]. There exists a third Chinese translation of the RPS, executed in 994 by the Song translator Dānapāla (*Huguo zunzhe suowen dasheng jing* 護國尊者所問大乘經 T 321). See BOUCHER (2008: xvii–xix).

[174] BOUCHER (2008: 109).

[175] RPS verses 84ab and 85 (FINOT (1901: 17.12 and 16–17)):

te ca parasparam eva ca dviṣṭā chidra-gaveṣaṇa-nitya-prayuktāḥ / …
evam asaṁyata paścima-kāle bhikṣava śīla-guṇeṣu sudūre /
te 'ntara-hāpayiṣyant' ima dharmaṁ[a] *bhaṇḍana-vigraha-īrṣyā-vaśena* // 85 //

[[a] Emendation (Sanderson, May 2010): *'ntara-hāpayiṣyant' ima dharmaṁ*; Ed.: *'ntara hāpayiṣyanti mad-harmaṁ*.] Translation BOUCHER (2008: 127).

erous, and fond of quarrelling. They are venerated as the Teacher by the people, but they will be consumed by pride and conceit … The destruction of the Dharma occurs during the very dreadful final period. And such undisciplined monks as these will cause the ruin of this teaching of mine.'[176]

2.4.1. There is at least some evidence to the effect that the chaotic final decades of the Gupta rule as well as the early post-Gupta period not only witnessed an increase in apocalyptic rhetoric, but also recorded significant shifts in strategy, contents and emphasis. In this regard, the tenth chapter (*sagāthaka*) of the *Laṅkâvatāra-sūtra* (LAS) provides a very interesting testimony. Whereas its chapters 2–8 had already been translated into Chinese in 443,[177] chapters 1, 9 and 10 are only recorded in Bodhiruci's 513 translation.[178] The late composition of the relevant passages can hardly be questioned since they refer explicitly to the Guptas. Most interesting is the fact that this text resorts exclusively to the Hindu cosmological and apocalyptic system of the four ages in order to account for the imminent demise of the Dharma. In verse 804, the former Buddha Viraja, who claims to belong to the 'golden age' or *kṛta-yuga*, speaks as follows:

> 'Neither in the *dvāpara*[-*yuga*], nor in the *tretā*[-*yuga*], nor afterwards in the *kali-yuga* do [Buddhas,] the protectors of the world, arise. They [only] get awakened in the *kṛta-yuga*.'[179]

With no fear of contradicting himself, Viraja proclaims, in verse 794:

> '[There are four ages:] the *kṛta-yuga*, the *tretā*[-*yuga*], the *dvāpara* [-*yuga*] as well as the *kali*[-*yuga*]. Myself and others [arose] in the *kṛta-yuga*, [whereas] the Lion of the Śākyas [will arise] in the *kali-yuga*.'[180]

---

[176] RPS verses 204 and 207 (FINOT (1901: 31.19–20 and 32.5–6)):

sada sat-kṛtā guṇa-vihīnā bheda-sūcakāḥ kalaha-kāmāḥ /
te śāstṛ-sammata janasya te ca bhaviṣyanti māna-mada-dagdhāḥ // 204 //
… etādṛśās[a] *carima-kāle dharma-vilopa vartati sughore*[b] */*
ta câpi bhikṣava adāntā nāśayitāra śāsanaṁ mamedam // 207 //

[[a] Emendation (BOUCHER < MS, Tib.): *etādṛśāś*; Ed.: *etādṛśaś*; [b] Emendation (BOUCHER < MS): *sughore*; Ed.: *sughoraḥ*.] Translation BOUCHER (2008: 140) (slightly modified).

[177] *Lengqie abaduoluo baojing* 楞伽阿跋多羅寶經 T 670.

[178] *Rulengqiejing* 入楞伽經 T 671.

[179] LAS 10.804:

na dvāpare na tretāyāṁ na paścāc ca kalau yuge /
sambhavo loka-nāthānāṁ sambudhyante kṛte yuge //

[180] LAS 10.794:

kṛta-yugaś ca tretā ca dvāparaṁ kalinas tathā /
ahaṁ cânye kṛta-yuge śākya-siṁhaḥ kalau yuge //

On *kalina*, see BHSD 172[b].

No less contradictory but still more interesting is, however, the properly apocalyptic kernel of the passage:

> 'Once I [shall] have passed away, afterwards, there will be [teachers] such as Vyāsa, Kaṇāda, Ṛṣabha, Kapila and the Guide of the Śākyas. Once I have passed away, within one hundred years there will be Vyāsa as well as [his] *Bhārata*, the Pāṇḍavas, the Kauravas, Rāma and, afterwards, Kṛṣṇa.[181] [There will be] the Mauryas, the Nandas and the Guptas, and then, the *mleccha*s [will be] the vilest among rulers. At the end of the *mleccha*s, [there will be] an armed conflagration (*śastra-saṅkṣobha*), and at the end of the warfare (*śastrânte*), the *kali-yuga* [will open up]. And at the end of the *kali-yuga*, the Good Law will no longer be cultivated by people.'[182]

Although the sequence hinted at is in itself perfectly clear, it is of course difficult to assess the identity of the *mleccha*s (Hūṇas?) as well as the exact circumstances presiding over the *sad-dharma-vipralopa*. One may tentatively interpret the sequence linking *mleccha* invasion–fight–demise of the Dharma along the lines of the 'Prophecy of Kauśāmbī', in which the sequence of events is the following: foreign invasion–victory over invaders–demise of the Dharma due to the agency of strictly internal disruptive forces.[183]

---

[181] According to BHSD 441^{b}, the MS reads here *saurī* and not *maurī*, 'and this or *śauriḥ* is surely to be read (Skt. Śauriḥ = Kṛṣṇaḥ).'

[182] LAS 10.784–786:

> *vyāsaḥ kaṇāda ṛṣabhaḥ kapilaḥ śākya-nāyakaḥ /*
> *nirvṛte mama paścāt tu bhaviṣyanty evam-ādayaḥ* // 784 //
> *mayi nirvṛte varṣaśate vyāso vai bhāratas tathā /*
> *pāṇḍavāḥ kauravā rāmaḥ paścāc [ch]aurī bhaviṣyati* // 785 //
> *mauryā nandāś ca guptāś ca tato mlecchā nṛpâdhamāḥ /*
> *mlecchânte śastra-saṅkṣobhaḥ śastrânte ca kalir yugaḥ /*
> *kali-yugânte lokaiś ca sad-dharmo hi na bhāvitaḥ* // 786 //

Let it be noted that the events following the disappearance of the Good Law, and more specifically what is likely to be interpreted as the final cataclysm and rise of a new *kṛta-yuga*, betray a strong alignment with non-Buddhist standards; see LAS 10.787cd–789ab:

> *vahny-āditya-samāyogāt kāma-dhātur vidīryate //*
> *punaḥ saṁsthāsyate divyaṁ tasmiṁl lokaḥ pravartsyate /*
> *cātur-varṇā nṛpêndrāś ca ṛṣayo dharmam eva ca //*
> *vedāś ca yajñaṁ dānaṁ ca dharma-sthā vartsyate punaḥ* / —
>
> —'Due to the conjunction of fire and sun, the realm of desire is [then] torn to pieces. [But] heaven will come again, and within it the world proceeds [again]. The four [social] classes, the kings, the *ṛṣi*s and the Dharma, the *Veda*s, the sacrifice and giving will re-arise conformable to Dharma.'

[183] The same pattern can be seen in a prophecy translated and most probably adapted by Narendrayaśas. See below, § 2.4.3.

2.4.2. But the *Laṅkâvatāra-sūtra* is not the only late fifth-century to sixth-century *sūtra* to reflect a Buddhist appropriation of the Brahmanical *yugas*.[184] In an extremely suggestive passage,[185] the *Kāraṇḍa-vyūha-sūtra* (KVS), a Mahāyānist text dealing with Avalokiteśvara's miraculous endeavours for the sake of the living beings, Hindu deities, most importantly Śiva Mahêśvara, are reported to originate from Avalokiteśvara. To Śiva, the great Bodhisattva delivers the following prophecy:

> 'O Mahêśvara, you will be [active] when the *kali-yuga* arrives.
> Born as the foremost of the gods in the realm of suffering beings,

[184] The *kali-yuga* is indeed the subject matter of a thirteen-verse work (*Kali-yuga-parikathā*, KYP) ascribed to the famous second-century Buddhist scholar Mātṛceṭa. According to DIETZ (2000: 173), '[d]ie Authentizität der Autorschaft des Mātṛceṭa läßt sich nicht mit Sicherheit nachweisen', and no parallel to the Stotras of Mātṛceṭa can be identified. In my opinion, this short text is strongly indebted to Epic and Purāṇic accounts of the *kali-yuga* due to its strong emphasis on the cosmological, social, political and ethical conditions that are supposed to characterise the *kali-yuga*. Cosmic and natural disorder is best represented (KYP 3, 4b, 6d, 7cd, 8cd, 9ac, 10cd), at times even caused by human immorality and disregard for Dharma (in its Brahmanical version!). Second in number are the references to the humans' vices and depravities, ignorance and immorality (KYP 1, 5cd, 8b, 11b and d, 12b, 13a). Issues recurring in the Brahmanical sources include women's misbehaviour (KYP 9d, 11a), plagues and illnesses (KYP 4a, 8a), the injustice of kings (KYP 7a, 10a, 10d), warfare and other threats (KYP 5b, 6c, 7ab), breaks in social and family order (KYP 10a, 11a), the importance of money and wealth (KYP 2b, 5a), and misplaced veneration (KYP 2a, 5ab, 6d, 9d). While these purely secular concerns represent more than 90 per cent of the whole, allusions to Buddhist motifs (*bhadra-kalpa*, KYP 4c, 4d, 11bc, 12; Māra KYP 13) and to the decline of the Buddhist law are remarkably few in number: (1) 'Die Betrüger werden die Wahre Lehre (*saddharma*) zugrunde richten' (KYP 5d: *g.yon can rnams kyis dam chos bsnub par 'gyur*; translation DIETZ (2000: 180)); (2) 'Nur wenig sind es, die in Zucht lebend sich der höchsten Lehre zuwenden. Zweifellos wird die Lehre der Seher nach kurzer Zeit verfallen' (KYP 6ab: *gaṅ źig sdom pa la gnas bstan pa'i mchog la'jug par byed pa ñuṅ / the tshom yod min draṅ sroṅ bstan pa riṅ por mi thogs nub par'gyur /* ; translation DIETZ (2000: 180–181)); (3) 'Zusammen mit dem Dharma fliehen die Parivrājakas und Asketen' (KYP 10c: *chos daṅ rab byuṅ dka' thub rnams'bros*; translation DIETZ (2000: 183)). I am inclined to consider the *Kali-yuga-parikathā* as a rather late (?) work modelled on Brahmanical prophecies and providing a very weakly 'buddhicised' account of the *kali-yuga*, one, at any rate, that lacks an equivalent in Buddhist literature. The earliest Buddhist reference to the *kali-yuga* I am aware of is Vasubandhu's AKBh 266.25–267.2 (ad AK 4.110d), though it does not occur in an apocalyptic context: *śākyamunir nāma samyak-sambuddhaḥ pūrvaṁ babhūva. yatra bhagavatā bodhisattva-bhūtenâdyaṁ praṇidhānaṁ kṛtam. evam-prakāra evâhaṁ buddho bhaveyam iti no 'py evaṁ kali-yuga evôtpannavān āryavat tasyâpy evaṁ varṣa-sāhasrântaṁ śāsanaṁ babhūva.*—'Formerly there was a perfectly awakened [Buddha also] named Śākyamuni under whom [our] Blessed One, [still] in the state of a Bodhisattva, made his initial vow [, saying]: "May I become a Buddha of exactly this kind!" Just like ours, he also arose during a *kali-yuga*, [and] like the Noble One his teaching also lasted one thousand years.' According to AKVy 432.7–8 the Bodhisattva was named Prabhāsa and was the son of a potter (*kumbha-kāra-kumāra*). On this earlier Śākyamuni, see AK_2 III: p. 228.

[185] I owe this reference to GONZÁLEZ-REIMANN (2002: 171–172). On the *Kāraṇḍa-vyūha-sūtra* in general, see STUDHOLME (2002).

> you will be called the creator and the agent [of the world]. All beings who hold the following discourse to(/among) ordinary people will be deprived of the path to enlightenment: "It is said that space is [Mahêśvara's] *liṅga*, [and that] the earth is [his] pedestal; it is the receptacle of all beings, [and it is] because [they] merge(/fuse) [into it that it] is called *liṅga*".'[186]

This passage somehow echoes the later Buddhist tantric apologetic strategies, according to which even the non-Buddhist, Śaiva esoteric procedures (which readers or practitioners of the *Mahā-vairocanâbhisambodhi-sūtra* or the *Mañjuśriya-mūla-kalpa* might suspect as hiding behind these Tantras) were actually revealed by the Buddha.[187] Most telling is our passage's explicit association of Śiva and Śaivism to the *kali-yuga*. Indeed, as recent and ongoing research by SANDERSON shows, Śaivism appears to be the most successful Indic religion from at least the sixth century onwards, with its increasing 'appeal to royal patrons by extending and adapting its repertoire to contain a body of rituals and theory that legitimated, empowered, or promoted key elements of the social, political and economic process that characterizes the early medieval period.'[188] To put it in other words, from this period Śaivism is the most dangerous religio-political challenge to Buddhism. Buddhism does not respond to this challenge on a philosophical level (at least not until its tenth-century confrontation with Kashmir Śaivism), but by developing an esoteric synthesis of its own (if one may describe it this way!). As the *Kāraṇḍa-vyūha-sūtra* makes clear, contact with Śaivas is as detrimental to a Buddhist's soteriological expectations as the contact with *pāṣaṇḍin*s is to a pious Brahmin's purity and religious merit.

---

[186] KVS 265.4–8: *bhaviṣyasi tvaṁ mahêśvara*[a] *kali-yuge pratipanne. kaṣṭa-sattva-dhātu-samutpanna ādi-deva ākhyāyase sraṣṭāraṁ kartāram. te sarva*[b]*-sattvā bodhi-mārgeṇa viprahīṇā bhaviṣyanti ya īdṛśaṁ pṛthag*[c]*-janeṣu sattveṣu*[d] *sāṅkathyaṁ kurvanti. ākāśaṁ liṅgam ity āhuḥ pṛthivī tasya pīṭhikā. ālayaḥ sarva-bhūtānāṁ līyanāl*[e] *liṅgam ucyate.*

[[a] Emendation (< KVS_{Tib} P *chu* 231b3): *mahêśvara*; 265.4: *mahêśvaraḥ*; [b] *sarva-* with no equivalent in KVS_{Tib} P *chu* 231b4; [c] Emendation: *īdṛśaṁ pṛthag-*; 265.5: *īdṛśa-pṛthag-* (*īdṛśa* with no equivalent in KVS_{Tib} P *chu* 231b4); [d] *sattveṣu* with no equivalent in KVS_{Tib} P *chu* 231b4–5 (*so so'i skye bo'i naṅ du*); [e] Emendation (REGAMEY (1971: 431)): *līyanāl*; 265.8: *līlayā*.] Translation (slightly modified) GONZÁLEZ-REIMANN (2002: 172). On this passage, see STUDHOLME (2002: 30–31, 44–45 and 123–124); on the verse quoted here (and especially *līyana*), see STUDHOLME (2002: 19–20 and 28–29) and REGAMEY (1971).

[187] See SANDERSON (2009: 128–132, and *passim*).

[188] SANDERSON (2009: 253). See, more generally, SANDERSON's (2009: 252–303) extremely detailed account. Note also DAVIDSON (2002: 86): 'Overall, Buddhist institutions could not effectively compete for patronage from militaristic princes, who increasingly found that they were best represented by Śaiva values and rhetoric. Śaiva systems made allowance for forms of behavior that Buddhist syntheses could not support, since even the most syncretic Buddhist systems were not as open to negotiation about issues of violence, power, and self-aggrandizement as were the medieval Śaiva representatives.'

2.4.3. Worth mentioning in connection with late Gupta prophecies of decline is the Buddhist monk and translator Narendrayaśas.[189] Born in Uḍḍiyāna (in 490 or 516), Narendrayaśas has often been credited with the transmission of Indian Buddhist prophetic/apocalyptic literature from India (where he travelled for many years) to Central Asia and China.[190] And indeed, Narendrayaśas did not only provide new Chinese translations of the *Sūrya-garbha-sūtra* and the *Candra-garbha-sūtra* (which form the fourteenth and fifteenth sections of the *Mahā-sannipāta-sūtra*[191]), but is also reported to have translated works such as the *Dehu zhangzhe jing*[192] and the *Lianhua mian jing*.[193] Narendrayaśas has long been noted for his 'tendance à naturaliser les *sūtra* dans le monde hindou-chinois.'[194] And since ZÜRCHER's more recent studies, it has become increasingly clear that the zealous translator was inclined to add very significant interpolations when it came to legitimising Central Asia and especially China as the new repositories of the Good Law, thus engaging in 'religious propaganda'.[195] These interpolations are best understood against the background of Buddho-Taoist eschatology, a 'typically hybrid complex of ideas'[196] mixing up the ideology of *mofa*, the imminent advent of a saviour 'rescuing the true believers from the impending holocaust'[197] (generally Maitreya, transformed from a future Buddha to a messiah, but also the Bodhisattva Candraprabhakumāra, in this case rather a 'great revivalist' or 'temporary saviour'[198]) and '*kalpa*-disasters' or cosmic crises 'heralded by countless signs of clerical corruption, political chaos, and natural disasters.'[199] This is especially true of our monk's translation of the *Dehu zhangzhe jing*, in which Narendrayaśas borrows from, and expands upon considerably, a prophecy already contained in the anonymous *Shenrijing*[200] but nowhere to be found in the earlier translations of Dharmarakṣa and Guṇabhadra. According to Narendrayaśas' version of this

[189] On Narendrayaśas, see ZÜRCHER (1982: 22–33), YAMADA (1988), KUWAYAMA (1989: 97–111) and WANG-TOUTAIN (1994: 75–78). Parts of Yamada's hypothesis have been challenged by NATTIER (1991: 112–117).

[190] See LÉVI (1905: 292–305), KUWAYAMA (1989: 91), WANG-TOUTAIN (1994: 70), HUBBARD (2001: 62, n. 24).

[191] *Daji jing* 大集經 T 397.

[192] *Dehu zhang zhe jing* 德護長者經 T 545.

[193] *Lianhua mian jing* 蓮華面經 T 386.

[194] LÉVI (1905: 292).

[195] ZÜRCHER (1981: 48). A few lines below ZÜRCHER adds, concerning the *Dehu zhangzhe jing*: 'Needless to say that such legitimistic masquerades are not more than artificial constructions made for propagandistic purposes.' See also LÉVI (1905: 295).

[196] ZÜRCHER (1982: 1).

[197] ZÜRCHER (1981: 44).

[198] ZÜRCHER (1982: 27).

[199] ZÜRCHER (1981: 44).

[200] *Shenrijing* 申日經 T 535, 'probably fifth century' (ZÜRCHER (1981: 46)).

prophecy, Candraprabhakumāra will be reborn as King Daxing (大行) and 'patronize Buddhism on a grandiose scale, notably by the reproduction and spread of holy texts, the making of Buddha images of every kind, and the establishment of countless sanctuaries in all parts of the empire.'[201] The prophecy is built on the popular but also politically legitimising story of the Buddha's travelling alms bowl (*pātra*) (coming now from Kashgar to China). Faxian (法顯) was already familiar with this story, which he puts, without the least hint of embarrassment, in the mouth of a Buddhist teacher of Śrī Laṅkā.[202]

Much more interesting, however, is Narendrayaśas' translation of the *Lianhua mian jing*. As already suggested by LÉVI, the text is replete with the same kind of Buddho-Taoist hybridisation. One part of the prophecy, however, deserves closer attention. In NATTIER's (1991: 113) short depiction, the *sūtra* records 'the story of Mihirakula in a *jātaka*-style text in which the Hephthalite ruler is portrayed as a devotee of the *Purāṇa*s … who vows to destroy the Buddhist religion in a future lifetime. He is reborn as an Indian king, and succeeds in overturning the Buddha-Dharma and in smashing the Buddha's begging bowl. Karmic justice must be done, however, and Mihirakula is reborn in the Avīci hell in recompense for his actions.' Contrary to NATTIER's interpretation, the *Lianhua mian jing* is more likely to allude to the rival teacher

---

[201] ZÜRCHER (1982: 26). On the rise and religio-political uses of Candraprabhakumāra ('Prince Moonlight'), see ZÜRCHER (1981) and (1982). The close association between Candraprabhakumāra and the Buddha's *pātra* (on the alms bowl, see below) is attested in China as early as 365 CE. As for this (hitherto obscure) Bodhisattva's 'special relation to China, [it] is for the first time alluded to around the middle of the fourth century' (ZÜRCHER (1982: 24)). According to ZÜRCHER (1982: 26–27) and WANG-TOUTAIN (1994: 76), the king hinted at is Yang Jian, the founder of the Sui Dynasty, who adopted the name Wendi, became king in 581 and emperor in 589. According to ZÜRCHER (1982: 26), '[i]t may well be that Narendrayaśas himself was responsible for inserting this passage into his translation, which he made only one year after he had been summoned by Yang Jian himself to the Daxing shan si …—the most prestigious Buddhist institution in the empire …—to perform his translation work under imperial auspices.' The *Dehu zhangzhe jing* was translated in 584 and the *Lianhua mian jing* in 585.

[202] See KUWAYAMA's original translation (1989: 106–107). Note that ZÜRCHER (1982: 31) seems not to call the authenticity of Faxian's testimony into question, though he describes it as a 'curious passage'. This is, in Faxian's version of the story, the itinerary of the precious relic: Vaiśālī–Yuezhi state–Khotan–Kucha–Han China–Śrī Laṅkā–mid-India–Tuṣita heaven …–newly awakened Maitreya. On the historically well-attested relic in Gandhāra (Puruṣapura), see KUWAYAMA (1989: 105–111) and WANG-TOUTAIN (1994: 63–64). On the alms bowl as a symbol of the Sad-dharma and an instrument of political legitimisation in newly converted countries, see WANG-TOUTAIN (1994). As WANG-TOUTAIN (1994: 69) remarks, the appearance of the alms bowl 'étant liée à la venue d'un Buddha en ce monde, il était donc logique d'affirmer qu'avec la disparition de la Loi, le bol disparaîtrait lui aussi … Plus précisément, c'est la disparition du bol qui annoncera le déclin de la Loi.' See also DEEG (1999).

Pūraṇa Kāśyapa than to the *purāṇas*:[203] Pūraṇa is often portrayed as closely related to Śrīgupta (by the way, the father of Candraprabhakumāra), who attempted to murder the Buddha and committed suicide as a consequence of the Śrāvastī miracle. Note should also be made that the text does not prophesise the final demise of the Sad-dharma ('Good Law'), but its gradual degradation in India in the aftermath of Mihirakula's 'harshly anti-Buddhist activities',[204] and its revival in Serindia and China. The *Lianhua mian jing*'s account of the ensuing degeneration is worth quoting in full:

> 'Après la mort de cette brute d'homme, il y aura sept *devaputra* successivement qui renonceront à leur corps pour naître dans le royaume de Ki-pin. Et ils consolideront à nouveau la droite loi du Tathâgata et ils feront de grandes offrandes. Ô Ānanda, à cause de la destruction du *pātra*, mes disciples peu à peu souilleront les défenses pures. Aux premiers temps que mon *pātra* sera détruit, les *bhikṣu*, quoique violant les défenses pures, sauront encore assez pour pouvoir, comme le taureau, détruire les hérésies. Mais, les premiers temps une fois passés, les *bhikṣu* dans le Jambudvîpa détruiront les défenses pures, ils ne se plairont qu'à faire le mal. Eux-mêmes, ils pilleront, voleront, laboureront les champs, cultiveront la terre. Ils convoiteront et entasseront en masse le bétail, les bons vêtements, les bons vases; ils n'aimeront pas à réciter les *Sūtra*, le *Vinaya*, l'*Abhidharma*. Oui, ô Ānanda, les hommes qui aiment à lire, qui aiment à réciter, les hommes qui savent auront tous disparu. Et alors il y aura beaucoup de *bhikṣu* qui flatteront, qui envieront, qui pratiqueront l'impiété. Et comme les *bhikṣu* n'agiront plus selon la loi, les rois eux aussi ne se conformeront pas aux lois des rois; et comme les rois ne gouverneront plus selon les lois des rois, le peuple en masse accumulera les dix mauvaises actions (*akuśala*). Et, par suite de ces mauvaises actions, la terre produira en abondance des plantes épineuses, des plantes vénéneuses, du sable et des cailloux.'[205]

As we can see, this prophecy of decline closely conforms to the narrative patterns already encountered above. Like the 'Prophecy of Kauśāmbī' and the *Laṅkâvatāra-sūtra*, the text 'translated' by Narendrayaśas does not make political events directly responsible for the decline/demise of the Good Law, but, rather, for an intra-monastic degeneration accounted for in terms of moral and disciplinary laxity and/or internecine quarrels leading in turn to the decline/

[203] YAMADA (1989: 80): 'In the future, there will appear ... a disciple of the heretic Fu-lanna [Pūraṇa]', as well as WANG-TOUTAIN (1994: 71): 'Après le nirvāṇa de ces cinq hommes apparaîtra un disciple du maître hérétique Pūraṇa.' See T 386, 12.1075b16–c21.

[204] HUBBARD (2001: 62, n. 24).

[205] Translation LÉVI (1905: 298–299).

demise. The present state of research does not allow a decision to be made as to whether Narendrayaśas made use of a pre-existing Indian text/story/*sūtra* prophesising the decline/demise of the Dharma after Mihirakula's allegedly violent anti-Buddhist campaigns,[206] adapting it in order to have it fit the Chinese religio-political context.

2.5. Indian Buddhists seem never to have made external events or persons directly responsible for the demise of the Dharma (in spite of their drive to regard external, mainly political causes as launching the process). Their apocalyptic rhetoric rather mirrors the warnings of Mahāyānist and non-Mahāyānist 'rigorist' (BOUCHER) and 'contestant' (ZÜRCHER) sectarian fractions within the Buddhist communities. In this context, the factors most frequently alluded to are internecine quarrels, moral and disciplinary laxity, decline in knowledge and spirituality, and, in early Mahāyāna especially, excessive concessions to secular society and its values. This is true of the Pāli canon, the 'Prophecy of Kauśāmbī' and early Mahāyāna scriptures such as the *Rāṣṭra-pāla-paripṛcchā-sūtra*, but also of late Gupta and early post-Gupta sources such as late interpolations and/or additions in the *Rāṣṭra-pāla-paripṛcchā-sūtra*, the *Laṅkâvatāra-sūtra*, and some among Narendrayaśas' 'translations'. Note should also be made that, contrary to contemporary Brahmanical rhetoric (Kalkin) and Chinese eschatological beliefs (Maitreya, Candraprabhakumāra), Indian Buddhists seem not to have resorted to messianism in the hope of an at least provisional

[206] Together with Meiji YAMADA (1989), I am strongly inclined not to accept the almost systematic (since Fleet, Stein and Marshall) but uncritical association of the Hūṇas of Indian inscriptions with the Hephthalites of northwestern India. According to the Japanese scholar, the Hūṇas who enter Indian history around 455–456 and were defeated by Bhānugupta (around 512) and Yaśodharman (531–532) came (*via* the Kāthiāwār, like the Śakas before them) from eastern Iran or southern Afghanistan and ruled over central India (Mālwā, including Eraṇ, Gwālior, Mandasor), i.e. a territory entirely different from the one ruled by the Hephthalites. The issue of Mihirakula's strong anti-Buddhist leaning is not without problems either. YAMADA suspects Xuanzang's description of Mihirakula's anti-Buddhist atrocities in Śāgala/Sialkot (Siyālkoṭ) as mixing up narrative elements borrowed from the legends of the Indo-Greek King Menander and the Śuṅga (and anti-Buddhist) ruler Puṣyamitra. Considering that Kalhaṇa's *Rāja-taraṅgiṇī* does not hold Mihirakula's cruelty to have been specifically directed against the Buddhists, we must conclude that the only descriptions of Mihirakula as a persecutor of Buddhism are Chinese apocryphs strongly indebted to *mofa* ideology (the *Lianhua mian jing* and the *Fufazangyinyuanchuan* 付法藏因緣傳 T 2058, see YAMADA (1989: 81–82) as well as MASPERO (1911)). Moreover, as KUWAYAMA (1989) has pointed out, Xuanzang never associates this king with the bad condition he witnessed of Buddhist institutions in northwest India. KUWAYAMA has made a strong case that the Hephthalites cannot be made responsible for this decay, which must, then, have taken place sometime in between the Hephthalites' disappearance around 550–560 and Xuanzang's account roughly 80 years later. As Deborah Klimburg-Salter kindly informs me, Giuseppe Tucci drew the hypothesis of a massive natural disaster (an earthquake?) having occurred during the mid-sixth century, a hypothesis that seems to have been confirmed by the IsIAO (= Istituto Italiano per l'Africa e l'Oriente) team after fifty years of archaeological excavation in Swat.

restoration of Buddhism. As we have seen, Gupta and early post-Gupta Brahmanical apocalypticism exhibits significant shifts in emphasis. Though to a lesser extent, the Buddhist prophecies of decline seem to undergo an analogous evolution. First, at least two important *sūtra*s testify to the fact that certain Buddhist *literati* took up the four *yuga*s pattern, and especially the *kali-yuga*, in order to account for their historical environment. As NATTIER rightly points out, Indian Buddhists who, contrary to their East Asian coreligionists, lacked any structured periodisation of decline, might have borrowed the ready-made and widespread *yuga* scheme in order to make up for this lack. But they are no less likely to have taken up a scheme whose gloomily flavoured fourth item, the *kali-yuga*, strongly appealed to imagination. Interestingly enough, these two occurrences are explicitly associated with well identifiable historical circumstances. Whereas the *Laṅkâvatāra-sūtra* locates the *kali-yuga* at the end (brought about through the agency of *mleccha*s who might be interpreted as the Hūṇas) of a sequence of dynasties (Mauryas, Nandas, Guptas) well disposed, or at least not hostile, towards Buddhism, the *Kāraṇḍa-vyūha-sūtra* links the *kali-yuga* to the Śaiva threat. Now, these features recur with only minor changes in one among the prophecies adapted by Narendrayaśas. There, the Hūṇa king Mihirakula is made responsible for the process that eventually leads to the disappearance of Buddhism from India. Interestingly, Narendrayaśas locates the non-Buddhists both upstream and downstream from Mihirakula. The ferocious king owes his anti-Buddhist leaning to having been, in a former life, a disciple of Pūraṇa Kāśyapa, a rival master noted for his attempt to murder the Buddha. In this connection, it would be extremely interesting to inquire whether the fifth and sixth centuries record any significant increase in iconic representations of the Buddha's great 'Miracle at Śrāvastī', for which Pūraṇa Kāśyapa was ultimately responsible. But Narendrayaśas also alludes to the Buddhists' increasing difficulty in resisting the outsiders' hostility after the defeat of Mihirakula. Both the *Kāraṇḍa-vyūha-sūtra* and Narendrayaśas, then, bear witness to the Buddhists' awareness of *one* external factor never alluded to before, i.e. the *tīrthika*s in the form of Śaivas, followers of Pūraṇa Kāśyapa (a metaphor of hostile non-Buddhists in general), and outsiders *lato sensu*. In a way, this provides an interesting echo of the Brahmanical animosity exhibited in the *Viṣṇu-purāṇa* and the *Tantra-vārttika*. To sum up, late Gupta and early post-Gupta Buddhist apocalypticism seems to reflect, though rather sparsely, a Buddhist awareness of otherwise clearly identifiable threats: a loss of political footing (if not political hostility) and the enmity of non-Buddhist orthodox and sectarian *milieux*.

Does this have any bearing on sixth-century philosophy as we know it from the works that have come down to us? In my opinion, sixth-century Buddhist philosophy entertains no connection whatsoever with political power, and thus this is very unlikely to have been its intended audience. But, as I mentioned earlier, it undergoes the same heresiological turn as its Brahmanical counterpart. And although this heresiological (as well as apologetic) endeavour is mainly directed towards the philosophical expressions of orthodox Brahmanism (Mīmāṁsā, Nyāya), it is not without a few critical hints at sectarian Hinduism. Dharmakīrti in particular criticises Śaiva doctrines and practices on at least two occasions.[207] In a way, this philosophical shift matches the Buddhist experience as reflected in apocalyptic prophecies. Note, however, that I am aware of no Buddhist philosophical text alluding to apocalyptic beliefs. Contrary to what can be observed in Kumārila's *Tantra-vārttika*, apocalypticism does not provide philosophy with any explicit ideological or rhetorical background. And other, more classic features of Buddhist apocalypticism might have played no less prominent a role in the development of Buddhist philosophy during the sixth century, at least as far as Dharmakīrti (whose works would, after all, dominate the philosophical landscape until the demise of Buddhism in India) is concerned: internecine quarrels make Buddhism incapable of resisting the outsiders' attacks on Buddhism. In other words, Buddhism needs a supersectarian identity, a need that might have played its part in the contemporaneous decline in Abhidharmic creativity and polemics and in the concomitant appearance, in doctrinal texts, of such supersectarian self-denominations as *bauddha*, *śākya*, and *saugata* (all of them meaning: Buddhist). There is, however, a more satisfactory explanation: Buddhism attempted to answer the strongly interrelated political and Śaiva threats by reformulating its symbolic, ritual and soteriological identity. This would be the 'Buddhist esoteric synthesis' (to which most later Buddhist intellectuals in the epistemological tradition came to be associated), which has been noted by both DAVIDSON and SANDERSON for its intrinsic connection with political power. At any rate, Dharmakīrti's works make it a compelling case that Buddhist epistemology and esotericism *in statu nascendi* are contemporaneous phenomena, and most likely two different answers to the same socio-historical challenge.

[207] See SANDERSON (2001: 11–13) and ELTSCHINGER (forthcoming: § 1.3.2). The Mīmāṁsā chapter (= 9) of Bhāviveka's *Madhyamaka-hṛdaya-kārikā* (MHK) is replete with allusions to and criticism of sectarian Hindu beliefs and practices. Alexis Sanderson kindly informs me that MHK 9.62 and 9.114–115 paraphrase *Pāśupata-sūtra*s 5.20, 4.4–5, 5.37–38, 5.24 and 25, and 5.40.

BIBLIOGRAPHY

AGRAWALA 1963 = Agrawala, Vasudeva S.: *Matsya Purāṇa. A Study*. All-India Kashiraj Trust, Varanasi 1963.

AK = Vasubandhu: *Abhidharma-kośa*. (1) Prahlad Pradhan (ed.): *Abhidharmakośabhāṣyam of Vasubandhu*. Tibetan Sanskrit Works Series 8, Kashi Prasad Jayaswal Research Institute, Patna 1975 [first edition: Patna 1967]. (2) Louis de la Vallée Poussin (tr.).: *L'Abhidharmakośa de Vasubandhu*. Mélanges Chinois et Bouddhiques 16, Institut Belge des Hautes Études Chinoises, Bruxelles 1980 [first edition: P. Geuthner–J.B. Istas, Paris–Louvain 1923–31].

AKBh = Vasubandhu: *Abhidharma-kośa-bhāṣya*. See: AK.

AKVy = Yaśomitra: *Abhidharma-kośa-vyākhyā*. Unrai Wogihara: *Sphuṭārthā Abhidharmakośavyākhyā, the work of Yaśomitra*. Sankibo Buddhist Book Store (The Publishing Association of Abhidharmakośavyākhyā), Tokyo 1989 [first edition: 1936].

ALLCHIN 1957 = Allchin, F.R.: 'Sanskrit Eḍūka—Pāli Eluka', *Bulletin of the School of Oriental and African Studies* 20 (1957) 1–4.

AmK = Amarasiṁha: *Amara-kośa* (*Nāma-liṅgānuśāsana*). M.M. Pandit Sivadatta Dādhimatha (ed.): *Nāmaliṅgānuśāsana alias Amarakośa of Amarasiṁha, with the commentary Vyākhyāsudhā or Ramśramī of Bhānuji Dīkṣita*. Edited with noted by … . Revised by Pt. Vāsudeva Laksmana Panaīkara. Krishnadas Sanskrit Series 179, Chowkhamba Krishnadas Academy, Varanasi 2002 [first edition: 1905].

AN III = *Aṅguttara-nikāya*. E. Hardy (ed.): *The Aṅguttara-Nikāya*. Part III. Text Series 5, The Pali Text Society, London 1976 [first edition: 1897].

BAKKER 2007 = Bakker, Hans T.: 'Monuments to the Dead in Ancient North India', *Indo-Iranian Journal* 50,1 (2007) 11–47.

BḍP = *Brahmâṇḍa-purāṇa*. Jagdish L. Shastri (ed.): *Brahmāṇḍa Purāṇa of Sage Kṛṣṇa Dvaipāyana Vyāsa*. Motilal Banarsidass, Delhi 1973.

BHSD = Edgerton, Franklin: *Buddhist Hybrid Sanskrit Grammar and Dictionary*. Vol. II: *Dictionary*. Motilal Banarsidass, Delhi 1970 [first edition: New Haven 1953].

BIARDEAU 1994 = Biardeau, Madeleine: *Études de mythologie hindoue II: Bhakti et avatāra*. Publications de l'École Française d'Extrême-Orient 171, École Française d'Extrême-Orient, Pondichéry 1994.

BIARDEAU 2002 = Biardeau, Madeleine: *Le Mahābhārata. Un récit fondateur du brahmanisme et son interprétation*. 2 Vols., Éditions du Seuil, Paris 2002.

BLOOMFIELD 1924 = Bloomfield, Maurice: 'On False Ascetics and Nuns in Hindu Fiction', *Journal of the American Oriental Society* 44 (1924) 202–242.

BOUCHER 2008 = Boucher, Daniel: *Bodhisattvas of the Forest and the Formation of the Mahāyāna. A Study and Translation of the Rāṣṭrapāla-paripṛcchā-sūtra*. Studies in the Buddhist Traditions, University of Hawai'i Press, Honolulu 2008.

BRONKHORST 2007 = Bronkhorst, Johannes: 'Modes of Debate and Refutation of Adversaries in Classical and Medieval India: A Preliminary Investigation', *Antiquorum Philosophia* 1 (2007) 269–280.

BRONKHORST 2009 = Bronkhorst, Johannes: 'Hendrik Kern and the Body of the Buddha', *Études Asiatiques/Asiatische Studien* 63,1 (2009) 7–27.

BRONKHORST forthcoming = Bronkhorst, Johannes: 'Manu and the Mahābhārata', forthcoming in Leonid Kulikov (ed.): *Festschrift Elizarenkova*.

CABEZÓN 2008 = Cabezón, José Ignacio: 'Buddhist Narratives of the Great Debates', *Argumentation* 22 (2008) 71–92.

CarS = *Caraka-saṁhitā*. Vaidya Jādavaji Trikamji (ed.): *Carakasaṁhitā by Agniveśa revised by Charaka and Dṛidhabala, with the Āyurvedadīpikā Commentary of Chakrapāṇidatta*. Vārāṇasī 1984 [first edition: Bombay 1941].

CHOUDHARY 1956 = Choudhary, Radhakrishna: 'Heretical Sects in the Purāṇas', *Annals of the Bhandarkar Oriental Research Institute* 37 (1956) 234–257.

CHURCH 1971 = Church, Cornelia D.: 'The Purāṇic Myth of the Four Yugas', *Purāṇa* 13,2 (1971) 151–159.

COHN 1970 = Cohn, Norman: *The Pursuit of the Millenium. Revolutionary Millenarians and Mystical Anarchists in the Middle Ages*. Revised and Expanded Edition. Oxford University Press, New York 1970 [first edition: 1957].

COLLINS 1982 = Collins, Steven: *Selfless Persons. Imagery and Thought in* Theravāda *Buddhism*. Cambridge University Press, Cambridge–New York 1982.

DANDEKAR 1997 = Dandekar, R.N.: 'Heretical Doctrines in the Purāṇas', in: Siegfried Lienhard; Irma Piovano (eds.): *Lex et Litterae. Studies in Honour of Professor Oscar Botto*. Edizioni dell'Orso, Turin 1997: 141–160.

DAVIDSON 2002 = Davidson, Ronald M.: *Indian Esoteric Buddhism. A Social History of the Tantric Movement*. Columbia University Press, New York 2002.

DEEG 1999 = Deeg, Max: 'Das Ende des Dharma und die Ankunft des Maitreya. Endzeit- und Neue-Zeit-Vorstellungen im Buddhismus mit einem Exkurs zur Kāśyapa-Legende', *Zeitschrift für Religionswissenschaft* 7 (1999) 145–169.

DIETZ 2000 = Dietz, Siglinde: 'Mātṛceṭas *Kaliyugaparikathā*', in: Christine Chojnacki; Jens-Uwe Hartmann; Volker M. Tschannerl (eds.): *Vividharatnakaraṇḍaka. Festgabe für Adelheid Mette*. Indica et Tibetica 37, Indica et Tibetica Verlag, Swisttal-Odendorf 2000: 173–186.

DONIGER O'FLAHERTY 1971 = Doniger O'Flaherty, Wendy: 'The Origin of Heresy in Hindu Mythology', *History of Religion* 10,4 (1971) 271–331.

DONIGER O'FLAHERTY 1983 = Doniger O'Flaherty, Wendy: 'The image of the Heretic in the Gupta *Purāṇas*', in: Bardwell L. Smith (ed.): *Essays on Gupta Culture*. Motilal Banarsidass, Delhi 1983: 107–127.

DONIGER–SMITH 1991 = Doniger, Wendy; Smith, Brian K.: *The Laws of Manu*. Penguin Classics, Penguin Books, London etc. 1991.

DWIVEDI 1977 = Dwivedi, R.K.: 'A Critical Study of the Changing Social Order at Yugānta or the End of the Kali Age: With Special Reference to the Mahābhārata', in: Lallanji Gopal (ed.): *D.D. Kosambi Commemoration Volume*. Banaras Hindu University, Varanasi 1977: 276–297.

ELTSCHINGER 2012 = Vincent Eltschinger: 'Debate, Salvation and Apologetics. On the Institutionalization of Dialectics in the Buddhist Monastic Environment', in: François Voegeli; Vincent Eltschinger; Danielle Feller; Maria Piera Candotti; Bogdan Diaconescu; Malhar Kulkarni (eds.): *Devadattīyam. Johannes Bronkhorst Felicitation Volume*. Worlds of South and Inner Asia 5, Peter Lang, Bern etc. 2012: 429–489.

ELTSCHINGER forthcoming = Vincent Eltschinger: 'Buddhist Esoterism and Epistemology', to be published in: Eli Franco (ed.): *Proceedings of the Panel on the Periodization and Historiography of Indian Philosophy (XIVth World Sanskrit Conference, Kyōto, September 1–5, 2009).*

FALK 2006 = Falk, Harry: 'The Tidal Waves of Indian History. Between the Empires and Beyond', in: Patrick Olivelle (ed.): *Between the Empires. Society in India 300 BCE to 400 CE.* Oxford University Press / The University of Texas South Asia Institute, New York 2006: 145–166.

FINOT 1970 = Finot, Louis: *Rāṣṭrapālaparipṛcchā. Sūtra du Mahāyāna*. Biblio Verlag, Osnabrück 1970 [first edition: Saint-Petersburg 1901].

FITZGERALD 2004 = Fitzgerald, James: *The Mahābhārata, 11: The Book of Women; 12: The Book of Peace, Part One*. The University of Chicago Press, Chicago–London 2004.

FITZGERALD 2006 = Fitzgerald, James: 'Negotiating the shape of "scripture". New Perspectives on the Development and Growth of the *Mahābhārata* between the Empires', in: Patrick Olivelle (ed.): *Between the Empires. Society in India 300 BCE to 400 CE.* Oxford University Press, New York 2006: 257–286.

FLÜGEL 2008 = Flügel, Peter: 'Jaina Relic Stūpas', *Jaina Studies, Newsletter of the Centre of Jaina Studies, SOAS, University of London* 3 (2008) 18–23.

FRAUWALLNER 1984 = Frauwallner, Erich: 'Erkenntnistheorie und Logik der klassischen Zeit', in: Erich Frauwallner: *Nachgelassene Werke. I. Aufsätze, Beiträge, Skizzen*. Herausgegeben von Ernst Steinkellner. Verlag der Österreichischen Akademie der Wissenschaften, Vienna 1984: 67–87.

GAIL 1969 = Gail, Adalbert J.: 'Buddha als Avatāra Viṣṇus im Spiegel der Purāṇas', *Zeitschrift der Deutschen Morgenländischen Gesellschaft*, Supplementa I, Teil 3 (1969) 917–923.

GONZÁLEZ-REIMANN 2002 = González-Reimann, Luis: *The Mahābhārata and the Yugas. India's Great Epic Poem and the Hindu System of World Ages.* Asian Thought and Culture 5, Peter Lang, New York etc. 2002.

HACKER 1960 = Hacker, Paul: 'Zur Entwicklung der Avatāra-Lehre', *Wiener Zeitschrift für die Kunde Süd- und Ostasiens* 4 (1960) 47–70.

HAZRA 1937 = Hazra, Rajendra Chandra: 'The Date of the Viṣṇu Purāṇa', *Annals of the Bhandarkar Oriental Research Institute* 18 (1937) 265–275.

HAZRA 1940 = Hazra, Rajendra Chandra: *Studies in the Purāṇic Records on Hindu Rites and Customs*. Motilal Banarsidass, Delhi 1988 [first edition: Dacca 1940].

HILTEBEITEL 2005 = Hiltebeitel, Alf: 'Buddhism and the *Mahābhārata*. Boundary Dynamics in Textual Practice', in: Federico Squarcini (ed.): *Boundaries, Dynamics and Construction of Traditions in South Asia*. Firenze University Press / Munshiram Manoharlal, Firenze 2005: 107–131.

HUBBARD 1993 = Hubbard, Jamie: 'Review' of NATTIER 1991. *The Eastern Buddhist* 24,1 (1993) 139–146.

HUBBARD 2001 = Hubbard, Jamie: *Absolute Delusion, Perfect Buddhahood. The Rise and Fall of a Chinese Heresy.* Nanzan Library of Asian Religion and Culture, University of Hawai'i Press, Honolulu 2001.

HUNTINGTON 1964 = Huntington, Ronald M.: 'Avatāras and Yugas: An Essay in Purāṇic Cosmology', *Purāṇa* 6,1 (1964) 7–39.

JAYASWAL 1917 = Jayaswal, K.P.: 'The Historical Position of Kalki and His Identification with Yaśodharman', *The Indian Antiquary* 46 (1917) 145–153.

JOSHI 1987 = Lalmani Joshi: *Studies in The Buddhistic Culture of India During the Seventh and Eighth Centuries A.D.* Motilal Banarsidass, Delhi 1987 [first edition: 1967].

KANE 1993 = Kane, Pandurang Vaman: *History of Dharmaśāstra (Ancient and Mediaeval Religious and Civil Law)*. Vol. III. Government Oriental Series Class B, 6, Bhandarkar Oriental Research Institute, Pune 1993 [first edition: 1930–1962].

KANE 1997 = Kane, Pandurang Vaman: *History of Dharmaśāstra (Ancient and Mediaeval Religious and Civil Law)*. Vol. II, Part II. Government Oriental Series Class B, 6, Bhandarkar Oriental Research Institute, Pune 1997 [first edition: 1930–1962].

KANG 2003 = Kang, Sung Yong: *Die Debatte im alten Indien. Untersuchungen zum Sambhāṣāvidhi und verwandten Themen in der Carakasaṁhitā Vimānasthāna 8.15–28*. Philosophia Indica, Einsichten/ Ansichten 6, Dr. Inge Wezler, Verlag für Orientalistische Fachpublikationen, Reinbek 2003.

KANG 2006 = Kang, Sung Yong: 'Die Carakasaṁhitā in der Geschichte der indischen Philosophie I. Nyāya und Carakasaṁhitā', *Wiener Zeitschrift für die Kunde Südasiens* 50 (2006) 143–176.

KHER 1979 = Kher, Citrarekha V.: 'Buddhism and the Non-Philosophical Brahmanical Literature', in: A.K. Narain (ed.): *Studies in Pali and Buddhism. A Memorial Volume in Honor of Bhikkhu Jagdish Kashyap*. B.R. Publishing Corporation, Delhi 1979: 208–216.

KLOSTERMAIER 1989 = Klostermaier, Klaus K.: *A Survey of Hinduism*. State University of New York Press, Albany 1989.

KOSKIKALLIO 1994 = Petteri Koskikallio: 'When Times Turn: Yugas, Ideologies, Sacrifices', *Studia Orientalia* 73 (1994) 253–271.

KRASSER 2011 = Krasser, Helmut: 'Bhāviveka, Dharmakīrti, and Kumārila', in: Toru Funayama: *Chūgoku-Indo syūkyō-shi tokuni bukkyō-shi ni okeru syomotsu no ryūtsū-denpa to jinbutsu-idō no chiiki-tokusei* [*Regional characteristics of text dissemination and relocation of people in the history of Chinese and Indian religions, with special reference to Buddhism*]. A Report of Grant-in-Aid for Scientific Research (B): Project Number 19320010. March, 2011: 193–242.

KUWAYAMA 1989 = Kuwayama, Shoshin: 'The Hephtalites in Tokharistan and Northwest India', *Zinbun* 24 (1989) 89–134.

KVS = *Kāraṇḍa-vyūha-sūtra*. P.L. Vaidya (ed.): *Mahāyānasūtrasaṁgraha*. Part 1. Buddhist Sanskrit Texts 17, The Mithila Institute of Post-Graduate Studies and Research in Sanskrit Learning, Darbhanga 1961: 256–308.

KVS_{Tib} = Tibetan version of the *Kāraṇḍa-vyūha-sūtra*. P no. 784, *Chu* 224a7–274b4.

KYP = Mātr̥ceṭa: *Kali-yuga-parikathā*. See: DIETZ (2000).

LAMOTTE 1976 = Lamotte, Étienne: *Histoire du bouddhisme indien. Des origines à l'ère Śaka*. Publications de l'Institut Orientaliste de Louvain-la-Neuve 14, Institut Orientaliste, Louvain-la-Neuve 1976 [first edition: 1958].

LAS = *Laṅkâvatāra-sūtra*. Bunyiu Nanjio: *The Laṅkāvatāra Sūtra*. Bibliotheca Otaniensis 1, Ōtani University Press, Kyōto 1956 [first edition: 1923].

LÉVI 1905 = Lévi, Sylvain: 'Notes chinoises sur l'Inde, V: Quelques documents sur le bouddhisme indien dans l'Asie centrale (première partie)', *Bulletin de l'École française d'Extrême-Orient* 5,1 (1905) 253–305.

LINGAT 1961 = Lingat, Robert: 'Dharma et temps. À propos de Manu, I, 85–86', *Journal Asiatique* 249 (1961) 487–495.

MAHALINGAM 1988 = Mahalingam, T.V.: *Inscriptions of the Pallavas*. Indian Council of Historical Research, Agam Kala Prakashan, Delhi 1988.

ManuBh = Medhātithi: *Manu-bhāṣya*. See: $MDhŚ_1$.

MASPERO 1911 = Maspero, Henri: 'Sur la date et l'authenticité du *Fou fa tsang yin yuan tchouan*', in: *Mélanges d'indianisme*. Paris 1911: 129–149.

MBh = *Mahā-bhārata*. Vishnu S. Sukthankar; S.K. Belvalkar; et al. (ed.): *The Mahābhārata for the First Time Critically Edited*. 19 Vols., Bhandarkar Oriental Research Institute, Poona 1933–1966.

MCGINN 1998 = McGinn, Bernard: *Visions of the End. Apocalyptic Traditions in the Middle Ages*. Records of Western Civilization, Columbia University Press, New York 1998 [first edition: 1979].

MCGINN 2000 = McGinn, Bernard: *Antichrist. Two Thousand Years of the Human Fascination with Evil*. Columbia University Press, New York 2000 [first edition: 1994].

MDhŚ = *Mānava-dharma-śāstra* [*Manu-smr̥ti*]. (1) Vishvanāth Nārāyaṇ Mandlik (ed.): *Mānava-Dharma Śāstra [Institutes of Manu], with the Commentaries of Medhātithi, Sarvajñanārāyaṇa, Kullūka, Rāghavānanda, Nandana, and Rāmachandra*. Munshiram Manoharlal, Delhi 1992 [first edition: Bombay 1886]. (2) See: OLIVELLE (2005).

MHK 9 = Bhāviveka/Bhavya: *Madhyamaka-hṛdaya-kārikā* (*Tarka-jvālā*). *Madhyamakahṛdayakārikā(tarkajvālā)* Chapter 9. Christian Lindtner: 'Bhavya on Mīmāṁsā', *Studia Indologiczne* 4 (1997) 91–124.

MICHAELS 1998 = Michaels, Axel: *Der Hinduismus. Geschichte und Gegenwart.* Verlag C.H. Beck, München 1998.

MITCHINER 1986 = Mitchiner, John E.: *The Yuga Purāṇa. Critically Edited, with an English Translation and a Detailed Introduction.* Bibliotheca Indica—A Collection of Oriental Works, The Asiatic Society, Calcutta 1986.

MS = Jaimini: *Mīmāṁsā-sūtra*. See: TV.

MŚV = Kumārilabhaṭṭa: *Śloka-vārttika*. Gaṅgā Sāgar Rāy: *Ślokavārttika of Śrī Kumārila Bhaṭṭa with the Commentary Nyāyaratnākara of Śrī Pārthasārathimiśra*. Ratnā Publications, Vārāṇasī 1993.

NATTIER 1991 = Nattier, Jan: *Once Upon a Future Time. Studies in a Buddhist Prophecy of Decline.* Nanzan Studies in Asian Religions 1, Nanzan Institute for Religion and Culture, Asian Humanities Press, Berkeley 1991.

NSmṛ = *Nārada-smṛti*. Quoted from: SHASTRI (2002).

OLIVELLE 2005 = Olivelle, Patrick: *Manu's Code of Law. A Critical Edition and Translation of the Mānavadharmaśāstra.* With the Editorial Assistance of Suman Olivelle. Oxford University Press, Oxford 2005.

P = Peking edition of the Tibetan canon.

PARASHER 1991 = Parasher, Aloka: *Mlecchas in Early India. A Study in Attitudes towards Outsiders upto AD 600.* Munshiram Manoharlal, Delhi 1991.

PATHAK 1997 = See: ViP.

PINGREE 1963 = Pingree, David: 'Astronomy and Astrology in India and Iran', *Isis* 54,2 (1963) 229–246.

PRZYLUSKI 1923 = Jean Przyluski: *La légende de l'Empereur Açoka.* Paul Geuthner, Paris 1923.

REGAMEY 1971 = Regamey, Constantin: 'Motifs vichnouites et śivaites dans le Kāraṇḍavyūha', in: *Études tibétaines dédiées à la mémoire de Marcelle Lalou.* Adrien Maisonneuve, Paris 1971: 411–432.

RENOU 1985 = Renou, Louis: 'Le brahmanisme. 1. Les sources sanskrites', in: Louis Renou; Jean Filliozat: *L'Inde classique, manuel des études indiennes.* Vol. I: Librairie d'Amérique et d'Orient, Adrien Maisonneuve, Paris 1985: 381–445 [first edition: Hanoi 1947].

ROCHER 1986 = Rocher, Ludo: *A History of Indian Literature. Volume II, Fascicule 3: The Purāṇas.* Otto Harrassowitz, Wiesbaden 1986.

RPS = *Rāṣṭra-pāla-paripṛcchā-sūtra*. See: BOUCHER (2008) and FINOT (1970).

SAINDON 2004 = Saindon, Marcelle: 'Le Buddha comme *avatāra* de Viṣṇu et le mythe de Raji', *Indo-Iranian Journal* 47 (2004) 17–44.

SANDERSON 2001 = Sanderson, Alexis: 'History through Textual Criticism in the Study of Śaivism, the Pañcarātra and the Buddhist Yoginītantras', in: François Grimal (ed.): *Les sources et le temps. Sources and Time. A Colloquium, Pondicherry, 11–13 January 1997.* Publications du Département d'Indologie 91, École Française d'Extrême-Orient, Pondicherry 2001: 1–47.

SANDERSON 2009 = Sanderson, Alexis: 'The Śaiva Age—The Rise and Dominance of Śaivism during the Early Medieval Period', in: Shingo Einoo (ed.): *Genesis and Development of Tantrism*. Faculty of Letters, Tokyo 2009: 41–349.

SCHOPEN 2004 = Schopen, Gregory: *Buddhist Monks and Business Matters. Still More Papers on Monastic Buddhism in India*. Studies in the Buddhist Traditions, University of Hawai'i Press, Honolulu 2004.

SCHOPEN 2004/1994 = Schopen, Gregory: 'Doing Business for the Lord: Lending on Interest and Written Loan Contracts in the *Mūlasarvāstivāda-vinaya*', in: SCHOPEN (2004: 45–90) [first published: *Journal of the American Oriental Society* 114,4 (1994) 527–553].

SCHOPEN 2004/1995 = Schopen, Gregory: 'Deaths, Funerals, and the Division of Property in a Monastic Code', in: SCHOPEN (2004: 91–121) [first published in: D.S. Lopez: *Buddhism in Practice*. Princeton 1995: 453–502].

SHARMA 1982 = Sharma, R.S.: 'The Kali Age: A Period of Social Crisis', in: S.N. Mukherjee (ed.): *India: History and Thought, Essays in Honour of A.L. Basham*. Subarnarekha, Calcutta 1982: 186–203.

SHARMA 2001 = Sharma, R.S.: *Early Medieval India. A Study in Feudalisation*. Orient Longman Limited, Kolkata 2001.

SHASTRI 2002 = Shastri, Sunanda Y.: *Nāradasmṛti (Historical, Sociological, Political And Legal Study)*. Bharatiya Kala Prakashan, Delhi 2002.

SN = *Saṁyutta-nikāya*. Léon Feer: *Saṁyutta-Nikāya*. Part II: *Nidāna-vagga*. Pali Text Society, London 1888.

STUDHOLME 2002 = Studholme, Alexander: *The Origins of Oṁ Maṇipadme Hūṁ. A Study of the Kāraṇḍavyūha*. State University of New York Press, Albany 2002.

T = Takakusu, Junjirō; Watanabe, Kaigyoku; Ono, B. (eds.): *Taishō Shinshū Daizōkyō*. 100 volumes, Taishō Issaikyō Kankōkai, Tokyo 1924–1934.

THAPAR 1971 = Thapar, Romila: 'The Image of the Barbarian in Early India', *Comparative Studies in Society and Humanity* 13,4 (1971) 408–436.

Thera-gāthā = Oldenberg, Hermann; Pischel, Richard: *The Thera- and Therī-Gāthāḥ (Stanzas Ascribed to Elders of the Buddhist Order of Recluses)*. Second Edition with Appendices by K.R. Norman and L. Alsdorf, The Pali Text Society, London 1966 [first edition: 1883].

TV = Kumārilabhaṭṭa: *Tantra-vārttika*. Kāśīnātha Vāsudevaśāstrī Abhyankara; Gaṇeśaśāstrī Aṁbādāsa Jośī (eds.): *Śrīmaj-jaimini-praṇītaṁ Mīmāṁsā-darśanam*. 7 Vols. (Vol. 1 *Śābara-bhāṣya*; vols. 2–4 *Śābara-bhāṣya* and *Tantra-vārttika*; vols. 5–7 *Śābara-bhāṣya* and *Ṭup-ṭīkā*). Second Edition, Ānandāśrama Sanskrit Series 97, Ānandāśrama Press, Poona 1970–1977.

VāP = *Vāyu-purāṇa*. H.N. Āpte (ed.): *Mahā-muni-śrīmad-vyāsa-praṇītaṁ Vāyupurāṇam*. Ānandāśrama Sanskrit Series 49, Ānandāśrama Press, Pune 1983 [first edition: Pune 1905].

VERARDI 2011 = Verardi, Giovanni: *Hardships and Downfall of Buddhism in India*. Appendices by Federica Barba, Manohar, Delhi 2011.

VIELLE 2005 = Vielle, Christophe: 'From the *Vāyuprokta* to the *Vāyu* and *Brahmāṇḍa Purāṇas*: Preliminary Remarks towards a Critical Edition of the *vāyuprokta Brahmāṇḍapurāṇa*', in: Petteri Koskikallio (ed.): *Epics, Khilas, and Purāṇas: Continuities and Ruptures. Proceedings of the Third Dubrovnik International Conference on the Sanskrit Epics and Purāṇas, September 2002*. Croatian Academy of Sciences and Arts, Zagreb 2005: 535–560.

ViP = *Viṣṇu-purāṇa*. M.M. Pathak (ed.): *The Critical Edition of the Viṣṇupurāṇam/ Viṣṇupurāṇam (samīkṣitā vṛttiḥ)*. 2 Vols., Oriental Institute, Vadodara 1997.

VON STIETENCRON 1986 = von Stietencron, Heinrich: 'Kalkulierter Religionsverfall: Das Kaliyuga in Indien', in: Hartmut Zinser (ed.): *Der Untergang der Religionen*. Dietrich Reimer Verlag, Berlin 1986: 135–150.

WANG-TOUTAIN 1994 = Wang-Toutain, Françoise: 'Le bol du Buddha. Propagation du bouddhisme et légitimité politique', *Bulletin de l'École Française d'Extrême-Orient* 81,1 (1994) 59–82.

WINTERNITZ 1981 = Winternitz, Maurice: *A History of Indian Literature*. Vol. I, Motilal Banarsidass, Delhi 1981 [first edition: *Geschichte der indischen Literatur*. Leipzig 1909].

YADAVA 1978–1979 = Yadava, B.N.S.: 'The Accounts of the Kali Age and the Social Transformation From Antiquity to the Middle Ages', *The Indian Historical Review* 5,1–2 (1978–1979) 31–63.

YAMADA 1960 = Yamada, Ryūjō: 'The Logic of Crisis: The Mappō Theory in India, China and Japan', in: *Proceedings of the IXth International Congress of the History of Religions, Tokyo and Kyoto 1958*. Maruzen, Tōkyō 1960: 459–462.

YAMADA 1988 = Yamada, Ryūjō: 'Rengemen-gyō ni tsuite', in: Gadjin M. Nagao (ed.): *Yamaguchi Hakashi Kanreki Kinen Indogaku Bukkyōgaku ronshū*. Hōkōkan, Kyōto 1988: 110–123.

YAMADA 1990 = Yamada, Meiji: 'Hūṇa and the Hephtal', *Zinbun* 23 (1989) 79–113.

YDhŚ = *Yājñavalkya-dharma-śāstra* [*Yājñavalkya-smṛti*]. Umesh Chandra Pāndey (ed.): *Yājñavalkyasmṛti of Yogīśvara Yājñavalkya With the Mitākṣarā Commentary of Vijñāneshwar, Edited with the 'Prakash' Hindī Commentary*. The Kashi Sanskrit Series 178, The Chowkhamba Sanskrit Series Office, Vārāṇasī 1967.

YuP = *Yuga-purāṇa*. See: MITCHINER (1986).

ZÜRCHER 1981 = Zürcher, Erik: 'Eschatology and Messianism in Early Chinese Buddhism', in: W.L. Idema (ed.): *Leyden Studies in Sinology. Papers Presented at the Conference held in Celebration of the Fiftieth Anniversary of the Sinological Institute of Leyden University, December 8–12, 1980*. E.J. Brill, Leiden 1981: 34–56.

ZÜRCHER 1982 = Zürcher, Erik: 'Prince Moonlight: Messianism and Eschatology in Early Medieval Chinese Buddhism', *T'oung Pao* 68 (1982) 1–75.

Parmenides and the *Sat-kārya-vāda* Doctrine of Sāṁkhya

EMILIO GARCÍA BUENDÍA

1. Introduction

Parmenides' thought brought about a dramatic change in the development of Greek philosophy inasmuch as the world view of Presocratic philosophers conceived all realities as *physis*. With the arrival of Parmenides, however, the reflection shifted to being. A new philosophical landscape opened up with the Eleatic thinker.

If the importance of Parmenides itself is beyond doubt, it is still possible to ask some relevant questions: Is there any parallelism between Parmenides' thought and other concepts? If the core of the discussion on Parmenides is that it is impossible to pass from the being into nonbeing, was that idea as such present within Indian philosophy? If that were indeed the case, how could such an idea have evolved? And, finally, could Parmenides have had any knowledge or been exposed to some kind of influence of an idea that came from India?

The *sat-kārya-vāda* doctrine known from India shows enough similarities with the problem whether it is possible to change from nonbeing to being. But also, the doctrine is linked to the problem of causality because the topic under discussion concerns the question whether the effect is something entirely new, i.e. *creatio ex nihilo,* or not. In the latter case, the effect pre-exists in the cause and therefore a new creation can never be understood as a transition from non-being to being or, in other words, its transition from non-existence to existence is not conceivable.

That being the case, the causality is the other face of the same coin: it involves both (a) a metaphysical question about the nature of the existence and non-existence, and (b) the issue of the origin of the effect, if there is anything new in its production or it reflects anything already pre-existing.

The aim of this paper is to explore the topic of causality in Greek philosophy, with a focus on Aristotle and Plato, and to demonstrate to what degree causality is linked to the problem of existence. Further, the *sat-kārya-vāda* doctrine will be revisited as an exposition of the impossibility of *creatio ex nihilo*. Finally, the paper demonstrates how the discussion between the possibility to pass from existence into non-existence is already present in the *Upaniṣad*s in a clear form, and parallels the argumentation found in the famous

World View and Theory in Indian Philosophy
Warsaw Indological Studies 5 (2012) 87–99.

poem of Parmenides. Finally, a hypothesis will be put forward about a possible relationship between the *sat-kārya-vāda* doctrine, the exposition of the being and the nonbeing in the *Upaniṣad*s, and the thesis found in Parmenides' poem. In addition, the paper suggests that a transmission of ideas by the influence of Orphism and its wandering priests, the Orphéotélestas, was equally possible.

2. The causality in Plato and Aristotle

Let us take our path into the past, searching for the similarities between the core of Parmenides' argument and similar topics in Indian philosophy.

In Sanskrit, the word that designates the cause is kāraṇa which is a neutral noun that means 'cause, reason, the cause of something, motive, origin, beginning' (principle) and, in philosophy a cause is 'which is invariably antecedent to some product'.[1] From the etymological point of view, as every Indologist knows, the word *kāraṇa,* in origin, is a verbal adjective derived from the verbal root √*kṛ* of the II, V or VIII class that means 'to do, to make'.

The issue of causality has been one of the fundamental problems of thought from antiquity. In Western thought the question of causality is exposed in *Phaedo* 96a 6–10: 'Listen then, and I will tell you. When I was young, Cebes, I was tremendously eager for the kind of wisdom which they call investigation of nature. I thought it was a glorious thing to know the causes of everything, why each thing comes into being and why it perishes and why it exists.'[2] The passage confirms that Plato links the question of causality with the problem of existence.

Aristotle continues the investigation on the problem of the causality in the same line of the Greek tradition, always with the horizon of trying to comprehend the world that surrounds us and its modifications. This important question is studied by Aristotle in his *Physics* and *Metaphysics*. As indicated by Andrea FALCON (2008), the Stagirite elaborates his doctrine of the four causes with the above-mentioned purpose though his study on the causality does not only include the ontological aspect about the reason for the existence of things, but also includes the epistemological aspect.

In the *Analytica Posteriora* (71b 9–12 and 94a 203)[3] Aristotle affirms that the real knowledge is only such that answers the question of the why. Only the knowledge of the causes is real knowledge, as reaffirmed in *Physics* 194b 17–204[4]. Thus, in *Physics* 194b 245[5] and *Metaphysics* 1013a–1025[6], he offers a presentation of his theory of the causality based on four causes: (a) the mate-

[1] MONIER-WILLIAMS (1997: 300).

[2] FOWLER (2005: 331).

[3] ROSS (1928: 71b 9–12; 94a 203).

[4] ROSS (1930: 194b 17–204).

[5] ROSS (1930: 194b 245).

[6] ROSS (1940: 1013a–1025).

rial, (b) the formal, (c) the efficient, and (d) the final cause. The important thing to mention is that if in Plato the question on the causality was turning around the problem of existence, in Aristotle it is transformed into the problem of why of things, or their causes.

The explanation of the phenomena of nature, from this moment onwards, will be tied to the question of the why (*Physics* 198a 21–237);[7] the causality will allow the enquirer not only to explain the phenomena of the natural world but also to acquire the knowledge of such a world. To explain will be equivalent to knowing the causes. Therefore, ontology, with Aristotle, develops into an onto-epistemology.

3. The Causality and Parmenides

Let us step backward, and reflect on Parmenides' thought. In his famous poem *On Nature* (Περὶ Φΰσεως) the topic of the causality is not treated expressly but its mention is found in verses 8.1–8.20:

> a ‘One path only is left for us to speak of, namely, that it is. In it are very many tokens that what is, is uncreated and indestructible, alone, complete, immovable and without end. Nor was it ever, nor will it be; for now it is, all at once, a continuous one. For what kind of origin for it will thou look for ? In what way and from what source could it have drawn its increase ? … I shall not let thee say nor think that it came from what is not; for it can neither be thought nor uttered that anything is not. And, if it came from nothing, what need could have made it arise later rather than sooner? Therefore must it either be altogether or be not at all. Nor will the force of truth suffer aught to arise besides itself from that which is not. Wherefore, Justice doth not loose her fetters and let anything come into being or pass away, but holds it fast. Our judgement thereon depends on this: “Is it or is it not?” Surely it is adjudged, as it needs must be, that we are to set aside the one way as unthinkable and nameless (for it is no true way), and that the other path is real and true. How, then, can what is be going to be in the future? Or how could it come into being? If it came into being, it is not; nor is it if it is going to be in the future. Thus is becoming extinguished and passing away not to be heard of.’[8]

---

[7] ROSS (1930: 198a 21–237).

[8] DIELS–KRANZ (1903: 122–123):

8.1 […] μοῦνος δ᾽ ἔτι μῦθος ὁδοῖο

The core argument of Parmenides is based on the reasoning (8.20) that being cannot change to nonbeing as well as it is impossible to accomplish a transition from nonbeing to being. His influence is twofold: (a) one should not speak about *physis* but about being, (b) the possibility of passing from nonbeing to being and reverse is not possible because whole reality is only being.

Precisely this is the argument on which the doctrine of the *sat-kārya-vāda* ('the doctrine of the existing effect') is based, or the impossibility for an effect to be a new creation *ex nihilo* and, therefore, its necessity to pre-exist in its cause.

4. The Doctrine of the Causality in Sāṁkhya and Yoga

Let us continue on our path into the past, searching for the similarities between the core of Parmenides' argument and similar cases in Indian philosophy.

As regards the problem of the causality, the Sāṁkhya system defends the doctrine known as *sat-kārya-vāda* which holds that the effect already is contained in the cause as a pre-existing form. This doctrine, also known as *pariṇāma-vāda* ('the doctrine of change'), is defended not only by Sāṁkhya but also by the Śaiva Siddhānta.

This exposition of the theory is found in an explicit form in the *Sāṁkhya-kārikā* of Īśvarakṛṣṇa:[9]

> 'The effect is existent (in its cause), since non-existent cannot be produced, since the material (cause) is selected, since everything cannot be produced (from anything), since a potent (cause) pro-

---

λείπεται ὡς ἔστιν· ταύτῃι δ᾽ ἐπὶ σήματ᾽ ἔασι
πολλὰ μάλ᾽, ὡς ἀγένητον ἐὸν καὶ ἀνώλεθρόν ἐστιν,
ἐστι γὰρ οὐλομελές τε καὶ ἀτρεμὲς ἠδ᾽ ἀτέλεστον·
οὐδέ ποτ᾽ ἦν οὐδ᾽ ἔσται, ἐπεὶ νῦν ἔστιν ὁμοῦ πᾶν,
ἕν, συνεχές· τίνα γὰρ γένναν διζήσεαι αὐτοῦ;
πῆι πόθεν αὐξηθέν; * * * οὐδ᾽ ἐκ μὴ ἐόντος ἐάσσω
φάσθαι σ(ε) οὐδὲ νοεῖν· οὐ γὰρ φατὸν οὐδὲ νοητόν
ἔστιν ὅπως οὐκ ἔστι. τί δ᾽ ἄν μιν καὶ χρέος ὦρσεν
ὕστερον ἢ πρόσθεν, τοῦ μηδενὸς ἀρξάμενον, φῦν;
οὕτως ἢ πάμπαν πελέναι χρεών ἐστιν ἢ οὐχί.
οὐδέ ποτ᾽ ἐκ μὴ ἐόντος ἐφήσει πίστιος ἰσχύς
γίγνεσθαί τι παρ᾽ αὐτό· τοῦ εἵνεκεν οὔτε γενέσθαι
οὔτ᾽ ὄλλυσθαι ἀνῆκε Δίκη χαλάσασα πέδῃισιν,
ἀλλ᾽ ἔχει· ἡ δὲ κρίσις περὶ τούτων ἐν τῶιδ᾽ ἔστιν·
ἔστιν ἢ οὐκ ἔστιν· κέκριται δ᾽ οὖν, ὥσπερ ἀνάγκη,
τὴν μὲν ἐᾶν ἀνόητον ἀνώνυμον οὐ γὰρ ἀληθής
ἔστιν ὁδόσ, τὴν δ᾽ ὥστε πέλειν καὶ ἐτήτυμον εἶναι.
πῶς δ᾽ ἂν ἔπειτ᾽ ἀπόλοιτο ἐόν; πῶς δ᾽ ἄν κε γένοιτο;
εἰ γὰρ ἔγεντ᾽, οὐκ ἔστὶ, οὐδ᾽ εἴ ποτε μέλλει ἔσεσθαι.
[…]

Translation: BURNET (1930: 174–175).

[9] SK 9, p. 14:

asad-akaraṇād upādāna-grahaṇāt sarva-sambhavâbhāvāt /
śaktasya śakya-karaṇāt kāraṇa-bhāvāc ca sat-kāryam // 9 //

> duces that of which it is capable and since (the effect is) of the same nature as the cause.'[10]

The commentary of Gauḍapāda clarifies this doctrine:[11]

> 'Since non-existent cannot be produced: non-existent is that which does not exist. Since there can be no production of a non-existent thing, so an effect does exist (in its cause). In this world we do not see the production of a non-existent object, as oil cannot be produced from sand (wherein oil is non-existent). So, since only an existent object can be produced, the Manifest does exist before its production in Nature. Therefore, the effect is existent.'[12]

The central argument receives a clear exposition in this part of the commentary: 'In this world we do not see the production of a non-existent object'. Given this empirical fact, one concludes that the effect has to be contained already in the cause; *sensu opposite*, that something that exists cannot cease to exist. To admit the opposite would imply a *creatio ex nihilo*, which turns out to be unacceptable.

If we examine Yoga, the twin system of Sāṁkhya in the scheme of the six orthodox *darśana*s, we will discover that such position on causality does not find such explicit an expression in the *Yoga-sūtra* (YS) attributed to Patañjali as it does the *Sāṁkhya-kārikā*. It is, however, the *Yoga-bhāṣya* (YBh) ad *Yoga-sūtra* 4.11 which expressly discusses the same idea: 'There is no coming into being of that which does exist and there is no destruction of that which exists …'.[13]

The commentary on *Yoga-sūtra* 4.12[14] represents a pinnacle of the metaphysical reflection in so far as the author attempts to apply the doctrine of causality to time, and speculates on its nature as well as on the reality of the past and the future. The *sat-kārya-vāda* doctrine reaches its zenith given that it is applied to any type of reality with a degree of maximum abstraction and in absolute coherence. One might think that the commentary to YS 4.12 is one of the best exponents of Indian metaphysics since its author reflects on the nature of substance in general and in relation to the problem of change, causality and time; the concepts of, say, the future or past are not new realities but they exist already in the present. It is from the point of view of such view of causality, that YS 4.12 can be understood completely: 'Therefore the past and the future

[10] DUTT SHARMA (1933: 13).

[11] SKBh 9, p. 14: *asad-akaraṇāt. na sad asat. asato 'karaṇaṁ tasmāt sat-kāryam. iha loke 'sat-karanaṁ nâsti. yathā sikatābhyas tailôtpattiḥ. tasmāt sataḥ karaṇād asti prāg utpatteḥ pradhāne vyaktam. ataḥ sat-kāryam.*

[12] DUTT SHARMA (1933: 13).

[13] RUKMANI (1999: 40): *nâsty asataḥ sambhavaḥ; na câsti sato vināśaḥ.*

[14] RUKMANI (1999: 40 ff.).

exist in essence.'[15] The commentator applies the *sat-kārya-vāda* doctrine to the problem of time and defines the past, present and future:

> 'The "not-as-yet-manifest" is of the nature of the future. The "past" is of the nature of that which has been experienced. The present is that which has started its activity (is in active operation). ... Therefore, the past and the future exist in essence (*yadi câtat svarūpatas*).'[16]

The passage confirms again that the rational basis to sustain the *sat-kārya-vāda* doctrine is that whatever does not exist can never be produced and that whatever exists can never perish.

If the doctrine of causality is conceived in this way, only two classes of causes are enough to explain the evolution and change: (a) the material cause (*upādāna*) and (b) the efficient cause (*nimitta*).

For example, in the *Tattva-vaiśāradī* ad YS 3.14, Vācaspatimiśra says:

> 'For instance, Kashmir is the place of saffron-plant. Because although these [causes] exist in Pañcala and other countries, there is no coming actively forth [of the plant]. Accordingly there is no manifestation of the saffron-plant in a place such Pañcala. 2. Likewise during the hot season, since no rain moves actively forth, there is no manifestation of rice-plants. ... Therefore because of connexion [or] separation by place or time or form or cause, things [that is] forms of being do not manifest themselves at the same time.'[17]

In the Sāṁkhya-Yoga system it is not the efficient cause which puts into action the material cause generating an effect of the same nature as the cause.[18] The role of the efficient cause simply implies the removal of that which prevents the manifestation of the latent effect which exists in the material cause. This idea of the role of different causes is clearly exposed in YS 4.3:

> 'The efficient cause does not impel the creative causes to action, it only removes the obstruction [to the creative causes] and then [the mutation] follows as it happens with the farmer.'[19]

---

[15] RUKMANI (1999: 40): *atītânāgataṁ svarūpato 'sti*. Translation: RUKMANI (1999: 41).

[16] YBh 4.12, p. 314: *bhaviṣyat-vyaktikam anāgatam anubhūta-vyaktikam atītam sva-vyāpārôpārūḍham vartamānam*. Translation: RUKMANI (1999: 314–316).

[17] WOODS (1998: 228–229).

[18] For example, an apple seed will produce an apple tree and not a pear tree; a rice seed will produce a rice plant and not a saffron plant etc.

[19] YS 4.3, p. 5: *nimittam aprayojakaṁ prakṛtīnāṁ varaṇa-bhedas tu tataḥ kṣetrikavat*. Translation: RUKMANI (1999: 5).

In *Yoga-bhāṣya* 4.3[20] an example is given of a peasant who wants to irrigate a field below by pouring water to an upper field, which then flows down, after the peasant removes a barrier separating an upper field with a lower field by making a groove to allow the water flow, and then he repeats the action once more, so that the water unimpeded flows from one upper field to another lower one and so on.

Thus, causes do not generate or produce anything new that did not exist previously but simply obstruct or permit the manifestation of the effects which are found latent in the material cause (YBh 4.12 and 3.14)[21]. Such effects are already present in material causes which assume a new form, being merely a modification (*vṛtti*) consisting, as expressly stated in YBh 4.3[22], of something that has previously existed. For such a production it is necessary the occurrence of certain circumstances which are called efficient causes (*nimitta*). Those circumstances or efficient causes are: (a) location, (b) time, and (c) form.

5. The Doctrine of Being and Nonbeing in *Upaniṣads*

Continuing our journey backward in the search for the conception of being and nonbeing and the relationship between existence and non-existence, we reach the *Chāndogyôpaniṣad*:

> 'In the beginning, son, this world was simply what is existent—one only, without a second. Now, on this point some do say: "In the beginning this world was simply what is non-existent—one only, without a second. And from what is non-existent was born what is existent".'[23]
>
> '"But, son, how can that possibly be?" He continued. "How can what is existent be born from what is non-existent? on the contrary, son, in the beginning this world was simply what is existent one only, without a second".'[24]

---

[20] WOODS (1998: 301–302).

[21] YBh 4.12: *siddhaṁ nimittaṁ naimittikasya viśeṣânugrahaṁ kurute nâpūrvam utpādayatîti* (RUKMANI (1999: 40)) and YBh 3.14: *sa ca phala-prasava-bhedânumita ekasyânyo 'nyaś ca paridṛṣṭaḥ* (RUKMANI (1998: 49)).

[22] YBh 4.3: *tasmin bhinne svayam eva prakṛtayaḥ svaṁ svaṁ vikāram āplāvayanti* (RUKMANI (1999: 5)). Translation: WOODS (1998: 301–302): 'and after this cut, the evolving-causes themselves overflow each its own appropriate evolved-effect (*vikāra*).'

[23] ChU 6.2.1, p. 246: *sad eva somyêdam agra āsīd ekam evâdvitīyam. tad dhâika āhur asad evêdam agra āsīd ekam evâdvitīyam. tasmād asataḥ saj jāyata.* Translation: OLIVELLE (1998: 247).

[24] ChU 6.2.2, p. 246: *kutas tu khalu somyâivaṁ syād iti hôvāca. katham asataḥ saj-jāyetêti. sat tv eva somyêdam agra āsīd ekam evâdvitīyam.* Translation: OLIVELLE (1998: 247).

The author(s) of this passage radically refused the possibility of a transition from nonbeing to being, and the argument shows a great deal of parallelism with Parmenidean reflections referred to above in the verse 8.20 of his poem. Both, Parmenides and the authors of *Upaniṣads*, are located in the ontological field of being, and share the same idea that nothing can emerge from nowhere and return to it.

The *Śvetâśvatarôpaniṣad*, intimately related to the tradition of Yoga, seems to capture the same idea that being is already within all things, even if it cannot be seen, in the same way as the effect is already contained in cause:

> 'Like oil in sesame seeds and butter in curds, like water in the riverbed and fire in the fire-drills, so, when one seeks it with truth and austerity, one grasps that self (*ātman*) in the body (*ātman*) that all-pervading self, which is contained [in the body], like butter in milk. That is *brahman*, the highest object of the teachings on hidden connections (*upaniṣad*), an object rooted in austerity and the knowledge of the self.'[25]

The passage of the *Chāndogyôpaniṣad* has another peculiarity. ChU 6.2.1 uses the term 'some say' (*eka āhuḥ*) which implies a group of thinkers who upheld a contrary view. A natural question is who these others referred to in this *Upaniṣad* actually were.

Perhaps a reply to the puzzle can be found in the following passage of the *Taittirīyôpaniṣad* of cosmogonic connotations:

> 'In the beginning this world was the non-existent, and from it arose the existent....'[26]

As we can see, there are indeed some who claim that it is possible to move from nonbeing to being. Probably those 'some' referred to in ChU 6.2.1 were the followers of the *Taittirīyôpaniṣad*.

This clear ontological confrontation, as reflected in these *Upaniṣads*, could suggest a revision of our assessment of the seemingly world view upheld of by their authors: the *Upaniṣads* should not be considered a monolithic thought system, instead there is evidence that various explanatory theories of the world confronted one another within these circles.

The evidence of the controversy about the transition from nonbeing to being and the denial of such possibility reveals the existence of, at least, two major ontological world views within the *Upaniṣads* which differed on something as

---

[25] ŚvU 1.15–16, p. 416: [1.15] *tileṣu tailam dadhinîva sarpir āpaḥ srotaḥsv araṇīṣu câgniḥ. evam ātmâtmani gṛhyate 'sau satyenâinam tapasā yo 'nupaśyati.* [1.16] *sarva-vyāpinam ātmānaṁ kṣīre sarpir ivârpitam. ātma-vidyā-tapo-mūlam tad brahmôpaniṣat-param.* Translation: OLIVELLE (1998: 417).

[26] TaiU 2.7.1, p. 305: *asad vā idam agra āsīt tato vā sad ajāyata. tad ātmānam svayam akuruta tasmāt tat sukṛtam ucyate.* Translation: OLIVELLE (1998: 305)

basic as the ultimate essence of reality and causality. There is no doubt, from this new perspective, that *Upaniṣad*s do not constitute in any way a uniform thought but do contain conflicting ontologies.

6. Parmenides and Orphism

Having completed our journey into the past of certain ideas that relate to causality and cosmogonic origins, it is necessary to return to the point from which we departed, to Parmenides. The question that arises is how Parmenides could have developed a doctrine that so greatly baffled his fellow thinkers and those in centuries to come.

Certainly there is no single reference in any text about a possible relation between Parmenides and Indian philosophy. When we consider transmission of ideas, we can speak of, on one hand, the diffusion, and, on the other, indigenous development independent of an external influence. Here, we would only like to point to a mere possibility grounded in the diffusion of religious and philosophical ideas inside certain religious groups in antiquity. A plausible option seems to think of Orphism as a mechanism for such diffusion. No doubt, the relationship between Indian philosophy and Greek thought is an open issue for debate. As rightly pointed out by BERNABÉ (2004: 14),

> 'there is some tendency … , [exemplified by] some scholars of Greek philosophy, to isolate philosophers from their surroundings, as if enclosed in a sealed compartment, unrelated to the culture of their time, the ideas expressed elsewhere. … And above all, as if they had to be separated strongly from the religion.'[27]

BERNABÉ (2004) emphasises a possible link between the thought of many Presocratic philosophers and Parmenides with Orphism, and alludes to a mutual relationship between Orphic poetry such as Hieronymus–Hellanicus' *Theogony* or the Orphic *Rhapsodies* and the philosophy of that time. His work demonstrates formal parallels between Parmenides' poem *On Nature* and Orphic literature, which can be summed as follows:

1. Personification of the goddess of Justice, Diké.
2. Literary parallels between the preface of the Parmenides' poem with the *Theogony* of the Derveni papyrus.

---

[27] This citation is from a handout of a paper that was read at a meeting of the Iberic Society of Greek Philosophy held on 10th October 2003.

This citation was read in a meeting of the Iberic Society of Greek Philosophy held on 10th October, 2003. The text of that lecture was to be included as a chapter in BERNABÉ (2004) but, eventually, this citation does not appear in the printed form exactly as has been quoted above, nevertheless the final text of that chapter retrieves the same idea.

3. Formal and thematic parallels between the text of Parmenides and the Orphic poetry.

But BERNABÉ does not only show the above-mentioned formal parallelism between Parmenides' poem and the Orphic corpus but also highlights the conceptual similarities which consider philosophy a way of initiation. Parmenides' poem is a journey into another world, a place now governed by the goddess Justice, where only a very few humans can go, the initiated ones. The knowledge Parmenides could have had of the Orphic thought was noticed by GUTHRIE (1980: 10): 'There are also hints that he was acquainted with the Orphic poems.' GUTHRIE shows several examples of other characters of the early Greek religious thought to whom the ability of travelling for a long time in a state of dream or ecstasy was attributed. A sample of these faculties is attributed to Aethalides, Aristeas, Abaris, Epimenides and others.

A striking example of such parallelism is discussed by BERNABÉ (2004: 135–136), who brings to notice an observation already made by Simplicio commenting on the *Physics* of Aristotle:

> 'And if he says (Parmenides 28 B 8, 43 DIELS–KRANZ) that what is one is "everywhere even the mass of a round ball", do not be surprised because it is adapted to poetry and it obeys a mythical fiction. Well looking, what is different from saying that about "the silver egg" as Orpheus said? ... For this commentator of Aristotle [Simplicio—E.G.B.] there does not seem to be much difference between the image of the Parmenidean spherical being and the Orphic egg.'

The above parallel, noticed by Simplicio, between the Parmenidean conception and the Orpheus' egg reminds us of the cosmogonic hymn that appears in *R̥g-veda* 10.121[28] in which all creation raises from a primeval golden egg (*hiraṇya-garbha*).

Among the various cosmogonies of antiquity, only those contained in the passage of *R̥g-veda* 10.121 and the Orphic cosmogony coincide in asserting that the universe emerged from an egg, *hiraṇya-garbha* in one case and from Fanes in the other. The similarities between the thought embodied in the R̥g-vedic hymn, the *sat-kārya-vāda* conception, and the Parmenidian system analysed in this paper may point to some exchange or connection between Indian world views and the Greek one. The formal similarities as well as the material content could constitute a valid evidence about the route of transmission.

So far we have argued that, accepting the hypothesis of BERNABÉ (2004: 14) and the supposition of GUTHRIE (1980: 10), there was a mutual influence between the thought of Parmenides and the Orphics although we do not necessarily suggest a direct relationship between the Orphics and the thought of

[28] WILSON (1888: 335).

India. We simply note that BERNABÉ's intuition should be taken seriously and pursued since, basically, it defends the idea, which I think is correct, that religious movements of ancient Greece were among the main vehicles of thought and reflection on the nature of reality, its origin and a range of philosophical problems that have troubled man since he emerged as a species.

We should not lapse into anachronism by considering the religious label the way it is understood nowadays; in antiquity the adjective 'religious' was associated with the manner of human thinking about certain issues. The reflection on these matters manifested itself successively through different languages such as iconography, myth, concepts etc., philosophy being a by-product of the discussion of problems such as causality, cause and effect, the relationship between existence and non-existence, and their expression through the use of a conceptual language.

These religious groups of ancient Greece, consisting of Orphics, Pythagoreans and many others, constitute a repository of human thought which existed in constant interchange with other world views. As noted by Ana Isabel JIMÉNEZ (2008: 782), within the Orphic tradition there existed the so-called Orphéotélestas (Ὀρφεοτελεστής, initiating hierophant), who played the role of Orphic wandering officiants that travelled from town to town, leading a mendicant life. The existence of such errant Orphic priests was behind the wide dissemination of ideas within these initiatic circles.

7. Conclusions

Modern conception of the world held by physics is based on the conservative principles as the law of conservation of mass and energy, which are clearly Parmenidean. The core of Parmenides' thought is that is impossible to move from being to nonbeing and *vice versa*, and constitutes a fundamental twist in Greek philosophy, marking a transition from the philosophy of *physis* to the philosophy of being. The *sat-kārya-vāda* doctrine expresses the same point of view, according to which the effect is nothing new because it pre-exists in its cause; there is no *creatio ex nihilo*. That doctrine specifically belongs to the milleux of the *darśana* systems but it is possible to track it back to its origins. We could point to a similar position expressed in such *Upaniṣad*s as the *Chāndogya-upaniṣad* or the *Śvetâśvatarôpaniṣad.* The *Chāndogyôpaniṣad* mentions the 'others' who claim that it is possible to move from nonbeing to being, although it rejects such possibility. The 'others' seem to the followers of the *Taittirī-yôpaniṣad*, which expresses the idea that the world comes into existence from nothingness. This reveals two different and opposite ontologies within the body of the Upaniṣadic literature, which in turn compels one to re-examine the idea of the Upaniṣadic thought as a monolithic system.

Likewise, the Greeks shared two opposite ontologies: (a) one which goes in a straight line from Parmenides to Plato and Aristotle, which assumes the existence of a substance, (b) another one, represented by Heraclitus and Protagoras, which is based on the idea of a becoming and represents a kind of phenomenic ontology. The former succeeded in that ontological battle. In ancient Indian thought it seemed that a similar ontological confrontation took place.

As regards the problem of the diffusion of ideas, ancient religious groups such as Pythagoreans, Orphics and others could have played a very important role in the spread of new concepts and views, specially through the Orphéotélestas, Orphic wandering priests.

BIBLIOGRAPHY

AGRAWAL 2001 = Agrawal, Mohan Madan: *Six Systems of Indian Philosophy*. Chaukhamba Sanskrit Pratishthan, Delhi 2001.

BERNABÉ 2004 = Bernabé, Alberto: *Textos órficos y filosofía Presocrática: materiales para una comparación*. Trotta, Madrid 2004.

BERNABÉ 2008 = Bernabé, Alberto: 'Ex Oriente. Paralelos próximos orientales de mitos y creencias órficos', in: BERNABÉ–CASADESÚS (2008: 899–933).

BERNABÉ–CASADESÚS 2008 = Bernabé, Alberto; Casadesús, Franscec (eds.): *Orfeo y la tradición órfica*. Vol. II. Akal, Madrid 2008.

BURNET 1930 = Burnet, John: *Early Greek Philosophy*. Adam & Charles Black, London 1930.

ChU = *Chāndogyôpaniṣad*. See: OLIVELLE (1998: 532–570).

DIELS–KRANZ 1903 = Diels, Hermann; Kranz, Walther: *Die Fragmente der Vorsokratiker Griechisch und Deutsch*. Weidmannsche Buchhandlung, Berlin 1903.

DUTT SHARMA 1933 = Dutt Sharma, Har: *The Sāmkhya Kārikā. Īśvara Kṛṣṇa's Memorable Verses on Sāṁkhya Philosophy with the Commentary of Gauḍapādācārya*. Poona Oriental Series nº 9, The Oriental Book Agency, Poona 1933.

ESNOUL 1964 = Esnoul, Anne Marie: *Les strophes de Sāṁkhya (Sāṁkhya-kārikā) avec les commentaires du Gauḍapāda. Texte sanskrit et traduction annotée*. Societé d'edition «Les belles lettres», Paris 1964.

FALCON 2008 = Falcon, Andrea: 'Aristotle on Causality', Edward N. Zalta (ed.): *The Stanford Encyclopedia of Philosophy*, 2008: <http://plato.stan ford.edu/entries/aristotle-causality>.

FOWLER 2005 = Fowler, Harold North: *Plato. Euthyphro. The Apology. Crito. Phaedo. Phaedrus*. Loeb Classical Library, Harvard University Press/ W. Heinemann, Cambridge (Mass.)/ London 2005 [first edition: 1914].

GUTHRIE 1980 = Guthrie, W.K.C.: *A History of Greek Philosophy*. Vol. II. Cambridge University Press, Cambridge 1980 [first edition: 1969].

JIMÉNEZ 2008 = Jiménez, Ana Isabel: 'Los *orfeotelestas* y la vida órfica', in: BERNABÉ–CASADESÚS (2008: 771–801).

MONIER-WILLIAMS 1997 = Monier-Williams, M.: *A Sanskrit-English Dictionary*. Motilal Banarsidas, Delhi 1997 [first edition: Oxford 1899].

OLIVELLE 1998 = Olivelle, Patrick: *The Early Upaniṣads: Annotated Text and Translation*. Oxford University Press, New York 1998.

Phaedo = See: FOWLER (2005).

ROSS 1928 = Ross W.D.: *The Works of Aristotle*. Volume I: *Categoriae and de interpretatione. Analytica priora, Analytica posteriora, Topica and the sophisticis elenchis*. Clarendon Press, Oxford 1928.

ROSS 1930 = Ross W.D.: *The Works of Aristotle*. Volume II: *Physica, De caelo, De generatione et corruptione*. Clarendon Press, Oxford 1930.

ROSS 1940 = Ross W.D.: *The Works of Aristotle*. Volume VIII: *Metaphysica*. 2th edition, Clarendon Press, Oxford 1940.

RUKMANI 1998 = Rukmani, T.S.: *Yogavārttika of Vijñānabhikṣu. Text with English Translation and Critical Notes along the Text and English Translation of the Pātañjala Yogasūtras and Vyāsa-bhāṣya*. Vol. 3: *Vibhūtipāda*. Munshiram Manoharlal Publishers, New Delhi 1998 [first edition: 1987].

RUKMANI 1999 = Rukmani, T.S.: *Yogavārttika of Vijñānabhikṣu. Text with English Translation and Critical Notes along the Text and English Translation of the Pātañjala Yogasūtras and Vyāsabhāṣya*. Vol. 4: *Kaivalyapāda*. Munshiram Manoharlal Publishers, New Delhi 1999.

RV = *Ṛg-veda*. See: WILSON (1888).

SK = Īśvarakrṣṇa: *Sāṁkhya-kārikā*. See: ESNOUL (1964).

SKBh = Gauḍapāda: *Sāṁkhya-kārikā-bhāṣya*. See: ESNOUL (1964).

ŚvU = *Śvetâśvatarôpaniṣad*. See: OLIVELLE (1998: 614–628).

TaiU = *Taittirīyôpaniṣad*. See: OLIVELLE (1998: 571–577).

TVai = Vācaspatimiśra: *Tattva-vaiśāradī*. See: WOODS (1988).

VS = Kaṇāda: *Vaiśeṣika-sūtra* (*Upaskāra*). See: AGRAWAL (2001: 85–139).

WILSON 1888 = Wilson, H.H.: *Ṛg Veda Sanhitā. A collection of Ancient Hindu Hymns*. W.F. Webster, MA. Trübner & Co. Ludgate Hill, London 1888.

WOODS 1998 = Woods, James Haughton: *The Yoga System of Patañjali or the Ancient Hindu Doctrine of Concentration of Mind*. Motilal Banarsidas, Delhi 1998 [first edition: 1914].

YBh = [Vyāsa (ascribed):] *Yoga-bhāṣya*. See: RUKMANI (1999).

YS = Patañjali: *Yoga-sūtra*. See: RUKMANI (1999).

World Views And Systems

Doxography and Boundary-Formation in Late Medieval India

ANDREW J. NICHOLSON

In recent years I have spent some time examining South Asian doxographies, texts concerned with cataloguing the tenets of the various schools of philosophy in India. Of course, the word doxography is not Indian in origin—it is actually a Latin neologism, coined in 1879 by the philologist Hermann Diels. He was primarily concerned with Greek and Roman texts, but his term doxography has been adopted to refer to a group of texts produced in pre-modern India, usually but not always in Sanskrit. The earliest example of Indian doxography we have, from Cāttaṉār's Tamil poem *Maṇi-mekalai*, dates to approximately the sixth century CE. But doxography really began to take off between the fourteenth and seventeenth centuries, when a slew of these doxographies was produced. The most familiar of these to western scholars is certainly Mādhava's *Sarva-darśana-saṁgraha* ('Compendium of all Philosophical Systems'), but there were many others, with names like *Sarva-siddhânta-saṁgraha*, *Sarva-mata-saṁgraha*, *Sarva-darśana-kaumudī*, *Ṣaḍ-darśana-samuccaya*, *Ṣaḍ-praveśaka*.[1] There are some similarities in the names of these texts: they are frequently labelled with the word *samuccaya* (collection) or *saṁgraha* (compendium), and they often claim to cover either 'the six philosophical systems' (*ṣaḍ-darśana*) or 'all philosophical systems' (*sarva-darśana*). Also remarkable is that most of the doxographies composed in the fourteenth century and later are by Advaita Vedāntins.

I am interested in these texts for what they tell us about the construction of boundaries between different groups based on their systems of belief. Specifically, the evidence suggests that by the fourteenth century, there was a new urgency to categorise philosophical and theological doctrines, and particularly to engage in a discourse of 'othering', creating clear boundaries between insiders and outsiders. One of the most important binaries for understanding these 'othering' practices in the late medieval period is the word-pair *āstika* and *nāstika*. Certainly these two terms have had an important life in texts other than doxographies, but I believe it is in these late medieval Vedāntic doxogra-

[1] See HALBFASS (1988: 350–1).

World View and Theory in Indian Philosophy
Warsaw Indological Studies 5 (2012) 103–118.

phies where the various earlier interpretations of these two terms gave way to the understanding of them that is now current among scholars of Indian philosophy.

After working for some time with these late medieval doxographies and with a number of earlier Sanskrit texts that theorise the difference between *nāstika* and *āstika*, it became increasingly clear to me that the evidence from these texts corroborates the thesis of a well-known article by David LORENZEN (2005). He states that the creation of a unified Hindu identity occurred not in the nineteenth century, but rather in the medieval period:

> '… the claim that Hinduism was invented or constructed by European colonizers, mostly British, sometime after 1800 is false. The evidence instead suggests that a Hindu religion theologically and devotionally grounded in texts such as the *Bhagavad Gītā*, the Purāṇas, and philosophical commentaries on the six *darśanas*, gradually acquired a much sharper self-conscious identity through the rivalry between Muslims and Hindus in the period between 1200 and 1500, and was firmly established long before 1800.'[2]

For his evidence, LORENZEN cites a number of medieval poets who composed their works in Indian vernacular languages. Since my focus today is not these vernacular poets but rather Sanskrit doxographers, I will right now cite just one of these authors, the celebrated fifteenth century poet Kabīr. Like other *nirguṇa bhakti* poets, Kabīr ridicules Hindus and Muslims, faulting them for their pettiness and possessive attitude toward God:

> 'If the mosque is the place where God resides,
> then who owns the rest of the land?
> Ram lives in images and holy locations?—
> Then why has no one ever found him there?
> Hindus, Muslims—Where did they come from?
> Who got them started down this road?'[3]

Kabīr's mockery of the small-mindedness of the two religions can only be possible if he and his readers do perceive two groups worthy of ridicule, each presenting a distinct and unified set of religious claims. Kabīr's object seems to have been to satirise all of the manifestations of organised religion that he saw in these two competing groups, and remarks time and again that both fail to bring worshippers any closer to God.[4]

---

[2] LORENZEN (2005: 53).

[3] HAWLEY–JUERGENSMEYER (1988: 41).

[4] For evidence of Kabīr as an equal-opportunity reviler of Islam and Hinduism, see complaints against him recorded by the sixteenth century author Anantadās: 'He has abandoned the customs of the Muslims and has broken the touchability rules of the Hindus…' (cited in LORENZEN 2005: 71).

In the remainder of this paper, I will go into some detail about the historical development of the binary opposition between *āstika* and *nāstika,* and its relevance to the concept of Hinduism as a unified group of beliefs. The idea that, for instance, the Yoga, Nyāya, and Vedānta schools of philosophy are essentially compatible is itself a product of this late medieval period of unification. Indeed, in the earliest formulations of the six *āstika* schools, Yoga and Vedānta do not even appear. Furthermore, Advaita Vedānta philosophers writing before this period of consolidation, such as the eighth century thinker Śaṅkara, take great pains to criticise and emphasise the defects in Sāṁkhya and Yoga. By contrast, the later Advaitins Mādhava and Madhusūdana emphasise Advaita's compatibility with Sāṁkhya and Yoga, and save their harshest critiques for the *nāstika* schools, which by then included Buddhists and Jainas.

So, how is it that a school of philosophy qualifies as *āstika*? What essential property must it have to avoid being *nāstika*? The etymology of these terms is important: the *āstika* is someone who says that 'there is' (*asti*), while the *nāstika* says 'there is not' (*nāsti*). The central question, then, is what precisely is being affirmed or denied. Historically, commentators have given a number of different answers to this question. When attempting to justify their own use of these terms, modern introductory texts on Indian philosophy generally cite the *Laws of Manu*: 'Any twice-born who disregards the two roots of [Śruti and Smṛti] on the basis of the science of logic should be excluded by the righteous as a *nāstika*, a reviler of the *Veda*.'[5] This definition, however simple it may appear, requires further analysis.

The southern Indian commentator Medhātithi (ninth century) provides a thoughtful gloss on some of the terms in Manu's famous verse. He is concerned to identify precisely what it means to scorn the *Veda* on the basis of the science of logic (*tarka-śāstra*). Does this imply that those who follow the injunctions of the *Veda* are being illogical?[6] He understands the 'science of logic' just to refer to 'the works on logic written by *nāstika*s, namely the works of the Buddhists, Cārvākas, and so forth, in which it is proclaimed again and again that the *Veda* is contrary to *dharma*'.[7] Medhātithi understands Manu's injunction primarily in the context of ritual action. If someone does something forbidden by the *Veda*s and the Smṛti, and even when warned that it is prohibited by the *Veda* he says that he does not care since the *Veda*s lack authority, then he should be excluded (e.g. excluded from officiating at sacrifices). It is

---

[5] MDhŚ 2.11:

yo 'vamanyeta te tūbhe hetu-śāstrâśrayād dvijaḥ /
sa sādhubhir bahiṣ-kāryo nāstiko veda-nindakaḥ //

(OLIVELLE (2006: 404)).

[6] See GANERI's (2001: 7 ff.) analysis of this passage and the dangers of reason 'ungrounded' and functioning as an end in itself.

[7] ManuBh *ad* MDhŚ 2.11, I: p. 72: *nāstika-tarka-śāstraṁ bauddha-cārvākâdi-śāstraṁ yatra vedo 'dharmāyêti punaḥ punar uddhuṣyate.*

important to note here that 'the reviler of the *Veda*' is not someone who says that the *Veda* is untrue, but someone who says that the *Veda* is immoral. Medhātithi's gloss of the word *nāstika* itself reflects his preoccupation with ritual action. Commenting on another passage of the *Laws of Manu* (MDhŚ 8.309), he writes that 'a *nāstika* is one who says, "there is no other world; there is no [purpose in] gift-giving; there is no [purpose in] sacrificing".'[8] For Medhātithi, a *nāstika* is someone who refuses to participate in Vedic rituals because he sees them as pointless or even as immoral.

Medhātithi seems to have in mind in particular the Buddhist and Jaina critiques of Vedic ritual on the basis of the doctrine of non-violence (*ahiṁsā*). Elsewhere in his commentary on Manu, he explicitly argues for the necessity of violence in certain contexts.[9] Yet it was not only the Buddhists and Jainas who opposed the tradition of Vedic ritualism and its practice of animal sacrifice; the Sāṁkhya and Yoga schools were also at the forefront of this debate.[10] The most well-known expression of the Sāṁkhya-Yoga rejection of Vedic sacrifice, and by extension the rejection of the sanctity of the *Veda*s, comes at *Sāṁkhya-kārikā*: 'Scripture, like perception, [is ineffective in relieving suffering,] since it is associated with impurity, destruction, and excess ...'[11] From a very early period, philosophical schools were split on the question of animal sacrifice. While the Sāṁkhya position on non-violence may have originally been the minority opinion, it eventually gained credence, even among Brahmins who specialise in ritual performance. The acceptance of the principle of non-violence has been so thorough that animal sacrifice among Hindus today is uncommon, and many Indians are of the opinion that such things as cow slaughter were never practised in ancient India.[12]

Late-medieval Advaita doxographies typically rank Sāṁkhya and Yoga very high on the list of *āstika* schools, likely because they had been thoroughly tamed and their terminology co-opted as part of a larger Vedāntic cosmology. Yet of all systems later listed as *āstika*, it is Sāṁkhya that comes closest to Manu's description of a 'reviler of the *Veda*'. Certainly, Sāṁkhya accepts scriptural authority as one of the means of valid knowledge, and if the minimum requirement for being an *āstika* is only this, Sāṁkhya qualifies.[13] But

---

[8] ManuBh *ad* MDhŚ 8.309, II: p. 203: *nâsti para-loko nâsti dattaṁ nâsti hutam iti nāstikaḥ.*

[9] See ManuBh *ad* MDhŚ 8.350 and 4.162.

[10] *Vide* HALBFASS (1983: 1–26).

[11] SK 2, p. 256:

dṛṣṭavad ānuśravikaḥ sa hy aviśuddhi-kṣayâtiśaya-yuktaḥ /
tad-viparītaḥ śreyān vyaktâvyakta-jña-vijñānāt //

[12] One indication of this is the furore surrounding Dwijendra Narayan Jha's *Myth of the Holy Cow* (JHA 2002), a book banned by a court in Hyderabad for its thesis that ancient Indians slaughtered and ate cows.

[13] According to Sāṁkhya commentators, 'reliable testimony' (*āpta-vacana*) refers both to the testimony of reliable persons and to the testimony of scripture (*Vide* Vācaspatimiśra, TK).

Sāṁkhya is unlike Vedānta, which saw reason as only able to function properly when anchored to the truths revealed by scripture.[14] Sāṁkhya denies that reason by itself is inherently aimless and unstable. On the contrary, for Sāṁkhya it is scriptural authority which needs to be checked by reason, since blind adherence to Vedic injunctions without critical evaluation leads to immorality and demerit. Therefore, Medhātithi's description of a *nāstika* text as one 'in which it is proclaimed again and again that the *Veda* is contrary to *dharma*', fits the *Sāṁkhya-kārikā* and its early commentaries perfectly. By the standards of the Vedic ritualist tradition, the tradition whose principles the authors of the *Laws of Manu* had internalised, the Sāṁkhya is a *nāstika* school.

The earlier meaning of *nāstika*, reviler of the *Veda*, was primarily an issue of orthopraxy (correct ritual performance) instead of orthodoxy (correct opinion). Over time, however, the second meaning displaced the first. This coincided, I believe, with the gradual rise of the Vedānta school and decline of Vedic ritual theory, represented especially by the Pūrva Mīmāṁsā school. We see evidence of the lack of general acknowledgement of a school known as 'Vedānta' in early doxographies like the Jaina *Ṣaḍ-darśana-samuccaya* and the Buddhist *Maṇi-mekalai*. This corroborates Hajime NAKAMURA's observation that before the tenth century, Vedānta was rarely acknowledged by Jainas, Buddhists, or other Brahmanical schools.[15] By the late medieval period the situation had changed completely. Mīmāṁsā weakened and lost influence, although it never lost its fundamental interpretive importance. To the extent that it did survive, it took on theistic ideas from the other schools.[16] However, the Vedāntic understanding of the *Veda* as imparting information about ultimate truths became the primary model for scriptural interpretation, just as Nyāya logical principles became common currency for any school that sought to engage in rigorous logical argumentation. By this period, the word *nāstika* was understood in terms or orthodoxy rather than orthopraxy. Thus, a reviler of the *Veda* was someone who denied that the *Veda*s' depiction of ultimate reality was accurate.

Besides Advaita Vedāntins, the Jainas are the other group of authors who wrote a large number of doxographies. The first of these Jaina doxographies, Haribhadra's *Ṣaḍ-darśana-samuccaya* ('Compendium of the Six Philosophical Systems') uses the enumeration of six schools as an ordering principle. Haribhadra lived in approximately the eighth century, according to traditional sources in not far from the town of Chitrakoot (Citrakūṭ, currently in northern Madhya Pradesh). For Haribhadra, the six *āstika* schools are: Buddhism, Nyāya, Sāṁkhya, Jainism, Vaiśeṣika and Mīmāṁsā. This list is remarkable because it is among the earliest lists of six *āstika-darśana*s, and because these

[14] *Vide* CLOONEY (1993: 29), GANERI (2001: 7 ff.).

[15] NAKAMURA (1989: 206–16).

[16] By the 15th century this process of adaptation had gone so far that some Mīmāṁsakas even accepted the existence of God, *vide* AS 69.

six *āstika* schools do not correspond to the later accounts of the six schools. Specifically, Haribhadra and the even earlier Buddhist list of six schools in Cāttaṉār's *Maṇi-mekalai* include Buddhism and Jainism. Haribhadra does this by defining the term *āstika* differently than it is understood by Mādhava or Madhusūdana. He says that his enumeration of the six schools, including Buddhism and Jainism, is a 'summary of all the *āstika* views'.[17] The commentator Maṇibhadra elucidates this by defining the *āstika* views as those views which affirm the existence of another world (*para-loka*), transmigration (*gati*), virtue (*puṇya*), and vice (*pāpa*).[18] Jainism and Buddhism qualify under this definition just as much as Nyāya, Vaiśeṣika, Sāṁkhya and Mīmāṁsā. And, here and elsewhere, *āstika* does not mean 'theist', or 'affirming the existence of a world-creating God'. If it did, the only of Haribhadra's six systems to qualify would arguably be the Nyāya.

The label *āstika* would be meaningless without the existence of its antithesis, *nāstika*. Haribhadra only identifies one school, the materialist Lokāyata school, as *nāstika*. After he lists the six *āstika* schools, he mentions the Lokāyata school in a kind of appendix:

> '[78] Others do not accept that there is a difference between the Naiyāyika doctrine and the Vaiśeṣikas. In their opinion, there are only five *āstika* schools. [79] In their opinion, the number of the six schools of philosophy is completed by adding the doctrine of the Lokāyatas. Therefore, that doctrine will be described.'[19]

This passage helps clarify just how the enumeration of the six schools functions. Haribhadra is not simply adding up all of the schools that he can find and then presenting this number as the total. Rather, the number six is a pregiven total for the number of possible schools. Haribhadra's job is to look at all of the possible candidates and to see how they can be most reasonably categorised to number six.[20] Like Cāttaṉār, Haribhadra was familiar with many

---

[17] ṢDSa 77cd, p. 62:

evam āstika-vādānāṁ kṛtaṁ saṁkṣepa-kīrtanam /

[18] ṢDSaLV 77, p. 62: *āstika-vādinām iha para-loka-gati-puṇya-pāpâstikya-vādināṁ …*

[19] ṢDSa 78–79, p. 62–63:

naiyāyika-matād anye bhedaṁ vaiśeṣikaiḥ saha /
na manyante mate teṣāṁ pañcâivâstika-vādinaḥ //
ṣaḍ-darśana-saṁkhyā tu pūryate tan-mate kila /
lokāyata-mata-kṣepāt kathyate tena tan-matam //

[20] This tendency to first establish the number of doctrines or sects and then to fit known sects into this schemes was a widespread technique in the pre-modern world. For instance, Islamic scholars used the number of the 72 heretical sects as established by the prophet in the *hadith* as the principle for evaluating the sects of their own eras. To do this, in some cases they double-counted the same sect by using two different names; in other cases they excluded sects on the rationale that these sects were so heretical that they no longer could be considered Muslims, see HENDERSON (1998: 125–126).

more than six schools. Perhaps because the Lokāyata was frequently mentioned as one of the six schools, he cannot simply pass over the materialist school in silence. Instead he offers an acknowledgement that there are other possible ways of counting the schools—not as numbering five or seven, but as adding up to six in some different combination. And he suggests one possible way of doing so, by combining two closely related schools such as the Nyāya and Vaiśeṣika into one. But Haribhadra personally prefers to leave the Lokāyata out of his enumeration.

The Jaina understanding of *āstika* and *nāstika* seems worlds apart from the *Laws of Manu*, since it does not consider reverence for the *Veda* to be the marker of the *āstika* schools. Yet Maṇibhadra's commentary shows the same concern with orthopraxy that we find in Medhātithi, a commentator on the *Laws of Manu*. It is in the context of this earlier, orthoprax sense of 'reviler of the *Veda*' that we can best make sense of the term *nāstika* as presented by the Jainas Haribhadra and Maṇibhadra. Medhātithi defines a *nāstika* as one who says, 'there is no other world; there is no [purpose in] gift-giving; there is no [purpose in] sacrificing'.[21] Compare this to Maṇibhadra's understanding of *āstika* views as those which affirm the existence of another world, transmigration, virtue, and vice.[22] For both authors, these two designations have to do with ritual-ethical action (*karman*). They agree that some actions lead to merit, while others result in demerit. The significance in belief in 'other worlds' (*para-loka*) is also in the context of ritual-ethical action: other worlds are important because only by acknowledging the existence of other worlds can we acknowledge that actions in this life have future consequences.

Besides the interpretations of the word *nāstika* represented by Medhātithi and Maṇibhadra, a third definition from the Sanskrit grammatical tradition complicates our understanding of both. The words *āstika* and *nāstika* are both derived from Pāṇini's rule at *Aṣṭādhyāyī* 4.4.60.[23] Pāṇini simply provides the derivation of the two words without suggesting what exactly is being accepted by the *āstika* or rejected by the *nāstika*. The first substantive definition of two words in the Pāṇinian tradition comes in the *Kāśikā-vṛtti*, a commentary by the seventh century authors Jayāditya and Vāmana. They write, 'The *āstika* is the one who believes that "there exists another world." The opposite of him is the *nāstika*.'[24] This definition has obvious similarities to Maṇibhadra's and Medhātithi's interpretations, since both include existence of another world (*para-loka*) as one of the affirmations of the *āstika*. But the stripped-down definition from the grammatical tradition omits the belief in the efficacy of ritual action found in Medhātithi, and the belief in merit and demerit found in both Maṇibhadra and Medhātithi.

---

[21] ManuBh *ad* MdhŚ 8.309 (II: p. 203): *nâsti para-loko nâsti dattaṁ nāsti hutam iti nāstikaḥ.*

[22] ṢDSaLV 70, p. 62: *āstika-vādinām iha para-loka-gati-puṇya-pāpâstikya-vādinām …*

[23] A 4.4.60: *āsti-nāsti-diṣṭaṁ matiḥ.*

[24] KāśV 1801, vol. V, p. 265: *para-loko 'stîti yasya matiḥ sa āstikaḥ. tad-viparīto nāstikaḥ.*

We should not conclude from a single seventh century passage that the grammarians' definition was the original understanding of the two words, and that Maṇibhadra's and Medhātithi's interpretations were further developments. But this passage does offer proof that there were multiple, related but competing definitions of these terms, and that Maṇibhadra's definition was not simply a bastardisation of the *Laws of Manu* or an example of wishful thinking among the Jainas.[25] After all, Pāṇini's school of grammar is considered an *āstika-darśana* by late medieval doxographers. Although there is no conclusive evidence to rule in favour of any of these three interpretations as the oldest meaning of the term *nāstika*, these ambiguities should lead historians to re-examine the certainty with which they proclaim *Manu-smṛti* 2.11 to be the original and authentic source for the meaning of the term *nāstika*.

Among the most influential of the Advaita Vedānta doxographers who wrote in the late medieval period are Mādhava (fourteenth century) and Madhusūdana Sarasvatī (sixteenth century). I will here discuss only the latter. Among the many texts he authored are the *Prasthāna-bheda* ('The Various Religious Sources', PrBh) and the *Vedānta-kalpa-latikā* ('The Creeper Vine of Vedāntic Views', VKT). The latter is a lengthy point-by-point refutation of the views of the non-Advaita schools.[26] The former, the *Prasthāna-bheda*, is a doxography organised around the eighteen 'sciences' (*vidyā*) or 'sources' (*prasthāna*). This was an alternative scheme employed by some Advaita doxographies, including the *Sarva-mata-saṁgraha* and the *Sarva-siddhânta-saṁgraha*.

Outside of the 18 *āstika* sources, Madhusūdana writes that the *nāstika*s have their own six sources (*prasthāna*). These are the four sects of Buddhists, the Cārvākas, and the Jainas. Although when speaking of the *āstika*s, Madhusūdana takes *prasthāna* to mean 'foundational text', the word *prasthāna*'s semantic fluidity allows him to understand it simply as a synonym for *darśana* when he refers to *nāstika* schools. Indeed, his standard enumeration of Cārvākas, Jainas, and the four schools of Buddhists (Mādhyamika, Yogācāra, Sautrāntika, and Vaibhāṣika) seems to be based on Mādhava's *Sarva-darśana-saṁgraha* or Pseudo-Śaṅkara's *Sarva-siddhânta-saṁgraha*, not on original works from the schools in question. He is the first doxographer explicitly to associate the beliefs of the *nāstika*s with those of foreigners (*mleccha*): 'To sum up, the *nāstika*s

---

[25] Possible scriptural evidence for the grammarians' understanding occurs at *Kaṭha-upaniṣad* 1.20: 'There is this doubt about a man who is dead. "He exists," (*asti*) say some, others, "He exists not" (*nāyam asti*)'—*yêyaṁ prete vicikitsā manuṣye astîty eke nâyam astîti câike* (translation in OLIVELLE (1998: 379), Sanskrit text in OLIVELLE (1998: 378)).

To the best of my knowledge no pre-modern commentator has cited this passage as justification for the definition of *nāstika* and *āstika*.

[26] Madhusūdana actually enumerates 21 viewpoints, including the Advaita Vedānta. Although opponents' views are first presented in brief, most of Madhusūdana's text is devoted to lengthy refutations of some of these views, including rejection of *bhedâbheda* arguments (VKP, p. 36).

have six sources (*prasthāna*). We disregard them because, like the teachings of the foreigners, they are external to the *Veda*s (*veda-bāhya*), and because they are useless even for the indirect attainment of human moral ends.'[27] Madhusūdana's criteria for classifying a text as *nāstika* are in part pragmatic—while the texts of foreigners and *nāstika*s are wholly useless for any human end (*puruṣârtha*), he claims that all *āstika* texts do lead to these ends, either directly or indirectly.

Madhusūdana concludes the *Prasthāna-bheda* by organising the *āstika* schools into three hierarchical categories, based on their theories of the creation of the world. The Nyāya, Vaiśeṣika, and Mīmāṁsā belong to the *ārambha-vāda,* an atomistic theory of creation.[28] The Sāṁkhya, Yoga, and the theistic schools belong to the *pariṇāma-vāda*, the theory of the real transformation of primal matter. The highest of the three cosmogonies is the *vivarta-vāda*, the theory of the unreal manifestation of Brahman. This theory is held only by the Vedāntins:

> 'According to the third viewpoint, that of the *brahma-vādin*s, Brahman, which is self-luminous, supreme bliss, and without a second, arranges itself by means of its own illusory power (*māyā*) in the form of the world in a way that is ultimately false (*mithyā*). The true purpose of all the sages who have created the systems is in the central purport, the unique, highest Lord, since all the systems ultimately issue into the *vivarta-vāda*. Those sages cannot just be confused, because they are omniscient. However, the access to human moral ends is not immediately possible for those who are preoccupied with external objects. The sages teach the various systems so that such people will not become *nāstika*s. Not knowing the true purport (*tātparya*) of the sages, people follow those various paths, grasping for ends that are contrary to the *Veda*s and overlooking the true purport of the *Veda*s.'[29]

---

[27] PrBh 13: *evaṁ militvā nāstikānāṁ ṣaṭ prasthānāni. tāni kasmān nôcyante. satyam. veda-bāhyatvāt teṣāṁ mlecchâdi-prasthānavat paramparayâpi puruṣârthânupayogitvād upekṣanīyam eva.*

It is not clear whether Madhusūdana also considers *mleccha* teachings as completely useless for any human end. He might possibly acknowledge, as the Mīmāṁsaka Śabara does, that foreigners' knowledge is often useful in some instrumental way, such as their skill in the breeding and capturing of birds (ŚBh 1.3.10).

[28] Of course, most Mīmāṁsakas would be very surprised to find that they subscribe to *ārambha-vāda*.

[29] PrBh 23, p. 23–24: *sva-prakāśa-paramânandâdvitīyaṁ brahma sva-māyā-vaśān mithyâiva jagad-ākāreṇa kalpata iti tṛtīyaḥ pakṣo brahma-vādinām. sarveṣām prasthāna-kartṝṇāṁ munīnāṁ vivarta-vāda-paryavasānenâdvitīye parameśvara eva pratipādye tātparyaṁ na hi te munayo bhrāntāḥ sarva-jñatvāt teṣām kiṁtu bahir-viṣaya-pravaṇānām āpātataḥ puruṣârthe praveśo na saṁbhavatîti nāstikya-vāraṇāya taiḥ prakāra-bhedāḥ pradarśitāḥ. tatra teṣāṁ tātparyam abuddhvā veda-viruddhe 'py arthe tātparyam utprekṣamāṇās tanmatam evôpādeyatvena gṛhṇanto janā nānā-patha-juṣo bhavanti.*

Madhusūdana claims that all of the great sages of the *āstika* schools besides the Advaita knew that some of the doctrines they taught were false. They taught what they did in order to keep humans from gravitating toward *nāstika* doctrines, and instead taught systems designed gradually to lead these people to the ultimate truths of Advaita Vedānta. The sages saw their teachings as useful in helping an audience with limited understanding avoid more serious pitfalls. Such a strategy is one possible way of solving a vexing problem to any thinker who seeks to value the *āstika* schools over the *nāstika*s in an unambiguous way. For Śaṅkara and thinkers of his era who had no particular concern with showing that the *nāstika* schools were inferior to all of the *āstika* schools, the simple solution was simply to deny, for instance, that Kapila, the sage of the Sāṁkhyas, was truly a reliable source. For Madhusūdana approximately 800 years later, discrediting Kapila, Patañjali and the other *āstika* sages was not a viable alternative. Instead, he adopted an explanatory strategy commonly found in the *Purāṇa*s by which these sages could both be said to be omniscient and that the schools they founded could be said to be flawed.

Sanskrit doxographers in the late medieval period were concerned with the concordance of the *āstika* systems in a way that pre-twelfth century authors were not. The corollary of this was an increasing concern with and systematisation of the category of *nāstika*. For Madhusūdana, this means accepting all *āstika* schools as having some heuristic value, although only Vedānta contains the ultimate teachings. For him, Buddhism and Jainism are completely without value. By the late medieval period, of course, Buddhism was virtually nonexistent in India, and Jainism hardly a threat. It would therefore seem that the need to unify *āstika* doctrines would have been less urgent, not more. So why should the late-medievals have been more concerned with defining the boundaries of the *āstikas* than their predecessors?

One answer to this question—the single most pronounced historical change between the eighth and sixteenth centuries—was the migration of Muslims into India that led to the rule of northern India first by the Delhi Sultanate (1206–1526) and later by the Mughal Empire (1526–1707). Living in northern India as subjects of the Mughal Empire, Madhusūdana Sarasvatī and other Advaita doxographers could not but have encountered Islam. There is even a widely disseminated story of Madhusūdana's visit to the Emperor Akbar's court at Fatehpur Sikri.[30] Yet in Madhusūdana's *Prasthāna-bheda*, ostensibly an exhaustive catalogue of all doctrines, Islam is never mentioned.[31] Among Islamic intellectuals, Akbar and Dārā Shikoh went to great efforts to try to understand the systems of Indian philosophy, and had the *Mahā-bhārata, Rāmāyaṇa, Purāṇa*s, and *Upaniṣad*s translated into Persian.[32] But from the other side there

[30] Halbfass (1988: 186–187).

[31] Halbfass (1988: 186–187).

[32] Ahmad (1999: 167–181, 191–196, 218–223).

was a complete lack of effort to translate works from Persian and Arabic into Sanskrit, indicative of a world view that did not see any value or purpose in intercultural or interreligious understanding.[33] For Akbar and other like-minded rulers, there was obvious practical benefit to create a court religion that combined Hinduism and Islam. By creating a distinctively Indian religion that incorporated symbols that resonate with all of his subjects, Akbar would have been able to strengthen allegiances and solidify his support among groups that may have been uneasy submitting to a Muslim ruler. No similar utility existed for śāstric scholars. The traditions of Sanskrit grammar, Mīmāṁsā, and *Dharma-śāstra* indeed teach of the *a priori* uselessness of foreign traditions. At the same time, among Sanskrit authors there was no explicit ideological resistance to Islam. Unlike later Hindu nationalist intellectuals, who sometimes recorded their fantasies of heroic and violent resistance to Muslim oppression, Sanskrit intellectuals of the sixteenth and seventeenth centuries responded with silence.[34]

Is it possible that the Cārvākas, Jainas, and Buddhists function as place-holders for Islam in late medieval Sanskrit doxographies? After all, the Buddhist philosophers had ceased to offer any meaningful competition to the school of Vedānta for 500 years before Madhusūdana wrote—what could possibly be the use of vilifying a school that had disappeared almost completely from the Indian subcontinent? The answer to this question requires an understanding of doxography as a genre, and as part of the larger śāstric world view. The frustration many modern scholars have had in dealing with the Indian doxographies comes from a misunderstanding of their purpose. They were not empirical accounts of a state of affairs, upon which we can base reliable and comprehensive accounts of the Indian philosophical schools. Rather, they were an idealised vision of the way the doctrines should be, clear, unambiguous, distinct, and leading inevitably in a progression from lower to higher.

The purpose of doxography in India was not the cataloguing of all existent schools of philosophical thought, or for that matter all of the schools that existed throughout history. In spite of Haribhadra's assertion that 'there are only six schools of philosophy'[35] and of the doxographers' titles holding out the apparent promise of surveying 'all systems', these doxographers were quite aware that there were other systems that fell outside of their descriptive pur-

---

[33] HALBFASS (1988: 172 ff.).

[34] The main exception to this silence seems in to be in Jaina texts such as *Hīra-saubhāgya,* a biography of Hīravijaya Sūri (1527–1595), see DUNDAS (1999). In the modern period, Bankim Chandra Chatterjee's *Ānanda-maṭha* (1882) tells a story of violent *saṁnyāsin* resistance against Muslim soldiers working for the British East India Company. *Vande Mātaram,* now the national song of India, appeared for the first time in this work.

[35] ṢDSa 3:

> *darśanāni ṣaḍ evâtra mūla-bheda-vyapekṣayā /*
> *devatā-tattva-bhedena jñātavyāni manīṣibhi //*

view. The late-medieval doxographers naturalise a state of affairs that is many centuries beyond their own historical situation, in what amounts to a suppression of historical change.[36] Only a fundamental shift in the understanding of the purpose of doxography could have eliminated the Buddhists from their fixed place among *nāstika* schools. They serve an important function in doxography as the prototypical *nāstika* school, allowing *āstika*s to define themselves over and against the Buddhists.

The near-total lack of mention of Muslims in Sanskrit texts has led some historians to suggest that there was little contact between Sanskrit intellectuals and Muslims, or if there was contact, there was no awareness of Islam as a religion or system of belief. Sanskrit texts were very late to adopt the word *musulmāna*, instead often describing Muslims with the names of other foreigners who had arrived over a millennium before: *yavana*s ('Ionians') or *śaka*s ('Scythians').[37] In other cases, the Sanskrit authors were more accurate, labelling the foreigners they encountered as *turuṣka*s ('Turks'), yet still there was no acknowledgement that many of these foreigners shared a single religious identity. Sanskrit intellectuals focused on their (imagined) place of origin, not their beliefs. The logic of medieval Indian xenology followed the patterns of doxography and *śāstra* generally, applying categories from a millennium earlier to changing sociocultural conditions without concern for their descriptive adequacy.

However, there is ample evidence from medieval texts in Indian vernacular languages to falsify the thesis that medieval Indians in general were unaware of the general tenets of a religion shared by the group of people called Muslims. That this conventional wisdom has stood for so long is an indication of heavy reliance on Sanskrit texts among historians of Indian religions, accompanied by ignorance or lack of interest in works in other Indian languages. In particular, the evidence David LORENZEN cites from medieval *bhakti* texts suggests that Hindus and Muslims were quite aware of their mutual differences, and even indicates a lively tradition of theological debate between the two groups.

One remarkable text of this sort comes from the Marathi poet Eknāth (1553–1599). In his *Hiṇdu-Turk Saṁvād* ('Dialogue Between Hindu and Turk'), Eknāth expresses not only an awareness of the differences in practice between Muslims and Vaiṣṇava Hindus, but also an awareness of theological differences. His goal, like many other late medieval *bhakti* poets, is to transcend sectarian differences in order to realise the truth of the one universal god wor-

---

36 On the logic of *śāstra*, see POLLOCK (1985: 516).

37 THAPAR (1989: 223). Obviously, *yavana* came to be regarded as a generic term for 'foreigner' or 'barbarian.' On *yavana* and *śaka*, see HALBFASS (1988: 176 ff.). Cases where Muslims are recognised as such in Sanskrit texts generally seem to be nineteenth century interpolations. For instance, the *Bhaviṣya-purāṇa* refers to *mahāmada* (Mohammedans), and alludes to the story of Adam and Eve, see HALBFASS (1988: 194).

shipped by all people, Hindu and Muslim alike. I will quote one memorable exchange from his two characters, whom he calls 'the Turk' and 'the Brahmin':

> 'Turk: O Brahmin, listen to what I have to say:
> Your scripture is a mystery to everyone.
> God has hands and feet, you say—
> This is really impossible!
>
> Brahmin: Listen, you great fool of a Turk!
> See God in all living things.
> You haven't grasped this point
> And so you have become a nihilist (*śūnya-vādka*).'[38]

The Brahmin labels his opponent with the especially remarkable Marathi epithet 'nihilist' (*śūnya-vādka*). This pejorative term hints at a vestigial cultural memory of a much earlier debate between Vedāntins and Mādhyamika Buddhists. The Mādhyamikas, also known in Sanskrit as *śūnya-vādins*, maintained the doctrine of emptiness (*śūnyatā*), teaching that there is no ultimately existent reality, no God or ultimate principle serving as the foundation of the world's existence. This passage should not be taken to indicate that Eknāth really believes the Muslims share the atheist doctrines of the Mādhyamika Buddhists. Rather, this word is another example of the extraordinary adaptability of Indian terms employed for othering. These words, emptied of all historical and doctrinal specificity, in time become little more than vague pejoratives. This is what also happens to the term *nāstika*, whose meaning varied widely across historical epochs. Even a Muslim, who affirms the existence of a supreme God, a life after death, and a specific path of ethical behaviour, can be categorised alongside Buddhists as a nihilist.

'Hindu' was not originally a Sanskrit word. It was first a Persian term used by Muslims to describe not a religious but a regional or ethnic identity: the people living near the Indus, or Sindhu, river.[39] Only at a relatively late date was the term adopted by Indians to refer to themselves, typically to distinguish themselves from outsider groups known as *turuṣka*s ('Turks') or *mleccha*s ('barbarians'). Cynthia TALBOT (1995: 700) has recorded the earliest usage of the word Hindu in an Indian language from inscriptions in mid-fourteenth century Andhra Pradesh. There, some Vijayanagara kings were described with the epithet 'Sultan among Hindu kings' (*Hindu-raya-suratrana*). TALBOT cautions that in these inscriptions, 'Hindu meant Indic as opposed to Turkish, not "of the Hindu religion" as opposed to "of the Islamic religion".'[40] In Gauḍīya Vaiṣṇava texts written in Bengali in the sixteenth and seventeenth centuries,

---

[38] ZELLIOT (1982: 178).

[39] *Vide* HALBFASS (1988: 192–193), THAPAR (1989: 222). The only authors to deny this are Hindu nationalists such as Savarkar, Golwalkar, and their followers.

[40] TALBOT (1995: 700).

'Hindu' was occasionally used to distinguish natives from *yavana*s or *mleccha*s.[41] Although from context it was clear that these foreigners were Muslims, this was not stated explicitly by Gauḍīya Vaiṣṇava authors until the eighteenth century, when the term *musulmāna* finally enters common usage in Bengali. In this case too, the word may have designated ethnicity generally, not a specific set of religious beliefs.

And yet, although early instances of the word 'Hindu' in fourteenth century inscriptions seem to use the word in a geographical or ethnic sense, TALBOT (1995: 720) acknowledges that ethnicity is a composite of many factors—including 'language, costume, marriage customs and fighting styles'—some of which do have their basis in religious practice. Just as observation would lead authors of vernacular texts to remark on differences of food or dress, eventually this led to an appreciation of the principled religious differences underlying some of these more superficial differences in custom. 'Hindu' was originally an ethnic designator. But the ample evidence from fifteenth and sixteenth century authors shows that by that time, the word 'Hindu' had been adopted by vernacular poets in a more specifically religious sense.

According to David LORENZEN (2005: 53), the period from 1200 to 1500 was a time in which rivalry between Hindu and Muslim created a newly self-conscious religious identity among Hindus. In this paper I have focused on a group of texts from the same time period and slightly later, doxographies written in Sanskrit between the fourteenth and seventeenth centuries. The evidence from medieval philosophy and doxography corroborates the thesis that LORENZEN has advanced. In philosophical texts before the twelfth century, the category of 'affirmer' (*āstika*) is a blurry one, potentially admitting groups such as Buddhists and Jainas who affirm the existence of worlds after death. But sometime during the late medieval period, the category of *āstika* hardens, and the well-known classification of the 'six systems' develops as it is known today. At the same time, Buddhists and Jainas become permanently classified as *nāstika*s in influential Advaita doxographies. Also in the late medieval period, the category of *nāstika* undergoes a subtle blurring with categories such as 'barbarian' (*mleccha*), allowing foreigners to be classed together with Buddhists and Jainas.[42] Pre-modern philosophical authors writing in Sanskrit never acknowledge Islam explicitly. But the perceived threat of Islam motivates them to create a strictly defined category of *āstika* philosophical systems, systems that profess belief in the authority of the *Veda*. This category, in turn, is later reformulated according to further developments in the nineteenth

[41] *Vide* O'CONNELL (1973: 341).

[42] At MDhŚ 2.11, *nāstika*s are defined as twice-borns who revile the *Veda*. Since twice-borns (members of the three highest *varṇa*s) are only indigenous to India, this excludes foreigners from the category of *nāstika*. In later definitions, this stipulation seems to have been dropped.

century. The medieval list of *āstika darśana*s becomes known as the 'schools of Hindu philosophy. Also in the modern period, Hinduism becomes a 'world religion', and in the eyes of many Hindus, Advaita Vedānta is the highest among the schools of philosophy. These developments were only possible due to the efforts of the late medieval doxographers, who may have been surprised if they had been able to see the fruits of their labours today.

BIBLIOGRAPHY

A = Pāṇini: *Aṣṭādhyāyī*. Śrisa Chandra Vasu (ed., tr.): *The Aṣṭādhyāyī of Pāṇini*. Motilal Banarsidass, Delhi 1962.

AHMAD 1999 = Ahmad, Aziz: *Studies in Islamic Culture in the Indian Environment*. Oxford University Press, Delhi 1999.

AS = Laugākṣi Bhāskara: *Artha-saṁgraha*. A.B. Gajendragadkar; R.D. Karmarkar (eds.): *The Arthasaṁgraha of Laugākṣi Bhāskara*. Motilal Banarsidass, Delhi 1998.

CLOONEY 1993 = Clooney, Francis X. *Theology After Vedānta: An Experiment in Comparative Theology*. State University of New York Press, Albany 1993.

DUNDAS 1999 = Dundas, Paul: 'Jain Perceptions of Islam in the Early Modern Period', *Indo-Iranian Journal* 42,1 (1999) 35–46.

GANERI 2001 = Ganeri, Jonardon: *Philosophy in Classical India*. Routledge, London 2001.

HALBFASS 1983 = Halbfass, Wilhelm: *Studies in Kumārila and Śaṅkara*. Verlag für Orientalistische Fachpublikationen, Reinbek 1983.

HALBFASS 1988 = Halbfass, Wilhelm: *India and Europe*. State University of New York Press, Albany 1988.

HAWLEY–JUERGENSMEYER 1988 = Hawley, John Stratton; Juergensmeyer, Mark: *Songs of the Saints of India*. Oxford University Press, New York 1988.

HENDERSON 1998 = Henderson, John B.: *The Construction of Orthodoxy and Heresy*. State University of New York Press, Albany 1988.

JHA 2002 = Jha, Dwijendra Narayan: *The Myth of the Holy Cow*. Verso, New York 2002.

KāśV = Vāmana and Jayāditya: *Kāśikā-vṛtti*. Tripathi, Jaya Shankar Lal; Malaviya, Sudhakar (eds.): *Kāśikā: A Commentary on Pāṇini's Grammar*. Vols. 1–10. Tara Printing Works, Varanasi 1985.

KU = *Kaṭhôpaniṣad*. See: OLIVELLE (1998).

LARSON 1998 = Larson, Gerald: *Classical Sāṁkhya*. Motilal Banarsidass, New Delhi 1998.

LORENZEN 2005 = Lorenzen, David: 'Who Invented Hinduism?', in: J.E. Llewellyn (ed.): *Defining Hinduism: A Reader*. Routledge, New York 2005: 52–80.

ManuBh = Medhātithi: *Manu-bhāṣya*. See: MDhŚ.

MDhŚ = *Mānava-dharma-śāstra* [*Manu-smṛti*]. (1) Ganganath Jha (ed.): *Manusmṛti with the Manubhāṣya of Medhātithi*. Motilal Banarsidass, Delhi 1999. (2) See: OLIVELLE (2006).

NAKAMURA 1989 = Nakamura, Hajime: *A History of Early Vedānta Philosophy, Part One*. Motilal Banarsidass, Delhi 1989.

O'CONNELL 1973 = O'Connell, Joseph T.: 'The Word "Hindu" in Gauḍīya Vaiṣṇava Texts', *Journal of the American Oriental Society* 93,3 (1973) 340–344.

OLIVELLE 1998 = Olivelle, Patrick: *The Early Upaniṣads: Annotated Text and Translation*. Oxford University Press, New York 1998.

OLIVELLE 2006 = Olivelle, Patrick: *Manu's Code of Law: A Critical Edition and Translation of the Mānava-Dharmaśāstra*. Oxford University Press, New Delhi 2006.

POLLOCK 1985 = Pollock, Sheldon. 'The Theory of Practice and the Practice of Theory in Indian Intellectual History', *Journal of the American Oriental Society*, 105,3 (1985) 499–519.

PrBh = Madhusūdana Sarasvatī: *Prasthāna-bheda*. Albrecht Weber (ed.): 'Madhusûdana-Sarasvatî's encyklopädische Uebersicht der orthodoxen brahmanischen Literatur', *Indische Studien*, Ferd Dümmler's Buchhandlung, Berlin 1850: 1–24.

ṢDSa = Haribhadra-sūri: *Ṣaḍ-darśana-samuccaya*. Dāmodar Lāl Gosvāmī Śāstrī (ed.): *Śrī-Haribhadra-sūri-viracitaḥ Ṣaḍdarśanasamuccayaḥ*. The Chowkhamba Sanskrit Series 95, Chowkhamba Sanskrit Book Depot, Benares 1905.

ṢDSaLV = Maṇibhadra: *Ṣaḍ-darśana-samuccaya-laghu-vṛtti*. See: ṢDSa.

ŚBh = Śabarasvāmin: *Śābara-bhāṣya*. Jha, Ganganatha (tr.). *Śābarabhāṣya*. Oriental Institute, Baroda 1933.

SK = Īśvarakṛṣṇa: *Sāṁkhya-kārikā*. See: LARSON (1998).

TALBOT 1995 = Talbot, Cynthia: 'Inscribing the Other, Inscribing the Self: Hindu-Muslim Identities in Pre-colonial India', *Comparative Studies in Society and History* 37,4 (1995) 692–722.

THAPAR 1989 = Thapar, Romila: 'Imagined Religious Communities? Ancient History and the Modern Search for a Hindu Identity', *Modern Asian Studies* 23,2 (1989) 209–231.

TK = Vācaspatimiśra: *Tattva-kaumudī*. Ganganath Jha (ed.): *The Tattva-kaumudī: Vācaspati Miśra's Commentary on the Sāṁkhya-kārikā*. Oriental Book Agency, Poona 1965.

VKP = Madhusūdana Sarasvatī: *Vedānta-kalpa-latikā*. Karmarkar, R.D. (ed.). *Vedantakalpalatika*. Bhandarkar Institute Press, Poona 1962.

ZELLIOT 1982 = Zelliot, Eleanor: 'A Medieval Encounter Between Hindu and Muslim: Eknath's Drama-Poem Hindu-Turk Samvad', in: Fred W. Clothey (ed.): *Images of Man: Religious and Historical Process in South Asia*. New Era Publications, Madras 1982: 171–195.

Rationalisation and Sincerity in Mīmāṁsā Hermeneutics

LAWRENCE McCREA

Indian philosophy has often, reasonably enough, been characterised as basically scholastic in character. While philosophers of various schools of thought often exercise considerable originality in formulating their arguments, this originality typically takes place within fairly well established and well recognised limits. A Buddhist philosopher, for instance, may exercise considerable freedom in formulating his theory of inference, but he cannot really accept the existence of a permanent self without in effect ceasing to be a Buddhist philosopher in both his own eyes and those of his interlocutors. Similarly, a Mīmāṁsaka, whatever his position on specific matters of epistemological or interpretive theory, must uphold both the eternality and the validity of the *Veda*s in matters of Dharma if he is to remain a Mīmāṁsaka. Ordinarily, then, an author working in any of the well established Sanskrit philosophical traditions will spend part of his time defending theses and developing arguments that are entirely his own, while at other times he will be arguing in support of positions he did not himself formulate or choose, but that he is not able to comfortably alter or discard.

In most of the more rigorous and theoretically ambitious works of Indian philosophy it is, I think, possible to trace out a dynamic interplay between these two conflicting tendencies: to push one's own premises as far as they will go and follow the line of one's own argument wherever it leads, and to make the best case one can for positions one has inherited from one's tradition even where they are superfluous or constitute an impediment to making the strongest possible philosophical argument.

It would be a mistake, I think, to see this tension as operative exclusively in the Indian philosophical tradition, or in other such overtly scholastic traditions. It could certainly be argued that philosophers in all traditions not infrequently feel constrained by larger cultural imperatives to uphold certain positions even where they are unsupported by or inconsistent with their philosophical arguments. Still, the structure of the field of philosophical debate in the Sanskrit tradition—where nearly all authors explicitly situate their own texts in an already established philosophical text tradition committed to a well defined set of epistemological and ontological positions—makes this dynamic more acute and more easily traced, for the most part.

World View and Theory in Indian Philosophy
Warsaw Indological Studies 5 (2012) 119–135.

I would like here to briefly examine certain aspects of this dynamic as it plays out in the works of the great seventh century Mīmāṁsā theorist Kumārilabhaṭṭa and some of his successors in the Mīmāṁsā tradition. Mīmāṁsā is often held up as the most 'traditional' or 'orthodox' of the Indian philosophical traditions, but Kumārila in particular can be surprisingly radical at times, taking bold and unprecedented stands on a variety of key issues. He is prepared, when occasion warrants, to openly challenge the arguments and interpretations taken by Śabara, his most important predecessor, on whose *Mīmāṁsā-sūtra-bhāṣya* all Kumārila's works comment. More typically, however, he simply pushes his arguments into areas unmentioned by Śabara, and it is here that he very often develops his most daring positions. This is perhaps nowhere more strikingly evident than in the *Sambandhâkṣepa-parihāra* section of the *Śloka-vārttika* (MŚV; his commentary on the first section of the first chapter of Śabara's *Bhāṣya*).

The *Sambandhâkṣepa-parihāra* ('rejection of the denial of a connection'—the name is Kumārila's coinage) comes as part of the long commentary on *Mīmāṁsā-sūtra* 1.1.5, and forms the conclusion of the argument for the eternality of language.[1] It responds to arguments that there is no natural connection between words and their meanings and that, if this connection does exist, it must have been produced at some time by some personal agent and hence is not eternal, as the Mīmāṁsā argument demands. Śabara argues that if word-meaning connections were really created by some person or persons, these creators would have to be remembered (just as we remember Pāṇini and Piṅgala as the creators of the technical terms belonging to the grammatical and metrical systems they devised).[2] Even if we were to admit as a theoretical possibility that some person created ordinary words such as 'cow' and was later forgotten, we cannot simply a s s u m e the existence of such a creator in the absence of any evidence. To the opponent's contention that we can, through

[1] See ŚBh in MD, I: pp. 62–69 and MŚV *Sambandhâkṣepa-parihāra*, pp. 453–482.

[2] ŚBh on MS 1.1.5 (MD, I: pp. 64–65): *yadi hi puruṣaḥ kṛtvā saṁbandhaṁ vyavahārayet, vyavahāra-kāle 'vaśyaṁ smartavyo bhavati. saṁpratipattau hi kartṛ-vyavahartror arthaḥ sidhyati, na vipratipattau. na hi vṛddhi-śabdenâpāṇiner vyavahārataḥ ād-aicaḥ pratīyeran pāṇini-kṛtim ananumanyamānasya vā. tathā ma-kāreṇâpiṅgalasya na sarva-gurus trikaḥ pratīyeta. piṅgala-kṛtim ananumanyamānasya vā. tena kartṛ-vyavahartārau saṁpratipadyete. tena vede vyavaharadbhir avaśyaṁ smaraṇīyaḥ saṁbandhasya kartā syāt, vyavahārasya ca.*— 'For if a person were to create a connection and establish a verbal usage, then at the time of usage that person would certainly have to be remembered. For the meaning is established only when there is agreement between the creator and the user, not when there is disagreement. For people would not understand by the word "vṛddhi" the sounds "ā" "ai" and "au" if the speaker were either not Pāṇini, or someone who does not accept Pāṇini's work; likewise a set of three heavy syllables would not be understood by the letter "ma" if the speaker were not Piṅgala, or someone who accepted Piṅgala's work. It is only by virtue of this that the creator and the user [of the expression] could be in agreement. Thus, in the case of the *Veda*, the creator of the connection and of the verbal expression would have to be remembered by its users.'

arthâpatti, presume the existence of such a creator even without specific evidence, Śabara responds as follows:

> 'If the meanings of words could definitely not be apprehended due to the absence of a creator, then we could understand, through *arthâpatti*, that there is a creator. But there is another way: Children are seen, visibly, to learn meanings upon hearing their elders using words in their own senses. Those elders too, when they were children, [learned] from other elders, and they again from others. It could be that there is no beginning.'[3]

This is a key passage, as it provides the template not only for the argument for the eternality of language, but for the eternality of the *Veda*s as well. So long as it is possible to believe that others in the past acquired knowledge of words and their meanings, and likewise of the Vedic texts, in the same manner we have always seen them to be acquired—by learning them from people who already know them, and who themselves learnt them from similarly knowledgeable elders earlier in their own lives—we have no basis for simply assuming a beginning to this chain of transmission, in the absence of any record or memory of an originator.

In his own commentary on and elaboration of this discussion, Kumārila extends Śabara's basic line of argument far beyond anything found in the *Bhāṣya*. Kumārila's *Sambandhâkṣepa-parihāra*, begins with the same problem—explaining how it is that particular words are connected with their meanings—and offers essentially the same answer—that such connections are uncreated and always learnt from those who already know them, but it reaches, in the course of its argument, far more sweeping and dramatic conclusions. Kumārila's argument for the beginninglessness of language is a kind of *tour de force* incorporating an absolute denial of the existence of God, and of the periodic dissolution and recreation of the world, and leads him to adopt at the very least a sceptical position on both the possibility and desirability of *mokṣa* (liberation), which had of course come by his time to be seen as the principle spiritual objective by adherents of nearly all religious and philosophical traditions both inside and outside the Vedic fold.

There are many adjectives that might be applied to this rather extraordinary document, but it seems to me that 'orthodox' is not really among them. It is true that there is nothing in what Kumārila has to say here that directly contradicts anything in the earlier Mīmāṁsā tradition. The *Mīmāṁsā-sūtra* and Śabara's *Bhāṣya*—the only pre-Kumārila Mīmāṁsā works that survive—are,

[3] ŚBh on MS 1.1.5 (MD, I: pp. 66–67). *yadi sambandhur abhāvān niyogato nârthā upalabhyeraṁs tato 'rthâpattyā sambandhāram avagacchāmaḥ. asti tv anyaḥ prakāraḥ. vṛddhānāṁ svârthena saṁvyavahāramāṇānām upaśṛṇvanto bālāḥ pratyakṣam arthaṁ pratipadyamānā dṛśyante. te 'pi vṛddhā yadā bālā āsaṁs tadā 'nyebhyo vṛddhebhyas te 'py anyebhya iti nâsty ādir ity evaṁ vā bhavet.*

as BRONKHORST (2007a: 4 ff.) and others have noted, entirely silent on the question of *mokṣa*, as well as on the existence of a creator God and the periodic dissolution and creation of the universe.[4] Nevertheless, in place of this silence, Kumārila has introduced a direct, frontal assault on a set of key cosmological and soteriological beliefs widely held in his time, and held precisely by those who regarded themselves as followers of the Vedic tradition the Mīmāṁsakas make it their business to uphold. It is a tremendous act of provocation, and was unmistakably meant to be so.

Still, provocative though Kumārila no doubt means to be, the arguments he makes against God and against creation are firmly grounded in epistemological and interpretive principles already set forth in Śabara's *Bhāṣya*. The real achievement of the *Sambandhâkṣepa-parihāra* is to spell out clearly and unflinchingly the implications of these principles, and to see them through to their logical conclusions.

Such attention as has been devoted to Kumārila's arguments against God[5] has focused primarily on the ontological (and, to a lesser extent, psychological and ethical) problems he finds in the notion of a creator God: How could God create the world if there were no pre-existing matter with which to create it (MŚV *Sambandhâkṣepa-parihāra* 45, 50–51), or if he himself had no body with which to act (MŚV *Sambandhâkṣepa-parihāra* 47)? What need or want could an all powerful and self-sufficient deity have that would lead him to create the world (MŚV *Sambandhâkṣepa-parihāra* 54–55)? And, the ever familiar problem of theodicy: How could a compassionate God create suffering and sin (MŚV *Sambandhâkṣepa-parihāra* 49, 52–53)? But, as is very often the case, the heart of Kumārila's argument is really more to do with epistemology than ontology. He seeks above all to exclude any possible evidence—perceptual, testimonial or inferential—for the existence of God. His argument is concerned as much or more with the impossibility of knowing God as with the impossibility of His existing. If he can establish this effectively, then he will be able to argue, by the very same principle Śabara enunciated in his rejection of a creator of word/meaning relations, that the world itself has no creator either. In the absence of any evidence for a creator, or for a radical break in the ordinary course of worldly events as they are known to us, it is most reasonable to assume that the world has always existed more or less as it is now (*adyavat*, see MŚV *Sambandhâkṣepa-parihāra* 113).

One of the reasons that the epistemological side of Kumārila's case has garnered less attention than the ontological is that it relies at several points on allusions or elliptical references to arguments made more extensively elsewhere, either by himself or by Śabara. For example, Kumārila notes at several

[4] Śabara does argue against the idea that the deities to which sacrificial offerings are dedicated derive any sustenance from these offerings or play any role in the distribution of sacrificial rewards (see 9.16–10 in MD, VI: pp. 72–81).

[5] See KRASSER (1999).

points in the *Sambandhâkṣepa-parihāra* that the existence of God is 'unprovable, like that of an omniscient person' (*sarva-jñavat tu duḥsādhaṁ*).[6] This alludes to Kumārila's earlier argument, in his comments on *Mīmāṁsā-sūtra* 1.1.2, against the use of claims of authorial omniscience to guarantee the validity of scripture.[7] There he argued that, even it were possible for a person such as the Buddha to acquire omniscience, his statements about matters beyond ordinary experience could hold no validity for other people; it would be impossible for them to know his claim of omniscience to be true unless they themselves were omniscient:

> 'In his own time, how could people who wished to know determine that he was omniscient, without being aware of his own knowledge and its objects? And you [the upholder of omniscience] would need to postulate many omniscient persons—anyone who is not himself omniscient cannot know an omniscient person. And, if a person does not know him to be omniscient, then his statements would have no authority for that person, since he would not know their source, just as with the statements of any other person.'[8]

As ordinary people, lacking any direct access to matters beyond the scope of ordinary human knowledge, we are in no position to assess the accuracy of those (now or in the past) who claim such knowledge themselves, and we have no grounds for putting faith in them. In the *Sambandhâkṣepa-parihāra* Kumārila makes essentially the same point regarding claims for the existence of a Creator:

> 'He could not be known by anybody, at any time. Even if he were perceived with his own form, the fact of his being the Creator would not be known. How could even the first beings in creation know this? They would not know how they were born here, or what the prior state of the world was, or that Prajāpati is the creator. Nor could they have certain knowledge of this due to His

[6] MŚV *Sambandhâkṣepa-parihāra* 44cd, p. 461:

sarva-jñavat tu duḥsādham ity atrâitan na saṁśritam /

See also MŚV *Sambandhâkṣepa-parihāra* 114ab, p. 477:

sarva-jñavan niṣedhyā ca sraṣṭuḥ sadbhāva-kalpanā /

[7] On which, see McCrea (2009).

[8] MŚV *Codanā* 134–136, p. 64:

sarva-jño 'sāv iti hy eva tat-kāle tu bubhutsubhiḥ /
taj-jñāna-jñeya-vijñāna-rahitair gamyate katham? // 134 //
kalpanīyāś ca sarva-jñā bhaveyur bahavas tava /
ya eva syād asarva-jñaḥ sa sarva-jñaṁ na budhyate // 135 //
sarva-jño 'nava-buddhaś ca yenâiva syān na taṁ prati /
tad-vākyānāṁ pramāṇatvaṁ mūlâjñāne 'nya-vākyavat // 136 //

> own statement; for He might say it even if he hadn't created them, in order to promulgate His own lordship.'[9]

Just as no one who is not omniscient is able to know that another person is omniscient, no one who was not present at the Creation is in a position to know that another being is the Creator.

An obvious notion for those seeking to validate the notion of a Creator God would be to turn to scripture itself. This is, after all, the source from which the most commonly accepted accounts of creation, dissolution, and the divine beings who superintend them, are derived. But here too, Kumārila has a ready-made answer—one which is firmly grounded in already well-established Mīmāṁsā principles:

> 'The *Veda* too, if it came after [the Creator], being doubtful, would not be an authority concerning His existence and the like. [But,] if it were eternal, how could it have any bearing on him? If it existed before he did, then it would follow that it could not be connected with him. Therefore it [the *Veda*] has another purpose [in speaking of a Creator]: to motivate others. And the mental confusion people have [about the mention of a Creator in the *Veda*] is produced by these eulogistic speeches. The words [of the *Veda*], considered out of their proper sequence, produce a mistaken idea. And, for us, the operation of texts like the *Mahā-bhārata* with regard to Dharma and the like, through the medium of stories and so on, is just like that of the *Veda*. Therefore the error comes about from these texts as well. And, since the stories [in and of themselves] are of no use, in all these cases there is some Vedic text or something enjoined by one, which is made an object of praise or blame.'[10]

---

[9] MŚV *Sambandhâkṣepa-parihāra* 57cd–60, pp. 463–464:

na ca kaiścid asau jñātuṁ kadācid api śakyate // 57 //
svarūpeṇôpalabdhe 'pi sraṣṭṛtvaṁ nâvagamyate /
sṛṣṭy-ādyāḥ prāṇino ye ca budhyantām kiṁ nu te tadā // 58 //
kuto vayam ihôtpannā iti tāvan na jānate /
prāg-avasthāṁ ca jagataḥ sraṣṭṛtvaṁ ca prajāpateḥ // 59 //
na ca tad-vacanenâiṣāṁ pratipattiḥ suniścitā /
asṛṣṭvâpi hy asau brūyād ātmâiśvarya-prakāśanāt // 60 //

[10] MŚV *Sambandhâkṣepa-parihāra* 61–65, pp. 464–465:

evaṁ vedo 'pi tat-pūrvas tat-sadbhāvâdi-bodhane /
sāśaṅko na pramāṇaṁ syāt; nityasya vyāpṛtiḥ kutaḥ? // 61 //
yadi prāg apy asau tasmād arthād āsīn na tena saḥ //
sambaddha iti tasyānyas tad-artho 'nya-prarocanā // 62 //
stuti-vākya-kṛtaś câiṣa janānāṁ mati-vibhramaḥ /
paurvāparyâparāmṛṣṭaḥ śabdo 'nyāṁ kurute matiṁ // 63 //
upākhyānâdi-rūpeṇa vṛttir vedavad eva naḥ /
dharmâdau bhāratâdīnāṁ bhrāntis tebhyo 'py ato bhavet // 64 //

Kumārila is appealing here to the Mīmāṁsā notion of '*artha-vāda*', or 'eulogistic description', already discussed in detail by Śabara in his commentary on *Mīmāṁsā-sūtra* 1.2.1–18. The Mīmāṁsakas famously hold that the *Veda*s are authoritative precisely because they are eternal texts, not produced by any author, and hence not subject to doubt on the grounds of authorial untrustworthiness, as in the case of the Buddhist and Jaina scriptures. But, precisely because they are eternal, the Mīmāṁsakas deny that the *Veda*s can ever refer to specific historical events or persons, as they themselves must always precede them in time. All apparent historical and factual content in the *Veda*s—the stories of Indra's battles with demons and the like—must be interpreted instead as *artha-vāda*s—as passages meant to praise elements to be used in the rituals prescribed in the *Veda*s, or to dispraise those whose use is to be avoided. So the stories of 'Indra's' battles, for example, are to be understood as praising Indra as the nominal dedicatee of certain sacrificial offerings, and hence as encouraging sacrificers to fulfil the prescribed injunctions to make offerings to Indra, but they cannot be taken to be factual accounts of real acts undertaken by an actual person. All such seemingly factual statements must be interpreted figuratively in this way, and must be read as subordinate to one or more injunctions to perform ritual actions which will produce a desirable result for the sacrificer. Essentially, the *Veda* speaks only in if/then statements—'If you perform such and such an act, you will obtain such and such a result'. Wherever it appears to do otherwise, we must conclude that it does not and cannot really mean what it says.

This interpretive principle is extremely effective in safeguarding the *Veda* against any empirical critique, essentially rendering its claims immune to falsification. But this safety comes at what might be seen, by some at least, as a heavy cost. It entirely precludes any attempt to extract information about either the past or the present state of the world from the *Veda*, the only potential source of knowledge the Mīmāṁsakas will allow for matters beyond the scope of ordinary human apprehension. Moreover, as Kumārila makes clear if Śabara does not, this same stricture must be seen as applying not only to the eternal *Veda* itself, but to all those texts whose authority derives from it: that is to say, Smṛti texts, whose claims on matters of Dharma are understood to be based on lost or inaccessible Vedic texts—a category which includes texts such as the *Mahā-bhārata*, the *Rāmāyaṇa*, all the *Purāṇa*s. All of these texts, precisely in so far as they bear on matters outside the domain of normal human experience, are incapacitated from giving us any factual information about cosmology, cosmogony, or anything of the sort.

ākhyānânupayogitvāt teṣu sarveṣu vidyate /
stuti-nindâśrayaḥ kaścid vedas tac-codito 'pi vā // 65 //

As Kumārila explains in the passage quoted above, the belief in a Creator God (and much else besides) is founded on a systematic misinterpretation of Śruti and Smṛti texts. It is an outgrowth of the 'mental confusion' of those who attempt to read such texts without a proper understanding of the theory of *artha-vāda*, and of the functional role of the narrative portions of such texts as motivational adjuncts to the injunctions which are the integral component of all such literature. Kumārila discusses the specific case of the epics in more detail in his *Tantra-vārttika*, commenting on the full discussion of *artha-vāda* in Śabara's *Bhāṣya* on *Mīmāṁsā-sūtra* 1.2.7:

> 'Statements such as those in the *Mahā-bhārata* are to be explained in this way. For them also, since one seeks some human purpose for them in accordance with the injunctions such as "One should teach them to the four *varṇa*s" (*Mahā-bhārata* 12.314.45c), there should be some result, above and beyond the sounds of the texts, [in the form of] the understanding the means to ends—such as meritorious action, profit, pleasure, liberation, demeritorious action, injury, suffering, and spiritual bondage—which would aid in the attainment or avoidance of them. Even there, some [statements], in the sections concerning the Dharma of giving, or of kings, or of liberation, are direct injunctions, some [statements], however, are *artha-vāda*s, in the form of [stories of] other persons' deeds and past ages. But, since, if this were their actual purport, the injunction to "teach [them to the four *varṇa*s]" would become useless, in all these stories we must accept that praise or blame [of elements connected with these prohibitions and injunctions] is somehow understood. And, because they are directed toward this [praise and blame], one should not worry too much about the truth in connection with these stories.'[11]

All the narrative content in these texts, then, becomes subsumed within the category of *artha-vāda*, and, if we grasp the principles of interpretation properly, we must understand that the truth or falsity of such narratives is irrelevant to their real function. They are all 'just stories', and the entire system of beliefs that some people have formed on the basis of the narrative content of the epics, the *Purāṇa*s, and the *Veda*s—beliefs in the gods and their deeds, and in the

---

[11] TV on MS 1.2.7 (MD, II: pp. 14–15): *evaṁ bhāratâdi-vākyāni vyākhyeyāni. teṣām api hi "śrāvayec caturo varṇān"* (MBh 12.314.45c) *ity evam-ādi-vidhy-anusāreṇa puruṣârthatvânveṣaṇād akṣarâdi vyatikramya dharmârtha-kāma-mokṣâdharmânartha-duḥkha-saṁsāra-sādhya-sādhana-pratipattir upādāna-parityāgâṅga-bhūtā phalam. tatrâpi tu dāna-rāja-mokṣa-dharmâdiṣu kecit sākṣād vidhayaḥ, kecit punaḥ para-kṛti-purā-kalpa-rūpeṇârtha-vādāḥ. sarvôpākhyāneṣu ca tātparye sati śrāvayed iti vidher ānarthakyāt kathaṁcid gamyamāna-stuti-nindā-parigrahaḥ. tat-paratvāc ca nâtīvôpākhyāneṣu tattvâbhiniveśaḥ kāryaḥ.*

periodic creation and destruction of the world—is simply the result of a massive and widespread error. Hence, while upholding the 'validity' of the *Veda*s, and of Smṛti texts such as the epics and the *Purāṇa*s, Kumārila has managed to discard out of hand what were surely the central beliefs of the vast majority of those who saw themselves as followers and adherents of these texts.

This flat out rejection of the narrative and factual content of the entire Vedic, epic, and Purāṇic corpus extends, of course, to such accounts of their own transmission as are found within these texts. A key part of Kumārila's defence of the both the eternality and the validity of the *Veda*s is his insistence that they must have always been transmitted by entirely ordinary means. He absolutely rejects any notion that these texts can ever have been 'seen' or intuited by *ṛṣi*s who are responsible for propagating them among ordinary people:

> 'The intuition of an eternal scripture is likewise to be rejected in [the same] manner [as an omniscient person]: For even here one cannot be certain whether [this person] has "seen" the text, or made it. And, at all times, people are liars, for the most part. Just as there can be no confidence in them now, in the same way there is no confidence in statements of things past. And, this person's awareness of the text and its meaning could be like a dream awareness: for people who have this doubt, how could the validity [of these texts] be understood?'[12]

If anyone were to claim that he or she had 'seen' a Vedic text, this would be no more dependable than the claims to supernatural knowledge of purportedly omniscient persons such as the Buddha. For Kumārila, the trustworthiness of the Vedic tradition depends on its always being transmitted by entirely ordinary, human means. At no point in its unbroken train of transmission has anyone been required to take on faith the knowledge claims of a purported *yogin* or *ṛṣi*:

> 'Because it exists in many people, and because it is learned and remembered within a single lifetime, there is nothing to impair independent authority in the case of the *Veda*. And, if there were any alteration [of the Vedic text], it would be prevented by many people. Whereas if [the text] were revealed to one person, it would be no different from one created [by that person]. So, in

[12] MŚV *Codanā* 143–145, p. 66:

nityâgamâvabodho 'pi pratyākhyeyo 'nayā diśā /
na hi tatrâpi visrambho dṛṣṭo 'nena kṛto 'tha vā // 143 //
sarvadā câpi puruṣāḥ prāyeṇânṛta-vādinaḥ /
yathâdyatve na visrambhas tathâtītârtha-kīrtane // 144 //
svapnâdi-jñānavac câpi pratyayo 'syâgamârthayoḥ /
bhaved iti saśaṅkānāṁ prāmāṇyaṁ gamyate katham // 145 //

> this tradition, no one person is required. Many people can be dependent [on it]; for they are all men, just like nowadays.'[13]

But, for just this reason, Kumārila's rejection of *sarga* and *pralaya*, the periodic creation and dissolution of the universe, is key to his defence of the *Veda*. He cannot allow for the kind of breaks in its transmission that would be necessitated by the periodic disappearance and reappearance of communities of human reciters. For Kumārila, the *Veda* is 'eternal' not in some mystical or transcendent sense, but in a completely everyday manner—it has always been recited by ordinary, human reciters, each of whom has learned it from an ordinary, human, Brāhmaṇa teacher. This is a compelling vision, one which, as I have argued elsewhere,[14] effectively exploits the difference between the Vedic tradition and the Buddhist and Jaina traditions which Kumārila sees as its main rivals, and which necessarily look back to a visionary founder as the source of their doctrines, but it is a vision which requires an ontology and a cosmology far more restricted than many upholders of the *Veda* would wish to admit.

As an example in Kumārila's work of what I have here called 'rationalisation'—that is to say, the advocacy of a position which is neither philosophically compelling nor necessary, but which is effectively forced on one by one's tradition—I think theory of the eternality of sound (*śabda-nityatā*) can serve fairly well. This had been one of the signal doctrines of the Mīmāṁsā tradition from its earliest period. The theory of the eternality of the *Veda*s was seen to be crucially linked with the idea that the very sounds that make them up are likewise eternal. This theory was hotly contested in the earlier period of Mīmāṁsā, and much intellectual energy was devoted to its defence. Yet, given Kumārila's insistence on the perpetual embeddedness of the *Veda* in ordinary human recitational practices, it would seem that for him the doctrine of *śabda-nityatā* has become entirely unnecessary. He makes the point himself in the *pūrva-pakṣa* that opens his discussion of the issue:

> 'If, even on the view [that sound is] not eternal, meanings are understood from words, and linguistic practice is beginningless, then why bother to establish this eternality [of sound]?'[15]

---

[13] MŚV *Codanā* 149–151, p. 67:

aneka-puruṣa-sthatvād ekatrâiva ca janmani /
grahaṇa-smaraṇād vede na svātantryaṁ vihanyate // 149 //
anyathā-karaṇe câsya bahubhiḥ syān nivāraṇam /
ekasya pratibhānaṁ tu kṛtakān na viśiṣyate // 150 //
ataś ca saṁpradāye ca nâikaḥ puruṣa iṣyate /
bahavaḥ paratantrāḥ syuḥ sarve hy adyatvavan narāḥ // 151 //

[14] See McCREA (1999).

[15] MŚV *Śabda-nityatā* 1, p. 515:

yady anityatva-pakṣe 'pi śabdād artho 'vagamyate /
anādir vyavahāraś ca nityatvaṁ kiṁ nu sādhyate //

Kumārila does attempt to provide an answer to this objection by claiming, for instance, that an eternal tradition of linguistic practice could not be founded on something which is itself transient (MŚV *Śabda-nityatā* 5). Still, there is something rather forced about his argument here, and the very fact that he raises the question of its uselessness reflects a certain unease about the topic. I think it is fairly clear that for him the theory of the eternality of sound has become a distraction at best, and an embarrassment at worst. Yet, given the prominence of this doctrine in both the *Sūtra* and the *Bhāṣya*, it would appear that the theory of *śabda-nityatā* is what one might, in contemporary terms, call 'too big to fail'. However unnecessary it may have become within Kumārila's system, and however tortured the manoeuvres needed to uphold it, it is simply too firmly rooted in the Mīmāṁsā philosophical and textual tradition to be cast aside.

A better example of rationalisation, of a rather different sort perhaps, can be seen in the later Mīmāṁsakas' treatment of Kumārila's arguments against God. For three or four centuries after Kumārila's time, his rather militant atheism appears to have been adopted without reservation by nearly all prominent Mīmāṁsakas, not only Kumārila's own followers, but also those of the rival Prābhākara school, one of whose main proponents, Śālikanāthamiśra, incorporates the essentials of Kumārila's argument in his own discussion of the *Sambandhâkṣepa-parihāra* section of the *Bhāṣya* and Prabhākara's commentary thereon.[16] But, beginning around the middle of the eleventh century, this shifts rather suddenly, and nearly all Mīmāṁsakas suddenly become self-proclaimed theists. They all begin their works, for instance, with benedictions or invocations to one or more deities. Some directly address the tension between this theistic stance and the Mīmāṁsā tradition of atheism. Bhavanātha, for example, an eleventh century Prābhākara author, contends that the arguments advanced in the *Sambandhâkṣepa-parihāra* are not really arguments against God as such, but only against inferential proofs for the existence of God, and still allow for belief in God on scriptural grounds.[17] The same line of argument is taken up by later followers of Kumārila who take up the question of theism,[18] though I think it is clear from what I have said above that this represents an obvious betrayal of Kumārila's position, and one which, if taken seriously, would totally undermine the case for Vedic authority as he understands it. A more typical approach to the question of God taken by later theistic followers of Kumārila is simply a kind of embarrassed silence. After the eleventh century, Kumārila's *Śloka-vārttika*, the text in which he advances his anti-theistic arguments, was never again commented upon, and the vast majority of post-eleventh century Mīmāṁsā authors, whether writing commentaries or independent works, simply skip over the opening chapter of the *Mīmāṁsā-sūtra*,

[16] Ṛju on 1.1.5 in Bṛ, : pp. 190–191.

[17] MNV, pp. 188–199.

[18] E.g. NTĀ, pp. 182–193.

where the non-existence of God is discussed. For whatever reason, it appears that from about the beginning of the second millennium, atheism simply became an unacceptable stance, regardless of the arguments that could be marshalled in its favour, and despite its crucial importance in the argument for Vedic authority as developed in the Mīmāṁsā tradition. This turn away from atheism seems obviously to be driven by extra-systemic and extra-philosophical concerns.

In concluding, I would like to examine, in the light of the foregoing discussion, one particular aspect of Kumārila's philosophy which has drawn considerable attention recently, namely his apparently shifting position on the nature of *mokṣa*. This is not a major topic in any of Kumārila's works, but he does address it at least in passing in all of them. In 1994, Roque MESQUITA noticed certain discrepancies between Kumārila's discussion of *mokṣa* in the *Śloka-vārttika*, and in two presumably later works, the *Tantra-vārttika* and *Bṛhaṭ-ṭīkā* (the latter of which survives only in a few brief fragments).[19] In the *Śloka-vārttika*, *mokṣa* is presented as a purely negative state, consisting neither of pain nor pleasure and achieved by the exhaustion of one's own *karman*, rather than by any kind of 'knowledge of the self', while in the later works it is presented as a state that can be acquired by a combination of ritual action and self-knowledge (*jñāna-karma-samuccaya*). MESQUITA (1994: 481) characterises this as a shift from a Nyāya-like position to a 'Vedāntic view of liberation'. More recently, question of Kumārila's different accounts of *mokṣa* has been taken up by John TABER (2007) and Kiyotaka YOSHIMIZU (2007), who reexamine the data considered by MESQUITA and reach rather different conclusions. TABER (2007: 172–173) feels that the inconsistency between Kumārila's statements on liberation in the *Śloka-vārttika* and the *Tantra-vārttika* is 'an insufficient basis for establishing a shift or evolution in Kumārila's thought', and can be accounted for by the fact that in the more ritual centred *Tantra-vārttika* Kumārila's concern is mainly with 'what is actually prescribed and not prescribed in the *Veda* and *Dharma-śāstra*s' whereas in the *Śloka-vārttika* he is 'thinking as a philosopher' and 'is guided mainly by principles of reason'. YOSHIMIZU (2007: 202), on the other hand, essentially endorses MESQUITA's position, that Kumārila's theory of *mokṣa* as developed in the *Śloka-vārttika* is closely akin to that of the Naiyāyikas, while in the *Tantra-vārttika* he 'advocates a position of the Vedānta'.

If one accepts MESQUITA and YOSHIMIZU's general account of the shift in Kumārila's views, this might look like another example of rationalisation—a reworking of Kumārila's original position on *mokṣa* to accommodate an increasingly popular and prestigious Vedānta theory. But I think this impression is misleading, and it can be shown that, while (contra TABER) Kumārila's position on *mokṣa* did shift significantly between the *Śloka-vārttika* and the *Tantra-vārttika*, this shift can be accounted for entirely as the result of an increasingly

[19] MESQUITA (1994).

perspicuous application of existing Mīmāṁsā hermeneutic principles to the analysis of Vedic passages where *mokṣa* is discussed, and in no way represents a shift toward a Vedāntic position.

In the *Śloka-vārttika* (*Sambandhâkṣepa-parihāra*), Kumārila briefly discusses the question of *mokṣa*, primarily in response to a Sāṁkhya opponent who contends that knowledge of the self can bring release from *saṁsāra*. He begins with an epistemological argument—that there is no *pramāṇa* warranting a belief that knowledge can lead to liberation, and only secondarily considering the nature and possible causes of *mokṣa*:

> 'That knowledge is a means of *mokṣa* is not understood by perception or any such [*pramāṇa*]; nor is *mokṣa* enjoined by the *Veda* as coming from knowledge of Sāṁkhya or the like. [The Vedic statement that] "The self should be known" is not enjoined for the sake of *mokṣa*; knowledge of the self is characterised as being for the sake of [motivating one] to perform ritual actions. And, since it is known to be for the sake of something else, whatever statement of results there is [in connection with it] is an *artha-vāda*; there is no result apart from heaven. And, if *mokṣa* is supposed to consist in the enjoyment of pleasure, it would simply be heaven by another name, and it would be perishable. For nothing that has a cause is understood to be imperishable. Therefore, one is liberated due to the a b s e n c e of a cause, precisely through the elimination of *karman*. For there is no reason for the eternality of *mokṣa*, apart from its having the form of an absence, and we do not accept that an absence can be the result of any action.'[20]

He goes on to suggest that one who desires *mokṣa* could exhaust his *karman* by the continued performance of obligatory actions (failure to perform which would produce bad *karman*) while ceasing to perform optional, desire-based rituals (which, if performed, would produce good *karman*); in doing so, one could in theory eventually exhaust all of one's good and bad *karman* after

[20] MŚV *Sambandhâkṣepa-parihāra* 102–107, pp. 474–475:
jñānaṁ mokṣa-nimittaṁ ca gamyate nêndriyâdinā /
na ca sāṁkhyâdi-vijñānān mokṣo vedena codyate // 102 //
"ātmā jñātavya" ity etan mokṣârthaṁ na ca coditam /
karma-pravṛtti-hetutvam ātma-jñānasya lakṣyate // 103 //
vijñāte câsya pārārthye yâpi nāma phala-śrutiḥ /
sârtha-vādo bhaved eva; na svārgâdeḥ phalântaram // 104 //
sukhôpabhoga-rūpaś ca yadi mokṣaḥ prakalpyate /
svarga eva bhaved eṣa paryāyeṇa, kṣayī ca saḥ // 105 //
na hi kāraṇavat kiṁcid akṣayitvena gamyate /
tasmāt karma-kṣayād eva hetv-abhāvena mucyate // 106 //
na hy abhāvâtmakaṁ muktvā mokṣa-nityatva-kāraṇam /
na ca kriyāyāḥ kasyāścid abhāvaḥ phalaṁ iṣyate // 107 //

which, due to the absence of any cause which would condition birth, one would cease to be reborn.

The most important thing to note about this argument is the claim, in the first three verses, that there is no warrant for the belief that self-knowledge leads to *mokṣa*. All apparent statements to this effect in the *Veda* (which for Kumārila includes the *Upaniṣads*, of course) are to be understood as *artha-vāda*s—they are made in connection with injunctions to know the self which are themselves subordinate to other ritual actions—and are therefore not to be taken as literally true. The phrasing Kumārila employs here—that 'since it is known to be for the sake of something else' (*vijñāte pārārthye*) the 'statement of results is an *artha-vāda*' (*phala-śrutiḥ artha-vādaḥ*)—is a deliberate echo of *Mīmāṁsā-sūtra* 4.3.1: 'In the case of substances, *saṁskāra*s ('preparatory actions'), and [subordinate] actions, a statement of results would be an *artha-vāda*.'[21] This sets forth the general rule that anything which plays a subordinate role in a ritual action exists exclusively for the sake of that action, and that any result mentioned in connection with it by a Vedic sentence should not be understood as an actual result, but only as a figurative way of praising that element so as to encourage its use in the larger ritual. For Kumārila, the Vedic injunctions to know the self are subordinate to rituals producing otherworldly results such as heaven, since it is only when one knows that one has a permanent self that will continue to exist after death that one will be motivated to perform such sacrifices. And hence, by the foregoing rule, statements to the effect that one can attain *mokṣa* by knowing the self must be understood as *artha-vāda*s.

In the *Tantra-vārttika* discussion of *mokṣa*, Kumārila takes quite a different stand. He now asserts that self-knowledge is enjoined in the *Veda* both 'for the sake of the ritual' (*kratv-artha*) and 'for the sake of the person' (*puruṣârtha*), due to its 'possession of separate connections' (*saṁyoga-pṛthaktva*).[22] This

---

[21] MD, V: p. 59: *dravya-saṁskāra-karmasu parârthatvāt phala-śrutir artha-vādaḥ syāt.*

[22] TV on MS 1.3.27 (MD, II: p. 227): *ātma-jñānaṁ hi saṁyoga-pṛthaktvāt kratv-artha-puruṣârthatvena jñāyate tena vinā para-loka-phaleṣu karmasu pravṛtti-nivṛtty-asambhavāt. tathā "ya ātmā 'pahata-papmā vijaro vimṛtyur viśoko vijighatso 'pipāsaḥ satya-kāmaḥ satya-saṁkalpaḥ so 'nveṣṭavyaḥ sa vijijñāsitavyaḥ" tathā "mantavyo bodhavyaḥ" tathā "ātmānam upāsīta" iti kāma-vāda-loka-vāda-vacana-viśeṣair jijñāsā-manana-sahitâtma-jñāna-kevalâvabodha-paryanta-spaṣṭâtma-tattva-jñāna-vidhānâpekṣita-vākyântarôpātta-dvividhâbhyudaya-niḥśreyasa-rūpa-phala-sambandhaḥ, "sa sarvāṁś ca lokān āpnoti sarvāṁś ca kāmān āpnoti" "tarati śokam ātma-vit" tathā "sa yadi pitṛ-loka-kāmo bhavati saṁkalpād evāsya pitaraḥ samuttiṣṭhanti tena pitṛ-lokena saṁpanno mahīyate" ity-ādinā yoga-janyâṇimâdy-aṣṭa-guṇâiśvarya-phalāni varṇitāni. tathā "sa khalv evaṁ vartayan yāvad-āyuṣaṁ brahma-lokam abhisaṁpadyate na sa punar āvartate" ity apunar-āvṛtty-ātmaka-parâtma-prāpty-avasthā-phala-vacanam. aprakaraṇa-gatatvenânaikāntika-kratu-saṁbandhâsaṁbandhāc ca nâñjana-khādira-sruva-vākyâdi-phala-śrutivad artha-vādatvam.*—'For knowledge of the self is understood to be both for the sake of the person and for the sake of the ritual, since it possesses a separate connection [with each]; for without it there would be no possibility of activity or inactivity with respect to actions whose results are beyond this world. Thus in sentences such as these—"That self, from which all sin is expelled, which is

alludes to *Mīmāṁsā-sūtra* 4.3.5: 'When one element has both, there is separateness of connection.'[23] This is an exception to the general rule stated in *Mīmāṁsā-sūtra* 4.3.1, and holds that when a subordinate element—a substance, *saṁskāra*, or subordinate action—is enjoined as connected with a ritual in one sentence, and as connected with a specific result in a different sentence, then it should be understood as aiding the completion of the ritual, but also as producing the specified result for the sacrificer; the mentioned result, in such cases, is n o t to be taken as an *artha-vāda*, but as an accurate statement of the result that will follow if the performer employs this element, rather than some other, in completing the ritual. It is this principle that Kumārila now applies to the injunctions to know the self: they subserve both the ritual, by prompting the performance of sacrifices with otherworldly goals, and the person, by leading him to a state of liberation.

Briefly, between the time Kumārila wrote the *Śloka-vārttika* and the time he wrote the *Tantra-vārttika* (which, if only for this reason, must certainly be the later work) he arrived at a more sophisticated application of pre-existing Mīmāṁsā hermeneutical rules to the injunctions of self-knowledge—one which allowed them to both subserve the general class of ritual actions, by promoting an awareness of a transmigratory self that will be able to experience sacrificial results beyond this life, but can also be understood to subserve the individual directly as a means to liberation. This represents a quite dramatic shift in Kumārila's stand on *mokṣa*, but one which, far from representing a capitulation or 'conversion' toward a specifically Vedāntic position, is actually a principled outgrowth of long established Mīmāṁsā interpretive principles.

---

from old age, free from death, free from grief, free from hunger, free from thirst, having true desires and true intentions—that should be sought after, and be investigated" (ChU 8.7.1), "It should be contemplated, it should be understood", and "one should meditate on the self"—there is connection with two sorts of result, namely prosperity and the supreme good [liberation], mentioned in other sentences which are required for these explicit injunctions to know the true nature of the self (which culminates in the exclusive experience of self-knowledge, together with investigation and contemplation), through specific statements regarding desires and regarding other worlds. "He obtains all worlds, he obtains all desires" (ChU 8.7.1), "He who knows the self passes beyond grief" (ChU 7.1.3), and "If he desires the world of the ancestors then, by his sheer will, his ancestors rise up and, by this, endowed with the world of the ancestors, he becomes great"—These sentences describe as results mastery of the eight qualities such as "minuteness" which are achieved through *yoga*. "Indeed he, acting in this way for as long as he lives, attains the world of *brahman*, and does not return." (ChU 8.15.1)—This sentence states as a result the state of attaining the supreme self, which consists in not returning [to this world]. And, since its connection or non-connection with any particular ritual cannot be unequivocally determined, as it is not mentioned in the context [of any particular action], it is not a eulogistic description, like the statements of results in the sentences connected with the smearing [of the eyes] or with the ladles made of khadira-wood.'

[23] MD, V: p. 65: *ekasya tûbhayatve saṁyoga-pṛthaktvam*.

BIBLIOGRAPHY

Bṛ = Prabhākaramiśra: *Bṛhatī*. S.K. Ramanatha Śastrī (ed.): *Bṛhatī of Prabhākara Miśra [on the Mīmāṁsāsūtrabhāṣya of Śabarasvāmin] with the Ṛjuvimalāpañcikā of Śālikanātha [Tarkapāda]*. 2 Vols., Madras University Sanskrit Series, n°3, The University of Madras, Madras 1934.

BRONKHORST 2007a = Bronkhorst, Johannes: 'Vedānta as Mimāṁsa', in: BRONKHORST (2007b: 1–91).

BRONKHORST 2007b = Bronkhorst, Johannes (ed.): *Mīmāṁsā and Vedānta: Interaction and Continuity*. Motilal Banarsidass, Delhi 2007.

ChU = *Chāndogyôpaniṣad*. E. Röer (ed.): *Chāndogya-upaniṣad. With the Commentary of Śaṅkara Ācārya and the Gloss of Ānanda Giri*. Bibliotheca Indica, Asiatic Society, Calcutta 1850.

KRASSER 1999 = Krasser, Helmut: 'Dharmakīrti's and Kumārila's Refutations of the Existence of God: A Consideration of Their Chronological Order', in: Shoryu Katsura (ed.): *Dharmakīrti's Thought and its Impact on Indian and Tibetan Philosophy: Proceedings of the Third International Dharmakīrti Conference, Hiroshima, November 4–6, 1997*. Österreichische Akademie der Wissenschaften, Vienna 1999: 215–223.

MBh = *Mahā-bhārata*. Vishnu S. Sukthankar; S.K. Belvalkar; et al. (ed.): *The Mahābhārata for the First Time Critically Edited*. 19 Vols., Bhandarkar Oriental Research Institute, Poona 1933–1966.

MCCREA 2009 = McCrea, Lawrence: '"Just Like us, Just Like Now": The Tactical Implications of the Mīmāṁsā Rejection of Yogic Perception", in: Eli Franco; Dagmar Eigner (eds.): *Yogic Perception, Meditation, and Altered States of Consciousness*. Österreichische Akademie der Wissenschaften, Vienna 2009: 55–70.

MD = *Mīmāṁsā-darśana*. Kāśīnātha Vāsudevaśāstrī Abhyankara; Gaṇeśaśāstrī Aṁbādāsa Jośī (eds.): *Śrīmaj-jaimini-praṇītaṁ Mīmāṁsā-darśanam*. 7 Vols. (Vol. 1 *Śābara-bhāṣya*; vols. 2–4 *Śābara-bhāṣya* and *Tantra-vārttika*; Vols. 5–7 *Śābara-bhāṣya* and *Ṭup-ṭīkā*), 2nd Edition, Ānandāśrama Sanskrit Series 97, Ānandāśrama Press, Poona 1970–1977.

MESQUITA 1994 = Mesquita, Roque: 'Die Idee der Erlösung bei Kumārilabhaṭṭa', *Wiener Zeitschrift für die Kunde Südasiens* 38 (1994) 485–507.

MNV = Bhavanāthamiśra: *Mīmāṁsā-naya-viveka*. S. Subrahmaṇya Śāstrī (ed.): *Mimamsa Naya Viveka*. Rastriya Sanskrit Samsthan, New Delhi 1977.

MS = Jaimini: *Mīmāṁsā-sūtra*. See: MD.

MŚV = Kumārilabhaṭṭa: *Śloka-vārttika*. Dvārikādāsa Śāstrin (ed.): *Ślokavārttika of Śrī Kumārila Bhaṭṭa with the Commentary Nyāyaratnākara of Śrī Pārthasārathi Miśra*. Prācyabhāratī Grantha-mālā 10, Tara Publications, Varanasi 1978.

NTĀ = Cidānanda: *Nīti-tattvâvir-bhāva*. P.K. Narayana Pillai (ed.): *Nititattvavirbhava of Cidanandapandita*. Trivandrum Sanskrit Series 168, Trivandrum 1953.

Ṛju = Śālikanāthamiśra: *Ṛju-vimala-pañcikā*. See: Bṛ.

ŚBh = Śabarasvāmin: *Śābara-bhāṣya*. See: MD.

TABER 2007 = Taber, John, 'Kumārila the Vedāntin?', in: BRONKHORST (2007b: 159–184).

TV = Kumārilabhaṭṭa: *Tantra-vārttika*. See: MD.

YOSHIMIZU 2007 = Yoshimizu, Kiyotaka: 'Kumārila's Reevaluation of the Sacrifice and the Veda from a Vedānta Perspective', in: BRONKHORST (2007b: 201–253).

On the Variety of Commentarial Approaches among the Commentators of the *Padârtha-dharma-saṁgraha*: A Reconsideration of the Notion of the 'Vaiśeṣika School'

TAKANORI SUZUKI

1. Indian philosophy developed its theories through commentarial activities surrounding the authoritative texts of each of its philosophical systems. It is common behaviour for modern researchers to call the scholarly current of each system a 'school', or to identify a certain scholar as 'one who belongs to a specific school', such as a Vedāntin or a Naiyāika.

This activity may sometimes mislead us into having the impression that there were historically and socially established entities that correspond to the English word 'school'. In reality, however, it was not rare for Indian thinkers to comment on the texts of several different systems, as typically seen in, for example, Vācaspati. Upon closer inspection, the meaning of the word 'school', used for understanding Indian philosophy, becomes vague. Indian researchers have often emphasised, as has already been quoted and clarified by Wilhelm HALBFASS (1988: 26–28), that 'in India, different schools ... flourished together during many centuries and pursued parallel courses of growth.'[1] Considering this, it seems important for modern researchers to consider the possibility that each commentarial tradition, which we conventionally call a 'school', did not operate, for Indian thinkers, as a binder of their commentarial activities but rather served as a field in which they tried to reflect their perspective toward Indian philosophy as a whole.

This paper presents evidence that there were a variety of commentarial approaches toward the *Padârtha-dharma-saṁgraha* (or *Praśastapāda-bhāṣya*, PBh), one of the authoritative texts of the Vaiśeṣika system, among its three commentators. In so doing, the necessity of reconsidering the notion of the 'Vaiśeṣika', which is often categorised as 'one school', will be confirmed as an example of the argument of this paper.

2. Earlier academic approach to the three commentaries of the *Padârtha-dharma-saṁgraha*.

When we aim to clarify the history of the Vaiśeṣika system, three commentaries of the *Padârtha-dharma-saṁgraha*—i.e. Vyomaśiva's V*yomavatī* (VyV),

[1] The quotation is from CHATTERJEE–DATTA (1968: 9).

World View and Theory in Indian Philosophy
Warsaw Indological Studies 5 (2012) 137–153.

Śrīdhara's *Nyāya-kandalī* (NKan), and Udayana's *Kiraṇâvalī* (KĀ)—are often used with the *Padârtha-dharma-saṁgraha* itself. These three commentaries, which were composed in the comparatively close period of ninth–eleventh centuries CE, are recognised as useful clues not only to the history of Vaiśeṣika but also to the Indian philosophy as a whole, especially the ontology and epistemology of that period. However, it is quite rare that researchers, especially Western and Japanese, investigate the differences between these three commentaries and consider unique features of each of these texts, which have usually been dealt with in a collective manner.

In contrast to the above attitude of most modern researchers towards the three commentaries, some Indian researchers have pointed out that there are a number of passages found in the *Nyāya-kandalī* which seem to oppose opinions voiced by Vyomaśiva. Already D.C. BHATTACHARYA (1958: 12) pointed out some phrases of the *Nyāya-kandalī* in which Śrīdhara critically refers to Vyomaśiva by the word *eke* etc. V. PARIKH (1991: iii) asserted in the same spirit that 'Śrīdhara preferred to differ from Vyomaśiva'. In recent research, A. THAKUR (2003: 268–275) enumerates eighteen points critical of Vyomaśiva found in the *Nyāya-kandalī*. These researchers attribute the evidence of Śrīdhara's criticism directed against Vyomaśiva to some passages of the *Nyāya-kandalī* which are introduced in order to object to 'somebody' (*kaścid*), whom Rājaśekhara in his commentary *Nyāya-kandalī-pañjikā* (NKanP) identifies as Vyomaśiva.[2] Since Śrīdhara himself does not refer to Vyomaśiva by name, it cannot be concluded that the former criticised the latter on this basis. In addition, some passages referred to as 'somebody' by Śrīdhara cannot be traced in the *Vyomavatī*. Nevertheless, the *Nyāya-kandalī-pañjikā*'s identification should be noted because it tells us how much these two were considered to have different opinions by later thinkers. In fact, there are indications that Vyomaśiva and Śrīdhara held quite different views when they commented on the *Padârtha-dharma-saṁgraha*, as we will see.

3. Difference of opinion between Vyomaśiva and Śrīdhara regarding the classification of verbal cognition among *pramāṇa*s.

Most of Śrīdhara's criticism directed against the 'somebody', and identified by Rājaśekhara as Vyomaśiva, concerns the difference in interpretation regarding categories, such as characteristics of conjunction (*saṁyoga*) or disjunction (*vibhāga*). This type of criticism deals with, so to speak, internal topics of the Vaiśeṣika system which seem quite subtle to outsiders. However, not all criticisms were directed only at the above-mentioned kind of argument.

One of these criticisms that is essential to the whole of Indian philosophy pertains to the classification of authoritative grounds of knowledge

[2] For example, NKan 30.18, NKanP 32.3 etc.

(*pramāṇa*)[3]. It is well-known that the Vaiśeṣika system traditionally admitted only perception (*pratyakṣa*) and inference (*anumāna*) as *pramāṇa*s and included verbal cognition (*śabda*) as a type of inference. Probably observing this traditional Vaiśeṣika tenet regarding *pramāṇa*s, the *Padârtha-dharma-saṁgraha* includes verbal cognition into inference and attributes the reason for this inclusion to the sameness of the cognitive process between these two cognitions.[4] Vyomaśiva, however, reveals that there was a difference of opinion among Vaiśeṣikas in his time regarding the location of verbal cognition, with some holding that it should be included in inference and others claiming that it is an independent *pramāṇa*. While commenting on the enumeration of four types of knowledge presented in the *Padârtha-dharma-saṁgraha* (*vidyā api catur-vidhā, pratyakṣa-laiṅgika-smṛty-ārṣa-lakṣaṇā*), Vyomaśiva argues as follows:

> '[Opponent:] Verbal cognition also has the form of knowledge (*vidyā*). Why, then, is it not examined here [in the section of *vidyā*]? [Vyomaśiva's reply:] To let the difference of opinions be known. Precisely, the difference of opinions that some (*kecid*) include verbal cognition within inference, whereas others (*anye*) consider it as an separate *pramāṇa*, exists among Vaiśeṣikas. Thus, verbal cognition is not mentioned here [in the section on *vidyā*].'[5]

---

[3] As is well-known the word '*pramāṇa*' has two aspects, i.e. a means of knowledge and an authoritative ground of knowledge. To avoid confusion and inconvenience, the latter translation is coherently used in this paper.

[4] VS(C) 9.18–21: [18] *asyêdaṁ kāryaṁ kāraṇaṁ sambandhy ekârtha-samavāyi virodhi cêti laiṅgikam.* [19] *etena śābdaṁ vyākhyātam.* [20] *hetur apadeśo liṅgaṁ nimittaṁ pramāṇaṁ kāraṇam ity anārthântaram.* [21] *asyêdam iti buddhy-apekṣatvāt.*—'[18] Inference [occurs in the following forms:] "This one is an effect of this, [this one is] a cause [of this], [this one is] a related object [of this], [this one is] a thing inhered in one and the same substratum [with this], or [this one is] a thing contradicted [with this]. [19] By the above [*sūtra*], verbal cognition is [also] explained. [20] The word «logical reason», «indication», «inferential mark», «sign» and «ground» have the same meaning. [21] Because [verbal cognition] anticipates the cognition that «This one is of that», [it is considered as a type of inference]"'; PBh, p. 498.2–3: *śabdâdīnāṁ apy anumāne 'ntar-bhāvaḥ samāna-vidhitvāt. yathā prasiddha-samayasya liṅga-darśana-prasiddhy-anusmaraṇābhyām atīndriye 'rthe bhavaty anumānam; evaṁ śabdâdibhyo 'pîti.*—'Verbal cognition etc. are also included as a type of inference because they have one and the same cognitive pattern (*vidhi*) with that of inference. In inference, one who knows very well the rule [that a certain inferential mark is invariably related to another specific object] infers an unseen object through perception of the inferential mark and remembrance of the well-known rule. Just like inference, [he/she] cognates, through a certain word, [the meaning invariably related to the word].'

[5] VyV_2, II: p. 137.10–12: *nanu śābda-jñānasyâpi vidyā-rūpatvād ihânupanyāse kiṁ prayojanam? vipratipatti-jñāpanam iti. tathā hi śābdam anumāne 'ntar-bhavatîti kecit, anye tu pramāṇântaram iti vaiśeṣikāṇāṁ vipratipattis tenêhânabhidhānam.* The difference of opinions was recognised also by Guṇaratna, a later Jaina scholar, who makes the following remark in TRD ad ṢDSa 67, pp. 281.20–282.1: *śabdâdīnāṁ tu pramāṇām anumāna evântar-bhāvāt kandalī-kārâbhiprāyeṇa etat-pramāṇa-dvitayam avocad ācāryaḥ. vyomaśivas*

In the section on the examination (*parīkṣā*) of verbal cognition, Vyomaśiva introduces two ways to interpret the *Padârtha-dharma-saṁgraha*'s statement 'Verbal cognition is also included in inference' or 'Verbal cognition is included also in inference' (PBh, p. 498.2: *śabdâdīnām apy anumāne 'ntarbhāvaḥ*): one which allows verbal cognition to be included in inference and the other claiming that verbal cognition should be differentiated from it. However, after a longer argument with opponents regarding the validity of the *Veda*, Vyomaśiva eventually admits verbal cognition as an independent *pramāṇa*, conceding that he follows an opinion of his teacher[s] (*guru*/ *guravaḥ*) who discussed the topic in detail before him.[6] As has been mentioned in my pr research,[7] the very word *guru*, to whom Vyomaśiva refers in several places of his book, possibly denotes some of the commentators of Nyāya texts.[8] Thus, it can be assumed that he admitted verbal cognition as an independent *pramāṇa* because of his commitment to the Nyāya theory, which had classified inference and verbal cognition as two separate *pramāṇa*s against the Vaiśeṣika traditional tenet.[9] Similarity between Vyomaśiva's opinion and Nyāya tenets can also be demonstrated in the theory of the cognitive process of inference (*anumāna*). While Praśastapāda held that inferential knowledge occurs directly from remembrance of invariable concomitance,[10] Vyomaśiva distinguished

tu pratyakṣânumāna-śabdāni trīṇi pramāṇāni procivān. upasaṁharann āha "vaiśeṣika-matasya" ity-ādi.—'In fact, the word as a means of knowledge is nothing but inference, because the former is included as a type of the latter. Based on this intension of the author of the *Nyāya-kandalī*, the teacher (Haribhadra) stated that the means of knowledge is of two-kinds. On the other hand, Vyomaśiva proclaimed the means of knowledge to be of three-kinds, i.e. perception, inference, and the word.'

[6] VyV_2, II: p. 170.12–13: *śeṣaṁ câtra dūṣaṇa-pratisamādhānam asmad-gurubhir vistareṇâbhihitam iti nêhôktam. ataḥ śabdasyâptôktatvena prāmāṇyān nânumāne 'ntarbhāvaḥ.*—'Since the rest of the reply to the refutations [regarding the authority of verbal cognition] has already been explained by our teacher(s) in detail, it is not discussed here. Accordingly, words are established as an authoritative ground due to the property of being spoken by a trustworthy person, and should not be included as a type of inference.' The fact that Vyomaśiva accepted verbal cognition as an authoritative ground of knowledge has been pointed out also by THAKUR (2003: 273–275) etc.

[7] SUZUKI (2010: 162, n. 15).

[8] For example, he refers to his teacher(s) at the end of his criticism against three conditions whereby a sound reason is satisfied (*trairūpya*; VyV_2, II: p. 149.17: *vistareṇa ... asmad-gurubhir nirasta iti nêha pratanyate.*—'Since it has already been discussed in detail by our teacher(s), we will not expand the argument here.'), which is quite similar to the one which appears in NV, p. 51.19–53.5. The same type of expressions can be found in the VyV_2, II: p. 130.13, 140.25, 149.18, 171.12, 173.18–19 etc.

[9] A detailed discussion regarding the classification of verbal cognition is found already in NS 2.1.49–56. Here, Gautama introduces the opponents' opinion that verbal cognition is to be included into inference, and he provides three reasons for this, to which the *Nyāya-vārttika* (NV) adds another three. Among these six reasons, four correspond to the ones which the VSV(C) presents; cf. NV 2.1.49, p. 246.16–20 and VSV(C) 9.19–21, p. 69.19–70.9.

[10] PBh, p. 477.2–3: *vidhis tu yatra dhūmas tatrâgnir agny-abhāve dhūmo 'pi na bhavatîti. evam prasiddha-samayasyâsandigdha-dhūma-darśanāt sāhacaryânusmaraṇāt tad-anantaram*

still another cognitive stage, *liṅga-parāmarśa* ('reflection of inferential mark'), before the occurrence of inferential knowledge, by forcibly interpreting the compound '*agny-adhyavasāya*' which appears in the Praśastapāda's statement.[11] The same line of interpretation can be seen also in Udayana.[12]

Śrīdhara, on the other hand, objects to 'somebody's' opinion differentiating verbal cognition from inference, which is similar to Vyomaśiva's view.[13] His objection is however based on the reason presented in the VS(C) 9.18–21 and the *Padârtha-dharma-saṁgraha* (PBh, p. 498.2–3), which seems to have come out of fashion in Śrīdhara's time.[14] In addition, there are indications that Śrīdhara knew of the new argument regarding verbal cognition.[15] The fact that he avoids mentioning the new point of view despite his knowledge of it leads us to hypothetically assume that he had a stronger commitment to defending the traditional Vaiśeṣika tenet than to implanting new theoretical current into the *Padârtha-dharma-saṁgraha*'s statement. On the other hand, we could also suppose that he preferred distancing himself from Nyāya scholarly current rather than approaching it because his basic standpoint differed.[16] This as-

---

agny-adhyavasāyo bhavatîti.—'The [cognitive] pattern [of inference] is as follows: When an agent of inference who has already ascertained the well-known rule that "wherever there is smoke, there is fire; wherever there is no fire, there is no smoke, either" perceives smoke without any doubt [that the smoke may be something else], decisive knowledge of fire (*agny-adhyavasāya*) immediately occurs for the agent of inference after the remembrance of the rule of co-existence [of smoke and fire].'

[11] Vyomaśiva interprets the compound *agny-adhyavasāya* in the above PBh's statement, as a *bahu-vrīhi* compound to mean 'that which has the definitive knowledge of fire', which means 'knowledge by which fire can certainly be known', i.e. *liṅga-parāmarśa* of fire, see VyV_2, II: p. 156.3–4: … *agnir adhyavasīyate anenêty agny-adhyavasāyaḥ parāmarśa-jñānam.*

[12] KĀ, p. 198.7.243.21.

[13] NKan, pp. 498.11–505.10. The opinion of *pūrva-pakṣa* summarised by Śrīdhara is similar to the description of Vyomaśiva (VyV_2, II: p. 164.6–165.6). For detailed discussion, see SUZUKI (2010: 162–165).

[14] As the ground for inclusion of verbal cognition in inference, the two authoritative texts hold the sameness of the cognitive process between two cognitions in terms of a single word. Kumārila, in his *Śloka-vārttika*, dismissed this justification before Śrīdhara by reasoning that knowledge of a sentence, apart from that of a single word, is not acquired by the same cognitive process of inference (MŚV 5.5.108–111, p. 194). Similar discussion is found also in the NMa, pp. 403–409. The *Tarka-saṁgraha*, a manual of the later Nyāya-Vaiśeṣika system, defines verbal cognition as cognition of sentence-meaning (TS, p. 54.17: *vākyârtha-jñānaṁ śābda-jñānam. tat-karaṇaṁ śabdaḥ*).

[15] In the beginning section of the *Nyāya-kandalī* (NKan, p. 18.4), Śrīdhara refers to mutual-dependence (*ākāṅkṣā*), proximity (*sannidhi*), and consistency (*yogyatā*), three necessary factors for sentence cognition. Nevertheless, he does not mention them at all when he tries to protect the inclusion of verbal cognition in inference in the section on verbal cognition.

[16] In SUZUKI (2010) I have suggested two hypotheses regarding Śrīdhara's orientation *vis-à-vis* the Vaiśeṣika tenets regarding verbal cognition. One concerns his conservatism, in which he tries to go back to the original Vaiśeṣika tenets of verbal cognition resisting influences from Nyāya theories, and the other concerns his inclination to Prābhākara

sumption is strengthened by the fact that Śrīdhara clearly dismissed the necessity of *liṅga-parāmarśa* ('reflection of inferential mark'), unlike Vyomaśiva and Udayana.[17]

4. Relationship between Vyomaśiva, Śrīdhara, Udayana regarding the valid knowledge towards the existence of emancipation.

Śrīdhara thus denies verbal cognition as an independent *pramāṇa*, but his denial is limited to that of secular language. He clearly states that the *Veda* is nothing but independent *pramāṇa*.[18] His acceptance of the *Veda*'s authority itself is not surprising because this acknowledgement must have been the critical condition for the orthodox Hindu philosophical systems. Yet, this description of Śrīdhara deserves more attention. The *Padârtha-dharma-saṁgraha* seems to indirectly admit the authority of the *Veda*, since it states: 'The scripture (*āmnāya*) characterised to contain Śruti and Smr̥ti anticipates the *prāmāṇya* ('authority') of their author, for [VS(C) 1.1.3] says "Because it is the word of a trustworthy person, the scripture has *prāmāṇya* ('authority') [and the scripture, as the word of a trustworthy person, is included in inference]".'[19] On the other hand, Śrīdhara accepts the *Veda* as an independent *pramāṇa* on the ground that it is the words of a special person.[20] Another conspicuous indication that shows his strong commitment to the Vedic scriptures will be discussed below.

Commenting on the opening section of the *Padârtha-dharma-saṁgraha*, Śrīdhara focuses on the word *mahodaya* (lit. 'great rising') in the *Padârtha-dharma-saṁgraha*'s description, introducing different points of view regarding

---

Mīmāṁsā, which held that cognition of secular language is inference. As has been pointed out by THAKUR (2003: 251–256), Śālikanātha, who flourished in Bengal, shows his intimacy with Vaiśeṣika, often quoting the VS(C) with the phrase *bhagavān kāśyapaḥ* in his *R̥ju-vimalā* (R̥ju) and *Prakaraṇa-pañcikā* (PrP). For example, he quotes the VS(C) 9.18–19 to advocate the inclusion of verbal cognition in inference (PrP, pp. 244.20–245.9). It is well-known that Bengal was also Śrīdhara's academic base.

[17] In the *Vyomavatī* and the *Kiraṇâvalī*, there are several cases of evidence that the authors imported the theory of *liṅga-parāmarśa* ('reflection of inferential mark') from Nyāya into their Vaiśeṣika system, whereas Śrīdhara neglected the need to introduce the theory in NKan; cf. SUZUKI (2010: 177–178).

[18] NKan, p. 508.7–8: *pramāṇaṁ vedaḥ sarveṣām avisaṁvādi-jñāna-janakatvāt pratyakṣavat.*—'The *Veda* is an authoritative ground of knowledge, for it produces consistent knowledge in [the mind of] every person, like perception.'

[19] PBh, p. 506.2–5: *śruti-smr̥ti-lakṣaṇo 'py āmnāyo vaktr̥-prāmāṇyâpekṣaḥ, tad-vacanād āmnāya-prāmāṇyam ... ity uktatvāt.*

[20] NKan, p. 507.6: *tad-vacanāt tena viśiṣṭena puruṣena praṇayanād āmnāyasya vedasya prāmāṇyam.*—'"Because [it is] his word", [which means] because [the *Veda* is] conveyed by the special person, "the scripture" i.e. the *Veda* has authority.' Here Śrīdhara uses the wording of the VS(C) 1.1.3 '*tad-vacanād āmnāya-prāmāṇyam*' as the ground that the *Veda* is authoritative ground of knowledge (*pramāṇa*), whereas the *Padârtha-dharma-saṁgraha* uses the same phrase as the ground for the *Veda*'s inclusion in inference.

the definition of emancipation.[21] After establishing his own definition of emancipation as absolute cessation of suffering, he next criticises the Tārkikas' ('logicians') opinion that the existence of emancipation can be established by inference, which is different from an opinion held by another group with which he himself identified (*asmad*). Śrīdhara, then, points out the invalidity of such inference and asserts that the existence of emancipation is to be established by sentences of the *Upaniṣads* (*vedântāḥ*), particularly those of the *Chāndogya-upaniṣad*. He says as follows:

> '[Śrīdhara:] Therefore, it is reasonable to conclude that *mahodaya* (lit. 'great rising') is absolute cessation of disadvantage. [Opponent:] What is the *pramāṇa* ('authoritative ground') to prove its existence? [Śrīdhara:] T ā r k i k a s present [the following inference as their authoritative ground]: "The continuation of suffering has absolute cessation, because it is a continuation, like the continuation of the light of a lamp". However, their opinion is not reasonable because this reason deviates to the colour of an earthen atom. On the other hand, w e take Upaniṣadic sentences such as "Indeed, both of pleasure and pain never touch the bodiless entity" (ChU 18.12.1) as its authoritative ground.'[22]

This comment of Śrīdhara, which tries to establish the existence of emancipation by Upaniṣadic sentences, looks very peculiar when we consider the specific features of the Vaiśeṣika system. It is said to have had a close connection with the Nyāya system, which investigated questions of logic from its early phase and aimed to establish its own pluralism through proofs using syllogism. However, the background of this 'theological' attitude of Śrīdhara, which establishes the ontological ground of transempirical existence more via the Upaniṣadic sentences than from inference, can be found in Candrānanda's *Vṛtti* ad the VS(C) 1.1.1.[23]

---

[21] The followings are the opinions criticised by Śrīdhara and his commentators' identifications with particular philosophical schools: (1) NKan, p. 13.6: *savāsana-kleśasam ucchedo jñānôparam ity eke.*—NKanṬ: *eke = mādhyamikāḥ*; NKanP: *eke = mādhyamikâkhyā caturtha-bauddhāḥ*; (2) NKan, p. 14.2: *nikhila-vāsanôcchede vigata-vividha-viṣayâkārôpa-plava-viśuddha-jñānôtpādo mahodaya ity apare.*—NKanP: *apare = vaibhāṣika-sautrāntika-yogācārâkhyā ādyas trayo bauddha-bhedāḥ*; (3) NKan, p. 15.5: *prakṛti-puruṣa-viveka-darśanād uparatāyāṁ prakṛtau puruṣasya svarūpeṇâvasthānaṁ mahodaya ity anye.*—NKanP: *anye = sāṁkhyāḥ*; (4) NKan, p. 16.5: *nitya-niratiśaya-sukhâbhivyaktir muktir ity apare.*—NKanP: *apare = jaiminīyāḥ*.

[22] NKan, p. 16.6–17.4: *tasmād ahita-nivṛttir ātyantakī mahodaya iti yuktam. tasyāḥ sadbhāve kiṁ pramāṇam? duḥkha-santatir dharmiṇy atyantam ucchidyate santatitvāt pradīpa-santativad iti tārkikāḥ. tad ayuktam, pārthiva-paramâṇu-rūpâdi-santānena vyabhicārāt. "aśarīraṁ vāva santaṁ priyâpriye na spṛśataḥ" ity-ādayo vedântāḥ pramāṇam iti tu vayam.*

[23] Commenting on VS(C) 1.1.1: *athâto dharmaṁ vyākhyāsyāmaḥ*, Candrānanda explains the reason why Dharma ('merit') is going to be discussed in the beginning of the VS(C) by way of narrating a story, according to which a student who has become convinced of the

Udayana's comment on the same part of the *Padârtha-dharma-saṁgraha* makes a perfect contrast with Śrīdhara's. He says as follows:

> '[Opponent:] What is, then, the authoritative ground [to prove the existence of emancipation]? [Udayana:] Ācāryas present [the following inference as its the authoritative ground:] "Continuation of suffering has absolute cessation, because it is continuation, like the continuation of the light of a lamp". [Opponent:] This reason deviates with respect to the colour of an earth atom. [Udayana:] [Their charge is] wrong, because the continuation of suffering, which exists in all souls, constitutes the inferential subject in this inference, and therefore, the colour of an earthen atom is consequently included in the inferential subject.'[24]

Udayana quotes the opinion of the 'Ācāryas', which is almost the same as that of the 'Tārkikas' of the *Nyāya-kandalī*, and defends it against the criticism, which resembles that of Śrīdhara. Udayana himself does not identify the specific *ācārya*(s) and his (their) critic.[25] However, the picture emerges in which Śrīdhara is on one side as a critic of 'Tārkikas', whereas Udayana is on the other side as a supporter or follower.

5. Who are the 'Tārkikas'?

Ganganatha JHA (1982: 5), in his translation of the *Nyāya-kandalī*, identifies the 'Tārkikas' with Naiyāyikas, whereas THAKUR (2003: 268) regards Vyomaśiva as one of them. The former does not present any sources and, even more so, seems to have literally interpreted the word '*tārkika*', which means 'logi-

existence of emancipation thanks to a sentence from the *Chāndogyôpaniṣad* (ChU 18.12.1: *aśarīraṁ vāva santaṁ priyâpriye na spṛśataḥ*), asks Kaṇāda about the means of achieving emancipation. To this Kaṇāda replies that the means is *dharma*; see VSV(C), p. 1.7: *kasyacid brāhmaṇasya vedâbhyāsa-vaśena vyapagata-kalmaṣasyêdaṁ veda-vākyaṁ pratibabhau "aśarīraṁ vāva santaṁ priyâpriye na spṛśataḥ" iti. tata idaṁ vākyam ālocya kaṇabhakṣam ājagāma. tato 'bhyuvāca—bhagavan! anena vākyenâpahata-śarīrasya kṣema-sādhanatā kathyate, tad ucyatām—ka upāya iti. tato munir abhyuvāca—dharma iti.*—'To [the mind of] a certain Brāhmaṇa, who had become free from any sin by repeated reading of the *Veda*, flashed a sentence from the text: "Indeed, both pleasure and pain never touch the bodiless entity" (ChU 8.12.1). After that, having reflected upon this sentence, he approached Kaṇabhakṣa. Then he said toward [Kaṇabhakṣa]: "O Venerable [Kaṇabhakṣa], this sentence [of ChU 8.12.1] states that a being whose body is destroyed accomplishes emancipation. Now, the following [point] should be made clear: what is the way for emancipation?" Then the sage replied: "[It is] merit (*dharma*)".'

[24] KĀ, p. 7.6–8: *kiṁ punar atra pramāṇam? "duḥkha-santatir atyantam ucchidyate santatitvāt, pradīpa-santativad" ity ācāryāḥ. pārthiva-paramâṇu-gata-rūpâdi-santāne-nânaikāntikam idam iti cet, na, sarvâtmagata-duḥkha-santāne pakṣīkaraṇe phalatas tasyâpi pakṣe 'ntar-bhāvyāt.*

[25] The commentaries such as the *Kiraṇâvalī-prakāśa* (KĀPr) and the *Kiraṇâvalī-rahasya* (KĀR) do not discuss to whom the term *ācārya* refers.

cians', to mean 'Naiyāyikas'. However, this interpretation does not seem to have enough philological background because the same logical formula (*duḥkha-santatir dharmini atyantam ucchidyate santatitvāt, pradīpa-santativat*), not to mention a similar description of it, cannot be found in any texts of the Nyāya from the *Nyāya-sūtra* to the *Nyāya-vārttika-tātparya-pariśuddhi*.[26] THAKUR's opinion, on the other hand, is based on the description found in the *Nyāya-kandalī-pañjikā*.[27] Before THAKUR, M.K. SHASTRI (1941), in his explanation for PKM, and G. SHASTRI (1980), in his Hindi translation and explanation of the KĀ, searched out the passages corresponding with the opinion of Ācāryas found in the *Vyomavatī*. THAKUR's indication must be based on a common assumption among Indian scholars regarding the relationship between Vyomaśiva and Udayana. Yet, this fact should be more carefully re-examined because the condition of the corresponding part in the manuscripts of the *Vyomavatī* is incomplete, and accordingly, some characters were illegible in the editions available at the time of the original publication.[28] In this connection, the part of the *Vyomavatī* was reconstructed by Elliot STERN (2007) who reutilised the manuscripts which served as the source for the first and second volumes of Sampūrṇānanda editions (VyV_2), and referring to relevant texts

[26] It should be noted here, however, that the *Nyāya-bhāṣya* contains similar arguments which may have worked as the foundation of this logical formula (NBh ad NS 4.1.65–67, p. 255.7–256.4): [65] ***na, kleśa-santateḥ svābhāvikatvāt.*** *nôpapadyate kleśânubandha-vicchedaḥ. kasmāt? kleśa-santateḥ svābhāvikatvāt. anādir iyaṁ kleśa-santatiḥ. na cânādiḥ śakya ucchetum iti.* [66] *atra kaścit parīhāram āha—****prāg-utpatter-abhāvânityatvavat svābhāvike 'py anityatvam*** *yathânādiḥ prāg-utpatter abhāva utpannena bhāvena nivartyata ity anityaḥ, evaṁ svābhāvikī kleśa-santatir anityēti.* [67] *apare āha—****aṇuśyāmatā 'nityatvavad vā.*** *yathânādir aṇuśyāmatā, atha câgni-saṁyogād anityā, tathā kleśa santatir apīti...*—'[65] **It is not correct** [that one who abandoned worldly desires does not establish the connection with the next life], **for continuation of worldly desires is natural and essential**. Bondage with worldly desires cannot be destroyed. Why? Because continuation of worldly desires is natural and essential. Continuation of worldly desires does not have a beginning. Anything that does not have a beginning cannot be destroyed. [66] Somebody raises an objection against this [opinion]—**Like the antecedent non-existence is impermanent, something natural and essential can be impermanent [in some cases].** Just like the antecedent non-existence, which does not have a beginning is impermanent because it can be destroyed when something is produced, continuation of worldly desires, which is natural and essential, is impermanent. [67] Some say—**Or, like the color black residing in earth atoms, [continuation of worldly desires is impermanent.]** Just like the color black residing in an earth atom, which does not have a beginning, is proven to be impermanent when it is linked with fire, continuation of worldly desires also [does not have a beginning but is impermanent] ...' Vātsyāyana here denies the opinion of some people (*apare*) who try to prove that continuation of worldly desire is non-eternal by taking 'black colour of an atom' as its similar example.

[27] NKanP, p. 19.13: *tārkikā iti = vyomaśivâpādāḥ. upahāsaś cāyam.*—'[The word] "*tārkika*" means Vyomaśiva and his followers. This word is [used for] derision.'

[28] VyV_1, p. 1.4–2.25 and VyV_2, I: p. 19(ka).21–p. 20 (kha).10.

such as the PKM, which has come to allow us to read it to a further extent.[29] The passage in question reads as follows:

> '[Opponent:] What is the authoritative ground for the existence of emancipation? (12–13 characters are unreadable.) Precisely, [the following inference is the authoritative ground.] "The continuation of the nine special qualities of the soul has absolute cessation, because it is a continuation. All kinds of continuation are observed to have absolute cessation, like the continuation of the light of a lamp. This continuation is also like that. Therefore, it has absolute cessation." The reason property of this inference does not fall into the fallacy of inconclusiveness (*asiddha*), because property [being the reason] resides in the inferential subject due to its existence in [special qualities such as] knowledge etc. Nor [does it fall] into the fallacy of contradiction (*viruddha*), because the reason property is perceived in the substrata which have the common quality [with the inferential subject], such as the light of a lamp etc. Nor [does it fall] into the fallacy of discrepancy (*anaikāntika*), because continuation does not exist in the dissimilar example such as the atom etc. Nor [does it fall] into the fallacy of mistiming (*kālâtyayâpadiṣṭa*), because neither perception nor scripture can be found leading to the opposite conclusion. And the reason property does not fall into the fallacy of counter balance (*sat-pratipakṣa*), either. Therefore, since the reason of this inference satisfies the five conditions [required for the valid reason], this inference is the authoritative ground [for the existence of emancipation].'[30]

A direct reply to the question which asks for the authoritative ground for the existence of emancipation is still unreadable even after STERN's reconstruction. However, there is nearly no doubt that Vyomaśiva presented the same proof which Śrīdhara criticised, and which Udayana supported, as the opinion

[29] For detailed information on the manuscript, see STERN (2007).

[30] STERN (404: 18–25) = VyV_2, I: p. 2.5–14: *atha niḥśreyasâstitve kiṁ pramāṇa{m astī* plus 12–13 characters}*vi. tathā hi navānām ātma-viśeṣa-guṇānāṁ santāno 'tyantam ucchidyate. santānatvād. yo yaḥ santānaḥ sa so 'tyantam ucchidyamāno dṛṣṭaḥ. yathā pradīpa-santānas. tathā câyaṁ santānas. tasmā{d atyanta}m ucchidyata iti. santānatvasya ca vyāptyā buddhy-ādiṣu sambhavāt pakṣa-dharmatayā asiddhatvâbhāvaḥ tat-samāna-dharmaṇi dharmiṇi pradīpa-ādāv upalambhād aviruddhatvam. na ca vipakṣe paramāṇv-ādāv asti san{tānatva}m ity anaikāntikatvâbhāvaḥ. viparītârthôpasthāpakayoḥ pratyakṣâgamayor anupalambhān na kālâtyayâpadiṣṭaḥ. na câyaṁ sat-pratipakṣa iti pañca-rūpatvāt pramāṇam.*

Curled brackets {} indicate damaged portions of the manuscript and their contents signify the number of letters or reading estimated by STERN. I basically follow his style of Roman transcription and punctuation, though I omit folio and line numbers and add additional spaces, periods, and *avagraha*s according to my own understanding.

of Ācāryas. Summarising the above, we now have a framework for the three commentators' standpoints. Vyomaśiva and Udayana, taking the Tārkikas' position, held that inference is the authoritative ground for existence of emancipation, whereas Śrīdhara rejected this opinion and followed the Tārkikas, holding that Upaniṣadic sentences are the authoritative ground for it.[31]

6. Logic-orientation and scripture-orientation among the Vaiśeṣikas.

It is noteworthy that we find a logic-oriented approach with Vyomaśiva and Udayana, whom we are likely to identify with the 'Tārkikas', and a scripture-oriented approach by Śrīdhara, who explicitly puts himself into a separate category, opposed to the former.[32] Although we have a difficulty, at this stage, to determine who the 'Tārkikas' are and what Śrīdhara's exact identity is, it is significant to consider the following points for further investigation.

Relying on the account of the *Yaśas-tilaka-campū* (tenth century CE), THAKUR (1957: 'Introduction', p. 16) argued that there were two groups, i.e. the Tārkikas and the Saiddhāntikas, in the Vaiśeṣika school.[33] While doxographically listing viewpoints regarding the means of emancipation, this Jaina text mentions the Vaiśeṣika system as their first example in which these two groups are classified. According to it, the Tārkikas are the Vaiśeṣikas who accept distinctive knowledge regarding the six categories (*tattva-jñāna*) as the

[31] The word *tārkika* is used by Śrīdhara at least once more in the section on sound (NKan, p. 639.10–11: *atīvāyaṁ mārgas tārkikaiḥ kṣuṇṇas tenâsmābhir iha bhāṣya-tātparya-mātraṁ vyākhyātam nâparā yuktir uktā.*). We find extensive discussion of this topic in VyV_2, II: p. 237–244. It is unfortunate that any commentary on this phrase of the NKan is not available as well as the correspondent discussion in KĀ.

[32] While Śrīdhara clearly dismisses the logical formula suggested by the Tārkikas, Vyomaśiva and Udayana mention the very sentence of the *Chāndogyôpaniṣad* presented by Śrīdhara (see n. 24). However, the following discussion in the *Vyomavatī* (VyV_2, p. 1.11 ff.) is unreadable also in STERN's reconstruction. As for Udayana, he does mention the Upaniṣadic sentence, but does not seem to attach much importance to it, when he says: *aśarīraṁ vāva santaṁ priyâpriye na spṛśataḥ ity-ādy āgamāc câyam artho 'dhyavaseyaḥ* ('Through the Upaniṣadic sentence: "Indeed, both pleasure and pain never touch the bodiless entity" the meaning of [the inference to prove the existence of emancipation] is ascertained.'), after a discussion regarding the validity of the inference in question (KĀ, p. 8.4).

[33] Although THAKUR himself does not single out the relevant passages, he uses the following passage of the *Yaśas-tilaka-campū* as evidence (YTC, p. 2.5–7): *sakala-niṣkalâpta-prāpta-mantra-tantrâpekṣa-dīkṣā-lakṣaṇāc chraddhā-mātrânusaraṇān mokṣa iti saiddhāntika-vaiśeṣikāḥ, dravya-guṇa-karma-sāmānya-samavāyântyaviśeṣâbhāvâbhidhānānāṁ padârthānāṁ sādharmya-vaidharmyâvabodhâtantrāj jñāna-mātrāt iti tārkika-vaiśeṣikāḥ.*—'[Vaiśeṣikas who hold] that emancipation [is attained] only as a consequence of strong belief in Śiva, which is characterised by religious practices based on mystical formulas and doctrines attained through the one, whose body [simultaneously] consists of parts or does not have parts, are called Saiddhāntika-Vaiśeṣikas. [Whereas, the ones who] hold that [emancipation is attained] only through knowledge characterised by the awareness of similarity and dissimilarity between six categories: substance, quality, motion, universal, inherence, particularity, and non-existence are called Tārkika-Vaiśeṣikas.'

cause of emancipation, whereas the Saiddhāntikas claim that devotion (*śraddhā*) to Śiva is the means of emancipation. Needless to say, these two groups cannot be directly linked with the above framework of the three commentators, which we illustrated according to their descriptions regarding the authoritative ground for the existence of emancipation. However, it is of note that Vyomaśiva provides a rational explanation of the process of emancipation, which is in accordance with the *Padârtha-dharma-saṁgraha*,[34] in order to advocate that emancipation is acquired through *tattva-jñāna* (lit. 'knowledge of truth'), whereas Śrīdhara emphasises the necessity of knowledge and action (*jñāna-karma-samuccaya*) for the acquisition of emancipation within a context in which he uses such expressions as *śravaṇa, manana, nididhyāsana*.[35] Śrīdhara, in the opening section of the *Nyāya-kandalī*, refers to another of his own no longer extant books named *Advaya-siddhi*, the title of which could suggest that it is a text regarding Advaita Vedānta philosophy.[36] When we classify his criticism of the 'Tārkika' under the Vedāntic context, we can recall that Śaṅkara criticised the Mīmāṁsaka and the 'Tārkika' for their false reliance on human reasoning in his *Bṛhad-āraṇyakôpaniṣad-bhāṣya*.[37]

Relevance with the widely accepted assumption that the Vaiśeṣika merged with the Nyāya to become the Nyāya-Vaiśeṣika school should also be considered. In the KĀ, there are several descriptions found that Udayana probably intended to embed the Nyāya theories into the *Padârtha-dharma-saṁgraha*. The fact that Udayana, who is known as the initiator of the fusion of these two schools, may have identified Vyomaśiva with his *ācārya* allows us to suppose that this word would, at least partly, have referred to a group among Vaiśeṣikas which eventually merged with the Nyāya school. If so, we can consequently

[34] *Tattva-jñāna* ('knowledge of truth') is a means of emancipation also in the Nyāya system although its contents is different from that of the Vaiśeṣika. The former concerns the knowledge of the sixteen categories regarding the debate (NS 1.1.1: *pramāṇa-prameya-saṁśaya ... nigraha-sthānānāṁ tattva-jñānān niḥśreyasa- adhigamaḥ*), while the latter involves the six ontological categories.

[35] NKan, p. 631.14–631.16: *sa câivam āvir-bhūta-jijñāsa ācāryam upagacchati, tasya câcāryôpdeśāt ṣaṇṇāṁ padārthānāṁ śrautaṁ tattva-jñānaṁ jāyate. tad anu śravaṇa-manana-nididhyāsanâdi-krameṇa pratyakṣaṁ bhavati.*—'Thus, a student who has evident desire for knowledge of the truth approaches his teacher. In the student's mind, then, the true knowledge of the six categories, which was heard by ancient sages (*śrauta*), arises. After that, the true knowledge of the categories manifests itself before his eyes, according to the order of *śravaṇa* (hearing), *manana* (reflection) and *nididhyāsana* (meditation).'

[36] MESQUITA (1995) demonstrates that Śrīdhara's theory of emancipation contains many layers of thought, especially those borrowed from Vedānta.

[37] BĀUBh, p. 8.7–12: *śrutyâtmâstitve liṅgasya darśitatvāt liṅgasya ca pratyakṣa-viṣayatvān nêti cen na, janmântara-sambandhasyâgrahaṇāt. āgamena tv ātmâstitve 'vagate veda-pradarśita-laukika-liṅga-viśeṣaiś ca tad-anusāriṇo mīmāṁsakās tārkikāś câham-pratyaya-liṅgāni ca vaidikāny eva svamati-prabhavāṇîti kalpayanto vadanti pratyakṣaś cânumeyaś ca ātmā iti*. Cf. HALBFASS (1991: 35).

suppose that the indications of the movement of unification can be found already in Vyomaśiva, and that Śrīdhara did not involve himself in this movement.[38]

7. Conclusion.

It has been confirmed by the above investigation that there are different perspectives in interpreting the *Padârtha-dharma-saṁgraha* among its commentators. With reference to the question of location of verbal cognition, Vyomaśiva did not avoid differing from the Vaiśeṣika authoritative texts to accept verbal cognition as an independent *pramāṇa*, whereas Śrīdhara seems to have rejected this commentarial approach. As for the topic of *pramāṇa* toward the existence of emancipation, Vyomaśiva explicitly made a logic-oriented interpretation which Udayana followed, while Śrīdhara stood against this movement in holding that the scripture are more authoritative than inference. The difference between the set of Vyomaśiva and Udayana, and Śrīdhara could be found also in the topic of the cognitive process of inference.

The above facts may show, as an example, how vague the notion of a 'Vaiśeṣika school' is. We modern researchers are more or less apt to categorise commentators according to which authoritative texts they commented on when we try to draw the history of Indian philosophy using the word 'school' as a device. However, the possibility should be considered that a specific entity with which commentators identified themselves, at least in some extreme cases, did not exist, not only in the sense that they wrote commentaries for several systems, but also in the sense that they seem to have input, into authoritative texts of a certain system, interpretations closer to that of other systems.[39]

---

[38] In this connection, it should be noted that Jayanta may have regarded the Vaiśeṣikas as followers of the Nyāya school, as THAKUR (2003: 381) argues, see NMa, I: p. 9.5–6: *vaiśeṣikāḥ punar asmad-anuyāyinaḥ evêty evam asyāṁ janatāsu prasiddhāyām api ṣaṭ-tarkyāṁ idam eva tarka-nyāya-vistara-śabdābhyāṁ śāstram uktam.*—'Vaiśeṣikas are, on the other hand, nothing but the followers of us (Naiyāyikas). Thus, even though these six philosophical systems are well known by people, this [Nyāya system] alone is called "speculation (*tarka*, *nyāya*)" or "intensive logic (*nyāya-vistara*)".'

[39] In his recent work, OETKE (2009: iii–viii) urged researchers not to abuse the idea of 'deconstructing the notion of school or tradition' by critically referring to SJÖDIN (2006) and my own review of it (SUZUKI (2008)). I agree with his suggestion that it is impossible to investigate a certain text without any assumption or framework, such as 'school' or 'tradition', even if it is somewhat prejudicial. His criticism is, however, at least in my understanding, directed against researchers' perspective in which the popular idea of deconstruction etc. precedes faithful reading of texts, not against the reconsideration of assumptions or framework which has traditionally been accepted. He says, 'Inasmuch as the Sjödin–Suzuki position embodies merely the empirical claim that in the Indian context views of authors and texts commonly grouped together as representing some individual tradition or school can be pretty divergent one can assent to it ...' I believe that this paper confirms that one can present, even if preliminarily, some indication of the necessity of reconsidering the traditional notion of the 'Vaiśeṣika school' in a manner which does not contradict with OETKE's suggestions.

If there had been a 'Vaiśeṣika school' as a social fact which bound individual commentators' activities, perhaps we would be able to reach the conclusion that the former two and Śrīdhara were Vaiśeṣikas who held largely different opinions. However, considering the above, we should, at this stage, refrain not only from categorising them into the 'Vaiśeṣika' group, but also from simply connecting them with some of the six philosophical schools. For instance, Vyomaśiva may have belonged also to the Nyāya school, or Śrīdhara may have been a Vedāntin. At any rate, what has been made clear in this paper is the necessity of reconsidering the fact that the conventional, and unexamined, use of 'Vaiśeṣika school' may obscure important distinctions in the historical situation in which the three commentators actually acted.

BIBLIOGRAPHY

BĀUBh = Śaṅkara: *Bṛhad-āraṇyakôpaniṣad-bhāṣya*. Edward Röer (ed.): *Collection of Oriental Works, Brihad Aranyaka upanishad*. Reprinted, Biblio Verlag, Osnabrük1980 [first edition: Vol. 2, Part 1: 5–9, Bibliotheca Indica, Calcutta 1849].

BHATTACHARYA 1958 = Bhattacharya, D.C.: *History of Navya-Nyāya in Mithilā*. Mithilā Institute of Post-Graduate Studies and Research in Sanskrit Learning, Darbhanga 1958.

CHATTERJEE–DATTA 1968 = Chatterjee, S.C.; Datta, D.M.: *An Introduction to Indian Philosophy*. seventh edition, University of Calcutta, Calcutta 1968.

ChU = *Chāndogyôpaniṣad*. Sarvepalli Radhakrishnan (ed.): *The Principal Upaniṣads* Introduction, text, translation and notes. Reprinted, Oxford University Press, Delhi–Bombay–Calcutta–Madras 1989 [first edition: 1953].

HALBFASS 1988 = Halbfass, Wilhelm: *India and Europe: An Essay in Understanding*. State University of New York Press, Albany 1988.

HALBFASS 1991 = Halbfass, Wilhelm: *Tradition and Reflection: Explorations in Indian Thought*. State University of New York Press, Albany 1991.

JHA 1982 = Jhā, Gaṅgānātha: *Padārthadharmasaṅgraha of Praśastapāda with Nyāyakandalī of Śrīdhara Translated into English*. Reprinted, Chaukhambha Oriental Studies 4, Chaukhambha Orientalia, Varanasi/Delhi 1982 [first edition: 1902, 1915].

KĀ = Udayana: *Kiraṇâvalī*. Jitendra S. Jetly (ed.): *Praśastapādabhāṣyam with the Kiraṇāvalī of Udayanācārya*. Gaekwad's Oriental Series 154, Oriental Institute, Baroda 1991 [first edition: 1971].

KĀPr = Vardhamāṇa: *Kiraṇâvalī-prakāśa*. Narendra Chandra Vedantatirtha (ed.): *Kiraṇāvalī of Udayanācārya*. Fasciculus 2, Bibliotheca Indica, Asiatic Society, Calcutta 1956.

KĀR = Mathurānātha Tarkavāgīśā: *Kiraṇâvalī-rahasya*. Gaurīnātha Śāstri (ed.): *Kiraṇāvalīrahasyam of MM Mathurānātha Tarkavāgīśa*. MM Śivakumāraśāstī-granthamālā Vol. 4, Sampurnanand Sanskrit Vishvavidyalaya, Varanasi 1981.

Ṛju = Śālikanāthamiśra: *Ṛju-vimālā*. A. Chinnaswami Sastri (ed.): *Bṛhatī with the Commentary the Ṛjuvimalā*. Chowkhamba Sanskrit Series 391, Chowkhamba Sanskrit Series Office, Benares 1929.

MESQUITA 1995 = Mesquita, Roque: 'Der Apavarga-Begriff bei Śrīdhara. Eine vedāntische Erlösungslehre?', in: Mirja Juntunen, William L. Smith, Carl Suneson (eds.): *Sauhṛdayamaṅgalam. Studies in Honour of Siegfried Lienhard on his 70th Birthday*. The Association of Oriental Studies, Stockholm 1995.

MŚV = Kumārilabhaṭṭa: *Śloka-vārttika*. Ganga Sagar Rai (ed.): *Śloka-vārttika of Śrī Kumārila Bhaṭṭa with the Commentary Nyāyaratnākara of Śrī Pārthasārahi Miśra*. Ratnabharati Series 4, Ratna Publications, Varanasi 1993.

NBh = Vātsyāyana Pakṣilasvāmin: *Nyāya-bhāṣya*. See: NS.

NKan = Śrīdharamiśra: *Nyāya-kandalī*. J.S. Jetly; V.G. Parikh (ed.): *Nyāyakandalī, being a commentary on Praśastapādabhāṣya, with three subcommentaries [Tippaṇa, Panjikā, and Kusumodgama]*. Gaekwad's Oriental Series 174, Oriental Institute, Vadodara 1991.

NKanP = Rājaśekhara: *Nyāya-kandalī-pañjikā*. See: NKan.

NKanṬ = Naracandra-sūri: *Nyāya-kandalī-ṭippaṇa*. See: NKan.

NMa = Jayantabhaṭṭa: *Nyāya-mañjarī*. K.S. Varadacharya (ed.): *Nyāya-mañjarī of Jayantabhaṭṭa with Ṭippaṇi—Nyāyasaurabha by the Editor*. 2 Vols., Oriental Research Institute Series 116, 139, Oriental Research Institute, University of Mysore, Mysore 1969, 1983.

NS = Akṣapāda Gautama: *Nyāya-sūtra*. Anantalal Thakur (ed.): *Gautamīyanyāyadarśana with Bhāṣya of Vātsyāyana*. Nyāya-catur-granthikā Vol. I, Indian Council of Philosophical Research, New Delhi 1997.

NV = Bhāradvāja Uddyotakara: *Nyāya-[bhāṣya]-vārttika*. Anantalal Thakur (ed.): *Nyāyabhāṣyavārttika of Bhāradvāja Uddyotakara*. Nyāya-catur-granthikā Vol. II, Indian Council of Philosophical Research, New Delhi 1997.

OETKE 2009 = Oetke, Claus: *Some Aspects of Vyāpti and Upādhi in the Nyāyalīlāvatī*. Acta Universitatis Stockholmiensis, Stockholm Oriental Studies, Stockholm University, Stockholm 2009.

PARIKH 1991 = Parikh, V.: 'Introduction' to NKan.

PBh = Praśastapāda: *Praśastapāda-bhāṣya* (*Padârtha-dharma-saṁgraha*). See: NKan.

PKM = Prabhācandra-sūri: *Prameya-kamala-mārtaṇḍa*. Mahendra Kumar Shastri (ed.): *Prameyakamal Mārtand by Shri Prabha Chandra*. Nirnaya Sagar Press, Bombay 1912 [second edition: 1941].

PrP = Śālikanāthamiśra: *Prakaraṇa-pañcikā*. Mīmāṁsā Ratnam; Subrahmanya Sastri (ed.): *Prakaraṇa Pañcikā of Śrī Śālikanātha Miśra with the Nyāya-siddhi of Jaipuri Nārāyaṇa Bhaṭṭa*. Banaras Hindu University Daraśana Series No. 4, Banaras Hindu University, Banaras 1961.

ṢDSa = Haribhadra-sūri: *Ṣaḍ-darśana-samuccaya*. Luigi Suali (ed.): *Ṣaddarśana-samuccaya (A Review of the Six Systems of Hindu Philosophy) with Guṇaratna's Commentary Tarkarahasyadīpikā by Haribhadra*. The Asiatic Society, Calcutta 1905–1914 [reprinted: 1986].

SHASTRI 1980 = Gaurīnāth Śāstrī (ed.) *Kiraṇāvalī of Udayanācārya*. [Hindi Translation]. Gaṅgānāthajhā-Granthamālā 8, Sampurnanand Sanskrit Vishvavidyalaya, Varanasi 1980.

SHASTRI 1941 = Shastri, M.K.: 'Introduction' to PKM. See: PKM.

SJÖDIN 2006 = Sjödin, Anna-Pya: *The Happening of Tradition: Vallabha on Anumāna in Nyāyalīlāvatī*. Acta Universitatis Upsaliensis: South Asian Studies 1, Uppsala University, Uppsala 2006.

STERN 2007 = Stern, Elliot M.: 'Padārthadharmasaṅgrahaṭīkā of Vyomaśiva: A Partial Reconstruction of Folia 2–3a', in: Karin Preisendanz (ed.): *Expanding and Merging Horizons Contributions to South Asian and Cross-Cultural Studies in Commemoration of Wilhelm Halbfass*. Osterreichishe Akademie der Wissenchaften Philosophisch-Historische Klasse Denkshriften 351, Austrian Academy of Sciences Press, Vienna 2007: 401–413.

SUZUKI 2008 = Suzuki, Takanori: Book Review of SJÖDIN (2006). *Nagoya Studies in Indian Culture and Buddhism: Saṁbhāṣā* 27 (2008) 192–194.

SUZUKI 2010 = Suzuki, Takanori: 'Text, Context, and Author's Intention: Two Frames of Reference in the Vaiśeṣika School', in: Toshihiro Wada (eds.): *Indian Philosophy and Text Science*. Motilal Banarsidass, Delhi 2010: 157–181.

THAKUR 1957 = Thakur, Anantalal: 'Introduction' to: Anantalal Thakur (ed.): *Vaiśeṣikadarśana of Kaṇāda with an Anonymous Commentary*. Mithila Institute, Mithila 1957.

THAKUR 2003 = Thakur, Anantalal: *Origin and Development of the Vaiśeṣika System*. In the Series: *History of Science, Philosophy and Culture in Indian Civilization* (General Editor: D.P. Chatttopadhyaya), Volume II, Part 4. Centre for Studies in Civilizations, New Delhi 2003.

TRD = Guṇaratna-sūri: *Tarka-rahasya-dipikā*. See: ṢDSa.

TS = Annambhaṭṭa: *Tarka-saṁgraha*. Yashwant Vasudev Athalye (ed.): *Tarka-Saṁgraha of Annaṁbhaṭṭa with the Author's own Dīpikā, and Govardhana's Nyāya-bodhinī*. Introduction and English translation of the text by the late Mahadev Rajaram Bodas, Bhandarkar Oriental Research Institute, Poona 1974 [first edition: Government Central Press, Bombay 1918].

VS(C) = Kaṇāda: *Vaiśeṣika-sūtra*. Muni Jambuvijaya (ed.): *Vaiśeṣika-sūtra of Kaṇāda with the Commentary of Candrānanda*. With the Introduction by Anantalal Thakur. Gaekwad's Oriental Series, Oriental Institute 136, Baroda 1961.

VSV(C) = Candrānanda: *Vaiśeṣika-sūtra-vṛtti*. See: VS(C).

VyV = Vyomaśiva: *Vyomavatī*. (1) Gopinath Kaviraj; Dhundhiraj Shastri (eds.): *The Prasastapādabhāshyam by Praśastadevācārya with Commentaries: Sūkti by Jagadisa Tarkālankāra, Setu by Padmanābha Misra, and Vyomavatī by Vyomaśivacharya*. Chowkhambā Sanskrit Series 316, Chowkhamba Sanskrit Series Office, Benares 1924. (2) Gaurinath Sastri (ed.): *Vyomavatī of Vyomaśivācārya*. 2 Vols., M.M. Śiva-kumāra-śastri Grantha-mālā 6, Sampurnanand Sanskrit University, Varanasi 1963.

YTC = Somadeva-sūri: *Yaśas-tilaka-campū*. Kailāśacandra Śāstrī (ed.): *Upāsakādhyayana of Somadevasūri, a Portion of Yaśastilaka-campū of Somadeva Sūri with Hindi Translation, Sanskrit Ṭīkā, Introduction & Indices etc*. Jnānapīṭha Mūrtidevī Jain Granthamālā: Sanskrit Grantha 28, Bhāratīya Jñānapīṭha Prakāśana, Varanasi 1964.

A Review of the Early Nyāya Fragments*

ERNST PRETS

The early school of Nyāya, as one of the orthodox Hindu philosophies, is mainly represented by commentaries on the school's founding text, the *Nyāya-sūtra*, which is ascribed to the sage Akṣapāda (? second century CE) and was most probably finalised in its classical form by anonymous redactors in the first half of the fifth century.[1] The four main preserved commentaries and sub-commentaries, the so-called *Nyāya-catur-granthikā*, are the *Nyāya-bhāṣya* of Pakṣilasvāmin Vātsyāyana (fifth century CE), the *Nyāya-vārttika* of Bhāradvāja Uddyotakara (second half of the sixth century), the *Nyāya-vārttika-tātparya-ṭīkā* of Vācaspatimiśra (tenth century), and the *Nyāya-vārttika-tātparya-pariśuddhi* of Udayana (eleventh century). Jayantabhaṭṭa's *Nyāya-mañjarī* (ninth century) and Bhāsarvajña's *Nyāya-bhūṣaṇa* (tenth century) are not direct commentaries on the *Nyāya-sūtra*. The *Nyāya-mañjarī* is a synopsis of the sixteen Nyāya topics, and the *Nyāya-bhūṣaṇa* is an auto-commentary on Bhāsarvajña's *Nyāya-sāra*. In addition to these, however, there must have been a considerable corpus of other works within the Nyāya tradition written during the second half of the first millennium that have not survived. We know for example that the *Nyāya-bhāṣya* was commented on by a number of early Naiyāyikas of whom only their names, titles of works, or fragments have survived.

These fragments have not been studied as a whole, nor have the fragments from individual periods been examined from the viewpoint of their historical interdependence or mutual dependence as based on their contents. They have only been studied with regard to either single authors, or within the framework of a particular group of authors.

An analysis of the fragments and doxographies would be highly important, since relevant developmental steps in the Nyāya system's concepts are often documented only indirectly in the four major commentaries. These basic concepts often seem to be related to authors whose works are lost. This assump-

---

* Work on this paper has been generously supported by the Austrian Science Fund (FWF) in the context of the FWF project P 20935–G15 ('Fragments of the Nyāya School of Philosophy'). I would like to express my gratitude to Cynthia Peck-Kubaczek for having taken a close look at my English.

[1] Cf. PREISENDANZ (2005: 56).

World View and Theory in Indian Philosophy
Warsaw Indological Studies 5 (2012) 155–171.

tion is substantiated by the fact that such concepts are often referred to in the works of authors of opposing schools and systems. The great Buddhist philosopher Dharmakīrti (*ca.* 600–660), for example, refers apart from Uddyotakara to lost Nyāya works in the polemical sections of his *Vāda-nyāya*, as does Śāntarakṣita in his commentary thereon.[2] As another example, it has been shown that Jayantabhaṭṭa bases his work on two Nyāya branches that are different from the extant commentaries of Pakṣilasvāmin and Uddyotakara. Accordingly, it is clear that lost Nyāya works were important for the philosophical development of Nyāya before the time of Jayantabhaṭṭa.

The first Indological study dealing with a more differentiated history of Nyāya was carried out already in 1936 by Erich Frauwallner.[3] In this article he convincingly shows that Jayantabhaṭṭa's *Nyāya-mañjarī* is mainly based on sources by later Nyāya authors from the time of Dharmakīrti. FRAUWALLNER reveals two sources of the *Nyāya-mañjarī*, namely the works of the so-called *ācāryāḥ* ('the teachers') and *vyākhyātāraḥ* ('the explainers'). These works are different from the preserved commentaries, both written before Dharmakīrti, the *Nyāya-bhāṣya* and the *Nyāya-vārttika*.

Amongst other authors presenting studies on Nyāya fragments,[4] Anantalal Thakur, in particular, contributed in 1953 to a differentiated history of Nyāya with his article 'Some Lost Nyāya Works and Authors',[5] as well as in his later series of studies on different 'lost' authors and works.[6]

In 1961, Ernst Steinkellner summarised earlier research results and presented a number of new consolidated findings in his article 'Die Literatur des älteren Nyāya'.[7] In addition, he tried to develop a chronology of the Naiyāyikas. He acted on the assumption that such a classification could be based on the discussions of the respective Naiyāyikas with the Buddhist teachers Dignāga (480–540 CE) and Dharmakīrti.[8] Accordingly, he restructured the Nyāya School into three groups: (1) teachers and their works before Dignāga, to which he counted the legendary Akṣapāda's *Nyāya-sūtra* (NS) and Pakṣilasvāmin's *Nyāya-bhāṣya* (NBh); (2) teachers between Dignāga and Dharma-

[2] Cf. e.g. Vip 142.28: *uddyotakara-prīticandra(?-)bhāvivikta-prabhṛtiḥ* in commenting on 'uneducated people' in VN 68.12: *durvidagdho jano*.

[3] FRAUWALLNER (1936).

[4] Cf. Benoytosh Bhattacharyya's introduction to his edition of the *Tattva-saṁgraha* (v. TSa); BHATTACHARYA (1946) on Śrīvatsâcārya; BHATTACHARYA (1958); KAVIRAJ (1961).

[5] Cf. THAKUR (1953).

[6] Cf. THAKUR (1947) on Trilocana; THAKUR (1955) on Trilocana as the teacher of Vācaspati; THAKUR (1958–1959) on Viśvarūpa. Cf. also Thakur's introductions to the works of Jñānaśrī (*Jñānaśrīmitra-nibandhâvali*; JNA) and Ratnakīrti (*Ratnakīrti-nibandhâvali*; RNA), which contain many fragments, mainly of discussions between the Nyāya School and Dharmakīrti.

[7] STEINKELLNER (1961).

[8] STEINKELLNER (1961: 150).

kīrti, whose discussions were shaped by their debates with Dignāga and also with his teacher Vasubandhu, to whom he counted Uddyotakara with his *Nyāya-vārttika* (NV), Bhāvivikta, and Aviddhakarṇa; (3) teachers after Dharmakīrti, who discussed Dharmakīrti's teachings in detail, to which he counted in chronological order the following authors: Śaṅkarasvāmin,[9] Trilocana, his pupil[10] Vācaspatimiśra (NVTṬ), Viśvarūpa, Jayantabhaṭṭa (NMa), Bhāsarvajña (NSā, NBhūṣ), Aniruddha (NBhVṬVi), Adhyayana, Vittoka, Narasiṁha, Śrīvatsâcārya, and Udayana (NVTP). In connection with his study of Nyāya fragments, STEINKELLNER also alluded to important aspects regarding the quotations in Kamalaśīla's *Tattva-saṁgraha-pañjikā* (TSaP), aspects that should generally be observed when working with fragments.[11]

About the same time, Gerhard Oberhammer was engaged in extracting and identifying the sources, no longer extant, of Jayantabhaṭṭa and Uddyotakara with regard to inference (*anumāna,* ad NS 1.1.5) and the members of proof (*avayava,* ad NS 1.1.32–39).[12] In his comparison of the two authors' sources, he concluded that Dignāga's logical ideas must have been extensively discussed in Nyāya circles already during Uddyotakara's lifetime. Uddyotakara must therefore have been only one individual in a group of Naiyāyikas of his time, and was probably not even the most important among them. Oberhammer observed further that Jayantabhaṭṭa's sources may be identified with the Nyāya *ācāryāḥ* and the *vyākhyātāraḥ*, even though they are not explicitly mentioned in the context under consideration. He guessed that both sources must have been known to Uddyotakara, which would lead to the assumption that they must have lived before him. He further guessed that the *vyākhyātāraḥ* might be identical with the Nyāya author Bhāvivikta.

In his dissertation of 1963 on the concept of perception in the *Nyāya-mañjarī* (NMa), Brahmānanda Gupta thoroughly investigated Jayantabhaṭṭa's Nyāya sources.[13] He concluded that these sources can be identified with two authors from the period after Pakṣilasvāmin, namely an *ācārya* (teacher) and a *vyākhyātṛ* (explainer). He further argued that it is likely that they both wrote commentaries on the *Nyāya-bhāṣya* (*Bhāṣya-ṭīkā*),[14] these commentaries then becoming

---

[9] In the context of the mentioned study, Steinkellner, with his unpublished dissertation, undertook an attempt, as yet the first, at a critical study of one of the important Nyāya teachers after Dharmakīrti.

[10] Cf. THAKUR (1947); SOLOMON (1986).

[11] Cf. STEINKELLNER (1963); cf. also the comments of Eli FRANCO (1991: 156) on Cārvāka fragments.

[12] Cf. OBERHAMMER (1962); cf. also OBERHAMMER (1964), in which he deals with the theory of logical nexus of another 'lost' Naiyāyika, namely Trilocana.

[13] Cf. GUPTA (1963).

[14] Cf. GUPTA (1963: 24 and 97 ff.).

the starting point of two different Nyāya sub-schools.[15] In addition, he assumed that Uddyotakara was an adherent of the Vyākhyātṛ School, whereas Śaṅkarasvāmin must have been an adherent of the Ācārya School.

The first editions of the only known commentary on the *Nyāya-mañjarī*, the *Nyāya-mañjarī-granthi-bhaṅga* (NMaGBh) of Cakradhara (twelfth century), and Bhāsarvajña's *Nyāya-bhūṣaṇa* (NBhūṣ) have shed some light on the problem of Jayantabhaṭṭa's sources. On the basis of these new editions, Albrecht Wezler[16] in 1975 was able to confirm GUPTA's assumption that the expressions *ācārya* and *vyākhyātṛ* referred to two different authors, since Cakradhara explains that the *ācāryāḥ*, beginning with Rucikāra, were commentators on Uddyotakara, and the *vyākhyātāraḥ*, beginning with a certain Pravara,[17] were commentators on the *Nyāya-bhāṣya*. GUPTA's theory was only to be corrected in so far as the *ācāryāḥ* were not commentators on the *Nyāya-bhāṣya*, but rather commentators on the *Nyāya-vārttika*. The name Rucikāra could thus only refer to Adhyayana, also known as Adhyayanapāda, who wrote a *Rucitīkā*.[18] According to the *Nyāya-bhūṣaṇa*, Adhyayana is referred to as *ācārya*, and fragments of Viśvarūpa and other commentators of the *Nyāya-bhāṣya* are quoted by using the verb *vyācakṣate*, a fact that at least could hint to their identification with *vyākhyātāraḥ*.[19]

In the 1970s and 1980s it was mainly Indian scholars who contributed to the history of early so-called lost Naiyāyikas,[20] foremost among them Esther Solomon, who in a series of short articles[21] dealt with numerous fragments of

---

[15] GUPTA (1963: 24). This assumption has been criticised by H. von Stietencron. He doubted this opinion and presumed that possibly not individual teachers are meant, but the teachings of different teachers who could even belong to different schools. Cf. the review of GUPTA's study by Heinrich von STIETENCRON (1969).

[16] Cf. WEZLER (1975).

[17] Cf. Wezler's translation of the first instance of the *ācāryāḥ* as mentioned by Cakradhara (NMaGBh 44.12–14: *atrâcāryās tāvad iti vakṣyamāṇa-vyākhyātṛ-matâpekṣayā tāvac chabda-prayogaḥ. iha ca sarvatrâcārya-śabdena uddyotakara-vivṛti-kṛto rucikāra-prabhṛtayo vivakṣitāḥ, vyākhyātṛ-śabdena ca bhāṣya-vivaraṇa-kṛtaḥ pravara-prabhṛtaya iti.*) in WEZLER (1975: 137): 'In Bezug darauf vertreten die Lehrer—um mit ihnen zu beginnen—die [folgende] Ansicht: [Jayanta] gebraucht das Wort *tāvat* ("um mit ihnen zu beginnen") im Hinblick auf die Anschauung der "Erklärer", die er [anschließend] darlegen wird. Und hier (d.h. in der NMa) sind in jedem einzelnen Fall mit dem Wort "die Lehrer" die Verfasser von Kommentaren [zum *Nyāya-vārttika*] des Uddyotakara, voran der Rucikāra, gemeint, und mit dem Wort "die Erklärer" die Verfasser von Kommentaren zum [*Nyāya-*]*Bhāṣya*, von denen Pravara der erste ist.'

[18] Cf. STEINKELLNER (1961: 160).

[19] WEZLER (1975: 140).

[20] Cf. HEGDE (1981) on Udbhaṭa; HEGDE (1983) on Bhāvivikta. In the latter article, HEDGE (1981: 30 ff.) is of the opinion that there must have been two Bhāviviktas, one a Naiyāyika who wrote a commentary on the *Nyāya-bhāṣya*, and an earlier Bhāvivikta who was a Cārvāka.

[21] Cf. SOLOMON (1970), (1971) and (1972) on Aviddhakarṇa; SOLOMON (1974b) on Adhayayna; SOLOMON (1974a) on Bhāvivkta; SOLOMON (1976) on Viśvarūpa; SOLOMON

authors of the Nyāya School, albeit without referring to the European discussion on the topic.[22] In her article on Aviddhakarṇa, she supports the opinion that he must have been an adherent of a tradition of commentators other than the tradition of Uddyotakara or Bhāvivikta, because his name is never mentioned together with the latter two. His *Tattva-ṭīkā* might have been written before Uddyotakara and probably is a commentary on the *Nyāya-bhāṣya*.[23] She conjectures further that, in addition to his commentary on the Lokāyata works *Lokāyata-sūtra* and *Paurandara-sūtra*, Bhaṭṭodbhaṭa probably wrote a commentary on the *Nyāya-sūtra*.[24]

The second volume of the *Encyclopedia of Indian Philosophies* (EIPh II) should also be mentioned, as it also includes articles on the Nyāya-Vaiśeṣika tradition, although the editor, Karl Potter, does not give much attention to fragments of lost works. He summarises chronologically the history of Nyāya as follows: Bhāvivikta before Uddyotakara; Prīticandra, Aviddhakarṇa, Śaṅkara(svāmin), Viśvarūpa and Dhairyarāśi before Jayantabhaṭṭa; Trilocana and Sānātani before Vācaspati; Adhyayana, Vittoka, Narasiṁha and Śrīvatsa between Vācaspati and Udayana.

Finally, a recent article by Hiroshi MARUI (2006) contributes to the discussion concerning the *ācāryāḥ* and the *vyākhyātāraḥ*. Here, he carefully examines the respective passages of the *Nyāya-mañjarī* in which the *ācāryāḥ* and *vyākhyātāraḥ* are quoted. His methodologically and philologically interesting study provides new evidence to support the plural *ācāryāḥ* as being a line of Nyāya scholars who must be seen as having been Jayanta's main sources.

Summarising the above, under the presupposition that the Buddhist authors Dignāga and Dharmakīrti can help us determine the chronology of the Nyāya authors, one can suppose the following situation: Aviddhakarṇa, the author of a *Bhāṣya-ṭīkā* and a *Tattva-ṭīkā*, and Bhāvivikta, the author of again a *Bhāṣya-ṭīkā*, must have lived with certainty before Dharmakīrti and most probably after Dignāga. Also included in this period is Prīticandra, about whose identity nothing is known other than Śāntarakṣita's statement that Dharmakīrti understood him to be an opponent.[25] The early fragments of the *ācāryāḥ* and the *vyākhyātāraḥ* should, in any case, be placed before or, at the latest, at the time of Dharmakīrti. Of the *ācāryāḥ* who are said to have written commentaries on

(1978) on Bhaṭṭa Udbhaṭa; SOLOMON (1978a) and (1979) on Śaṅkara; SOLOMON (1979a) on Vittoka; SOLOMON (1980) and (1986) on Trilocana.

[22] Since Solomon does not mention any articles published by European scholars before (1986), it may be ruled out that she considered them.

[23] SOLOMON (1972: 351f.).

[24] SOLOMON (1978: 990 ff.).

[25] Cf. Vip 142.27 f.: … *ity āha durvidagdhaḥ samyag-viveka-rahitatayā jano 'yam uddyotakara-prīticandra(?)-bhāvivikta-prabhṛtiḥ*. According to Śāntarakṣita, Dharmakīrti refers in his *Vāda-nyāya* to three Nyāya authors, namely Uddyotakara, Bhāvivikta, and Aviddhakarṇa. It seems that Śāntarakṣita may refer to Aviddhakarṇa by the name Prīticandra (?).

the *Nyāya-vārttika*, at least Adhyayana[pāda], who wrote the *Ruci-ṭīkā* and therefore was also called Rucikāra, can be identified. Head of the *vyākhyātāraḥ*, most probably commentators on the *Nyāya-bhāṣya*, is according to Cakradhara's *Nyāya-mañjarī-granthi-bhaṅga* a certain Pravara, who might be identical with one of the other known authors of his tradition. Bhaṭṭodbhaṭa, author of a *Tattva-vṛtti*, a commentary on the Lokāyata *Paurandara-sūtra*, must have lived before Jayantabhaṭṭa. Whether he should be considered part of the wider circle of Naiyāyikas or not cannot be decided with any degree of certainty. Śaṅkarasvāmin certainly belongs to the period after Dharmakīrti. He is said to be the author of a **Kṣaṇa-bhaṅga-siddhi-dūṣaṇa* and an **Īśvara-siddhi*. According to STEINKELLNER (1977), he most probably lived between 720/30 and 780/90. Trilocana, the teacher of Vācaspati, is the author of another *Nyāya-mañjarī*, which is probably identical to his *Nyāya-bhāṣya-ṭīkā*. Moreover, he is the author of a work called *Nyāya-prakīrṇaka*. Viśvarūpa, who also wrote a *Nyāya-bhāṣya-ṭīkā*, and Dhairyarāśi may have been contemporaries of Jayantabhaṭṭa, or may have lived and worked shortly before his lifetime. A certain Tausala is quoted by Bhāsarvajña in his *Nyāya-bhūṣaṇa*. Śrīvatsâcārya, who wrote a *Līlāvatī,* and Sānātani are quoted by Udayana. The earliest quotes of Narasiṁha, Śatānanda, Vittoka, Vatseśvara and Śaśāṅkadhara (who wrote a commentary on Viśvarūpa's *Viśva-rūpa-ṭīkā = Nyāya-bhāṣya-ṭīkā*) can be found in the works of Jñānaśrī and Ratnakīrti (cf. Appendix, p. 163).

A critical investigation of the fragments of this eminent period of Nyāya should also clarify the branching of the various traditions within the school, a question that to date has not been sufficiently considered by the international scholarly community. The collected fragmentary material of lost works will probably also shed some general light on questions of chronology, not only within the Nyāya School, but also on authors of other traditions who refer to this body of thought.

Uddyotakara's *Nyāya-vārttika* is the first extant Nyāya work that offers an interesting insight into the discussions of his period, because he responds to the new epistemological, logical, and dialectical activities of Vasubandhu and Dignāga. The Nyāya scholars found themselves forced to argue against these Buddhist teachers, developing and adapting the innovative Buddhist ideas for their own purposes.[26] Uddyotakara is not only engaged in adapting and refuting the Buddhist authors, but also refers to deviant opinions of Nyāya teachers following Pakṣilasvāmin.

The two Nyāya authors Bhāvivikta and Aviddhakarṇa must have been close contemporaries of Uddyotakara. They are both said to have written commentaries on the *Nyāya-bhāṣya*. There were probably also other representatives of the *vyākhyātāraḥ* during this period, the first said to be Pravara, as well as at least one author of the *ācāryāḥ*, namely Adhyayana, who as mentioned above

---

[26] Cf. e.g. WEZLER (1969).

wrote a *Ruci-ṭīkā*. And, there are other authors of whom we know little more than their names, such as Prīticandra (see above), who definitely lived before Dharmakīrti.

All these studies and investigations have yielded new results concerning the lost Naiyāyikas' works, but have also uncovered a number of difficulties that present themselves when working with fragments of lost works. Methodologically, working with fragments poses a challenge. When examining 'quotations' of authors whose works have been lost, it is often necessary to consider fragments from various sources, including other religious and philosophical traditions. In order to deal with the material of a particular tradition—and often, even each author within a particular tradition—an awareness must be maintained of the historical circumstances surrounding that tradition, as has been pointed out by STEINKELLNER in his remarks concerning methodology when examining the Buddhist *pramāṇa* tradition.[27] Determining the authenticity of a fragmentary text passage, even if the quoting author has identified it as a quotation, can only be undertaken with caution, not only with respect to the wording, but also the contents. Since it is exceedingly rare to find the favourable case of the same passage quoted in more than one place, it must be assumed the original intentions may have been distorted. There can be various reasons for such distortions, including the author being consentient or hostile, how the passage fits into the context, or how it relates to the polemical discussion in which the passage is quoted. It has been clearly shown by STEINKELLNER, in his article concerning the manner of Uddyotakara's *Nyāyavārttika* being quoted in Kamalaśīla's *Tattva-saṁgraha-pañjikā*,[28] that in some cases Kamalaśīla quotes verbatim, but in others he adapts the wording to the context. In still other cases, he quotes equivalent passages of several Nyāya authors, or sources that are common to Uddyotakara and others, and he always includes a discussion of the meaning of such citations.[29] Under such circumstances, an evaluation of fragment material must be based on many factors, including the wording, content, authenticity, personal and historical classification etc. For this reason, a collection of fragments requires minute and systematic documentation. The manner in which authors quote other material is often unique to the work in question, and therefore when evaluating these quotes one must also provisionally rely on external criteria, such as the formal style of quoting, the order of the quotations,[30] the manner in which other authors or schools are designated or left anonymous etc. Indeed, leaving a

---

[27] Cf. STEINKELLNER (1988: 103).

[28] Cf. STEINKELLNER (1963).

[29] STEINKELLNER (1963: 144 f.).

[30] Cf. e.g. TSaP 188.10 in STEINKELLNER (1963: 119): *udyotakara-bhāviviktâdayo ... udbhāvayanti*.

quote anonymous sometimes provides information concerning the degree to which the opinion being quoted is accepted.[31]

Another specific feature is to differentiate between the various ways that lost works are attested to. In some cases, the diction of a lost work has been preserved as a quote or it is paraphrased, in other cases, a thought from a lost work is merely alluded to. The term 'fragment' is understood as a text passage that not only reflects a thought or an idea from a lost work, but also most likely retains the distinct wording of an earlier theory, this having been incorporated verbatim into the work that preserves it.

The identification of external textual material in a certain work requires a high degree of familiarity not only with the compositional style of its author, but also, especially, with how the same author clarifies particular topics in other works, and how these same topics are discussed within his tradition and by its opponents. In-depth knowledge of these aspects is an indispensable prerequisite for judging whether an author has included a passage from another work into his text. In the process of collecting the information needed for identifying fragments, it is helpful to systematically classify the different types of embedded textual material according to quantitative or qualitative criteria.[32]

[31] Cf. THIEME (1956: 587): 'Now, there is a difference between the expression *kecit* "certain [scholars]", which the Kāśikā uses ... and *apare* "others". ... The first, quite commonly with the later Pāṇinīyas, refers to scholars whose opinion is not accepted, the second to those whose opinion is considered, if not always definitely correct, at least preferable to the one stated before. We should, if wishing to be quite precise, translate *kecit* by "certain [scholars, whose opinion I do not accept]", *apare* by "others [whose opinion is preferable]".'

[32] Quantitative assessment of corresponding passages pertains to the various degrees of verbatim correspondence. Qualitative assessment of correspondence pertains to the mode of reference to an embedded passage and to the succession of transmission.

APPENDIX

Synopsis of 'lost' Nyāya authors' works

The list contains a synopsis of who are known only through fragments. Listed below are the respective names of such authors, and the works, with their authors, that contain fragments, as based on the current stage of research.

Adhyayana / Adhyanapāda / Rucikāra:

Tattva-bodha-vidhāyinī (Abhayadeva)
Dharmottara-pradīpa (Durvekamiśra)
Nyāya-bhūṣaṇa (Bhāsarvajña)
Nyāya-mañjarī-granthi-bhaṅga (Cakradhara)
Pramāṇa-vārttika-sva-vṛtti-ṭīkā (Karṇakagomin) Adhyanapāda

Aviddhakarṇa:

Tattva-bodha-vidhāyinī (Abhayadeva)
Tattva-saṁgraha (Śāntarakṣita)
Tattva-saṁgraha-pañjikā (Kamalaśīla)
Pramāṇa-vārttika-sva-vṛtti-ṭīkā (Karṇakagomin)
Vāda-nyāya (Dharmakīrti)
Vipañcitârthā = *Vāda-nyāya-ṭīkā* (Śāntarakṣita)
Siddhi-viniścaya-ṭīkā (Anantavīryâcārya)

Ācāryāḥ / Vyākhyātāraḥ:

Nyāya-bhūṣaṇa (Bhāsarvajña)
Nyāya-mañjarī (Jayantabhaṭṭa)
Nyāya-mañjarī-granthi-bhaṅga (Cakradhara)
Vyomavatī (Vyomaśiva)

Tausala:

Nyāya-bhūṣaṇa (Bhāsarvajña)

Trilocana:

Abhisamayâlaṅkārâloka (Haribhadra)
Ātma-tattva-viveka (Udayana)
Ṛju-vimalā-pañcikā (Śālikanātha)
Jñānaśrīmitra-nibandhâvali: *Apoha-prakaraṇa*, *Īśvara-vāda*, *Kṣaṇa-bhaṅgâdhyāya*, *Vyāpti-carcā* (Jñānaśrīmitra)
Tarka-bhāṣā (Mokṣākaragupta)
Tārkika-rakṣā (Varadarāja)

Daśa-sāhasrikā (Prajñāpāramitā)
Dharmottara-pradīpa (Durvekamiśra)
Nyāya-kaṇikā (Vācaspati)
Nyāya-nibandha-prakāśa (Vardhamāna)
Nyāya-bhāṣya-vārttika-ṭīkā-vivaraṇa-pañjikā (Aniruddha)
Nyāya-bhūṣaṇa (Bhāsarvajña)
Nyāya-mañjarī (Jayantabhaṭṭa)
Nyāya-ratna-mālā (Pārthasārathimiśra)
Nyāya-vārttika-tātparya-ṭīkā (Vācaspati)
Nyāya-vārttika-tātparya-pariśuddhi (Udayana)
Nyāya-viniścaya-vivaraṇa (Vādirāja-sūri)
Nyāya-sāra-vicāra (Bhaṭṭa Rāghava)
Prakaraṇa-pañcikā (Śālikanātha)
Pramāṇa-mīmāṁsā (Hemacandra)
Ratnakīrti-nibandhâvali: *Apoha-siddhi*, *Citrâdvaita-prakāśa-vāda*, *Īśvara-sādhana-dūṣaṇa*, *Kṣaṇa-bhaṅga-siddhi*, *Pramāṇântar-bhāva-prakaraṇa*, *Sarvajña-siddhi*, *Sthira-siddhi-dūṣaṇa*, *Vyāpti-nirṇaya* (Ratnakīrti)
Śloka-vārttika-vyākhyā/Tātparya-ṭīkā (Uṁbeka)
Subhāṣita-ratna-kośa (Vidyākara)
Syād-vāda-ratnâkara (Vādideva-sūri)

Dhairyarāśi:

Āgama-ḍambara (Jayantabhaṭṭa)

Narasiṁha:

Jnānaśrīmitra-nibandhâvali
Ratnakīrti-nibandhâvali: *Īśvara-sādhana-dūṣaṇa* (Ratnakīrti)
Khaṇḍanôddhāra (Vācaspati II)
Sārâvalī (Vāsudevasārvabhauma)

Pravara / Prāvarāḥ:

Nyāya-mañjarī (Jayantabhaṭṭa)
Nyāya-mañjarī-granthi-bhaṅga (Cakradhara)

Prīticandra:

Vipañcitârthā = *Vāda-nyāya-ṭīkā* (Śāntarakṣita)

Bhaṭṭodbhaṭa:

Nyāya-mañjarī (Jayantabhaṭṭa)
Nyāya-mañjarī-granthi-bhaṅga (Cakradhara)
Syād-vāda-ratnâkara (Vādideva-sūri)

Bhāvivikta:

Tattva-saṁgraha (Śāntarakṣita)
Tattva-saṁgraha-pañjikā (Kamalaśīla)
Nyāya-mañjarī (Jayantabhaṭṭa)
Nyāya-mañjarī-granthi-bhaṅga (Cakradhara)
Vāda-nyāya (Dharmakīrti)
Vipañcitârthā = *Vāda-nyāya-ṭīkā* (Śāntarakṣita)

Rucikāra (see Adhyayana):

Vatseśvara:

Tattva-cintā-maṇi (Gaṅgeśa)
Nyāya-siddhānta-mālā (Jayarāmanyāyapañcānana)
Tattva-cintā-maṇy-āloka-kaṇṭhakôddhāra (Madhusūdanamiśra)
Tattva-cintā-maṇy-āloka (Pakṣadharamiśra)
Tattva-cintā-maṇi-ṭīkā (Pragalbhamiśra)

Vittoka:

Jñānaśrīmitra-nibandhâvali (Jñānaśrīmitra)
Ratnakīrti-nibandhâvali: *Īśvara-sādhana-dūṣaṇa* (Ratnakīrti)

Viśvarūpa:

Nyāya-bhāṣya-vārttika-ṭīkā-vivaraṇa-pañjikā (Aniruddha)
Dharmottara-pradīpa (Durvekamiśra)
Āgama-ḍambara (Jayantabhaṭṭa)
Vivaraṇa-prameya-saṁgraha (? Mādhava/Vidyāraṇya/Bhāratītīrtha)
Nyāya-viniścaya-vivaraṇa (Vādirāja-sūri)
Tarkika-rakṣā (Varadarāja)
Tārkika-rakṣā-sāra-saṁgraha
Vibhāvanā (Vedātman)

Vyākhyātāraḥ (see Ācāryāḥ):

Śaṅkarâcārya / Śaṅkara:

Āpta-parīkṣā (Vidyānanda)
Khaṇḍanôddhāra (Vācaspati II)
Jñānaśrīmitra-nibandhâvali: *Kṣaṇa-bhaṅgâdhyāya* (Jñānaśrīmitra)
Tattva-bodha-vidhāyinī (Abhayadeva)
Tattva-saṁgraha (Śāntarakṣita)
Tattva-saṁgraha-pañjikā (Kamalaśīla)
Dharmottara-pradīpa (Durvekamiśra)
Nyāya-mañjarī (Jayantabhaṭṭa)

Nyāya-mañjarī-granthi-bhaṅga (Cakradhara)
Nyāya-vārttika-tātparya-ṭīkā (Vācaspati)
Nyāya-vārttika-tātparya-pariśuddhi (Udayana)
Pramāṇa-vārttika-bhāṣya (Prajñākaragupta)
Pramāṇa-vārttika-sva-vṛtti-ṭīkā (Karṇakagomin)
Bṛhat-kathā-mañjarī (Kṣemendra)
Ratnakīrti-nibandhâvali: *Īśvara-sādhana-dūṣaṇa*, *Kṣaṇa-bhaṅga-siddhi*, *Sthira-siddhi-dūṣaṇa* (Ratnakīrti)
Vāda-nyāya (Dharmakīrti)
Vipañcitârthā = *Vāda-nyāya-ṭīkā* (Śāntarakṣita)
Syād-vāda-ratnâkara (Vādīdeva)
Hetu-bindu-ṭīkā (Arcaṭa)

Śatānanda:

Jñānaśrīmitra-nibandhâvali (Jñānaśrīmitra)

Śaśāṅkadhara:

Nyāya-mañjarī-granthi-bhaṅga (Cakradhara)

Śrīkaṇṭha:

Ṣaḍ-darśana-samuccaya (Guṇaratna)

Śrīvatsâcārya:

Nyāya-siddhānta-mālā (Jayarāmanyāyapañcānana)
Nyāya-kandalī-ṭīkā (Rājaśekhara)
Nyāya-vārttika-tātparya-pariśuddhi (Udayana)

Sānātani:

Nyāya-siddhānta-mālā (Jayarāmanyāyapañcānana)
Vādi-vinoda (Śaṅkaramiśra)
Nyāya-vārttika-tātparya-pariśuddhi (Udayana)

BIBLIOGRAPHY

BHATTACHARYA 1946 = Bhattacharya, D.C.: 'Śrīvatsācārya, a long forgotten Naiyāyika', *The Historical Quarterly* 22 (1946) 152–154.

BHATTACHARYA 1958 = Bhattacharya, D.C.: *History of Navya-Nyāya in Mithilā*. Mithila Institute Series 3/2, Darbhanga Press, Darbhanga 1958.

DhPr = Durvekamiśra: *Dharmottara-pradīpa*. Dalsukhbhai Malvania (ed.): *Paṇḍita Durveka Miśra's Dharmottarapradīpa [Being a Sub-Commentary on Dharmottara's Nyāyabinduṭīkā, a Commentary on Dharmakīrti's Nyāyabindu*]. Kashi Prasad Jayaswal Research Institute, Patna 1955.

EIPh II = Potter, Karl H. (ed.): *Encyclopedia of Indian Philosophies. Indian Metaphysics and Epistemology*. Vol. II: *The Tradition of Nyāya-Vaiśeṣika up to Gaṅgeśa*. Motilal Banarsidass, Delhi 1977.

FRANCO 1991 = Franco, Eli: 'Paurandarasūtra', in: M.A. Dhaky (ed.) *Pt. Dalsukhbhai Malvaniya Felicitation Volume, Aspects of Jainology* 3, Varanasi: P.V. Research Institute 1991, Vol. 1: 154–163.

FRAUWALLNER 1936 = Frauwallner, Erich: 'Beiträge zur Geschichte des Nyāya. I. Jayanta und seine Quellen', *Wiener Zeitschrift für die Kunde des Morgenlandes* 43 (1936) 263–278 [= *Kleine Schriften*. Hrsg. von Gerhard Oberhammer und Ernst Steinkellner, Franz Steiner Verlag, Wiesbaden 1982: 145–160].

GUPTA 1963 = Gupta, Brahmānanda: *Die Wahrnehmungslehre in der Nyāyamañjarī*. Verlag für Orientkunde Dr. H. Vorndran, Walldorf-Hessen 1963.

HBṬ = Arcaṭabhaṭṭa: *Hetu-bindu-ṭīkā*. Pandit S. Sanghvi, Muni Shri Jinavijayaji (eds.): *Hetubinduṭīkā of Bhaṭṭa Arcaṭa with the Subcommentary Entitled Āloka of Durveka Miśra*. Baroda Oriental Institute, Baroda 1949.

HEGDE 1981 = Hegde, R.D.: 'Identity of Udbhaṭa and His Infinity Theory of Epistemological Proofs', *The Mysore Orientalist* 14 (1981), 103–114. = *ABORI* 67 (1987) 35–45.

HEGDE 1983 = Hegde, R.D.: 'Bhāvivikta and His Metaphysical Objectivism', *Glory of India. A Quarterly on Indology* 6 (1983) 29–36.

JNA = Jñānaśrīmitra: *Jñānaśrīmitra-nibandhâvali*. Anantalal Thakur (ed.): *Jñānaśrīmitra-nibandhâvalī—Buddhist Philosophical Works of Jñānaśrīmitra*. Tibetan Sanskrit Works Series 5, Kashi Prasad Jayaswal Research Institute, Patna 1987 [first edition: Patna 1956].

KAVIRAJ 1961 = Kaviraj, G.: *Gleanings from the History and Bibliography of the Nyāya-Vaiśeṣika Literature*. Indian Studies, Past & Present, Distributors, Firma K.L. Mukhopadhyaya, Calcutta 1961 (Reprinted).

MARUI 2006 = Marui, Hiroshi: 'Some notes on the controversies between the "*ācāryāḥ*" and the "*vyākhyātaraḥ*" in the Nyāyamañjarī', *Journal of Indian and Buddhist Studies* 54,3 (2006) 1145–1153 (33–41).

NBh = Pakṣilasvāmin Vātsyāyana: *Nyāya-bhāṣya*. Anantalal Thakur (ed.): *Gautamīyanyāyadarśana with Bhāṣya of Vātsyāyana*. Nyāya-catur-granthikā Vol. I, Indian Council of Philosophical Research, New Delhi 1997.

NBhūṣ = Bhāsarvajña: *Nyāya-bhūṣaṇa*. Svāmī Yogīndrānanda (ed.): *Śrīmad-ācārya-Bhāsarvajña-praṇītasya Nyāya-sārasya svopajñaṁ vyākhyānaṁ Nyāya-bhūṣaṇam*. Ṣaḍ-darśana-prakāśana-granthamālā 1, Ṣaḍ-darśana Prakāśana Pratiṣṭhānam, Vārāṇasī 1968.

NBhVṬVi = Aniruddha: *Nyāya-bhāṣya-vārttika-ṭīkā-vivaraṇa-pañjikā*. Anantalal Thakur (ed.): *Nyāyabhāṣyavārttikaṭīkāvivaraṇapañjikā [II-V] of Aniruddhācārya*. Mithila Institute Series, Ancient Text 19, Darbhanga Press, Darbhanga 1969.

NKan = Śrīdharamiśra: *Nyāya-kandalī*. Vindhyeśvarīprasāda Dvivedin (ed.): *The Bhāshya of Praśastapāda together with the Nyāyakandalī of Śrīdhara*. Vizianagram Sanskrit Series 6, Benares 1895.

NMa = Jayantabhaṭṭa: *Nyāya-mañjarī*. K.S. Varadacharya (ed.): *Nyāyamañjarī of Jayantabhaṭṭa with Ṭippaṇi—Nyāyasaurabha by the Editor*. 2 Vols. Oriental Research Institute Series 116 & 139, University of Mysore, Mysore 1969, 1983.

NMaGBh = Cakradhara: *Nyāya-mañjarī-granthi-bhaṅga*. Nagin J. Shah (ed.): *Cakradhara's Nyāyamañjarīgranthibhaṅga*. L.D. Series 35, L.D. Institute of Indology, Ahmedabad 1972.

NS = Akṣapāda Gautama: *Nyāya-sūtra*. Walter Ruben: *Die Nyāyasūtra's. Text, Übersetzung, Erläuterung und Glossar*. Abhandlungen für die Kunde des Morgenlandes, XVIII/2, Deutsche morgenländlische Gesellschaft, Leipzig 1928.

NSā = Bhāsarvajña: *Nyāya-sāra*. See: NBhūṣ.

NV = Bhāradvāja Uddyotakara: *Nyāya-vārttika*. Anantalal Thakur (ed.): *Nyāyabhāṣyavārttika of Bhāradvāja Uddyotakara*. Nyāya-caturgranthikā Vol. II, Indian Council of Philosophical Research, New Delhi 1997.

NVTP = Udayana: *Nyāya-vārttika-tātparya-pariśuddhi*. Anantalal Thakur (ed.): *Nyāyavārttikatātparyapariśuddhi of Udayanācārya*. Nyāya-catur-granthikā Vol. IV, Indian Council of Philosophical Research, New Delhi 1996.

NVTṬ = Vācaspatimiśra: *Nyāya-vārttika-tātparya-ṭīkā*. Anantalal Thakur (ed.): *Nyāyavārttikatātparyaṭīkā of Vācaspatimiśra*. Nyāya-caturgranthikā Vol. III, Indian Council of Philosophical Research, New Delhi 1996.

OBERHAMMER 1962 = G.Oberhammer, On the Sources in Jayanta Bhaṭṭa and Uddyotakara. *Wiener Zeitschrift für die Kunde Süd- und Südostasiens* 6 (1962) 91–150.

OBERHAMMER 1964 = G.Oberhammer, 'Der *svābhāvika-sambandha*, ein geschichtlicher Beitrag zur Nyāya-Logik', *Wiener Zeitschrift für die Kunde Süd- und Südostasiens* 8 (1964) 131–181.

PREISENDANZ 2005 = Preisendanz, Karin: 'The Production of Philosophical Literature in South Asia During the Pre-Colonial Period (15th to 18th Centuries): The Case of the Nyāyasūtra Commentarial Tradition', *Journal of Indian Philosophy* 33 (2005) 55–94.

PVSVṬ = Karṇakagomin: *Pramāṇa-vārttika-(sva)vṛtti-ṭīkā*. Rāhula Sāṁkṛtyāyana (ed.): *ācārya-Dharmakīrteḥ Pramāṇavārttikam (svārthānumānaparicchedaḥ) svopajñavṛttyā Karṇakagomiviracitayā Taṭṭīkayā ca sahitam*. Kitāb Mahal, Ilāhābād [Allahabad] 1943.

RNA = Ratnakīrti: *Ratnakīrti-nibandhāvali*: Anantalal Thakur (ed.): *Ratnakīrti-Nibandhāvaliḥ (Buddhist Nyāya Works of Ratnakīrti)*. Second edition, Tibetan Sanskrit Works Series 3; Kashi Prasad Jayaswal Research Institute, Patna 1975.

SOLOMON 1970 = Solomon, Esther A.: 'Aviddhakarṇa—A Forgotten Naiyāyika', *Vidya. The Journal of the Gujarat University* 13/1 (1970) 18–40.

SOLOMON 1971 = Solomon, Esther A.: 'A Further Note on Aviddhakarṇa', *Vidya. The Journal of the Gujarat University* 13/2 (1971) 19–24.

SOLOMON 1972 = Solomon, Esther A.: 'Aviddhakarṇa—A Forgotten Naiyāyika', in: *Proceedings of the All-India Oriental Conference, Twenty-Fifth Session, Jadavpur University, Calcutta, October 1969*. Bhandarkar Oriental Research Institute, Poona 1972, 337–352.

SOLOMON 1974a = Solomon, Esther A.: 'Forgotten Nyaiyāyikas: Bhāvivikta', *Vidya. The Journal of the Gujarat University* 17/1 (1974). (foliation not legible).

SOLOMON 1974b = Solomon, Esther A.: 'Forgotten Nyaiyāyikas: Ācārya Adhayana', *Vidya. The Journal of the Gujarat University* 17/2 (1974). [foliation not legible].

SOLOMON 1976 = Solomon, Esther A.: 'Forgotten Nyaiyāyikas: Viśvarūpa', *Vidya. The Journal of the Gujarat University* 18/1 (1976) 13–28.

SOLOMON 1978 = Solomon, Esther A.: 'Bhaṭṭa Udbhaṭa', *Annals of the Bhandarkar Oriental Research Institute* 58–59 (1978) 985–992.

SOLOMON 1978a = Solomon, Esther A.: 'Śaṅkara—A Forgotten Naiyāyika', *Vidya. The Journal of the Gujarat University* 21/2 (1978) 218–234.

SOLOMON 1979 = Solomon, Esther A.: 'Śaṅkara—A Forgotten Naiyāyika (continued)', *Vidya. The Journal of the Gujarat University* 22/2 (1979) 1–23.

SOLOMON 1979a = Solomon, Esther A.: 'Vittoka—Poet and Logician', *Indica 16 (Fr. Esteller Felicitation Volume)*. Heras Institute, Bombay 1979, 177–183.

SOLOMON 1980 = Solomon, Esther A.: 'Trilocana—A Forgotten Naiyāyika', *Vidya. The Journal of the Gujarat University* 23/1 (1980) 17–46.

SOLOMON 1986 = Solomon, Esther A.: 'Trilocana—A Forgotten Naiyāyika', in: *Schriften zur Geschichte und Kultur des Alten Orients* 18. *Sanskrit and World Culture. Proceedings of the Fourth World Sanskrit Conference of the International Association of Sanskrit Studies, Weimar May 23–30, 1979*. Ed. by W. Morgenroth. 1986: 560–566.

STEINKELLNER 1961 = Steinkellner, Ernst: 'Die Literatur des Älteren Nyāya', *Wiener Zeitschrift für die Kunde Süd- und Südostasiens* 5 (1961) 149–162.

STEINKELLNER 1963 = Steinkellner, Ernst: 'Zur Zitierweise Kamalaśīla's', *Wiener Zeitschrift für die Kunde Süd- und Südostasiens* 7 (1963) 116–150.

STEINKELLNER 1977 = Steinkellner, Ernst: 'On the Date and Works of the Naiyāyika Śaṅkarasvāmin', *Wiener Zeitschrift für die Kunde Südasiens* 21 (1977) 213–218.

STEINKELLNER 1988 = Steinkellner, Ernst: 'Methodological Remarks on the Constitution on Sanskrit Texts from the Buddhist *Pramāṇa*-Tradition', *Wiener Zeitschrift für die Kunde Südasiens* 32 (1988) 103–129.

von STIETENCRON 1969 = von Stietencron, Heinrich: Review of GUPTA (1963), *Zeitschrift der Deutschen Morgenländischen Gesellschaft* 119 (1969) 215–216.

STP = Siddhasena Divākara: *Saṁmati-tarka-prakaraṇa*. Sukhlāl Saṅghavi; Becardās Dośi (ed.): *Saṁmatitarka-Prakaraṇa by Siddhasena Divākara. With Abhayadevasūri's Commentary, Tattvabodhavidhāyinī*. 2 Vols. Reprinted, 2 Vols., Rinsen Buddhist Text Series VI–1, 2; Kyoto 1984 [first edition: Gujarāt-purā-tattva-mandir-granthāvalī 10, 16, 18, 19, 21, Gujarāt-purā-tattva-mandir, Amdāvād 1924–1931].

SVR = Vādideva-sūri: *Syād-vāda-ratnâkara*. Motīlāl Lādhājī (ed.): *Śrīmad-Vādideva-sūri-viracitaḥ Pramāṇa-naya-tattvâlokâlaṅkāraḥ tad-vyākhyā ca Syād-vāda-ratnâkaraḥ*. Ārhata-mata-prabhākara 4, Puṇyapattana (Poona) 1926–1930 [*vīra-saṁvat* 2453–57].

SVṬ = Akalaṅkabhaṭṭa: *Siddhi-viniścaya-ṭīkā*. Mahendrakumār Jain (ed.): *Siddhivinishchayatika of Shri Anantavirya, the Commentary on Siddhivinishchaya and its Vritti of Bhatta Akalanka Deva*. Ed. with 'Aloka' and Introduction etc. by.... 2 Vols., Bhāratīya Jñānapīṭha Prakāśana, Varanasi 1959.

TBV = Abhayadeva: *Tattva-bodha-vidhāyinī*. See: STP.

THAKUR 1947 = Thakur, Anantalal: 'The Naiyāyika Trilocana as Teacher of Vācaspati', *Indian Culture* 14/1 (1947) 36–40.

THAKUR 1953 = Thakur, Anantalal: 'Some Lost Nyāya Works and Authors', *Proceedings and Transactions of the All-India Oriental Conference* 17, *Ahmedabad, October-November 1953*. Ahmedabad 1953: 385–394.

THAKUR 1955 = Thakur, Anantalal: 'Nyāyamañjarī of Guru Trilocana—a Forgotten Work', *Journal of the Bihar Research Society* 41 (1955) 507–511.

THAKUR 1958–59 = Thakur, Anantalal: 'Viśvarūpa the Naiyāyika', *Journal of Oriental Research, Madras* 28 (1958–59) 29–37.

THIEME 1956 = Thieme, Paul: 'Pāṇini and the Pāṇinīyas', *Journal of the American Oriental Society* 76 (1956) 1–23

TSa = Śāntarakṣita: *Tattva-saṁgraha*. Embar Krishnamacharya (ed.): *Tattvasaṅgraha of Śāntarakṣita. With the Commentary of Kamalaśīla*. Ed. with an Introduction in Sanskrit, with a Foreword by [Benoytosh Bhattacharyya]. 2 Vols. Gaekwad's Oriental Series 30 & 31, Oriental Institute, Baroda 1926.

TSaP = Kamalaśīla: *Tattva-saṁgraha-pañjikā*. See: TSa.

Vip = Śāntarakṣita: *Vipañcitârthā*. Rāhula Sāṁkṛtyāyana (ed.): *ācārya-Dharmakīrtteḥ Vādanyāyaḥ ācārya-Śāntarakṣitapraṇītayā Vipañcitârthâbhidhayā ṭīkayā saṁvalitaḥ*. Appendix to J.B.O.R.S. Vols. XXI & XXII, Patna 1935–1936.

VN = Dharmakīrti: *Vāda-nyāya*. Michael Torsten Much: *Dharmakīrtis Vādanyāyaḥ. Teil I: Sanskrit-Text.* Veröffentlichungen der Kommission für Sprache und Kulturen Südasiens 25, Verlag der Österreichischen Akademie der Wissenschaften, Wien 1991.

WEZLER 1969 = Wezler, Albrecht: 'Dignāga's Kritik an der Schlußlehre des Nyāya und die Deutung von Nyāyasūtra 1.1.5', *Zeitschrift der Deutschen Morgenländischen Gesellschaft*, Supplementa I.3. (1969) 836–842.

WEZLER 1975 = Wezler, Albrecht: 'Zur Identität der "*Ācāryāḥ*" und "*Vyākhyātāraḥ*" in Jayantabhaṭṭas Nyāyamañjarī', *Wiener Zeitschrift für die Kunde Südasiens* 19 (1975) 137–146.

When Yoga is not Yoga. The Nyāya-Vaiśeṣika Tradition and the *Artha-śāstra*

PIOTR BALCEROWICZ

1. The tradition of Ānvīkṣikī, which features at the beginning of the *Artha-śāstra*, has attracted the attention of a number of scholars ever since the work of (the collective author known as) Kauṭilya was discovered (or rather a manuscript of it was acquired from a Paṇḍit of the Tanjore District) by R. Shamasastry in 1902, the then librarian of the Mysore Government Oriental Library, provisionally translated in 1906 by him and subsequently published in 1909 (AŚ$_3$). The significance of Ānvīkṣikī and its supposedly philosophical dimension as well as its relation to sciences and philosophical schools have been investigated, among others, by Hermann JACOBI (1911), Satish Chandra VIDYABHUSANA (1920: 4–39), Moritz WINTERNITZ (1929), Paul HACKER (1958), Madhumati CHATTERJEE (1978), Harsh NARAIN (1979), Wilhelm HALBFASS (1988: 263–286, esp. 273 ff.), Bruce PERRY (1997), Karin PREISENDANZ (2000). The present paper re-examines what has been frequently analysed before, viz. the relationship between Ānvīkṣikī of the *Artha-śāstra* and the Nyāya-Vaiśeṣika tradition. The conclusion of the paper may seem an expression of what many scholars must have felt but, surprisingly, no one has formulated it explicitly, and emerges as something so obvious that the subtitle of the paper given in the conference handout in Barcelona read: 'All we all knew but we didn't dare say it aloud...'. We should also remember that my thesis cannot rest on irrefutable foundations for the simple fact that available materials on Ānvīkṣikī are extremely scarce and all we can say about the system is actually based on several lines found here and there. In the passages translated in this paper, I will often render the term 'Ānvīkṣikī' as methodology.

2. The *locus classicus* for Ānvīkṣikī are the actual opening passages Kauṭilya's *Artha-śāstra*:

> '[1] These are the disciplines of learning: methodology (*ānvīkṣikī*), the triple *Veda*, economics[1] and political science. [8] According

[1] The term *vārttā* comprises triple economic activity: agriculture (*kṛṣi*), cattle breeding (*pāśu-pālya*) and trade (*vaṇijyā*), see AŚ 1.4.1: *kṛṣi-pāśu-pālye vaṇijyā ca vārttā*.

World View and Theory in Indian Philosophy
Warsaw Indological Studies 5 (2012) 173–245.

> to Kauṭilya there are exactly four disciplines of learning. [9] Particular disciplines of learning [acquire] a genuine status of discipline of learning when with their help one can know moral law (*dharma*) and [the means to accomplish] life goals (*artha*).'[2]

Ānvīkṣikī is counted by Kauṭilya—in which he expressly differs from other traditions, mentioned by him in the sequel—among four sciences, or disciplines of learning (*vidyā*). Further, we learn that, according to Kauṭilya, Ānvīkṣikī as well as the other three disciplines carry moral implications, broadly understood, in the sense that it is with their help that one can live a life which is both meritorious and satisfactory as well as one complies with the rules and injunctions of moral law (*dharma*), understood as a device that regulates social life,[3] and one is also capable of satisfying material needs of his own and of his family. Therefore, just like all the other disciplines, such as the Vedic soteriological and religious reflection (*trayī*), theoretical reflection on economy and its practical implementation as well as the reflection on how to successfully and effectively seize, maintain and exercise political power, Ānvīkṣikī is said to be of relevance both for religious or moral life and for social and individual welfare. The goals defined in this way could hardly be compatible with the idea of Ānvīkṣikī as 'philosophy', taken as abstract and rational reflection, of little direct practical application, that emancipates itself from the limits of religious and mythical thinking, as it was once suggested by JACOBI (1911) and subsequently questioned by WINTERNITZ (1929), and systematically disproved by HACKER (1958).

Kauṭilya cites some other classifications of disciplines of learning which either include or exclude Ānvīkṣikī. What is symptomatic, even some of those who do not include Ānvīkṣikī in their typology of disciplines of learning do it not because, in their opinion, Ānvīkṣikī does not count as a separate branch of learning of its own, but only because it can be subsumed under soteriological and religious reflection (*trayī*):

> 'The representatives of the school of Manu [maintain] that the triple *Veda*, economics and political science [are the only disciplines of learning], because methodology is a special branch of the triple *Veda*.'[4]

[2] AŚ$_1$ 1.2.1.8–9: [1] *ānvīkṣikī trayī vārttā daṇḍa-nītiś cêti vidyāḥ*. [8] *catasra eva vidyā iti kauṭilyaḥ*. [9] *tābhir dharmârthau yad vidyāt tad vidyānām vidyātvam*.

[3] Kauṭilya takes obligations and duties that are derived from the concept of moral law (*dharma*) primarily in a social and political sense, certainly not a religious one, see AŚ 1.3.4: *eṣa trayī-dharmaś caturṇāṁ varṇānāṁ āśramāṇāṁ ca sva-dharma-sthāpanād aupakārikaḥ*.— 'This moral law [prescribed] in the triple *Veda* is wholesome because it helps establish respective roles for the four social strata and for the four life stages.'

[4] AŚ$_1$ 1.2.3: *trayī vārttā daṇḍa-nītiś cêti mānavāḥ. trayī-viśeṣo hy ānvīkṣikîti*.

Even though Ānvīkṣikī is not separately mentioned in this classification, nevertheless the passage establishes a direct connection between Ānvīkṣikī and the *Vedas*, understood to incorporate the *Upaniṣads*.

This association was from time to time voiced and recollected in the *Mahābhārata* (e.g. MBh 3.149.32–33; 12.59.33), *Manu-smṛti*, and in some *Purāṇas*[5]. The memory or deep conviction that Ānvīkṣikī was, at least to some extent, closely related to the orthodox tradition and to the *Vedas* is articulated as late as in the *Nyāya-sāra* (NSā, pp. 71–72) in a passage in which Bhāsarvajña (who, in fact, follows Pakṣilasvāmin Vātsyāyana in this respect, see p. 194 and n. 50) discusses why there are only four disciplines of learning, and whether the division is because each of the f o u r disciplines has a different subject matter (*viṣaya-bhedāt*) or whether because each has a different purpose (*prayojana-bhedāt*). He eventually subscribes to the opinion that

> 'Because human goals are primary and secondary, one should recognise four disciplines of learning, namely: the discipline of moral law, welfare, sensual satisfaction and of liberation.'[6]

In this context, the following opinion is expressed to which Bhāsarvajña accedes:

> '[Objection:] "Since both the triple *Veda* and methodology have liberation as their purpose, it turns out that there is no difference [between them, and the number of disciplines cannot be four]." That is true, nevertheless [one can distinguish] the primary classification and subdivisions with respect to all sciences, because a discipline can be a sphere for an enquirer and it can be something that stimulates all other disciplines.'[7]

The reason why Bhāsarvajña finds it justified to classify Ānvīkṣikī as a separate branch of learning is pragmatic, and not due to the system's salvific purpose. Bhāsarvajña thereby emphasises the role of Ānvīkṣikī, which was still remembered at his times as a discipline that stimulates other branches, viz. provides them with methodology and analytic tools applicable in their respective fields of enquiry, but which can also become an object of enquiry in its own right.

---

[5] BhāgP 3.12.44 (*vide infra* p. 180, n. 21), BhāgP 11.16.24 (*vide infra* p. 217, n. 97), and BrP 187.43:

> *ānvīkṣikī trayī vārttā daṇḍa-nītis tathâparā /*
> *vidyā-catuṣṭayaṁ tv etad vārttām atra śṛṇuṣva me //*

[6] NSā, p. 72.3–4: *tasmāt mukhya-gauṇa-puruṣârtha-bhedena catasro vidyā draṣṭavyāḥ, dharmârtha-kāma-mokṣa-śāstrāṇîti.*

[7] NSā, p. 72.5–7: *nanu evaṁ tarhi trayy-ānvīkṣikyor apavargârthatvād abhedaḥ prāpnoti. satyam tathâpi vicāraka-viṣayatvena sarva-vidyânugrāhakatvena câsyāḥ sarva-vidyābhyaḥ prādhānyam avāntara-bhedaś câsti.*

3. Much has been said by researchers on the nature of what Ānvīkṣikī actually was and was not.[8] JACOBI's (1911) interpretation of Ānvīkṣikī as philosophy has been eventually dismissed on various accounts and most researchers would now agree that Ānvīkṣikī is some kind of theoretical reflection on effective, successful and consistent procedures both in the sphere of reasoning and of practical actions, or—to use Paul HACKER's expression—'the art of thinking' (*Denkkunst*), however with both theoretical and pragmatic implications. This methodical, systematic analysis is, as we shall see, what we could tentatively call methodology. That also is why, in my translations of Sanskrit passages throughout, the term 'methodology' is used interchangeably with 'Ānvīkṣikī'.

3.1. What is, therefore, the nature of Ānvīkṣikī? We should start with the first mention of the system in extant Indian literary sources. Kauṭilya enumerates the disciplines comprised by Ānvīkṣikī, or methodology, and thereby provides some important information on the nature of Ānvīkṣikī:

> 'Methodology [comprises three schools]: Sāṁkhya, Yoga and the materialists (*lokāyata*).'[9]

This is the frequently discussed passage that once led some researchers, e.g. JACOBI's (1911), to see, wrongly as it were, in Ānvīkṣikī an Indian counterpart of philosophy, i.e. a rational, theoretical enterprise which is instantiated through specific philosophical schools.

Instead, the passage can rather be taken as a case of an enumerative or a typological definition that demarcates a notion by mentioning specimens to which the definiendum is a p p l i c a b l e, either in a selective way, by mentioning just a few examples (similar to, e.g., 'The cat (*Felis*) is: the domestic cat (*Felis catus*), the jungle cat (*Felis chaus*), the African wildcat (*Felis silvestris lybica*)', without mentioning all the seven members of the genus), or in an exhaustive way, by specifying all the varieties subsumed by the definiens (similar to, e.g. 'The chimpanzee is *Pan troglodytes* and *Pan paniscus*', no more no less). In the case of Ānvīkṣikī, as we will see, it is most probably the former case: Kauṭilya enumerates all the branches of thought and analysis he considers to be most significant representatives of the philosophical-methodological current, but his enumeration does most probably not exhaust all instantiations. What Kauṭilya proposes is not, therefore, a definition proper which would describe the character and essential aspects or intrinsic characteristics of a thing, or the definiendum.

Further, the passage does not postulate Ānvīkṣikī, the way JACOBI (1911) wanted, as a kind of meta-level generic term (*der übergeordnete Artbegriff*) which encompasses, or rather is instantiated in, the three remaining disciplines

---

[8] See esp. GLASENAPP 1940: (110 f.), HACKER (1958: 4–13, 29–30), HALBFASS (1988: 263–286), PREISENDANZ (2000).

[9] AŚ$_1$ 1.2.10: *sāṁkhyaṁ yogo lokāyataṁ cêty ānvīkṣikī.*

of learning, especially in the sense of 'philosophy', to which the three other branches would be subordinated, but what we have here is merely a list of philosophical strands which apply the same pattern of reasoning and analysis approach or betray the same investigative, methodological approach.[10] Rather, the definition shows what the three other disciplines have in common and what is the theoretical and practical method they share, irrespective of their incompatible world views and irreconcilable differences in metaphysics and ethics.

In the next step, Kauṭilya proceeds to define the role of Ānvīkṣikī as an indispensable instrument for all the remaining disciplines of learning, and this can be treated as something that approximates a definition proper:

> '[Ānvīkṣikī] first investigates (*anvīkṣamāṇā*) with the help of logical tools (*hetu*): (1) in the sphere of the triple *Veda*, what conforms to moral law (*dharma*) and what does not conform to moral law (*adharma*), (2) in the sphere of economics, what is profitable and what is not profitable, (3) in the sphere of political science, what is conducive [to political power] and what is not conducive [to political power], (4) what is effective and what is ineffective for these [three disciplines of learning, and thereby] it serves people, it keeps the reason steady in misfortune and in prosperity as well as generates / sustains expertise in judgement, speech and action.'[11]

The defining characteristic of Ānvīkṣikī, derived from the verbal root *anu√īkṣ* 'to observe, investigate methodically, examine, enquire', as it is described by Kauṭilya, is thus a certain procedure through which one methodically investigates a given object with the help of logical tools and reasoning (*hetubhir anvīkṣamāṇā*). This investigative methodical approach is the main object of the investigation of Ānvīkṣikī, but not exclusively. It is not merely a reflection on how to reason, argue, analyse etc. correctly, but it has a very practical dimension, which is its inherent feature: one applies theoretical methodology to all practical issues that one considers important and relevant to attain one's goals, and thereby can take a course of action most suited for one's objectives. And these practical goals can be as divergent as, for instance, how to live morally, viz. what criteria make one judge that a particular deed complies with moral law (*dharma*) or not (*adharma*), what considerations one has to take into account in order to be able to determine whether the adopted course of action may bring wealth and profit or not, or which stratagems and actions of the monarch are beneficial to the maintenance of his political power and which are not. In fact, as we have seen, Kauṭilya explicitly mentions three such spheres

[10] See HACKER (1958: 4–14), HALBFASS (1988: 263 ff.).

[11] AŚ 1.2.11: *dharmâdharmau trayyām arthânarthau vārttāyāṁ nayâpanayau daṇḍanītyāṁ balâbale câitāsāṁ hetubhir anvīkṣamāṇā lokasyôpakaroti vyasane 'bhyudaye ca buddhiṁ avasthāpayati prajñā-vākya-kriyā-vaiśāradyaṁ ca karoti*.

of application of the Ānvīkṣikī method, and always consistently along the same pattern: the method allows one to distinguish (1) the virtue (*guṇa*), or the appropriate strategy and positive course of reflection or action that leads to desirable results, i.e. what conforms to moral law (*dharma*), what is profitable (*artha*), what is conducive to political power (*naya*) and what is effective (*bala*), and (2) the vice (*doṣa*), or the negative procedure that might bring undesired effects, which one should avoid, i.e. what does not conform to moral law (*adharma*), what is not profitable (*anartha*), what is not conducive to political power (*apanaya*) and what is ineffective (*abala*).

3.2. This idea of advancing a successful activity which eventually leads to the achievement of one's goals and, at the same time, of avoiding any activity which is counterproductive to one's goals and which should therefore be discarded, at least with respect to the three spheres of religion, economics and political science in Kauṭilya's account, seems to have been at the root of the Ānvīkṣikī enterprise. This strikes a close resemblance with Nyāya, esp. Pakṣilasvāmin Vātsyāyana's, account of reasonable activity and purposefulness of human existence. In a passage[12] we read:

> '"What should be avoided, what keeps one that [to-be-avoided] away, absolute avoidance [of that to-be-avoided and] the means [to accomplish] this [avoidance which] should be realised"—having understood these four beneficial statements properly, one attains the ultimate (sc. liberation).'[13]

In the same spirit and using similar terms, Uddyotakara Bhāradvāja emphasises the role of reflection or reasoning in achieving desired and commendable goals and in avoiding activities which would result in something undesirable:

> 'These two, i.e. reasoning (*tarka*) and determination (*nirṇaya*) sustains the progress of people. People, having reflected again and again [by means of reasoning and determination], undertake activities, namely: they avoid what should be avoided and appropriate what should be appropriated thanks to reasoning and determination.'[14]

Further, while discussing the typology of cognitive criteria (*pramāṇa*), Pakṣilasvāmin Vātsyāyana notes that 'Whenever cognition occurs, the result is the discernment the nature of which is avoidance, appropriation or indiffer-

[12] This is directly influenced by the four noble truths of Buddhism, see WEZLER (1984) and BALCEROWICZ (2003: 296–301).

[13] NBh on NS 1.1.1: *heyam, tasya nirvartakaṁ, hānam ātyantikaṁ, tasyôpāyo 'dhigantavya ity etāni catvāry artha-pādāni samyag buddhvā niḥśreyasam adhigacchati.*

[14] NV_1 1.1.1, p. 18.8–10 = NV_2, p. 17.8–9: *tāv etau tarka-nirṇayau loka-yātrām udvahata*[a] *iti. buddhvā buddhvā lokaḥ pravartamānaḥ tarka-nirṇayābhyām heyam jahāti upādeyam côpādatte.* [[a] NV_2: *vahata.*]

ence,'[15] and the cognition meant here is not just any cognitive state or cognitive act, but a cognitively valid procedure or true cognition that fulfils the criteria of a cognitive criterion (*pramāṇa*) proper. What is thus characterised as cognition by Pakṣilasvāmin Vātsyāyana is not necessarily limited to perception (the passage occurs between a short definition of perception and definitions of inference, analogy and verbal knowledge) but should be understood as underlying the results of the other three cognitive criteria recognised by the Nyāya school. This is precisely the same approach which is so manifest in the Ānvīkṣikī account of successful action and unsuccessful, unproductive one which should not be undertaken, except perhaps for the third element, namely indifference (*upekṣā*), introduced by Pakṣilasvāmin. This third element, in fact, does not run counter the Ānvīkṣikī approach to successful action, for it merely typologises all those activities which are not irrelevant, i.e. such that neither lead to success not bring loss.

Akṣapāda Gautama defines the result (*phala*) as 'the object (circumstances / situation) which is generated by activities and faults'[16], while understanding the activity as 'the causal effort by means of speech, mind and body'[17] and faults as 'characterised by the effectuating activity'.[18] While commenting on the definition, Pakṣilasvāmin Vātsyāyana remarks:

> 'The result is the sensation of happiness or of suffering. And the *karman* is the fruition [in the form] of happiness as well as the fruition [in the form] of suffering. ... Thus, this result is what should be avoided [but is] appropriated again and again; [this result is also] what should be appropriated [but is] discarded again and again; in such a way there is no end or termination of avoidance and appropriation [of results]. This very world, as one should realise, is jostled by the torrent of avoidance and appropriation of the result.'[19]

Again in this passage Pakṣilasvāmin directly refers to activities which should be carried out or which should be abandoned, and places the idea of the result (either success or failure) in a wider context of rebirth (mentioned in NS 1.1.19). These are general circumstances or existential predicaments in which everyone is doomed to act: people habitually follow objectives which should be discarded or renounce goals which should be striven for. This lack of con-

---

[15] NBh.1.1.3: *yadā jñānaṁ tadā hānôpādānôpekṣā-buddhayaḥ phalam.*

[16] NS 1.1.20: *pravṛtti-doṣa-janito 'rthaḥ phalam.*

[17] NS 1.1.17: *pravṛttir vāg-buddhi-śarīrârambhaḥ.*

[18] NS 1.1.18: *pravartanā-lakṣaṇā doṣāḥ.*

[19] NBh 1.1.20: *sukha-duḥkha-saṁvedanaṁ phalam. sukha-vipākaṁ karma duḥkha-vipākaṁ ca. ... tad etat phalam upāttam upāttaṁ heyam, tyaktaṁ tyaktam upādeyav iti nâsya hānôpādānayor niṣṭhā paryavasānaṁ vâsti, sa khalv ayaṁ phalasya hānôpādāna-srotasôhyate loka iti.*

sistence in action—viz. avoiding what should be avoided and appropriating what should be appropriated—emphasises the role of proper reflection on the nature of the result and the means to achieve it, if it is desirable, or the means to avoid it, if it is objectionable.

If, as Pakṣilasvāmin Vātsyāyana himself sees it, Nyāya was the successor of Ānvīkṣikī at least in some sense, this throws additional light on the original characterisation of Ānvīkṣikī by Kauṭilya and its role for the monarch: since humans, including monarchs, often act inconsistently, i.e. not in consonance with what is desirable or proper and with acceptance for what is objectionable or harmful, one should follow the method of Ānvīkṣikī which sets things right and helps one be fully consistent in one's actions.

To recapitulate, Ānvīkṣikī should be interpreted as some kind of theoretical reflection on what constitutes effective, successful and consistent procedures, both in reasoning and practical activity, which prompts one to undertake an appropriate course of action and reach conclusive judgement in order to achieve desirable and commendable goals, while discouraging one from engaging in activities which bring undesirable results, incompatible with accepted values. This methodical, systematic analysis is what we could call 'methodology', or reason-based methodological enquiry and approach.

4. The very few ideas encapsulated in the *Artha-śāstra* by Kauṭilya are later recapitulated in Kāmandaki's *Nīti-sāra* (fifth century?), hardly adding any new material. First, Kāmandaki repeats *verbatim* the classification of the disciplines of learning, which is identical with that of the *Artha-śāstra* (AŚ 1.2.1):

> 'Methodology, the triple *Veda*, economics and everlasting political science constitute exactly the four disciplines of learning. These are the causes of stability of the world.'[20]

Exactly the same enumeration is also repeated in the *Bhāgavata-purāṇa*.[21] Another verse echoes the spheres of application, which is the contents of AŚ 1.2.11:

> 'Methodology, being the knowledge of the self, [investigates] (1) what conforms to moral law (*dharma*) and what does not conform to moral law (*adharma*) in the sphere of the triple *Veda*, (2) what is profitable and what is not profitable in the sphere of economics, (3) what is conducive [to political power] and what is not conducive [to political power] in the sphere of political science;'[22]

---

[20] NīSā 2.2:

ānvīkṣikī trayī vārttā daṇḍa-nītiś ca śāśvatī /
vidyāś catasra evâitā loka-saṁsthiti-hetavaḥ //

[21] BhāgP 3.12.44ab: *ānvīkṣikī trayī vārttā daṇḍa-nītis tathâiva ca /*

[22] NīSā 2.7:

whereupon follows an explanation why Ānvīkṣikī is so vital:

> 'Methodology is a discipline teaching about the self, because it investigates happiness and suffering. The one who investigates the reality through this [methodology] abandons excitement and grief.'[23]

Most importantly, the verse emphasises the purposefulness of Ānvīkṣikī, which is in accord with what Pakṣilasvāmin Vātsyāyana has to say above about the investigation of the purpose and result (*phala*) of human actions which end with the sensation of happiness or of suffering (*sukha-duḥkha-saṁvedanaṁ phalam*),[24] and thereby stresses the link between liberation and Ānvīkṣikī.

5.1. To conclude his brief introduction of Ānvīkṣikī as a separate discipline, Kauṭilya emphasises both its importance and its unique character as a branch that is useful in a l l other disciplines of learning, irrespective of particular world view and particular theoretical presuppositions:

> 'Methodology has always been considered to be the lamp for disciplines of learning, the means to [accomplish] all actions, the fundament of all moral laws.'[25]

This characterisation is significant because Kauṭilya himself shows that he does not limit the scope of application of Ānvīkṣikī to a selected sphere of the monarch's activities but treats it as a method which can serve anyone in any theoretical or practical discipline, not necessarily in the three mentioned by Kauṭilya.

5.2. A direct trace of the method of Ānvīkṣikī precisely in the sense of its successful application in a range of fields with a view of achieving one's goals is found in the *Mahā-bhārata*, which contains a few stray references to the current in a contaminated passage in which the place of Ānvīkṣikī is taken by political science (*daṇḍa-nīti*), the main proponent of which was Kauṭilya. The passage, however, must have been influenced by Kauṭilya's account of Ānvīkṣikī whose ideas are here expanded at great length (emphasised/in bold are phrases that occur also in AŚ 1.2.11):

ānvīkṣiky ātma-vijñānaṁ dharmâdharmau trayī-sthitau /
arthânarthau tu vārttāyāṁ daṇḍa-nītyāṁ nayêtarau //

[23] NīSā 2.11:

ānvīkṣiky ātma-vidyā syād īkṣaṇāt sukha-duḥkhayoḥ /
īkṣamāṇas tayā tattvaṁ harṣa-śokau vyudasyati //

[24] NBh 1.1.20, see n. 19.

[25] AŚ 1.2.12:

pradīpaḥ sarva-vidyānām upāyaḥ sarva-karmaṇām /
āśrayaḥ sarva-dharmāṇāṁ śaśvad ānvīkṣikī matā //

'[23] Political science is what holds the world [in balance], for the political force contains numerous measures. [24] [It is about] what is profitable and what is not profitable; happiness and unhappiness; what conforms to moral law and what does not conform to moral law; what is effective and what is ineffective; misfortune and prosperity; merit and demerit; virtue and fault; [25] sensual satisfaction and sensual dissatisfaction; dividing [time into] season, month, night, days and a moment; rudeness and kindness; excitement and fury; peace and control; [26] fate and human agency; liberation and want of liberation; fear and lack of fear; injury and non-injury; asceticism, sacrifice and constraint; what is poisonous and what is not poisonous; [27] end, beginning and middle stage as well as maintenance of duties; rapture, joy, insolence, hypocrisy and fortitude; what is conducive [to one's aims] and what is not conducive [to one's aims]; [28] power and powerlessness; similarly self-conceit and arrogance; decay and absence of decay; discipline and emancipation; proper time and improper time, O Bhārata; [29] falsehood, truth, state of knowing and of not knowing; also faith and lack of faith; passiveness and activity; profit and want of profit; victory and defeat; [30] sharpness and softness; death as well as acquisition [of new life] and no acquisition [of new life any more] (?); contradiction and lack of contradiction;[26] obligation and lack of obligation; what is effective and what is ineffective; [31] indignation and lack of indignation as well as what conforms to moral law and what does not conform to moral law; embarrassment and absence of embarrassment as well as modesty; success and failure; [32] ardour, skill in deeds, [convincing] power of speech, discernment of the true nature [of things]—in such a manner the political power is manifold in this world of the descendants of Kuru.'[27]

---

[26] MBh_2 and MBh_1 the apparatus, p. 572 (10 mss): *virodhaś câvirodhaś ca*. Alternatively, 'failure and success', MBh_1: *virāddhiś câiva rādhiś*.

[27] MBh 12.121.23c–32:

> ***daṇḍa-nītir*** *jagad-dhātrī daṇḍo hi bahu-vigrahaḥ* // 23 //
> ***arthânarthau*** *sukhaṁ duhkhaṁ* ***dharmâdharmau balâbale*** /
> *daurbhāgyaṁ bhāga-dheyaṁ ca puṇyâpuṇye guṇâguṇau* // 24 //
> *kāmâkāmāv ṛtur māsaḥ śarvarī divasaḥ kṣaṇaḥ* /
> *aprasādaḥ prasādaś ca harṣaḥ krodhaḥ śamo damaḥ* // 25 //

The passage, which clearly is an expanded account taken from the *Artha-śāstra* and which was apparently reworked more than once as testified by its repetitive character, contains all the dilemmas and alternatives listed by Kauṭilya but includes a lot more. In fact, it is very unlikely that the above was originally a characterisation of political science (*daṇḍa-nīti*) or divine or royal power and dominance (*daṇḍa*); it seems rather that the term *daṇḍa-nīti* simply replaced *ānvīkṣikī*—with basically no metrical change in 23c[28]—at the time when Ānvīkṣikī was already looked down upon, being strongly associated with unorthodox views and smacked of heresy.

The passage demonstrates that Ānvīkṣikī was thought of as a discipline which is not limited to the three main spheres delineated in the *Artha-śāstra* but the scope of its application was much wider: it is also pertinent to other aspects of life and human actions, including devising the calendar and the count of time (division of time), individual behaviour and conduct, one's emotional and mental states, i.e. the domain of psychology, sensual (sexual) satisfaction and the lack thereof etc. Most significantly, however, in this account Ānvīkṣikī is portrayed as being relevant also to the fields of epistemology and rhetorics—falsehood (*anṛta*), truth (*satya*), state of knowing and of not knowing (*jñâjñatā*), contradiction (*virodha*) and lack of contradiction (*avirodha*), convincing power of speech (*vāk-śakti*), that is to the branches so closely related to Nyāya and to the argumentative and debate-related portions of the *Caraka-saṁhitā* (CarS, esp. *Sūtra-sthāna*, *Vimāna-sthāna*]).

Another, this time indirect mention of Ānvīkṣikī in the same spirit, i.e. as a discipline that helps one achieve one's goals, and here merely applied to the preservation of royal power, reverberates in what the sage Nārada says in the

daivaṁ puruṣa-kāraś ca mokṣâmokṣau bhayâbhaye /
hiṁsâhiṁse tapo yajñaḥ saṁyamo 'tha viṣâviṣam // 26 //
antaś câdiś ca madhyaṁ ca kṛtyānāṁ ca prapañcanam /
madaḥ pramādo darpaś ca dambho dhairyaṁ ***nayânayau*** *// 27 //*
aśaktiḥ śaktir ity evam māna-stambhau vyayâvyayau /
vinayaś ca visargaś ca kālâkālau ca bhārata // 28 //
anṛtaṁ jñâjñatā satyam śraddhâśraddhe tathâiva ca /
klībatā vyavasāyaś ca lābhâlābhau jayâjayau // 29 //
tīkṣṇatā mṛdutā mṛtyur āgamânāgamau tathā //
virāddhiś câiva rādhiś ca kāryâkārye ***balâbale*** *// 30 //*
asūyā cânasūyā ca ***dharmâdharmau*** *tathâiva ca /*
apatrapânapatrape hrīś ca sampad vipac ca ha // 31 //
tejaḥ karmaṇi pāṇḍityaṁ vāk-śaktis tattva-buddhitā /
evaṁ daṇḍasya kauravya-loke 'smin bahu-rūpatā // 32 //

[28] I.e. **ānvikṣikī jagad-dhātrī* (with the second syllable long and third short, instead of the second short and third long). One might argue that what remains slightly problematic is *daṇḍo* in *daṇḍo hi bahu-vigrahaḥ* of 23d, if we suppose that *ānvīkṣikī* was the original reading of 23c; if it was, then *daṇḍo* should rather not occur in the passage. However, *daṇḍa*, the power or dominance, is a general theme or framework in a longer account (beginning with MBh 12.121.13) into which this Ānvīkṣikī interpolation seems to have been inserted.

Mahā-bhārata, the context of which is, again, the examination of the conduct and qualities of the monarch:

> A'O Impeccable [ruler], I hope you similarly [resort to] the seven expedients with six royal virtues[29]? Do you properly analyse what is conducive and what is not conducive [to political power] and the fourteen [secret measures][30]? O supreme among conquerors, I hope you that after you have examined yourself and your enemies, you pursue the eight occupations in order to have peace?'[31]

[29] The expression *rāja-guṇaiḥ ṣaḍbhiḥ* does not really seem originally to refer to any established sixfold set of royal virtues but rather to the list of the monarch's virtues found in the Sixth Chapter of the *Artha-śāstra* (AŚ 6.1.3–6), which enlists the following four categories of the virtues a monarch should possess: virtues of good social interaction (*ābhigāmika-guṇa*), intellectual virtues (*prajñā-guṇa*), virtues of vigour (*utsāha-guṇa*), personal perfections (*ātma-sampad*). And that would explain the number 'six' in the expression, which occurs here not because of the actual number of virtues but because of the chapter number ('six'), just like in the case of the expression *catur-daśa* (see below). The expression *rāja-guṇaiḥ ṣaḍbhiḥ* (through the compound *rāja-guṇa*) seems to conflate the list of the monarch's virtues of AŚ 6.1.3–6 with the sixfold character of foreign policy (*ṣāḍguṇya*) of the king *vis-à-vis* his neighbours, mentioned a view lines later in AŚ 6.2.4, and enumerated in full in AŚ 7.1.2 (*saṁdhi-vigrahâsana-yāna-saṁśraya-dvaidhī-bhāvāḥ ṣāḍguṇyam ity ācāryāḥ*; these are: peace, aggression, wait, march, retreat for shelter, dual policy; further in NSā 27.3ab).

Similarly, the idea of the seven expedients (*saptôpāya*) seems to be an extended version of an original concept of four expedients the monarch may avail himself of in order to maintain his power in the kingdom and blended with some other classification. The four expedients are enumerated in AŚ 2.10.47 (*upāyāḥ sāmôpapradāna-bheda-daṇḍāḥ*; these are conciliation, gifts, sowing dissent, outright force), with more details and subvarieties given in AŚ 2.48–56. Seven kinds of treatises are mentioned in AŚ 7.5.11, and these could be treated as means of subduing an enemy. However, the seven expedients are mentioned in the 27th Chapter on the Varieties of Expedients (*Upāya-vikalpa-prakaraṇa*) of the *Nīti-sāra* by Kāmandaki (NSā), who first mentions three basic expedients (NSā 27.2), i.e. buying off (*kośa* = *upapradāna, dāna*), counsel (*mantra* = *sāma*), the use of the fourfold army (*caturaṅga-bala* = *daṇḍa*), and then expands it, first, to four (with *iti catuṣṭayam* being a clear reference to AŚ) and then to seven (NSā 27.3): *sāma dānaś ca daṇḍaś ca bhedaś cêti catuṣṭayam / māyôpekṣêndra-jālaṁ ca saptôpāyāḥ prakīrtitāḥ //* , i.e. conciliation, gifts, outright force, sowing dissent, deceit, political indifference, magical practices (this is, again, a reference to AŚ, Chapter 14). On the six virtues and seven means, comp. SCHARFE (1989: 206–210), who does not consider all the sources (e.g. NSā) though.

[30] This seems to be an allusion to Chapter 14 (*Aupaniṣadikam*) of the *Artha-śāstra*.

[31] MBh 2.5.11:

kac cid rāja-guṇaiḥ ṣaḍbhiḥ saptôpāyāṁs tathânagha /
***balâbalam** tathā samyak catur-daśa parīkṣase //*
*kaccid ātmānam **anvīkṣya** parāṁś ca jayatām vara /*
tathā saṁdhāya karmāṇi aṣṭau bhārata sevase //

The wording (emphasised/ in bold)—*balâbalam* and *anvīkṣya*—cannot be co-incidental. The compound *balâbala* refers to *daṇḍa-nītyāṁ balâbale* of AŚ 1.2.11, whereas the gerund *anvīkṣya* invokes the very name of the Ānvīkṣikī current.

Such importance and a vital role to play by Ānvīkṣikī in the qualifications and general education of the king which transpires from the questions posed by Nārada in the above passage is also highlighted in the advice contained in the *Gautama-dharma-sūtra*:

> '[The king] should be trained in the triple *Veda* and methodology.'[32]

As is well known, Kauṭilya who also emphasises the importance of the current, wrote his practical manual with the purpose of imparting comprehensive knowledge system to a future king. The reference to Ānvīkṣikī in the *Gautama-dharma-sūtra* is also important because it attests to a positive perception of the current at an early phase, i.e. around and after the collapse of the Mauryas.[33] The current was viewed positively in some circles even in at least the first two centuries of the common era, i.e. around the time of the composition of the *Yājñavalkya-smṛti*[34], which refers to it as well:

> 'The king who is versed in methodology, political science, economics and the triple *Veda* [knows how to] conceal his own weaknesses.'[35]

In a creation myth about the beginnings of the royal sovereignty when, after all the virtues, rites etc. in the world disintegrated, Brahmā composes and imparts a mythical text in a hundred thousand chapters which was believed to allegedly contain a section on norms, customs, observances and social rules alongside the following reference to the same four basic disciplines, including Ānvīkṣikī, encapsulated in a separate chapter:

> 'Likewise, O the Bull of the Bharata, such extensive disciplines of learning as the triple *Veda*, methodology (*ānvīkṣikī*), economics and political science were laid down [in the work].'[36]

---

[32] $GDhS_1$ 11.3 = $GDhS_2$ 2.2.3 = $GDhS_3$ 11.3: *trayyām ānvīkṣikyā vâbhivinītaḥ*.

[33] The text was composed in the period corresponding to the decline of and posterior to the Mauryan Empire, see OLIVELLE (2000: 8): 'I think that there is sufficient evidence to conclude that Āpastamba is older than Gautama' and OLIVELLE (2000: 10): 'There is no compelling reason at too great a distance in time from Gautama, we would not be far wrong in placing his upper limit around the beginning of the third century BCE.'

[34] KANE (1930–1962 I^2: 443, 447), DUNCAN–DERRETT (1973: 34).

[35] YDhŚ 1.311:

sva-randhra-goptânvīkṣikyāṁ daṇḍa-nītyāṁ tathâiva ca /
vinītas tv atha vārttāyāṁ trayyāṁ câiva narâdhipaḥ //

[36] MBh 12.59.33:

trayī cânvīkṣikī câiva vārttā ca bharata-ṛṣabha /
daṇḍa-nītiś ca vipulā vidyās tatra nidarśitāḥ //

Ānvīkṣikī is mentioned here as one of the disciplines to sustain the life and welfare of people, one considered so important that it had to be included in the sacred text laying down all the rules for the humankind and being a foundation of culture.

The positive image of Ānvīkṣikī as a theoretical discipline of learning one should master is occasionally emphasises even in such texts as the *Bhāgavata-purāṇa*, albeit the canonical fourfold list of sciences gets expanded:

> '[The teacher Sāndīpani imparted to the gods] the science of archery and law treatises as well as the path of methodical reasoning (*nyāya-pathin*) and the methodological knowledge (*ānvīkṣikī-vidyā*), and the sixfold royal conduct (political science).'[37]

These and other stray references in the epic to Ānvīkṣikī as a methodological discipline show that the current was, at least for some centuries and in certain milieux, positively associated with the proper royal conduct, preservation of moral law (*dharma*) etc., even among orthodox Brahmanic circles. The references can also serve as a good illustration of how the methodology of Ānvīkṣikī was used or believed to be used in actual or epic life and in the way Kauṭilya recommended.

5.3. At least one reference in the *Mahā-bhārata* is conspicuous in explicitly leaving Ānvīkṣikī out of the enumeration of the four main branches through which the world is regulated and maintained, thus reducing the list to three:

> 'There are three disciplines of learning for the learned ones: the triple *Veda*, economics and political science. It is through them, correctly applied, that the course of the world is regulated.'[38]

Interestingly, the *pāda*s ab (***trayī vārttā daṇḍa-nītis*** ... ***vidyā***) look almost like a quotation from *Artha-śāstra* 1.2.1 (*ānvīkṣikī* ***trayī vārttā daṇḍa-nītiś*** *cêti* ***vidyāḥ***) or *Nīti-sāra* 2.2a–c (*ānvīkṣikī* ***trayī vārttā daṇḍa-nītiś*** *ca śāśvatī /* ***vidyāś*** *catasra evâitā*), except for the term *ānvīkṣikī* absent. Despite the obvious omission of Ānvīkṣikī in this enumeration—additionally emphasised through the mention of only 'three disciplines of learning' (*tisro vidyā*), not four—the verse might nevertheless contain a hidden reference to the methodological current: it apparently reproduces a list of three disciplines which is associated with 'the school of Manu' in the *Artha-śāstra* (whatever that school was, certainly it was

---

[37] BhāgP 10.45.34:

sarahasyaṁ dhanur-vedaṁ dharmān nyāya-panthāṁs tathā /
tathā cânvīkṣikīṁ vidyāṁ rāja-nītiṁ ca ṣaḍ-vidhām //

[38] MBh 3.149.31:

trayī vārttā daṇḍa-nītis *tisro vidyā vijānatām /*
tābhiḥ samyak-prayuktābhir loka-yātrā vidhīyate //

not the school of the *Manu-smṛti*), and according to which Ānvīkṣikī is simply included in the Vedic soteriological and religious reflection (*trayī*):

> 'The representatives of the school of Manu [maintain] that the triple *Veda*, economics and political science [are the only disciplines of learning], because methodology is a special branch of the triple *Veda*.'[39]

If indeed, as Kauṭilya informs us, there were certain authoritative Brāhmaṇic traditions which ostensibly recognised the triple classification such as the representatives of the school of Manu (*mānava*), but included Ānvīkṣikī as a sub-variety of the Vedic learning (*trayī-viśeṣa*), then it is quite likely that the above verse simply replicates such a view.

There is one more verse which either directly or indirectly refers to Ānvīkṣikī:

> 'In this world the livelihood of people is [provided for through] agriculture, tending cattle and trade, [viz. economics; further, there is also] political science, the triple *Veda*, the knowledge—through that people fully exist.'[40]

What it presents is, likewise, the enumeration of the same four—or three, depending on the interpretation of the terms *trayī vidyā* either as two separate words or as a compound *trayī-vidyā* —disciplines. In the first place, economics is here disguised in the three economic activities (*kṛṣi*, *go-rakṣya* and *vāṇijya*) which are identical with the components (*kṛṣi*, *pāśu-pālya* and *vaṇijyā*) of economy (*vārttā*) enumerated in AŚ 1.4.1 (n. 1). The verse allows for two interpretations: either a fourfold classification ([*vārttā*] *daṇḍa-nītis trayī vidyā*), in which Ānvīkṣikī features merely as 'the knowledge', or a treefold classification ([*vārttā*] *daṇḍa-nītis trayī-vidyā*), i.e. 'political science, the knowledge of the triple *Veda*'.

Furthermore, the latter hemistich of the first of the *Mahā-bhārata* verses (MBh 3.149.31) explains that these three disciplines are relevant to people provided 'they are correctly applied' (*tābhiḥ samyak-prayuktābhir*). It seems that, first, the fact that the three disciplines become relevant (i.e. 'the course of the world is regulated … through them') means that they 'acquire a genuine status of disciplines of learning' (*vidyānām vidyātvam*), to use Kauṭilya's expression of AŚ 1.2.9, and indeed the implication of the passage corresponds in spirit to the Kauṭilya's expression. Secondly, the idea of the disciplines being correctly applied (*samyak-prayuktābhiḥ*) calls for an explanation of what criteria or procedures are thereby indicated. And that could possibly be a reference to proper methodology, i.e. to Ānvīkṣikī.

---

[39] $AŚ_1$ 1.2.2–3: *trayī vārttā daṇḍa-nītiś cêti mānavāḥ. trayī-viśeṣo hy ānvīkṣikîti.*

[40] MBh 3.198.23:

kṛṣi-go-rakṣya-vāṇijyam iha lokasya jīvanam /
daṇḍa-nītis trayī-vidyā *tena lokā bhavanty uta //*

Both verses in their last *pāda*s emphasise the role of the chief disciplines of learning, Ānvīkṣikī included, in maintaining the order and proper course of the world and human actions: *loka-yātrā vidhīyate* and *tena lokā bhavanty uta*, precisely the way it is done by Kāmandaki in NīSā 2.2d: these are the causes of stability of the world (*loka-saṁsthiti-hetavaḥ*). This additionally establishes the link between the two verses and the tradition described by Kauṭilya and Kāmandaki.

A passage that immediately follows *Mahā-bhārata* 3.149.31 both gives some additional explanation as to why the three disciplines are so vital and reiterates that the condition of their relevance is their proper implementation:

> 'Indeed, the execution of moral law (*dharma*) would not be possible on earth without the standard of the triple *Veda*. And also without political science, this [whole world] would be without moral limits. Further, [all] these people who do not practice the standard of economics would perish. Indeed, through these three standards, when implemented correctly, people are truly stimulated.'[41]

Thus, also the exemplification of the importance of the three disciplines of learning highlighted in the passage, analogous to *Mahā-bhārata* 3.149.31, allocates a fourth category, without mentioning it by name, which is necessary for the three disciplines to make any practical sense at all. This unnamed discipline which furnishes a proper methodological knowledge cannot but be, I would claim, Ānvīkṣikī.

At the same time, as it transpires from rather rare direct references to Ānvīkṣikī, from the fact that the references which would show it in a favourable light are even more scarce and from its omission in the classification of main disciplines of learning, it was indeed the case that for some reasons Ānvīkṣikī became at a certain point, probably in the centuries towards the end of the final compilation of the *Mahā-bhārata* (*ca.* second to fourth century CE), a current which was either neglected or looked down upon, while an explicit association with it was not particularly ennobling and was rather to be avoided.

6. Let us return to the actual essence of Ānvīkṣikī, of which we know that it was regarded as a successful investigative procedure and methodology associated with proper reasoning, determination of truth and effective course of conduct. But there is more than this. The pivotal, albeit very laconic statement of *Artha-śāstra* 1.2.11 (*vide supra* p. 177 and n. 11), reiterated by Kāmandaki (*vide*

[41] MBh 3.149.32–33:

sā ced dharma-kriyā na syāt trayī-dharmam ṛte bhuvi /
daṇḍa-nītim ṛte câpi nirmaryādam idam bhavet //
vārttā-dharme hy avartantyo vinaśyeyur imāḥ prajāḥ /
supravṛttair tribhir hy etair dharmaiḥ sūyanti vai prajāḥ //

supra p. 180 and n. 22), is, as a matter of fact, the only tangible feature of Ānvīkṣikī as we find it in Kauṭilya's and later in Kāmandaki's, and as much as we can attempt to reconstruct its nature we can see that the starting point for such a practical application of the Ānvīkṣikī methodology presented in the *Artha-śāstra* is the following question:

> Is a particular deed (*x*)
> good (P) or bad (not-P)
> in the realm of:
> —religion,
> —economic activity,
> —social coherence and political power?[42]

Accordingly, is a particular deed (*x*) profitable (*artha*, P) or not profitable (*anartha*, not-P) in the field of agriculture, cattle breeding and trade? Is a particular deed (*x*) conducive (*naya*, P) or not conducive (*apanaya*, not-P) to the maintenance of one's political power? Is a particular deed effective (*bala*, P) or ineffective (*abala*, not-P) in implementing other disciplines of learning? Correspondingly, the starting point for each cases of the application of Ānvīkṣikī which Kauṭilya enumerates is consistently a dilemma whether a particular deed possesses characteristics desired in a given field of application or not: 'Is *x* P or not-P?' In other words, it is consistently a dilemma whether a particular deed possesses characteristics desired in a given field of application or not: 'Is *x* P or not-P?'

And this seems to be precisely a classical case of doubt so vital for the epistemology of the Nyāya system, engrafted in the sixteen epistemological categories of the system as the third one, which opens the whole process of questioning, enquiry and analysis (see NS 1.1.1: *pramāṇa-prameya-**saṁśaya**-*° etc.). As we shall see (§ 8), Ānvīkṣikī is known also to the proponents of Nyāya specifically as a system in which analysis of doubt and its resolution plays a vital role, a system whose 'unique realms are the [epistemological] categories such as doubt etc.' (Pakṣilasvāmin Vātsyāyana: *tasyāḥ pṛthak-prasthānāḥ saṁśayâdayaḥ padârthāḥ*) which 'is guided by the categories such as doubt etc.' (Uddyotakara: *saṁśayâdi-bhedânuvidhāyinī ānvīkṣikī*). Doubt as a starting point of methodological analysis is therefore one of the thematic points of both the current of Ānvīkṣikī and the school of Nyāya.

6.1. The idea of doubt is of extreme importance to the system of Nyāya and it is defined in the *Nyāya-sūtra* in the following manner:

---

[42] Where P, to be exact, stands for: 'conforming to moral law' (*dharma*), 'economically profitable' (*artha*), 'conducive to political power' (*naya*), 'effective' (*bala*), and where non-P stand for: 'not conforming to moral law' (*adharma*), 'not economically profitable' (*anartha*), 'not conducive to political power' (*apanaya*), 'ineffective' (*abala*)—with respect to the three main spheres of application religion (*trayī*), economic activity (*vārttā*) and social coherence maintained through political power (*daṇḍa-nīti*).

> 'Doubt is an inquisitive reflection that depends on a particular characteristic [about which one is not certain and it is] due to perceived possibility of a property common [to different loci], due to perceived possibility of numerous properties, contradictory apprehension, incongruity of apprehension or incongruity of non-apprehension.'[43]

The *Locus classicus* for the nature of doubt (*saṁśaya*) is a the following passage of the *Nyāya-bhāṣya*:

> 'First one sees a property common to a pillar and a person, say, a [particular] height or a [particular] circumference [which could be a feature of both], and becomes curious as regards that particular characteristic [which can be applicable] to both [a pillar and a person] which he has seen before. Then he cannot determine any of the two [possibilities and decide] what it is. Doubt is such a cognition that fails to determine what it is. "I apprehend a property which is common to both [but] I do not apprehend a particular characteristic which belongs only to one of these two"—such a reflection is the basis [of doubt]. This [reflection] emerges as [a cause] that prompts doubt. Such an inquisitive reflection that depends on [this] particular characteristic [which one needs to determine what object one actually sees] is doubt.'[44]

A particular object x subject to doubt is first determined to have a property Q, of which it is known that only a certain set of things possesses it, and out of these things some are P and some are non-P. Thus, doubt for Vātsyāyana assumes a slightly more complex form of reasoning:

x ix Q
(P and not-P) $\in$ Q
———————
Is x P or not-P?

Further, the importance of doubt is emphasised by Vātsyāyana who considers doubt as a starting point of an enquiry, which is for him called '*nyāya*':

---

[43] NS 1.1.23: *samānâneka-dharmôpapatter vipratipatter upalabdhy-anupalabdhy-avyavasthātaś ca viśeṣâpekṣo vimarśaḥ saṁśayaḥ.*

[44] NBh 1.1.23: *sthāṇu-puruṣayoḥ samānaṁ dharmam āroha-pariṇāhau paśyan pūrva-dṛṣṭaṁ ca tayor viśeṣaṁ bubhutsumānaḥ kiṁsvid ity anyataraṁ nâvadhārayati, tad-anavādharaṇaṁ jñānaṁ saṁśayaḥ. samānam anayor dharmam upalabhe viśeṣam anyatarasya nôpalabha ity eṣā buddhir apekṣā. sā saṁśayasya pravarttikā vartate. tena viśeṣâpekṣo vimarśaḥ saṁśayaḥ.* For NS 1.1.23, see n. 43.

> 'Methodical reasoning (*nyāya*) is carried out n o t with respect to an object which has been perceived or which has been determined [conceptually], but with respect to an object under doubt.'[45]

This is clearly an approach which is a continuation of the process of analysis weighing the pros and cons of a particular action or value in the three realms of ritual / religion, economic activity and political power, emphasised, as we have seen, in the *Artha-śāstra*, albeit in a form much more advanced.

6.2. The idea of doubt also significantly features in the *Caraka-saṁhitā*, where it is characterised in quite similar terms:

> 'Now, [we describe] doubt. What is called doubt is a lack of certainty concerning things with respect to which one entertains a systemic doubt because of a characteristic of suspicion, for instance: we see people who are endowed with characteristics of an old age and people who are not endowed with characteristics of an old age, similarly people who are active and who are inactive, who get older quickly and those who are long-lived—because one has seen these two [categories, one entertains] doubt: Does untimely death exist or not?'[46]

The quintessence of doubt, according to the *Caraka-saṁhitā* is precisely of the same nature: 'Is *x* P or not-P?', or 'Is the quality of P ascribable to the object *x* or is the quality of non-P ascribable to the object *x*?' Clearly, the realm of application in this case which is diagnosis and medical treatment is quite different for obvious reasons, and the instance just quoted is the doubt which concerns death, its actual causes and additional factors which can lead to it as well as, by implication, the natural duration of life and the causes of its prolongation. In other words it is the question: Which of possible ways of life and of possible kinds of medical treatment may preserve life, i.e. rescue one from untimely death?

We notice that the same kind of doubt and subsequent reasoning is behind the idea of Ānvīkṣikī in Kauṭilya's passage (and subsequently in Kāmandaki's), albeit cast in a different environment: one entertains doubt whether a particular course of action is beneficial to, or at least compatible with the goals of religion, economics or political science: 'Is conduct *x* P or not-P?', where 'P' is 'beneficial / profitable / serviceable', in the sphere of religion, moral law, economics and political science. Ānvīkṣikī, the reasoner behind the *Caraka-*

---

[45] NBh$_1$ 1.1.1, p. 35.4 = NBh$_2$ p. 3.3: *tatra nânupalabdhe na nirṇīte 'rthe nyāyaḥ pravartate, kiṁ tarhi? saṁśayite 'rthe.*

[46] CarS 3.8.43: *atha saṁśayaḥ—saṁśayo nāma sandeha-lakṣaṇânusandigdheṣv artheṣv aniścayaḥ, yathā dṛṣṭā hy āyuṣmal-lakṣaṇair upetāś cânupetāś ca tathā sakriyāś câkriyāś ca puruṣāḥ śīghra-bhaṅgāś cira-jīvinaś ca, etad ubhaya-dṛṣṭatvāt saṁśayaḥ—kim asti khalv akāla-mṛtyur uta nâstîti.*

saṁhitā, Akṣapāda Gautama and Pakṣilasvāmin Vātsyāyana all share the same concern in their epistemic method: how to resolve the doubt so defined. And that does not seem coincidental.

7.1. Kauṭilya comes to mention Ānvīkṣikī once again but in a different context:

> 'Political science is the means of securing the pursuit of (lit. acquisition and maintenance) of methodology (*ānvīkṣikī*), the triple *Veda* and economics...'[47]

In the passage the relations between Ānvīkṣikī and other disciplines, or at least one of them, i.e. political science, is reversed. Before Kauṭilya maintained that Ānvīkṣikī is an indispensable tool to effective political rule. Here he says that the relation is reciprocal: political power is vital for the preservation of Ānvīkṣikī as well as other disciplines of learning.

This emphasises the importance of political and social stability as well as economic welfare for an unrestrained cultivation of Ānvīkṣikī, which in turn reminds us of what Aristotle in his *Metaphysics* says of philosophy and philosophers who for the practice of their philosophical vocation require a society which has reached a certain level of economic development that can enable an elite of intellectuals to focus on philosophical reflection rather than on mundane pursuit of activities indispensable merely for material or biological survival.

The passage also suggests that Kauṭilya treated political science and actual political power based on the theoretical analysis and enlightened advice as a precondition for unrestrained theoretical pursuit of the other three disciplines and practical implementation of their conclusions, which were to serve the preservation of political power. Thus the relation between the two disciplines was reciprocal and that of symbiosis: Ānvīkṣikī, alongside the other two, helped the monarch guide the society, use force, exercise the control in the sphere of social interaction and moral conduct, stimulate economy, stabilise the country etc., and thereby maintain power in a relatively peaceful manner without excessive violence. Political science applied through actual royal rule facilitated the development of the three other disciplines, including Ānvīkṣikī, for its own goals.

7.2. Kauṭilya also mentions how the knowledge of the four disciplines of learning could be acquired, i.e. what its legitimate sources are:

> 'After he has gone through the initiation rite, [the prince] should learn the triple *Veda* and methodology from the experts, economics from supervisors of departments, political science from theoreticians and practitioners.'[48]

[47] AŚ 1.4.3: *ānvīkṣikī-trayī-vārttānāṁ yoga-kṣema-sādhano daṇḍaḥ...*

[48] AŚ 1.5.8: *vṛttôpanayanas trayīm ānvīkṣikīṁ ca śiṣṭebhyo vārttām adhyakṣebhyo daṇḍa-nītiṁ vaktṛ-prayoktṛbhyaḥ.*

This implies that Ānvīkṣikī was a separate discipline that should be learnt from specialists (*śiṣṭebhyaḥ*) in this particular field and not from experts in any other field. We may assume, that is, that if a student wished to study Ānvīkṣikī, he should clearly not turn to experts in economics or in political science, but exclusively to those learned in the methodology of Ānvīkṣikī, i.e. experts in this particular field in its own right.

That is distantly echoed in the *Mahā-bhārata*, where probably the *traividyāḥ* ('experts in three disciplines'/'triple-discipline' experts') is a short hand for experts in respective fields:

> 'From the experts in three disciplines [the prince] should learn the triple *Veda*, the everlasting political science, methodology as well as the knowledge of the self, whereas from ordinary people [he should learn] economics.'[49]

8.1. The crucial question, therefore, arises who these 'triple-discipline experts' (*traividyāḥ*) who taught and practised Ānvīkṣikī actually were? As I pointed our earlier (p. 176), Kauṭilya includes three schools under the current of methodology under the names: *sāṁkhya*, *yoga* and *lokāyata*. However, the question is whether these designations really stand for what one may think they do, when one reads the passage and seems justified in taking them at their face value?

Let us first turn our attention to a philosophical school of Nyāya, which is not explicitly mentioned in the *Artha-śāstra* but whose proponent Pakṣilasvāmin Vātsyāyana, nevertheless, attempts to explicitly establish a historical link between his own school and the tradition of Ānvīkṣikī. Interestingly, it is not only Nyāya but also its associate school of Vaiśeṣika which is not mentioned as a school related to Ānvīkṣikī in the *Artha-śāstra*, *Mahā-bhārata* and other sources. A question immediately follows why they two not, despite the evidence of Vātsyāyana? Alternatively, what would be the rationale behind Vātsyāyana's attempt to equate, as we shall see, Nyāya with Ānvīkṣikī and to establish a link between these two, even though Kauṭilya completely ignored to mention either Nyāya or Vaiśeṣika in his account Ānvīkṣikī?

As it is well known, the text of the Nyāya tradition in which the term '*ānvīkṣikī*' features for the first time is the *Nyāya-bhāṣya*:

> '[Opponent's objection]: "As regards these [epistemological categories mentioned in NS 1.1.1,] a separate mention of [such categories] as doubt etc. is purposeless, because they—as far as they are legitimately included in [the two categories of] cognitive criteria and the cognoscibles—are not distinct [from one of these two]." [Reply.] This is true. However, the following four disci-

[49] MDhŚ 7.43:

traividyebhyas trayīṁ vidyāṁ daṇḍa-nītiṁ ca śāśvatīm /
ānvīkṣikīṁ câtma-vidyāṁ vārttârambhāṁś ca lokataḥ //

> plines of learning, each having its unique realm, are specified for the benefit of living beings, of which the fourth one is methodology (*ānvīkṣikī*), i.e. the discipline of methodical reasoning (*nyāya-vidyā*). Its unique realms are the [epistemological] categories such as doubt etc. Without a separate mention of these [categories] this [methodology] would merely be a discipline teaching about the highest self, like the *Upaniṣads*. Therefore, on account of [epistemological] categories such as doubt etc. [methodology] is established as a distinct [discipline of learning].'[50]

Clearly, 'the following four disciplines of learning' (*imās tu catasro vidyāḥ*) are precisely the same disciplines as those mentioned by Kauṭilya. In this passage Vātsyāyana equates his own school with Ānvīkṣikī and emphasises that the defining characteristic of Nyāya/Ānvīkṣikī is the fourteen epistemological categories out of sixteen enumerated in NS 1.1.1 that begin with doubt (*saṁśaya*) and end with points of defeat (*nigraha-sthāna*). Of particular notice is the fact that he singles out doubt as the defining feature of Ānvīkṣikī which was, it seems, indeed the case (*vide supra* § 6). It is doubt as a separate category that is crucial both in this passage as well as in the list of the fourteen categories of Nyāya inasmuch as it is a starting point of any enquiry and analysis. And this is exactly what also seems so important for Ānvīkṣikī in evaluating particular course of action that is beneficial to accomplish religious, economic or political goals. But for doubt etc., Nyāya—and apparently Ānvīkṣikī—would end up as being reduced merely to a salvific doctrine that teaches about the highest self (*adhyātma-vidyā*/*ātma-vidyā*), restricted to the Brāhmaṇic orthodox tradition. Further, in the passage Vātsyāyana treats Ānvīkṣikī as primary, while explaining how it differs from *adhyātma-vidyā*, 'a discipline studying the highest self', and how it is established as separate branch in its own right (*pṛthak prasthāpyate*); surprisingly, Nyāya is subordinate to Ānvīkṣikī and treated as secondary: it is not Nyāya which is mentioned as the fourth among the main disciplines of learning but Ānvīkṣikī. We can, therefore, see that Vātsyāyana's reference to Ānvīkṣikī is not simply coincidental but concerns the very nature of both traditions, which are historically equated by Vātsyāyana: the fourth discipline is in its true essence the discipline of methodical reasoning (*yāsāṁ caturthīyam ānvīkṣikī nyāya-vidyā*), which is what Nyāya is and does.

[50] NBh_1 1.1.1, p. 34–35 = NBh_2, p. 2.18–3.2: *tatra saṁśayâdīnāṁ pṛthag-vacanam anarthakam—saṁśayâdayo* {*hy*}[a] *yathā-sambhavaṁ pramāṇeṣu prameyeṣu cântar-bhavanto na vyatiricyanta iti. satyam etat. imās tu catasro vidyāḥ pṛthak-prasthānāḥ prāṇa-bhṛtām anugrahāyôpadiśyante, yāsāṁ caturthīyam ānvīkṣikī nyāya-vidyā. tasyāḥ pṛthak-prasthānāḥ saṁśayâdayaḥ padârthāḥ. teṣāṁ pṛthag-vacanam antareṇâdhyātma-vidyā-mātram iyaṁ syāt, yathôpaniṣadaḥ. tasmāt saṁśayâdibhiḥ padârthaiḥ pṛthak prasthāpyate.* [[a] NBh_2.]

Subsequently, Vātsyāyana raises a crucial question that concerns the very nature of his own school of thought and, at the same time, the foundations of Ānvīkṣikī:

> 'What is then this methodical reasoning (*nyāya*)? Methodical reasoning is an examination of an object by means of cognitive criteria. Inference relies on perception and testimony. This is systematic enquiry. Systematic enquiry is a systematic query into [an object] which has already become known by means of perception and testimony. What proceeds by means of this [systematic enquiry] is methodology (*ānvīkṣikī*), i.e. the discipline of methodical reasoning (*nyāya-vidyā*), or the science of methodical reasoning (*nyāya-śāstram*).'[51]

In this short account, he draws a direct link between the essential features of his own school and Ānvīkṣikī, which not only is treated as tantamount to the discipline known as *nyāya-vidyā* or *nyāya-śāstra*, or 'discipline of methodical reasoning', but determines the method of analysis adopted by Nyāya itself. For all practical purposes, Vātsyāyana clearly equates the method and quintessence of Ānvīkṣikī with the discipline of methodical reasoning (*nyāya-vidyā*), which lies at the core of Nyāya.[52]

In his *Nyāya-vārttika*, Uddyotakara recapitulates and elucidates on all the main points made by Vātsyāyana as follows:

> 'Thus, these [main] disciplines of learning are four. Each of them has its own unique realm. The triple *Veda* has as its unique realm fire sacrifice, fire oblation etc. Economics has as its unique realm a [farmer's] plough, a [merchant's] carriage etc. Political science is guided by the categories such as the ruler, ministers etc. Methodology is guided by the categories such as doubt etc. Without its own unique realm such as doubt etc. it would merely be a discipline teaching about the highest self. Why so? Because being merely a discipline teaching about the highest self it would be like the *Upaniṣad*s, and thus it would be included into the triple *Veda*, and the fourfold division [of disciplines] would cease.'[53]

---

[51] NBh_1 1.1.1, p. 39.1–2 = NBh_2, p. 3.11–13: *kaḥ punar ayaṁ nyāyaḥ? pramāṇair artha-parīkṣaṇaṁ nyāyaḥ. pratyakṣâgamâśritam anumānam. sânvīkṣā. pratyakṣâgamābhyām īkṣitasyânvīkṣaṇam anvīkṣā. tayā pravartata ity ānvīkṣikī nyāya-vidyā nyāya-śāstram.*

[52] Comp. also Jayantabhaṭṭa's account in the same spirit, NMa_1 I: 9.10–11: *pratyakṣâgamābhyām īkṣitasyânvīkṣaṇaṁ anvīkṣā anumānam ity arthaḥ tad-vyutpādakaṁ śāstraṁ ānvīkṣikī.*

[53] NV_1 1.1.1., p. 12.10–16 = NV_2 1.1.1., p. 11.17–22: *catasra imā vidyā bhavanti* {*iti*}[a]. *tāś ca pṛthak-prasthānāḥ. agni-hotra-havanâdi-prasthānā trayī. hala-śakaṭâdi-prasthānā vārttā. svāmy-amātya-*{*ādi*}[b]*-bhedânuvidhāyinī daṇḍa-nītiḥ. saṁśayâdi-bhedânuvidhāyinī*

We can see that indeed each of the four disciplines has its unique realm of interest and application, and that of Ānvīkṣikī is precisely doubt and other epistemological categories, i.e. epistemology and general enquiry. Neither Vātsyāyana nor Uddyotakara in their brief definitions of the nature of Ānvīkṣikī mentions any particular practical field of application where it could be employed, apart from a broad theoretical realm of methodical reasoning and examination of an object by means of cognitive criteria, which can practically be applied to almost any field one chooses. The unique subject matter (*prasthāna*) for Ānvīkṣikī is therefore methodological enquiry, epistemology and related issues, and soteriology seems to be merely o n e of its additional fields of application.

By way of summary of his comments on the enumeration of all the sixteen epistemological categories listed in opening aphorism of the *Nyāya-sūtra*, Vātsyāyana returns to Ānvīkṣikī and cites a verse already known from *Artha-śāstra*, albeit with a significant change:

> 'This methodology in question, which is differentiated [as a separate science from all other disciplines of learning] through categories, such as cognitive criteria etc.,
>
> is declared, in the catalogue of disciplines of learning, to be the lamp for disciplines of learning, the means to [accomplish] all actions, the fundament of all moral laws.'[54]

This is by no means an insignificant statement: Vātsyāyana offers a brief description of the categories which found the cornerstone of the Nyāya philosophical project and at the same time recapitulates the nature of his own system with the verse which speaks of nothing else but Ānvīkṣikī, and doing so, he consciously replaces the original *pāda* 4 (*śaśvad ānvīkṣikī matā*) of the *Artha-śāstra* with a new phrase (*vidyôddeśe prakīrtitā*), which additionally emphasises the primary role of the current. 'The catalogue of disciplines of learning' (*vidyôddeśe*) of Vātsyāyana's verse in which Ānvīkṣikī 'is declared … to be the lamp for disciplines of learning' can be a n y fourfold division of disciplines of learning, not necessarily the same as Kauṭilya's, but most likely it is indeed the *Artha-śāstra*, for the simple reason that the verse itself is a quotation, with a minor change, from this work.

ānvīkṣikī. tasyāḥ saṁśayâdi-prasthānam antareṇâ{dhyā}[c]*tma-vidyā-mātram iyaṁ syāt. tataḥ kiṁ syāt? adhyātma-vidyā-mātratvād upaniṣad-vidyāvat trayyām evântar-bhāva iti catuṣṭvaṁ nivartate.* [[a] NV_2. [b] NV_2. [c] NV_2.]

[54] NBh_1 1.1.1, p. 64 = NBh_2, p. 5.18–20: *sêyam ānvīkṣikī pramāṇâdibhiḥ padârthair vibhajyamānā*

> *pradīpaḥ sarva-vidyānām upāyaḥ sarva-karmaṇām /*
> *āśrayaḥ sarva-dharmāṇāṁ vidyôddeśe prakīrtitā //*

Cf. RUBEN's (1926: 354) idea that the change within the verse does not stem for Vātsyāyana himself, unconvincing for the simple fact that the verse is grammatically embedded in the structure of the NBh passage and its grammatical subject is outside of the verse.

Also Uddyotakara's gloss contained in the *Nyāya-vārttika* emphasises the fact that Ānvīkṣikī, in its method, is applicable to all domains of learning and is serviceable to all other sciences, which means that the soteriological aspect does exhaust its multidimensional character and philosophical concerns:

> 'Therefore, these categories, such as doubt etc., which are included in [the two categories of] cognitive criteria and the cognoscibles, have been described separately in order to emphasise the [fourfold] division of the disciplines of learning. This methodology in question, which is the discipline of methodical reasoning and which is differentiated [as a separate science from all other disciplines of learning] through categories, such as cognitive criteria etc., is declared to be the lamp for disciplines of learning, because it illuminates [its object, i.e. unique realm,] like a lamp, and so it is a lamp [for other disciplines of learning]. Its object has been explained to consist in cognitive criteria and other [categories]. Other disciplines are explained, too. Why cognitive criteria and other [categories] are not [an object] for these other disciplines of learning?'[55]

There can be no doubt that Vātsyāyana, and Uddyotakara following him, view themselves and their own school of Nyāya as direct successors of Ānvīkṣikī. How far, however, does their claim hold validity in a historical sense? And could Nyāya be a genuine successor of Ānvīkṣikī at all, if it was not even contained in Kauṭilya's list comprising the three schools (p. 176)?

8.2. We find a partial confirmation of the accuracy of Kauṭilya's classifying the materialists (*lokāyata*) among the followers of Ānvīkṣikī in a passage from the *Rāmāyaṇa* in which Rāma addresses Bhārata as follows:

> 'I hope, dear friend, that you do not associate with Brahmins who are materialists, for they are fools whose competence is useless and they consider themselves experts. These malignant people acquire their intelligence in the form of Ānvīkṣikī and then talk nonsense, even when principal law treatises are there at hand.'[56]

---

[55] NV_1 1.1.1, p. 21.8–14 = NV_2 1.1.1., p. 20.2–7: *tasmād ete saṁśayâdayḥ padârthāḥ pramāṇe prameye cântar-bhavanto vidyā-prasthāna-bheda-jñāpanârthaṁ pṛthag-upadiṣṭāḥ{iti}*[a]. *sêyam ānvīkṣikī nyāya-vidyā* ***pramāṇâdibhiḥ padârthaiḥ vibhajyamānā pradīpaḥ sarva-vidyānāṁ*** *bhavati prakāśakatvāt pradīpavat {pradīpaḥ}*[b]. *pramāṇâdi-pratipāditam artham itarā vidyāḥ pratipadyanta iti. kim itarāsu vidyāsu pramāṇâdīni na santi?* [[a] NV_2. [b] NV_2 omits.]

[56] R_1 2.100.38–39 = R_2 2.94.32–33:

kaccin na lokāyatikān brāhmaṇāṁs tāta sevase /

Clearly, the verses confirm what Kauṭilya stated that at least some of the followers of Ānvīkṣikī were materialists (*lokāyatika*, *lokāyata*).

Further, in these two verses Rāma warns Bhārata to stay away from mischievous followers of Ānvīkṣikī, who ignore tradition, law and order established through *Dharma-śāstra*s and speak against the sacred lore. They are not outcasts, however, being legitimate Brahmins. What precedes these verses is also quite informative:

> 'I hope, dear friend, that plans devised by you or your ministers, when not divulged, are never known [to anybody], even while applying all kinds of reasoning.'[57]

The verse refers to methods which can be used against the king and his policy and with which one can uncover royal plans and stratagems. These are the tools of reasoning which belong to the domain of Ānvīkṣikī, referred to explicitly a few verses later. Thus, we obtain quite a different picture of the same Ānvīkṣikī, which is for Vātsyāyana primarily a method and knowledge concerned with the highest self (*adhyātma-vidyā*; see also §§ 8.1, 9.3, 10).

The verses also demonstrate that the attitude towards both Ānvīkṣikī and its methods and subject matter of rational enquiry was viewed among certain circles with suspicion and animosity. This opens a possibility that the threefold—instead of the fourfold (depending on the interpretation)—enumeration of the foremost sciences of the *Mahā-bhārata* (§ 5.3.), which would leave out Ānvīkṣikī and could thereby be a voice against the high status of the current, was not necessarily either an innocuous omission or a concealed reference to Ānvīkṣikī, comprised among the three sciences as a subvariety of one of them, but may have been a deliberate expression of disavowal and disregard for the followers of the current. Clearly, Ānvīkṣikī was not a current everyone would like to subscribe to and be known to be associated with.

---

anartha-kuśalā[a] *hy ete bālāḥ paṇḍita-māninaḥ* //
dharma-śāstreṣu mukhyeṣu vidyamāneṣu durbudhāḥ /
buddhim ānvīkṣikīṁ[b] *prāpya nirarthaṁ pravadanti te* //

[[a] POLLOCK (2005: 510): *anartha kuśalā*. [b] POLLOCK (2005: 510): *buddhimān vīkṣikīṁ*. Interstingly, Internet-accessible TITUS machine-readable e-text of the *Rāmāyaṇa*, prepared by Muneo Tokunaga (Kyōtō, 1993) with adaptations by John D. Smith (Cambridge, 1995) on the basis of edition R_2, on which apparently also POLLOCK's edition is based, all contain the same mistranscription of the Sanskrit text. In the reading adopted by them, *buddhimān* would not relate gramatically to anything in the sentence and would have to be emended to *buddhimantaḥ*. Besides, *vīkṣikīṁ* is meaningless. The correctness of parsing *buddhim ānvīkṣikīṁ prāpya* is confirmed by the commentary *Bhūṣaṇa* of Govindarāja in R_1 *ad loc.*, p. 95.26–27: *ānvīkṣikīṁ buddhim prāpya śuṣka-tarka-viṣayāṁ buddhim āsthāpya nirarthaṁ niṣprayojanaṁ pravadanti.*]

[57] R_1 2.100.21 = R_2 2.94.16:

kaccin na tarkair yuktvā vā ye câpy aparikīrtitāḥ /
tvayā vā tava vâmātyair budhyate tāta mantritam //

There is a range of other equally negative references to Ānvīkṣikī, either *verbatim* critical of it or of its method of rational enquiry and subject matter, which confirm that the attitude among various circles towards the current was ambiguous, to say the least. One of these is found in the *Manu-smṛti*:

> '[10] «Scripture» should be recognised as the *Veda*, whereas «tradition» as the law treatise. These two should never be questioned with respect to any matter,[58] because it is from these two that moral law has emanated. [11] A twice-born who would look down upon these two by reason of the science of argumentation (*hetu-śāstra*) should be cast out by righteous people as a nihilist and a denigrator of the *Veda*.'[59]

The nihilist (*nāstika*) here is clearly a materialist, the term being often associated and synonymous with materialism (Cārvāka, Lokāyata), as numerous references indicate.[60] Followers of Ānvīkṣikī, associated with materialism and nihilism, are censured with quite similar words in the *Mahā-bhārata* on a few occasions:

> '[11] The rejection of the authority of the *Veda*s and the scriptures is a serious transgression; [to maintain that] inconsistency is everywhere brings one's own destruction. [12] If a Brahmin, claiming to be an expert, would be a denigrator of the *Veda*, would be fond of methodology, i.e. a discipline of reasoning,

---

[58] For an alternative reading and interpretation of the *pāda* C (*te sarvârtheṣu mīmāṁsye*) see OLIVELLE (2006: 244–5, note 2.10).

[59] MDhŚ 2.10–11:

śrutis tu vedo vijñeyo dharma-śāstraṁ tu vai smṛtiḥ /
te sarvârtheṣv amīmāṁsye tābhyāṁ dharmo hi nirbabhau //
yo 'vamanyeta te tūbhe[a] *hetu-śāstrâśrayād dvijaḥ /*
sa sādhubhir bahiṣ-kāryo nāstiko veda-nindakaḥ //

[[a] Varia lectio: *sarvârtheṣu mīmāṁsye*, see n. 58. [b] Varia lectio: *mūle*, and the translation: '...who would look down upon these two fundaments'.]

[60] See e.g. TS 1960–61; Bhā 3.3.53; TRD ad ṢDSa 80–87; p. 452–462; esp. p. 452.3 (*lokyāyatā nāstikā evam itthaṁ vadanti*); MŚVṬ, *Autpattika-sūtra* 10, Part II, p. 4.15 (*lokāyataṁ nām nāstikānām tantram*); NBh ad NS 3.2.61 (*atra nāstika āha:* ***bhūtebhyo mūrty-upādānavat tad-upādānam***).

Another type of reference of the term *nāstika* is to a sceptic who accepts neither the Vedic tradition, the existence of soul, karmic retribution etc., just a Lokāyata, nor the validity of argument or enquiry, and doubts all; see e.g. $CarS_1$ 1.11.14–15:

na parīkṣā na parīkṣyaṁ na kartā kāraṇam na ca /
na devā na ṛṣayaḥ siddhāḥ karma karma-phalaṁ na ca //
nāstikasyâsti naîvâtmā yadṛcchôpahatâtmanaḥ //
pātakebhyaḥ paraṁ câtat pātakaṁ nāstika-grahaḥ //

In the above verse, the *nāstika* cannot be such a 'sceptic' who rejects valid methods and objects enquiry (*na parīkṣā na parīkṣyaṁ*), because he clearly applies *hetu-śāstra*.

> which is useless, [13] if he would propound theories based on logical arguments, negated facts, but in reality would argue with logical arguments, permanently calumniate and criticise Brahmins, [14] and would put everything to doubt, such a person should be acknowledged to be a fool and idiot, of harsh and primitive language, and people should know, dear friend, that those like him are like dogs among humans.'[61]

In another passage, god Indra, in the guise of a jackal, addresses the sage Kāśyapa, in front of whom undergoes a kind of 'self-criticism' session for sins apparently committed as a follower of Ānvīkṣikī and vows never to fall back in case he would assume a human form again, for from now on he would eventually know what is good and what is wrong:

> '[44] Others, of inauspicious descent, who are born at evil moments under demonic constellations, fall into the demonic race, destitute of sacrifice and progeny. [45] I used to be such a pseudo-expert, a reasoner, a denigrator of the *Veda*, fond of methodology, i.e. a discipline of reasoning, which is useless, [46] I formulated doctrines based on logical reason, in assemblies I spoke about what is based on logical reason, I calumniated and verbally assaulted the twice-born during Vedic sacrifices. [47] I was a nihilist, putting everything to doubt, a thickhead, considering myself an expert. This [present] life of mine as a jackal, O Twice-Born, is a consequence of all this. [48] May I, even after hundreds of days and nights that I am a jackal, obtain a human birth again. Then I would be content and observant, taking pleasure in sacrifices, donations and asceticism, I would know what is to be known, and would avoid what is to be avoided.'[62]

---

[61] $MBh_1 = MBh_2$ 13.37.11–14:

aprāmāṇyaṁ ca vedānāṁ śāstrāṇāṁ câtilanghanaṁ /
sarvatra cânavasthānaṁ[a] *etan nāśanaṁ ātmanaḥ* // 11 //
bhavet paṇḍita-mānī yo brāhmaṇo veda-nindakaḥ /
ānvīkṣikīṁ tarka-vidyāṁ anurakto nirarthikāṁ // 12 //
hetu-vādān bruvan satsu vijetā hetu-vādikaḥ[b] /
ākroṣṭā câtivaktā ca brāhmaṇānāṁ sadâiva hi // 13 //
sarvâbhiśankī mūḍhaś ca bālaḥ kaṭuka-vāg api /
boddhavyas tādṛśas tāta nara-śvānaṁ[c] *hi taṁ viduḥ* // 14 //

[[a] MBh_2: *avyasthā ca sarvatra.* [b] MBh_1 reads: *vijetâhetu-vādikaḥ*. If we read '*ahetu-vādikaḥ*', the translation would be: 'would be talking without logical arguments'. [c] MBh_2: *naraṁ śvānaṁ*.]

[62] MBh_1 12.173.44–49 = MBh_2 12.180.46–51:

nakṣatreṣv āsureṣv anye dustīrthā durmuhūrta-jāḥ /
saṁpatanty āsurīṁ yoniṁ yajña-prasava-varjitāṁ // 44 //
ahaṁ āsaṁ paṇḍitako haituko veda-nindakaḥ /

In the passages associating the 'useless' (*nirarthikā*) Ānvīkṣikī with nihilistic materialists, the current is called a 'discipline of reasoning' (*tarka-vidyā*) and a 'theory based on logical arguments' (*hetu-vāda*), 'a discipline whose subject matter is vain reasoning' (*śuṣka-tarka-viṣayā* in the *Bhūṣaṇa* on *Rāmāyaṇa*, see n. 56), whereas its follower is labelled an 'arguer with logical arguments' (*hetu-vādika*), 'reasoner' (*haituka*), but also a 'fool', 'idiot', 'of harsh and primitive language', a 'thickhead' who 'brings his own destruction' and negates facts.

In the same vein, Sāndīpani of Kāśī, Kṛṣṇa's teacher, provides in the *Bhāgavata-purāṇa* the following rule for a wandering ascetic (*saṁnyāsin*):

> 'He should not be fond of [critical] disputes about the *Veda*s, should not be a heretic or reasoner (*haituka*), he should not engage in a dry debate or verbal contest (*śuṣka-vāda-vivāda*).'[63]

The stipulation rules that the orthodox wandering ascetic should not participate in any activity normally associated with Ānvīkṣikī and the social-philosophical context in which it evolved.

The epithets *sarvâbhiśaṅkin* and *sarva-śaṅkin* ('someone who puts everything in doubt') in the *Mahā-bhārata* quoted above should not be understood literally intimating a sceptical attitude. They rather imply that the person would not accept anything without a proper reason and logic, which is so frequently shown in negative light here. The opposite of the Ānvīkṣikī way of life is 'to know what is to be known, and to avoid what is to be avoided', i.e. to know what is good and what is wrong from an orthodox traditional point of view, apparently something the followers of Ānvīkṣikī are incapable of. The passages incidentally paint a picture of a conflict between belief, dogmatism and religious attitude, on the one hand, and reason, reasoning and intellectual openness, on the other, while the side is taken on the former: Ānvīkṣikī and its followers should be ostracised, being the public enemies in view of their critical approach to traditionally and uncritically accepted values.

ānvīkṣikīṁ tarka-vidyām anurakto nirarthikāṁ // 45 //
hetu-vādān pravaditā vaktā saṁsatsu hetumat /
ākroṣṭā câbhivaktā ca brahma-yajñeṣu vai[a] *dvijān* // 46 //
nāstikaḥ sarva-śaṅkī ca mūrkhaḥ paṇḍita-mānikaḥ /
tasyêyaṁ phala-nirvṛttiḥ sṛgālatvaṁ mama dvija // 47 //
api jātu tathā tat syād aho-rātra-śatair api /
yad ahaṁ mānuṣīṁ yoniṁ sṛgālaḥ prāpnuyāṁ punaḥ // 48 //
saṁtuṣṭaś câpramattaś ca yajña-dāna-tapo-ratiḥ /
jñeya-jñātā bhaveyaṁ vai varjya-varjayitā tathā // 49 //

[[a] MBh$_2$: *brahma-vākyeṣu ca*.]

For an alternative translation of MBh$_2$ 12.180.46–47ab see PREISENDANZ (2000: 243).

[63] BhāgP 11.18.30:

veda-vāda-rakto na syān na pākhaṇḍī na haitukaḥ /
śuṣka-vāda-vivāde na kañcit pakṣaṁ samāśrayet //

8.3. The epithets mentioned just above, despite the unequivocally negative connotations they carry, along with other references to Ānvīkṣikī such as *nyāya-vidyā* (NBh, NV, MDhŚ) and *hetu-śāstra* (MDhŚ) or *nyāya-pathin* (BhāgP) attest to a direct link between Ānvīkṣikī and its methods of enquiry based on reasoning (*tarka*) and logical argumentation (*hetu*). Independent lexicographic sources[64] also confirm that reasoning was the essence of Ānvīkṣikī, known under its second name 'discipline of reasoning' (*tarka-vidyā*).

What Uddyotakara has to say on the essence of Ānvīkṣikī being *anvīkṣā*, while discussing the nature of suppositional knowledge (*ūha*) and inference, is also quite significant in this context:

> 'Others say that inference is [the same as] reasoning (*tarka*). They call inference: logical reason (*hetu*), reasoning (*tarka*), methodical reasoning (*nyāya*) or systematic enquiry (*anvīkṣā*).'[65]

Such designations prove that investigation of the highest self (*adhyātma-vidyā*) and liberation (*mokṣa*) was neither the main nor the sole concerns of the current en masse. Further, if all the proponents of Ānvīkṣikī were to pursue the salvific path, Kauṭilya and others could not have listed the materialists among its followers. And, indeed, we see no suggestion in the passages of the *Artha-śāstra* that Ānvīkṣikī was in any way concerned with any kind of salvific theory and the hereafter. Furthermore, Kauṭilya, who places much emphasis on Ānvīkṣikī as a primary science and who most probably himself subscribed to the current, does not seem bother much about eschatology and emancipation. As Johannes BRONKHORST (2007: 168) notices, '... the Artha Śāstra, in spite of explicitly enumerating the four *āśrama*s, shows no interest whatsoever in liberation'. One possible candidate for a reference to liberation (*mokṣa*) could be the expression *vyasane 'bhyudaye ca* ('in misfortune and in prosperity') in AŚ 1.2.11, but clearly it is not. The concept of liberation may also be implied in AŚ 1.3.14 (*sva-dharmaḥ svargāyânantyāya ca*—'One's own moral duty [serves] the [attainment of] heaven and immortality (or: the [attainment of] immortality in heaven') with the term *ānantya* (immortality), as one of the two main goals (beside heaven, *svarga*) which can be achieved by following one's own moral duty (*sva-dharma*), but this seems to be rather a mere attestation of commonly accepted view (also by those—the monarch and his retinue—for whom the *Artha-śāstra* was composed) at that time, whereas 'immortality' (*ānantya*) does not have to imply the acceptance of the ideal of liberation by Kauṭilya himself but solely a reproduction of a general belief in the afterlife widespread in (at least some circles of) the society.

---

[64] ACM 251c: *ānvīkṣikī tarka-vidyā*.

[65] NV_1 1.1.40, p. 141.17–18 = NV_2, p. 133.113–14: *apare tv anumānam tarka ity āhuḥ. hetus tarkaḥ nyāyo 'nvīkṣā iti anumānam ākhyāyata iti.*

9.1. In his important paper, HACKER (1958: 19–20) maintains that it was Vātsyāyana who identified Nyāya with Ānvīkṣikī for the first time and before the *Nyāya-bhāṣya* there was no such connection:

> 'Since Vātsyāyana managed to pass off his science [i.e. Nyāya—P.B.] as Ānvīkṣikī, which had been identified by some with Sāṁkhya and other systems, it was therefore possible that the classification of Kauṭilya had not won any wider recognition. ... Perhaps Kauṭilya's classification [of four sciences—P.B.] was forgotten precisely because Sāṁkhya had gradually become extinct, Yoga had been philosophically totally dependent on Sāṁkhya and Lokāyata had become radically materialistic. ... Since there were no more teachers of Sāṁkhya, or not in sufficient numbers, other systems had to be designated, at the guidance of which one could learn the art of methodical reflection. Since Vātsyāyana's times the system of Nyāya offered its service in this respect.'

This approach in main points is taken over by HALBFASS (1988: 274–277), albeit with some reservation and hesitation. Indeed, there apparently seems to be a kind of 'historical succession gap': there is no mention of Nyāya, or its twin system Vaiśeṣika, in the *Artha-śāstra*, on the one hand, and, on the other, it is Vātsyāyana who seems first to establish a connection between Ānvīkṣikī and Nyāya.

HACKER's, and to some extent HALBFASS', is the thesis that I now want to challenge.

9.2. The most obvious counter-question that automatically comes to one's mind is this: Why should, in the first place, Vātsyāyana want to 'pass off his science, i.e. Nyāya, as Ānvīkṣikī' if already at his time Ānvīkṣikī triggered negative associations in wider popular reception, or at least any association with it was not particularly dignifying? Would he rather not dissociate himself at any price from a current whose name would carry negative connotations? Why should we doubt the credibility of Vātsyāyana's account and not take what he says about the direct link between the tradition of Ānvīkṣikī and his own school of Nyāya for what it stands for, i.e. as an expression of a genuine historical continuity, even though the absence of any explicit mention of Nyāya and Vaiśeṣika by Kauṭilya may be disturbing? After all, we could argue, there existed no school of Nyāya of which we knew at the time when Kauṭilya's manual was composed, i.e. in the period of second–first centuries BCE (after the disintegration of the Mauryan empire), and the first Nyāya text know to us, ascribed to Akṣapāda Gautama, was composed from *ca.* the middle of first century CE onwards (till its final redaction in fifth century), so Kauṭilya could not possibly refer to it by name.[66]

---

[66] Comp. the remark of HACKER (1958: 19): 'Had Kauṭilya known Nyāya, which is a science of reflection par excellence, and for which both reflection and argumentation constitute

In my opinion we can easily see that Ānvīkṣikī was not a well-established and celebrated tradition which was at the outset unrelated to Nyāya but to which Vātsyāyana w a n t e d t o subscribe, without any historical justification, and it is not the case that he intended Nyāya to take the place of Ānvīkṣikī in the u n i v e r s a l l y e s t a b l i s h e d classification of four disciplines of learning outlined by Kauṭilya, as HACKER (1958: 19–20) maintains. First of all, neither had the fourfold classification of the *Artha-śāstra* become a standard one universally accepted at the times of Vātsyāyana as HACKER himself noticed, nor was it the case that all the four disciplines were universally regarded as pre-eminent and celebrated in all circles. There were other classifications which were even more popular: the six limbs of the *Vedas* (*ṣaḍ-vedâṅga*), but also fourteenfold[67], eighteenfold, nineteenfold[68] and even much longer lists as attested e.g. by the seventy-twofold list of arts and skills (*kalā*) in 'the Story of Paesi' (*Paesi-kahāṇayaṁ*)[69] of the *Rājapraśnīya-sūtra* (RP 806[211]), the sixty-fourfold list of supplementary sciences and disciplines (*aṅga-vidyā*) of the *Kāma-sūtra* (KS 1.3.15).[70]

A more popular classification was probably the fourteenfold division of sciences which could have diversified contents, but it never included Ānvīkṣikī. It is mentioned by Jayantabhaṭṭa in the *Nyāya-mañjarī*,[71] who describes the four *Vedas* (in a rather unusual sequence: *Atharva-veda*, *Ṛg-veda*, *Yajur-veda*, *Sāma-veda*), the legendary-mythological lore (*itihāsa–purāṇa*), the six supplementary sciences (*vedâṅga*), law treatises (*dharma-śāstra*), Mīmāṁsā and Nyāya. Jayanta himself refers to other fourteenfold classifications:

> '"The *Vedas* rely on legendary-mythological texts (*purāṇa*), reasoning, Mīmāṁsā, law treatises (*dharma-śāstra*)—these are the fourteen supports of disciplines of learning and moral law."
>
> And it is said with regard to other [disciplines]:
>
> "the supplementary texts, the [minor] *Vedas*, Mīmāṁsā, the realm of Nyāya, legendary-mythological texts (*purāṇa*) and law

not only the method but also the subject matter, as a separate discipline in its own right, he would certainly have mentioned it by whatever name on the occasion of the examination of the nature of Ānvīkṣikī; what follows, it could not have existed as such at his time.'

67 This division is mentioned even in the tradition of Nyāya, see e.g. NMa_1 I: 9.12 = NMa_2 I: 9.25: *nanu catasraś ced vidyāḥ tat kathaṁ catur-daśa darśitāḥ nâiṣa virodhaḥ* ... or NBhū p. 71 ad NBh 1.1.1 (*sêyam ānvīkṣikī...*): ... *na tarhi catasra eva vidyāḥ catur-daśānāṁ vidyānāṁ bhinna-viṣayatvāt...*

68 Mil_1, p. 3–4, Mil_2 3.4: *suti sammuti sanhkyā yogā nīti visesikā gaṇikā gandhabbā tikicchā cātubbedā purāṇā itihāsā jotisā māyā hetu mantaṇā yuddhā chandasā muddā, vacanena ekūnavīsati.*

69 BOLLÉE (2002).

70 For a brief overview of such lists see: Willem B. BOLLÉE (2002: 192–193, § 806).

71 NMa_1 I: p. 5–8 = NMa_2 1, I: p. 7–9.

treatises (*dharma-śāstra*)—this is the fourteen disciplines of learning".'[72]

It is difficult to determine the exact date when the tradition to distinguish fourteen sciences and disciplines of learning was settled down and became widespread. It must have been current and well known already at the time of the composition of the *Nyāya-bhāṣya*, for it mentioned by Kālidāsa (fifth century) in the *Raghu-vaṁśa* (RghV 5.21). It is further mentioned by Kumārila-bhaṭṭa in the *Tantra-vārttika* (TV 1.3.6), the *Viṣṇu-purāṇa*[73], *Yajñavālkya-smṛti*[74], the *Sarva-darśana-siddhānta-saṁgraha* (SDSS 1.2–25) and even by Madhusūdana Sarasvatī in the *Prasthāna-bheda* ($PrBh_1$ 13.4–14 = $PrBh_2$ 1.6–12: *...iti catur-daśā vidhāḥ*), who tries to combine it with the eighteenfold classification. The constitutive elements of the classification were not universal and would change from text to text, albeit with some elements uniform, but the number 'fourteen' remained the same. Why should therefore Vātsyāyana wish to equate Nyāya with Ānvīkṣikī, had such a connection not existed, and to classify his philosophical school under the guise of Ānvīkṣikī among the four disciplines in the way which has almost become obsolete by his times?

Second, by the 400–450 CE Sāṁkhya was not dead yet, as HACKER (1958: 19–20) claims: their proponents, Īśvarakṛṣṇa, Vārṣagaṇya and Vindhyavāsin, were just composing the *Sāṁkhya-kārikā* and other texts, no longer extant, and some century or so later was also the *Yukti-dīpikā* to come. Therefore, the place for reasoners within the folds of Ānvīkṣikī—beside Yoga and the materialists (*lokāyata*)—as HACKER wanted, occupied so far by Sāṁkhya was still occupied by it. Third, granted that the place of the followers of Sāṁkhya and of the Lokāyata had become empty by the time of Pakṣilasvāmin Vātsyāyana, there was still the place occupied by the followers of Yoga (which hardly had anything to do with methodology in the sense of rational enquiry), who had just produced the *Pātañjala-yoga-śāstra* comprising the *Yoga-sūtra* and the *Yoga-bhāṣya*, if we follow the reasoning of HACKER. Fourth, what is most important, when we read the surviving few references to Ānvīkṣikī, especially

---

[72] NMa_2 I: 5–8 = NMa_2 1, I: 7–9, and the verses NMa_1 1, I: 9.5–9 = NMa_2 1: *Vidyā-sthāna-rūpa-vicāra*, I: 9.4–8:

> *purāṇa-tarka-mīmāṁsā-dharma-śāstrâṅgam iśritāḥ /*
> *vedāḥ sthānāni vidyānāṁ dharmasya ca catur-daśa iti /*

anyatrâpy uktam:

> *aṅgāni vedāś catvāro mīmāṁsā nyāya-vistaraḥ /*
> *purāṇaṁ dharma-śāstraṁ ca vidyā hy etāś catur-daśa iti //*

[73] ViP 3.6.28:

> *aṅgāni vedaś catvāro mīmāṁsā nyāya-vistaraḥ /*
> *purāṇaṁ dharma-śāstraṁ ca vidyā hy etāś catur-daśa //*

[74] YDhŚ 1.3:

> *purāṇa-nyāya-mīmāṁsā-dharma-śāstrâṅgam iśritāṁ /*
> *vedān sthānāni vidyānāṁ dharmasya ca catur-daśa //*

those in the *Mahā-bhārata*, they are not at all favourably disposed to Ānvīkṣikī. As I pointed out earlier (§ 5, esp. § 5.3), Ānvīkṣikī was rarely mentioned in literary sources and often left out of classifications of the fundamental disciplines of learning, even though its methodological impact was felt in the classifications and descriptions of sciences. Had Vātsyāyana wanted to upgrade the status of his own school of Nyāya in the eyes of, say, orthodox Brahmins he would certainly not have equated it with the tradition of Ānvīkṣikī, because the result would be counterproductive.

In the light of the above, there seems to be no reason to read Vātsyāyana the way proposed by HACKER and HALBFASS, who seems to accept the former's arguments, in the sense that Vātsyāyana fills in an empty space left by the tradition of Sāṁkhya as a discipline of reasoning, and Vātsyāyana comes to equate his own Nyāya with an older tradition. Further I find no justification why we should not take what Vātsyāyana himself says of his own tradition at its face value. What he actually says merely emphasises that his tradition of Nyāya developed from the tradition of Ānvīkṣikī and it is the latter's legitimate and direct successor. I claim, therefore, that it was precisely the other way round—in contrast with the development suggested by HACKER and HALBFASS: Nyāya, along with its twin system of Vaiśeṣika, was closely associated with Ānvīkṣikī from its very beginnings to the extent that it actually developed directly from that tradition. And it was a natural move for Vātsyāyana to equate, in the verse taken from Kauṭilya (AŚ 1.2.12), the term *ānvīkṣikī* with his own tradition, called just before the verse *nyāya-vidyā*.

As Karin PREISENDANZ (2000: 230–237) successfully argued, certain Naiyāyikas included two sequences of *sūtra*s at the conclusion of *Nyāya-sūtra* 4.2—viz. NS 4.2.38–45, 46–50—which specifically concern some self-oriented yogic practices, in order to align their system with certain salvific tenets of the *Upaniṣad*s that focused on the *adhyātma-vidyā*. These two inclusions were clearly intended to shift the focus from debate and rational enquiry, i.e. the chief preoccupation of Ānvīkṣikī, to which the original *Nyāya-sūtra* was devoted, to the extramundane and salvific, and subsequently 'Vātsyāyana, next to anchoring his philosophical tradition in a prestigious secular classification of science and in the most excellent position to boot, is concerned to accommodate it with the established religious tradition and place it, so to say, in line with the *Upaniṣad*s. The *Nyāyasūtra* does not address the topic specifically and explicitly…' (PREISENDANZ (2000: 230)).

9.3. There are a number of additional points, apart from Vātsyāyana's own testimony, that strengthen the thesis of direct historical link between the two traditions.

First of all, as I have indicated above, there is conspicuously a very close affinity in the approach of Ānvīkṣikī and Nyāya to problems they investigate, mainly—from what we can say on the basis of the laconic account in the *Artha-*

śāstra—concerning the idea of doubt, brought to the fore by Kauṭilya in his highly condensed exposition of Ānvīkṣikī.

Further, it seems that the *Caraka-saṁhitā*, which stands in the line of development of Indian epistemology and methodology which eventually led to the Nyāya school, contains a passage that could have been influenced by the metaphor of Ānvīkṣikī as the lamp for disciplines of learning. The passage runs as follows:

> '[13] It is not accepted that the creation of beginningless element of consciousness [within a living body] is created through something else [such as matter]. If this "something else" is the highest self, it is accepted as the cause [of consciousness in the body and rebirth]; it must [therefore] be accepted that the creation is caused by something else, [which is the highest self]. ... [16] Therefore, a wise person, having abandoned [heretic] opinions which have gone the wrong way, should view the whole [world] correctly with the help of the lamp of reason of the good [people].'[75]

The context of the second verse is delineated by the first verse that concerns the highest self, here called *para ātmā*, which is precisely the domain of *adhyātma-vidyā*, later mentioned by Vātsyāyana as a field of investigation common to *Upaniṣad*s and to Nyāya. What this verse expresses is a belief that behind the whole world there must be 'the highest self'. Then comes the conclusion that the wise person should apply 'the lamp of reason' (*buddhi-pradīpa*) to see the whole world the way it really is (*yathātatham*). This metaphor betrays close affinity to the metaphor of 'the lamp of Ānvīkṣikī' mentioned in the verse by Kauṭilya (n. 25) and, later on, by Vātsyāyana (n. 54).

Of importance is the fact the immediate context in which these verses, which seem to relate to stand in some relation to Ānvīkṣikī, occur betrays close affinity to some ideas characteristic of Nyāya. First, it is the discussion and enumeration of cognitive criteria (*pramāṇa*), without the term *pramāṇa* itself being mentioned:

> 'Everything is only twofold: either true or false. Its examination is fourfold: the teaching of an authoritative person, perception, inference and argumentation.'[76]

---

[75] CarS$_1$ 1.11.5, pp. 488, 490= CarS$_2$ 1.11.13, 16, pp. 208–209:
anādeś cetanā-dhātor nêṣyate para-nirmitiḥ /
para ātmā sa ced dhetur iṣṭo 'stu para-nirmitiḥ // 13 //
tasmān matiṁ vimucyâitām amārga-prasṛtāṁ budhaḥ /
satāṁ buddhi-pradīpena paśyet sarvaṁ yathātatham // 16 //

[76] CarS$_1$ 1.11, pp. 490–491 = CarS$_2$ 1.11.17, p. 210: *dvividham eva khalu sarvaṁ sac câsac ca. tasya caturvidhā parīkṣā—āptôpadeśaḥ pratyakṣam anumānaṁ yuktiś cêti.*

This list in most elements overlaps with the classification of the four cognitive criteria of Nyāya, except for argumentation (*yukti*)—replaced with the reasoning based on analogy (*upamāna*) in Nyāya—which is defined by Caraka as follows:

> 'Such a cognition which apprehends entities originating as a result of a combination of numerous causes and which refers to the three times is known as argumentation, and thereby the three aims of life can be achieved.'[77]

Even though overridden by *upamāna*, *yukti* is still referred to in Nyāya as a methodical devise of reasoning: 'The argumentation of one's system is this: another person's view, when it is not contradicted, is accepted,'[78] and has not been totally eliminated from the system.

Secondly, the author of the *Caraka-saṁhitā* passage understands the nature of perception exactly the way Nyāya and Vaiśeṣika did:

> 'Such a cognition which proceeds as a result of the contact of the self, sense-organ, the mind and the object, which is manifested at the same time, is defined as perception.'[79]

The idea evoked in the verse draws on the contact (*sannikarṣa*) of the four elements for ordinary sensory perception to take place: the self (*ātman*) which is believed to be the ultimate cognitive subject, a sense organ (*indriya*) grasping the physical data, the mind (*manas*) which connects the sense organ with the self, and the external object (*artha*) being cognised.

This is identical with what is regarded as a quasi-definition of perception in the *Vaiśeṣika-sūtra*:

> '[Perception] which arisen from the contact of the self, a sense organ, the mind and an object is still another [reason to prove the existence of the self].'[80]

Even the wording in both the sources matches, except for minor metrical differences: *ātmêndriya-mano-'rthānāṁ sannikarṣāt* in the *Caraka-saṁhitā* and *ātmêndriya-mano-'rtha-sannikarṣāt* in the *Vaiśeṣika-sūtra*. The formulation also corresponds to the definition of perception found in the *Nyāya-sūtra*:

---

[77] $CarS_1$ 1.11, pp. 518 = $CarS_2$ 1.11.25, p. 213:
buddhiḥ paśyati yā bhāvān bahu-kāraṇa-yoga-jān /
yuktis tri-kālā sā jñeya tri-vargaḥ sādhyate yayā //

[78] NBh 1.1.3: *para-matam apratiṣiddham anumatam iti hi tantra-yuktiḥ.*

[79] $CarS_1$ 1.11, pp. 501 = $CarS_2$ 1.11.20, p. 211:
ātmêndriya-mano-'rthānāṁ sannikarṣāt pravartate /
vyaktā tadātve yā buddhiḥ pratyakṣaṁ sā nirucyate //

[80] VS(C) 3.1.13: *ātmêndriya-mano-'rtha-sannikarṣād yan niṣpadyate tad-anyat.*

> 'Perception is cognition which is produced by the contact of an object with a sense organ, which is non-verbal, which is non-deviant, which consists in determination;'[81]

It also seems that the idea expressed in the *Caraka-saṁhitā* agrees with the notion of non-simultaneity of acts of perception, which involve all the four elements, the description of which is found in the *Nyāya-bhāṣya*:

> '[NS] [Skin] is not [the only sense organ], because [different] objects are not simultaneously perceived. [NBh] [In the case of perception] the self comes into contact with the mind, the mind with [one] sense organ, the sense organ is conjoined with all objects. Therefore, [if we were to accept the opponent's thesis], there should be simultaneous acts of perception [of all the objects, such as the colour, taste, smell, touch and sound,] because of the contact of the self, sense organs, the mind and the objects. But [such numerous objects as] the colour etc. are not perceived simultaneously. Therefore, it is not the case that there is one sense organ which grasps all sensory data.'[82]

Also the process of inference described in the *Caraka-saṁhitā* passage which may be related to Ānvīkṣikī bears resemblance to the ideas of the Nyāya, including some formulations which are close to the wording of the *Nyāya-sūtra*:

> 'One infers in a threefold manner and in three times something that is preceded by perception. A concealed fire [at present is inferred] from smoke. A sexual intercourse [in the past is inferred] from the observation of the foetus (sc. pregnancy)—in this way [people] determine something that happened in the past. The wise, having seen a fruit that has already been produced from a seed, similarly infer in the present situation (*iha*) a future fruit [produced] from a seed.'[83]

---

[81] NS 1.1.4: *indriyârtha-sannikarṣôtpannaṁ jñānam avyapadeśyam avyabhicāri vyavasāyâtmakaṁ pratyakṣam.*

[82] NS_1 3.1.54 = NS_1 3.1.53: *na yugapad-arthânupalabdheḥ.* NBh *ad loc.*: *ātmā manasā sambadhyate, mana indriyeṇa, indriyaṁ sarvârthaiḥ sannikṛṣṭam iti ātmêndriya-mano-'rtha-sannikarṣebhyo yugapad-grahaṇāni syuḥ. na ca yugapad rūpâdayo gṛhyante. tasmān nâikam indriyaṁ sarva-viṣayam astîti.*

[83] $CarS_1$ 1.11, pp. 514 = $CarS_2$ 1.11.2–12, p. 212:

pratyakṣa-pūrvaṁ tri-vidhaṁ tri-kālaṁ cânumīyate /
vahnir nigūḍho dhūmena maithunaṁ garbha-darśanāt //
evaṁ vyavasyanty atītaṁ bījāt phalam anāgatam /
dṛṣṭvā bījāt phalaṁ jātam ihâiva sadṛśaṁ buddhāḥ //

These three kinds of inference correspond to a threefold obsolete classification of ancient origin and preserved in *Nyāya-sūtra* 1.1.5,[84] which is extremely ambiguous in itself and allows for more than one interpretation. The *Caraka-saṁhitā* may even resemble the *Nyāya-sūtra* classification especially in the form of the first interpretation offered by Pakṣilasvāmin Vātsyāyana, who himself was no longer certain as to the actual meaning of the three terms: *pūrvavat* (inference *a priori*), *śeṣavat* (inference *a posteriori*) and *sāmānyato-dṛṣṭa* / *sāmānyato-'dṛṣṭa* (inference based on general (non-)observation).

> 'Inference *a priori* is when one infers an effect from a [present] cause, for instance: from the accumulation of clouds [one infers that] it will rain. Inference *a posteriori* is when one infers a [past] cause from [a present] effect, [for instance]: having seen [the high level of] water which stands in contrast with [low] water [level] seen previously as well as swollenness and swiftness of the river, one infers from its current that it has rained [up the river]. Inference based on general observation is the following: one observes in one place an object, when there is motion, seen before in another place; and so is the case with the sun; therefore the sun is in motion, albeit invisible.'[85]

We cannot be sure whether the explanations offered by Vātsyāyana were accurate any more than he was uncertain, because he offered two parallel interpretations (the latter logically and structurally more advanced). However, Vātsyāyana's inference *a priori* corresponds to *Caraka*'s inference of a future fruit from the present seed, inference *a posteriori* matches *Caraka*'s inference of a sexual intercourse in the past from present pregnancy, and the final inference based on general observation conforms to the inference of the movement of the sun. Even if Vātsyāyana's interpretations were not faithful in every detail to what Akṣapāda Gautama had in mind, they do reflect the general spirit of the nature of the three kinds of inference defined in the *Caraka-saṁhitā*.

The above is, in fact, the only 'lamp metaphor' found in the oldest *Caraka-saṁhitā* sections that relates to epistemology and logical enquiry in any way and that may lead us to believe that this does not have to be coincidental. The only other occurrence of a metaphor of a lamp in the treatise concerns medicine, but even then it is 'the lamp of knowledge and understanding', being an

---

[84] NS 1.1.5: *atha tat-pūrvakaṁ tri-vidham anumānaṁ pūrvavac cheṣavat sāmānyato-dṛṣṭaṁ ca.*

[85] NBh 1.1.5: *pūrvavad iti. yatra kāraṇena kāryam anumīyate. yathā meghônnatyā bhaviṣyati vṛṣṭir iti. śeṣavat tad yatra kāryeṇa kāraṇam anumīyate. pūrvôdaka-viparītam udakaṁ nadyāḥ pūrṇatvaṁ śīghratvaṁ ca dṛṣṭvā srotaso 'numīyate bhūtā vṛṣṭir iti. sāmānyato-dṛṣṭam vrajyā-pūrvakam anyatra dṛṣṭasyânyatra darśanam iti, tathā câdityasya, tasmād asty apratyakṣâpy ādityasya vrajyêti.*

instrument of knowledge to investigate the inner self (*antar-ātman*), which looks like an offshoot of the 'study of the (highest) self', i.e. (*adhy*)*ātma-vidyā*:

> 'The one who knows the truth but does not enquire into the inner self of the sick one with the help of the lamp of knowledge and understanding cannot cure any diseases.'[86]

We can see that the same metaphor that makes use of the lamp which is a particular kind of knowledge and insight in the nature of things and illuminates a respective sphere of reference occurs in the *Artha-śāstra*, *Caraka-saṁhitā* (strongly modified) and in the *Nyāya-bhāṣya*.

To recapitulate, the verses from the *Caraka-saṁhitā* contain references to the study of (*adhy*)*ātma-vidyā*, known to be related to Ānvīkṣikī, and to the metaphor of 'a lamp of reason' that allows one to see things the way they really are, a metaphor which informed Kauṭilya's way of describing Ānvīkṣikī as the lamp for disciplines of learning and was probably later adopter by the authors of the *Caraka-saṁhitā*. These two elements entitle us, in view of otherwise extreme scarcity of material related to Ānvīkṣikī, to tentatively link the verses to the current of Ānvīkṣikī and to its successor Nyāya. There seems to be much in the way of support of the claim that the systems of Nyāya and Vaiśeṣika were related to Ānvīkṣikī—both through the rational method of enquiry (*tarka*, *nyāya*) and the specific subject matter of liberation (*adhyātma-vidyā*/*ātma-vidyā*)—perhaps even more than the systems of Sāṁkhya and Yoga, but what is indeed puzzling is that Kauṭilya did not bother to mention neither Nyāya nor Vaiśeṣika in his catalogue of the representatives of Ānvīkṣikī.

10. Let us now see how far Pakṣilasvāmin Vātsyāyana's (see p. 194 and n. 50), but also Bhāsarvajña's (see p. 175 and n. 7), assertions to the effect that Ānvīkṣikī is a discipline which, apart from its systemic concerns and methodological applications, investigates the highest self (*adhyātma-vidyā*) and, by implication, the means of liberation (*mokṣa*), find their justification in other sources, external to the system of Nyāya-Vaiśeṣika, which could confirm their veracity. These are not plenty, but fortunately there are a few.

The *Nīti-sāra* has already been mentioned (n. 22) as a source describing Ānvīkṣikī as investigation or knowledge of the self (NīSā 2.7a: *ānvīkṣiky ātma-vijñānaṁ*; NīSā 2.11a: *ānvīkṣiky ātma-vidyā syād*), and so has the *Manu-smṛti* to the same effect (MDhŚ 7.43c: *ānvīkṣikīṁ câtma-vidyāṁ*). With the expressions such as *ātma-vijñāna* or *ātma-vidyā*, these passages clearly understand Ānvīkṣikī as a discipline engaged in the examination of the self, and the compounds do not constitute just a reference to a separate fifth discipline *ātma-vijñāna*, different from Ānvīkṣikī, but the terms *ātma-vijñāna* or *ātma-*

---

[86] Car 3.4.12:

jñāna-buddhi-pradīpena yo nâviśati tattvavit /
āturasyântar-ātmānaṁ na sa rogāṁś cikitsati //

vidyā are attributive and qualify Ānvīkṣikī. There can be no doubt that in the verse of *Manu-smṛti* 7.43 the authors do not enumerate five but only four disciplines of learning. Similarly, Vijñeśvara in his *Mitâkṣarā* (YDhŚM), a mediaeval South-Indian commentary on the *Yājñavalkya-smṛti*, equates Ānvīkṣikī with the salvific doctrine that teaches about the highest self in exactly the same manner as all other texts, attesting to the fact that salvific reflection of the current was well remembered all over India even at a later date.[87]

There is an interesting passage in the *Mahā-bhārata* (MBh 12.306.27–55) which directly concerns Ānvīkṣikī, its methods and its subject matter.[88] The story presents a conversation between the sage Yājñavalkya and Viśvāvasu, a king of Gandharvas, recounted by the former. Viśvāvasu asks Yājñavalkya a number of questions on various subjects, until he comes to the final broad theme he wants to enquire about, which is Ānvīkṣikī, a theme which culminates a series of twenty-five questions. The number twenty-five is not a coincidence: it concerns the self (*puruṣa*), the twenty-fifth and highest principle of Sāṁkhya-Yoga, and the numeric placement of Ānvīkṣikī which culminates the series of enquires and corresponds to the rank of the self in the system of Sāṁkhya-Yoga thereby reflecting the hierarchical primacy and importance of Ānvīkṣikī. The beginning of the passage runs as follows:

> '[27] O King, thereupon, [desirous to know the highest knowledge and what is beneficial, Gandharva] Viśvāvasu, well-versed in the knowledge of Vedānta, asked [me, Yājñavalkya,] twenty-four questions relating to the *Vedas*. And then he asked me about methodology (*ānvīkṣikī*) as the twenty-fifth question: [28] What is that made of the universe and the non-universe? What is the mare and the stallion? What is Mitra and Varuṇa? What is cognition, what is the cognoscible? Similarly, what is the one who knows? What is the one who does not know? What is Ka? What is the one who engages in asceticism and what is the one who does not engage in asceticism? What is the devourer of the sun and what is the sun? What is [salvific] knowledge and what is nescience? [29] What is the object of knowledge? What is that which cannot be known, O King? What is the movable? What is the immovable? What is that which is without a beginning? What is that which is indestructible? What is that which is destructible?—These are the profound questions [about Ānvīkṣikī asked by the Gandharva Viśvāvasu]. [30] Then, O King, I replied to the king, most virtuous of Gandharvas, who asked one profound question after another, of deep significance: [31] "Forgive

[87] MiA *ad loc.*, p. 98.10–11: *ānvīkṣikyāṁ ātma-vidyām*.

[88] See also DAHLMANN (1895: 225 ff.) who points out to the relationship between the salvific doctrine about the highest self (*ātma-vidyā*) and Ānvīkṣikī in the *Mahā-bhārata*.

> me for a while, till I reflect on these [questions]." "So be it", having so assented, the Gandharva remained quiet. [32] Then, I again summoned the goddess Sarasvatī with my mind. [As a result, the replies to] these questions arose, like butter drawn up [by churning milk]. [33] O King, taking recourse to supreme methodology (*ānvīkṣikī*), I churned with my mind the *Upaniṣad*s and ancillary [Vedic] texts. [34] The fourth discipline of learning, O Tiger-King, treats of eschatology (liberation)—I explained it [to you,] O King [already]: it is concerned with the twenty-fifth [principle, viz. the self (*puruṣa*)]. [35] Then, I said the king Viśvāvasu: Listen, O Lord, about the questions you asked me here. [36] [Out of] the universe and the non-universe, which you, O Gandharva King, asked me about, notice that the universe is the unmanifest [primordial factor (*prakṛti*)], the highest [principle] which brings existence and fear to living beings.'[89]

The subsequent verses (MBh 12.306.37–55) explain the nature of *prakṛti* and *puruṣa* in the spirit of Sāṁkhya-Yoga, and map all the terms that appear in Viśvāvasu's questions onto the principles of *prakṛti* and *puruṣa*.

---

[89] MBh 12.306.27–36:

viśvāvasus tato rājan vedānta-jñāna-kovidaḥ /
catur-viṁśatikān praśnān pṛṣṭvā vedasya pārthiva /
pañca-viṁśatimaṁ praśnaṁ papraccha ***ānvīkṣikīṁ*** *tathā // 27 //*
viśvâviśvaṁ tathâśvâśvam mitraṁ varuṇam eva ca /
jñānaṁ jñeyaṁ tathā jño 'jñaḥ[†] *kas tapā atapās tathā /*
sūryâdaḥ sūrya iti ca vidyâvidye tathâiva ca // 28 //
vedyâvedyaṁ tathā rājann acalaṁ calam eva ca /
apūrvam akṣayaṁ kṣayyam etat praśnam anuttamam // 29 //
athôktaś ca mayā rājan rājā gandharva-sattamaḥ /
pṛṣṭavān anupūrveṇa praśnam uttamam arthavat // 30 //
muhūrtam mṛṣyatām tāvad yāvad enam vicintaye /
bāḍham ity eva kṛtvā sa tūṣṇīm gandharva āsthitaḥ // 31 //
tato 'nvacintayam ahaṁ bhūyo devīṁ sarasvatīm /
manasā sa ca me praśno daghno ghṛtam iva uddhṛtam // 32 //
tatrôpaniṣadaṁ câiva pariśeṣaṁ ca pārthiva /
mathnāmi manasā tāta dṛṣṭvā ***cânvīkṣikīṁ*** *parām // 33 //*
caturthī rāja-śārdūla vidyâiṣā sāṁparāyikī /
udīritā mayā tubhyam pañca-viṁśe 'dhi dhiṣṭhitā // 34 //
athôktas tu mayā rājan rājā viśvāvasus tadā /
śrūyatām yad bhavān asmān praśnaṁ saṁpṛṣṭavān iha // 35 //
viśvâviśvêti yad idaṁ gandharvêndrânupṛcchasi /
viśvâvyaktaṁ paraṁ vidyād bhūta-bhavya-bhayaṁkaram // 36 //

[†] The edition reads: *tathâjño 'jñaḥ*, however it should be emended as *tathâjño jñaḥ* (in accordance with MBh 12.306.39c: *ajñaś ca jñaś ca*) or, less likely, *tathā-jño 'jñaḥ*, to the same effect.

The philosophical and conceptual setting is clearly that of Sāṁkhya-Yoga, which rather unsurprisingly reveals the link between these and Ānvīkṣikī already known from the *Artha-śāstra*. This link with the classification of sciences in the *Artha-śāstra* is highlighted by the expression 'the fourth discipline' (*caturthī vidyā*) in Kauṭilya's catalogue, which clearly is Ānvīkṣikī. Like Sāṁkhya-Yoga, Ānvīkṣikī is presented here as a discipline engaged in the study of the human fate and with the passage from this world into the other (*sāṁparāyikin*), i.e. eschatology, which in the Upaniṣadic context cannot but be the enquiry of liberation. The questions about the ultimate posed by Viśvāvasu were apparently considered quite esoteric and challenging, and that difficulty and profundity is emphasised by the sage Yājñavalkya's initial silence and consequent supplication to Sarasvatī, the goddess of learning and wisdom. Such profound questions required extraordinary tools and methodology, and Ānvīkṣikī was considered to be the answer. The structure of Viśvāvasu's most questions follows a similar binary pattern of doubt based on two contrary attributes: what is P and what is non-P, which resembles the structure typical of Ānvīkṣikī enquiry discussed above in § 6, which additionally confirms that the passage is an echo of the method of Ānvīkṣikī.

Towards the end of the whole passage, strongly rooted in Sāṁkhya-Yoga terminology, we come across another explicit mention of Ānvīkṣikī, which repeats the same information about its subject matter and method:

> [44] … [The wise] call the unmanifest [primordial factor (*prakṛti*)] the unborn, because it is indestructible among the created things; [the wise] call the conscious principle (*puruṣa*) indestructible, because there exists no destruction for it; [45] [indestructible is likewise] the primordial factor (*prakṛti*), because it is the qualities (*guṇa*) which undergo destruction, and because [the primordial factor (*prakṛti*)] is active; the wise [call] it the indestructible. All that precisely is the fourth discipline of learning [known as] m e t h o d o l o g y (*ānvīkṣikī*), which treats of eschatology (liberation). [46] When one has assigned the wealth acquired through [the application of] the discipline of learning (i.e. Ānvīkṣikī) for [the performance] of obligatory rites through one's ritual acts, all the *Veda*s, with their individual schools, are regularly studied, O Viswavasu.'[90]

[90] MBh 12.306.44–46:

akṣayatvāt prajanane 'jam atrâhur avyayam /
akṣayaṁ puruṣaṁ prāhuḥ kṣayo hy asya na vidyate // 44 //
guṇa-kṣayatvāt prakṛtiḥ kartṛtvād akṣayaṁ budhāḥ /
*eṣā te '**nvīkṣikī** vidyā caturthī sāṁparāyikī // 45 //*
vidyôpetaṁ dhanaṁ kṛtvā karmaṇā nitya-karmaṇi /
ekānta-darśanā vedāḥ sarve viśvāvaso smṛtāḥ // 46 //

Verse 46 underscores the link with the *Artha-śāstra*: Ānvīkṣikī serves here to accumulate wealth and to regulate Vedic ritual and tradition, which are the realms of economics and religious reflection respectively, and correspond to Kauṭilya's *vārttā* and *trayī*. The only missing discipline of learning is political science (*daṇḍa-nīti*). This is not so surprising in an epic verse on Sāṁkhya-Yoga which neither strives to be philosophically accurate nor attempts to give a reliable account of Ānvīkṣikī as known to Kauṭilya.

The concluding verse of the whole discourse on Ānvīkṣikī ends with explicitly ascribing the views expressed in it to the followers of Sāṁkhya-Yoga treated jointly:

> 'Therefore, the followers of Yoga and the followers of Sāṁkhya, who strife for the highest goal, do not regard this collection of twenty-five principles as imperishable.'[91]

The placing of Ānvīkṣikī in the context of the exposition of the doctrine of the system of Sāṁkhya-Yoga and treating it as an indispensable analytical tool to investigate its fundamental principles is a clear indication of immanent relation between the two. The passage also confirms what the proponents of Nyāya, such as Vātsyāyana and Bhāsarvajña, claimed that Ānvīkṣikī investigated into eschatological matters and one—but not necessarily the only one—of its foci was liberation.

The link between yogic practice of meditation (*dhyānâbhyāsa*), the focus on the highest self (*adhyātman*) and methodical examination finds incidental mention in a passage of the *Mahā-bhārata* about

> … '[the wind Parivaha] which is favourable to immortality of those who examine (*anvīkṣant*) properly [and] happily engage in continuous practice of meditation with tranquil minds which are constantly focused on the highest self (*adhyātman*).'[92]

Another evidence is provided by the *Bhāgavata-purāṇa* which, despite some verses inimically disposed *vis-à-vis* Ānvīkṣikī, mentions the term on a few occasions, and undoubtedly in a favourable light. In one passage, the sage Nārada, while describing the forest recluse (*vāna-prastha*) of the four orthodox life stages (*āśrama*), advises:

> 'When [the forest recluse] is not able to perform his duties with respect to the m e t h o d o l o g i c a l k n o w l e d g e

---

[91] MBh 12.306.55:

tenâtan nâbhijānanti pañca-viṁśakam acyutam /
janma-mṛtyu-bhayād yogāḥ sāṁkhyāś ca paramâiṣiṇaḥ // 55 //

[92] MBh 12.315.50:

samyag ***anvīkṣatāṁ*** *buddhyā śāntayâdhyātma-nityayā /*
dhyānâbhyāsâbhirāmāṇām yo 'mṛtatvāya kalpate //

> (*ānvīkṣikī vidyā*), either because of disease or old age, he should refrain from food etc.'[93]

Clearly, Ānvīkṣikī is put on in this verse par with such important religious duties as maintaining one's own personal fire sacrifice to an extent that a failure to rehearse it should incur special sanction. Nārada comes to speak of Ānvīkṣikī again, and again in clearly positive terms:

> 'Through methodology [one can conquer (*jayet*)] sorrow and delusion, through worship [one can overcome] deceit, through silence [one can remove] other obstacles to [the practice of] *yoga*, through indifference to sensual pleasures etc. [one can triumph over] the harming [of other beings].'[94]

Ānvīkṣikī is seen here as essential means to overcome mundane distress and ignorance by providing adequate forms of worship and ascetic rigourous methods suitable to accomplish mystical and religious goals.

In addition, the *Bhāgavata-purāṇa* also contains a warning against forsaking Ānvīkṣikī, which is superior to sacrifices and is apparently understood to be instrumental in crossing the ocean of rebirth, i.e. to lead to liberation:

> '[The renegade cowherds] abandon the methodological knowledge (*ānvīkṣikī vidyā*) and wish to cross the ocean of rebirth with what is relatively mighty sacrificial rites, consisting of ritual actions, resembling boats [to cross waters].'[95]

The 'renegades' are those who denounce the righteous path and erroneously take rituals for something they cannot provide: the path to liberation, in which Ānvīkṣikī, by implication, can apparently be advantageous.

Ānvīkṣikī even turns out to be one of three kinds of crucial spiritual practice through which an adept of *yoga* maintains inner equilibrium on the path to ultimate self-realisation:

> 'One should remember [to maintain one's] mind fit through the stages of the *yoga* practice such as restraint etc., and through the

---

[93] BhāgP 7.12.23:

yadâkalpaḥ svakriyāyāṁ vyādhibhir jarayâthavā /
ānvīkṣikyāṁ vā vidyāyāṁ kuryād anaśanādikam //

[94] BhāgP 7.15.23:

ānvīkṣikyā śoka-mohau dambhaṁ mahad-upāsayā /
yogântarāyān maunena hiṁsāṁ kāmâdy-anīhayā //

[95] BhāgP 10.25.4:

yathā-dṛḍhaiḥ karma-mayaiḥ kratubhir nāma nau-nibhaiḥ /
vidyām ānvīkṣikīṁ hitvā titīrṣanti bhavârṇavam //

> methodological knowledge (*ānvīkṣikī vidyā*), or through the worship and adoration of my self, not through any other means.'[96]

In another verse Kṛṣṇa, the protagonist of the *Bhāgavata-purāṇa*, while presenting his pivotal role and supreme status, comes to speak of Ānvīkṣikī as the foremost among all kinds of skills and disciplines of learning:

> '[Kṛṣṇa said:] I am the most profound self-control among all kinds of *yoga*, I am the sacred incantation for all those who strive after victory, I am the methodology among all kinds of proficiencies, I am the conceptualisation for the propounders of the theory of presentation.'[97]

In some of these verses we can easily observe that the term *ānvīkṣikī* has undergone a metamorphosis and changed both its meaning and grammar: it is no longer associated with rational enquiry and rigorous reasoning (*tarka*, *nyāya*) and further, in addition to its substantive meaning, it assumes an adjectival aspect qualifying salvific knowledge (*vidyā*), hence 'the methodological knowledge' (*ānvīkṣikī vidyā*). The current has thus escaped oblivion, managed to elevate its status and come to serve religious and sectarian purposes in a new fashion, providing a method to cross the *saṁsāra*, or being the method *per se*, and thus retaining, in a way, its eschatological dimension of which Pakṣilasvāmin Vātsyāyana spoke.

11.1. I have briefly indicated above that the Yoga we know was a discipline primarily concerned with meditative practice and mystical exercise that is believed to be instrumental in achieving final liberation from the mundane world and suffering and hardly had anything to do with rational and analytical enquiry. Hence arises the difficulty: Yoga as we know it does not fit well into Kauṭilya's classification of the branches that apply the reasoners' methods of Ānvīkṣikī, albeit in its essence it is concerned primarily with liberation. In its epistemology, especially as far as inference (*anumāna*) is concerned, Yoga hardly developed its own approach and was heavily reliant on the legacy of Sāṁkhya in this respect. To find its name among the sciences enumerated by Kauṭilya under such circumstances is rather surprising.

At the same time, the compound *sāṁkhya-yoga* was well established in Indian literature. Whether we can speak of an undifferentiated / composite Sāṁkhya-Yoga tradition or of two distinct traditions more or less closely related, it seems that basically all occurrences of the compound *sāṁkhya-yoga* refer to the tra-

---

[96] BhāgP 11.20.24:
yamâdibhir yoga-pathair ānvīkṣikyā ca vidyayā /
mamârcôpāsanābhir vā nânyair yogyaṁ smaren manaḥ //

[97] BhāgP 11.16.24:
yogānām ātma-saṁrodho mantro 'smi vijigīṣatām /
ānvīkṣikī kauśalānāṁ vikalpaḥ khyāti-vādinām //

dition of Sāṁkhya and Yoga, whatever their exact relation in a given case was.[98] Alone the *Mahā-bhārata* contains approximately 25 occurrences of the compound, and I have counted about 50 verses in which the terms *sāṁkhya* and *yoga* are mentioned side by side, not necessarily in a compounded form *sāṁkhya-yoga*. We could easily conclude, as all translators of the *Artha-śāstra* and an overwhelming majority of researchers did, that the Yoga of Kauṭilya is the same branch as the Yoga related to Sāṁkhya as the latter's correlate. The only problem with such interpretation is that all we know of the nature of the system of Yoga does not quite fit into the general picture of Ānvīkṣikī and, on the basis of this incompatibility, the obvious meaning of the term as it features in the *Artha-śāstra* should be treated at least with suspicion. Or rather, as I will demonstrated in the following, it should be rejected. So, what is actually the Yoga of *Artha-śāstra*?

11.2. In view of all the interpretative difficulties related to the problem what systems were actually included in the list of the *Artha-śāstra*, I propose that the *yoga* in Kauṭilya's list refers to an early form of Vaiśeṣika-Nyāya, a kind of 'proto-Nyāya-Vaiśeṣika', which later evolved into two distinct schools, whereas the *sāṁkhya* of the list is a shorthand for the conjoint systems of Sāṁkhya–Yoga. The identification of Sāṁkhya as one of the schools comprised in the *Artha-śāstra* list is beyond any controversy. Its link to Ānvīkṣikī confirms general knowledge preserved in external sources such as the *Bhāgavata-purāṇa*, which reports a myth of the beginnings of Sāṁkhya:

> '[10] Fifth, [god Brahmā] under the name of Kapila, the lord of the accomplished ones, passed on to Āsuri [the doctrine of] Sāṁkhya, which is an exposition of an array of ontological principles but which had gone astray in the course of time. [11] Sixth, when he gained birth as the son of Atri from Anasūyā, he taught about methodology (*ānvīkṣikī*) to Alarka, Prahlāda and others.'[99]

As we read there, it was precisely the knowledge of Ānvīkṣikī which was passed on by the mythical or legendary founders of the system to their disciples, and it seems that the rational reflection and enquiry representative of Ānvīkṣikī constituted an important part of the system.

There are some scholars who have questioned the identification of *yoga* in Kauṭilya's list with the system of Yoga before, although without giving any

---

[98] For various shades and occurrences of the term *sāṁkhya-yoga* and its tradition see, e.g. LARSON (1979: 44, 72, 88, 95, 99, 107, 121–122, 127–128, 137, 288 f.).

[99] BhāgP 1.3.10–11:

pañcamaḥ kapilo nāma siddhêśaḥ kāla-viplutam /
provācâsuraye sāṅkhyaṁ tattva-grāma-vinirṇayam //
ṣaṣṭham atrer apatyatvaṁ vṛtaḥ prāpto 'nasūyayā /
ānvīkṣikīm alarkāya prahlādâdibhya ūcivān //

well-founded justification for their reservations, and suggested to interpret the expression *yoga* in Kauṭilya's list in the sense of Vaiśeṣika.

Perhaps the first one in this line was Rājeśvara Śāstrī Draviḍa (b. 1899), an author of a modern Sanskrit commentary *Vaidika-siddhānta-saṁrakṣiṇī* (AŚ$_2$) on the then recently discovered *Artha-śāstra*. He comments on the term *yoga* in Kauṭilya's classification of branches that practise methodology and says that the term *yoga* has been explained as Vaiśeṣika in a subcommentary on the *Nyāya-vārttika* as follows: '«of the Yogas», means «of the followers of Vaiśeṣika».'[100] The 'subcommentary' *Nyāya-vārttika-ṭippaṇī* he refers to is in fact a note by Pt. Vindhyeśvarī Prasāda Dvivedin in the 1915 edition to NV$_1$ 1.1.29, p. 105: *yogānāṁ—vaiśeṣikāṇām*. That short footnote brings to our attention a passage of the *Nyāya-vārttika* which is not directly related to Ānvīkṣikī, but is of much importance as an internal evidence that the followers of Vaiśeṣika were called *Yoga*s within the system of Nyāya-Vaiśeṣika. A suggestion in this direction was also made by CHAṬṬOPĀDHYĀYA (1927: 858): 'it is possible that "Yoga" here means the Nyāya system and not the Pātañjala, which is more practical and speculative. However, I must leave this question undecided at present.'

The starting point for Pt. Vindhyeśvarī Prasāda Dvivedin's footnote is a passage of the *Nyāya-sūtra* explaining the notion of 'a system's distinctive tenet' (*pratitantra-siddhānta*), which in fact concerns a well-known principle that all propositions, except for those which are explicitly rejected, of the Nyāya system are tacitly accepted in the Vaiśeṣika system, and *vice versa*:

> 'A system's distinctive tenet is such which is upheld in a similar (*sc.* allied) system (similar, allied systems) but is not upheld in other systems.'[101]

This is what is nicely explained by Guṇaratna in the *Tarka-rahasya-dīpikā*:

> 'All this [description of the Naiyāyikas] in the form of the *liṅga* [worship], the outfit, [the worship] of the deity etc. should also be applied to the system of Vaiśeṣika, because there is really a very small difference between the Naiyāyikas and the Vaiśeṣikas, even though there is some divergence as regards the number of cognitive criteria and categories, but the categories are mutually accepted. That is why their views are in general identical. And both [groups] are called ascetics (*tapasvin*).'[102]

---

[100] *Vaidika-siddhānta-saṁrakṣiṇī* in AŚ$_2$, p. 124: *yogo vaiśeṣikam iti vyākhyātaṁ nyāya-vārttika-ṭippaṇyām. tad yathā—yogānāṁ vaiśeṣikāṇām (a° 1 ā° 1 sū° 28) iti.*

[101] NS 1.1.29: *samāna-tantra-siddhaḥ para-tantrâsiddhaḥ pratitantra-siddhântaḥ.*

[102] TRD ad ṢDSa 12, p. 77.16–78.1: *etat sarvaṁ liṅga-veṣa-devâdi-svarūpaṁ vaiśeṣika-mate 'py avasātavyam. yato naiyāyika-vaiśeṣikāṇāṁ hi mithaḥ pramāṇa-tattvānām saṁkhyā-bhede saty apy anyonyaṁ tattvānām antar-bhāvane 'lpīyān eva bhedo jāyate, tenâiteṣāṁ prāyo mata-tulyatā. ubhaye 'py ete tapasvino 'bhidhīyante.*

A similar principle would for instance hold valid in the case of the twin systems of Sāṁkhya and Yoga. The aphorism of Akṣapāda Gautama is commented by Vātsyāyana as follows:

> 'For example, [the distinctive tenets] of the representatives of the Sāṁkhya system [also upheld in an allied system] are the following: something non-existent does not acquire existence; something existent does not abandon its existence; conscious beings do not possess any unique feature [that distinguishes one from the other]; distinctive character [occurs] in the body, the sense organs and the mind as well as in the objects [of the sense organs] and in their respective causes. [The distinctive tenets] of the representatives of « Y o g a » [also upheld in an allied system] are the following: the creation [of the word] from material elements is occasioned by the *karman* etc. of humans; defects and activity are the causes of *karman*; conscious selves are characterised by their qualities; the non-existent comes into existence; what has come into existence ceases to exist.'[103]

A more detailed discussion of the passage is provided by Kṣetreśacandra CHAṬṬOPĀDHYĀYA (1927), who was the source of the note of H.N. RANDLE (1930: 3, n. 1) and draws the reader's attention to the fact that 'Pandits say that *Yogāḥ* (plural) was used as an early designation of the *Vaiśeṣika* school', who in turn becomes a source for F.W. THOMAS (1960: 7, n. 1).

It does not require much discussion here to demonstrate that the tenets of 'Yoga' in the passage are by no means compatible with anything what we know of the Yoga school and in fact they run counter basic doctrinal fundaments of the Sāṁkhya-Yoga system.[104] Instead, they neatly correspond to familiar doctrines of Vaiśeṣika, but are also accepted by Nyāya. The first tenet postulates that the world in not a creation of some kind of transformation (*pariṇāma*) of a primeval substance caused by some additional supramundane factors, say, a relation between the consciousness principle (*puruṣa*) and the primordial factor (*prakṛti*) (see SK 21), but rather a result of the cumulated *karman* of living beings. In the process of creation, the world and all aggregate, composite things are created from material elements (*mahā-bhūta*) under the influence or 'supervision' of the karmic results of previous deeds of hu-

[103] NBh 1.1.29: *yathā nâsata ātma-lābhaḥ, na sata ātma-hānam, niratiśayāś cetanāḥ dehêndriya-manaḥsu viṣayeṣu tat-tat-kāraṇeṣu ca viśeṣa iti sāṁkhyānām. puruṣa-karmâdi-nimitto bhūta-sargaḥ, karma-hetavo doṣāḥ pravṛttiś ca, sva-guṇa-viśiṣṭāś cetanāḥ, asad utpadyate utpannaṁ nirudhyata iti yogānām*. For an alternative translation of the passage see BHATTACHARYA (1974: 39–40), JACOBI (1930: 608 ff.) and THAKUR (1963: 81); for a structrued discussion of its contents see CHAṬṬOPĀDHYĀYA (1927: 854–856).

[104] Comp. CHAṬṬOPĀDHYĀYA (1927: 854–855), BHATTACHARYA (1974: 39–41).

mans. This is indeed an important tenet of the developed[105] Vaiśeṣika, according to which it is the invisible moral principle (*adṛṣṭa*), being the cumulated deeds of living beings (*dharmâdharma*), which is responsible for a number of events in the world that could not otherwise be explicable, including the moment of the creation of the word, i.e. putting all the separate and immovable atoms in motion and thereby in composite perceivable structures.[106] This was also a tenet tacitly adopted by Nyāya and not so pronounced as in Vaiśeṣika, albeit hardly ever discussed with respect the creation of the whole world, but rather restricted to the discussion of the creation of the new human body[107]. The second tenet fits very well into the ideology of Nyāya; the activity (*pravṛtti*) and defects (*doṣa*), such as passion (*rāga*), aversion (*dveṣa*) and confusion (*moha*), are discussed in NS 4.1.1–9, and are explicitly said to be the causes of the circle of birth, being the causes of activity.[108] The idea is also very well at home in the system of Vaiśeṣika, and the defects, albeit not called *doṣa*s, such

[105] That was not the idea of the earliest form of Vaiśeṣika, and the meaning of *adṛṣṭa*—initially understood without any moral or 'karmic' implications—changed to incorporate the moral aspect of cumulated human deeds around fourth–fifth century CE. Comp. THAKUR (2003: 14–19), BRONKHORST (2000: 34).

[106] See VS(C) 5.2.14: *agner ūrdhva-jvalanaṁ vāyoś ca tiryak-pavanam aṇu-manasoś câdyaṁ karmêty adṛṣṭa-kāritāni.*—'The upward movement of the flame of fire, the sideward movement of the wind and the initial movement of the atom and the atomic mind are initiated by the invisible moral principle (*adṛṣṭa*)' and VSV(C) *ad loc.*: *agner avasthāne tiryag vā gamane pacyamānasyâbhasmī-bhāvaḥ syād apāṁ vā, tathā vāyor atiryag-gamane pūyamāna-dravyāṇāṁ pavanâbhāvo agneś câprabodhaḥ, vinaṣṭa-śarīrāṇām ātmanāṁ sargâdau pṛthivy-ādi-paramâṇuṣv ādyaṁ parasparôpasarpaṇa-karma na syāt, tathā labdha-bhūmīnāṁ yogināṁ kalpânte 'bhisaṁdhāya prayatnena manaḥ śarīrād vyatiricyâvatiṣṭhamānānāṁ sargâdau nava-śarīra-sambandhāya manasa ādyaṁ karma na bhavet adṛṣṭād ṛte. tasmād agner ūrdhva-jvalanaṁ vāyoś ca tiryak-pavanam aṇūnāṁ ca upasarpaṇa-karma manasaś ca ādyaṁ karma etāni prāṇināṁ adṛṣṭena kṛtāni.* See also PBh 359–360, p. 80: ... *tathā sarga-kāle pratyagreṇa śarīreṇa sambandhârtham karmâdṛṣṭa-kāritam.* [360] *evam anyad api wmahā-bhūteṣu yat pratyakṣânumānābhyām anupalabhyamāna-kāraṇam upakārâpakāra-samartham ca bhavati tad apy adṛṣṭa-kāritam. yathā sargâdāv aṇu-karma, agni-vāyvor ūrdhva-tiryag-gamane mahā-bhūtānāṁ prakṣobhaṇam...*

[107] See NS 3 2.60: *pūrva-kṛta-phalânubandhāt tad-utpattiḥ*, and NBh *ad loc.*, esp.: NBh_1 3.2.60, p. 210.4–1 = NBh_2, p. 900.2–901.4: *yad-adhiṣṭhāno 'yam ātmā yad*[a] *aham iti manyamāno yatrâbhivyakto*[b] *yatrôpabhoga-tṛṣṇayā viṣayânupalabhamāno dharmâdharmau saṁskaroti tad asya śarīram, tena saṁskāreṇa dharmâdharma-lakṣaṇena bhūta-sahitena patitenāsmin*[c] *śarīre niṣpadyate śarīrântaram*[d]*, niṣpannasya câsya pūrva-śarīravat puruṣârtha-kriyā, puruṣasya ca pūrva-śarīravat pravṛttir iti karmâpekṣebhyo bhūtebhyaḥ śarīra-sarge saty etad upapadyata iti. dṛṣṭā ca puruṣa-guṇena prayatnena prayuktebhyo bhūtebhyaḥ puruṣârtha-kriyā-samarthānāṁ dravyāṇāṁ ratha-prabhṛtīnām utpattiḥ. tathânumātavyaṁ śarīram api puruṣârtha-kriyā-samartham utpadyamānaṁ puruṣasya guṇântarâpekṣebhyo bhūtebhya utpadyata iti.* [[a] NBh_2: *ayam.* [b] NBh_2: *yatrâbhiyukto.* [c] NBh_2: *bhūta-sahite patite 'smin.* [d] NBh_2: *śarīra uttaraṁ niṣpadyate.* [e] NBh_1: *tayânumātavyaṁ.*] See also NS_1 4.1.22–24, p. 229–230 = NS_2 21–23, p. 958–961, and NBh *ad loc.*

[108] NBh 4.1.2: *pravṛtti-hetutvāt punar-bhava-pratisandhāna-sāmarthyāc ca saṁsāra-hetavaḥ*. Cf. See BRONKHORST (2000: 33 ff.).

as desire (*icchā*), aversion (*dveṣa*), ignorance (*avidyā*), as well as activity, are discussed as causes of good and bad deeds (*dharmâdharma*), which make up the *karman* (the term preferred is *adṛṣṭa*) on a number of occasions.[109] It may be the case—in fact, it is the most plausible explanation—that Vātsyāyana uses more familiar terms of his own school to refer to the idea common to both Nyāya and Vaiśeṣika, which does not prejudge that what he meant was indeed the tenet of Nyāya. Also the third tenet is a clear reference to the *viśeṣaṇa-viśeṣya-bhāva* relation ('qualifier-qualified relation'), constitutive of Vaiśeṣika ontology, but also adopted by and well grounded in Nyāya. The qualities which qualify the souls are frequently mentioned in Vaiśeṣika literature,[110] but also by Nyāya authors.[111] In the formulation of the fourth tenet the passage clearly refers to theory of causality which treats the effect as an entirely new entity (*asat-kārya-vāda*), which stands in clear opposition to the theory of the effect pre-existent in the cause (*sat-kārya-vāda*), promulgated by Sāṁkhya and Yoga. The theory is fundamental to both schools. A bit hesitant on the identification is THAKUR (1963: 81–82), who eventually subscribes to the original connection of the 'Yogas' with the Vaiśeṣikas:

> 'The Yogas mentioned here are Ārambhavādins and as such, cannot be indentified with the followers of Patañjali. MM. Phaṇībhūṣaṇa Tarkavāgīśa took the word to mean the Naiyāyikas and the Vaiśeṣikas, as both accept creation from the conjunction between *paramāṇus* etc. The title of these philosophers may also be due to their association with the Pāśupatas who had their own system of Yoga. Vidyānandasvāmin (*Patraparīkṣā*, p. 4) and Śālīkanātha (*Ṛjuvimalā*, p. 209) take the word "yoga" to mean the Vaiśeṣika alone. The tenets mentioned may thus originally be associated with the Vaiśeṣikas and the acceptance thereof in the Nyāya system might be a later event.'

---

[109] See for instance VS(C) 6.217: *icchā-dveṣa-pūrvikā dharmâdharmayoḥ pravṛttiḥ.* and VSV(C) *ad loc.*: *icchā-pūrvikā dharme pravṛttiḥ, anyena dhana-madād abhibhūtasya vā dveṣa-pūrvikâpi grāma-kāmêṣṭy-ādau. adharme picchā-pūrvikā para-dārâdiṣu dveṣa-pūrvikā. evaṁ dharmâdharmayoḥ samcayaḥ*; PBh 292, 294: [*icchā*] *prayatna-smṛti-dharmâdharma-hetuḥ.* [*dveṣaḥ*] *prayatna-smṛti-dharmâdharma-hetuḥ.*

[110] VS(C) 6.1.7: *ātma-guṇeṣv ātmântara-guṇānām akāraṇatvāt*; VS(C) 9.17: *ātma-samavāyād ātma-guṇeṣu*; VS(C) 10.1: *ātma-samavāyaḥ sukha-duḥkhayoḥ pañcebhyo 'rthântaratve hetus tad-āśrayibhyaś ca guṇebhyaḥ*; VSV(C) 2.1.25: *ye khalv ātma-guṇās te sukhâdaya ivāntar-śarīram upalabhyante*; PBh 79: *sukha-duḥkhêcchā-dveṣa-prayatnaiś ca guṇair guṇy anumīyate, te ca na śarīrêndriya-guṇāḥ. ... tasya guṇāḥ buddhi-sukha-duḥkhêcchā-dveṣa-prayatna-dharmâdharma-saṁskāra-saṁkhyā-parimāṇa-pṛthaktva-samyoga-vibhāgāḥ.*

[111] E.g. NBh$_2$ 1.1.5, p. 12.16–19: *sāmānyato-dṛṣṭaṁ nāma yatrâpratyakṣe liṅga-liṅginoḥ sambandhe kenacid arthena liṅgasya sāmānyād apratyakṣo liṅgī gamyate. yathêcchâdibhir ātmā, icchâdayo guṇāḥ. guṇāś ca dravya-saṁsthānāḥ. tad yad eṣāṁ sthānaṁ sâtmêti.*

We thus see that all the four tenets of the 'Yogas' fit well in both the doctrines of Nyāya and Vaiśeṣika and it is not possible to determine solely on the basis of ideas who the 'Yogas' who upheld these theories were. The terminology actually employed by Vātsyāyana in the passage is of no help for us, because it cannot be treated as an indicator of the system from which the original ideas and terms stem. In no way should we be misled by the nomenclature of the *Nyāya-bhāṣya*: obviously Vātsyāyana would have the natural systemic propensity to use the terms of his own school rather than the terminology of Vaiśeṣika to denote the same phenomena and ideas. However, he also uses terminology which is not necessarily characteristic specifically of either Nyāya or Vaiśeṣika or terms which are technical in neither of them, e.g. *cetana*. Solely on the basis of Vātsyāyana's description and vocabulary it seems impossible to decide whether he considered these tenets to belong primarily to the Nyāya system and secondarily accepted by the Vaiśeṣikas or *vice versa*. To judge either way we cannot apply historical criteria as regards which of these schools developed these tenets first, because Vātsyāyana would not have applied such historical criteria himself.

Uddyotakara adds two more examples in his gloss to illustrate the idea of a system's distinctive tenet (*pratitantra-siddhānta*):

> 'A system's distinctive tenet [also upheld in an allied system] is invariably the acceptance of the universals, the particulars (individuators) and the like. For instance, it is for the «Yogas» that the sense-organs are material (*sc.* derived from the material elements), whereas for the followers of Sāṁkhya it is that they are non-material (*sc.* derived not from the material elements but from the psychic faculty of self-identity, *ahaṁ-kāra*).'[112]

As against the opinion of Pt. Vindhyeśvarī Prasāda Dvivedin and other *paṇḍit*s, Kṣetreśacandra CHAṬṬOPĀDHYĀYA's (1927: 858) conclusion of the passage is that 'From all this it is clear that Vātsyāyana and Uddyotakara meant the Naiyāyikas when they used the term *Yogānam* in the passages quoted above ... The meaning of the term *yoga* in Vātsyāyana and Uddyotakara is certainly "Naiyāyika".' And that is an opinion to which Kamaleswar BHATTACHARYA (1974: 42) apparently subscribes. But is such assessment really accurate?

Let us analyse Uddyotakara's examples. The first of them refers to the idea of *sāmānya* and *viśeṣa* understood as distinct entities. Both are recognised in Nyāya and Vaiśeṣika alike, albeit they primarily constitute the hard-core ontological structure of the Vaiśeṣika set-up of the world as universals and individuators, or a category which introduces the ultimate difference among indi-

[112] NV_1, p. 105.7–9 = NV_2, p. 100.3–4: *sāmānya-viśeṣa-tadvatāṁ niyamenâbhyupagamaḥ pratitantra-siddhānta iti. yathā bhautikānîndriyāṇîti yogānām abhautikānîti sāṁkhyānām iti.*

vidual entities which can be differentiated irrespective of their qualities (*guṇa*) solely through their unique individuators. However, the *viśeṣa*s are not necessarily technically used in Nyāya in this sense; they may also stand for what is generally understood as particulars. Further, *sāmānya* and *viśeṣa* are recognised as two separate categories of the system of Vaiśeṣika, besides mere four (or five) others, and they do not enjoy a status of separate categories of the Nyāya system: Nyāya does not list them among the sixteen categories, which are primarily of epistemological character. This could be a hint. The second example is rather straightforward and lucidly explained by CHAṬṬOPĀDHYĀYA's (1927: 856): 'The Sāṁkhya system derives the sense-organs directly from *Ahaṁ-kāra*, from which are also produced in a different line the Five Subtle Elements (*Sā. K.* 22); consequently they are "non-elemental". But the Nyāya-Vaiśeṣikas believed in the "elemental" origin of the *indriyas*.' Since the view is so intimately related to both the school, it is not possible to draw any conclusions from this example.

Let us take still another look at the passage. The very nature of the notion of 'a system's distinctive tenet' (*pratitantra-siddhānta*) is that the thesis is shared by both school and, naturally, it is not possible to draw any conclusions as regards the affiliation of the thesis to one school or another solely on the basis of its contents. Indeed, the very idea is that it is a tenet of one school which is at the same time shared by an allied school. How should Vātsyāyana's latter four examples be treated? Are these tenets primarily of the Nyāya school also shared by the Vaiśeṣikas, called 'Yogas', or tenets primarily of the Vaiśeṣika school also shared by the Naiyāyikas, i.e. 'Yogas'?

It is of note that nowhere in his text does Vātsyāyana use the name *vaiśeṣika* to refer to his fellow school, whereas he does use the terms *nyāya* and *naiyāyika* on a few occasions.[113] It would be quite untypical for him to unexpectedly, on this singular occasion, chose a different locution to refer to his own school, if

---

[113] The only reference to fellow school representatives is in NBh 1.1.32: *daśâvayavān eke naiyāyikā vākye sañcakṣate*. The number of occurrences of the term *nyāya* in the *Nyāya-bhāṣya* is about two dozen, though most of them do not necessarily refer to the system of Nyāya but to the method of logical-epistemological enquiry. Some of them do contain a possible reference to the school itself, understood via its method: NBh_1 1.1.1, p. 35.1 = NBh_2 p. 2.20: *nyāya-vidyā*; NBh_1 1.1.1, p. 35.4 = NBh_2 p. 3.3: *tatra nânupalabdhe na nirṇīte 'rthe nyāyaḥ pravartate* (?); NBh_1 1.1.1, p. 35.6 = NBh_2 p. 3.6: *nyāya-pravṛttiḥ* (?); NBh_1 1.1.1, p. 38.2 = NBh_2 p. 3.9–10: ... *nyāyaḥ pravartate. kaḥ punar ayaṁ nyāyaḥ. pramāṇair artha-parīkṣaṇaṁ nyāyaḥ*; NBh_1 1.1.1, p. 39.1–2 = NBh_2, p. 3.11–13: *kaḥ punar ayaṁ nyāyaḥ? pramāṇair artha-parīkṣaṇaṁ nyāyaḥ. ... sânvīkṣā. pratyakṣâgamābhyām īkṣitasyânvīkṣaṇam anvīkṣā. tayā pravartata ity ānvīkṣikī nyāya-vidyā nyāya-śāstram*; NBh_1 1.1.1, p. 45.2 = NBh_2 p. 4.4: *tad-āśrayā ca nyāya-pravṛttiḥ* (?); NBh_1 1.1.1, p. 52.1 = NBh_2 p. 4.16: *so 'yaṁ paramo nyāya iti*; NBh_1 1.1.41, p. 330.6–7 = NBh_2 p. 38.6–7: *so 'yaṁ vimarśaḥ pakṣa-pratipakṣāv avadyotya nyāyaṁ pravartayatîty upādīyata iti*; NBh_1 2.2.17, p. 613 = NBh_2 p. 108.16–17: *śāstra-siddhāntas tu nyāya-samākhyātam anumataṁ bahu-śākham anumānam*; NBh_1 colophon, p. 1200 = NBh_2 p. 320.17: *yo 'kṣapādam ṛṣiṁ nyāyaḥ pratyabhād vadatāṁ varam.*

he does not do it in other cases. Further, while referring to the views of his own school Vātsyāyana does it directly with verbs in the first person plural.[114]

Further, it is crucial to remember that the notion of *pratitantra-siddhānta* means a tenet of our system which is acceptable also in a fellow, allied school. Vātsyāyana, while explaining the idea, directs the message primarily to the representatives of his own school. That being the case, it would be rather surprising if he referred to himself and other representatives of his own school with the unusual 'Yogas'. Rather, he would either say *iti asmākam* or simply *iti*, without mentioning the systemic affiliation of the tenets. The views referred to by Vātsyāyana are therefore the tenets of his own school which are acceptable also to the school of the 'Yogas', as the genitive plural indicates. This is exactly what transpires from all comments, including the elucidation, slightly confrontational in nature, by Bhāsarvajña in his *Nyāya-bhūṣaṇa*, where the genitives plural denote the proponents of a fellow, allied school:

> '[Now follows a comment on the aphorism]: «A system's distinctive tenet is such which is upheld in a similar (sc. allied) system (or similar, allied systems) but is not upheld in other systems». A similar system for the followers of Kapila (*sc.* Sāṁkhya system) is [the system] of Patañjali's Yoga, and for the followers of [the system] of Patañjali's Yoga is the system of Kapila—of this sort is the example accepted by some [.e.g. by Uddyotakara etc., *vide supra* p. 223, n. 112]. The author of the gloss (i.e. Jayantabhaṭṭa?) does not accept it however, because he maintains that [he rejects this] because it cannot be argued for with a rational argument. In his opinion, the following is the [proper] example: A similar system for the followers of the Naiyāyikas is the system of Vaiśeṣika, and for the Vaiśeṣikas it is the school of Nyāya. In contradistinction to that, we will explain as follows: One system (sc. set of believes (*tantra*)) which is fundamental and common to many authors of commentaries and for those who listen to the commentators is called similar (i.e. common), like a similar (i.e. common) house, similar (i.e. common) wealth. A thesis which is established in such a similar (common) system but is not established in another system or in no other system at all that is a system's distinctive tenet. And in such a way it follows that a thesis which is not established in one's own system, even though it is established in a similar system, is not a system's

[114] Such cases are indeed rare, see NBh_1 1.1.4, p. 124 = NBh_2 p. 11.19–20: *asannidhiṁ câsya yugapaj-jñānânutpatti-kāraṇaṁ vakṣyāma iti*; NBh_1 3.1.60, p. 793 = NBh_2 p. 168.7–8: *tena bhūta-guṇa-viśeṣôpalabdher manyāmahe bhūta-prakṛtînīndriyāṇi nâvyakta-prakṛtīnîti*; NBh_1 3.2.22, p. 854 = NBh_2 p. 186.14–15: *nâtrôtpatti-kāraṇam apadiśyate yenâitat pratipadyemahîti*; NBh_1 5.1.1, p. 1102 = NBh_2 p. 283.9–10: *aviśeṣaṁ tatra tatrôdāhariṣyāmaḥ.*

> distinctive tenet. And, accordingly, even though it contradicts it (sc. one's own system), it does not follow that it becomes schismatic tenet.'[115]

The conclusion which obviously follows is that the 'Yogas' of the *Nyāya-bhāṣya* cannot but be the proponents of Vaiśeṣika, to whom a number of the Naiyāyikas' tenets are likewise acceptable.

Interestingly, the sequence of the school names given *verbatim* by Vātsyāyana as examples is: Sāṁkhya-Yoga, and the names correspond to the first two schools mentioned by Kauṭilya; furthermore, what they really mean is: Sāṁkhya, the co-system (*samāna-tantra*) of which was Yoga, and Vaiśeṣika, the co-system of which was Nyāya.

It is nothing new that the name Yoga was a customary designation of the systems of Nyāya and Vaiśeṣika, as Debiprasad CHATTOPADHYAYA and Mrinalkanti GANGOPADHYAYA (1992, I: 102) aptly noted:

> 'The theses mentioned by Vātsyāyana are the *pratitantra-siddhānta* of the followers of Yoga are characteristic of both the Naiyāyikas and the Vaiśeṣikas. ... The Naiyāyikas were known as *yogin*-s belonging to the Śaiva and the Pāśupata sects. This is evident from the statement of the Jaina philosopher Guṇaratna (*Tarka-rahasya-dīpikā*, p. 51). In any case, the Vaiśeṣika system was known as Yoga even in ancient times and the Vaiśeṣika philosophers were accordingly characterised as the "followers of *yoga*". The Jaina philosopher Vidyānanda Svāmi, in his work *Patra-parīkṣā*, quotes a sūtra of Kaṇāda (viz. *Vaiśeṣika-sūtra* iv. 1.1.) and adds, "As it is said by the followers of *yoga*". Further, Guṇaratna opens his discussion of the Nyāya view with the words: "The Naiyāyaikas, also known as the *yauga*-s". Therefore, according to the ancient tradition, Vātsyāyana mentions the theses of the Vaiśeṣikas as characteristic of the followers of *yoga*. ... The thesis referred to here as that of the follower of *yoga* is shared alike by the Naiyāyikas and Vaiśeṣikas. By the followers

[115] NBhū 66.17–26: "*samāna-tantra-prasiddhaḥ para-tantrâprasiddhaḥ pratitantra-siddhântaḥ*". *samānaṁ tantraṁ kāpilānāṁ pātañjalam, pātañjalānāṁ ca kāpilam ity evaṁ prakārakam udāharaṇaṁ kecid icchanti. ṭīkā-kārās tu nêcchanti, apramāṇôpapannatvād iti manyamānāḥ. tan-mate tv etad evôdāharaṇam—samānaṁ tantraṁ naiyāyikānāṁ vaiśeṣika-śāstram, vaiśeṣikāṇāṁ nyāya-śāstram iti. vayaṁ tv anyathā vyācakṣmahe—anekeṣām upanibandha-kārāṇāṁ vyākhyātṛ-śrotṝṇāṁ ca mūla-bhūtam ekaṁ tantraṁ sādhāraṇaṁ samānam*[a] *ity ucyate. yathā samānaṁ gṛhaṁ samānaṁ dhanam iti. tasmin samāna-tantre yaḥ siddho 'rthaḥ para-tantre tu kvacit sarvatra vā na siddhaḥ, sa pratitantra-siddhāntaḥ. evaṁ ca sva-śāstrâsiddho 'rthaḥ sadṛśa-tantra-siddho 'pi pratitantra-siddhānto na bhavatîti gamyate. tataś ca tad-virodhe 'pi nâpasiddhāntaḥ prasajyate iti*. [[a] NBhū: *sāmānam*.]

> of *yoga* are thus to be understood the followers of both Nyāya and Vaiśeṣika systems. …'

The same approach of Rājeśvara Śāstrī Draviḍa to identify Yoga of Kauṭilya with Vaiśeṣika was taken, although with much caution, by Wilhelm HALBFASS (1988: 278), who says with respect to the problematic term *yoga*:

> 'What Kauṭilya means by *yoga*, the second item in his list, is not easy to determine. In a general sense, it is important to remember that the words *yoga* is by no means exclusively associated with the Yoga system of Patañjali, or with other doctrines and techniques of meditation and inner discipline. Its root *yuj-* also accounts for the word *yukti*, "reasoning"; and likewise, the word *yoga* itself is occasionally used to refer to disciplines of "reasoning" and "argumentation," such as Nyāya and Vaiśeṣika. This usage is documented in older as well as in more recent texts.'

In the same verve, Johannes BRONKHORST (2007: 171) relies here on the opinion of HALBFASS (1988: 278), and writes:

> 'Yoga, as is common in early texts, may refer to Nyāya. It follows that Sāṁkhya, Lokāyata and p r o b a b l y (emphasis—P.B.) Nyāya are presented here as investigative sciences (*ānvīkṣikī*).'

The nature of HALBFASS' arguments in favour of his equation of Yoga with Vaiśeṣika is that it is n o t i m p o s s i b l e t h a t a l s o Vaiśeṣika could be implied by the term *yoga*. In other words, these arguments, indirect in nature, simply do n o t e x c l u d e such a possibility. But we do not find any direct arguments with these authors that could effectively help establish a link between the 'Yoga' of Kauṭilya and Vaiśeṣika. HALBFASS (1988: 278), clearly following the above remark of CHATTOPADHYAYA–GANGOPADHYAYA (1992, I: 102), vaguely says that 'In the doxographic literature of the Jainas, the *Naiyāyikas* and *Vaiśeṣikas* are often referred to as "Yogins" or, more specifically, as *Śaiva* and *Pāśupata* Yogins; and their teachings are presented as doctrines of "Yoga",' and merely draws our attention (1988: 540 n. 66) to one passage from a late mediaeval commentary of Guṇaratna-sūri (*ca.* 1343–1418) on Haribhadra-sūri's *Ṣaḍ-darśana-samuccaya*, in order to substantiate the claim that 'Yoga' of Kauṭilya is Vaiśeṣika, not the Yoga of meditation.

These arguments are not entirely convincing, albeit attractive. Still, the major problem remains: how to account for such a strong relation between the tradition of Nyāya and the current of Ānvīkṣikī given an apparent absence of any reference to it by name in Kauṭilya's enumeration of branches that practise methodology (*ānvīkṣikī*)? Further, how to link Nyāya with the Yoga of the *Artha-śāstra*, a text composed perhaps two centuries before the emergence of Nyāya and the composition of an early version of the *Nyāya-sūtra* (*vide supra* § 9.2)?

12. The passage from Guṇaratna's *Tarka-rahasya-dīpikā* referred to by Debiprasad CHATTOPADHYAYA and Mrinalkanti GANGOPADHYAYA and, following him, by HALBFASS, opens a separate section on Nyāya in the doxographic treatise *Ṣaḍ-darśana-samuccaya*:

> 'Now, [the author] describes the specific features, such as *liṅga* etc. of the Naiyāyikas, whose another designation is «Yaugas».'[116]

Since the designation of the school representatives was Yauga, it follows that the school's name was Yoga.

The structure of the doxographic treatise of Haribhadra-sūri (*ca.* 740–800), known as Yākinī-putra, is quite revealing in that it subsumes the discussion of Vaiśeṣika under the heading of Nyāya, and in fact treats the former as a subvariety of the latter, which is confirmed the commentator Guṇaratna (*vide supra* p. 219, n. 102), who in addition emphasises the nature of the religious-sectarian division between the two:

> 'Further, in treatises the Naiyāyikas are always called the Śaivas, because they worship Śiva, whereas the Vaiśeṣikas are called the Pāśupatas. Hence, the teaching of the Naiyāyikas is called Śaivism, whereas the doctrine of the Vaiśeṣikas Pāśupatism.'[117]

Such a treatment is by no means an invention of Haribhadra himself but rather a reflection of a continuous centuries-long tradition in which the systems of Nyāya and Vaiśeṣika were seen, both within and outside the systems, as complementary.

The close relationship of the systems finds confirmation on many occasions, e.g. in Malliṣeṇa-sūri's *Syād-vāda-mañjarī* who says:

> 'Since the schools of the Vaiśeṣikas and the Naiyāyikas are generally similar, one should understand that when the system of the Aulūkyas (Vaiśeṣikas) has been refuted also the system of Yaugas (Naiyāyikas) is refuted.'[118]

Of note is that Malliṣeṇa calls the propounders of the system of Nyāya 'Yauga',[119] and by implication the system itself 'Yoga'.

Despite the claims to the contrary, the cases when the term *yoga* is taken to refer to either Nyāya or Vaiśeṣika in Indian philosophical literature are few and

---

[116] TRD ad ṢDSa 12, p. 76.5: *athâdau naiyāyikānām yaugâparâbhidhānānāṁ liṅgâdi-vyaktir ucyate.*

[117] TRD ad ṢDSa 12, p. 78.8–10: *paraṁ śāstreṣu naiyāyikāḥ sadā śiva-bhaktatvāc chaivā ity ucyante, vaiśeṣikās tu pāśupatā iti. tena naiyāyika-śāsanaṁ śaivam ākhyāyate, vaiśeṣika-darśanaṁ ca pāśupatam iti.*

[118] SVM 10.1–2, p. 54.16–17: *vaiśeṣika-naiyāyikayoḥ prāyaḥ samāna-tantratvād aulūkya-mate kṣipte yauga-matam api kṣiptam evâvaseyam.*

[119] See also SVM 14.138, p. 89.19: *yaugair.*

far between. Despite their scarcity, they do seem sufficient to provide satisfactory evidence to enable certain conclusions. In addition to the cases discussed above, some occurrences of the term *yoga* in the sense of Nyāya or Vaiśeṣika are provided by CHAṬṬOPĀDHYĀYA (1927: 856) who follows MM. Paṇḍit Phaṇībhūṣaṇa Tarkavāgīśa's discussion on pp. 227–230 of the edition of the *Nyāya-bhāṣya* with Bengali translation (Calcutta 1917), which is not available to me. These are the *Patra-parīkṣā* (PaP, p. 4.30?) of Vidyānanda Pātrakesarisvāmin, the *Parīkṣâmukha-sūtra* (PA 6.57) of Māṇikyanandin, and two sources already referred to, viz. the *Tarka-rahasya-dīpikā* of Guṇaratna (TRD ad ṢDSa 12; *vide supra* p. 219, n. 116) and the *Syād-vāda-mañjarī* of Malliṣeṇa-sūri (SVM 10.1–2, *vide supra* p. 228, n. 118).

An analysis of how Vidyānanda Pātrakesarisvāmin uses the terms *yoga*/*yauga* in his two works the *Patra-parīkṣā* and the *Āpta-parīkṣā* will reveal that what he has in mind is the system of the Vaiśeṣika and its followers. In the *Patra-parīkṣā* he uses the term *yoga* at least twice,[120] and in both cases in the same context to designate those who assert that 'The [ultimately] existent [particular] is without a cause and eternal' (*sad akāraṇavan nityam*) which is nothing else but a quote from the *Vaiśeṣika-sūtra* (VS(C) 4.1.1). Similarly, in his other work, the *Āpta-parīkṣā*, Vidyānanda comes to speak of the 'Yaugas'.[121] Also in this case there is no slightest shade of doubt that what he has in mind are again the followers of the Vaiśeṣika system whose founder is referred to by name just a few lines before: *īśvara-kaṇādayor* (ĀpP 6 § 42, p. 29.1).

On the other hand, in an aphorism of Māṇikyanandin's *Parīkṣâmukha-sūtra*[122] which enumerates a range of cognitive criteria (*pramāṇa*) and states that each of the succeeding systems recognises one criterion more, the Yaugas represent a system which admits of four such cognitive criteria, which cannot be Vaiśeṣika, recognising either two or three *pramāṇa*s, but Nyāya. On the other had, in his commentary *Parīkṣâmukha-laghu-vṛtti*, also known under the title *Prameya-ratna-māla*, Anantavīrya clearly distinguishes in one passage between the Naiyāyikas[123] and the Yaugas[124], who cannot but be the Vaiśeṣikas. On an-

---

[120] PaP, p. 4.30: *yogasya sad akāraṇavan nityam ity ādivat*, and PaP 21cd, p. 5.24: *sad akāraṇavan nityam iti yoga-vaco 'pi ca*.

[121] $\bar{A}pP_1$ 5, p. 7. 25–27 = $\bar{A}pP_2$ 6 § 43, p. 29.7–8: *tatra teṣu mokṣa-mārga-praṇetṛtva-karma-bhū-bhṛd-bhetṛtva-viśva-tattva-jñātṛtveṣu karma-bhū-bhṛtāṁ bhetṛtvam asiddham. munîndrasya viparyāsāt tad-abhetṛtvāt karma-bhū-bhṛd-asambhavāt sadā-śivasya ye vadanti yaugāḥ…*

[122] PA_1 6.56_1 = PA 6.57_2: *saugata-sāṁkhya-yauga-prābhākara-jaiminīyānām pratyakṣânumānâgaôpamānârthāpatty-abhāvair ekâikâdhikair vyāptivat.*

[123] $PALV_1$ 1.1, p. 9.17–19 = $PALV_2$ 1.1, p. 3.5–6: *tasya ca jñānam iti viśeṣaṇam ajñāna-rūpasya sannikarṣâder naiyāyikâdi-parikalpitasya pramāṇatva-vyavacchedârtham uktam.*

[124] $PALV_1$ 1.1, p. 9.23–25 = $PALV_2$ 1.1, p. 3.11–14: *tathā parokṣa-jñāna-vādināṁ mīmāṁsakānām asvasaṁvedana-jñāna-vādināṁ sāṁkhyānāṁ jñānântara-pratyakṣa-jñāna-vādināṁ yaugānāṁ ca matam apākartuṁ sva-padôpādānam ity avyāpty-ativyāpty-asambhava-doṣa-parihārāt suvyavasthitam eva pramāṇa-lakṣaṇam.*

other occasion[125] the same Anantavīrya enumerates, and subsequently refutes, the five members of the proof formula (*pañcâvayava*) and ascribes the view to the 'Yauga', in the wording well-known from the tradition of Nyāya:[126] *pratijñā-hetûdāharaṇôpanaya-nigamana*. Indeed, also the Vaiśeṣikas recognised the five-membered proof-formula, but named the members differently: *avayavāḥ punaḥ pratijnâpadeśa-nidarśanânusandhāna-pratyāmnāyāḥ* (PBh 265, p. 49). Such terms as *upanayana* and *nigamana* do not even occur in the *Vaiśeṣika-sūtra*, Candrānanda's commentary or in the *Praśastapāda-bhāṣya*. This may imply that *yauga* in the passage refers, in turn, to the Naiyāyikas, not to Vaiśeṣikas as in the preceding passage. Then again in a passage directly related to the ontology of Vaiśeṣika, which discusses the relation between the universal (*sāmānya*) and the particular (*viśeṣa*) as absolutely different from each other we come across the following remark: 'Neither the opinion of the «Yaugas» that the universal and the particular are independent of each other seems to be justified through argumentation.'[127] The idea of the universal and the particular as absolutely different from each other typically forms a favourite butt of Jaina criticism which is usually directed against the Vaiśeṣika, not necessarily against the Nyāya, but not always, as in the case of Siddharṣigaṇin, who indicates that this was the claim of both the schools: 'The Naiyāyika and the Vaiśeṣika [consider the domain of the cognitive criterion to be] «the universal and the particular as [absolutely] separate from each other».'[128] Apparently, Anantavīrya uses the same term *yauga* still in a third meaning which covers both. He does the same while commenting on Māṇikyanandin's aphorism which asserts that the resultant cognition is both different and non-different from the cognitive procedures which led to it.[129] Anantavīrya mentions the opinion of the 'Yaugas' to the effect that the result of the cognitive process (cognitive criterion) is absolutely different form the process (criterion) itself[130], and such is an opinion is shared by both the Naiyāyikas[131] and

---

[125] PALV$_1$ 3.32, p. 29.37–30.2 = PALV$_2$ 3.37, p. 33.11: *pratijñā-hetûdāharaṇôpanaya-nigamana-bhedāt pañcâvayavam iti yaugaḥ*.

[126] NS 1.1.32: *pratijñā-hetûdāharaṇôpanaya-nigamanāni avayavāḥ*.

[127] PALV$_1$ 4.1, p. 44.27–28 = PALV$_2$ 4.1, p. 57.1–2: *nâpi sāmānya-viśeṣau parasparânapekṣāv iti yauga-matam api yukti-yuktam avabhāti*.

[128] NAV 0.7: *paraspara-vibhaktau sāmānya-viśeṣāv iti naiyāyika-vaiśeṣikāḥ*.

[129] PA 5.2: *pramāṇād abhinnaṁ bhinnaṁ ca*.

[130] PALV$_1$ 5.2, p. 29.37–30.2 = PALV$_2$ 5.2, p. 62.18–19: *tad dvividham api phalaṁ pramāṇād bhinnam evêti yaughāḥ*.

[131] See for instance: NBh 1.1.1: *tatra yasyêpsā-jihāsā-prayuktasya pravṛttiḥ sa pramātā, sa yenârthaṁ pramiṇoti tat pramāṇam, yo 'rthaḥ pramīyate tat prameyam, yad artha-vijñānaṁ sā pramitiḥ*; NBh 1.1.1: *pramāṇato 'rtha-pratipattiḥ*; NBh 1.1.1: *pramāṇair artha-parīkṣaṇam; pramāṇam* NBh 1.1.1: *antareṇa nârtha-pratipattiḥ*; NBh 1.1.3: *akṣasyâkṣasya prativiṣayaṁ vṛttiḥ pratyakṣam. vṛttis tu sannikarṣaḥ jñānaṁ vā. yadā sannikarṣas tadā jñānaṁ pramitiḥ, yadā jñānaṁ tadā hānôpādānôpekṣā-buddhayaḥ phalam*; NV$_1$ 1.1.1, p. 18.3 = NV$_2$, p. 17.4: *nirṇayaḥ tattva-jñānaṁ pramāṇānāṁ phalam*.

the Vaiśeṣikas.[132] This is one more case when the term *yauga* comprises both systems. We can observe that one and the same author uses one and the same term either to refer to the followers of Nyāya, or the Vaiśeṣika or both, and when the followers of one of the schools are mentioned explicitly by their standard name, say 'the Naiyāyikas', 'the Yaugas' will refer to the other, e.g. 'the Vaiśeṣikas'.

As we could see so far, the term *yoga* is never used unequivocally as referring just to one and the same school in philosophical literature. On some occasions it refers to Nyāya, on others to Vaiśeṣika. The external evidence shows that the term *yoga* was predominantly used with reference to Vaiśeṣika, but sometimes (e.g. Guṇaratna) also to Nyāya. Also the system's internal evidence (NBh 1.1.29) reveals that the term was current as another name for Vaiśeṣika, the older of both schools. Further, followers of Nyāya are sometimes called also *yoga*s or *yauga*s (e.g. SVM), but sometimes—as we shall see—also the followers of Vaiśeṣika are known as such.

Even though his judgement is based on an assessment of a much narrower pool of samples, CHAṬṬOPĀDHYĀYA (1927: 857) seems generally right in concluding that 'All these passages show that the Naiyāyika or the Vaiśeṣika, more often the former, was known as Yoga or Yauga', except for his conclusion regarding the frequency of references to either of the schools. Certainly it is not the case that 'the balance of evidence is in favour of the Naiyāyika' (1927: 857). As we have seen, the term *yoga* is used to designate both the systems of Nyāya and Vaiśeṣika, whereas the terms *yauga* or *yoga* alike denote the followers of either of the systems or of both the systems jointly.

The fact that both the schools were here and there referred to by the same name *yoga* should be interpreted as a reflection of their common origin which was grounded in the primary meaning of the verbal root √*yuj*—'to connect', esp. 'to rationally establish a connection between two things', i.e. 'to reason', 'to be consistent', 'to justify' etc., and its substantive derivative *yukti*—'argumentation' or 'reasoning', 'logical congruity' etc. This line of interpretation is confirmed in a comment by Raghūttama in his *Bhāṣya-candra*, a commentary on the *Nyāya-bhāṣya*:

> 'Those who primarily have (sc. practice) *yoga*, i.e. argumentation (*yukti*) or reasoning (*tarka*) are the Yogas, according to [Pāṇini's rule 5.2.127 stipulating that the *taddhita* affix] aC [A 3.1.1 is in-

---

[132] See e.g. PBh 243, 245, p. 45: [243] *tatra sāmānya-viśeṣeṣu svarūpâlocana-mātraṁ pratyakṣaṁ pramāṇam, prameyā dravyâdayaḥ padârthāḥ, pramātâtmā, pramitir dravyâdi-viṣayaṁ jñānam.* … [45] *athavā sarveṣu padârtheṣu catuṣṭaya-sannikarṣād avitatham avyapadeśyaṁ yaj jñānam utpadyate tat pratyakṣaṁ pramāṇam, prameyā dravyâdayaḥ padârthāḥ, pramātâtmā, pramitir guṇa-doṣa-mādhyasthya-darśanam iti.*

> troduced] after [the class of stems] beginning with *arśas* ["hemorrhoids"].'[133]

In addition, we have also seen above that the current of Ānvīkṣikī was methodologically linked to the epistemological, investigative and analytic tradition preserved in the *Caraka-saṁhitā*, which was in its turn linked to the school of Nyāya. I would claim it was not a coincidence but a gradual development of the tradition of Nyāya and Vaiśeṣika, which did not yet exist as separate schools at the time of 'Kauṭilya' (the collective author of the *Artha-śāstra*) in the second–first centuries BCE, but which gradually evolved out the methodical reflection cultivated by the representatives of various groups subsumed under Ānvīkṣikī. These common roots of Nyāya and Vaiśeṣika in the current of Ānvīkṣikī are most probably responsible for the fact that the term *yoga* was applied to both schools or to the followers of both schools.

Early epistemology, e.g. the theory of perception (see § 9.3), developed within the circles of the epistemologists of the *Caraka-saṁhitā*, the authors of *Nyāya-sūtra* and the *Vaiśeṣika-sūtra* are very similar and point to their common origins. All three shared the same concerns of epistemology, analysis, rational enquiry, methodology and reason-based debate as Ānvīkṣikī. Furthermore, the assurances of Pakṣilasvāmin Vātsyāyana and Uddyotakara Bhāradvāja to the effect that there exists a historical link between Nyāya and Ānvīkṣikī and one can genuinely speak of Nyāya's successorship cannot be disregarded, because they reflect the actual historical development, it seems. What Vātsyāyana did was not artificially equate his own school with Ānvīkṣikī and create a new link, but rather he reaffirmed an existing connection with a current of which Nyāya was a direct successor and, in addition, stressed the orthodox character of his own school as the study of the self (*ātma-vidyā*) so that it should not be confused with other systems which once belonged to and were directly associated with Ānvīkṣikī, such as the materialists, who outspokenly rejected any sort of eschatology:

> 'Thus, this knowledge of truth [mentioned in the *sūtra*] as the accomplishment of the highest goal should be known according to respective disciplines of learning. And in this particular discipline, i.e. the study of the highest self, the knowledge of truth means the knowledge of the self etc., and the attainment of the highest goal means the attainment of liberation.'[134]

[133] BhC, p. 133: *yogo yuktiḥ tarkaḥ pradhānatayā vidyate yeṣāṁ te yogāḥ, arśa-āditvāt ac.* [A 5.2.127: *arśa-ādibhyo 'C*]. BHATTACHARYA (1974: 43) draws attention to this passage.

[134] NBh_1 1.1.1, p. 65 = NBh_2, 6.2–3: *tad idaṁ tattva-jñānaṁ niḥśreyasâdhigamaś ca*[a] *yathā-vidyaṁ veditavyam. iha tv adhyātma-vidyāyām ātmâdi-jñānaṁ tattva-jñānam, niḥśreyasâdhigamo 'pavarga-prāptiḥ.* [[a] NBh_1: *niḥśreyasâdhigamârthaṁ.*]

Apart from shared epistemological concerns, we can see a consistent line of evolution of a system which applied methodological skills and analytical and epistemological tools to the investigation of the highest human goals, i.e. of what they labelled *adhyātma-vidyā*, the study of the highest self. At this stage my initial claim that the Yoga of the *Artha-śāstra* is precisely an early form of Nyāya and Vaiśeṣika seems well grounded. Certainly, it was not the Nyāya and the Vaiśeṣika we now know. It was a tradition which only gradually assumed its later name of Nyāya, perhaps a tradition which was not clearly distinguished from the Vaiśeṣika, a tradition which I would here call 'proto-Nyāya-Vaiśeṣika'. That could explain why the term *yoga* is later used, also by the Naiyāyikas, with reference to the proponents of the Vaiśeṣika, but still an early tradition of Nyāya is included in Kauṭilya's classification of Ānvīkṣikī.

The above conclusion decidedly speaks against theories which would try to explain the name *yoga* for the system of Nyāya by trying to link it to spiritual practices of the system of (Pātañjala) Yoga. Such an explanatory conjecture is found with CHAṬṬOPĀDHYĀYA (1927: 857–858), subscribing to the view of Paṇḍit Gopīnātha Kavirāj (*Sarasvatī Bhavana Studies*, vol. III) who allegedly

> 'shows the intimate connexion between Nyāya and Yogic practices. He (Gopīnātha Kavirāj—P.B.) writes, "though Yoga in its wider form has been practically accepted by every system of Indian philosophy, its relation with Nyāya is in some manner more special and, perhaps, fundamental." The *Sarva-siddhānta-saṁgraha*, he points out, "affords distinct proof in support of a relation existing between Nyāya and Yoga; for it is maintained there that according to Nyāya *mokṣa* follows directly from Yoga, a doctrine which it shares in common with the Patañjali system (as distinguished from the Sāṅkhya, where *jñāna* is held to be the immediate cause of Mukti)." "The Nyāya Darśana, in its present form," Mr. Kavirāj adds, "contains some *Sūtras* (4–2, 38–49) where the practices of Yoga are strongly recommended."'

In view of the fact that in Kauṭilya's work, 'Yoga' does not encompass a proto-Nyāya, but also a proto-Vaiśeṣika alike, this theory cannot not explain how also Vaiśeṣika, substantially related to Nyāya, could be linked to the practice of Yoga at the time when it was clearly atheistic and rejected any paranormal explanations and supramundane practices, such as extrasensory perception[135] and meditation was not the concern of the system. The ties between earliest form of Vaiśeṣika and probably also Nyāya, on the one hand, and the system of Yoga were rather relaxed, to say the least. Further, what the theory referred to above actually claims is that early Nyāya was called Yoga

[135] A good attestation is the fact that the discussion of supernatural perception in the *Vaiśeṣika-sūtra* (VS(C) 9.13–17) is clearly a later interpolation, see WEZLER (1982), HONDA (1988), ISAACSON (1993) and BALCEROWICZ (2010: 292 f., 308 ff.).

simply because it was associated with Pātañjala Yoga, which in itself is an ahistoric statement: Pātañjala Yoga in the form and texts we know is a product of a turn fourth and fifth centuries CE.[136] Along these lines, one could as well argue that any school of thought in India could deserve the name 'Yoga' simply because of its association the system of Pātañjala Yoga. And, as we know, the influence of Yoga practice on various systems in India was indeed enormous, and still these did not come to be occasionally known as Yoga: clearly, not everything related to Yoga becomes a Yoga.

Our understanding of what systems Ānvīkṣikī comprised and what Kauṭilya's 'Yoga' stood for finds an indirect confirmation in the *Kāvya-mīmāṁsā*, a work on poetics composed by Rājaśekhara (*ca.* 880–920 CE). In Chapter Two *On Disciplines of Learning* (*Śāstra-nirdeśa*),[137] the author summarises various divisions of sciences and disciplines, and Ānvīkṣikī features in a number of such typologies. The list opens an eighteenfold classification, which comprises Ānvīkṣikī, just as several other lists, including the well-known fourfold classification of Kauṭilya, but also, many of them including Ānvīkṣikī. Of particular interest is a passage (KM 2, p. 4.11–23) commenting on and expanding or updating the *Artha-śāstra* classification:

> 'According to Kauṭilya there are four disciplines of learning: methodology (*ānvīkṣikī*), the triple *Veda*, economics and political science. The triple *Veda*, explored with the help of methodology, surpasses both economics and political science. ... Out of these the triple *Veda* has already been discussed. Methodology is twofold in view of being a preliminary position (*pūrva-pakṣa*) and

[136] See e.g. BRONKHORST (1984: 191–203), Philipp André MAAS (2006: xii–xix) and (2010: 383 f.) according to whom for the date of the *Pātañjala-yoga-śāstra* and the *Yoga-bhāṣya* 'a time span reaching from 325 to 425 CE seems to be most likely' (2010: 383).

[137] KM 2 (*śāstra-nirdeśa*), pp. 2.16–5.17, esp. the passages 3.11–12, 20–21, 4.5–24: *pauruṣeyaṁ tu purāṇam ānvīkṣikī mīmāṁsā smṛti-tantram iti catvāri śāstrāṇi. ... ānvīkṣikī tu vidyâvasare vakṣyāmaḥ. ... tad dhi śāstrāṇy anudhāvanti. "vārttā kāma-sūtraṁ śilpi-śāstraṁ daṇḍa-nītir iti pūrvaiḥ sahâṣṭā-daśa vidyā-sthānāni" ity apare. ānvīkṣikī trayī varttā daṇḍa-nītiś cêti vidyāḥ. "daṇḍa-nītir evâikā vidyā" ity auśanasāḥ. daṇḍa-bhayād dhi kṛtsno lokaḥ sveṣu sveṣu karmasv avatiṣṭhate. "vārttā daṇḍa-nītir dve vidye" iti bārhaspatyāḥ. vṛttir vinaya-grahaṇaṁ ca sthiti-hetu-loka-yātrāyāḥ. "trayī-vārttā-daṇḍa-nītayas tisro vidyāḥ" iti mānavāḥ. trayī hi vārttā-daṇḍa-nītyor upadeṣṭrī. ānvīkṣikī trayī-vārttā-daṇḍa-nītayaś catasro vidyā" iti kauṭilyaḥ. ānvīkṣikyā hi vivecitā trayī vārttā-daṇḍa-nītyoḥ prabhavati. "pañcamī sahitya-vidyā" iti yāyavarīyaḥ. sā hi catasṝṇāṁ api vidyānāṁ niṣpandaḥ. ābhirddharmârthau yad vidyāt tad vidyānām vidyātvam. tatra trayī vyākhyātā. dvidhā cânvīkṣikī pūrvôttara-pakṣābhyām. arhad-bhadanta-darśane lokāyataṁ ca pūrvaḥ pakṣaḥ. sāṁkhyaṁ nyāya-vaiśeṣikau côttaraḥ. ta ime ṣaṭ tarkāḥ. tatra ca tisraḥ kathā bhavanti vādo jalpo vitaṇḍā ca. madhyasthayos tattvâvabodhāya vastu-tattva-parāmarśo vādaḥ. sva-pakṣasyâparigrahitrī para-pakṣasya dūṣayitrī vitaṇḍā. kṛṣi-pāśu-pālye vaṇijyā ca vārttā. ānvīkṣikī-trayī-vārttānāṁ yoga-kṣema-sādhano daṇḍas tasya nītir daṇḍa-nītiḥ. tasyām āyattā loka-yātrêti śāstrāṇi.*

an antithetical position (*pūrva-pakṣa*). The view of the Jainas and Buddhists but also of the materialists constitute a preliminary position. Sāṁkhya and the systems of Nyāya and Vaiśeṣika are an antithetical position. All these constitute six schools of reasoning (*tarka*). These also for three kinds of debate: debate proper (*vāda*), paradialectical dispute (*jalpa*) and eristic disputation (*vitaṇḍā*). ... Economics comprises agriculture, cattle breeding and trade. Political power (*daṇḍa*) is the means of securing the pursuit of (lit. acquisition and maintenance) of methodology (*ānvīkṣikī*), the triple *Veda* and economics (AŚ 1.4.3), the application of this [political power] is political science.'

In the above classification based on the well-known Kauṭilya's division of disciplines of learning, Ānvīkṣikī is divided into two sections. The first section, called a preliminary position (*pūrva-pakṣa*), groups non-Brahmanic schools, among which the original materialistic school (*lokāyata*) is still preserved. Furthermore, the system of the materialists is in fact grammatically distinguished in the enumeration as a separate locution, not a part of a compound **arhad-bhadanta-lokāyatika-darśanāni*, which may suggest that the original *lokāyataṁ ca* of *Artha-śāstra* 1.2.10 (*sāṁkhyaṁ yogo lokāyataṁ cêty ānvīkṣikī*) was expanded by the insertion of the additional two systems *arhad-bhadanta-darśane*. The second section, called an antithetical position (*pūrva-pakṣa*), comprises Brahmanic schools such as Sāṁkhya, Nyāya and Vaiśeṣika, the latter two schools being a later development of the 'Yoga' current of Kauṭilya. Thus, the *pūrva-pakṣa* exactly corresponds to the enumeration *sāṁkhyaṁ yogaḥ* of *Artha-śāstra* 1.2.10. All in all, except for the inclusion of Jainas and Buddhists, the original list of Kauṭilya is preserved, except for Nyāya-Vaiśeṣika explicitly replacing 'Yoga'.

Again, in Chapter Eight *On the Sources of the Meaning of Poetry* (*Kāvyârtha-yonayaḥ*, p. 35 ff.), Rājaśekhara discusses how different schools of thought and disciplines can contribute to the understanding of poetical meaning and what their theories of meaning are. In a passage he says that there are two kinds of thinkers who rely on cognitive criteria (*prāmāṇika*), being the representatives of the discipline of (*pramāṇa-vidyā*):[138] the *maimāṁṣika*s, i.e. those who follow *mīmāṁsā* (reasoned hermeneutics) and the reasoners (*tārkika*), i.e. those who follow *tarka* (reasoning).[139] Among those who follow reason (*tarka*), are the followers of Sāṁkhya,[140] and their thought is exemplified with a verse from the chapter on Sāṁkhya-Yoga of the *Bhagavad-gītā* (BhG 2.16). Further,

---

[138] KM 8, p. 35.2.

[139] KM 8, p. 36.19–20: *dvividhaḥ prāmāṇiko maimāṁṣikas tārkikaś ca.*

[140] KM 8, p. 37.1: *tarkeṣu sāṁkhīyaḥ*. We should probably read *tārkikeṣu* instead of *tarkeṣu*.

among the reasoners are the representatives of Nyāya and Vaiśeṣika[141], the Buddhists[142], the materialists[143] and the Jainas[144]. This is, no doubt, an updated (to the intellectual conditions of the turn of the ninth and tenth centuries) classification of currents which examine the foundations of our cognition: what we have here is the term *pramāṇa-vidyā* which replaced the outdated *tarka-vidyā*, synonymous to *ānvīkṣikī*, and also the list of systems is expanded by the inclusion of Mīmāṁsā, Buddhism and Jainism. (In fact, Jayantabhaṭṭa indicates that another name for Ānvīkṣikī is *pramāṇa-vidyā*.[145])

What we really have here is precisely Kauṭilya's typology of Ānvīkṣikī in a new garb adopted to new requirements of Rājaśekhara's times. Also this updated and extended classification agrees with the core typology of sciences of *Artha-śāstra* 1.2.10, and all the three original representatives of Ānvīkṣikī are preserved in the enumeration.

13. To conclude, in the debated passage of the *Artha-śāstra*, which enumerates the three schools—*sāṁkhya*, *yoga* and *lokāyata*—which were comprised within the current of Ānvīkṣikī, Kauṭilya refers, respectively, (1) with the name *sāṁkhya*, to a joint school of Sāṁkhya-Yoga, regularly mentioned under this double name in the epic literature, (2) with the name *yoga*, to an early form of epistemological method and rational enquiry which we could here call a 'proto-Nyāya-Vaiśeṣika', which gradually developed into the school of Nyāya, from its beginnings associated with Vaiśeṣika and the tradition of rational enquiry and debate preserved in the medical treatise *Caraka-saṁhitā*, and (3) to the materialistic tradition of the Lokāyatas/Cārvākas. What united all these three traditions was not the subject matter of enquiry, being so disparate as dualistic ontology of Sāṁkhya-Yoga, pluralistic ontology of Nyāya-Vaiśeṣika and monistic ontology of the materialists, or the salvific concerns of the representatives of Sāṁkhya-Yoga and early Naiyāyikas, on the one hand, and purely materialistic interests of the Cārvākas. We would probably be not far from truth assuming that the current of Ānvīkṣikī comprised also other minor traditions which subscribed to similar methods of rational enquiry and participated in the debates in the circles of Ānvīkṣikī. What all these three main branches, and probably a range of minor ones, shared was the method they applied in their respective fields of particular ontologies and axiologies. In the course of its development, Ānvīkṣikī was 'highjacked' by the tradition of Nyāya, which eventually grew out of it and appropriated the name for itself, but it remained in popular memory as a system which focused on rational argument and enquiry and used or—in the eyes of some: misused—logic (*hetu*) and reason

[141] KM 8, p. 37.7: *nyāya-vaiśeṣikīyaḥ*.

[142] KM 8, p. 37.13: *bauddhīyaḥ*.

[143] KM 8, p. 37.19: *laukāyatikaḥ*.

[144] KM 8, p. 37.24: *ārhataḥ*.

[145] NMa_1 II: 136.1 = NMa_2 II: 100.11: *pramāṇa-vidyā cêyam ānvīkṣakī*.

(*tarka*), and therefore not always triggered positive associations in religious circles. The fear of reason for pious religion-oriented minds is not just a modern phenomenon.

The current of Ānvīkṣikī comprised various philosophical schools and systems which represented divergent ontologies—dualism of Sāṁkhya–Yoga, pluralism of 'Yoga' (later developed into Nyāya–Vaiśeṣika) and monism/materialism of the Lokāyata—and axiologies but were united by a common interest in investigative methods, methodological solutions, epistemological concerns and rational enquiry which could be adopted to their respective ontologies and ethical systems. The current of 'Yoga' represented a tradition whose main preoccupation was the pursuit of the ultimate goal, which involved both the insight into the ultimate human nature, or the highest self (*adhyātma-vidyā*/ *ātma-vidyā*), and its corollary the liberation from mundane bonds and material limitations. Its direct successors were the schools of Nyāya and, to a lesser extent, Vaiśeṣika. Both 'Yoga' and Nyāya shared the same salvific concerns and the same method which reflected the name of the schools: *yoga* (as a synonym to *yukti*) and *nyāya* indicated the method of Ānvīkṣikī, i.e. argumentation or methodical reasoning, which in turn were actually synonymous with still another term *anvīkṣā*, or systematic enquiry (*vide supra* NV 1.1.40, p. 202, n. 65). Interestingly, all these three technical terms *anvīkṣā*, *yoga*/*yukti* and *nyāya*—of more or less the same meaning, gave rise to three separate currents or schools: Ānvīkṣikī, Yoga and Nyāya.

BIBLIOGRAPHY

A = Pāṇini: *Aṣṭādhyāyī*. Sumitra Mangesh Katre: *Aṣṭādhyāyī of Pāṇini in Roman Transliteration*. University of Texas Press, Austin 1987 [reprinted: Motilal Banarsidass, Delhi 1989].

ACM = Hemacandra-sūri: *Abhidhāna-cintā-maṇi*. Vijaya Kastūra-sūri: *Kali-kāla-sarvajña-śrīmad-Hemacandrâcārya-viracitaḥ Abhidhāna-cintā-maṇi-kośaḥ*. Sarasvatī Pustak Bhaṇḍār, Ahmadābād Vī. Saṁ. 2483 [= 1958].

ĀpP = Vidyānanda Pātrakesarisvāmin: *Āpta-parīkṣā*. (1) Gajādharalāl Jain: *1 Āpta-parīkṣā 2 Patra-parīksā ca*. Sanātana Jaina Granthamālā 1, Pannālāla Jaina, Kāśī 1913. (2) Darabārī Lāl Jain Koṭhiyā (ed., tr.): *Tārkika-śiromaṇi śrīmad-Vidyānanda-svāmi-viracitā Āpta-parīkṣā Svopajñâpta-parīkṣâlaṅkṛti-ṭīkâyutā* (*Hindī-anuvāda-prastāvanâdi sahita*). Vīra-sevā-mandir, Sahāranpur 1949 [reprinted Bhāratavarṣīya Anekānta Vidvat Pariṣad, 1992].

AŚ = Kauṭilya: *Artha-śāstra*. (1) R.P. Kangle (ed., tr.): *The Kauṭilīya Arthaśāstra*. Part I: *A Critical Edition with a Glossary*. Part II: *An English Translation with Critical and Explanatory Notes*. Part III: *A Study*. University of Bombay, Bombay 1960, 1963, 1965 [reprinted: Delhi 1986–1988]. (2) Viśvanātha Śāstrī Dātāra (ed.): *Kauṭalīyam Arthaśāstraṁ of Ācārya Viṣṇugupta [Volume One, Part One] With Five Commentaries: 'Śrimūlā' by T. Gaṇapati Śāstrī, 'Vaidikasiddhāntasaṁrakṣiṇī' & 'Jayamaṅgalākroḍapatram' bt Śrī Paṇḍitarāja Rājeśvara Śāstrī Draviḍa, 'Jayamaṁgalā' by Śrī Śaṁkarārya & 'Nītinirṇīti' by Śrī Yogghamācārya*. Sampurnanand Sanskrit University, Varanasi 1991. (3) Rudrapatna Shama Sastry (ed.): *Kauṭilya Arthaśāstra*. Bibliotheca Sanskrita 37, Government Oriental Library Series, Mysore 1909.

BALCEROWICZ 2003 = Balcerowicz, Piotr: *Historia klasycznej filozofii indyjskiej. Część pierwsza: początki, nurty analityczne i filozofia przyrody* [*History of Classical Indian Philosophy. Part One: Beginnings, Analytical Trends and Philosophy of Nature*]. Wydawnictwo Akademickie Dialog, Warszawa 2003.

BALCEROWICZ 2003 = Balcerowicz, Piotr: *Jaina Epistemology In Historical And Comparative Perspective—A Critical Edition And An Annotated Translation Of Siddhasena Mahāmati's Nyāyâvatāra, Siddharṣigaṇin's Nyāyâvatāra-vivṛti And Devabhadrasūri's Nyāyâvatāra-ṭippana*. Volume I & II. Second revised edition. Motilal Banarsidass, Delhi 2009. [first edition: Stuttgart 2001].

BALCEROWICZ 2010 = Balcerowicz, Piotr: 'What Exists for the Vaisesika?', in: Piotr Balcerowicz (ed.): *Logic and Belief in Indian Philosophy*. Motilal Banarsidass, Delhi 2010: 241–348.

BALCEROWICZ–MEJOR 2000 = Balcerowicz, Piotr; Mejor, Marek (eds.): *On the Understanding of Other Cultures. Proceedings of the International Conference on Sanskrit and Related Studies to Commemorate the Centenary of the Birth of Stanisław Schayer (1899–1941). Warsaw University, Poland, October 7–10, 1999. Studia Indologiczne* 7, Warsaw 2000 [Re-edited as: *Essays in Indian Philosophy, Religion and Literature*. Edited with the help of Anna Trynkowska (assistant editor). Motilal Banarsidass, Delhi 2004].

Bhā = Vācaspatimiśra: *Bhāmatī*. (1) Anantakṛṣṇa Śāstrī (ed.): *The Brahmasūtra Śāṅkara Bhāṣya, with the Commentaries Bhāmatī, Kalpataru and Parimala*. Re-edited by Bhārgav Śāstrī, Nirṇāya Sāgara Press, Bombay 1938. (2) Jagadīśa Śāstrī (ed.): *Brahmasūtra-śāṅkara-bhāṣyam, With the Commentaries: Bhāṣya-ratnaprabha of Govindānanda, Bhāmatī of Vācaspatimiśra, Nyāyanirṇaya of Ānandagiri*. Motilal Banarsidass, Delhi 1980 [reprinted: Delhi 1988].

BhāgP = *Bhāgavata-purāṇa*. [no editor's name:] *Maha-ṛṣi-veda-vyāsa-praṇītaṁ śrīmad-bhāgavata-purāṇam*. Gītā-pres, Gorakhpur [no date].

BHATTACHARYA 1974 = Bhattacharya, Kamaleswar: 'A Note on the Term Yoga in Nyāyabhāṣya and Nyāyavārttika on I, 1, 29', *Indologica Taurinensia* 2 (1974) 39–44.

BhC = Raghūttama: *Bhāṣya-candra*. Ganganatha Jha (ed.): *The Nyāya-darshana. The sūtras of Gautama and Bhāshya of Vātsyāyana with two commentaries, Khadyota by Mahāmahopādhyāya Gangānātha Jha, and Bhāshyachandra by Raghūttama*. Caukhambā-Saṁskṛta-granthamālā, Chowkhamba Sanskrit Series Office, Benares 1925.

BhG = *Bhagavad-gītā*. Sarvepalli Radhakrishnan: *The Bhagavadgītā*. George Allen & Unwin Ltd., London 1948.

BOLLÉE 2002 = Willem B. Bollée: *The Story of Paesi (Paesi-kahāṇayaṁ). Soul and Body in Ancient India. A Dialogue on Materialism. Text, Translation, Notes and Glossary*. Harrassowitz Verlag, Wiesbaden 2002 [Reprinted: Hindi Granth Karyalay, Mumbai 2005].

BRONKHORST 1984 = Bronkhorst, Johannes: 'Patañjali and the Yoga Sūtras', *Studien zur Indologie und Iranistik* 10 (1984) 191–212.

BRONKHORST 2000 = Bronkhorst, Johannes: *Karma and Teleology. A problem and its solutions in Indian philosophy*. Studia Philologica Buddhica, Monograph Series XV, The International Institute for Buddhist Studies, Tokyo 2000.

BRONKHORST 2007 = Bronkhorst, Johannes: *Greater Magadha—Studies in the Culture of Early India*. E.J. Brill, Leiden–Boston 2007.

BrP = *Brahma-purāṇa*. Peter Schreiner; Renate Söhnen (ed.): *Sanskrit Indices and Text of the Brahma-purāṇa. Purāṇa Research Publications–Tübingen* 1, Otto Harrassowitz Verlag, Wiesbaden 1987.

CarS = *Caraka-saṁhitā*. (1) Narendra Nātha Senagupta, Balāicandra Senagupta (eds.): *The Carakasaṇhitā of Mahāmuni Agniveśa. Revised by Charaka and Dṛḍhabala. With the 'Āyurveda-Dīpikā' Commentary of Cakrapāṇidatta and 'Jalpakalpataru' by Gaṅgadhara*. Calcutta 1927 [reprinted: Vidya Vilas Press, Varanasi 1983]. (2) R.K. Sharma, Bhagwan Dash (ed., tr.): *Caraka Saṁhitā. Text with English Translation and Critical Exposition Based on Cakrapāṇi Datta's Āyurveda Dīpikā*. Vol. 1 (*Sūtra Sthāna*), Chowkhambā Sanskrit Series, Vārāṇasī 2001 [1. ed.: 1972].

CHATTERJEE 1978 = Chatterjee, Madhumati: 'Notes on philosophy, *darśana* and ānvīkṣikī', *Calcutta Review* 4,1–2 (1978) 135–138.

CHAṬṬOPĀDHYĀYA 1927 = Chaṭṭopādhyāya, Kṣetreśacandra: 'A Peculiar Meaning of "Yoga"', *Journal of the Royal Asiatic Society* (New Series) 59.4 (1927) 854–858.

DAHLMANN 1895 = Dahlmann, Joseph: *Das Mahābhārata als Epos und Rechtsbuch. Ein Problem aus Altindiens Cultur- und Literatur-Geschichte*. Verlag von Felix L. Dames, Berlin 1895.

DUNCAN–DERRETT 1973 = Duncan, John; Derrett; Martin (eds.): *Dharmaśāstra and Juridical Literature*. [in the series: J. Gonda (ed.): *A History of Indian Literature*. Vol. V, fasc. 1], Otto Harrassowitz Verlag, Wiesbaden 1973.

CHATTOPADHYAYA –GANGOPADHYAYA 1992 = Gangopadhyaya, Mrinalkanti; Chattopadhyaya, Debiprasad (tr.): *Nyāya Philosophy. Literal Translation of Gautama's Nyāya-sūtra with Vātsyāyana's Bhāṣya. Indian Studies* (*Indian Philosophy in its Sources*). Vol. 1, Reprinted, Firma KLM Private Limited, Calcutta 1982 [first edition: Indian Studies Past & Present, Calcutta 1967].

GDhS = *Gautama-dharma-sūtra*. (1) A.F. Stenzler (ed.): *The Institutes of Gautama* (*Gautama-dharma-sūtra*). London 1876. (2) *Gautama-dharma-sūtra*. Ānandâśrama-saṁskṛta-granthāvaliḥ 61, Ānandāśrama (Anandasrama), Poona (Pune) 1966. (3) See: OLIVELLE (2000: 116–189).

GLASENAPP 1940 = Glasenapp, Helmuth von: *Entwicklungsstufen des indischen Denkens. Untersuchungen über die Philosophie der Brahmanen und Buddhisten*. Niemeyer, Halle (Saale) 1940.

HACKER 1958 = Hacker, Paul: 'Ānvīkṣikī', *Wiener Zeitschrift für die Kunde Süd- und Ostasiens* 2 (1958) 54–83 [reprinted in: *Kleine Schriften*: 137–166].

HALBFASS 1988 = Halbfass, Wilhelm: *India and Europe. An Essay in Philosophical Understanding*. State University of New York Press, Albany 1988 [reprinted: Motilal Banarsidass Publishers, Delhi 1990]: 263–286.

HONDA 1988 = Honda, Megumu: 'Vaishēshika Sūtora oboegaki II. [Notes on the Vaiśeṣikasūtra II]', *Indogaku Bukkyōgaku Kenkyū* (*Journal of Indian and Buddhist Studies*) 37,1 (1988) 472–467 [cited after ISAACSON (1993)].

ISAACSON 1993 = Isaacson, Harunaga: 'Yogic perception (yogipratyakṣa) in early Vaieṣika', *Studien zur Indologie und Iranistik* 18 (1993) 139–160.

JACOBI 1911 = Jacobi, Hermann: 'Zur Frühgeschichte der indischen Philosophie', Sitzungsberichte der Preussischer Akademie der Wissenschaften, B 1911: 733 ff. [English translation: 'A Contribution Towards the Early History of Indian Philosophy (tr. V.A. Sukthankar)', *Indian Antiquary* 57 (1918) 101–109.

JACOBI 1930 = Jacobi, Hermann: 'Über das ursprüngliche Yogasystem', *Sitzungsberichte der preussischen Akademie der Wissenschaften*, philosophisch-historische Klasse 1929 (1930) 581–624 [in: *Kleine Schriften*, hrsg. Bernhard Kölver, Franz Steiner Verlag, Wiesbaden 1970: 682–725].

KANE 1930–1962 = Kane, Pandurang Vaman: *History of Dharmaśāstra*. 5 Vols., Bhandarkar Oriental Research Institute, Poona 1930–1962 [reprinted: 1968–1977 and 1990–1997].

KM = Rājaśekhara: *Kāvya-mīmāṁsā*. C.D. Dalal; R. Anantakrishna Shastry (eds.): *Kāvyamīmāṁsā of Rājaśekhara*. Gaekwad's Oriental Series 1, Oriental Institute, Baroda 1916.

KS = Vātsyāyana: *Kāma-sūtra*. Gosvamī Dāmodar Shastri: *The Kāma-sūtra by Śrī Vātsyāyana Muni*. Kāshi Sanskrit Series 29, Jai Krishnadas-Haridas Gupta, Benares 1929.

LARSON 1979 = Larson, Gerald J.: *Classical Sāṁkhya—An Interpretation of its History and Meaning with The Sāṁkhya-kārikā of Īśvarakṛṣṇa (romanized text with translation)*. Second revised ed., Motilal Banarsidass, Delhi–Varanasi–Patna 1979.

MAAS 2006 = Maas, Philipp André (ed.): *Sāmadhipāda. Das erste Kapitel des* Pātañjalayogaśāstra *zum ersten Mal kritisch ediert./The First Chapter of the* Pātañjalayogaśāstra *for the first Time Critically Edited.* Studia Indologica Universitatis Halensis, Geisteskultur Indiens: Texte und Studien 9, Shaker Verlag, Aachen 2006.

MAAS 2010 = Maas, Philipp André: 'Valid Knowledge and Belief in Classical Sāṁkhya-Yoga', in: Piotr Balcerowicz (ed.): *Logic and Belief in Indian Philosophy*. Motilal Banarsidass, Delhi 2010: 383–392.

MBh = *Mahā-bhārata*. (1) Vishnu S. Sukthankar; S.K. Belvalkar; et al. (ed.): *The Mahābhārata for the first time critically edited*. 19 Vols., Bhandarkar Oriental Research Institute, Poona 1933–1966. (2) Rāmanārāyaṇadatta Pāndeya Śāstrī (ed. tr.): *Śrīmad-mahārṣi veda-vyāsa-praṇīta mahā-bhārata*. 4 Parts (*Khaṇḍa*), Gīta-pres Gorakhpur 1911–1964.

MDhŚ = *Mānava-dharma-śāstra* [*Manu-smṛti*]. See: OLIVELLE (2006).

Mil = *Milinda-pañho*. (1) V. Treckner (ed.): *The Milindapañho: Being Dialogues between King Milinda and the Buddhist Sage Nagasena*. Williams and Norgate, Edinburgh 1880 [reprinted: 1962]. (2) Swami Dwarikadas Shastri (ed.): *Milinda-pañha (Questions of Milinda)*. Bauddha Bharati Series, Bauddha Bharati 13, Vārāṇasī 1979.

MŚVṬ = Sucaritamiśra: *Mīmāṁsā-śloka-vārttika-ṭīkā* [*Kāśikā*]. Sāmbaśiva Śāstri; V.A. Rāmasvāmi Śāstri (eds.): *Ślokavārttikaṁ Sucaritamiśra-praṇītayā Kāśikākhyayāṭīkayā sametam*. 3 Vols., *Trivandrum Sanskrit Series* 23, 29 and 31, CBH Publications, Trivandrum 1926–1943.

NARAIN 1979 = Narain, Harsh: '*Ānvīkṣikī* as dialectic', [in:] *Ludwik Sternbach Felicitation Volume*. 2 Vols., Lucknow 1979: 579–592.

NAV = Siddharṣi-gaṇin: *Nyāyâvatāra-vivṛti*. See: BALCEROWICZ 2003.

NBh = Vātsyāyana Pakṣilasvāmin: *Nyāya-bhāṣya*. See: NS.

NBhū = Bhāsarvajña: *Nyāya-bhūṣaṇa*. Svāmī Yogīndrānanda (ed.): *Śrīmad-ācārya-Bhāsarvajña-praṇītasya Nyāya-sārasya svôpajñaṁ vyākhyānaṁ Nyāya-bhūṣaṇam. Ṣad-darśana-prakāśana-granthamālā* 1, Ṣad-darśana Prakāśana Pratiṣṭhānam, V 1968.

NīSā = Kāmandaki: *Nīti-sāra*. T. Gaṇapāti Sāstrī: *The Nītisāra of Kāmandaka with the commentary, Jayamaṅgala of Sankarārya*. Trivandrum Sanskrit Series 14, Travancore Government Press, Trivandrum 1912.

NMa = Jayantabhaṭṭa: *Nyāya-mañjarī*. (1) K.S. Varadacharya (ed.): *Nyāyamañjarī of Jayantabhaṭṭa with Ṭippaṇi—Nyāyasaurabha by the Editor*. Vol. 1 & 2, *Oriental Research Institute Series* 116, 139, University of Mysore, Mysore 1969, 1983. (2) Gaurinath Sastri (ed.): *Nyāyamañjarī of Jayanta Bhaṭṭa with the Commentary of Granthi-bhaṅga by Cakradhara*. Part 1–3, M.M. Śivakumāraśāstri-Granthamālā, Sampūrṇānand Saṁskṛta Viśvavidyālaya 5, Vārāṇasī 1982, 1983, 1984.

NS = Akṣapāda Gautama: *Nyāya-sūtra*. (1) Taranatha Nyaya-Tarkatirtha; Amarendramohan Tarkatirtha; Hemantakumar Tarkatirtha (eds.): *Nyāyadarśanam. With Vātsyāyana's Bhāṣya, Uddyotakara's Vārttika, Vācaspati Miśra's Tātparyaṭīkā & Viśvanātha's Vṛtti*. 2 Vols., Calcutta Sanskrit Series 18, 19, Metropolitan Printing & Publishing House, Calcutta 1936, 1944. (2) Anantalal Thakur (ed.): *Gautamīyanyāyadarśana with Bhāṣya of Vātsyāyana*. Indian Council of Philosophical Research, New Delhi 1997.

NSā = Bhāsarvajña: *Nyāya-sāra*. See: NBhū.

NSā = Kāmandaki: *Nīti-sāra*. Raja Rajendra Lala Mitra (ed.): *The Nītisāra by Kāmandaki*. With English translation by Sisir Kumar Mitra. Bibliotheca Indica No. 179, The Asiatic Society, Calcutta 1861.

NV = Uddyotakara: *Nyāya-[bhāṣya]-vārttika*. (1) Pt. Vindhyeśvarī Prasāda Dvivedin (ed.): *Nyâyavârttika, A Critical Gloss on Nyàya Darśana, Vàtsyàyanabhàshya, by Bhâradwâja Uddyotakara*. The Chowkhamba Sanskrit Series Office, Benares 1915–18 [reprinted: Eastern Book Linkers, Delhi 1986]. (2) Anantalal Thakur (ed.): *Nyāyabhāṣyavārttika of Bhāradvāja Uddyotakara*. Indian Council of Philosophical Research, New Delhi 1997.

OLIVELLE 2000 = Olivelle, Patrick: *The Dharmasūtras: The Law Codes of Āpastamba, Gautama, Baudhāyana, and Vasistha*. Annotated Text and Translation. Motilal Banarsidass, Delhi 2000.

OLIVELLE 2006 = Olivelle, Patrick: *Manu's Code of Law. A Critical Edition and Translation of the Mānava-dharmaśāstra*. With the editorial Assistance of Suman Olivelle. Oxford University Press. Oxford—New York—Delhi 2006.

PA = Māṇikyanandin: *Parīkṣâmukha-sūtra*. (1) Satis Chandra Vidyābhūṣaṇa (ed.): *Parīkṣāmukha-sūtram (A Digambara Jaina Work on Logic (Nyāya)) by Māṇikya Nandi Together with the Commentary Called Parīkṣāmukha-laghu-vṛttiḥ by Ananta Vīrya*. Bibliotheca Indica 1209, Asiatic Society, Calcutta 1909. (2) Hira Lal Jain (ed.): *Prameyaratnamāla of Lahu Anantavīrya, A Commentary on Parīks'āmukha Sūtra of Māṇikyanandī. Edited with Chintamani Hindi Commentary*. Caukhambā Vidyābhavan, Vārāṇasī 1964.

PALV = Anantavīrya: *Parīkṣâmukha-laghu-vṛtti* [= *Prameya-ratna-māla*]. See: PA.

PaP = Vidyānanda Pātrakesarisvāmin: *Patra-parīkṣā*. See: $\bar{\text{A}}\text{pP}_1$.

PBh = Praśastapāda: *Praśastapāda-bhāṣya* (*Padârtha-dharma-saṁgraha*). Johannes Bronkhorst; Yves Ramseier (ed.): *Word index to the Praśastapādabhāṣya: a complete word index to the printed editions of the Praśastapādabhāṣya*. Motilal Banarsidass, Delhi 1994.

PERRY 1997 = Perry, Bruce: 'Early Nyāya and Hindu Orthodoxy: *ānvīkṣikī* and *adhikāra*', [in:] Eli Franco; Karin Preisendanz (eds.): *Beyond Orientalism: The Work of Wilhelm Halbass and its Impact on Cross-Cultural Studies*. Poznań Studies in the Philosophy of the Sciences and the Humanities, Vol. 59, Rodopi, Amsterdam–Atlanta 1997: 449–470.

POLLOCK 2005 = Sheldon I. Pollock (tr.): *Rāmāyaṇa, Book Two: Ayodhyā, by Valmīki*. The Clay Sanskrit Library, New York University Press, JJC Foundation, New York 2005.

PrBh = Madhusūdana Sarasvatī: *Prasthāna-bheda*. (1) Albrecht Weber (ed.): *Madhusūdana-Sarasvatī's encyklopädische Uebersicht der orthodoxen brahmanischen Literatur*. [no place of publication, a copy with a handwritting: 'Göttingen'] 1849 [reprinted: *Indische Studien I*, Berlin 1973]. (2) *Prasthāna-bhedaḥ Śrīmad-Madhusūdana-Sarasvatyā viracitaḥ*. Śrīraṅgam 1912.

PREISENDANZ 2000 = Preisendanz, Karin: 'Debate and Independent Reasoning vs. Tradition: On the Precarious Position of Early Nyāya', [in:] Ryutaro Tsuchida; Albrecht Wezler (eds.): *Harānandalaharī. Volume in Honour of Professor Minoru Hara on his Seventieth Birthday*. Dr. Inge Wezler, Verlag für Orientalistische Fachpublikationen, Reinbek 2000: 221–251.

PRETS 2000 = Prets, Ernst: 'Theories of Debate, Proof and Counter-Proof in the Early Indian Dialectical Tradition', [in:] BALCEROWICZ–MEJOR (2000: 369–382).

R = *Rāmāyaṇa*. (1) Shastri Shrinivasa Katti Mudholakara (ed.): *Rāmāyaṇa of Vālmīki, With the Commentaries Tilaka of Rāma, Rāmāyaṇaśirmaṇi of Śivasahāya and Bhūṣaṇa of Govindarāja*. 8 Vols., Parimal Publications, Delhi 1983. (2) G.H. Bhatt e.a. (eds.): *The Vālmīki-Rāmāyaṇa. The Ayodhya-kāṇḍa*. Oriental Institute, Baroda 1960–1975. (3) Sankrit text (following R_2) and English translation of *Ayodhyā-kāṇḍa*: POLLOCK (2005).

RANDLE 1930 = Randle, H.N.: *Indian Logic in the Early Schools. A Study of the Nyāyadarśana in Its Relation to the Early Logic of Other Schools*. Oxford University Press, London 1930 [reprinted: Oriental Books Reprint Corporation, Delhi 1796].

RghV = Kālidāsa: *Raghu-vaṁśa*. Shankar P. Pandit (ed.): *The Raghu-vam'sa of Kâlidâsa, with the Commentary of Mallinātha*. Part I, Cantos I–VI, Bombay Sanskrit Series V, Bombay 1897.

RP = *Rāyapaseṇiya* [*Rājapraśnīya-sūtra*]. (1) Yuvācārya Śrī Miśrīmalajī Mahārāj 'Madhukar' (ed.), Śrī Ratan Muni (tr.): *Rājapraśnīya-sūtra. Second Upāṅga Rājaprashniya Sūtram [Original Text, Hindi Version. Notes, Annotations and Appendices etc.]. Jināgama Grantha-mālā* 15, Śrī Āgam Prakāśan Samiti, Beawar (Byāvar/Rājasthān) 1982. See: BOLLÉE (2002).

RUBEN 1926 = Ruben, Walter: 'Zur Frühgeschichte der indischen Philosophie' (Review of JACOBI (1911), in: Willibald Kirfel (ed.): *Beiträge zur Literaturwissenschaft und Geistesgeschichte Indiens. Festgabe Hermann Jacobi zum 75. geburtstag (11. Februar 1925) dargebracht von Freunden, Kollegen und Schülern*. Kommissionsverlag F. Klopp, Bonn 1926: 346–357.

SASTRY 1967 = Sastry, R. Shama (tr.): *Kautilya's Arthaśāstra*. Mysore Printing and Publishing House, Mysore 1967.

SCHARFE 1989 = Scharfe, Hartmut: *The State in Indian Tradition*. E.J. Brill, Leiden—New York—København—Köln 1989.

ṢDSa = Haribhadra-sūri: *Ṣaḍ-darśana-samuccaya*. Mahendra Kumār Jain (ed.): *Śrī-Haribhadrasūri-viracita-Ṣaḍ-darśana-samuccaya Śrī-Guṇaratnasūri-kṛta-Tarka-rahasya-dipikā Somatilaka-sūri-kṛta-Laghu-vṛtti tathā ajñāta-kartṛka-Avacūrṇi*. With the Introduction of Pt. Dalsukh Malvania. Jñānapīṭha Mūrtidevī Jaina Grantha-mālā 36 [Sanskrit Grantha], Bhāratīya Jñānapīṭha Prakāśana, Vārāṇāsī 1981 [first edition: 1969].

SDSS = [Anonymous, ascribed to Śaṅkara]: *Sarva-darśana-siddhānta-saṅgraha*. Malur Raṅgācārya (ed.): *The Sarva-siddhānta-saṅgraha of Śaṅkarācārya*. Madras Government Press, Madras 1909.

SK = Īśvarakṛṣṇa: *Sāṁkhya-kārikā*. Nārāyaṇacaraṇa Śāstri and Śvetavaikuṇṭha Śāstri (eds.): *Sāṁkhya-kārikā of Īśvarakṛṣṇa, With the Commentaries of Svāmin Nārāyaṇa, Gauḍapādâcārya and Tattva-kaumudī of Vācaspati Miśra with Kiraṇâvalī of Kṛṣṇavallabhâcārya Svamināṛāyaṇa*. Banaras 1937 [Second Edition, Vyāsaprakāśan, Vārāṇasī 1989.]

SOLOMON 1976–1978 = Solomon, Esther A.: *Indian Dialectics. Methods of Philosophical Discussion*. 2 Vols. Ahmedabad 1976, 1978.

SVM = Malliṣeṇa-sūri: *Syād-vāda-mañjarī*. A.B. Dhruva (ed.): *Syād-vāda-mañjarī of Malliṣeṇa with the Anya-yoga-vyavaccheda-dvātriṁśikā of Hemacandra*. Bombay Sanskrit and Prakrit Series 83, Bombay 1933.

THAKUR 1963 = Thakur, Anantalal: 'Vātsyāyana and the Vaiśeṣika System', Vishveshwaranand Indological Journal 1,1 (1963) 78–86.

THAKUR 2003 = Thakur, Anantalal: *Origin and Development of the Vaiśeṣika System*. In the Series: *History of Science, Philospohy and Culture in Indian Civilization* (General Editor: D.P. Chatthopadhyaya), Volume II, Part 4. Centre for Studies in Civilizations, New Delhi 2003.

THOMAS 1960 = Thomas, F.W. (tr.): *Śrī Malliṣeṇasūrisūri: Syād-vāda-mañjarī—The Flower-spray of the Quodammodo Doctrine*. Translated and annotated. Akademie-Verlag, Berlin 1960 [reprinted: Motilal Banarsidass, Delhi 1968].

TRD = Guṇaratna-sūri: *Tarka-rahasya-dipikā*. See: ṢDSa.

TSa = Śāntarakṣita: *Tattva-saṁgraha*. (1) Embar Krishnamacharya (ed.): *Tattvasaṅgraha of Śāntarakṣita with the commentary of Kamalaśīla*. 2 Vols., Gaekwad's Oriental Series 30–31, Oriental Institute, Baroda 1926 [reprinted: 1984, 1988]. (2) Dvarikadas Shastri (ed.): *Tattvasaṅgraha of Ācārya Shāntarakṣita with the Commentary 'Pañjikā' of Shri Kamalashīla*. 2 Vols. Bauddha Bharati Series, Bauddha Bharati 1, Vārāṇasī 1981–1982.

TV = Kumārilabhaṭṭa: *Tantra-vārttika*. In: Kashinath Vasudev Abhyankar; G.A. Jośi (eds.): *Mīmāṁsā-darśanam*. 7 Vols., Ānandâśrama-saṁskṛta-granthāvaliḥ 17, Ānandāśrama (Anandasrama), Poona (Pune) 1970–1976.

VIDYABHUSANA 1920 = Vidyabhusana, Satish Chandra: *A History of Indian Logic (Ancient, Mediaeval and Modern Schools)*. Calcutta 1920 [reprinted: Motilal Banarsidass, Delhi 1988].

ViP = *Viṣṇu-purāṇa*. (1) *Śrī-śrī-viṣṇu-purāṇa*. Gita Press (Gītāpres), Gorakhpur 1957 [= Saṁ. 2033]. (2) *Viṣṇu-purāṇa*. Veṅk: no date.

VS(C) = Kaṇāda: *Vaiśeṣika-sūtra*. Muni Jambuvijaya (ed.): *Vaiśeṣikasūtra of Kaṇāda with the Commentary of Candrānanda*. With the Introduction by Anantalal Thakur. Gaekwad's Oriental Series, Oriental Institute 136, Baroda 1961.

VSV(C) = Candrānanda: *Vaiśeṣika-sūtra-vṛtti*. See: VS(C).

WEZLER 1982 = Wezler, Albrecht: 'Remarks on the definition of "yoga" in the Vaiśeṣikasūtra', in: L.A. Hercus et al. (eds.): *Indological and Buddhist Studies. Volume in Honour of Professor J.W. de Jong on His Sixtieth Birthday*. Australian National University, Faculty of Asian Studies, Canberra 1982: 643–686.

WEZLER 1984 = Wezler, Albrecht: 'On the Quadruple Division of the *Yogaśāstra*, the *Caturvyūhatva* of the *Cikitsāśāstra* and the «Four noble truths» of the Buddha', *Indologica Taurinensia* 12 (1984) 289–337.

WINTERNITZ 1929 = Winternitz, Moritz: '*Ānvīkṣikī* und *ātmavidyā*', *Indologica Pragensia* 1 (1929) 1–8.

YDhŚ = *Yājñavalkya-smṛti*. Wāsudev Laxmaṇ S'āstrī Pans'īkar (ed.): *Yādnyavalkyasmṛti of Yogīshvara Yādnyavalkya with the Commentary Mitākṣarā of Vidnyāneshvara, Notes, Variant readings, etc.* Pāndurang Jāwaji/Nirṇaya-sāgar Press, Bombay 1936.

YDhŚM = Vijñeśvara: *Mitâkṣarā*. See: YDhŚ.

World Views and Persons

Buddhist Individuals and Inward Empathy

JONARDON GANERI

Fundamental to Buddhism is the thesis that there is no self. I want to investigate whether this denial of self is compatible with a respect for the individual, their importance as loci of autonomy, responsibility, and demands for justice; or whether it entails impersonalism, which I define as the doctrine that the concept of the individual lacks explanatory function or normative role. Related to this first question is a second: where is the progressiveness seemingly inherent in the Buddhist world view to be located? Does it consist in the articulation of a conception of the individual which is free from the individualism and prudentialism of more European representations; or is its progressive radicalism rather in the envisioning of a wholly impersonal (and presumably radically consequentialist) ethics? Let me therefore distinguish two interpretations of Buddhist 'no self': as impersonalist denial of the moral or explanatory relevance of individuals *tout court*, and as anti-individualistic denial only of the moral or explanatory relevance of individualism.

While the idea of the individual is simply an idea of freedom from subjugation to community, caste, and social station, individualism represents an aspiration for personal fulfilment and self-development in the cultivation of one's uniqueness and difference from others. Georg SIMMEL (1901), (1904) famously distinguishes between 'quantitative' and 'qualitative' individualism; the first, which he associated with Kant and the eighteenth century Enlightenment in Europe, affirms the individual's independence from artificial constraints 'by stressing self-interests common to all human beings' (IZENBERG (1992: 3)), the second, associated with Goethe, Schleiermacher and Nietzsche, asserts a 'unique core of feeling and intuition in each person that must be developed if individuality is to be realized' (IZENBERG (1992: 3); cf. PODOKSIK (2010: 125–126)). SIMMEL observed rightly that the romanticism of qualitative individualism pulls against the collective concern for liberty, for each individual affirms their uniqueness against every other. I will argue that the same objection can be made against impersonalism, which seems unable to secure that freedom from outside constraint that the idea of the individual is meant to introduce. I do not deny that impersonalism exists within sectors of Buddhist Mahāyāna, perhaps especially in Madhyamaka, but what I want to argue here is for an alternative, associated more prominently with non-Mahāyana tradi-

World View and Theory in Indian Philosophy
Warsaw Indological Studies 5 (2012) 249–262.

tions. Contrary to what is sometimes claimed, 'Buddhist values' per se are not antithetical to notions of liberty, human rights, dignity, autonomy, and responsibility. Rather, if my argument is correct, there is a distinctively Buddhist, and consequently radically anti-Cartesian, approach to these very concepts. I will also argue, however, that any interpretation of Buddhist 'no self' more sympathetic to the idea of liberty must be distinguished sharply from the quantitative individualism of the Enlightenment. What is required for a progressive Buddhism is a conception of individuals that preserves liberty without grounding it in a domain of interiority, of private access, and of brute distinction between individual private wills. Buddhist 'no self' is, if nothing else, a complete rejection of these residually Cartesian notions of interior private space, however individuated. For while it is one's status as an individual which is the basis of one's claim to human rights and respect, the affirmation of those rights rests only on one's common ground with all other individuals, and prescinds from anything that makes one unique among them. This superficially paradoxical feature of the idea of the individual is precisely what makes that idea available to an exponent of Buddhist 'no self'.

Impersonalism: Dismantling the First Person Stance

I propose, first of all, that we should understand the fundamental Buddhist claim as stating a policy not as describing a fact, a policy that goes back to the Buddha's celebrated declaration, in the *Anatta-lakhaṇa-sutta*, that it is a mistake ever to identify oneself with any of the mental happenings in one's mind:

> 'Volitional formations (*saṅkhāra*) are nonself. For if, bhikkhus, volitional formations were self, they would not lead to affliction, and it would be possible to have it of volitional formations: "Let my volitional formation be thus; let my volitional formations not be thus." But because volitional formations are nonself, volitional formations lead to affliction, and it is not possible to have it of volitional formations: "Let my volitional formations be thus; let my volitional formations not be thus".'[1]

Impersonalists interpret the foundational claim of Buddhism as consisting in the recommendation that we aim to repudiate a first-personal stance on our own mental lives. The first person stance is the stance from which I am entitled to say that my desires and preferences 'are me', as opposed merely, as it were, to discovering them occurring within me; the stance from which they present

[1] SN_1 22.59, III: p. 67 §§ 8–9: [8] *saṅkhārā anattā. saṅkhārā ca hidaṁ bhikkhave attā abhavissaṁsu. na yidaṁ saṅkhārā ābādhāya saṁvatteyyum. labbhetha ca saṅkhāresu "evaṁ me saṅkhārā hontu evaṁ me saṅkhārā mā ahesunti*". [9] *yasmā ca kho bhikkhave saṅkhārā anattā tasmā saṅkhārā ābādhyāya saṁvattanti. na ca labbhati saṅkhāresu "evaṁ me saṅkhārā hontu evaṁ me saṅkhārā mā ahesunti*". Translation SN_2.

as 'mine'. The policy advice is that we should not adopt this stance, there is something erroneous about it, and that we do much better instead to adopt instead a spectatorial, third-personal view with regard to our mental lives. Vasubandhu, for example, executes the programme by analysing with exceptional insight precisely what the distinction between a first-person and a spectatorial position consists in, so as to locate exactly the nature of the error involved (AK, Triṁś, PSk). Qua philosopher, his role is to provide justification for the normative claim that assuming a spectator's stance on our mental lives is better than adopting the first-person stance, the stance naturally expressed in the words 'I am'. One way to pursue this is to argue that what is distinctive of a first-person stance is that thoughts are associated with a distinct phenomenology of ownership as agency. Ownership, Vasubandhu states explicitly, is a causal relation, a matter of how it is generated and not what its entitlements are.[2] The ownership of a thought is explained by the idea that the owner is a mental agent, the active thinker of the thought. The reason the Buddha gives for his claim that one should not identify oneself with any of the mental happenings in one's mind is exactly that they are not under one's control: there is no self because there is no agent of thinking; for to be the subject of an experience is to be its producer (cf. ADAM (2010); KUAN (2009)).

These considerations lead to a first formulation of the impersonalist reading of the Buddhist 'no-self' claim:

> No-Agency: The phenomenology of agency that accompanies thinking should be eradicated.

If philosophy is to have any practical consequence, it must also demonstrate that there is indeed a way to alter the stance we adopt, that this stance is not necessitated by our very nature or by the very nature of experience. It would be naive to think that the matter is entirely voluntary; clearly, I cannot simply choose to look upon my thoughts as if they are all alien presences (not least because, I could not regard that choice itself in the same way). So the Buddhist proposal implies that philosophy must be supplemented by techniques which are not themselves philosophical, techniques that a c h i e v e the transformation of stance that philosophy only a n n o u n c e s , techniques of contemplation and meditation under the direction of a spiritual teacher. The teacher trains the pupil using graded spiritual exercises to turn from being a participant to being a mere observer of their inner mental lives. This formulation understands 'no self' to consist in the advice to turn to forms of mental training whose outcome is that the trainee's thoughts no longer carry with them any sense that they have been generated by—authored by—the subject. That does not have to imply that they are felt as being someone else's thoughts, but rather that they are occurrences from the phenomenology of

[2] GANERI (2007: 175–17.

which any sense of agency—and so ownership—has been removed. It is important that the phenomenology is one of thoughts not felt as generated, rather than as one of thoughts felt as generated by someone else; for a sense that the thoughts to which one has first person access are generated by someone else soon leads to mental disintegration, via the pathology frequently called 'thought insertion', and that is not at all the aim of Buddhist therapy. We are in the grip of a false phenomenology whenever we have a sense that we ourselves have agency with respect to our thoughts. We need training to break that phenomenology, and if the training works, it will not be as if all our thoughts are insertions, but rather that they are as if arising unbidden, spontaneously.

So when a Buddhist describes himself as denying that there is a self, we are given to understand this as denying the existence of an agent of thinking, someone actively doing the thinking. Specifying mental action as the core ingredient in a first person stance is a plausible move, because it means that assuming such a stance is something we do, and so something we can, in principle, stop doing.

One way to clarify this account of what is distinctive about the first-person stance is to notice that the sense of agency is related to the idea that one makes up one's own mind. In the case of someone who is uncertain about what they will do, it is not that they are simply unaware what their intention is but rather that they have not yet formed any appropriate intention. We should therefore distinguish between what Richard MORAN calls 'theoretical questions' and 'deliberative questions', the point being 'to mark the difference between that inquiry which terminates in a true description of my state, and one which terminates in the formation of an attitude' (MORAN (2001: 63)). The difference is reflected in the often-noted fact that, if one is asked whether one believes something, for example that it will rain, one attends to the same facts as one would if one had been asked simply if it will rain. The question is not to be addressed by inspecting the inner contents of one's mind.

Later Buddhists do distinguish between these two dimensions of self-awareness: Vasubandhu speaks of *mano-vijñāna*, which is knowledge of the states of one's mind; and *manas*, which is an additional sense of being-mine.[3] The addition of *manas* marks the distinction between a merely spectatorial view of one's inner life, and a participant's view. Vasubandhu does not take the first-person stance to consist in the operation of anything like an inner sense, firmly rejecting anything like a Cartesian or perceptual model of self-knowledge. The refusal to identify oneself with any of one's thoughts (including especially

[3] Triṁś 5:

tasya vyāvṛtir arhatve tad-āśritya pravartate /
tad-ālambaṁ mano nāma vijñānaṁ mananâtmakam // —

—'Based on it [sc. the repository-consciousness], there functions the consciousness called *manas*, which consists in thinking (*manana*) having that [repository-consciousness] as its base.'

willings to do and intentions to act (*cetanā*)) is the denial of self as the owner of those thoughts qua their producer or agent.

The weight of the impersonalist interpretation of the Buddhist 'no-self' proposal rests on the idea that if we want to lead our lives well we should repudiate a first-person stance, and instead cultivate a detached third-personal stance. We should do this because only by so doing can we immunise ourselves against the temptations of egotism and self-pride, and thereby cultivate compassion. Again, Vasubandhu is explicit that *manas*, the distinguishing feature of a deliberative stance, is also *kliṣṭa*, 'afflicted', the source of all the vices associated with self-centredness. So a second formulation of the impersonalist reading of the Buddhist 'no-self' policy is this:

> No-Identification: The deliberative stance towards one's thinking should be suspended.

An impersonalist reading of Buddhist 'no self' says that we should give up a first-person stance and cultivate an entirely third-personal, empirical stance towards our mental lives. We should view our emotions, interests, and wishes as if from nowhere, with indifference and without involvement. There are no relevant asymmetries between the states of one individual and those of another, and the very idea of the individual ceases to do any explanatory work or to carry any normative significance. An altruistic principle about equality, that there is no good reason for someone to attach greater weight to the alleviation of their own pain than to that of someone else, is explained as being true because the very distinction a pain's being one's own and being that of another is dispensed with. If there is no real distinction between self and other, then the claim that this distinction is of ethical significance is necessarily false.

Three Arguments against Impersonalism

I will present three arguments against impersonalism: an argument from autonomy, an argument from self-defeat, and an argument from passivity.

N o A u t o n o m y . Autonomy rests on a preservation of the idea of ownership:

> 'The respect that individuals claim for their preferences, commitments, goals, projects, desires, aspirations, and so on is ultimately to be grounded in their being the person's own. It is because those preferences, commitments, and so on are a person's own that disregarding them amounts to disregarding him or her qua that distinctive individual. By contrast, disregarding preferences, commitments, and so on that are the product of coercion or deception does not seem to involve a violation in the same sense, raising the vexing issue of what makes some preferences, commitments, and so on "one's own", and others not' (CHRISTMAN (2005: 9)).

The impersonalist claim is that the only remedy for self-pride and other first-person involving vices is to refuse the first-person stance altogether. The cost of depriving the individual of discretion and judgement in the matter of moral psychology, however, is that one also deprives them of autonomy. So, for example, in order to resist the impositions of a tyrant, one needs a conception of moral boundaries that can sustain demands for one's autonomy and individual rights to be respected. A different, more moderate claim, is that with discretion and judgement one can separate out, among the various first-personal threads in one's moral psychology, those which harm and those which benefit. Among the beneficial virtues is authenticity, the state of being motivated by beliefs, values, desires and attitudes which can withstand self-scrutiny. The argument from autonomy is thus that if Buddhist 'no self' is interpreted in such a way that it implies the non-existence of the individual, then it places Buddhism entirely outside any engagement with liberal political theory, human rights discourses, and contemporary conversations in bio-ethics. Instead of offering a radical and progressive alternative, impersonalism situates Buddhism as having its roots in fundamentally pre-modern attitudes towards the person.

Self-Defeat. Someone who assumes an entirely empirical stance with regard to their mental life, who sees it only in its facticity and without endorsement or avowal, is in a state of alienation from themselves. Their resolutions do not bind them, their desires or fears do not motivate them; they are mere spectators and not involved participants. They have purged their moral psychology of affliction, but only at the very high cost of purging themselves of a moral psychology, indeed, some would say, of their humanity. MORAN (2001: 150) argues that the attempt wholly to disown one's thoughts is globally self-defeating:

> 'The problem with the idea of generalizing the theoretical stance toward mental phenomena is that a person cannot treat his mental goings-on as just so much data or evidence about his state of mind all the way down, and still be credited with a mental life to treat as data in the first place. For any given mental presentation of mine, just as for any utterance, it may be true that I can treat it as data, something which gives me a more or less good indication of my genuine belief. But for there to be judgments or deliberation in the first place, I cannot adopt this point of view on my mental life quite generally. At some point I must cease attempting to infer from some occurrence to my belief; and instead *stake* myself, and relate to my mental life not as something of symptomatic value, but as my current commitment to how things are out there. And so, for this reason the abrogation of first-person authority is not made up for by improving theoretical access to myself.'

The idea that there can be a stance from which one views one's entire mental life purely theoretically leads to an infinite regress, and the way to escape from this regress is not to make all thought reflexive (a move contemplated by post-Vasubandhu Buddhist philosophers beginning with Dignāga), but to notice the mistake that gives rise to it in the first place. The argument from self-defeat is that abandoning a view of human beings as engaged participants in a life but as mere witnesses leads to a conception of individuals as detached from the very possibility of forming a resolution to seek the improvement of their situation or enter into a binding commitment about their future has been denied them. To be alienated from one's wishes or desires is to fail to identify them as one's own.

Passivity. I have said that philosophy is not a way of life for a Buddhist practitioner, not the practice through which one leads one's life in order to achieve one's larger aims, according to the impersonalist view.[4] The goal is a radical altering in the practitioner's inner phenomenology, and the techniques which are needed to achieve that involve meditation and other forms of mind-training. The description of these practices as 'contemplative' tends to obscure the point: they do not involve contemplation in the philosophical sense of 'reflecting upon', but only in the religious sense of 'attending to'. Many religions, perhaps all, aim at a form of self-negation, at the destruction of the individual ego, and do so through techniques demanding the surrender of sovereignty in reason-giving and decision-making. The defining feature of philosophy is the thought that an individual's use of discriminative reason, rather than their guided use of spiritual techniques, is the path to be followed in the cultivation of mind. There is a discriminating rational endorsement of mental contents as one's own or not, rather than an indiscriminate refusal of avowal. The argument from passivity is that this turns selves into passive subjects, unable to participate in decisions that concern them or the formation of policies that affect them.

The impersonalist interpretation of the Buddhist 'no self' view started off sounding laudably egalitarian and altruistic but has turned out to be starkly disenfranchising. How can the proposal be seen as progressive, as providing a conception of subjects whose very humanity has not been negated? It will not help to fall back on a deflationary interpretation of Buddhist 'no self' as involving merely a metaphysical denial of substantial or enduring egos; for the deflationary reading likewise deprives Buddhism of a progressive potential: it renders it banal. I do think that there is a way both to preserve the insight that 'no self' is view not a theory—that it is a pragmatic and not a metaphysical recommendation—and also to save the theory from the allegation that it re-subjugates the subject by surrendering the individual. In the next section, I will present a suggestion as to where this alternative might be found.

[4] In terms of a helpful distinction in BALCEROWICZ (2011), philosophy is here a practice of second-level but not first-level rationality.

Inward Empathy: No-Self as a Second-Personal Stance

Empathy relates to a person's ability at some fundamental level to comprehend the emotions and other states of mind of another, to assume what can be called a 'second-personal' view, in which others appear not merely as bodies but as embodied 'you's. Such an ability has standardly been interpreted as consisting either in the individual's possession of a theory of mind that enables them to attribute states of mind in virtue of the other's behaviour (so-called 'theory-theory'), or else as involving a simulation of the other's states of mind by their own. Much of the contemporary discussion in social cognition concerns the respective merits of theory-theory and simulation. Recently, an interesting alternative proposal has been put forward, that empathy has to do rather with the direct experiencing of another's attitudes in and through their bodily expression (GALLAGHER (2005); ZAHAVI (2007), (2008)). Zahavi finds the view anticipated in Max Scheler's remark that 'we certainly believe ourselves to be directly acquainted with another person's joy in his laughter, with his sorrow and pain in his tears, with his shame in his blushing, with his entreaty in his outstretched hands...' (quoted in ZAHAVI (2010: 292)). According to this analysis, empathy is not a theory about others but a type of view on others' mental lives.

An idea at the heart of all of Buddhist ethics is the idea that moral value is constrained by the 'intention' (*cetanā*) with which an action is performed. From this it follows that it is possible to apprehend the intentions of others, for otherwise there could be no practice of moral appraisal. Some account of one's ability to know the mental states of others is presupposed by the very architecture of Buddhist ethics. If intentions were thought of on the model of private inner occurrences, however, it would hardly be possible reliably to know the intentions of another, and the practices of praise or blame would be without foundation. Empathy is the name given to this ability to discern the intention behind the act: we do not get angry with someone who pushes us if we see that it is done in error—unintentionally—or to move us out of danger—with good intentions.

The same is true of our knowledge of our own intentions. There could be no moral motivation, no revision of our action plans, unless we have some way to know what our intentions in acting are. The tradition of Early Modern European thinkers has been to postulate a faculty of immediate introspection or apperception, a faculty in virtue of which we know what thoughts we are the producers of and what our will inclines us to do. That postulate has begun to seem increasingly ad hoc, and an alternative account of self-knowledge is very much required. Indeed, as soon as we give up the idea of the self as hidden private space, there is no need to invent special faculties to access it.

Are we then able to assume an empathetic relation to our own mental lives, as well as to those of others? Can we direct empathy inwards? My proposal is that if we can make sense of the idea of empathy as able to be involved in self-self attitudes as well as self-other attitudes, then a new understanding of the 'no-self' stance can come to the fore: no-self is the advice to cultivate a second-personal attitude towards one's own mental states, in the process factoring out the first-personal.

> No-Interiority: A second-personal stance should be adopted with respect to one's mental life.

The idea is that just as one can distinguish between outward empathy as abductive inference from perceived bodily movement and empathy as experience facilitated by bodily movement, so one can distinguish between Rylean behaviourism about self-knowledge (that one makes inferences from perceiving one's own bodily behaviour) and an inward empathy account (that one's own body is the vehicle through which self-experience takes place). It seems to me that neither the theory-theory nor the simulation account can permit empathy directed towards one's own mental states, the former collapsing into a specatorial stance and the second into a form of cognitive dystopia. It is the third approach which offers a Buddhist analysis the greatest scope. What I am suggesting is that what the Buddhist stance advises is that one seeks to dissociate an element of subjectivity and first-personality normally associated with one's awareness of one's emotional and cognitive inner life; if this is indeed a live possibility, then what remains is still a direct relationship with one's inner life, but now having a phenomenological character analogous to that which the experiential model of empathy ascribes to one's comprehension of others. The bracketing of the subjectivity seemingly inherent in normal experience is a form of dissolution of the self–other distinction, and makes sense of 'no self' not as a metaphysical denial of selfhood but as a progressive practical recommendation. It is the abandonment of a false but seductive belief in first-person authority: there is no privileged access grounded in a purely interior awareness of one's mental states.

A demonstration that a bracketing of putative interiority is indeed a genuine possibility is the work of a substantive theory of subjectivity, and I suggest that later Buddhist analyses of mind, whether from Abhidharma, Yogācāra, or Madhyamaka authors, have precisely such a substantive theory as their principal end, and that for the reason just mentioned. Vasubandhu's analysis of ownership in terms of mental action is itself precisely such an account: *manas* is what explains the appearance to thought of a sense of mineness, grounded in the repository-consciousness or *ālaya-vijñāna*, and in principle separable from the flow of *skandha*s including *mano-vijñāna* (Triṁś 5; see GANERI (2012: 146–65) for details). It is therefore a mistake to read such theories as involving or committed to a metaphysical interpretation of no-self. What they do is to debunk the false promise of interior access and the concomitant idea of an epistemologically prior internal subject. There is no ghost in the machine. An empathy account of self-knowledge leaves the inner subject of Descartes or Kant as at best an epiphenomenon and certainly not at the centre of one's involvement.

None of this is to deny that there can exist asymmetries between self-knowledge and knowing the minds of others. What it does is to reject one particular and corrosive understanding of that asymmetry, replacing the old dichotomy between one's own mind pictured as something immediately accessible and other minds pictured as obscure and hidden with an asymmetry, still real but no longer wretched, between the way one can get the feel of one's own states of mind and the way one feels for those of others.

Empathetic beings are capable of recognising the distinction between their own embodied mental states and the embodied mental states of others. My hypothesis is that it is empathy rather than interior agents which sustains a notion of the individual and so underpins the commitment to rights in Buddhism. One's demand for access to palliative medication for example, will be understood as derived not from the self-interested claim that the pain is mine, but from the empathetic acknowledgement of its existence within oneself. In so far as one is entitled to be partial about one's own pain, to be differentially proactive in its alleviation, it is because one's understanding of it is unmediated by one's perception of others' bodily acts, and to that extent more sure and more insightful. One happens to be more effective in managing this pain rather than another, not least because one has control of the body that embodies it, but there is no claim that the treatment of this pain is privileged merely because it is my own. One can be justified in taking a special interest in one's health without it following that one regards one's own health as more important than that of any other.

On the account presented here, there is no type difference between the way I relate to my own states and the way I relate to yours: the relationship in both cases is one of experiential empathy. That is enough to encourage altruism and even-handedness, since my states do not present themselves to me as mine, mine, mine. In so far as there is a difference, it is that there are two modes of experiential empathy in play, and that asymmetry is sufficient to discriminate individuals. A detached impersonalist can raise no objection if their blood is drained to save the lives of five others, even without their consent (whether or not there is consent, it is not theirs). Now, however, individuals are defined by relations of inward empathy, and inward empathy is experiencing one's mental states by way of one's body, so the necessity of consent and the rights one has over one's own body both follow from what can be identified as the fundamental moral law in this view, that inward empathy takes precedence over outward. This law can, however, be restated as the right not to be harmed, which is to say that others must not do one harm any more than one should harm others (*ahiṁsā*), which is to say that one's own states take precedence over theirs. One has the right not to be harmed even if by being harmed many others will be healed. There are reasons to be partial which are not reasons to be proud.

The hypothesis that it is empathy not agency which defines an individual can serve as the target for empirical investigation within contemporary Buddhist communities, monastic and lay, in for example an examination of the kinds of reasons Buddhists are prone to give in circumstances where they defend a right to health or a right to participate in care-provision decisions, in attitudes towards advance directives and assisted suicide, and in resource allocation decisions. My conjecture is that what will be discovered is that the notion of Buddhist individuals as inward empathisers is operationally available while that of the Kantian inner self as an interior 'I think': accompanying thought is not. It will require a combination of textual research and empirical work to establish which of the three accounts of empathy is actually in play in Buddhist evaluative practices.

Conclusion

I have considered two interpretations of Buddhist 'no-self' considered as a policy and a stance, that is to say a view rather than a theory. I have rehearsed a range of objections to a third-personal, spectatorial, interpretation of the policy, specifically arguments from autonomy, from self-defeat, and from passivity. I have also suggested, however, that a better interpretation of the Buddhist position is available, one which brings into focus the idea that in assuming an empathetic stance towards one's conscious life one can break the attachments and cravings (*tṛṣṇā*) whose origins are located in the interiority of a first-personal view. In so far as there remains nevertheless an asymmetry between self–self and self–other forms of empathy, the hope is that it can serve to ground a consistent Buddhist account of rights, respect, and responsibility. The asymmetry is derived from two distinct modes of embodied experiential access to thought and emotion. Rights, for example, are to be seen as grounded in the concern one has for oneself as much as for others, a concern based on empathy towards oneself and not on the prioritisation of one's unique interior needs. I have diagnosed the basis of individualism as being an 'inner subject as agent of thinking' account of individuals, to which the 'No self' inward empathy of self-knowledge is a clear rival. It is the middle way between Descartes and Ryle: there are neither ghosts nor machines, but only empathetic human beings. The empathy account offers a way to retain a notion of partiality, and so permit at least a surrogate of ideas of autonomy, responsibility and justice, but without the vices of self-love, greed and pride that in normal circumstances accompany them. That is because, in the view I am presenting, self-knowledge consists in an experience of the mental by way of direct proprioceptive and perspectively situated acquaintance with a body, as opposed to the more mediated forms of acquaintance one has of other bodies. What is rejected is any interior point of view which presents itself as the author of my experience. 'My' states of mind are those which show up non-derivatively in their embodiment; 'your' states of mind are those which show up only derivatively in their embodiment. There is certainly a sense in which I am the owner of my states of mind, but the sense is not that of an interior subject who actively thinks them; rather, it is simply that I have sensori-motor control over my own body in ways that I do not have over others. There are reasons for me to take more interest in my states of mind than in others, but only such reasons as derive from this asymmetry of bodily control: the body through which mental states that show up non-derivatively is also the body over which one has most direct control. By and large, but not invariably, these will be the states one is best in a position to manipulate. What is completely absent from this picture are the needs and demands of an interior subject.

If a self is the producer of the thoughts it owns, then autonomy consists in the freedom to produce desires and intentions without coercion. One is alienated from those desires which one does not choose to have; one does not identify with them; they are not oneself. Of the two interpretations of 'no self' I have distinguished, the difference between them has to do with which step the above description is rejected. If one retains the identity between ownership and agency, then one is led to a no-ownership account of the mental, radical consequentialism, and a denial of free will; that is, to impersonalism, which I have claimed cannot provide even surrogates for the ideas of autonomy and rights, dignity and respect. What I am recommending instead is that the element in the description which should be rejected is the identity between ownership and agency. The denial of selves, qua producers of their own willings and intentions, is not the denial of individuals, the owners of thoughts. I have presented an alternative theory, in which ownership relations are defined in terms of empathy rather than agency. If nothing else, the existence of this alternative loosens the grip of the still-powerful agency account.

Rather than draw the conclusion that there is in Buddhism no distinction between freedom and coercion, between desires and intentions that one identifies with and ones from which one is alienated, and so conclude that one is effectively alienated from all one's desires and willings, my suggestion here is that a Buddhist conception of the individual can provide viable substitutes for the notions of autonomy and freedom, for *svātantrya*. For a desire to be one's own is for one to experience it in the special way afforded by one's own body, and the surrogates of the notions of autonomy and freedom will be notions that place the rights one has with respect to one's own body at the centre.

One possibility is that inward empathy will be regarded as a cultivated skill. Ordinary human beings live in a state of radical alienation from their desires and preferences, falsely imagining that an agency model of ownership is correct, and lacking in any other means for identifying with their experience. The gradual cultivation of empathetic cognitive skills is a move from alienation to involvement, grounded in a non-agentive model of ownership. Eliminating the phenomenology of agency from one's psychology is a 'preparatory condition' (GANERI (2007: 19)) for the cultivation of involvement and participation grounded in empathy. A hierarchical model might indeed permit a rapprochement between the two interpretations of 'no self': we might imagine the ordinary human being (*puthujjana*) to be entirely in the grip of the false phenomenology of agency, in a condition of alienation and vulnerability to coercion, the trainee (*sekha*) to be in a process of weakening this phenomenology and developing the skills of empathy, inwardly as well as externally, and the *arahat* to have completed the process and to occupy a fully engaged empathetic stance (see ADAM (2008); (2010: 261–4)). This picture would place policies for the cultivation of empathy at the centre of programmes for human development. Again, it seems to me an empirical question as to where actual human populations fall within this notional hierarchy.

Rather than reading Buddhist 'no self' as a medieval or post-modern alternative to the concept of the individual as the focal point of respect, autonomy, and human rights, my recommendation has been that we interpret it as providing the resources to identify a notion of the individual very different from the one which gained prominence in the Enlightenment. One can consistently reject individualism as a thesis about the normative priority of subjective uniqueness and still retain a role for self/other contrasts. Mahāyāna impersonalism thus does not usurp Theravāda commitment to the significance of the individual (and it is precisely because *nirvāṇa* is not the survival of an individual but the eradication of an illness that this commitment does not imply a form of individualism). Indeed I have argued that Theravāda individuals sustain a form of discourse in terms of which Buddhist ethical discussion can take place, a discourse in which it is empathy (*maitrī*, *karuṇā*) not agency which defines us as human beings.

BIBLIOGRAPHY

ADAM 2008 = Adam, Martin: 'Classes of Agent and the Moral Logic of the Pali Canon', *Argumentation* 22 (2008) 115–24.

ADAM 2010 = Adam, Martin: 'No self, no free will, no problem', *Journal of the International Association of Buddhist Studies* 33,1–2 (2010) 239–265.

AK = Vasubandhu: *Abhidharma-kośa* with *Abhidharma-kośa-bhāṣya*. (1) Prahlad Pradhan (ed.): *Abhidharmakośabhāṣyam of Vasubandhu*. 2nd Revised Edition with Introduction and Indices by Aruna Haldar, Tibetan Sanskrit Works Series 8, Kashi Prasad Jayaswal Research Institute, Patna 1975. [first edition: Patna 1967]. (2) Louis de la Vallée Poussin (tr.): *Abhidharma Kośa Bhāṣyam*. English translation by Leo M. Pruden, 4 Vols., Asian Humanities Press, California 1988–90.

BALCEROWICZ 2011 = Balcerowicz, Piotr: 'Rationality as a Common Public Domain', *Dialogue and Universalism* 1 (2011) 73–94 [draft available at: www.orient.uw.edu.pl/balcerowicz/texts/balcerowicz2011c.pdf].

CHRISTMAN 2005 = Christman, John and Anderson, Joel: 'Introduction', to: John Christman and Joel Anderson (eds.): *Autonomy and the Challenges to Liberalism*. Cambridge University Press, Cambridge 2005: 1–23.

GALLAGHER 2005 = Gallagher, Shaun: *How the Body Shapes the Mind*. Oxford University Press, Oxford 2005.

GANERI 2007 = Ganeri, Jonardon: *The Concealed Art of the Soul: Theories of Self and Practices of Truth in Indian Ethics and Epistemology*. Oxford University Press, Oxford 2007.

GANERI 2012 = Ganeri, Jonardon: *The Self: Naturalism, Consciousness, and the First-Person Stance*. Oxford University Press, Oxford 2012.

IZENBERG 1992 = Izenberg, Gerald: *Impossible Individuality: Romanticism, Revolution, and the Origins of Modern Selfhood*. Princeton University Press, Princeton NJ 1992.

KUAN 2009 = Kuan, Tse-fu: 'Rethinking Non-Self: A New Perspective from the Ekottarika-āgama', *Buddhist Studies Review* 26,2 (2009) 155–175.

MORAN 2001 = Moran, Richard: *Authority and Estrangement: An Essay on Self-Knowledge*. Princeton University Press, Princeton NJ 2001.

PODOKSIK 2010 = Podoksik, Effraim: 'Georg Simmel: Three Forms of Individualism and Historical Understanding', *New German Critique* 37,1 109 (2010) 119–45.

PSk = Vasubandhu: *Pañca-skandhaka*. (1) Xuezhu Li and Ernst Steinkellner (eds.): *Vasubandhu's Pañca-skandhaka*. Austrian Academy of Sciences Press, Vienna 2008. (2) Stefan Anacker (tr.): *Seven Works of Vasubandhu, the Buddhist Psychological Doctor*. Motilal Banarsidass, Delhi 1984: 65–74.

SIMMEL 1901 = Simmel, Georg: 'Die beiden Formen des Individualismus', in: Georg Simmel: *Gesamtausgabe in 24 Bänden*. Band 7: *Aufsätze und Abhandlungen 1901–1908*. Band I. Suhrkamp, Frankfurt am Main 1995: 49–56.

SIMMEL 1904 = Simmel, Georg: 'Sixteenth Lecture on Kant', in: Georg Simmel: *Gesamtausgabe in 24 Bänden*. Band 9: *Die Probleme der Geschichtsphilosophie*. Suhrkamp, Frankfurt am Main 1997: 9 215–26.

SN = *Saṁyutta-nikāya*. (1) Léon Feer (ed.): The *Saṁyutta-nikāya of the Sutta-piṭaka*. 5 Vols. Pali Text Society, London 1884–1898. (2) Bhikkhu Bodhi (tr.): *The Connected Discourses of the Buddha*. A New Translation of the *Saṁyutta Nikāya*. 2 Vols., Wisdom Publications, Boston 2000.

Triṁś = Vasubandhu: *Triṁśikā-vijñapti-kārikā*. Swati Ganguly (ed.): *Treatise in Thirty Verses*. Motilal Banarsidass, Delhi 1992.

ZAHAVI 2007 = Zahavi, Dan: 'Expression and Empathy', in D.D. Hutto; M. Ratcliffe (eds.): *Folk Psychology Re-Assessed*. Springer, Dordrecht 2007: 25–40.

ZAHAVI 2008 = Zahavi, Dan: 'Simulation, Projection and Empathy', *Consciousness and Cognition* 17 (2008) 514–22.

ZAHAVI 2010 = Zahavi, Dan: 'Empathy, Embodiment and Interpersonal Understanding: From Lipps to Schutz', *Inquiry* 53,3 (2010) 285–306.

Śāntarakṣita on the Emotions

JOERG TUSKE

In verses 1948–1953 in the *Lokāyata-parīkṣā* of the *Tattva-saṁgraha* (TS), Śāntarakṣita provides an argument for the existence of what his commentator, Kamalaśīla, calls the 'other world' (*para-loka*) in the *Pañjikā* (TSP):

> 'As a matter of fact, all these feelings of love, hatred and the rest become strong through habit and repetition, as has been ascertained by positive and negative concomitance. These feelings appearing for the first time [in the child], are essentially devoid of any habit and repetition during the present life; what then is the cause of their appearance, if there is no other life? Their appearance cannot be due to the presence of their [external] excitants; because even when these excitants are present, the feelings in question do not appear, if there is disgust; and when this disgust ceases, they are found to be strong, even in connection with past and future things, when the counter-feelings appear in intensified form. The feelings of love, hatred and the rest are found to proceed in regard to women and other things, when the man attributed to them goodness, devotedness and constancy and so forth; even though these qualities may not be actually there. For these reasons, these feelings appearing in this life must be regarded as appearing, without the excitants being actually present, through the force of habitual appearance of similar feelings in the past, because they are feelings of love etc., like these same feelings appearing subsequently.'[1]

---

[1] TS_1 1948–1953:

rāga-dveṣâdayaś câmī paṭavo 'bhyāsa yogataḥ /
anvaya-vyatirekābhyāṁ bhavantaḥ pariniścitāḥ // 1948 //
ihatyâbhyāsa-rahitās te ye prathama-bhāvinaḥ /
ko hetur janmanas teṣāṁ yadi na syād bhavântaram // 1949 //
na hy ālambana-sānnidhyāt teṣāṁ janmôpapadyate /
pratisaṅkhyāna-sad-bhāve tad-bhāve 'py atad-udbhavāt //1950 //
pratisaṅkhyā-nivṛttau ca teṣāṁ prābalya-darśanāt /
naṣṭâjāte 'pi viṣaye viparyāsâbhivṛddhitaḥ (-naḥ?) // 1951 //
śubhâtmīya-sthirâdīṁś ca samāropyâṅganâdiṣu /

World View and Theory in Indian Philosophy
Warsaw Indological Studies 5 (2012) 263–276.

In this argument, Śāntarakṣita claims that there has to be a previous birth because young children can feel love and hate before they have had any experience of these emotions in their present lives. The best possible explanation for this phenomenon is the existence of a previous life. In this paper, I will examine this argument and highlight some of its implications for the discussion about the status of the emotions in Western philosophy of mind. I will argue that Śāntarakṣita's view of love and hatred shows that his taxonomy of mental states differs from the taxonomy of Western philosophers and psychologists and suggest that this difference could be the starting point for new lines of inquiry into the philosophy of the emotions. First, in order to make sense of Śāntarakṣita's argument, it is important to put it into context.

The context

The *Tattva-saṁgraha* is a 'compendium' of arguments on a variety of philosophical topics and, more importantly, it contains responses to many philosophical views that are opposed to Śāntarakṣita's positions. In particular, there are several chapters devoted to refutations of arguments for the existence of a self (*ātman*) by different philosophical schools. In the *Lokāyata-parīkṣā*, however, Śāntarakṣita is trying to defend the view that there exists a non-physical momentary consciousness or chain of cognitions (*santāna vijñāna*) which carries over from former births into the present and future rebirths. Thus, Śāntarakṣita is trying to find a middle ground between a permanent non-physical self and the materialism of the Lokāyata school which argues that the self is purely the result of bodily processes. According to them, it comes into existence with the body and ceases to exist when the body ceases to exist.

Many of Śāntarakṣita's arguments, as well as the general objections to the Lokāyata school, can be found in the writings of earlier Buddhist philosophers. Throughout the whole *Lokāyata-parīkṣā*, Śāntarakṣita refers to arguments from the *Pramāṇa-siddhi*-chapter of Dharmakīrti's *Pramāṇa-vārttika*. There, Dharmakīrti argues that past lives exist. We can know this because of the authority of the Buddha and we have reason to accept his authority because of his infinite compassion. This compassion can only be the result of practice over many life times.[2] The Lokāyata philosophers argue that cognitions require the support of a body and therefore cease to exist when the body ceases to exist. Dharmakīrti objects to this by arguing that mental cognitions do not derive from any physi-

---

rāgâdayaḥ pravartante tad-rūpā viṣayā na ca // 1952 //
tad-anālambanā eva sadṛśâbhyāsa-śaktitaḥ /
ihatyā api varttante rāgâditvād yathôttare // 1953 //

[2] See PV 1.36 (i.e. *Pramāṇa-siddhi* 36; all references are to this chapter):
sādhanaṁ karuṇâbhyāsāt sā buddher deha-saṁśrayāt /
asiddhâbhyāsa iti cen nâśraya-pratiṣedhataḥ //

cal support.[3] Both Śāntarakṣita and Kamalaśīla state that the relationship between the support and what is supported can be analysed either as a causal relationship or as the relationship between an object and its capacity.[4] In this respect they do not deviate from Dharmakīrti who rejects this position of the Lokāyata philosophers by arguing that the body could be neither the cause of cognition nor could it have the capacity of cognition. FRANCO (1997: 134–135) explains Dharmakīrti's argument in the following way:

> 'If the body were one lasting and changeless entity from birth to death, it could not produce cognitions gradually, and thus all the cognitions one has throughout one's life would be produced at once. If the body were the material cause of the cognition, the cognition would last as long as the body, and thus there could be no dead body (v. 51). If the breaths are considered the cause of cognition, the same inadmissible consequence applies: Because the body is the material cause of the breaths, the breaths would last as long as the body and the cognition as long as the breaths (v. 53). All these inadmissible consequences do not apply if one admits that cognition is the cause of cognition.'

Of course, there is no reason why the Lokāyata philosophers should say that the body is changeless. It might precisely be the changes that appear in the body, for example the brain, which are responsible for cognition. Dharmakīrti argues that if cognition required the support of the body, there is no reason why it should not arise everywhere where there exists a body or matter.[5] The obvious objection to this argument is that not any form of matter supports cognition. It has to be a particular kind of matter, ordered in a particular way, as is the case in human beings and many animals.[6]

---

[3] See PV 1.49:

tad-dhī-vad grahaṇa-prāpter mano-jñānaṁ na sêndriyāt /
jñānôtpādana-sāmarthya-bhedān na sakalād api //

[4] See TS_1 1858–1859:

deha-buddhîndriyâdīnāṁ pratikṣaṇa-vināśane /
na yuktaṁ para-lokitvaṁ nânyaś câbhyupagamyate //1858 //
tasmād bhūta-viśeṣebhyo yathā śukta-surâdikam /
tebhya eva tathā jñānam jāyate vyajyate 'tha vā //1859 //

[5] See PV 1.37–38:

prāṇâpānêndriya-dhiyāṁ dehād eva na kevalāt /
sa-jāti-nirapekṣāṇāṁ janma janma-parigrahe // 37 //
atiprasaṅgāt yad dṛṣṭaṁ pratisandhāna-śaktimat /
kim āsīt tasya yan nâsti paścād yena na sandhimat //38 //

[6] According to FRANCO (1997: 135–139), Dharmakīrti, attributes the theory of the three humours (*doṣa*) as a way of accounting for bodily changes to the Lokāyata philosophers. Nagatomi does not translate *doṣa* as humour. He uses the terms 'disease' and 'damage' among others; see PV 1.54–59.

Dharmakīrti's arguments lead to a discussion about whether the purely bodily embryo can have cognition. The Lokāyata philosophers would have to say that cognition arises in the embryo whereas Dharmakīrti asks where cognition originates if not in cognition from a previous birth.

According to Buddhist 'psychology', love and hatred are two of the afflictions (*kleśa*) that befall human beings and that need to be removed in order to attain liberation. There are a number of sections in the *Yogācāra-bhūmi*, possibly written by either Asaṅga or Maitreya, that discuss these *kleśa*s.[7] The text provides several lists, most of which include love (*rāga*) and hatred or enmity (*pratigha*). Other *kleśa*s are: *sat-kāya-dṛṣṭi* (false view with regard to the *sat-kāya*, or the five *skandha*s),[8] attachment to extreme views, attachment to unwholesome views, attachment to practices and observances, pride, ignorance and doubt. These *kleśa*s could be associated with one or more of the five possible feelings: pleasant feeling (*sukha*), unpleasant feeling (*duḥkha*), neutral feeling (*upekṣā*), happy mood (*saumanasya*) or unhappy mood (*daurmanasya*).[9] A translation of the psychological categories of the *Yogācāra-bhūmi* into the categories of Western philosophy of mind would render the following distinctions: a *kleśa* is a mental phenomenon that consists of a representation of an object plus a certain feeling, sensation or affect.[10] For example, in the case of love, the *Yogācāra-bhūmi* states that we have the object of love plus either a pleasant sensation or a happy mood or indifference (neutral feeling).[11] In addition, the text acknowledges that a representation can be about a real object or an imagined object. In the latter case, the question arises in what way we can distinguish between an object and its representation.[12] This suggests that at least some Buddhist traditions distinguish between a cognition, the object of a cognition and the feeling accompanying a cognition. Śāntarakṣita mentions *kleśa*s in TS 1955[13] and it is clear that he operates within the context of this psychological distinction.[14] This is also the context in which we have to place

[7] See AHN (2003) for an edition and translation of these passages.

[8] For a discussion of this term see AHN (2003: 163, n. 18).

[9] See AHN (2003: 245).

[10] I use these terms interchangeably.

[11] See AHN (2003: 245).

[12] See AHN (2003: 246).

[13] TS_1 1955:

rāga-dveṣâdayaḥ kleśāḥ pratisaṅkhyāna-vidviṣām /
ayoniśo (sau) manaskāra-vidheyānāṁ yathā-balam //

Kamalaśīla mentions the term twice in his commentary to TS_1 5 and TS_1 6. Usually, Śāntarakṣita and Kamalaśīla refer to love and hatred as *doṣa*s. See, for example, TS_1 1502–1503 and commentary.

[14] For Śāntarakṣita, however, feelings have objects which would make them cognitive according to Western philosophy and psychology. See below for further discussion of this point.

Śāntarakṣita's discussion of love and hatred. Before doing so, I would like to lay out some of the main philosophical ideas of Western theories of cognition and emotion, as they provide an interesting comparison with Śāntaraksita's discussion.

Cognition, feeling and emotion

While the importance of the emotions for rational deliberation and decision making has been acknowledged in recent discussions in the philosophy of mind, the history of philosophy contains many views, which emphasise the potentially dangerous and destructive role of the emotions.[15] At the heart of this view lies a division of our mental lives into cognitions and feelings. Cognitions are representational thoughts. They are regarded as rational because they represent the external world and therefore provide us with access to the external world, based on certain evidence. So, according to this view of rationality, when I think that there is a book on the table based on my available evidence and there really is one, then my thought is rational. If I am hallucinating that there is a book on the table, my thought is not rational.[16] This means that, according to this view, cognitions are rational if I have evidence for believing them and if they represent the external reality correctly. By contrast, feelings are some of the non-representational attitudes one can have towards the objects of the representations of our thoughts. For example, when I think about my daughters, I have a cognition which represents my daughters. The objects of my thought are my daughters and my thought picks them out among various objects and subjects in the world. There are several ways in which these objects can be picked out. For example, I can simply have the thought that I have two daughters or my thought can be 'coloured' with love and affection. This 'colouring' of my thought is often regarded as an affect. Together with the thought, it accounts for an emotion. So, the emotion of love, for example, is the thought of the object of love plus an affect. The affect is non-representational and regarded as a 'mere' feeling.

The reason why many philosophers regard the emotions as an obstacle to rational thought is the influence of the non-representational feeling. The fact that feelings do not seem to have objects means, according to some views, that they can interfere with rational thought. According to these views, rational thought, which is representational and therefore object-directed, is subject to disturbing interferences from the feelings. The feelings themselves, however, are non-rational because they arise due to some physical imbalance in the body, for example through an imbalance of the various 'humours'. This imbalance can

[15] Plato and Aristotle are well-known examples of philosophers who held such views.

[16] For the sake of brevity, I am going to ignore the case where I have good reason to believe that something is the case when it is not.

negatively impact rational thought. An example is the person who acts against her better judgement because she is in the grip of some feeling. This is of course also the basis for the term 'passion' as something that we 'suffer'. Since rational thought is an ideal for many philosophers and the feelings can interfere with this ideal, the natural consequence seems to be to advocate for the extinction or at least the control of the feelings and, as a consequence, of the emotions. This is what many philosophers throughout the history of philosophy have done. While they often recognise that the emotions contain a cognitive, and therefore potentially rational, element, they try to uncover this element by advocating its separation from the affect. Of course, if the affect were to be purged from the emotion, the resulting cognition would cease to be an emotion.[17]

There is a parallel between this Western view and a prejudice that attaches to Indian and particularly Buddhist philosophy. The prejudice is that Buddhist philosophy, because of its soteriological nature with its emphasis on the attainment of *nirvāṇa*, is about freeing the mind from feelings and emotions because they constitute an attachment to the world. I would like to analyse Śāntarakṣita's views on love and hatred in order to determine in what way, if any, this prejudice corresponds to reality.

Śāntarakṣita on love and hatred

Śāntarakṣita argues that love and hatred exist due to habit and repetition which is ascertained by confirming and disconfirming concomitance. This means that they are learned through experience. For example, love is learned by a person being confronted with objects to which this feeling is attributed and thus reinforced the more of these objects a person encounters. However, we can observe the existence of love and hatred in babies who have not had the repeated experience of these objects in this life. Śāntarakṣita claims that the existence of love and hatred cannot be due to the first encounter with the object of love or hatred because it would be possible, as indeed happens according to him, to encounter this object without the respective feelings of love or hatred or to encounter it with another feeling, such as disgust. As an example, Śāntarakṣita mentions the attraction a man might feel towards a woman. He claims that men are attracted to women if they also attribute 'goodness' and 'devotedness' to them, even though a particular woman might not possess these qualities. So the qualities that make, for example, a woman 'loveable' do not have to exist in the woman and therefore, according to Śāntarakṣita, the woman cannot be said to be the cause of the feeling of love in the man. Love,

[17] While there are many objections one could raise against this view of feelings and cognitions, I do not want to discuss these in this paper. My aim is to contrast and compare this view of the emotions with Śāntarakṣita's view.

then is not an object of the senses (*viṣaya*). Therefore, the reason why these feelings exist is through force of habit in previous lives. We have learned over time that women are 'loveable'. This argument is meant to demonstrate that love and hatred could not exist if the materialists were right and mental life was simply the result of bodily processes.

Kamalaśīla explains this argument in his commentary on TS 1948–1953 in a rather straightforward way but adds a very helpful example:

> 'For the following reason also, the feelings of love etc. cannot be due to presence of the excitants: Because, if the feelings appeared exactly in accordance with the excitants, they would proceed from the excitant exactly in the same manner as the cognition of blue and other things (which always proceeds in accordance with these things); the feelings however do not proceed in this way; on the contrary, the said feelings appear in regard to the woman and other things, in men who attribute to the woman the form of their own lasting pleasure etc. which have not been experienced at all; and yet the objects (woman etc.) are not actually possessed of the said form of goodness etc.; and when a thing is devoid of a certain form, it cannot be the excitant or basis of the cognition of that form; otherwise it would lead to absurdity.'[18]

In this passage, Kamalaśīla draws a distinction between the cognition of blue and the feeling of love. His point is that the cognition of blue is a perception and therefore requires an object whereas a feeling of love does not. There is no basis for love in the way that there is a basis for our perception of blue. So, Śāntarakṣita's argument, as explained by Kamalaśīla, consists of two parts: (a) love, hatred etc. are learned through experience and reinforced by repetition and (b) love, hatred etc. are not perceptions.

At first glance, Śāntarakṣita's argument does not appear to be very convincing. With regard to (a), it is unclear that whatever feelings babies have are comparable to the adult feelings of love or hatred. It is possible that the feelings in babies are instincts from which the fully-fledged emotions of love and hatred develop. Secondly, even if babies could experience love and hate without any prior experience of these feelings, this could be due to a number of reasons, none of which necessarily imply a 'previous birth' or a continuing 'chain of cognitions', as Śāntarakṣita suggests. For example, it is possible that love and hatred are instincts themselves that are innate and therefore not

---

[18] TSP_1 1948–1953, p. 547.10–14: *ito 'pi nâlambana-vaśād bhāva-ādīnāṁ pravṛttiḥ. tathā hi yadi yathâlambanam eva pravartterann evam ālambana-vaśāt pravṛttāḥ syur yathā nīlâdi jñānaṁ na câivaṁ pravarttante. kiṁ tarhi ātmīya-nitya-sukhâdy ākārān anubhūtān evâropayanto 'ṅganâdiṣu pravarttante. na ca śubhâdi rūpā-viṣayāḥ na ca yad yad ākāra-śūnyaṁ tat tasyâlambanaṁ yuktam atiprasaṅgāt.* Translation: TSP_2, p. 931.

learned by prior experience.[19] Another possibility is that, rather than instincts, love and hate are innate ideas, i.e. ideas or cognitions which again are innate to human beings but which go beyond instinctual behaviour in that they are cognitive. By 'cognitive' I mean that they involve a mental representation.

In TS 1958, Śāntarakṣita provides a similar example of male animals that become 'perturbed' by the touch of female animals even though they do not know anything about any 'doings' (*vṛttānta*) or sexual intercourse, yet. His argument is that this feeling must be due to experiences in previous lives. Again he does not account for the possibility of instinctual behaviour. If Śāntarakṣita allowed for the existence of instinctual behaviour then his observation of babies and animals might have let him to believe that love and hatred are mental phenomena that are not learned through experi ence.

Śāntarakṣita needs to address the general question of how love and hatred can ever arise if they require a previous experience of love and hatred. While Śāntarakṣita, as a Buddhist, might not be particularly interested in answering this question, finding an answer would clarify the idea that feelings are reinforced through repetition and habit. The problem with this idea is that Śāntarakṣita clearly believes that there is something fundamental about the feelings of love and hatred. It is so fundamental that even babies feel it. At the same time, it requires experience. So the question is how was the first feeling of love acquired? There might have been a time when humans did not have the feeling of love and they only acquired it at some point in their lives through experience and subsequent repetition of the experience. This sounds like a strange idea precisely because love and hatred are so fundamental to our unenlightened lives that the existence of a time when they did not exist seems impossible. Yet, Śāntarakṣita's view implies either that there must have been such a time or that there is an infinite chain of these feelings stretching backwards. In TS 1872, Śāntarakṣita makes it clear that he believes in the latter option:

> 'As regards the "other world", there is no such [thing as] "other world" apart from the "chain of causes and effects, in the form of cognition and the rest". What is spoken of as "the other world" or "this world", that is only by way of a certain limit placed upon the said "chain" which is beginningless and endless.'[20]

---

[19] In this sense, the Lokāyata philosophers' response to Śāntarakṣita could be similar to that against Dharmakīrti's argument that the body cannot be the cause of cognitions. Against Śāntarakṣita the Lokāyata philosophers could argue that there are certain processes which are not themselves the emotions of love or hate but which could cause love or hate. Against Dharmakīrti they could argue that certain bodily processes which are not cognitions could cause cognitions.

[20] TS_1 1872:

tad atra para-loko 'yaṁ nânyaḥ kaścana vidyate /
upādāna-tad-ādeya-bhūta-jñānâdi santateḥ //

So, Śāntarakṣita might argue that love and hatred are just as much part of a 'chain of cognitions' that is beginningless and endless as all other cognitions. The reason why he postulates the existence of this eternal 'chain of cognitions' is the argument that no cognition could be caused by anything other than a previous cognition and hence there cannot be a first cognition for anything we call a particular being. If there was a first cognition for a particular being then, according to Śāntarakṣita (TS 1878–1885), there would be five options: (i) the first cognition does not have a cause; (ii) it is produced by an eternal cause; (iii) it is eternal and unchanging; (iv) it is caused by any other substance; and (v) it is caused by a cognition 'from another chain'.[21]

Śāntarakṣita rejects the first option because he argues that according to this idea the foetus would somehow receive the first cognition without any cause. This means that the cognition would be eternal, rather than momentary. Śāntarakṣita rejects the second option because if the cognition is produced by an eternal non-material cause then it should itself be eternal. The argument is that if something which exists eternally can bring about a cognition then there is no point in time at which this cause could have brought about the effect. So the effect is eternal in the same way as the cause. But an eternal effect cannot exist because something which is eternal does not have a cause. The third option that the cognition is eternal runs counter to our experience which tells us that cognitions are momentary. Śāntarakṣita also dismisses the Lokāyata position that cognitions are produced by physical substances because the Lokāyata philosophers argue that material substances are eternal. So, Śāntarakṣita makes a similar argument to the rejection of option two. An eternal cause has to have an eternal effect but cognitions are not eternal. Option five is rejected in TS 1893–1896 where Śāntarakṣita argues that the first cognition of one chain cannot be solely caused by a cognition from another chain because in that case we would expect the knowledge of parents to carry over into their babies.

It seems to me that the Lokāyata philosophers could argue for a version of the fourth option that even if physical substances are eternal, they could have non-eternal effects. Matter might well be eternal but could have effects which are non-eternal because these effects require matter to come together in a particular way. A more in-depth discussion of this argument would go beyond the scope of this paper.[22]

The second part (b) of Śāntarakṣita's argument, that love and hatred are different from perception, is intriguing in that he claims that there cannot be an external cause for love and hatred because whatever we might want to postulate as this external object can elicit different feelings in different people. The object of one person's love might be the object of another person's aversion.

[21] Compare Dharmakīrti's argument in PV 1.51–53.

[22] For an in-depth discussion of this argument in Dharmakīrti see FRANCO (1997: Ch. 5, esp. pp. 134–138).

For this reason, love and hatred cannot be acquired in this life, like perceptions. So the love and hatred that exist in a baby or young animal must be carried over from another life. This argument assumes that there could not be non-perceptual cognition that can arise without previous experience and therefore faces the same challenges as the claim that all feelings have to be learned through repeated experience. But it goes beyond this discussion in that it raises the question of what the object of love and hatred is. Kamalaśīla uses the term *vaśa* rather than *rāga* in his commentary on TS 1948–1953[23] which suggests that he does not clearly distinguish between desire and love. If it is true that *rāga* is a *kleśa* then it is plausible that there is no distinction between love and craving. So he could be making the obvious point that we can desire something without a basis in the external world, i.e. what I desire might not exist or that I might desire something for the wrong reasons. Love, hatred and desire all require the existence of an object. However, unlike a perceptual object, the objects of love and desire can be 'merely' mental. I can love the idea of equality or I can desire something which does not exist.[24] Perception, at least on a realist account, requires the object of perception to exist in the external world.

Cognitions, emotions and *kleśa*s

While the argument about the difference between perception and love does not show that love requires previous experience, it raises, (at least) two interesting questions: (i) why does Śāntarakṣita draw a distinction between perception and feeling on the basis of the non-existence of external objects in the case of love, hatred and desire? (ii) why does he make a specific argument about love and hatred when he has already argued in previous verses of the *Lokāyata-parīkṣā* that all cognitions require other cognitions as their causes?

I would like to discuss these questions briefly in reverse order. The second question raises the general problem of the translatability of the concept of feeling or emotion into Sanskrit. It is noticeable that Śāntarakṣita does not use a general term but talks about 'love and hatred etc.' (*rāga-dveṣa* + *ādi*). In the translation, Jha has taken the 'etc.' as referring to other feelings, assuming that Śāntarakṣita was operating with a psychological category such as 'feeling'. However, there is no single word in the text which would translate as feeling every time it appears in the translation.[25] In fact, it is clear that Śāntarakṣita

[23] See n. 18.

[24] This 'non-existence' can be twofold: (i) I can desire something which cannot exist either logically or physically, for example, I can desire that I had wings; (ii) if I desire something to be the case, then what I desire does not exist, yet. For example, if I desire an ice-cream then the state of affairs in which I have an ice-cream does not exist, yet.

[25] He does not use the terms *vedanā* or *bhāva* but one can assume that he recogniseds *vedanā* as one of the *skandha*s.

does not mean 'feelings' in the sense of non-representational attitudes towards objects because love and hatred have objects according to him, albeit mental objects. Since Śāntarakṣita remains within the context of Buddhist psychology and clearly refers to Dharmakīrti, it is plausible that he means 'other *kleśa*s' instead of 'other feelings' because love and hatred are *kleśa*s and have objects.

In this context, it is also important to discuss the translation of the term *vijñāna* as 'cognition'. Both terms refer to a mental phenomenon that provides knowledge. This means that they refer to a state of affairs that pertains in the world. Both terms presuppose an external or mental object they are directed towards. One important difference between these two terms, which shows the difficulty with translating *vijñāna* as cognition, is that, according to Śāntarakṣita, a *vijñāna* always has an object but it does not have to have conceptual content.[26] In this sense, even a sensation or feeling, such as the sensation of pleasure, is a *vijñāna* because it has an object but lacks conceptual content, according to Śāntarakṣita. The sensation has an object because it provides knowledge about mental states and therefore has to have an object of knowledge. However, this object is not conceptual.[27] So, according to Śāntarakṣita, a *vijñāna* includes affective mental states, such as feelings, sensations and emotions and therefore *kleśa*s. The Western term 'cognition', by contrast, excludes affective mental states.

The whole of the *Lokāyata-parīkṣā* is one argument for the existence of an infinite chain of *vijñāna*s that is independent of its physical manifestation. For Śāntarakṣita, 'love, hatred and the rest' are examples of *vijñāna*s. These *vijñāna*s are also *kleśa*s but not all *vijñāna*s are *kleśa*s. Love and hatred are especially useful for his argument because they are fundamental to our experience and emphasise the continuity of the 'chain of *vijñāna*s'.

According to Śāntarakṣita's 'world view', *vijñāna*s can include feelings and emotions whereas in Western psychology and philosophy cognitions are distinct from emotions and feelings. This means that the role of *vijñāna*s in Śāntarakṣita's system is different from the role of cognitions in Western psychology and philosophy. As I mentioned above, in the history of Western philosophy the distinction between feeling and cognition has often been used as the demarcation between feeling and rational thought with the ideal of affectless thought. Śāntarakṣita's ideal is not necessarily that of affectless thought. Instead, his ideal is that of an existence free from afflictions (*kleśa*). So, Śāntarakṣita also tries to extinguish one kind of mental phenomenon but his distinction is different from the distinction between feeling and thought. For him, all mental phenomena that provide an obstacle to liberation should be eliminated. This includes what Western psychologists would call emotions or feelings.

[26] See Śāntarakṣita's discussion in the *Pratyakṣa-lakṣaṇa-parīkṣā*, especially TS_1 1332–1339 plus Kamalaśīla's commentary.

[27] Of course, this raises the general question in what way an object can be non-conceptual, which I cannot discuss here.

However, it also includes many affectless cognitions. This means that the Western psychological category 'emotions' does not feature prominently in Śāntarakṣita's account of the mind. In fact, it is not clear that he would even recognise such a category. According to Buddhist psychology, some *kleśa*s straddle the Western divide between feeling and thought. They involve both feeling and thought and they are a mental phenomenon, called a *vijñāna*. Whereas for many philosophers in the history of Western philosophy, the ideal has been to purge feeling from thought, in order to attain a standard of rationality, the ideal for Śāntarakṣita and other Buddhist philosophers is to free our mental life from those *vijñāna*s which are *kleśa*s. The reason is not to attain some standard of rationality because, for Buddhists, most *vijñāna*s are suspect in that they involve an attachment to the present life and therefore pose an obstacle to liberation.[28]

One question that arises in this context is 'why does Śāntarakṣita single out love and hatred, instead of discussing *kleśa*s in general?' One answer might be that they are fundamental to our human experience and therefore lend themselves to Śāntarakṣita's argument that cognitions in general do not come into existence with the body.

In Western discussions of this topic, feelings are very often associated with some physical change, such as a quicker heartbeat or a change in the chemical make up of the brain. For this reason, emotions are very often regarded as providing some link between the mental and the physical. Śāntarakṣita mentions this link between feeling and physical changes in TS 1960. He claims that phlegm (*balāsa*) and other bodily changes are not responsible for love, hatred or perturbations through sexual arousal because there is no observed concomitance between them. While this claim might be true with regard to phlegm, it is obviously false with regard to other physical changes, especially changes in the brain.[29] However, it would be wrong to completely dismiss Śāntarakṣita's argument simply because he turned out to be wrong about this empirical claim. After all, the argument raises important questions about the status of mental phenomena, such as love and hatred. This becomes clear when we think about the other question I mentioned: why does Śāntarakṣita distin-

---

[28] The ideal for Śāntarakṣita is the attainment of luminous consciousness (*prabhāsvara citta*); see TS_1 3435.

[29] In TSP_1, p. 528 (translation TSP_2, pp. 900–901) Kamalaśīla states the Lokāyata argument that thinking is the result of bodily processes because love is a form of thinking which results from bodily processes. Kamalaśīla rejects this argument by stating that love is not necessarily the result of bodily processes but that it arises from the mind because love can cause certain bodily processes and it can be independent of bodily processes. Thus bodily processes cannot be the causes of love because there is no invariable concomitance between these processes and love. According to Kamalaśīla, the relationship of invariable concomitance has to hold between a cause and its effect. Compare also PV 1.77:

rāga-ādi-vṛddhiḥ puṣṭy-ādeḥ kadācit sukha-duḥkha-jā /
tayoś ca dhātu-sāmya-āder antar-arthasya sannidheḥ //

guish between perceptions, on the one hand, and love and hatred, on the other hand, based on the existence or non-existence of external objects? While Śānta-rakṣita often adopts an idealist position compatible with the Yogācāra stand-point in the *Tattva-saṁgraha*, he seems to switch to a realist position in this case which is compatible with a Sautāntrika standpoint. It seems to me that the best explanation for this switch is that Śāntarakṣita and Kamalaśīla are arguing against Lokāyata philosophers, who do not share the Yogācāra outlook on reality. This means that Śāntarakṣita and Kamalaśīla try to find common ground with these philosophers and therefore share their assumptions about the mind-independent existence of an external world. Śāntarakṣita's and Kamala-śīla's argument then is that even with this assumption in place, it does not follow that all cognitions are dependent on or even identical with the body. According to them, the Lokāyata philosophers would have to draw a distinc-tion between perceptions on the one hand and love and hatred on the other hand, and while they might be able to account for perceptions they are not able to account for love and hatred. As I demonstrated earlier, this argument is not cogent but it is interesting because it leaves open the possibility that Śānta-rakṣita (and perhaps other Indian thinkers) might not have operated with the psychological category 'emotion'. Śāntarakṣita and Kamalaśīla also might not have considered love and hatred to be irrational because they involve non-cognitive feelings that do not represent an external reality. Kamalaśīla in par-ticular makes it clear that for him love and hatred do not require a relationship to objects in the external world. He argues that not having an external object is a salient feature of love and hatred. In Western philosophy of mind we often use the presence or absence of an object of love in order to distinguish between rational and irrational love. Śāntarakṣita and Kamalaśīla, however, do not use this distinction in order to argue that love and hatred should be eliminated. As Buddhists, their concern lies with the afflictions that prevent the mind from becoming liberated and whatever mental state is an affliction ought to be eliminated. If this means that these Buddhist philosophers did not recognise the psychological category of the emotions then the repercussions of this are certainly worthy of further philosophical inquiry, because this psychological category impacts our world view with regards to concepts such as thought, rationality and ultimately reason.[30]

[30] I would like to thank the participants of the International Conference World View and Theory in Indian Philosophy (26–30 April 2009 in Barcelona, Spain), especially Piotr Bal-cerowicz, Vincent Eltschinger, Jonardon Ganeri, Brendan Gillon, Parimal Patil and Ernst Prets for some very helpful comments on an earlier version of this paper.

BIBLIOGRAPHY

AHN 2003 = Ahn, Sung-Doo: *Die Lehre von den Kleśas in der Yogācāra-bhūmi.* Alt- und Neu-Indische Studien, herausgegeben von der Abteilung für Kultur und Geschichte Indiens und Tibets des Asien-Afrika-Institutes an der Universität Hamburg, Band 55, Franz Steiner Verlag, Stuttgart 2003.

FRANCO 1997 = Franco, Eli: *Dharmakīrti on Compassion and Rebirth.* Wiener Studien zur Tibetologie und Buddhismuskunde, Heft 38, Arbeitskreis für Tibetische und Buddhistische Studien Universität Wien, Wien 1997.

PV = Dharmakīrti: *Pramāṇa-vārttika.* Rāhula Sāṅkṛtyāyana (ed.): *Ācārya-Dharmakīrteḥ Pramāṇa-vārttikam, Ācārya-Manoratha-nandi-kṛtayā vṛttyā saṁvalitaṁ* (*Dharmakīrti's Pramāṇavārttika with a Commentary by Manorathanandin*). Appendix to *The Journal of the Bihar and Orissa Research Society* 24, Bihar and Orissa Research Society, Patna 1938.

TS = Śāntarakṣita: *Tattva-saṁgraha.* (1) Embar Krishnamacharya (ed.): *Tattva-saṁgraha of Śāntarakṣita with the commentary (Pañjikā) of Kamalaśīla.* 2 Vols. Oriental Institute, Baroda 1984. (2) Ganganatha Jha (tr.): *The Tattva-saṁgraha of Śāntarakṣita with the Commentary (Pañjikā) of Kamalaśīla.* 2 Vols. Motilal Banarsidass, Delhi 1986.

TSP = Kamalaśīla: *Tattva-saṁgraha-pañjikā.* See: TS.

Some Aspects of *Ātman* According to Prabhākara and Śālikanātha

JEAN-MARIE VERPOORTEN

1. Historical and philological context.

Prabhākara and Śālikanātha are both thinkers of the Mīmāṁsā tradition, one of the six 'views' (*darśana*) well-known in Indian philosophy. In his *Bṛhatī* (Bṛ), Prabhākara (seventh century CE) has developed an original approach of the problems dealt with by his school. Śālikanātha, his disciple and commentator (750–820 CE), has, in turn, explained the *Bṛhatī* in his *Ṛju-vimala-pañcikā* (Ṛju).

Both Prabhākara and Śālikanātha have composed lengthy explanations of the commentary (*Bhāṣya*) on the fifth of the 2,745 *sūtra*s of Jaimini, written by their predecessors: Śabarasvāmin (ŚBh) and a mysterious Vṛtti-kāra ('Glossator'), whom ŚBh widely quotes.

The detailed explanation of the fifth *sūtra* of Jaimini's *Mīmāṁsā-sūtra* (MS) by ŚBh and the 'Glossator' is divided into 10 sections. The last one, called *Ātma-vāda* (MŚV 5.17), is devoted to the *ātman* or 'soul/self', and is followed by chapters setting forth grammatical and exegetical questions like the validity of the *Veda* etc.

The Sanskrit text of the *Bṛhatī* and *Ṛju-vimala-pañcikā* on the *Ātma-vāda* has been edited by S.K. Ramanatha Śastrī ($Bṛ_2$ / $Ṛju_2$), accompanied by the *Ātma-vāda* of ŚBh. There is also another edition of the *Bṛhatī* and *Ṛju-vimala-pañcikā* by A. Chinnaswami Sastri ($Bṛ_1$/$Ṛju_1$), partially reproduced by Kevalānanda Sarasvatī in his *Mīmāṁsā-kośa* (MK, II: pp. 900–907). As far as the *Bhāṣya* of Śabara (ŚBh) is concerned, the text can be read elsewhere also, either in the aforesaid *Mīmāṁsā-kośa* (MK, II: pp. 897–899 with the first lines in III: p. 1710a.27–30) or in the *Mīmāṁsā-darśana* (MS) published by Kāśīnātha Vāsudevaśāstrī Abhyankara and Gaṇeśaśāstrī Aṁbādāsa Jośī (MS, I: pp. 72–86).

In the English translation of Gangānātha Jhā ($ŚBh_3$), the passage studied below is found in Vol. I, pp. 26–31, 52–60, and the German translation is published (with the critical edition of the text) by E. Frauwallner ($ŚBh_1$). The references to page and lines are to the Madras edition ($Bṛ_2$), which has been used for *Bṛhatī* and *Ṛju-vimala-pañcikā*.[1] For the *Bṛhatī*, the references to *Mīmāṁsā-*

[1] I want to express my gratitude to Professor K. Yoshimizu, Sendai University, Japan, who kindly supplied me with photocopies of the text.

World View and Theory in Indian Philosophy
Warsaw Indological Studies 5 (2012) 277–298.

kośa have been added (page, column a or b and lines). The beginning of the *Śābara-bhāṣya* edited and translated by Frauwallner is cited as $ŚBh_1$, page and lines with mention of MS, volume, page and lines.

The following pages examine only the first part of the lengthy commentary[2] of Prabhākara and Śālikanātha, in which they seek to show that *ātman* is different from other components of the human being, such as breath, pleasure etc. Therein they define the self as *kartṛ–bhoktṛ*, possibly under the influence of the Sāṁkhya doctrine.

2. The question of the existence of *ātman*: the starting point of the debate.

There is a Vedic sentence which triggers the discussions of the *Ātma-vāda*, namely *Āpastamba-śrauta-sūtra* 31 2 21: 'The [deceased] institutor of the sacrifice instantly proceeds to the heavenly world, furnished with [his] sacrificial utensils.'[3] According to ŚBh, this phrase is a crux in that it contradicts what the eyes can see: actually, the late sacrificer does not proceed to heaven since his corpse surrounded by sacred objects is burning on the pyre. Now, if we do not want to acknowledge that the *Veda* is lying to us, we must presume that something else is going to heaven and discover what it is, which clues are available to trace this invisible '[wholly] other'[4] and which inferential marks should be used in the inference (*anumāna*) establishing its existence.

3. In the subsequent discussion, the Vedic sentence is no longer the focus; nevertheless, it is not totally forgotten. For instance, it occurs as a reminder by the end of the first part of the Prabhākara's commentary where it is qualified by *artha-vāda* or 'explanatory phrase'.[5]

---

[2] It expands on pp. 207–256 and contains 276 Sanskrit lines for the Bṛ and approximately 385 lines for the Ṛju *stricto sensu*, viz. without the long and numerous quotes of the Bṛ.

[3] Translated by SLAJE (2006:145). The text is found in $ŚBh_1$, p. 50.1–2 (*sa eṣa yajñâyudhī yajamāno 'ñjasā svargaṁ lokaṁ yāti*. In section 5 (*Citra-vāda*) of the ŚBh on 1.1.5, a disputant, already citing this sentence, emphasises the conflict arising thereby between the perception and the statement of the Revelation ($ŚBh_1$, p. 34.6: *dṛṣṭa-viruddham api bhavati kiṁcid vaidikaṁ vacanam* = MS, I: p. 49.1–3 where *vaidikam* is omitted). We find hints at this very sentence in Kumārila, MŚV *Ātma-vāda* 74:

> *yajamānatvam apy ātmā sakriyatvāt prapadyate /*
> *na parispanda eva ekaḥ kriyā naḥ kaṇa-bjojivat //* —
>
> —'On account of its active character, the soul comes to be the performer of sacrifices. We do not hold "motion" to be the only form of action, as held by the Vaiśeṣikas' (tr. $MŚV_2$, p. 395),

and in Śālikanātha, PrP, p. 329.11–12: *kartā bhoktā ca yajña-āyudhi-vākyenâkṣiptaḥ samarthayitavya ity upayuktaḥ pratyabhijñā-upanyāsaḥ.*—'Since it is necessary to consider that doer and enjoyer are implied in the sentence "equipped with the arms of the sacrifice", mention can be made of the recognition'.

[4] $ŚBh_1$, p. 50.5 = MS, I: p. 72.4: *āha: ko "sāv anyo"*.—'(An opponent) asks: "Who is this «other»?".' Throughout the text, the word *anya* is a way of talking of the self.

[5] $Bṛ_2$, p. 239.10 = MK, p. 905b.11–12: *tasmād yathârtho 'yam artha-vādaḥ: "sa eṣa yajñâyudhī yajamāna iti"*. $Ṛju_2$ glosses *yathârtha* ('correct') by *nâyathârtha* ('not incor-

Prabhākara and Śālikanātha prefer to devote themselves to an analysis of the human entity in order to discover:

—what this mysterious 'other' (*anya*) is which is different from body, breath, inner states (*sc.* feelings, such pleasure etc.) and which might be called *ātman*, or 'self',

—whether not only breath and feelings but also desire (*icchā*) and recollection (*smṛti*) can serve as inferential marks fit to aver (by *anumāna*) the existence of *ātman*.

4. The components of the human being which are not conducive to *ātman*.

In Śabara's work, an opponent states: 'We perceive it (*ātman*) with the help of breath (*prāṇa*).'[6] Both Prabhākara and Śālikanātha wonder whether *prāṇa* can lead us to *ātman* or whether it merely remains a material element, a product of the body, without link with the mysterious 'other one'.

The question remains unsettled because the nature of *prāṇa* is uncertain. *Prāṇa* is not a quality of the body[7] and is not tightly associated with it because it is not coeval with it (*ayāvad-śarīra/-bhūta*).[8] Whereas the body is still present, 'intact', 'not destroyed'[9] (even though it is now a corpse), breath has already vanished. Consequently, 'the *prāṇa*s cannot be material qualities since they do not last as long as their abode and are not seen in [material objects,] e.g. a jug.'[10] Further in the *Bṛhatī*, the non-coevality of the *prāṇa* is put aside by a disputant (unexpectedly a Mīmāṁsaka, Prabhākara himself) who prefers to talk of *(a)calanâtmakatva* '(im)mobility' (cf. n. 89).

Despite having a degree of independence from the body, breath cannot be the logical mark of the presence of *ātman*. On this point, Prabhākara and Śālikanātha are opposed to the Vaiśeṣikas[11] who claim that *sukha* (pleasure) and *prāṇa* (breath), being bereft of material support, are rightly named 'properties of *ātman*'.[12]

rect'). The semantic status of the *iti*-quote is uncertain: mandatory (*vidhi*) or explanatory (*artha-vāda*). The answer differs according to the authors. This aspect is not dealt with here in detail. *Vide infra* n. 111.

[6] ŚBh$_1$, p. 50.5–6: *nanu prāṇâdibhir enam upalabhāmahe* = MS, I: p. 72.4, where *nanu* is omitted. *Enam* = *asāv anyo*, i.e. 'that other one' of n. 4, finally identified with *ātman*.

[7] MŚV *Ātma-vāda* 97: *tasmān na deha-dharmatvaṁ prāṇâder.*

[8] Cf. ŚBh$_1$, p. 50.9 = MS, I: p. 73.4 (*ayāvac-charīra-bhāvitva*); Bṛ$_2$, p. 217.8 and 12 = MK, p. 902a.20, 25 and 27 (*ayāvad-bhūta-bhāvitva/tā*).

[9] *Dṛḍha*, *avinaṣṭa* as said in MŚV *Ātma-vāda* 94, 96.

[10] Bṛ$_2$, p. 217.8–9: *bhūta-guṇā hy amī (=prāṇa) na bhavanti ayāvad-bhūta-bhāvitvād ghaṭâdiṣv adarśanāt.* The last two words are not found in MK, p. 902a.20. They look like an explanation inspired by the debate around VS 3.2.4–6: VS$_1$, p. 173–174, tr. VS$_2$ (1868: 389–390), cf. n. 113.

[11] Ṛju$_2$, p. 218.15.

[12] Bṛ$_2$, p. 217.10–11 = MK, p. 902a.22–23: *ātma-guṇā hy ete ity yuktam evôktam*; Ṛju$_2$, p. 218.15: *nirasta-bhūtâśraya-bhāvāḥ samyag eva ātma-guṇatayā uktāḥ.*

5. In the subsequent passage (Bṛ / Ṛju, p. 217–218), both authors constantly mix up the accounts on *prāṇa* and on *sukha*. Although breath and pleasure are outside the material range, it would be preposterous to look upon them as *ātma-guṇa*, or the 'qualities of *ātman*'. To declare that the non-coevality of breath–body is not established—in other words, to opt for a tight relationship of both of them—would be tantamount to applying the idea of *ātman* to that which is material (*bhūta*) and, thus not *ātman*.[13] That would deny the latter's own existence, confining what is 'other' (*anya*/ *vyatirikta*), i.e. what is beyond the visible, to *prāṇa* alone and ultimately dismissing as false the aforesaid Vedic sentence (§ 2).

6. The inner states/ feelings (*sukha*, 'pleasure' etc.) and their inferential mark (*ceṣṭā*, 'the movements of the body'), i.e. the inference of the self on the basis of bodily movements (*ceṣṭā-anumāna*).

Of course, these states should not be seen as material features (*bhūta-dharma*),[14] for they are, unlike e.g. colour, imperceptible to anybody else except to their enjoyer.[15] Thus, with other people, they are reached by *anumāna* (inference).

On the other hand, they should not be regarded as qualities (*guṇa*) of the self, despite the claim of the Vaiśeṣikas,[16] because their inferential mark is a 'material change': *bhūta-vikāra-hetutva*, the first two elements of the compound being a synonym of *ceṣṭā*.

It would thus be erroneous to infer the presence of *ātman* from the movements of the body (*ceṣṭā*), for these movements only reveal the essence of the states that bring them about. If *sukha* etc. inferentially led us to *ātman* through *ceṣṭā*, the self would lose its immaterial essence.[17].

Earlier in the text of the *Ṛju-vimala-pañcikā*, a proponent stated that 'the existence of *ātman* is indeed demonstrated everywhere by the experience of pleasure [which is never without motion]'. But an opponent put that statement aside by pointing out: 'There is no proof that this [existence/ experience] is presently accompanied by a motion.'[18]

---

[13] $Bṛ_2$, p. 218.9–10 = MK, p. 902a.30: *tasmād ayāvad-bhūta-bhāvitvam asiddham. Sêyam anātmany ātma-buddhiḥ.*

[14] $Bṛ_2$, p. 211.4 = MK, p. 901b.18: *mā bhuvan bhūta-dharmāḥ sukhâdayaḥ*, glossed by $Ṛju_2$, p. 211.14: *kiṁ ca sukhâdayaś ca na bhūta-dharmāḥ śakyante vaktum.*

[15] $Ṛju_2$, p. 211.17: *na ca sukhâdayaḥ parêndriya-grāhyāḥ. tasmād na bhūta-dharmāḥ.*

[16] Are they Vaiśeṣikas those who think that the *sukha* etc are material qualities in $Ṛju_2$, p. 219.18.

[17] $Ṛju_2$, p. 246.23–24: *ātmano 'py anātmatā prasajyate.* Cf. n. 13 for a similar expression. To use material marks like *prāṇa* in order to infer the self could turn this latter into a 'material agreggate' (*bhūta-saṁghaṭa*), $Ṛju_2$, p. 217.16.

[18] $Ṛju_2$, p. 236.9 ff. (cited in MK II: p. 904b.30–34): *sattā tāvad ātmanaḥ sarvatra sukhôpalambhena siddhā. sêdānīṁ gamana-pūrvikā iti nâsti pramāṇam.* The point of these cumbersome passages ($Bṛ_2$, 235.10–12, 236/4–5 and $Ṛju_2$, 235.23–25, 236/9–11) is to show how *ātman*, by itself ubiquitous (*sarva-gata*) and therefore inactive and motionless (*niṣkriya*; cf. also *infra* §§ 18 and 20), can receive an amount of change from its objects

Seemingly, the Mīmāṁsakas accept as valid an *anumāna* which is based on the bodily movements (*ceṣṭā*)—a frown or a smiling face[19]—and reveals the states of pleasure etc., but they do not go to the extent of saying that that *anumāna* bears out the presence of *ātman*.

7. As seen just above, Śabara and his disciples are prepared to dismiss the logical marks such as *prāṇa* and *sukha* as incapable of making one infer the self. They prefer to confine this power to the Vedic Revelation alone. Putting one's trust in *prāṇa* etc. as a path to *ātman* leads us astray by inducing us to think that 'on account of them, the notion of *ātman* is in force for what is not *ātman*.'[20] However the Vaiśeṣika thinkers are guilty of this fallacy and they teach it to their students.[21]

8. Are desire (*icchā*) and recollection (*smṛti*) conducive to an invisible *ātman*?[22]

This question is dealt with from p. 215.14 (Prabhākara) and 216.16 f. (Śālikanātha) onwards.[23]

In this intricate issue, the Buddhist and the three Mīmāṁsakas (Śabarasvāmin, Prabhākara and Śālikanātha) agree on just one fact: desire and recollection are existing elements. However the Buddhist wants to confine human nature to the act of 'knowing' (*jānāti*), its ideas (*buddhi*) and their reciprocal causality (*paraspara-kāraṇatā*),[24] and he gives desire and recollection a minimal importance. Therefore he points out that *icchā* and *smṛti* bear only on the perceived objects and not on the so far unperceived ones, like the sweet fruits said

(*sukha* etc.), and how these latter, although or rather because they are not ubiquitous but localised in time and space (*prādeśika*), are the means of revealing it.

[19] *Bhrū-bhaṅga*, Bṛ2, p. 247.9 = MK, p. 906b.3; *prahṛṣṭa-vadanatva*, MŚV *Ātma-vāda* 99.

[20] Bṛ2, p. 216.9–10 = MK, p. 902a.14: *ebhir anātmanaḥ ātma-buddhiḥ prāpnoti.* For *anātman* (glossed *bhūta*, 'material', in Ṛju2, p. 218.20), cf.also Bṛ2, p. 217.11–12 = MK, p. 902a.23–24; 218.10 = MK, p. 902a.30–31; Ṛju2, 219.19 (cf. n. 113); Bṛ2, p. 224.7–8 = MK, p. 903a.22–23; 230.7 and 9 = MK p. 904a.3–4 and 6–7; 237.8 and 238.13 (MK, p. 905a.22 reads *ātmani* instead of *anātmani*, but p. 238.13, Ṛju2 quotes with *anātmani*); Ṛju2, p. 246.24 (*anātmatā*); 256.9 = MK, p. 907b.14.

[21] Ṛju2, p. 216.25–217.14–15: *asyārthaḥ: yady ete hetavo na niṣkriyeran tadā śiṣyānām eṣv api vaiśeṣikâdi-darśana-śravaṇa-vipralabdha-buddhināṁ samīcīna-ātma-hetv-abhimānaḥ syāt.*—'The meaning is as follows: if these [logical] grounds were not dismissed, there would be, for the students of these [topics] whose minds are deceived by hearing the Vaiśeṣika doctrines, the misconception that these grounds (*sukha, prāṇa*) are right [to infer] the Self'. Incidentally, Śālikanātha and Prabhākara come to target more personally some philosophical adversaries: Prabhākara (Ṛju2, p. 247.8 = MK, p. 906b.2) calls his opponent *anupāsita-guru*, 'a badly educated doctor', and some scholars believe that this word refers to Kumārila.

[22] ŚBh1, p. 52.17 (= MS, I: p. 76.6): *icchayā ātmānam upalabhāmahe*; p. 54.17 (= MS, I: p. 78.6): *smṛtir apîcchāvat.*

[23] Cf. also MŚV *Ātma-vāda* 103.

[24] Ṛju2, p. 216.15–16: *buddhy-ādibhyo 'nyasyânupalabdheḥ paraspara-kāraṇatayā côpapatter jānāti.*—'Due to the non-perception of another [entity] apart from the ideas and due to the possibility [for these latter to exist] under the form of a reciprocal causality, he knows'.

to grow north of Mount Meru[25] or, implicitly, a whimsical entity as *ātman*. With respect to desire and recollection, one should not ask who is their owner, since, like the sun and moon, they are things without 'possessor' (*tadvān*).[26]

Prabhākara and Śālikanātha argue that, on the contrary, desire and recollection are perceptible and consequently non-implausible;[27] they cannot be looked upon as negligible data. The Buddhist seems to endorse this approach when he states in an awkward phrase that 'one could not say that recollection etc. are impossible when/ if the 'other', the 'dissimilar' (*visabhāga*), is invisible'.[28] However he draws from there the following consequence: *icchā* and *smṛti* exist without being related to an imperceptible *ātman*. The self is not their support and thus does not deserve any attention or refutation.[29]

9. From p. 219–220 onwards, both Mīmāṁsakas proceed to ascertain their own positions against the Buddhists.[30] Prabhākara tauntingly portrays them as *kecit prajnâbhimāninaḥ*, or 'some people who overrate their intelligence/ discernment',[31] who dare, as Śālikanātha explains, to remove the relation of 'the supported and the support' (*āśrayâśrayitā*)[32] and to impede the inference of an invisible support (*ātman*) from the visibly supported (*sukha* etc.).

---

[25] ŚBh$_1$, p. 52.17–19: *upalabdha-pūrve hy abhiprete bhavatîcchā, nânupalabdha-pūrve, yathā merum uttareṇa yāny asmaj-jātīyair anupalabdha-pūrvāṇi svādūni vṛkṣa-phalāni na tāni praty asmākam icchā bhavati.*—'Desire appears when the desired object is one that has been perceived before [and not one not perceived before]; for instance we have no desire for those sweet fruits that grow to the north of the Meru mountains and which have never before been tested by people like us'. Frauwallner points out (Śbh$_1$, p. 52, no. 18), among the *variae lectiones*, the omission of the phrase '*nānupalabdhapūrve*' in three mss, what is evidenced in MS, I: p. 76.6–7, where the group is absent, and in Śbh$_3$, p. 27, where it is not translated by G. Jha.

[26] ŚBh$_1$, p. 50.18–19; p. 52.1 = MS, I: p. 74.6–8.

[27] Bṛ$_2$, p. 222.8 = MK, p. 903a.5–6: *dṛṣṭe hy anupapattir nâsti*; Ṛju$_2$, p. 223.14: *yat tu khalu dṛṣṭam, tatrânupapannaṁ nâsti.*

[28] Bṛ$_2$, p. 215.14–15 = MK, p. 902a.9–10: *na hy adṛṣṭe 'nyasmin visabhāge smṛty-ādayo nôpapadyanta iti śakyate vaktum. Visabhāga*, which occurs e.g. in *Abhidharma-kośa* 3.43 (tr. AK, III: p. 77, 196 ff.), possibly means that *ātman* is outside the cognitive series and not of the same nature as desire and recollection. Thus the self is not revealed by them and therefore non-cognisable.

[29] Ṛju$_2$, p. 216.21–22: *yadi prāṇâdīny ātmānam avagāmayitum īṣate, tatas tebhyo 'py ātma-pratītir astu; atha na, tadā anadāra eva yuktaḥ, kim-artham eṣāṁ nirākaraṇam.*—'If breath etc. are able to let know the self, let the knowledge of *ātman* be [produced] by them as well; but if not, then [to pay] no heed to them (*prāṇa* etc.) is right.What is the need to refute them?'

[30] *Bauddha*: Ṛju$_2$, p. 220.11, p. 224.12; *vijñāna-vāda*: p. 224.13, p. 229.12; *nairātmya-vādin*: Bṛ$_2$, p. 235.8 = MK, p. 904b.24.

[31] Bṛ$_2$, p. 219.11–220.5 = MK, p. 902b.9.

[32] Bṛ$_2$, p. 220.5 = MK, p. 902b.10; Ṛju$_2$, p. 220.12 seems to gloss this term by the Vaiśeṣika notion of *samavāyi-kāraṇa* ('inherent/necessary causality') in the sentence *kṣaṇikatvāt padârthānāṁ samavāyi-kāraṇaṁ na bhavati.*—'In view of the momentariness of [all] things, there is no necessary causality [between them]'.

Throughout both commentaries, the Buddhist pushes forward the view that it is useless to search for an invisible entity beyond and behind the sensorial data (*skandha*). Thus *anumāna* (inference), passing from the visible towards the invisible, is of no avail when perception has already taken place.[33] In other words, when perception takes place, *anumāna* becomes useless.[34] On the other hand, when perception is lacking, e.g. in the case of an invisible object, *anumāna* cannot work either.[35]

10. On the contrary, Prabhākara and Śālikanātha defend the *anumāna* which the Buddhist undermines so strongly that he could be regarded as a sheer materialist. The Mīmāṁsakas envisage the perceptive cognition (*pratyakṣa-(vi)jñāna*) as unsatisfactory in so far as it is momentary (*kṣaṇika*) and thus unable to prompt the 'epistemological jump' from the visible to the invisible. Accordingly, Prabhākara and Śālikanātha use the expression 'perception with recognition' (*sapratyabhijñaṁ pratyakṣam*)[36] to define their approach.

11. The crucial proof of the existence of the soul, or *ātman*, is obviously the process of recognition (*pratyabhijñā*) on which Buddhists and Mīmāṁsakas so radically disagree.

According to the latter, the notion of *aham* 'I' is necessarily linked with the recognition, because the recognizer is nobody else but the 'ego'.

As Śabarasvāmin says, *aham* denotes what is apart from—i.e. beyond—cognitions.[37] This statement is better understood in contrast, viz. if we remember that the aforesaid pronoun can also metaphorically denote a material element, e.g. in the phrase 'I am going', where *aham* takes the place of 'my body'.[38]

---

[33] This is what Prabhākara qualifies as 'a piece of recklessness' (*sāhasam*), Bṛ2, p. 225.10–11 = MK, p. 903a.28–29: *pratyakṣa-dṛṣṭe 'rthe 'numānaṁ na saṁbhavatîti sāhasam idam.*

[34] Bṛ2, p. 226.9 = MK p. 903b.4–5: *upalabdhaś cet svayam, kim anumānena.*—'If [*ātman*] is perceived by itself, what is the point of an inference?' Noteworthy is the fact that these words bear upon the important issue (not dealt with in these pages) whether the perception of one's own *ātman* can allow one to infer the existence of someone else's self.

[35] Bṛ2, p. 226.8–9 = MK, p. 903b.3–4: *svayam ātmānaṁ pratyakṣeṇânupalabhya nêdam anumānaṁ pravartate.*

[36] Ṛju2, p. 234.23 glossing Bṛ2, p. 235.7 = MK, p. 904b.23, where both words are attributed to the *bhāṣya-kāraḥ*, i.e. Śabarasvāmin, who however does not use them, at least in his *Ātma-vāda*. They are also present in Ṛju2, pp. 234.22–23 and 235.15–16.

[37] ŚBh1, p. 56.3–4 = MS, I: p. 79.5: *tasmāt tad-vyatirikto 'nyo 'sti yatrâyam ahaṁ-śabdaḥ.*—'Hence it follows that there is something apart from the [cognitions], and it is to this something that the term "I" is applied' (tr. ŚBh3, I: p. 28); p. 56.21 = MS, I: p. 80.13–14, the Buddhist demands that the 'other', i.e. the 'knower', be shown to him (*āha: yadi vijñānād anyad asti vijñātṛ ... tan nidarśyatām*); *vide infra* n. 96.

[38] The phrase *ahaṁ gacchāmi* is mentioned in ŚBh1, p. 56.6 = MS, I: p. 79.7, and commented by Prabhākara and Śālikanātha, Bṛ2, p. 230.5 and 14 = MK, p. 904a.1 ff. The complex relationship between *ātman* ('soul/self') and *aham* ('I') is scrutinised by M. HULIN (1978) and (2008: e.g. 98).

Further in the text, towards the end of the first part of his commentary, Prabhākara points out that 'the concept of *aham* is the support (*ālambana*) of *ātman,* provided this concept [of *aham*] is devoid of any notion of "this" (*asaṁbhinnêdaṁ-pratyaya*)', viz. of any thing of objective essence.[39]

For his part, Kumārila points out that *aham* must exclusively refer to the cogniser and its reference to a feature or an act concerning the body can safely be taken as a misconception (*bhrānti*).[40]

12. The nature of the recognition as set forth by our authors can be more easily realised with the help of some quotations of ŚBh which describe the phenomenon and the conclusions that might be drawn from it.

A (1) The first extract describes the standard recognition, the one caused by recollection, i.e. linked with the past:[41] 'It is only when a person has seen a thing on one day that he has the notion (remembrance/recollection) on the next day in the form "I have seen it", and this notion of recognition appears only in his own one's self and not otherwhere...'.[42] Hence it follows that there is something apart from both cognitions and it is to this "something" that the term "I" is applied'.[43]

Prabhākara and Śālikanātha cite words and excerpts from this passage more than once, when they thoroughly deal with the *aham-ātman* relationship.[44]

A (2) Elsewhere, we meet with a shortened picture of the same event: 'It was we who saw this thing on one day, and it is we who remember it today ... It is "we" that existed yesterday, and it is the same "we" that exists today.'[45]

---

[39] Bṛ₂, p. 239.1–2 = MK p. 905b.1–2 (where *ātmana* is omitted): *tasmād asaṁbhinnêdaṁ-pratyaya evâhaṁ-pratyaya ātmana ālambanam.* Ṛju₂, p. 239.14 glosses *asaṁbhinna* by *amiśrīkata* ('not mixed') and *ālambana* by *vyavasthitau kāraṇa* ('cause of distinction'). The compound *asambhinnêdaṁ-pratyayâhaṁ-pratyaya-viṣayatva* ('the fact of being the discriminated object of the notions of "this" and "I"') occurs already in Ṛju₂, p. 231.17–18.

[40] MŚV *Ātma-vāda* 125–27.

[41] ŚBh₁, p. 56.1 ff. = MS, I: p. 79.3 ff.: *anyedyur dṛṣṭe 'paredyur "aham idam adarśam" iti bhavati pratyayaḥ. «pratyag-ātmani câtad bhavati, na paratra» ... tasmād tad-vyatirikto 'nyo 'sti yatrâyam aham śabdaḥ.* The words *pratyag-° ... paratra* are the approximate quotation of VS (*vide infra* n. 42). It is quoted in Bṛ₂, p. 231.4–5 = MK, p. 904a.7 ff. and Ṛju₂, p. 230.21–22.

[42] The words in the guillemets « ... » in n. 41 are a quotation *lato sensu* of VS 3.2.14: *aham iti pratyag-ātmani bhāvāt paratrâbhāvād arthântara-pratyakṣaḥ.*—'Because the [intuition] "I" exists in one's own self, and because it does not exist elsewhere, it apprehends something else [than the body]'. English translation: RADHAKRISHNAN–MOORE (1960: 392); French translation and text: BIARDEAU (1968: 116). See also NOZAWA (1991: 35) and PREISENDANZ (1994: 228–29).

[43] Tr. ŚBh₃, I: p. 28 (modified).

[44] Bṛ₂ and Ṛju₂, p. 231.14 and 18, p. 236.5 ff., 237.8 and 238.13.

[45] ŚBh₁, p. 56.9–11 = MS, I: p. 80.2–3 (tr. ŚBh₃, I: p. 29). A shorter phrasing of the same statement occurs in Bṛ₂, p. 232.6 = MK, p. 904a.18–19 (and Ṛju₂, p. 232.13): *na ca—anya upalabdhā hyaḥ, adya cânyaḥ—ity etāvatā nairātmyam.*—'It is not as far as [we say] "other [was] the perceiver yesterday, other is he today" that there is non-existence of the self'.

B (1) The third example describes recognition as related to desire, i.e. to something rather linked with the future. It, too, occurs in the *Śābhara-bhāṣya*: 'For instance, we find that when on one day a man has left an action half-done, he tries to make up for it on the next day, and from this action it is inferred that the person regards himself as enduring (lasting) in relationship to things that are evanescent [or, on the basis of evanescent activities one comes to cognise the enduring self].'[46]

B (2) In the MŚV, *Ātma-vāda* 135, a somewhat similar example is given: 'In a case where only a half of a certain scripture etc. has been learnt, if one were not to have any idea that 'I have learnt this much', then (when taking up the study of the work after some time), he would have to learn from the beginning again'.[47]

It is clear to anyone that a number of human behaviours require, at least in the view of non-Buddhist thinkers, an underlying entity is in charge of recollection and desire. It is justified to call this entity *ātman*, or 'self/soul'.

13. At this point, Prabhākara makes several remarks with respect to the stock formula of the recognition *aham idam adarśam* ('I have seen it'), remarks which his disciple Śālikanātha does not let go unnoticed.

The former says: 'It is not intended here to dismiss the concept of momentariness. What then? The intention is to ascertain the existence of *ātman* as apart from the intellect, sensory organs and body.'[48] The latter takes up almost the same words but twice mentions the *ahaṁ-pratyaya* ('notion of "I"') to identify this *ātman* which escapes any additional description.[49]

It is with such a view that Śālikanātha and Prabhākara confront the Buddhist opponent who, twice in the *Śābara-bhāṣya*, challenges them as follows: 'Leaving cognition aside (*apāsya*) ... please point out the cogniser with the words: "Here it is, such it is".'[50] This sentence is the one of a man who sees no need

---

[46] ŚBh$_1$, p. 58.22–23 = MS, I: p. 83.8–10: *yadâsau puruṣaḥ pūrvedyuḥ sāmi-kṛtānām arthānām prati samādhāne śeṣa-anuṣṭhāne ca yatate. ataḥ pravṛttyâvagamyate: "nūnam asāv anityān nityam avagacchati" iti*; tr. ŚBh$_3$, I: p. 30.

[47] MŚV$_1$, *Ātma-vāda* 125–27:

śāstrâdāv ardha-vijñāte yady 'ham jñātavān iti /
nâvagacchet tataḥ sarvaḥ pravartetâditaḥ punaḥ //

Tr. MŚV$_2$, p. 406.

[48] Bṛ$_2$, p. 231.7–8 = MK, p. 904a.12–13: *na câtra kṣaṇikatva-nirākaraṇam abhipretam. kiṁ tarhi? buddhîndriya-śarīra-vyatiriktasyâtmanaḥ sadbhāva-pratipattir abhipretā.* Somewhat further (Bṛ$_2$, p. 232.7 = MK, p. 904a.20, repeated in Ṛju$_2$, p. 232.17), the second phrase is taken up in Sāṁkhya terms: 'apart from the body and its organs' (*kārya-karaṇa-vyatirikta*).

[49] Ṛju$_2$, p. 231.14, 18. Bṛ$_2$, p. 232.7 = MK, p. 904a.20 has the compound *ahaṁ-pratyaya-grāhya* to qualify *ātman*. According to HULIN (1978: 66): 'L'*ātman* [of Mīmāṁsā] est substrat inerte et muet, simple point de référence de la variété des expériences concrètes ... simple capacité abstraite de connaître, de jouir et d'agir ...'

[50] ŚBh$_1$, p. 56.21–22; 60.5 (partially) = MS, I: p. 80.13–14, 84.5 commented upon by Bṛ$_2$, p. 240.5–6, 250.4 = MK, p. 905b.13–14, 906b.25 and Ṛju$_2$, p. 240.15–16. Tr. ŚBh$_3$, I: p. 29.

of a support (*ātman*) for a quality like cognition etc.[51] *Ātman* is therefore useless; it can be replaced by the quality itself: cognition or a cognitive series (*saṁtāna*). The Buddhist thus asks his opponent Mīmāṁsaka to show the 'cogniser', personally convinced that it is impossible to do so.[52]

The Mīmāṁsaka skilfully answers that it is hardly possible to trace a sheer cogniser devoid of any cognition. With the words of the *Śābara-bhāṣya* Śālikanātha demonstrates this: 'Thus, if we leave cognition aside, we cannot indicate anything at all',[53] especially no cogniser.

By and large, the second section of Prabhākara's and Śālikanātha's explanation of the *Ātma-vāda* (*vide infra* § 22) is devoted to this question and contains statements, such as'outside knowledge, no knower is there', 'when cognition is not apprehended, there is no apprehension of *ātman*',[54] and also 'without apprehending cognition, no knowable [object] can be apprehended.'[55]

14. In addition to the Buddhists (*vide supra* § 9), other disputants (*apare*), i.e. the followers of the Sāṁkhya school, are brought to the foreground under the name of *brahma-vid*.[56] Their influence on our two authors is perceptible, if only slightly. Significant is the presence in the *Ṛju-vimala-pañcikā* of two stanzas of the *Sāṁkhya-kārikā*: 3 and 57.[57] More expressions, e.g. *kārya-*

[51] BIARDEAU (1968: 111): 'L'adversaire proteste que tout cela (that is body, cognition etc.—J.-M.V.) ne requiert aucun substrat permanent; son argument essentiel—et qui le restera jusqu'au bout—est qu'on ne peut voir ce substrat en lui-même. On le décrit toujours comme ce qui possède tel ou tel attribut (*guṇa*) mais on ne propose jamais d'écarter le voile de cet attribut pour le montrer lui-même. Pourquoi alors ne pas reconnaître qu'il se réduit à l'attribut".'

[52] HULIN (2008: 95).

[53] Tr. ŚBh$_3$, p. 30 of ŚBh$_1$, p. 60.10–11 = MS, I: p. 85.1–2: *tasmān na vijñānaṁ pratyākhyāya kasyacid rupaṁ nidarśayituṁ śakyam*, cited by Br$_2$, p. 229.14–15. In Śbh$_1$, p.60.5, Śabara uses *apāsya* as a synonym of *pratyākhyāya*.

[54] Ṛju$_2$, p. 228.15 and 17: *vijñānâgrahaṇe saty ātmano grahaṇaṁ nâsti; vijñānâgrahaṇe yadâtmano 'grahaṇam...*

[55] Ṛju$_2$, p. 229.11: *vijñānam agṛhītvā vijñeyaṁ nâiva grahītuṁ śakyate.*

[56] Bṛ$_2$, p. 220.8, 20 = MK, p. 902b.14 glossed by Śālikanātha, p. 220.21–22, as *eṣā hi sāṁkhyānāṁ prakriyā*—'for it is a designation of the Sāṁkhyas'. Cf. Bṛ$_2$, p. 230.6 = MK, p. 904a.2. In Bṛ$_2$, p. 230.9, the opponents of the *brahma-vid* are given the name of the *ātma-vid* (most probably the Naiyāyikas rather than the Vedāntins). The term *brahma-vid* still occurs in Bṛ$_2$, p. 239.8 = MK, p. 905b.8. In Ṛju$_2$, p. 209.20, the Vaiśeṣikas are called *padârtha-vid*.

[57] The *Sāṁkhya-Kārikā* is a collection dated of fourth–fifth century CE according to PELISSERO (2007: 327). SK 3 (p. 221.14–15) reads as follows: 'Primal Nature (*prakṛti*) is not an evolute; the seven, beginning with the Great one (*mahat*, i.e. the intellect) are both evolvents and evolutes; the sixteen (i.e. the five organs of sense, the five of action, the mind, and the five gross elements) are only evolutes; the spirit is neither evolvent nor evolute.' SK 57 (p. 222.16–17): As the insentient milk flows out for the growth of the calf, so does Nature act towards the emancipation of the spirit' [tr. RADHAKRISHNAN–MOORE(1960: 427 and 443)].

karaṇa ('the body and its organs'),[58] *pariṇati* ('transformation', a synonym of *pariṇāma*)[59], *kaivalya* ('absolute independence')[60] and so on are likely to stem from Sāṁkhya sources. But one of the most interesting terms is undoubtedly *bhoktṛ* ('experiencing person', 'enjoyer'), i.e. subject of perceptive and retributive experiences.

15. The *ātman* as *bhoktṛ* ('enjoyer').

The term *bhoktṛ* is predominantly met with from p. 232 onwards in the Madras edition of the *Bṛhatī* (Bṛ2).[61]

The notion of the 'enjoyer' has priority over that of the 'doer' in the demonstration of the *ātman* by Prabhākara and Śālikanātha. In other words, their argumentation, undertaken along the Mīmāṁsā lines, stresses the importance of the self as ritual agent, but still more as ritual beneficiary (*bhoktṛ*) of the sacrifice. Prabhākara and Śālikanātha are looking for an evidence to substantiate their views, namely that a sacrificer performs his long and weary ritual task in the hope of earning a benefit from it at the end, namely to become the *bhoktṛ* of heaven (*svarga*). Now, this is impossible if he is nothing but a body which will burn on a pyre and if, accordingly, someone else might go to heaven because the acting person is not the enjoying one.

The well-known stanza[62]—*Sāṁkhya-kārikā* 17—provides support to their position. The crucial passage therein is *puruṣo 'sti bhoktṛ-bhāvāt*—'...because there must be someone to experience, the spirit must be there...'.[63] This conception of the soul/self (*ātman*), here called 'spirit' (*puruṣa*), as the 'experiencing person' is accepted by the Brahminical systems: *ātman* enjoys either objects of one's senses and pleasure or the good and bad results of retributive action. The Buddhists, on the contrary, dismiss the notion of *bhoktṛ* (*bhoktṛ-grāha*) along with that of 'soul/self' (*ātman*) and speak instead of *āyatana* (the 'base [of cognition]').[64]

16. In the system of Prabhākara and Śālikanātha, the 'condition of *bhoktṛ*' (*bhoktṛtva*) is primarily required to support the thesis of the existence of the *ātman* and to protect the necessary identity of the doer of the sacrifice and the enjoyer thereof, jeopardised by the tenet of universal momentariness.

---

[58] Bṛ2, p. 238.8 = MK, p. 905a.32: *idaṁ-pratyaya-grāhyaṁ kārya-karaṇam.* The *dvandva*-compound *kārya-karaṇa* ('body and sense organs') is glossed in Bṛ2, p. 238.23 as follows: 'body' = *jñeya* ('the knowable') and 'sense organs' = *jñāna* ('cognitive instruments').

[59] Bṛ2, p. 234.6 = MK, p. 904b.16.

[60] Ṛju2, p. 239.26.

[61] It seems to be unknown to ŚBh. No reference to it is found in the MK.

[62] Also alluded to in MŚV *Ātma-vāda* 114.

[63] SK 17:

> *saṁghāta-parârthatvāt tri-guṇâdi-viparyayād adhiṣṭhānāt /*
> *puruṣo 'sti bhoktṛ-bhāvāt kaivalyârthaṁ pravṛtteḥ //*

Tr. RADHAKRISHNAN–MOORE (1960: 431).

[64] See e.g. Sthiramati's *Pañca-skandhaka-vibhāṣā* cited in KRAMER (2008: 154, n.17).

Prabhākara makes the following statement: 'Even if the existence [of the *ātman*] is established, its nature as *ātman* is totally (*eva*) lost in case of momentariness.'[65] And Śālikanātha explains: 'The nature of *ātman* is the nature as an experiencing subject, and precisely that nature as an experiencing subject in case of a momentary [entity] is forsaken.'[66]

Prabhākara previously stated[67] that the recognitive event (of the identity between performer and enjoyer of the sacrifice) was not designed to put momentariness aside but to assert the existence of a self/soul (*ātman*) as distinct from the mind, sensory organs and body. A similar statement is found in the *Śloka-vārttika*: 'Thus then, we would have a rejection of the theory of the non-existence of the soul, by means of the aforesaid recognition (of the soul) experienced by all persons.'[68]

Thus, when Prabhākara proclaims that the momentariness of the *skandha*s, i.e. the constituent parts of the human being, is caused by the absence of a *bhoktṛ*, his opponent confronts him by asking whether one is bound to accept this teaching like 'an order of the king', that is unconditionally and blindly. Prabhākara answers that his view is to be accepted not as an order of the king, but as an order of reason.[69]

Such a statement sounds like a reverse of the position of the Buddhist who points out that the *bhoktṛ* cannot exist because everything is and must be momentary.

17. Both Mīmāṁsakas have grounds of their own to emphasise the importance of the enjoying function of the self and thus look for arguments to support their position in the Sāṁkhya system as well. They might have reckoned in the first place *Sāṁkhya-kārikā* 19 and 20. Stanza 19 describes *ātman*, called here *puruṣa*, as 'having the qualities of witness and onlooker but without that of agent' (*sākṣitvam puruṣasya ... draṣṭṛtvam akartṛ-bhāvaś ca*)[70] and stanza 20 adds 'although [only] the strands (*guṇa*) are agents, the [*puruṣa*] indifferent (*udāsīna*) is, in similar manner, as if an agent (*kartā iva*).'[71]

Is it under the influence of the Sāṁkhya that Prabhākara and Śālikanātha are inclined to underrate the *kartṛ* side of the *ātman*.

18. *Bhoktṛ* and *kartṛ* ('active agent') in the *Sāṁkhya-pravacana-bhāṣya*.

A further testimony of the priority granted by the Sāṁkhya to the *bhoktṛ* over the *kartṛ* is that of the *Sāṁkhya-pravacana-bhāṣya*. This important but

---

[65] $Bṛ_2$, p. 232.8–9 = MK, p. 904a.22–23: *sādhite 'py astitve kṣaṇikatvād ātmatâiva hīyate.*

[66] $Ṛju_2$, p. 232.19–20: *bhoktṛtā hy ātmatā. sā bhoktṛtâiva kṣaṇikasya hīyate.*

[67] $Bṛ_2$, p. 231.6–8, cited *supra* n. 48.

[68] MŚV *Ātma-vāda* 136: *tenâsmāt pratyabhijñānāt sarva-lokâvadhāritān nairātmya-vāda-bādhaḥ syāt*; tr. $MŚV_2$, p. 406.

[69] $Bṛ_2$, p. 233.7 = MK, p. 904a.33–34: *bhoktur abhāve kṣaṇikatā skandhānām iti kim iyaṁ rājâjnā? nêyaṁ rājâjnā. nayâjnā hy eṣā.*

[70] SK 19: *sākṣitvam asya puruṣasya... draṣṭṛtvam akartṛ-bhāvaśca.*

[71] SK 20: *guṇa-kartṛtve ca tathā kartêva bhavaty udāsinaḥ.* Tr. BRONKHORST (2000: 12–13).

late Sāṁkhya treatise written by Vijñānabhikṣu (1550–1600) on the hardly more ancient *Sāṁkhya-sūtra* is of course not a source for Prabhākara and Śālikanātha, who lived more than seven centuries earlier. However it seems to be close to the positions of both Mīmāṁsakas in a number of cases.

In the very beginning of his work, Vijñānabhikṣu already points out the difference between Sāṁkhya and Nyāya the adepts of which—here named 'logicians' (*tārkika*)—champion the *ātman* as a *kartṛ*.[72]

Kapila's *Sāṁkhya-sūtra* 1.143 contains a wording of SK 17.[73] Later on, Vijñānabhikṣu, commenting on SS 1.143, states that *bhoktṛtva* (= *bhoktṛ-bhāva*) cannot belong to the (human) body, but to the *puruṣa*, and that *bhoga* is made up of thought (*cit*, cf. also SS 1.104). According to the Sāṁkhya doctor, the *puruṣa*, synonym of the *ātman* of Mīmāṁsā, primarily possesses *bhokṛtva*. Being motionless and actionless by nature, the *puruṣa* will be *bhoktṛ* ('the subject of experience (e.g. of pleasure etc.) and retribution')[74] and *draṣṭṛ* ('the onlooker')[75] rather than *kartṛ* ('active agent'). The *bhoktṛ* is operating by (immaterial) contact with the entities on which it exerts its control (*adhiṣṭhāna*), like a suzerain who is the beneficiary of the activities performed by those who abide by his orders.[76] For instance, the *bhoktṛ* manages to keep the body from putrefying with the help of the breath but the merit thereof accrues, not to the latter, but to the enjoyer himself.[77]

In fact, *bhoga* ('enjoyment') accrues to *bhoktṛ* ('the enjoyer'), provided the enjoyer possesses a material abode, which is the body, or *bhogâyatana* ('place of enjoyment').[78] But to locate enjoyment within the mere body would be a misconception like the converse fallacy which refers the pronoun 'I' in the statement 'I am bright (of skin)' to the *ātman* instead of to the body.[79] In both

[72] Cf. GARBE (1943: 2.5 = introduction to SS 1.1), where the Tārkika is qualified as *kartṛtvâbhimānin* 'who overrates the function of agent'; (1943: 65.6–7 *ad* SS 1.146), where the Tārkika's take the *kartṛ* function of the *ātman* for granted.

[73] This *sūtra* contains just the word *bhoktṛ-bhāvāt* (cf. GARBE (1943 : 63)), which is no doubt borrowed from SK 17 cited *supra* § 15. Cf. RAJU (1994: 143).

[74] SPrBh *ad* SS 1.75 and 106 = GARBE (1943: 39.12–13 and 51.35–37). *Puruṣa* has a synonym in the word *pumān* (see n. 75): 'male [principle]', i.e. 'spirit' as opposed to 'nature'.

[75] SS 1.139: *śarīrâdi-vyatiriktaḥ pumān*; SPrBh *ad loc.*: *tato* (= *śarīra*) *'tiriktaḥ pumān bhoktêty arthaḥ. bhoktṛtvaṁ ca draṣṭṛtvam iti* = GARBE (1943: 62.30–32).

[76] SPrBh *ad* SS 1.142 = GARBE (1943: 63.20–22). On the comparison of the *bhoktṛ* ('suzerain') and the *prāṇa* ('servants') cf. e.g. SS 5.115: *bhṛtya-dvārā svāmy-adhiṣṭhitiḥ…* = GARBE (1943: 142.35).

[77] SPrBh *ad* SS 5.114 and 6.60: *prāṇa-vyāpāra-abhāve śukra-śoṇitayoḥ pūti-bhāva-prasaṅgāt* and *bhoktr-anadhiṣṭhitasya śukrâdeḥ pūti-bhāva-prasaṅgāt* = = GARBE (1943: 142.29 and 160.27).

[78] SS 5.114: *bhoktur adhiṣṭhānāt bhogâyatana-nirmāṇam, anyathā pūti-bhāva-prasaṅgāt* = GARBE (1943: 142.28–29).

[79] SPrBh *ad* SS 5.64 *loke hi śarīra-śarīriṇor bhogya-bhoktroś câvivekena-abhedo vyavahriyate "ahaṁ gauro", "mamâtmā bhadrasena" ity-ādiḥ*—'For in the world no dis-

cases we come across a wrong view of reality. Thus the *bhogâyatana* is the place of the *bhoga* the owner of which is actually the self.

19. *Ātman* and *ahaṁ-kāra* ('the "I"-consciousness') according to the *Sāṁkhya-pravacana-bhāṣya*.

A survey of early Sāṁkhya documents shows that *ātman* gives birth to *ahaṁ-kāra* and that the one and unique act carried out by this unchangeable entity is to be aware of itself as *aham*. However, this 'utterance of "I"' (*ahaṁ-kāra*) has wide-ranging consequences.[80] Replacing its own source, *ahaṁ-kāra* becomes henceforth an agent,[81] not only in the individual range but even in the case of the creation and dissolution of the world.[82]

In principle, the agent benefits from the fruit of his own act,[83] but that does not hold true for the *ātman*/*puruṣa* that enjoys it without being its active cause, its agent.[84] And when agency is assigned to the *puruṣa*, it is due to a wrong transfer from the *buddhi*.[85] The genuine agent is *ahaṁ-kāra*[86] which is said to be independent from anything else, to be deprived of a creator, and to be 'caused by [the power of] time alone'.[87]

20. The position of Prabhākara and Śālikanātha concerning *ātman* as *bhoktṛ*.

As far as Mīmāṁsā is the philosophy of the ritual action, it cannot but deny a conception of the self as an omnipresent and everlasting entity which would be, accordingly, unable to act because it is unable to move and to change.

In several places in the *Bṛhatī* and the *Ṛju-vimala-pañcikā*, one or more opponents put forward suspicions and criticisms against the Mīmāṁsā approach

tinction is expressed between the body and its owner since no separation [is done] between what is enjoyed and the enjoyer as in the statements: "I am of bright skin"; "I am (*stricto sensu* my self is) Bhadrasena". = GARBE (1943: 130. 33–35); cf. § 11.

[80] Cf. Van BUITENEN (1957: 17) (°-*kāra*, like in *oṁ-kāra* etc., means 'cry, uttering, ejaculation'), and BIARDEAU (1965: 65), (1966: 115).

[81] SS 6.54: *ahaṁ-kāraḥ kartā, na puruṣaḥ*. = GARBE (1943: 159.23).

[82] SPrBh *ad* SS 6.64: *idānīṁ mahad-ahaṁ-kārayor eva tad-itaraṁ jagad kāryam* and *ahaṁ-kāra-rūpo yaḥ kartā, tad-adhinâiva kārya-siddhiḥ sṛṣṭi-saṁhāra-niṣpattir bhavati*. = GARBE (1943:162.3 and 8). But according to SPrBh *ad* SS 2.1: *pradhānasya jagat-kartṛtvam*. = GARBE (1943: 74.29), the role of agent of creation is ascribed to the *pradhāna* or 'primordial matter'; see van BUITENEN (1957: 19): 'the self-formulated being is the cosmos'.

[83] SPrBh *ad* SS 1.105: *nanu kartur eva loke kriyā-phala-bhogo dṛṣṭaḥ*. = GARBE (1943: 51.22).

[84] SPrBh *ad* SS 1.105: *buddhi-karma-phalasyâpi vṛtter upabhogas tad-akartur api puruṣasya yuktaḥ*. = GARBE (1943: 51.27 ff.).

[85] SPrBh *ad* SS 1.164: *puruṣasya yat kartṛtvam, tad buddhy-uparāgāt; buddheś ca yā cittā, sā puruṣa-sāṁnidhyāt* ('The agent quality of the *puruṣa* [arises] from the tinge of the *buddhi* and the thought [pertaining] to the *buddhi* [arises] from the proximity of the *puruṣa*'). = GARBE (1943: 74.2–3). *Buddhi* or *mahad* ('understanding') derives its active power out of its source, the *pradhāna*, cf. BALLANTYNE (1865: 63).

[86] SS 6.54 *ahaṁ-kāraḥ kartā, na puruṣaḥ*. = GARBE (1943: 159.23).

[87] SPrBh *ad* SS 6.65 = GARBE (1943: 162.18, 21–22 *kāla-mātra-nimitta*).

to the *ātman* as *kartṛ* by pointing out that the self is by nature inert (*niṣkriya*).[88] Furthermore, the *ātman* cannot be an agent on account of its immobility that results itself from its omnipresence (*sarva-gatatva*). In its turn, *sarva-gatatva* results from the universal experience of *sukha* ('well-being, pleasure').[89]

21. The aforesaid views seem to be those of opponents, but Prabhākara cannot endorse them on account of his allegiance to the main and obvious tenet of the Mīmāṁsa, that is that the mandatory operations of the Vedic ritual must be performed by a self provided with an amount of activity.

When Prabhākara returns to the first description by Śabarasvāmin of the recognition event,[90] he argues that it contributes to the demonstration of the 'enjoying nature' of the *ātman*. If indeed somebody else, he adds, were the *bhoktṛ* of the sacrifice instead *ātman* / *aham*, i.e. the person who has performed it, that would mean the ruin of *bhoktṛtva*,[91] since the fruit would not accrue to its expected beneficiary: the doer.

That the term *ātman* is a synonym of *bhoktṛ* is ultimately repeated by Prabhākara[92] as follows: 'We answer on this point: "It is said that the nature of *ātman* (*ātmatā*) is [synonymous to] enjoying (*bhoktṛtayā*)"', and Śālikanātha glosses this last word by *anubhavitatayā iti yāvat* ('in other words, [it is the synonym of] experiencing').[93]

For his part, Śālikanātha seeks to affirm his stance in face of the Sāṁkhya, and, in an eager argument, he reaffirms up to five times, that *ātman* is nothing else than the condition of acting a n d experiencing together. These are the relevant sentences:

---

[88] Bṛ₂, p. 221.7–8 = MK, p. 902b.21–22: *tasmāt siddha ātmā kartṛ-bhūtaḥ. nanu asau niṣkriya ity uktam* (MK: *abhyupagatam*)—'Therefore, the self is proved to be an agent. [Objection:] It is stated that it is inert/inactive'.

[89] Bṛ₂, p. 235.10–12 = MK, p. 904b.27–29: *yuktam bhoktṛtayā-evâtmā iti. kartṛtvôpanyāsas tu virudhyate, niṣkriyatvād ātmanaḥ.sarvagatatvāc ca. niṣkriyatvaṁ pratipannaṁ ca sarvagatatvam, sarvatra sukhôpalambhāt*—'To say that the self is sheer enjoyment is correct. The mention of its agency is contradictory because of its inactivity and its omnipresence. The inactivity and omnipresence [of *ātman*] occur because the experience of pleasure [exists] everywhere (')'. Bṛ₂, p. 238.6 = MK, p. 905a.28–29., *ātman* is again qualified as 'immovable by nature' (*acalanâtmakatva*).

[90] *Vide supra* § 12.

[91] *Vide supra* § 16; Bṛ₂, p. 237.3–4 = MK, p. 905a.13–15 (glossed *Ṛju*, p. 237.18–19): *yadi paro 'py ahaṁ-pratyaya-viṣayatām āpadyeta, tadā bhoktṛtva-hānam* [in MK °-*hānam* is replaced by °-*jñānam*] *prāpnoti. bhoktatā câtmêty uktam*: 'If somebody else became the object of the notion of 'I', the notion of *bhoktṛ* would go to ruin and it has been said that the self [has] the quality of *bhoktṛ*'.

[92] Bṛ₂, p. 248.10–249.14 (it is a passage which does not appear in the Bṛ₁ and consequently not in MK, II: p. 906b either): *atra brumaḥ: uktam eva bhoktṛtayā hy ātmatā iti*.

[93] Ṛju₂, p. 249.20–21.

1. 'Since agency and enjoyment are, by reasoning, co-ordinated within the self ...';
2–3. 'The self is nothing else than agency and enjoyment';
4. 'The meaning of the word "self" is based on agency and enjoyment';
5. 'Since the self is known as agency and enjoyment by nature ...'.[94]

22. In the second part of the commentary,[95] the topic is different. Prabhākara and Śālikanātha no longer look for a definition of the self; they encounter the Buddhist challenge, as stated in the *Bhāṣya* of Śabarasvāmin: 'If there is something apart from cognition, viz. a cogniser, [then] leaving aside the cognition, please point out the cogniser.'[96] Here the echoes of the Sāṁkhya thought are weaker and, therefore, we limit ourselves to a cursory survey of the most significant doctrinal features exposed from here on up to the end the *Ātma-vāda*.

The first development is based on BĀU$_1$ 4.3.6 which reads as follows: 'When the [Vedic] speech is silent, what light does the person possess?'[97] In answer, Śabarasvāmin points out that, in this case, the auto-luminosity (*svayaṁ-jyotiṣṭva*) of the *ātman* takes the place of the *Veda*.[98]

Thereupon another question arises: when the Śruti avers that *ātman* is non-perceptible (*agṛhya*) (BĀU$_1$ 3.9.26), does that mean that it is such for anyone including the owner of the self or is it such only for the other persons (*para*)?[99] In other words, is the *ātman*'s invisibility complete and necessary or is it contingent (*āpekṣika*), viz. just limited to somebody else?[100]

The fact that the self might escape the notice of somebody else does not prevent it from being grasped by its owner. But when it is indispensable to say something about it, one should have recourse to an apophatic method by defining it as 'not that, not that' like in the *Bṛhad-āraṇyakôpaniṣad*.[101]

Then our Mīmāṁsakas examine *ceṣṭā-anumāna*,[102] which enables one to discover, not the *ātman*, but only the inner states, such as *sukha*, traced by

[94] Ṛju$_2$, p. 236.18: *yasmād ātmanaḥ kartṛtvam bhoktṛtvam ca yuktyā saṁgachante*; Ṛju$_2$, p. 236.19–20: *kartṛtva-bhoktṛtve evâtmā*; Ṛju$_2$, p. 236.19: *kartṛtva-bhoktṛtva-nibandhanā ātma-śabda-vācyatā*; Ṛju$_2$, p. 236.20–21: *yasmāt kartṛtva-bhoktṛtva-svarupa ātmā siddhaḥ*.

[95] Bṛ$_2$/Ṛju$_2$, p. 240–256 = MK, p. 905b.13–p.907b.20.

[96] ŚBh$_1$, p. 56.21–22 = MS, I: p. 80.13–14: *yadi vijñānād anyad asti vijñātṛ, vijñānam apāsya tan nidarśyatām* (tr. ŚBh$_3$, I: p. 29 slightly modified). *Vide supra* n.37 and § 13, n. 50.

[97] *śāntāyāṁ vāci kiṁ-jyotir evâyaṁ puruṣaḥ?*, quoted in ŚBh$_1$, p. 58.8 = MS, I: p. 82.7.

[98] ŚBh$_1$, p. 58.11 = MS, I: p. 82.9 mentioned by Bṛ$_2$, p. 245.11 = MK, p. 906a.25, where Śabara quotes BĀU$_1$ 4.3.9 as well: *atrâyaṁ puruṣaḥ svayaṁ jyotir bhavati*.—'Then is this "person" light by his own light?' Tr. ZAEHNER (1972: 66).

[99] ŚBh$_1$, p. 58.9–10 = MS, I: p. 82.7–8 commented upon by Bṛ$_2$, p. 245.12–246.6 ff. = MK, p. 906a.26 ff.

[100] Bṛ$_2$, p. 245.8 = MK, p. 906a.21: *asyâgrahaṇa-śrutir āpekṣikī*.—'The mention of the [*ātman* by BĀU 3.9.26 and 4.3.9] as "non-perceptible" is contingent/occasional'.

[101] BĀU$_1$ 3.9.26: *sa eṣa nêti nêti ātmêti*, is quoted in ŚBh$_1$, p. 58.14 = MS, I: p. 83.1 and is commented upon by Bṛ$_2$, p. 246.9 ff. = MK, p. 906a.31 ff.

[102] Cf. supra § 6.

physical motions. Afterwards they question what help the *upamā* / *upamāna*,[103] or 'comparison-identification', may supply to discover *ātman*, and address a final theme:[104] the refutation of the Buddhist who is urging that there is nothing to grasp apart from cognition, neither an *ātman* that would be its support nor an entity *extra animam* that would be its object.[105]

Prabhākara and Śālikanātha answer that cognition contains an objective datum and not only a subjective one.[106] Moreover, *ātman* is part of all cognitions[107] and supplies each one (including an *anumāna*) with a quality of perceptive evidence (*sākṣāt-kāra*).[108]

Prabhākara and Śālikanātha conclude with three exegetical remarks. The baffling statement of Yājñavalkya in the *Bṛhad-āraṇyakôpaniṣad*: 'After death, there is no consciousness',[109] must be read in its context, namely at the light of the subsequent teaching of the seer: 'The Self is wholly indestructible; of its very nature (*dharma*) it cannot be annihilated'.[110] Yet with the modern reader, uncertainty remains. Does the first assertion mean that consciousness leaves the dead body? However, that would sound like a trivial assertion.

---

[103] ŚBh$_1$, p. 58.25–60.1 = MS I: p. 83.10–11, p. 84.1: *upamānāc côpadiśyate "yādṛśaṁ bhavān svayam ātmānaṁ paśyati, anenôpamānenâvagacha «aham api tādṛśam eva paśyāmi»" iti*. Tr. ŚBh$_3$, p. 30: 'By *upamāna* (*ātman*–self) is pointed out in the words: 'Just as you perceive your own self, so, on the same *upamāna*, [please] understand that I also perceive the self in the same manner', commented upon in Bṛ$_2$, p. 249, 14 ff. = MK, p. 906b.22 ff.: *upamānâpi atra kathanôpeyatayā eva upanyastā*.—'*Upamā* for its part is here mentioned in the function of means of naming'. Ṛju$_2$, p. 249.23–250.9 seems to criticise Śabara when he (i.e. Śālikanātha) says: *bhāṣye kathanôpāyatvenôpamābhimatā*.—'In the Bhāṣya, the *upamā* is wrongly considered as a means of naming'.

[104] Bṛ$_2$, p. 251.10 ff. = MK, p. 907a.2 ff.

[105] Bṛ$_2$, p. 251.9–10 = MK, p. 907a.3–4: *vijñāna-viviktasya tu grahaṇaṁ na prāpnoti vyāpṛtâvagamāt...*—'the grasping [of what is] apart from cognition is not in force because the comprehension is operated [by cognition alone]'; Ṛju$_2$, p. 252.13–14: *tataś cârtha-śūnyatā jñānānāṁ prāpnoti*.—'Therefore, the absence of an object is in force for the cognitions'.

[106] Ṛju$_2$, p. 252.17–18: *grāhyâkāraṁ vijñānam, na grāhakâkāram ity uktam śūnya-vāda-nirākaraṇe*.—'In the refutation of the doctrine of voidness, it is said that cognition is an aspect of the knowable [and] not an aspect of the knower'. The Śūnyavādin thinks the other way around: the knowledge rests upon the *grāhaka* ('knowing subject') and not on an external—*grāhya* or *bāhyârtha* (Ṛju$_2$, p. 252.14)—object, or an 'outside object'.

[107] Bṛ$_2$, p. 253.10–11 = MK, p. 907a.30–31: *tasmād sarva-vijñāna-jñeyatâtmanaḥ sthitā bhavati*.—'Therefore, the knowable nature of all cognitions is lying in the self'.

[108] Ṛju$_2$, p. 253.22–23: *sākṣāt-kāreṇa pratibhāsamānatvād ātmano 'numānâdiṣv api pratyakṣatâva*.—'Since the self is manifesting itself with evidence, there is actually (*eva*?) perception inside inference and so on'.

[109] BĀU$_1$ 4.5.13: *na pretya saṁjñâsti*. Tr. ZAEHNER (1972: 75).

[110] BĀU 4.5.14: *avināśī vā are 'yam ātmā anucchitti-dharmā*. Tr. ZAEHNER (1972: 75).

The Vedic passage which triggered the debate (*vide supra* § 2) is classified as an explanatory passage (*artha-vāda*) and not as a mandatory one (*vidhi*),[111] so that it can be interpreted in a metaphoric way.

Finally Prabhākara rounds off his explanation of the *Ātma-vāda* by quoting the *Bhagavad-gītā*: 'Let not "the wise man" split the mind (*buddhi*) of witless men attached to work',[112] suggesting to the reader that he knows, more than anyone, the limits of his hermeneutical labour.

23. General conclusion.

The explanations by Prabhākara and Śālikanātha of the *Ātma-vāda* section of *Śābara-bhāṣya* 1.1.5 show up as a lengthy and rambling text in which the main issue—the existence of a self/soul—is entangled in a variety of side problems and stock discussions (e.g. the relative value of perception and inference). Nonetheless, the portions analysed above allow us to pick out two basic problems: (1) Which human components are inferential marks purported to reveal the presence of the self; (2) Why it is important to regard the self as a *bhoktṛ*, an 'enjoyer' of the sacrificial outcome and not only as a *kartṛ*, a 'performer' of rites.

(1) Which human components are inferential marks of the self (§§ 4–5)? These are:

—neither breath (*prāṇa*). Admittedly *prāṇa* is something apart from the body since it does not last as long as the body (*ayāvad-bhūta-bhāvitva*, 'non-coevality'; § 4) and is already gone whereas the body is still intact in front of our eyes. But that does not mean that *prāṇa* is a clue to trace the existence of the *ātman,* because the jump from the perceptible breath to the invisible *anya*, 'the [wholly] other', i.e. the self, is logically not sound.[113]

[111] Cf. supra § 3 and n. 5. The fact that we face an *artha-vāda* and not a *vidhi* allows for a metaphoric explanation *Āpastamba-śrauta-sūtra* 31.2.21 (already cited in n. 3): *sa eṣa yajñâyuddhī yajamānaḥ…*—'This sacrificer equipped with the sacrificial utensils…' actually means 'this sacrificer whose body [is equipped]…' (*yasyâtac charīram…*), see Bṛ$_2$ and Ṛju$_2$, p. 207.11–12 and 22–24.

[112] BhG 3.26a: *na buddhi-bhedaṁ janayed ajñānāṁ karma-saṅginām*. Tr. ZAEHNER (1972: 264).

[113] The Vaiśeṣika inference (*anumāna*) is mentioned in VS 3.2.4 and is made up of a list of 12 'inferential marks' (*liṅga*) of the existence of an *ātman*. These *liṅga*s are inbreathing (*prāṇa*) and outbreathing (*apāna*), motions of the shutting (*nimeṣa*) and opening (*unmeṣa*) of eyes, life (*jīvana*), movement of the mind (*mano-gati*), alterations of the other senses (*indriyântara-vikāra*), pleasure (*sukha*), pain (*duḥkha*), desire (*icchā*), aversion (*dveṣa*) and volition (*prayatna*). Such a mechanistic conception is dismissed by Ṛju$_2$, p. 219.19 as follows: *prāṇâdibhir anātmany ātma-buddhir bhavati.*—'By [using the words] *prāṇa* and so on, the notion of self is [transferred towards] what is not the self'. Cf. somewhat further p. 220.17–18: *evaṁ tāvat abhyupagamyâpi prāṇâdi-sukhâdīnām abhūta-dharmatvaṁ nâtma-sādhakatvam ity upasamhṛtam.*—'So even if breathing etc. and pleasure etc. are obviously of immaterial nature, they are not means to demonstrate the [existence of] *ātman*. Such is the conclusion'. The issue is dealt with by Ṛju$_2$, pp. 210–211 = MK, p. 901a and b, with a quotation of VS 3.1.4–5–6. In a different context, the 'otherness' (*anyatā*) is defined

—nor inner states/feelings (*sukhâdi*, 'pleasure etc.'). Albeit looking immaterial, *sukhâdi* must not be regarded as leading towards the self, for fear of making the latter as transitory as themselves. To claim the contrary is nothing else than to call that which is material (*anātman*) '*ātman*' (cf. n. 20).

The situation is different for desire (*icchā*) and recollection (*smṛti*) because they are factors of recognition. According to Mīmāṁsā, *pratyabhijñā* is a decisive proof of the presence of *ātman*, for, without the self, there would be no connection between the past and the present (recollection) or between the present and the future (desire). And that would mean the victory of the Buddhist theory of momentariness. For the Buddhist indeed—at least such as he is depicted by his opponent, the Mīmāṁsaka—no one would remember today the experience of yesterday; nobody would wish to take up a task at the point he had let it the day before. So nobody performing a sacrifice could hope to benefit from its result, in the future or even after his death.

In order to ward off these disastrous consequences, Prabhākara and Śālikanātha put forward that the human self is together the doer (*kartṛ*) of the sacrifice and the enjoyer (*bhoktṛ*) of it.

(2) The self as *bhoktṛ*.

How can one demonstrate that the man, especially one who seeks heaven and sacrifices in order to get there, will manage to enjoy it? Prabhākara and Śālikanātha sought elements of the answer in the Sāṁkhya doctrine the adherents of which they call *brahma-vid* (§ 14). In the well-known collection of the *Sāṁkhya-kārikā*, it is said that the *puruṣa*—the Sāṁkhya equivalent of the *ātman* of Mīmāṁsā—exists to benefit the acts performed on the material factors, providing them with meaning and goal. Such an approach might have prompted the interest of both Prabhākara and Śālikanātha and induced them to apply the idea in the domain of the sacrifice.

A late treatise of Sāṁkhya, the *Sāṁkhya-pravacana-bhāṣya*, in which Vijñānabhikṣu comments upon the *Sāṁkhya-sūtra*, points out that the self as *kartṛ* is championed by the 'logicians' (*tārkika*).True to the teachings of the Sāṁkhya, Vijñānabhikṣu prefers to ascribe the function of *kartṛ* to the *ahaṁ-kāra* or 'I'-consciousness[114] and to reserve the role of *bhoktṛ* to the *puruṣa-ātman* (§ 19).

Whereas Prabhākara seems prone to rally the Sāṁkhya tradition on this point, but without crossing the line, his disciple Śālikanātha makes a choice, in keeping with his usual behaviour (e.g. in the *Prakaraṇa-pañcikā*): he reconciles both contrasting points of view and vindicates that *ātman* is *kartṛ* and *bhoktṛ* together (§ 21).

---

as 'complete disconnection' (*atyantâsaṁbandhatā*) by Ṛju$_2$, p. 219.18. Thus we could say that it is impossible to cross from the visible towards what is 'other': the invisible.

[114] The *ahaṁ-kāra* and its function within cognition are repeatedly mentioned in the Bṛ and Ṛju, but have not been explored in depth in this contribution.

BIBLIOGRAPHY

AK = Vasubandhu: *Abhidharma-kośa*. Louis de la Vallée Poussin (tr.).: *L'Abhidharmakośa de Vasubandhu traduit et annoté*. 6 Vols., Mélanges Chinois et Bouddhiques 16, P. Geuthner–J.B. Ista, Paris–Louvain 1923–31 [reprinted: Bruxelles 1971, 1980; English translation of the French version of La Vallée Poussin with an Index by Leo M. Pruden: 4 vols., Asian Humanities Press, California, Berkeley 1988–90].

ĀŚS = *Āpastamba-śrauta-sūtra*. Richard Garbe (ed.): *The Śrauta Sūtra of Āpastamba, belonging to the Taittirīya Saṁhitā with the commentary of Rudradatta*. 3 Vols., Bibliotheca Indica 92, 98, 110, Asiatic Society, Calcutta 1882–1902.

BALLANTYNE 1865 = Ballantyne, James R. (ed., tr.): *The Sa'nkhya Aphorisms of Kapila with Extracts from Vijn'ana Bhikshu's Commentary*. Bibliotheca Indica New Series 32, 81, Baptist Mission Press, Calcutta 1865.

BĀU = *Bṛhad-āraṇyakôpaniṣad*. (1) E. Senart (ed., tr.): *Bṛhad-āraṇyaka-upaniṣad traduite et annotée*. [With the Sanskrit text]. Société d'édition «Les Belles Lettres», Paris 1934; (2) English translation, see: ZAEHNER (1972: 33–82).

BhG = *Bhagavad-gītā*. (1) Sarvepalli Radhakrishnan (ed., transl.): *The Bhagavadgītā*, 6th Impression. Allen-Unwin, London 1960. (2) English translation, see: ZAEHNER (1972: 249–325).

BIARDEAU 1965–66 = Biardeau, Madeleine: 'Ahaṁkāra, the Ego principle in the Upanishads', *Contributions to Indian Sociology* 8 (1965) 62–84 and 9 (1966) 115.

BIARDEAU 1968 = Biardeau, Madeleine: 'L'ātman dans le commentaire de Śabarasvāmin', *Mélanges d'indianisme à la mémoire de L. Renou*. Publications de l'Institut de Civilisation Indienne Série in–8°, fascicule 28, De Boccard, Paris 1968: 109–126.

Bṛ = Prabhākaramiśra: *Bṛhatī*. (1) A. Chinnaswami Sastri (ed.): *Prabhākara's Bṛhatī's on Jaimini's Mīmāṁsāsūtras edited in Part with Śālikanātha Miśra's Ṛjuvimalapañcikā*. Chowkhamba Sanskrit Series 391, Benares 1929. (2) S.K. Ramanatha Śastrī (ed.): *Bṛhatī of Prabhākara Miśra [on the Mīmāṁsāsūtrabhāṣya of Śabarasvāmin] with the Ṛjuvimalāpañcikā of Śālikanātha [Tarkapāda]*. Madras University Sanskrit Series, n°3, Part I, The University of Madras, Madras 1934.

BRONKHORST 2000 = Bronkhorst, Johannes: *Karma and Teleology. A Problem and its Solutions in Indian Philosophy*. The International Institute of Buddhist Studies, Studia Philosophica Buddhica Monograph Series XV, Tokyo 2000.

ESNOUL 1964 = See: SK.

GARBE 1943 = Garbe, Richard (ed.): *The Sāṁkhya-pravacana-bhāṣya or Commentary on the Exposition of the Sāṁkhya Philosophy by Vijñānabhikṣu*. Harvard Oriental Series Vol. II, The Harvard Oriental University Press, Cambridge, Massachusetts 1943.

HULIN 1978 = Hulin, Michel: *Le principe de l'ego dans la pensée indienne classique. La notion d'ahaṁkāra*. Publications de l'Institut de Civilisation Indienne, fascicule 44, de Boccard, Paris 1978.

HULIN 2008 = Hulin, Michel: *Comment la philosophie indienne s'est-elle développée?' La querelle brahmanes-bouddhistes*, Éditions du Panama, Paris 2008.

KRAMER 2008 = Kramer, Jowita: 'On Sthiramati's Pañcaskandhakavibhāṣā: A Preliminary Survey', *Nagoya Studies in Indian Culture and Buddhism: Saṁbhāṣā* 27 (2008) 149–171.

MK = *Mīmāṁsā-kośa*. Kevalānanda Sarasvatī (ed.): *Mīmāṁsākośaḥ*. 7 Vols., Prājña-pāṭha-śālā-maṇḍala grantha-mālā, Prājña-pāṭha-śālā Maṇḍal, Wai (Dist. Satara) 1952–1976.

MS = Jaimini: *Mīmāṁsā-sūtra* [*Mīmāṁsā-darśana*]. See: ŚBh$_2$.

MŚV = Kumārilabhaṭṭa: *Śloka-vārttika*. (1) Dvārikādāsa Śāstrin (ed.): *Ślokavārttika of Śrī Kumārila Bhaṭṭa with the Commentary Nyāyaratnākara of Śrī Pārthasārathi Miśra*. Prācyabhāratī Grantha-mālā 10, Tara Publications, Varanasi 1978. (2) Gaṅgānātha Jhā (tr.): *Ślokavārtika Translated from the Original Sanskrit with Extracts from Commentaries of Sucarita Miśra (the Kāśikā) and Pārthasārathi Miśra (the Nyāyaratnākara)*. Sri Garib Das Oriental Series 8, Delhi 1983 [first edition: 1900–1908; second edition: 1909].

NOZAWA 1991 = Nozawa, Masanobu: 'Inferential Marks in the Vaiśeṣikasūtra', [*Nagoya Studies in Indian Culture and Buddhism*] *Saṁbhāṣā* 12 (1991) 25–38.

PELISSERO 2007 = Pelissero, Alberto: *Letterature classiche dell'India*. Editrice Morcelliana, Brescia 2007.

PREISENDANZ 1994 = Preisendanz, Karin: *Studien zu Nyāyasūtra III.1 mit dem Nyāyatattvāloka Vācaspati Miśras II*. 2 Vols., Alt- und Neu-Indische Studien 46, Franz Steiner Verlag, Stuttgart 1994.

PrP = Śālikanāthamiśra: *Prakaraṇa-pañcikā*. A. Subrahmanya Sastri (ed.): *Prakaraṇapañcikā of Śālikanātha Miśra with the Nyāyasiddhi of Jaipuri Nārāyaṇa Bhāṣya*. Banaras Hindu University Darśana Series 4, Varanasi 1961.

RADHAKRISHNAN–MOORE 1960 = Radhakrishnan, Sarvepalli; Moore, Charles Alexander (eds.): *A Sourcebook in Indian Philosophy*. Princeton University Press, Princeton, New Jersey 1960 [first edition: 1957].

RAJU 1994 = Raju, P.T.: 'Activism in Indian Thought', in: Dwivedi R.C. (ed.): *Studies in Mīmāṁsā. Dr. Mandan Mishra Felicitation Volume*. Motilal Banarsidass, Delhi 1994: 131–68.

Ṛju = Śālikanāthamiśra: *Ṛju-vimala-pañcikā*. See: Bṛ.

SK = Īśvarakṛṣṇa: *Sāṁkhya-kārikā*. Esnoul, Anne-Marie (ed., tr.): *Les strophes du Sāṁkhya (Sāṁkhya-kārikā) avec le commentaire de Gauḍapāda Texte sanskrit et traduction annotée*. Société d'édition «Les Belles Lettres», Paris 1964.

SLAJE 2007 = Slaje, Walter: 'Yājñavalkya-brāhmaṇas and the Early Mīmāṁsā', in: Johannes Bronkhorst (ed.): *Mīmāṁsā and Vedānta. Interaction and Continuity*. Papers of the 12th World Sanskrit Conference Vol. 10.3, Motilal Banarsidass, Delhi 2007: 115–158.

SPrBh = Vijñānabhikṣu: *Sāṁkhya-pravacana-bhāṣya*. See: GARBE (1943).

SS = Kapila: *Sāṁkhya-sūtra*. (1) See: BALLANTYNE (1865). (2) See: GARBE (1943).

ŚBh = Śabarasvāmin: *Śābara-bhāṣya*. (1) Erich Frauwallner (ed., tr.): *Materialien zur ältesten Erkenntnislehre der Karmamīmāṁsā*. [Edition and German translation of *Mīmāṁsā-sūtra* 1.1.1–5 and *Śābara-bhāṣya* ad loc.]. Österreichische Akademie der Wissenschaften, Wien 1968. (2) Kāśīnātha Vāsudevaśāstrī Abhyankara; Gaṇeśaśāstrī Aṁbādāsa Jośī (eds.): *Śrīmaj-jaimini-praṇītaṁ Mīmāṁsā-darśanam*. Part 1, Fourth edition, Ānandāśrama Sanskrit Series 97, Poona 1976. (3) Gangānātha Jhā (tr.): *Śabara-bhāṣya, Translated into English in Three Volumes*. (Vol. 1), Gaekwad's Oriental Series 66, Baroda 1973 [first edition: 1933, 1934, 1936].

van BUITENEN 1957 = van Buitenen, Johannes Adrianus Bernardus: 'Studies in Sāṁkhya (II)', *Journal of the American Oriental Society* 77,1 (1957) 15–25.

VS = Kaṇāda: *Vaiśeṣika-sūtra*. (1) Jayanārāyana Tarkapañcānana (ed.): *The Vaiśeṣika Darśana, with the Commentary of Śaṅkara Miśra and Jayanārāyana Tarkapañcanana*. Bibliotheca Indica 34, Asiatic Society, Calcutta 1861. (2) E. Röer (tr.): 'Die Lehrsprüche der Vaiçeshika Philosophie', ZDMG 21 (1867) 309–420; ZDMG 22 (1868) 383–442.

ZAEHNER 1966 = Zaehner, Robert Charles: *Hindu Scriptures*. Everyman's University Library, London–New York 1972 [first edition: 1966].

The Polity of the Philosopher-Bureaucrat: Brahmanical Virtue as a Qualification for Public Office*

TIMOTHY LUBIN

One of the most striking features of Indian social history is the success of the Brahmin castes in promoting the ideal of Brahmins as model candidates for appointment to ministerial or administrative office. The Brahmanical literature on personal virtue and social norms (*dharma-śāstra*) offers a systematic argument for the notion that Brahmanically defined virtues are inculcated and exhibited through observance of particular ritual norms, and ideally embodied in virtuous Brahmins. Scholastic discussions of political science (*artha-śāstra*, *nīti-śāstra*) and kingly virtue (*rāja-dharma*) further suggest that Brahmins, and by extension other 'twice-born' castes, viz. those eligible to observe Brahmanical ritual norms, and shaped by them) are best suited to high office, a policy often reflected in inscriptional records. Beginning from the conceit that the Brahmanical tradition offers an interesting contrast to the Platonic ideal of the 'philosopher-king', this article analyses a selection of data drawn from Indian inscriptions, read in light of (or against) the scholastic literature, to show the ways in which Brahmanical norms are reflected in actual records of public administration and statecraft in medieval India. It is observed that in inscriptions, Brahmins in public service were not explicitly identified as such (e.g. by *gotra* or school), as were Brahmins who were recipients of endowments (where such caste and religious qualifications justified the grant). However there are indications that the virtues and ideals associated with Brahmin settlements, as well as the writing practices inculcated in them, made them a prime field for recruiting officials.

In distinguishing the legitimate king from the tyrant, Plato's stranger from Eleas proposes to call 'the freely-accepted management of herds of free bipeds' *polity*,[1] contrasting it with the compulsion and violence of tyranny. Plato's ideal 'manager' or 'guardian' is a philosopher, that is, someone pos-

---

* The author gratefully acknowledges the support of a Fulbright-Hays FRA fellowship, a sabbatical fellowship from the American Philosophical Society, and a Lenfest summer research grant from Washington and Lee University. Part of the research was conducted under the auspices of the Institut français de Pondichéry.

[1] *Statesman* 276e.

sessed of knowledge of truth and virtue, and so capable of ensuring *eudaimonia* (well-being or human flourishing) for the populace. And the creation of such a 'philosopher-king' requires that would-be kings receive a philosopher's education.

The classical Indian works of *Artha-śāstra* (the principles of polity) and *Dharma-śāstra* (the principles of ethics and piety) develop an increasingly elaborate picture of the ideal polity that is analogous to Plato's model in some respects, combining extensive rules on moral education and personal conduct with increasingly detailed chapters on royal policy. This tradition defines the traits of legitimate rulership, and prescribes a comprehensive education or training that is supposed to inculcate both virtue and empowering knowledge. This education was at first treated as the province of a priestly (Brahmin) elite, but was soon extended also to kings and a broad swath of society.

Among the many differences between the two models, the most striking might be the role assigned to Brahmins as a class. A good king should be personally just, and preferably learned, in order to fulfil his executive and judicial functions, but the Brahmanical ideal has him ruling vicariously through Brahmins, who take upon themselves most of the burden of knowing truth, instructing others, embodying virtue, and—as appointed officials or royally supported experts—executing much of the work of governance: a polity of the 'philosopher-bureaucrat'. In this respect, Brahmanical political ideas are closer in spirit to Aristotle's retort to Plato, as expressed in a surviving fragment of his dialogue *On Kingship*: there, Aristotle argued that 'it was not only not necessary for a king to become a philosopher, but actually a hindrance to his work; that, however, it was necessary [for a good king] to listen to the true philosophers and to be agreeable to their advice'.[2] The classic authorities of *Dharma-śāstra* seem to concur: it is the duty of a king to seek and accept the guidance of learned virtuous Brahmins.

In his observations on Indian society (preserved fragmentarily in the works of Strabo, Arrian, and Diodorus Siculus), the Greek ethnographer Megasthenes—Seleucus I Nicator's ambassador to the Maurya court at Pāṭaliputra—distinguished between the *philosophoi* on the one hand,[3] by which he meant the Brahmin priesthood, and the 'councillors and assessors' (σύμβουλοι καὶ σύνεδροι) on the other.[4] While historiographical conventions may have helped shape his views, Megasthenes differs from many other Greek writers on other peoples in that he was an actually eye-witness to the matters he described, and much of what he says accords with what we otherwise know about the early

[2] As quoted by Hannah ARENDT (1958: 87 n. 5), based on FRITZ–KAPP (1950: 216).

[3] Or *sophistai*, according to Arrian's *Indica* 11–12.

[4] MCCRINDLE (1926: 43, 44–45, and 85–86) observes that Megasthenes' set of seven castes distinguishes the 'philosophers' from the 'councillors and assessors', seemingly blending a hereditary status with a merely professional one; he supposes that this model imitates Herodotus' description of Egyptian society.

Maurya world. So we ought to give some weight to his seemingly eccentric classification of the 'castes' (μέρη, 'classes') of India. For instance, he reports that the philosophers were summoned annually to what was known as the Great Synod (κατὰ τὴν μεγάλην λεγομένην σύνοδον), which seems to answer well to a *sabhā*, a Brahmin assembly.

Megasthenes may not have had a comprehensive or wholly accurate notion of the structure of Pāṭaliputra society, but his description certainly undercuts the currently fashionable notion that rigid observance of caste distinctions was a development of the British colonial era: 'No one is allowed to marry out of his own caste, or to exchange one profession or trade for another, or to follow more than one business. An exception is made in favour of the philosopher, who for his virtue is allowed this privilege'.[5]

The Ideal of the Brahmanical Administrator

Early India's standard ideal of the polity[6] is depicted in Sanskrit scholastic and literary works as a kingdom governed by a king assisted by appointed officials, with Brahmins in key positions. The core text of the 'political Brāhmin' tradition was the *Artha-śāstra* traditionally ascribed to Kauṭilya (AŚ). The appointment of ministers is dealt with in chapters 1.8–9. Chapter 8 consists entirely of contrasting opinions of earlier authorities, which seems designed to illustrate the cacaphony of conflicting advice that kings must hear from their councillors. At the end, Kauṭilya's voice is brought in to clear the confusion.

At the beginning of the next chapter (AŚ 1.9), the qualifications of the best sort of minister (*amātya*) are listed:

> 'Native of the country, of noble birth, easy to manage, trained in the crafts, insightful, intelligent, with a keen memory, skilled, articulate, bold, quick-witted, possessing energy and might, able to endure hardships, honest, friendly, firmly loyal, endowed with character, strength, health, and spirit, free of obstinacy and fickleness, amiable, and not a fomenter of enmities—these are the qualities of an exemplary Minister.'[7]

---

[5] Strabo's *Geography* XV.1.48 (49 in Loeb ed.) as translated in McCrindle (1926: 85–86); cf. Diodorus (II.41), who omits the exception.

[6] Rare exceptions include the 'tribal oligarchies' (*jana-pada*) mentioned in Pali Buddhist works, although the precise nature of these polities cannot be fully ascertained, given the nature of the sources available to us.

[7] AŚ 1.9: *jāna-pado abhijātaḥ svavagrahaḥ kṛta-śilpaś cakṣuṣmān prājño dhārayiṣṇur dakṣo vāgmī pragalbhaḥ pratipattimān utsāha-prabhāva-yuktaḥ kleśa-sahaḥ śucir maitro dṛḍha-bhaktiḥ śīla-balârogya-sattva-yuktaḥ stambha-cāpala-hīnaḥ sampriyo vairāṇām akartêty amātya-sampat*. Translated by Olivelle (2012).

We note immediately that among so many attributes Brahmin status is not mentioned. Indeed, the author of the *Jaya-maṅgalā* commentary specifically explains the word *abhijāta,* 'well-born' thus: 'whether a Brahmin or another, on account of stemming from a (good) family, he does not indulge in bad deeds or cause others to do so.'[8] Which is to say that others besides Brahmins may be considered well-born. At the same time, this clarification implies that many readers might have assumed the contrary, namely, that by 'well-born' Kauṭilya meant (or at least was likely to call to mind) a Brahmin. Apparently, the matter was debatable.

As regards the chief priest, of course, the *Artha-śāstra* calls for a well-trained Brahmin candidate:

> '[The king] should appoint as his personal priest one who is of noble family and conduct, skilled in the *Veda*s, their ancillary disciplines, portents, and the administration of justice, and able to counteract calamities of divine and human origin with the methods of the *Atharva-veda.*'[9]

The principle underlying his appointment is presented two stanzas on, in a formulation that plays on the double meanings of words describing Brahmin functions:

> 'Rule, augmented by the Brahmin, consecrated by the pronouncements of the counsellor, expertly guided by following the expert treatises, unconquered, conquers utterly.'[10]

Mantra is both the ritual utterance of the Brahmin priest and the advice of the minister (*mantrin*), roles that are thus conflated. The ruler's capacity to rule is magnified by the ministrations of an expert whose authority is inseparable from his sacred status. Moreover, Kauṭilya views preceptors or ministers (*ācāryān amātyān vā*) as a salutary check (*maryādā*) on the ruler's private conduct (AŚ 1.7.8), which again points to the overlapping of ritual, moral, and political responsibilities of some forms of royal service.

As in Kauṭilya, the *Dharma-śāstra*s emphasise the abilities and qualities of the individual candidate. However we hear much more about knowledge of Dharma and knowledge of *śāstra* as important qualifications; these probably

---

[8] AŚJM, p. 24: *brāhmaṇo 'nyo vā kula-putratvān na vikarmaṇi pravartate na pravartayati ca.* POHLUS (2011: 24). The word *brāhmaṇa* is set in bold as if cited from the *Artha-śāstra*, but this is a misprint; it belongs to the commentary.

[9] AŚ 1.9.9: *purohitam uditôdita-kula-śīlaṁ sāṅge vede daive nimitte daṇḍa-nītyāṁ câbhivinītam āpadāṁ daiva-mānuṣīṇām atharvabhir upāyaiś ca pratikartāraṁ kurvīta.* Translated by SANDERSON (2007: 52).

[10] AŚ 1.9.11:

brāhmaṇenâdhitaṁ kṣatraṁ mantri-mantrâbhimantritam /
jayaty ajitam atyantaṁ śāstrânugama-śastritam //

amount to the same thing: an education in the *Dharma-śāstras*. The *Mānava-dharma-śāstra* (attributed to the legendary sage Manu), the first work on *dharma* to discuss the administration of a state in any detail, borrows much from the *Artha-śāstra*. First, the king should himself be instructed in the *Vedas*, knowledgeable, and virtuous. He must also appoint various sorts of officials:

> '[7.54] The king should appoint seven or eight counsellors (*saciva*).[11] They must be individuals who are natives of the land, well-versed in the Treatises, brave, well-accomplished, and coming from illustrious families, individuals who have been thoroughly investigated.
> [7.56–59] He should confer with them daily on general matters relating to alliance and war, and about the state,[12] revenue, and security, as also the pacification of acquisitions. After ascertaining their views about his affairs, first from each individually and then from all of them as a group, he should do what is in his best interest. From the most distinguished and sagacious Brahmin among them, however, the king should seek the most important counsel, the one relating to the sixfold strategy. Trusting him completely, he should always entrust all his affairs to him and proceed with any task only after reaching a decision jointly with him.'[13]

Members of this cabinet of ministers must have various practical qualifications, and should be vetted carefully with background-checks and tests of moral rectitude, but the reference to their learning in the Śāstras implies a Brahmanical, Sanskrit education. From the last two sentences, but it is clear that some of the members of the king's cabinet should be Brahmins, and the chief minister especially:

---

[11] As OLIVELLE notes (2005: 295), Manu's *saciva* is just another name for what Kauṭilya (AŚ 1.7.9) calls *mantrin*, i.e. 'minister', the highest rank of royal officer.

[12] OLIVELLE (2005: 295) observes that the word *sthāna* here is taken by most of the commentators as a technical term denoting a political entity comprising army, treasury, fort, and territory.

[13] AŚ 7.54, 56–59:

maulāñ chāstra-vidaḥ śūrāṁl labdha-lakṣān kulôdgatān /
sacivān sapta câṣṭau vā prakurvīta parīkṣitān // 7.54 //
taiḥ sārdhaṁ cintayen nityaṁ sāmānyaṁ saṁdhi-vigraham /
sthānaṁ samudayaṁ guptiṁ labdha-praśamanāni ca // 7.56 //
teṣāṁ svaṁ svam abhiprāyam upalabhya pṛthak pṛthak /
samastānāṁ ca kāryeṣu vidadhyād dhitam ātmanaḥ // 7.57 //
sarveṣāṁ tu viśiṣṭena brāhmaṇena vipaścitā /
mantrayeta paraṁ mantraṁ rājā ṣāḍguṇya-saṁyutam // 7.58 //
nityaṁ tasmin samāśvastaḥ sarva-kāryāṇi nikṣipet /
tena sārdhaṁ viniścitya tataḥ karma samārabhet // 7.59 //

Translated by OLIVELLE (2005: 156–157).

> '[7.60–62] He should also appoint other officials. They must be individuals who are honest, intelligent, steadfast, and able to collect revenues properly, individuals who have been thoroughly investigated. He should appoint as many tireless, clever, and wise men as are required to carry out his obligations, employing the brave and the clever amongst them, individuals coming from illustrious families, in financial affairs; the honest in mines and factories; and the timid in the interior of his residence.
> [7.63–64] He should also appoint an envoy. He must be an expert in all the Treatises; able to grasp a hint, bearing, or gesture; be honest and clever; and come from an illustrious family. A man who is loyal, honest, and clever; who has a sharp memory and knows the right time and place; and who is handsome, fearless, and eloquent—such a man is recommended as the king's envoy.
> [7.141] When [the king] becomes tired of trying lawsuits filed by people, he should install on that seat a leading minister who knows the Law, is wise and self-disciplined, and comes from an illustrious family.'[14]

The qualifications for the offices of *amātya* ('officer'), *dūta* ('envoy'), and judge are similar to those for the counsellors, including both personal virtues and ascriptive status (*kulôdgatān*, 'stemming from a good family'), which in AŚ 7.54 implied Brahmin family in many cases. Here too, 'being learned in all *śāstra*s' (*sarva-śāstra-viśārada*) and 'knowing *dharma*' (*dharma-jña*) stand out as important qualifications; both of these imply a Sanskrit education under a Brahmin teacher, if not Brahmin status *per se*.

In addition, a council (*parṣad* or *pariṣad*) should be composed of learned Brahmins. Manu specifies their qualifications in detail (MDh 12.108–114): ideally, ten Brahmins, including a representative of each of the three *Veda*s, experts on logic, Mīmāṁsā, etymology, and *Dharma-śāstra*, and representatives of the three worldly *āśrama*s; or a representative of each of the three *Ve-*

---

[14] AŚ 7.60–64, 141:

anyān api prakurvīta śucīn prājñān avasthitān /
samyag artha-samāhartr̥̄n amātyān suparīkṣitān // 7.60 //
nirvartetâsya yāvadbhir iti-kartavyatā nr̥bhiḥ /
tāvato 'tandritān dakṣān prakurvīta vicakṣaṇān // 7.61 //
teṣām arthe niyuñjīta śūrān dakṣān kulôdgatān /
śucīn ākara-karmānte bhīrūn antar-niveśane // 7.62 //
dūtaṁ câiva prakurvīta sarva-śāstra-viśāradam /
iṅgitākāra-ceṣṭa-jñaṁ śuciṁ dakṣaṁ kulôdgatam // 7.63 //
anuraktaḥ śucir dakṣaḥ smr̥timān deśa-kāla-vit /
vapuṣmān vītabhīr vāgmī dūto rājñaḥ praśasyate // 7.64 //
amātya-mukhyaṁ dharma-jñaṁ prājñaṁ dāntaṁ kulôdgatam /
sthāpayed āsane tasmin khinnaḥ kāryêkṣaṇe nr̥ṇām // 7.141 //

Translated by OLIVELLE (2005: 157, 161).

das; or at least on learned Brahmin. In principle, ignorant and unobservant Brahmins cannot constitute a *pariṣad* no matter how numerous they may be.

The next landmark treatise of the tradition, the *Yājñavalkya-dharma-śāstra* (YDhŚ), is brief on these matters:

> '[1.312] He should appoint ministers that are wise, of good descent (*maula*), steadfast, and pure. With them, he should examine the affairs of state; then with a Brahmin; and then on his own. [1.313] He should appoint a chief priest (*purohita*) who knows divine portents (*daiva-jña*), possessed of recommended traits (*uditôdita*),[15] skilled in the administration of justice (*daṇḍa-nīti*),[16] and in Atharvāṅgirasa rites.'[17]

Authority in Dharma is vested by the *Dharma-śāstras* in Brahmins on the basis of their knowledge of the *Veda* or of spiritual matters:

> '[1.9] Four who know *Veda* and Dharma[śāstra] constitute an Assembly (*pariṣad*), or just a group representing the three *Vedas*; whatever it declares is Dharma—or one who has full knowledge of the Soul.'[18]

But while piety and learning are put forward as the criteria of virtue for Brahmins, and by extension what makes them suitable for royal service, there was a deep ambivalence within the tradition about such a role. In fact, the issue was really just a new permutation of the older ambivalence about all forms of paid service, even priestly service. Although to the outside observer, such service would seem to be the very *raison d'être* of Brahmin status, even in the exegeses of the *brāhmaṇa* passages in the *Veda*, it was sometimes stated that receiving pay for officiating at a sacrifice 'used up' a Brahmin's *Veda* and incurred sin, which had to be removed through penitential private recitation (as

---

[15] This translation of *uditôditam* reflects Aparāditya's explanation; Vijñāneśvara has something quite similar: '*uditôdita* means 'possessed of', i.e. endowed with, 'recommended traits' , i.e. those stated in the expert texts, such as knowledge, good birth, and initiative' (*uditôditaṁ vidyābhijanānṣṭhānādibhir uditaiḥ śāstroktaiḥ uditaṁ samṛddham*). However, the doubling of *udita* may originally have conveyed simply emphasis: '[very] noble'. Thus SANDERSON's translation of the parallel passage in AŚ 1.9.9, quoted above.

[16] Vijñāneśvara explains *daṇḍa-nīti* simply as the discipline of *Artha-śāstra*.

[17] YDhŚ 1.312–313:

> *sa mantriṇaḥ prakurvīta prājñān maulān sthirān śucīn* /
> *taiḥ sārdhaṁ cintayed rājyaṁ vipreṇâtha tataḥ svayam* // 1.312 //
> *purohitaṁ prakurvīta daiva-jñam uditôditam* /
> *daṇḍa-nītyāṁ ca kuśalam atharvâṅgirase tathā* // 1.313 //

[18] YDhŚ 1.9:

> *catvāro veda-dharma-jñāḥ parṣat traividyam eva vā* /
> *sā brūte yaṁ sa dharmaḥ syād eko vâdhyātma-vittamaḥ* //

taught in *Taittirīyâraṇyaka* 2).[19] Later, with the advent of temple worship, service as a temple priest was declared polluting, even so as to result in loss of caste. Śaiva-siddhānta *Śiva-brāhmaṇa*s were regarded by orthodox Smārta Brahmins as sub-Brahmin or even 'untouchable'.

So in the same way, without irony the *Aparârka* (YDhŚA, pp. 286–287) quotes Śātātapa's inclusion of Brahmins in the service of a king (a *rājâśraya*), or of a town or village (*bhṛtas teṣām grāmasya nagarasya ca*), among those persons who, though born to Brahmin families, do not deserve the name; they are no better than Brahmins who engage in trade, and those who hire themselves out to multiple clients or who neglect their own daily devotions. Yet this *Aparârka* is generally taken to be the work of none other than Aparāditya I Śilāhāra, who himself seems to have resumed the practice of most of his predecessors in appointing Brahmins to key posts in his administration.[20]

A similar example is that of Aparāditya's contemporary, Lakṣmīdhara, author of the encyclopaedic *Kṛtya-kalpa-taru*. When he completed this *magnum opus*, he held perhaps the highest post under King Govindacandra, ruler of Kanauj and Kāśī, that of *mahā-sāndhi-vigrahika* ('chief minister in charge of issuing documents'), which had been held earlier by his father.[21]

Aparāditya glosses the *Yājñavalkya* on the virtues of 'ministers' thus:

> '"He", a king with the aforesaid qualities, "should appoint", i.e. should carefully take into service, "ministers", i.e. those who know what must and must not be done, who are "wise", i.e. competent to deliberate and reason, "of [good] descent", i.e. coming in the tradition of their forefathers, "firm", i.e. unwavering in the interests of their master, "pure", i.e. [proven] faultless by the [four] tests of honesty. Then, "with them, he should attend to kingship", i.e. to a king's work which has six components, viz., dominion etc. In other words, he should deliberate, rejecting or accepting [possible courses of action]; then he should deliberate further "with a Brahmin" who knows the six components; and once again he should finally decide that same matter himself,

[19] On this, see MALAMOUD (1977: especially 78–84).

[20] YDhŚA 1.11–12 also accepts that the eight *saṁskāra*s (up to but excluding the *upanayana*) may be performed on a Śūdra. The commentary may rather have been the work of paṇḍits commissioned by the king. '*Aparârka*' and '*aparâditya*' are synonymous names.

[21] The office of *sāndhi-vigrahika* or *sandhi-vigraha-kārin* is often explained as 'minister of peace and war' (or the like), but his proper bailiwick was the production of royal documents, as pointed out by Vijñāneśvara in his *Mitâkṣarā* commentary (YDhŚM, p. 93) on YDhŚ 1.320. OLIVELLE (2011) has demonstrated that even in the *Artha-śāstra*, *saṁdhi* and *vigraha* meant not 'peace' and 'war', but 'pact' and 'declaration of war', that is, formal enactments as a feature of strategy or policy.

taking as the determining criterion those factors that are conducive or obstructive [to his aims].'[22]

Yājñavalkya's list of ministerial qualifications as understood in this period thus included (1) a pragmatic knowledge of the business of state, (2) a capacity for deliberation and sound argumentation, (3) good family background, (4) steadfastness, and (5) demonstrated integrity. Vijñāneśvara, writing just a few years before Aparāditya, in the nearby royal capital of the Cālukya king Vikramāditya VI, interprets 'steadfastness' differently: for him it is not loyalty but 'remaining unaffected even in a state of great joy or sorrow' (*mahaty api harṣa-viṣāda-sthānaṁ vikāra-rahitān*)[23]—the philosophical virtue of stoical equanimity, which is precisely the ideal quality of a sagacious Brahmin.

Again, neither the *Yājñavalkya-dharma-śāstra* nor Aparāditya actually says that these ministers should be Brahmins, but Vijñāneśvara quotes MDh 7.54, which says that ministers should be *śāstra-vidaḥ*, that is, conversant with Sanskrit treatises, *Dharma-śāstra* or *Artha-śāstra* in particular. By this period, Sanskrit learning was a courtly virtue, no longer to be found only among Brahmins. But Brahmins remain the authorities, the teachers, and the exemplars of such learning. Moreover, YDhŚ 1.313 gives the Brahmin privy counsellor greater authority than all the rest of the ministers in steering the final deliberations of the king.

By contrast, the role of the *purohita* (chief priest) is more explicitly a priestly one and so necessarily a Brahmin one, but Aparāditya treats it as a sort of ministerial position as well:

> 'He should appoint as *purohita* a Brahmin endowed with qualities such as "knowing divine portents". "Knowing divine portents (*daiva*)" means knowing astrology, for by means of that discipline, the destiny of living beings, i.e. the ripening of *karman*, can be known. He in whom there have arisen (*udita*)—i.e. developed—those qualities such as being wise which are "recommended" (*udita*)—i.e. stated—for ministers, is called "one who possesses the recommended traits" (*udita-udita*).'[24]

---

[22] YDhŚA 1.310 [= 312 in standard numbering], p. 577.18–23: ***sa** ukta-guṇo rājā **mantriṇaḥ** kāryâkārya-vidaḥ. **prājñān** ūhâpoha-samarthān. **maulān** pitṛ-pāramparyâgatān. **sthirān** svāmi-hiteṣv acañcalān. **śucīñ** śuddhôpadhān. prakurvīta prayatnād upādadīta. atha **taiḥ** saha **rājyaṁ** rāja-karma ṣāḍguṇyaṁ tad-aṅgāni ca svāmy-ādīni **cintayet**. heyôpādeyatayā vicārayed iti arthaḥ. atha ṣāḍguṇya-vidā punar **vipreṇa** saha vicārayet. punaś ca **svayaṁ** tam evârthaṁ sādhaka-bādhaka-pramāṇavat tayā niścinuyāt.*

[23] YDhŚM 1.312 (p. 91.12).

[24] YDhŚA 1.311 [=313], pp. 577.26–578.1: *daiva-jñatvâdi-guṇôpetaṁ brāhmaṇaṁ purohitaṁ kurvīta. **daiva-jño** jyotiḥ-śāstra-vit. tena hi śāstreṇa prāṇināṁ daivaṁ karma-vipāko jñāyate. ye mantriṇām uditā uktāḥ prājñâdayo guṇās te yasyôditā udbhūtāḥ sa **uditôditaḥ**.*

In this case, the operative virtues include expertise in mystical knowledge. But Yājñavalkya goes on to say that part of the *purohita*'s brief is to superintend the administration of criminal justice (*daṇḍa-nīti*).

Finally, Yājñavalkya notes the importance of his knowing the 'Atharvâṅgirasa', that is, the strategic magic taught in the *Atharva-veda*.[25] Vijñāneśvara explains that this body of wisdom enables the royal servant efficaciously to perform the six types of sorcery taught in that tradition: *śānti* (counteracting harmful forces, such as those caused by celestial bodies), *vaśya* (subjecting another to one's will), *stambhana* (rendering another immobile), *vidveṣaṇa* (causing enmity between others), *uccāṭana* (dislodging an enemy), and *māraṇa* (causing the death of another). Belief in Brahmin priests' supernatural powers appears to have been widespread, and to have contributed greatly to their influence on rulers. And while skills of this sort might not be deemed those of a philosopher in Plato's sense, they were taken as a sort of pragmatic ancillary to the central body of higher lore of *Veda* and Śāstra, and as an application of the sacred power of *mantra* that in any case requires an ritual agent of exemplary discipline and purity.

The *Yājñavalkya* goes on to recommend that kings endow Brahmins with lands and wealth, and that such generosity itself constitutes an imperishable 'treasure' for the king. Rules are given for the recording of such endowments on cloth and in inscriptions, detailing the contents of the record, and including the authorising 'signatures'. There is a close correspondence between the practice described in these rules and the actually surviving epigraphical records.

The Brahmanical Administrator in Practice

Did the normative vision projected by the *Dharma-śāstra* literature correspond in any way to actual practice? Our only real information on political administration in classical and medieval India can be extracted from inscriptions, mostly on copper plates or on stone. Inscriptions constitute permanent records of royal decrees, deeds conferring property rights, and administrative records. They give us a way of comparing evidence of two very different sorts: inscriptions providing something quite close to a record of the structure of royal administration; and contemporary scholastic interpretations of the classical authorities on the primordial relationship between Brahmins and rulers. Although these two bodies of information do not always 'speak to each other' in a clearly direct fashion, they at least allow us to see where the correspondences lie, and to what extent the textual sources had any direct bearing on political

[25] Yājñavalkya mentions the *Atharvan* corpus thrice, twice as *atharvâṅgiras* (1.44 and 313) and once simply as *atharva-* (1.101). Moreover, in the latter case, Yājñavalkya clearly distinguishes that corpus from the *Veda* in a list: *vedâtharva-purāṇāni*, 'the *Veda*s, the Atharvan [texts], and the Antiquities'. This may be taken to show that the notion of an '*Atharva-veda*' was still not accepted by the fourth or fifth century CE.

practice. In earlier scholarship, such influence was assumed and asserted more than it was demonstrated. A countervailing trend among more recent historians has been to claim that such influence has been overstated, and that an earlier generation of scholars uncritically, or even surreptitiously endorsed the Śāstric model, distorting the testimony of other forms of evidence in order to show that it supports that model.[26]

The caste affiliation of officials mentioned in epigraphs is often not discernible, but from a few exceptional cases we know that from early on Brahmins sometimes served as royal ministers, even in environments in which Buddhism was ascendant. For example, a Brahmin minister of a ruler in western India recorded his gift to a Buddhist community in 124 CE—the mention of his Brahmanical *gotra* (clan) indicates his caste:

> 'The charitable donation of a *maṇḍapa* (pavilion) and cistern by Ayama of the Vatsa *gotra*, minister of [the king,] the "great satrap" (*mahā-kṣatrapa*), lord Nahapāṇa, made for the sake of merit in the year 46.'[27]

We are also told that the famous Hīrahadagalli copper-plates of the fourth century were written by the ruler's Brahmin 'privy councillor' (*rahasâdhikata*) Bhaṭṭisama (Prakrit for Bhaṭṭiśarman, *-śarman* being a status title applied exclusively to Brahmins).[28]

There was certainly no requirement that royal officials in general should be Brahmins, but in certain functions, Brahmin status was deemed essential. These function include adjudicating what we might call 'religious' processes such as vows and ordeals. A temple inscription from Nandalūru Saumyanātha temple in Cuddapah District (SII 23, no. 577) describes how members of two families vowed to perform the ordeal in order to have hereditary privileges restored. The record is signed by Brahmin officials of the king with the Sanskrit titles *dharmâdhikārin* ('Dharma officer') and the *divyâdhikārin* ('ordeals officer'). Śāstric descriptions of these roles emphasise that learning in *Dharma-śāstra* was a prerequisite.

But even functions less narrowly associated with sacred or scriptural knowledge per se were often served by Brahmins. An inscription of Rajendra Coḻa I[29] on the Tirumala temple (*ca.* 1014–1015) illustrates the functions of an *adhikārin* ('officer') during that reign. The officer, called Koṟṟamaṅkalamuṭaiyān, conducted an enquiry to determine whether funds allocated by an earlier grant

---

[26] For Tamil inscriptions, NAGASWAMY's work (1978) is a rather stark example of this trend.

[27] BURGESS–INDRAJI (1881: 51 f.; no. 25): [*raño*] *mahā-khatapasa sāmi-nahapānasa* [*ā*]*mātyasa vachasa-gotasa ayamasa* [*de*]*ya-dhama ca* [*po?*]*ḍhi maṭhapo ca puñathaya vase 46 kato*.

[28] BÜHLER (1892: 7; lines 50–51 of the inscription).

[29] SUBRAHMANYA SASTRY (1930: 28–31; no. 19).

for the performance of certain services were actually being used as intended. His name, which suggests that he had authority over a Brahmin settlement (*maṅgala*), together with the Sanskrit title he bears, suggest that he was himself a Brahmin. He called as witnesses a subdistrict administrator titled Ciṟutanattuppaṇimakaṉ and some priests (*pūjāri*) and temple servants (*tēvar-kaṟmikaḷ*). The *sabhaiyār* or 'members of the assembly' of Tirumuṇṭiyam were found in breach of their duties to use the funds to keep lamps lit in the temple. The legal remedy imposed by the *adhikārin* was to recover the capital of the grant from the *sabhā*, and to transfer it to the general account of the temple to support the lighting of the lamps by the regular temple staff. In this example, the fact that the matter concerned temple business, the conduct of Brahmins in responsible positions, namely as members of a Brahmin village council, may have made it appropriate for a Brahmin officer to take charge.

A striking and well known example has often been cited in support of this notion. The famous Uttaramallūr inscriptions of Parāntaka I (Parakesarivarman, r. from 906) record the king's efforts to reform the management of funds in the Brahmin settlement of Uttaramerucaturvedimaṅgalam, which had been perverted by 'wicked men'. In a first attempt, in the twelfth year of his reign (918–919), the king sent an (apparently non-Brahmin) officer called Tattaṉūr Mūvēndavēḷāṉ to promulgate a set of statutes to regulate the selection of members of three separate committees in such a way that power could no longer be concentrated in the hands of a small, corrupt group. Two years later, the king had to send a second officer, this time a Brahmin (Karañcai Koṇṭayakramavitta-Bhaṭṭaṉ alias Cōmāci-perumāṉ), to greatly refine the regulations, presumably so that they would more effectively exclude the selection of corrupt or corruptible members (including recent past members). The inscriptions take the form of resolutions issued by the *sabhā*: 'We, (the members of) the assembly of Uttaramēru-caturvēdimaṅgalam, made (this) settlement [with the king's officer] sitting with us by royal order.'[30]

The rules stipulated that names of candidates from each of twelve streets in thirty wards should be written on leaves and placed in a pot. To qualify as a candidate, a man must be between the ages of 35 and 70, own at least a quarter *vēli* of taxable land and reside in a house thereon, know the *Mantra* and *Brāhmaṇa* portions of his *Veda*. If he has studied also a commentary he may own as little as one-eighth of a *vēli*—be conversant with business, virtuous, with honest earnings, not have served on any committee in the past three years and not be related in any of twelve specified ways to any former committee member who has not submitted his accounts, and not be guilty of theft or any of a list of unexpiated moral faults (or even expiated ones, in some cases). Explicit rules were also given for the public selection of names: in the presence of temple

[30] *śrī-āñaiyiṉāl Tattanūr-Mū[vē]nda[vē]lān-uḍaṉ-irukka nam grāmatt[u du]ṣṭai koṭṭu* (read: *keṭṭu*) *śiṣṭar varddhi[tti]ḍuvār-āga [vyava]sthai śey[dō]m [Ut]taramē[ru*]-cca[tur-vv]ēni-maṅgalat[tu] sabh[ai]yōm*; as edited and translated in Venkayya (1908: 138–139).

priests and the full assembly, ward by ward, the names are shaken in a pot and drawn out by an illiterate boy, then passed to the *madhyastha*, a state-certified 'mediator' in charge of documents, who receives the leaf on his open palm and reads the name aloud, and passes it to be read out by all the priests. Note the emphasis place on Sanskrit learning, not only for the committee members but also in the case of the king's second deputy sent to deal with the problem.

Two prominent participants in the efflorescence of *Dharma-śāstra* in the eleventh and early twelfth centuries were Aparāditya (a Śilāhāra king) and Vijñāneśvara, both commentators on the *Yājñavalkya-dharma-śāstra* hailing from western India. Administrative practices from roughly the same time and place can be observed in the inscriptions of the Śilāhāras of Kolhapur, early medieval rulers of the Konkan who produced an ample body of records, mostly land grants to recipients identified clearly as Brahmins, often including information on their liturgical and clan (*gotra*) affiliations, and their educational and ritual attainments. As usual, many of the other individuals mentioned in the records, including officials, are not identified by caste, and the status titles commonly appended to personal names can be unreliable as guides to caste. (*Gotra*-affiliation and information about Vedic learning is generally provided only in the case of Brahmins in their capacity of recipients of grants to support religious or scholarly activities. Where the grant is made for other considerations, such as in recognition of official service, such credentials appear to have been irrelevant.[31]) In spite of this ambiguity, we can make some cautious observations based on these records.

For instance, in a series of grants made by Mummuṇirāja in the mid-eleventh century, we first see him set aside several villages for a number of Brahmins, and the part of the produce and cash income from some other villages for another group of Brahmins including one Daddapaiya who is said to have come originally from Madhyadeśa, the heartland of orthodox Brahmanism.[32] The settlement is written by an officer named Joupaiya, bearing the title of treasury officer and minister, nephew of the previous treasury officer, the poet Nāgalaiya. The suffix *-aiya* (< *ārya*) is common among Brahmins, though it can occur in other castes. Given their functions, however, these two seem likely to have been Brahmins.

A grant made just a few months later refers to the royal administration (*śrī-karaṇa*) being presided over by apparently the same Daddapaiya, now bearing the title *mahâmātya* (high officer), and one Viṭṭhapaiya, the Minister of Peace and War. This grant confers a village on twelve Brahmins residing in an endowed Brahmin settlement (*agra-hāra*) called Brahmapurī, which was itself founded by Daddapaiya. The beneficiaries hail from distant places far to the

[31] So notes MIRASHI (1977: 194) in the case of the Brahmin Śaṅkamaiya, son of the military officer Nāgamaiya; Balipattana plates of Raṭṭarāja (1010), CII 6.42.

[32] Ṭhāṇā Plates of Mummuṇirāja, 1049, CII 6.14 (MIRASHI (1977: 82–98)).

north, including Madhyadeśa and Bhṛgukaccha (in modern Gujarat).[33] The charter was written by Nāgalaiya.

The third inscription is a charter (*vyavasthā*),[34] written by the aforementioned Joupaiya, who has now been promoted to *pradhāna* (chief minister). The charter records statutes protecting the village of Dīpakāgara, along with its surrounding hamlets, from any claims by members of the royal family or other powerful persons (*sāmantas*, *nāyakas*, *ṭhākuras*), and exempts the main village (but not the hamlets) from the village tax (*deṇaka*) and from having to supply room and board (*paḍaṇaka*) to travelling government officers. The Brahmins are made responsible for paying revenue on the village, as well as fines for offences would be set by a Brahmin assembly called the *smārikā*.

After the death of Mummuṇirāja, there was a war, including incursions by 'Yavanas' (foreigners from the West, perhaps Parthians). The succeeding king seems to have beaten them back with the aid of wealthy non-Brahmin merchants (*śreṣṭhins*), and a copper-plate grant issued by him not only confers special dispensations on shippers but also reveals that his administration was dominated by members of the merchant class.[35] The exigencies of circumstance and the need to reward allies evidently drove a shift in political appointments after the war.

However a grant issued by his successor Aparāditya I (the commentator) returns to conferring benefices on Brahmin ritualists—in this case, Trivikrama, son of Ananta Agnihotrin, a White Yajurvedin (Mādhyandina) of Vārṣeya *gotra*. During his reign, the administration was in the hands of officers named Lakṣmaṇanāyaka (*mahâmātya*), Lakṣmaṇaiyaprabhu (*sāndhi-vigrahika* and *mahā-pradhāna*), Chītamaiyaprabhu (junior treasury officer), Lakṣmaṇaiya (senior treasury officer and scribe).[36] The caste status of these individuals cannot be definitely ascertained: the suffixes *-nāyaka* and *-prabhu* might be considered typical of Kṣatriya names, but *nāyaka*, originally an official title, was also borne by many Brahmins, and three of these names include the Brahmanical-sounding *aiya,* as in the example of Daddapaiya, who appears first as a Brahmin beneficiary of an endowment, and then (if it is indeed the same person) as a founder of a village and a high government official.[37] Only on rare occasions are we given a clear indication. One such case is that of a Brahmin named Lokaṇanāyaka, who is mentioned as a munificent donor in one record.[38]

---

[33] Prince of Wales Museum Plates of Mummuṇirāja, 1049, CII 6.15 (MIRASHI (1977: 98–106)).

[34] Dive Āgar Plate of Mummuṇirāja, 1053, CII 6.16 (MIRASHI (1977: 107–110)).

[35] Khārepāṭaṇ Plates of Anantadeva I, 1095, CII 6.19 (MIRASHI (1977: 115–120)).

[36] Vaḍavalī Grant of Aparāditya I, 1127, CII 6.20 (MIRASHI (1977: 120–127)).

[37] TALBOT (2001: 58) notes the ambiguity of the label *nāyaka*.

[38] Kolhāpur stone inscriptions of Bhoja II (late twelfth century), CII 6.58–59 (MIRASHI (1977: 127–130)).

Conclusion

This sort of comparison has obvious constraints. The information we would like to have is in part provided only incidentally in the inscriptions; much needs to be inferred or deduced from what is actually recorded, and one must take account of the fact that messy realities and ambiguous statuses may to varying degrees get smoothed over and deliberately made to conform to classical norms when they get inscribed in stone or copper (as they do in the formulation of modern legal documents). Moreover, the Brahmin scholiasts almost always studiously avoid making direct reference to political realities of their own day, and only occasionally provide much information about themselves or their personal circumstances and reasons for writing. Hence, even more 'reading between the lines' is required to try to situate such texts in relation to the evidence from inscriptions.

Granting these caveats, though, such a comparison suggests that the scholastically expounded ideal was by no means pure fantasy. Although the educational or sacral credentials of Brahmin officials are not usually cited, the administrative framework discernible in the inscriptions corresponds in many respects with the models depicted in the scholastic sources.[39] Brahmins appear to have been represented in high administrative positions far beyond their numbers in the population; this is especially true of positions that involved record-keeping and other forms of writing (most prominently, the office of *sāndhi-vigrahika*). It is also clear, though, that Brahmins' fortunes at court could rise and fall depending on the needs or inclinations of the ruler. In spite of this, royal patronage of Brahmin communities was a sustained phenomenon in Indian history, attested in the land grants to Brahmins (*brahma-deya, agrahāra*) so common in the epigraphy.

Those communities, which enjoyed privileges and exemptions granted in order to support scriptural study and ritual practice, may in fact have provided a pool of candidates for royal service. Individual candidates may not personally have been selected for their Vedic learning, but they would still have represented the classical virtues of learning and self-discipline. These communities may have been nexus point of two seemingly distinct types of Brahmin: the 'religious' and the 'secular', where the public image of the former lent authority to the latter. In the case of Brahmin officials—those Megasthenes called 'councillors and assessors' and TALBOT calls 'secular brahmins'—their Brahminhood was not specially noted, and seemed not to require any elaboration.

[39] Direct quotations from *Dharma-śāstras* do not occur in inscriptions, but Sanskrit stanzas are often quoted in support of grants of land, and the protection of such grants are relatively common; less common, but still met with, are stanzas supporting the validity of judicial ordeals.

Vedic credentials seem to have been called for only where the Brahmins were the recipients of benefices justifiable on the basis of their learning and piety.

Even in the absence of direct quotations from Śāstra, the personal virtues cited in inscriptions as qualifications for royal office clearly reflect those taught in classical and scriptural sources. The Brahmanical ideal of how to live a 'good life'—learning in *Veda*, self-discipline, personal purity, moral rectitude, even the assumption that birth is the higher orders of society is indispensable—show many analogies with Plato's conception of the philosopher. Plato regarded philosophers as belonging to an altogether higher plane on account of their knowledge of the forms, and this is the basis of the hierarchy between ruler and ruled in his model.

But for all the overweening ambition of Brahmin apologists, it was never asserted that they themselves should act as rulers, and the (ostensibly) Brahmin early Kadamba kings (predecessors of the Cālukyas) remained an exceptional case requiring special pleading to justify their rule.[40] Rather, the Brahmanical model of statecraft channelled the political potential of the 'philosopher' through the king into official capacities, including some offices explicitly meant for Brahmins. This arrangement served and was perhaps designed to shield the pure moral authority of the Brahmin from being corrupted by the violence intrinsic to wielding the *daṇḍa* (sceptre) of sovereignty.[41] It became the unifying principle for the administration of royal states across India, and was even adopted for several centuries by royal states arising in mainland Southeast Asia and Indonesia, with the result that Brahmin lineages and priesthoods got transplanted and took root in those regions.

---

[40] The royal panegyric contained in the Tāḷaguṇḍa inscription (mid-fifth century) construct a myth of origin for the dynasty that justifies king Mayūraśarman's rise to power (early 4th century) in terms of a restoration in the current decadent age of the primordial superiority of Brahmins to Kṣatriyas (line 4, KIELHORN (1905–06: 24–36); see also LUBIN (2005: 98–99)). Mayūraśarman's own inscriptions were composed in increasingly Sanskritised Prakrit (see the discussion in POLLOCK (2006: 116–117)). Later Kadambas, however, adopted the Kṣatriya status suffix *-varman*, in deference to the conventional wisdom that Brahmins should not be kings. Some historians argue that the dynasty's actually originated in the Kadambu tribe.

[41] ARENDT (1958: 82–84) distinguished sharply between coercion (which relies on violence), authority (which is rooted in injunction), and persuasion (which relies on reason for its force), arguing that they are mutually incompatible. She accordingly cited Kant's 'reply to Plato': 'It is not to be expected that kings philosophise or that philosophers become kings, nor is it to be desired, because the possession of power corrupts the free judgement of reason inevitably' (KANT (1949: 456)).

BIBLIOGRAPHY

ARENDT 1958 = Arendt, Hannah: 'What Was Authority?', in: Carl J. Friedrich (ed.): *Authority* (*Nomos I*). Harvard University Press, Cambridge, Massachusetts 1958: 81–112.

AŚ = Kauṭilya: *Artha-śāstra*. See KANGLE (1969); OLIVELLE (2012).

AŚJM = *Jaya-maṅgalā* commentary on the *Artha-śāstra*. See POHLUS (2011).

BÜHLER 1892 = Bühler, Georg: 'A Prākrit Grant of the Pallava King Śivaskandavarman', *Epigraphia India*, Vol. 1, Archaeological Survey of India, New Delhi 1892: 2–10 [reprinted 1983].

BURGESS–INDRAJI 1881 = Burgess, James; Bhagwanlal Indraji: *Inscriptions from the Cave-Temples of Western India, with Descriptive Notes, &c.* Government Central Press, Bombay 1881.

CII = *Corpus Inscriptionum Indicarum*, Archaeological Survey of India, New Delhi 1877–1991.

Diodorus = (1) C.H. Oldfather (ed., tr.): *Diodorus Siculus: Library of History, Volume II, Books 2.35–4.58*. Loeb Classical Library. Harvard University Press, Cambridge, Mass. 1935. (2) Translated also in: MCCRINDLE (1926).

FRITZ–KAPP 1950 = Kurt von Fritz; Ernst Kapp: *The Constitution of Athens, and Related Texts*. Hafner Publishing Co., New York 1950.

Geography = Strabo: *Geography*. (1) Horace Leonard Jones (ed., tr.): *The Geography of Strabo*, Vol. VII. Loeb Classical Library, Harvard University Press, Cambridge, Mass. 1954. (2) Translated also in: MCCRINDLE (1926).

Indica = Arrian: *Indica*. (1) P.A. Brunt (ed., tr.): *Arrian*, Vol. II, *Anabasis Alexandri, Books V–VII, Indica*. Loeb Classical Library, Harvard University Press, Cambridge, Mass. 1983. (2) Translated also in: MCCRINDLE (1926).

KANGLE 1969 = R.P. Kangle (ed.): *The Kauṭilīya Arthaśāstra*. Part I: *A Critical Edition with a Glossary*. University of Bombay, Bombay 1969 [first edition: Bombay 1960].

KANT 1949 = Kant, Immanuel: 'Eternal Peace', in: *The Philosophy of Kant*, edited and translated by C.J. Friedrich, Modern Library, New York 1949.

KIELHORN 1905–06 = Kielhorn, F.: 'Talagunda Pillar Inscription of Kakusthavarman', *Epigraphia Indica* 8 (1905–06) 24–36.

LUBIN 2005 = Lubin, Timothy: 'The Transmission, Patronage, and Prestige of Brahmanical Piety from the Mauryas to the Guptas', in: *Boundaries, Dynamics and Construction of Traditions in South Asia*. Edited by Federico Squarcini, Kykéion studi e testi. I, Scienze delle religioni 3. Firenze University Press, Firenze 2005: 77–103.

MALAMOUD 1977 = Malamoud, Charles: *Le svādhyāya, récitation personnelle du veda. Taittirīya-Āraṇyaka, livre II.* Institut de civilixation indienne, Paris 1977.

McCRINDLE 1926 = McCrindle, John W.: *Ancient India as Described by Megasthenēs and Arrian*. Revised edition. Chatterjee & Co., Calcutta 1926.

MDh = *Mānava-dharma-śāstra* [*Manu-smṛti*]. (1) Edition and translation: OLIVELLE (2005).

MIRASHI 1977 = Mirashi, Vasudev Vishnu: *Corpus Inscriptionum Indicarum, vol. 6, Inscriptions of the Śilāhāras*. Archaeological Survey of India, New Delhi 1977.

NAGASWAMY 1978 = Nagaswamy, R.: *Studies in Ancient Tamil Law and Society*. Tamil Nadu State Department of Archaeology, Madras 1978.

OLIVELLE 2005 = Olivelle, Patrick: *Manu's Code of Law: A Critical Edition and Translation of the Mānava-Dharmaśāstra*, with the editorial assistance of Suman Olivelle. Oxford University Press, New York 2005.

OLIVELLE 2011 = Olivelle, Patrick: 'War and Peace: Semantics of *Saṁdhi* and *Vigraha* in the *Arthaśāstra*', in: Bertil Tikkanen; Albion M. Butters (eds.): *Pūrvāparaprajñābhinandanam, East and West, Past and Present. Indological and Other Essays in Honour of Klaus Karttunen*. Studia Orientalia 110. Finnish Oriental Society, Helsinki 2011: 131–139.

OLIVELLE 2012 = Olivelle, Patrick: *King, Governance, and Law in Ancient India: Kauṭilya's Arthaśāstra*. Oxford University Press, New York 2012.

POHLUS 2011 = Andreas Pohlus (ed.): *Two Commentaries on the Arthaśāstra: Jayamaṅgalā & Cāṇakyaṭīkā. Critically re-edited from Harihara Sastri's Fascicle Editions.* Universitätsverlag Halle-Wittemberg, Halle 2011.

POLLOCK 2006 = Pollock, Sheldon: *The Language of the Gods in the World of Men*. University of California Press, Berkeley 2006.

SANDERSON 2007 = Sanderson, Alexis: 'Atharvavedins in Tantric Territory: The Āṅgirasakalpa Texts of the Oriya Paippalādins and their Connection with the Trika and the Kālīkula, with critical editions of the *Parājapavidhi*, the *Parāmantravidhi*, and the **Bhadrakālīmantravidhiprakaraṇa*', in: Arlo Griffiths; Annette Schmiedchen (eds.): *The Atharvaveda and its Paippalāda Śākhā: Historical and Philological Papers on a Vedic Tradition*. Geisteskultur Indiens, Texte und Studien 11. = Studia Indologica Universitatis Halensis, Shaker Verlag, Aachen 2007: 81–139.

SII = *South Indian Inscriptions*. Archaeological Survey of India, New Delhi 1890–2001.

Statesman = Plato: *Statesman*. Edith Hamilton; Huntington Cairns (ed.,tr.): *The Collected Dialogues of Plato*. Princeton University Press, Princeton 1961.

SUBRAHMANYA SASTRY 1930 = Subrahmanya Sastry: *Early Inscriptions Translated and Edited with Introductions*. Tirumala Tirupati Devasthanams, Tirupati 1930 [reprinted: 1980].

TaiĀ = *Taittirīya-āraṇyaka*. Edition and translation of TaiĀ 2: MALAMOUD (1977).

TALBOT 2001 = Talbot, Cynthia: *Precolonial India in Practice: Society, Region, and Identity in Medieval Andhra*. Oxford University Press, New York 2001.

VENKAYYA 1908 = Venkayya, V.: 'Two Inscriptions at Uttaramallūr', *Archaeological Survey of India, Annual Report 1904–1905*. Government Printing, Calcutta 1908: 131–145.

YDhŚ = *Yājñavalkya-dharma-śāstra*. See YDhŚM.

YDhŚA = [Aparāditya I Śilāhāra (ascribed):] *Aparârka*. Hari Nārāyaṇa Āpaṭe (ed.): *Aparārkâparâbhidhâparāditya-viracita-ṭīkā-sametā Yājñavalkya-smṛtiḥ*. Ānandāśrama Sanskrit Series, 46, Ānandāśrama, Puṇe 1903.

YDhŚM = Vijñāneśvara: *Mitâkṣarā*. Jagannātha Raghunātha Ghārapure (ed.): *Yājñavalkya-smṛtiḥ, yogīśvareṇa maharṣiṇā Yājñavalkyena praṇītā śrī-Vijñāneśvara-praṇīta-Mitākṣarā-ṭīkayā sametā*, Vol. 1. Arya Bhusana Press, Poona 1914.

APPENDIX

Officials Named in North Konkan Śilāhāra Inscriptions

(extracted from Mirashi 1977)

Ins	*Reign*	*Date*	*Mahâmātya*	*Mahā-sāndhi-vigrahika*
4	Chadvaideva	ś 861–889		
5	Aparājita	ś 915	**Ammaṇaiya**	**Jhañjamaiya**
6	Aparājita	ś 915	**Keśapārya** (*amātya*)	**Jhañjamaiya**
7	Aparājita	ś 919	**Saṅgalaiya**	**Sīhapaiya**
8	Arikesarin	ś 939	**Vāsapaiya**	**Vārdhiyapaiya**
9	Chittarāja	ś 948	**Nāgaṇaiya**, *sarvâdhikārin*	**Sīhapaiya** and **Kapardin**, Karṇāṭa-sāndhi-vigrahika!
10	Chittarāja	ś 949		
11	Chintarāja		**Nāgaṇaiya**	**Nāüpaiya** = Vāüpaiya in no. 12?

	Mahā-pradāna/Śrīkaraṇin/ Sthapati/Bhāṇḍâgāra	*other officials*	*Donees*
4		*śaulkikas*, *gaulmikas*, *cauroddharaṇikas*	B Cāḍādevabhaṭṭa, ṚV, Kāśyapa, knowing the Vedas, Vedâṅgas, Vedānta, Purāṇa, Mīmāṁsā, Smṛti, Nyāya
5		*lekhaka*: Uddāma s. Chakkaiya, *kāyastha*	B Kolama, *krama-vid*
6		*lekhaka*: Uddāma s. Chakkaiya, *kāyastha*	B Kolama, *krama-vid* s. Harideva, Sāmavedin, ṚV, Kāśyapa, who has come here from Karahāṭa 'for *kārya*' (MIRASHI (1977: 23, line 60)
7		*lekhaka*: **Annapaiya**	the god Lonāditya-deva at Lavaṇetaṭa, through the Nagara of Guṇapura: Ambuśreṣṭhin, Vāppaiyaśreṣṭhin, Celapaiya (village official), B Govanaiya
8		*lekhaka*: **Joupaiya**, nephew of *mahā-kavi* **Nāgalaiya**; engraver was **Mānadharapaiya** s. Vedapaiya	B purohita Tikkapaiya s. Chintapaiya, Jāmadagnya g., of Sthānaka,
9		*lekhaka*: **Jogapaiya**	B Āmadevaiya s. Nodamaiya, Parāśara g., Chandoga ś., ever engaged in the ṣaṭkarma
10		**Nāgalaiya**, *bhā[ṇ]ḍāgāra-sena*	learned B Govinda, ṚV ś., Kāśyapa g., of Dīpakāgara, s. Saudapaiya of Tīpaka
11		*lekhaka*: **Joüpaiya**	Śaiva ascetic Jñānaśiva, d. Vāḍācārya of the Western Āmnāya

Ins	*Reign*	*Date*	*Mahâmātya*	*Mahā-sāndhi-vigrahika*
12	Chittarāja	ś 956	**Nāgaṇaiya**	**Vāüpaiya** = Nāüpaiya in no. 11?
13	Nāgārjuna	ś 961	**Daddhapaiya**	**Soḍhalaiya**
14	Mummuṇirāja	ś 970	**Joupaiya**	**Viṭhapaiya**
15	Mummuṇirāja	ś 971	**Daddapaiya**	**Viṭṭhapaiya**

<table>
<tr><th></th><th>Mahā-pradāna/Śrīkaraṇin/ Sthapati/Bhāṇḍâgāra</th><th>other officials</th><th>Donees</th></tr>
<tr><td>12</td><td colspan="2">Dhruva (revenue coll.) Mammalaiya
chief among artisans, traders, & karaṇikas = merchants: Alliya, Mahara, Mahumata etc.
Śreṣṭhin Kesari, goldsmiths Kakkala, Somaiya; merchant Uva;
Vevaalaiya, collector of the viṣaya;
śāla: Yājñika, Ratnamaiya Kṣitalakṣaiya, Delaiya, Kesavaiy etc.;
Mahāparṣad: Agasti, Śavī, Sīluva, Bhāskara, Arjuna, Dinakara, Deveti, Ārya Sindūra, Ādityavarṇa, et al.</td><td></td></tr>
<tr><td>13</td><td>Jogapaiya, nephew of Nāgalaiya</td><td></td><td>Mādhavapaṇḍita s. Gokarṇapaṇḍita, Pārāśara g., YV ś., from Hastigrāma in Madhya Pradesh</td></tr>
<tr><td>14</td><td></td><td>lekhaka: Nāgalaiya</td><td>as below:</td></tr>
<tr><td colspan="4">Two endowments:
(i) to 14 Brahmins from Karahāṭaka (a Kannada-speaking town): Nārāyaṇa P. s. Tikkapaiya g. Jāmadagnya-Vatsa ṚV (2x), Rāmba P. s. Tikkapaiya g. Jāmadagnya-Vatsa ṚV, Lakṣmīdhara P. s. Tikkapaiya g. Jāmadagnya-Vatsa ṚV, Karṇāṭa Keśavabh. ṚV, Gopati P. s. Rāmba P. g. Jāmadagnya-Vatsa ṚV, Dhāreśvarabh. s. Mādhavabh. g. Jāmadagnya-Vatsa ṚV, Nārāyaṇabh. s. Govardhanabh. g. Gārgya ṚV, Cakrapāṇibh. s. Droṇabh. g. Kapi ṚV, Mādhava Jyotirvid s. Dāmupaiya g. Ātreya ṚV, Vāmbadevabh. s. Risiyappabh. g. Ātreya ṚV, Vāvalaiya s. Dāmupaiya g. Kāśyapa ṚV, Divākaraiya s. Siddhapaiya g. Bhāradvāja ṚV (2x), Janārdana s. Vevala Ṣaḍaṅgavid g. Kāśyapa ṚV, Vāmbaṇa s. Tīkapaiya g. Ātreya ṚV;
(ii) to
7 Vāvailaka Brahmins: Daddapaiya s. Brahmanāyaka f. Madhyadeśa g. Gārgya ṚV, Vāpyaiya s. Dhālana Ṣaḍaṅgavid f. Karahāṭa g. Vāsiṣṭha ṚV, Dāmupaiya s. Risiyapaiya f. Karahāṭa g. Kāśyapa ṚV, Nāgadevaiya s. Risiyapaiya f. Karahāṭa g. Kāśyapa ṚV, Govindaiya s. Mahīdharaiya f. Karahāṭa g. Jāmadagnya-Vatsa ṚV, Nannapaiya s. Madhuvalaiya f. Purī g. Bhāradvāja Gobhila SV, Lokapaiya s. Vāvaṇaiya f. Karahāṭa g. Kāśyapa ṚV</td></tr>
<tr><td>15</td><td></td><td></td><td>as below:</td></tr>
<tr><td colspan="4">to 12 Brahmins from other regions residing in Brahmapurī agrahāra, which was founded by Daddpaiya, the Mahāmātya of Mummunirāja: Koko P. s. Pitāmaha f. Gauḍa g. Śāṇḍilya Kauthuma SV, Devadhara D. s. Yajña D. f. Muñjasthāna in Madhyadeśa g. Vatsa ṚV, Dāmodara s. Kesaiya D. f. Muñjasthāna in Madhyadeśa g. Bhāradvāja VSM, Sūdanaiya s. Someśvara U. f. Muñjasthāna in Madhyadeśa g. Bhārgava ṚV, Dāmodara s. Sūdana D. f. Bhṛgukaccha in Lāṭadeśa g. Upamanyu ṚV, Nārāyaṇa Upāsanī s. Damodara U. f. Bhṛgukaccha in Lāṭadeśa g. Ātreya Rāṇāyaṇiya SV, Śrīpati Agnihotrī s. Keśava U. f. Bhṛgukaccha in Lāṭadeśa g. Kuśika ṚV, Śrīpati s. Dugaiyā Upāsanī f. Bhṛgukaccha in Lāṭadeśa g. Ātreya ṚV, Kanakeśvara s. Velāditya U. f. Bhṛgukaccha in Lāṭadeśa g. Jāmadagnya ṚV, Velaiyā Upāsanī s. Dīgvaiyā Agnihotrī f. Bhṛgukaccha in Lāṭadeśa g. Ātreya ṚV, Sarvadevaiya s. Īśvara U. f. Bhṛgukaccha in Lāṭadeśa g. Lokākṣa [Yajña?], Viṭṭhapaiya s. Soḍhalaiya U. f. Bhṛgukaccha in Lāṭadeśa g. Ātreya ṚV</td></tr>
</table>

Ins	*Reign*	*Date*	*Mahâmātya*	*Mahā-sāndhi-vigrahika*
16	Mummuṇideva	ś 975	**Joupaiya**	**Viṭhṭhapaiya *nāyaka***
17	Maṁvāṇirāja	ś 982	**Bimbapaiya**	**Jogalaiya,** *lekha-sāndhi-vigrahika*: **Vakavaiya**
18	Anantadeva I	ś 982	**Rudrapaiya**	
19	Anantadeva I	ś 1016	Mahādevaiya-prabhu, Bhābhaṇaśreṣṭhin	**Ṛṣibhaṭṭa**, Dhaṇāmaśreṣṭhin
20	Aparāditya I	ś 1049	Lakṣmaṇanāyaka	Lakṣmaṇaiya-prabhu
21	Aparāditya I	ś 1059	Śrīmālī Khetaya Ṭhākura	Amuka
22	Aparāditya I	ś 1060	Soḍhala Nāyaka	Amuka
23	Vikramāditya	ś 1061	Khetama Ṭhākkura	
24	Haripāladeva	ś 1070		

	Mahā-pradāna/Śrīkaraṇin/ Sthapati/Bhāṇḍâgāra	***other officials***	***Donees***
16	pr.: **Nārāyaṇaiya** bhāṇḍāgārasena-pradhāna **Joupaiya**	*purohita*: **Vāsudeva, Nārāyaṇa Paṇḍita,** *jyotiṣika*: **Divākara**	[charter]
17	pr.: **Nāgaṇaiya;** bhānd. **Mahādevaiya,** (jr) **Bhailaiya**	rājagurus: **Nābhāta** and **Vilaṇḍaśivabhaṭṭa** *śakāna* (?): Paivayaka *mahā-sāmanta*: Tāsivarājala	[completion of construction on the Ambarnāth temple]
18			Ajyapanāyaka s. Māvaiya Viyāḍika
19		*nauvitaka*: Vāsaida *pradhāna*: Somaṇaiyaprabhu et al.	exemptions for 2 Balipattana merchants: Bhābhaṇaśreṣṭhin and Dhaṇāmaśreṣṭhin
20		*pradhānas*: Lakṣmaṇaiyaprabhu, Chitamaiyaprabhu	Trivikrama s. Ananta Agnihotrin g. Vārṣeya ś. YV (Madhya Pradesh)
21	Lakṣmaṇeyaprabhu, Amuka, Divākaranāyaka, Viṣṇubhaṭṭasena Mahalū Ṭhākura	[exemption from house tax for 13 houses of persons connected with the temple of the goddess Jogeśvarī, e.g. *maṭha-pati* & *pūjārī*]	
22	Lakṣmaṇeyaprabhu, Amuka		to the royal *pariṣad*
23	pr.: Lakṣmaṇaiyaprabhu	*lekhaka*: **Lakṣmīdhara Paṇḍita s. Nāgasvāmin Paṇḍita**	Rudrabhaṭṭopādhyāya s. Keśava Dvivedi-bhaṭṭopādhyāya Somayājin s. Vidyādhara-bhaṭṭopādhyāya g. Bhāradvāja TS
24			Viṣṇu Upādhyāya f. Māhara

Ins	*Reign*	*Date*	*Mahâmātya*	*Mahā-sāndhi-vigrahika*
29	Mallikārjuna	ś1083		Prabhākaranāyaka
30	Aparāditya II	ś1106	**Vyomaśambhu** [bhopaka, mahā-pradhāna]	Mādhava
31	Aparāditya II	ś1107	Lakṣmaṇanāyaka s. Bhāskaranāyaka	
32	Aparāditya II	ś1108	**Vyomaśambhu [?]**	Anantapaiprabhu
33	Anantadeva II	ś1120	Nāika Vrīhimaprabhu	
34	Keśideva II	ś1125	**Lakṣmīdhara [?]**	
36	Keśideva II	ś1161	Jhampaḍaprabhu	**Rājadevapaṇḍita**
38	Someśvara	ś1181	Jhampaḍaprabhu	Taijaparbhu
39	Someśvara	ś1182	Jhāmpaḍaprabhu	Maināku

Key to the Appendix:

B = Brahmin
bh. = -bhaṭṭa (Brahmin title)
D. = Dīkṣita (Brahmin title)
d. = disciple of
f. = from
g. = of the *gotra*
neph. = nephew of
P. = Paṇḍita (Brahmin title)
ṚV = belonging to the *Ṛg-veda*
s. = son of
ś. = *śākhā* (branch of the *Veda*)
ś861 = in the Śaka-era year 861 (etc.)
SV = belonging to the *Sāma-veda*
TS = Taittirīya-saṁhitā of the YV
YV = belonging to the *Yajur-veda*

	Mahā-pradāna/Śrīkaraṇin/ Sthapati/Bhāṇḍâgāra	*other officials*	*Donees*
29	Anantapaiprabhu Amuka	*rāja-guru*: **Vedaśiva** *bhopaka*: **Vyomaśiva** **Laṣaṇa Vaṅgaka s. Mahadugiva Jhā**	Lāṣaṇa Upādhyāya
30		scribe: Mādhava	
31			
32	Anantapaiprabhu	'2nd *sthapati*': Amuka	
33		?: Vāhimaprabhu *amātya*: Sāmantapai s. Lāhugiprabhu	
34			
36	Anantaprabhu		
38	Dādaprabhu		
39	Govenāku	Bebalaprabhu, **Pomadepaṇḍita**	

The Concept of Non-Possession in the *Mokṣa-dharma*

SHUJUN MOTEGI

1. The *Mokṣa-dharma* section, the latter half of the *Śānti-parvan* of the *Mahābhārata* (MBh), is a type of encyclopaedia of the religio-philosophical thought of the day before the systematisation of the orthodox philosophies of Brahmanism. In the present paper I shall examine the concept of non-possession found in this literature, which is often stressed in Buddhism and Jainism. In general, human beings cannot survive without possessing some material things for everyday usage. Life without possessing such things seems impossible in the literal sense of the word. But in the *Mokṣa-dharma-parvan* (MDhP; *ca.* second century BCE – second century CE), this concept appears in various contexts which indicates that it is an object of concern even for Brahmanism or Hinduism. In the current work, I shall examine the occurrences of this concept and the way in which it is viewed.

2. In the initial six chapters of the *Mokṣa-dharma,* the concept of non-possession and its related concepts appear in the discussion of how to attain happiness (*sukha*) in this world full of pain (*duḥkha*).[1]

In this world, human life is filled with pain caused by loss of wealth, separation from loved ones, old age, death and so on. How might we overcome grief and attain happiness if we encounter such a painful incident. Some ways of attaining happiness, in which the concept of non-possession is referred to, are presented in these chapters. They are:

[1] extinction of attachment (*tṛṣṇā*), the ultimate cause of pain (MDhP 168),
[2] the practice of one's own duty, together with the cognition of time (*kāla*) driving us to the end (MDhP 169),
[3] non-possession of things (MDhP 170),
[4] cognition of destiny and its acceptance as the highest principle (MDhP 171, 172),
[5] satisfaction and self-restriction (MDhP 173).

---

[1] Shinkan MURAKAMI (1979) discussed the concept of non-possession in these chapters in comparison with the parallel verses found in Buddhist and Jainist texts, translating MDhP 168 and 170 into Japanese with notes.

World View and Theory in Indian Philosophy
Warsaw Indological Studies 5 (2012) 327–347.

2.1. First I shall briefly give an outline of these chapters focusing on these methods.

[1] Extinction of attachment (*tṛṣṇā*), the ultimate cause of pain (MDhP 168).

In MDhP 168, as the second question,[2] Yudhiṣṭhira asks Bhīṣma about how to avoid grief caused by the loss of wealth, wife, child or father.

Bhīṣma quotes an episode from the life of King Senajit, which is the main story of this chapter. King Senajit asks a Brāhmaṇa how to be free from the grief caused by the death of his son (168.12). The preaching of the Brāhmaṇa may be roughly explained as follows: The world is full of pain. Meeting others presupposes parting from them. Therefore, we should not be attached to others.

Attachment is the ultimate cause of pain (168.18). Attachment (*tṛṣṇā*) causes consciousness of possession, that is, something belongs to me. The extinction of this attachment brings a happiness different from worldly happiness, known as the great happiness (*mahat sukham*). Those who have attained the great happiness are said to have become Brahman, the eternal being.

[2] The practice of one's own duty, with the cognition of time (*kāla*) driving us to the end (MDhP 169).

In MDhP 169, Bhīṣma quotes a dialogue between Medhāvin and his father in order to answer a question posed by Yudhiṣṭhira, namely, how we should react to being threatened by old age and death brought by time (*kāla*).

Medhāvin asks his father how we should react to the fact that we have a limited life span which is dominated by the fear of death. The father answers what to do as a Brāhmaṇa in an orderly succession, beginning with the study of the *Veda*.

To this answer, Medhāvin raises the objection that we must be aware that the rapid passage of time soon brings old age and death, and states his own view on this matter. Medhāvin maintains that, in a constantly changing world, the most important thing is the practice of duty (*dharma*), by which we accrue honour in this world and happiness after death (169.15). We should not form attachments to things which are deemed valuable in this world, such as children, wife, cattle and wealth. He maintains that, instead of forming an attachment to these things, we must pursue the self (*ātman*), by which we may arrive at the final end, immortality (*amṛta*). The practices which make it possible to attain immortality are: the pursuit of truth (*satya*), a consciousness of the equality (*sama*) of pleasure and pain, penance (*tapas*) and abandonment

[2] In MDhP 168, at the very beginning, Yudhiṣṭhira asks Bhīṣma the duty (*dharma*) of those who live in the order of life stage (*āśramin*). Bhīṣma answers that it is penance (*tapas*) which brings the true result (*satya-phala*) and non-attachment (*virāga*) by which we see the world as something lacking substance (*asāravat*). This question and answer have no connection with the following story.

(*tyāga*), and so on. We attain happiness after death and recognition of the true self through the practice of duty.[3]

[3] Non-possession of things.

The practice of abandonment (*tyāga*) is again valued highly in MDhP 170. A certain Brāhmaṇa, who practices abandonment, stresses the importance of non-possession (*ākiṁcanya*). Only the practice of non-possession, which is more valuable than the throne of the king, brings happiness. On the contrary, it is wealth that confuses people and directs them to greed and anger. In this chapter, the term *ākiṁcanya* is preferable to *tyāga* which regularly appears throughout the text of the *Mokṣa-dharma*. It is preached that only non-possession makes it possible to be free from fears and so attain happiness. We encounter the description that, for those who move around the world, old age and death do not exist. This is reminiscent of the figure of a wandering mendicant (*parivrājaka, saṁnyāsin*).

[4] Cognition of destiny and its acceptance as the highest principle (MDhP 171, 172).

Again in MDhP 171, Yudhiṣṭhira asks Bhīṣma how to attain happiness if one cannot gain wealth or if one places great value in wealth. Bhīṣma replies that one can attain happiness if one sees equality in everything and tells the truth, being reluctant to gain worldly knowledge. Then he quotes the story of Maṅki who becomes filled with disgust (*nirveda*) when he loses all his belongings.[4] Maṅki thinks that worldly affairs are predestined by acts done in a previous life, and that we cannot alter this predestination through our efforts. Therefore, he believes it is important to be indifferent to worldly affairs, and this attitude of disgust brings happiness.

He enumerates the faults arising from wealth, declaring that he has arrived at disgust and attained the highest happiness.[5]

---

[3] The preaching of Vyāsa to his son Śuka in MDhP 309 is almost the same as the preaching of Medhāvin here.

[4] Maṅki has to accept the overwhelming power of destiny, saying:

na câvâvihitaṁ śakyaṁ dakṣeṇâpîhituṁ dhanam /
yuktena śraddhayā samyag ihāṁ samanutiṣṭhatā // (MBh 12.171.9)

'We cannot obtain wealth which is not determined by destiny to be obtained, even if we, being pious and diligent, make an appropriate effort to obtain it.'

[5] Declaring this, he quotes the well known verses of Janaka who admires non-possession of wealth, by which he himself arrived at infinity (*ānantya*).

anantaṁ bata me vittaṁ yasya me nâsti kiṁcana /
mithilāyāṁ pradīptāyāṁ na me dahyati kiṁcana / (MBh 12.171.56)

'My wealth is infinite, because I possess nothing at all. When Mithilā was burnt, nothing belonging to me was burnt.'

Cf. MBh 12.170.18, 268.4, DhP 200, Uttar 9.14, *Jātaka* V: 252 (no. 529 *Sonaka-jātaka* v. 16); FRANKE (1906: 352–53); MURAKAMI (1979: 188–192); ARAMAKI (1989: 93–94); IRIYAMA (2000), (2001).

The preaching of destiny is again seen in MDhP 172, where Bhīṣma quotes the teaching of the Sage Ājagara. Prahlāda asks Sage Ājagara about happiness (*śreyas*) in this world. Sage Ājagara, who is indifferent to duty (*dharma*), wealth (*artha*) and love (*kāma*), stresses the acceptance of destiny. He teaches that, as living beings are predestined to die, we should not be moved by their death. Whatever we may obtain has again been predestined by destiny (*vidhi*). If we accept this as the truth, we shall naturally attain the attitude of self-control, sincerity and purity, through which we may attain happiness.

[5] Satisfaction and self-restriction.

In MDhP 173, Yudhiṣṭhira raises a question concerning the base of man among family, rite, wealth and wisdom (*prajñā*). Bhīṣma points out that wisdom is the base of man, and quotes a dialogue between Indra and Kāśyapa. When he lost his wealth, Kāśyapa considered his life to be meaningless and was determined to commit suicide. Indra tried to persuade him not to kill himself. Indra maintains that, so far as we intend to prosper in the world, we cannot escape from the chains of desire. We should be satisfied with our present situation by observing helpless animals or less fortunate people. According to Indra, wisdom appears in the attitude of satisfaction and abhorrence, which is the only source of happiness.[6]

3. The previously mentioned five arguments are used in the attainment of happiness in the life full of pain. We cannot avert the loss of loved ones. To avoid grief, we should resort to a type of unusual action which is different from acts performed to attain things of normal value. In the pursuit of such a course of action, there is a reference to the concept of non-possession to some degree. In these arguments, some important concepts are seen to be used in relation to the concept of non-possession, such as destiny, abandonment, consciousness of possession, disgust and emancipation. I shall now examine some of these concepts throughout the text of the *Mokṣa-dharma*, focusing on the concept of non-possession.

3.1. Disgust or indifference through the denial of attachment (*tṛṣṇā*).

The thinkers of the day grappled with the single and ultimate cause of grief or pain in the world. In MDhP 169, attachment (*tṛṣṇā*) is regarded as the ultimate cause of grief and pain in this world. If we extinguish attachment, we attain or reach something beyond worldly happiness, that is, the great happi-

[6] In his argument, Indra first said that Kāśyapa should be satisfied with the fact that he was born as a Brāhmaṇa, the highest form of human being, and not as an animal (MDhP 173.18). Indra further stated that the richer people become, the more desirous they are for things. As there is no end to desire, desire must always be growing. To stop the growth of desire, man must restrict the function of the sense-organs which are the cause of desire and action (MDhP 173.27). If people do not eat delicious meals, they are not reminded of them. Happiness consists of not-eating, not-touching and not-seeing. The restriction of the sense-organs brings about human happiness.

ness. In other chapters, we encounter the same kind of thinking which regards attachment (*tṛṣṇā*) as the ultimate cause, similar to Buddhist thought.

In MDhP 268, King Janaka teaches the meaninglessness of the possession of wealth or kingdom and the great happiness caused by the extinction of attachment (*tṛṣṇā*). The verses sung by Janaka are well known and frequently quoted in many places, not only in the literature of Brahmanism, but also in that of Buddhism and Jainism.[7]

If wealth grows, King Janaka says, the consciousness of attachment to it grows accordingly. The consciousness of attachment is called *tṛṣṇā* here as in MDhP 171. By the extinction of *tṛṣṇā*, we attain a happiness larger than anything else.

There is one happiness through obtaining desired things. But the larger happiness comes through extinguishing the desire of material things. The latter happiness is incomparably larger than the former. This happiness is infinite (*ānantya*). If we abandon the adherence to wealth which is restricted by our own property, we gain a position restricted by nothing. This position is called infinity (*ānantya*), because it has no end and cannot be restricted by something which has an end (*anta*). This happiness is larger than the happiness to be found in heaven. It is said that those who have extinguished attachment (*tṛṣṇā*) become calm, and that Māndavya, on hearing Janaka's teaching, arrived at emancipation (*mokṣa*) (MDhP 269.14).

3.2. Disgust by the recognition of time (*kāla*).

In these chapters, an important concept is that living beings are exposed to change caused by time. With this idea in mind, thinkers pursued the way of attaining happiness or averting pain in the uncertain conditions of human life. Living beings are cast into the stream of time, from which they may not be

---

[7] MBh 12.268.4:

susukhaṁ bata jīvāmi yasya me nâsti kiṁcana /
mithilāyāṁ pradīptāyāṁ na me dahyati kiṁcana //

'I, who have nothing, live in great happiness. When Mithilā was burned, nothing belonging to me was burned.'

(Cf. MBh 12.170.18, 171.56; DhP 200, Uttar 9.14.)

MBh 12.268.5:

arthāḥ khalu samaddhā hi bādhaṁ duḥhkhaṁ vijānatām /
asamṛddhās tv api sadā mohayanty avicakṣaṇān //

'You have to know that possession of a lot of wealth is nothing but pain. Wealth bewilders stupid people, even if it is only a little.'

MBh 12.268.6:

yac ca kāma-sukhaṁ loke yac ca divyaṁ mahat sukham /
tṛṣṇā-kṣaya-sukhasyâite nârhataḥ ṣoḍaśīṁ kalām //

'Whether it is the happiness of love in the world, or the large happiness in heaven, it is not worthy of one sixteenth of the happiness acquired by the extinction of attachment.' (Cf. HOPKINS (1978: 69, 428 (No.196)); patternised expression to denote the minimum quantity: 'less than one sixteenth').

freed. This leads to the question of what we can or should do in a life driven by rapidly passing time which finally brings us to death. In response to this question, we see at least two possible solutions in the aforementioned arguments. One of them is the acceptance of destiny in which time is the ultimate principle, as seen in MDhP 171, 172. It is time that governs and decides everything in the world. Another solution is the pursuit of acts based on one's own will, even though the existence of living beings is rigidly restricted by time.

The first alternative, namely, fatalism in which time is the ultimate principle, is seen in some chapters of the *Mokṣa-dharma*, as in MDhP 192 and so on. In this fatalism, the meaninglessness of attachment to worldly values is realised by the recognition of the world as changing.

In MDhP 220, Bhīṣma, when asked by Yudhiṣṭhira what brings happiness to those who are in sorrow through the loss of wife, child or wealth, answers that it is resolute patience (*dhṛti*) that brings happiness to them,[8] and quotes a long dialogue between Indra and Bali. Bali objects to Indra who is proud of his victory and despises Bali, stating his own recognition thus:

> 'Seeing the world passing, who can rely on the wealth and physical body in the world.'[9]
> 'Wealth decays. Comforts, social rank and power decay also. All things change and do not stay long. It is difficult to attain this conviction. But the truth is that growth ends in decay, existent beings lie in non-existence.[10]

Bali's point is that everything in the world is dominated by time. Those who are in sorrow need do nothing except be patient. But it is again time that rescues them, so we should wait in patience until then. We can avoid grief by the recognition of the fact that time governs everything. In these chapters, the total acceptance of destiny and patience is positively stressed.

In the *Mokṣa-dharma*, we find fatalism which is constructed on the basis of time, and requires us to feel disgust for worldly affairs or abandon them. However, this fatalism based on the concept of time seems to have less influence on

---

[8] MBh 12.220.3:

> *putra-dāraiḥ sukhaiḥ câiva viyuktasya dhanena ca /*
> *magnasya vyasane kacchre dhatiḥ śreyah-karī nṛpa //*

(Cf. BÖHTLINGK (1966: No.4108)).

[9] MBh 12.220.91:

> *ko hi viśvāsam artheṣu śarīre vā śarīra-bhṛt /*
> *kartum utsahate loke dṛṣṭvā saṁprasthitaṁ jagat //*

MBhAD *ad loc.* interprets *saṁprasthitaṁ* as *vinaśvaram.*

[10] MBh 12.220.100:

> *naśyanty arthās tathā bhogāḥ sthānam aiśvaryam eva ca /*
> *anityam adhruvaṁ sarvaṁ vyavasāyo hi duṣkaraḥ /*
> *ucchrāyā vinipātântā bhāvo 'bhāva-stha eva ca //*

later philosophical thought. In the six systems of the orthodox philosophy of Brahmanism, we do not encounter a system constructed on time as the basic concept.[11]

3.3. The practice of duty (*dharma*).

On the other hand, we encounter a system of thought which considers human effort to be effective in attaining happiness, even if living beings are exposed to rapidly passing time. If destiny is totally accepted, there is no room for human will or effort. But this belief pursues the possibility of attaining happiness through human effort. It is said that it is the practice of righteous acts or duty (*dharma*) that brings happiness in this world. If we accept this view, we should ask why the practice of Dharma makes it possible to attain happiness, and what kind of happiness is meant by this system of thought.

In MDhP 181, the origin of social strata (*varṇa*) is explained. At the beginning of the world, the creator god Brahmā is said to have created Brāhmaṇas shining like the sun, and ordained that, through the diligent practice of their duty, they may attain rebirth in heaven (MDhP 182.2).

Brāhmaṇas should perform virtuous acts such as truth (*satya*), duty (*dharma*), penance (*tapas*), study of the *Veda*, good conduct (*ācāra*) and purification (*śauca*). Good Brāhmaṇas or true Brāhmaṇas are those who perform these virtuous acts, as a result of which they attain glory and happiness in this world and rebirth in heaven after death. In MDhP 182, Bharadvāja asks how a man becomes Brāhmaṇa or Kṣatriya or Vaiśya or Śūdra. The sage Bhṛgu explains the acts which are expected to be done by each social class (*varṇa*). He enumerates the desirable acts of Brāhmaṇas in detail (MDhP 182.2–4).

The acts of a Brāhmaṇa and the specific features of a true Brāhmaṇa are slightly different in each chapter. Observing the usage of terms such as donation (*dāna*), renunciation (*tyāga*), not belonging to me (*nirmama*)[12] which are enumerated as the acts of Brāhmaṇa, we may point out that the possession of wealth in general is considered to be negative.[13] Related to the concept of non-possession, in the virtuous acts of Brāhmaṇas enumerated above, the practice of abandonment (*tyāga*) is considered important. In general the practice

[11] Cf. BEDEKAR (1961).

[12] Sometimes the consciousness that this is mine is denied by the reason that it belongs to immature childish persons (MBh 12.217.28, 220.43). On the other hand the term *nirmama* ('nothing belonging to me') is used as a description for an accomplished person (MBh 12. 215.29, 228.33).

[13] Moreover, in MDhP 188, there is an argument as to the nature of a true Brāhmaṇa. The central theme of the argument is penance (*tapas*), self-control (*dama*) and trustworthiness (*satya*) which should be performed by a true Brāhmaṇa for fame and respect.

Furthermore, Haṁsa, a swan who enumerates many elements of the true Brāhmaṇa, stresses the strong power of speech, anger and lust for possession. Haṁsa maintains that those who regulate these powers deserve to be a true Brāhmaṇa (MDhP 288.14), and declares that he himself avoids the anger and lust associated with possession (MDhP 288.19).

of abandonment (*tyāga*) is basically treated positively throughout the *Mokṣa-dharma*. Here I shall introduce the Teaching of the Sage Nārada who views abandonment in the most positive way. He teaches Śuka the behaviour of the wise Brāhmaṇa in MDhP 316–318. He stresses the practice of abandonment as the behaviour of the wise, saying that nothing is more pleasing than abandonment (316.6), and that one who abandons all is wise (316.14). The happiness of the wise is the highest happiness, which is brought about by various acts including non-possession, as follows:

> 'Non-possession, satisfaction, disgust, immorality. These bring the highest happiness for the one who knows himself and exercises self-restraint.'[14]

In this way Nārada stresses the abandonment of all worldly values. He even teaches the abandonment of good practice, because this is also of relative value:

> 'Cast off virtue and vice, and both of truth and falsehood. After casting off truth and falsehood, cast off that by which you cast off these.'[15]

This abandonment could be called the ultimate abandonment. To pursue the practice of abandonment, he arrives at the recognition that man must abandon all that has relative value, including the base on which the practice of abandonment becomes possible. With this practice of abandonment of all relative values, he might be able to reach something absolute. This final teaching of abandonment seems to aim to go beyond the system of thought in which Brāhmaṇas are supposed to be reborn in heaven.

3.4. The life stage of the householder (*gṛha-stha*)—contradiction with three purposes (*tri-varga*).

The acts mentioned above, which Brāhmaṇas are supposed to perform, have not been explicitly described in connection with life stages (*āśrama*), even though it might be presupposed that some particular acts must be done in a certain life stage.[16] We encounter acts of Brāhmaṇa described explicitly in connection to the system of life stages which regulates their whole lives. In

[14] MBh 12.316.19:

ākiṁcanyaṁ susaṁtoṣo nirāśīṣṭvam acāpalam /
etad āhuḥ paraṁ śreya ātma-jñasya jitâtmanaḥ //

(Cf. MBh 3.203.46.)

[15] MBh 12.316.40 = MBh 12.318.44:

tyaja dharmam adharmaṁ côbhe satyânṛte tyaja /
ubhe satyânate tyaktvā yena tyajasi taṁ tyaja //

[16] The first verse of MDhP 168 seems to presuppose the system of life stages which Brāhmaṇa should pass in succession. However, it is problematic whether or not this verse is original, because the question which it raises is not related to the theme of MDhP 168.

MDhP 184, Bharadvāja raises a question: What kind of good practice (*ācāra*) must be done in each life stage (184.7). Bhṛgu answers this question by describing in detail the good practices common to all life stages and to each life stage in particular. In his explanation, the life stage of the householder, being the base of all other life stages, should embody the realisation of three purposes of life, namely, duty (*dharma*), love (*kāma*), and wealth (*artha*).

With this recognition of the life stage of the householder, Bhṛgu enumerates the acts which Brāhmaṇas must perform. He admits that the possession of wealth is necessary, but only if it is gained by acceptable methods. A Brāhmaṇa at the stage of householder needs wealth in order to assist young Brāhmaṇas who are at the stage of student of the *Veda*, or for donation to Brāhmaṇas who are at the stage of wandering mendicant (12.184.10). The life stage of householder is the one where a Brāhmaṇa must manage his home, including a wife and children, by supporting them financially. Thus if wealth is prohibited for Brāhmaṇas, the essential meaning of the stage of householder will be lost.

The gain of wealth for its own sake is the role of merchants (*vaiśya*), not that of Brāhmaṇa. Hence, it is not recommended for Brāhmaṇa to gain wealth. However, we encounter the statement that the possession of wealth by Brāhmaṇa is justified. In MDhP 262, for example, the sage Kapila talks about the way of wealth, stating that it should be donated to good Brāhmaṇas (262.4).[17] In his teaching, what is important is practice of Dharma and abandonment of gained wealth. It is not discussed whether a Brāhmaṇa should be poor or wealthy. They are required not to be attached to wealth obtained through righteous acts. It is said in the *Veda*[18] that, for those who devote themselves to their acts sincerely and without desire and anger, everything is infinite (*ānantya*). Further in MDhP 265, Bhīṣma holds that good persons will acquire friends and wealth through their righteous acts. As the practice of righteous acts (*dharma*) makes it possible to possess things, the possession itself is agreeable. But there is the possibility of adherence to the things possessed. Thus good persons must

[17] MBh 12.262.4:

dharma ity eva ye yajñān vitanvanti nirāśisaḥ /
utpanna-tyāgino 'lubdhāḥ kṛpâsuyā-vivarjitāḥ /
dhanānām eṣa vai panthās tīrtheṣu pratipādanam //

'Those who perform the sacrificial rite without desire, saying "this is duty", are free from tenderness and unhappiness. They are not greedy, abandoning things gained. The path of wealth must direct the donation to worthy persons.'

[18] MBh 12.262.15:

apeta-kāma-krodhānāṁ prakṛtyā saṁśitâtmanām /
ṛjunāṁ śama-nityānāṁ sthitānāṁ sveṣu karmasu /
sarvam ānantyam eva āsīd iti naḥ śāśvatī śrutiḥ //

'The eternal *Veda* tells us that everything becomes infinite for those who have no desire and anger by nature, an immovable sense of self, sincerity and constant quietude, being steady in their own actions.'

not cling to them and arrive at disgust (*nirveda*).[19] As the result of the practice of righteous acts, we can acquire friends and wealth. Those who practice righteous acts or their own duty (*dharma*) in the true sense of the term are not satisfied with acquired things, and should arrive at disgust (*nirveda*) through the eyes of correct recognition (MDhP 265.17, 18),[20]

Again, the preaching of the sage Parāśara in MDhP 281–286 approves the gaining of wealth. He says that Brāhmaṇas should protect wealth which is righteously obtained, even though the attainment of wealth is the duty of merchants (*vaiśa*).[21]

He maintains that, although the most important act for Brāhmaṇa is self-control (*dama*),[22] the possession of wealth is positively approved, as the prosperity in the world is the result of the former penance (*tapas*) (284.19–23). The possession of wealth itself is approved, but the adherence to wealth must be abandoned, says Parāśara. Finally Parāśara places importance on disgust (*nirveda*) through which one can extinguish adherence to things of worldly value.

---

[19] MBh 12.265.16:

dharmâtmā bhavati hy evaṁ mitraṁ ca labhate śubham /
sa mitra-dhana-lābhāt tu pretya cêha ca nandati //

'A virtuous person gets good friends. As he gets good friends and wealth, he is pleased in this world and in the next world.'

[20] MBh 12.265.17:

śabde sparśe tathā rūpe rase ca bhārata /
prabhutvaṁ labhate jantur dharmasyâitat phalaṁ vidhuḥ //

'He attains control of sound, touch, colour, taste and smell, o Bhārata. This is known as the result of righteous acts.'

MBh 12.265.18:

sa dharmasya phalaṁ labdhvā na tapyati yudhiṣṭhira /
atapyamāno nirvedam ādatte jñāna-cakṣuṣā //

'He is not satisfied with the result of righteous acts, o Yudhiṣṭhira. Being not satisfied, he attains disgust [for acquired things] through the eye of recognition.'

[21] MBh 12.281.4:

nyāyâgataṁ dhanaṁ varṇair nyāyenâiva vivardhitam /
saṁrakṣyaṁ yatnam āsthāya dharmârtham iti niścayaḥ //

'The truth is that wealth, which is rightly acquired by each *varṇa* and rightly increased, must be guarded with effort for the sake of (acquiring) virtue (*dharma*).'

[22] MBh 12.282.21:

damena śobhate vipraḥ kṣatriyo vijayena tu /
dhanena vaiśyaḥ śūdras tu nityaṁ dākṣyena śobhate //

'The Brāhmaṇa shines by self-control, the Kṣatriya by victory, the Vaiśya by wealth, and the Śūdra always by dexterity in serving.'

In MDhP 188, there is an argument as to the essence of a true Brāhmaṇa. There it is penance (*tapas*), self-control (*dama*) and trustworthiness (*satya*) that should be performed by true Brāhmaṇa for fame and respect.

In summary, there are two reasons to justify the possession of wealth even for Brāhmaṇas: (1) for the realisation of the essential purpose of a householder, (2) as a result of righteous acts in the past. In both cases, the concept of non-possession is not forgotten. In the life stage of householder it is important that they are conscious of adherence to things, not that they really possess wealth. They often argue about the inner consciousness of adherence, and treat it negatively. It is not real possession of wealth, but conscious lust that must be denied. In the life of the householder, non-possession itself seems to be less strongly emphasised, as it is not the chief purpose of this life stage.[23]

3.5. The practice of gleaning (*uñcha-vṛtti*), a unique practice for the householder.

In the description of the life of a householder, we come across another regulation that governs his life, that is, storage of food. In MDhP 235, the life of the householder is divided into four categories by means of the amount of stored food as follows:

> 'The poets talk about four kinds of householders. The first is those who have a granary full of food. The second is those who have a pot full of food.'[24]

The next is those who do not think of tomorrow. The last is those who live after the manner of pigeons. The last is the most excellent. Those who belong to the last category will be the greatest winners in the world thanks to righteous acts.[25]

Through these verses, we know that good Brāhmaṇas should not be concerned about food in the future, even if they are householders. Nīlakaṇṭha in-

---

[23] In these arguments, they pursue the cause of adherence or lust for possessions, and identify the ultimate cause of lust (MDhP 199.6) to be bewilderment (*moha*, MDhP 205.4) rather than attachment (*tṛṣṇā*). It is the ultimate cause of consciousness of possession that should be eliminated. The lust for possessions is not at all positive, but it is not something ultimate.

[24] MBh 12.235.2:

> *gṛha-ṣṭha-vṛttayaś caiva catasraḥ kavibhiḥ smṛtāḥ /*
> *kusūla-dhānyaḥ prathamaḥ kumbhī-dhānyas tv anantaram //*

GANGULI (1981–82, IX: 189–90) translates the verse as:

> 'The first consists of keeping a store of grain sufficient to last for three years. The second consists of keeping a store to last for one year.'

Cf. MDhŚ 4.7ab.

[25] MBh 12.235.3:

> *aśvastano 'tha kāpotīm āśrito vṛttim āharet /*
> *teṣāṁ paraḥ paro jyāyān dharmato loka-jittamaḥ //*

Cf. MDhŚ 4.7cd, 8cd; BDhS 3.2.14–15.

MDhŚ 4.7 tells us the following four kinds: *kusūla-dhānyaka, kumbhī-dhānyaka, tryahaihika* ('those who have food for three days') *aśvastanika* ('those who do not care about food for tomorrow'). Here the life of those who only think of a period shorter than *aśvastanika*, that is, who never think of the future at all, is referred to by the simile of a pigeon.

terprets the word *kāpotī* in verse 235d as *uñcha-vṛtti*, the life of those who sustain themselves only by gleaning.[26] The life of gleaning is often referred to in the *Mokṣa-dharma* as a desirable attribute of a householder.

In general living beings cannot live without consuming food or something edible. Generally, one of the most important issues for human beings is how to sustain life through eating. In ancient India, there was a protracted argument about meat-eating, as it necessarily sacrifices the lives of animals. It is also argued, as part of the good conduct expected of Brāhmaṇa, how much or little they should eat. Although food unlike wealth cannot be preserved for a long time, it might be possible to regard as another type of non-possession the virtue of keeping food for a short time or eating as little as possible. I shall next examine the concept of living through gleaning found in the *Mokṣa-dharma*.[27]

The term *uñcha-vṛtti* first appears in the last verse of MDhP 184, which describes the relief of those who do not achieve the essential purpose of the householder. It runs:

> 'It is not difficult to arrive at heaven for the householder who lives the life of gleaning, being satisfied with the practice of his own duty, even if he abandons the happiness of love and setting to do (his work).'[28]

Here it says that those who live the life of gleaning and gain satisfaction from doing their duty can reach heaven, even if they do not achieve the main purposes of the householder. Living the life of gleaning itself is supposed to be an independent method of rescue for the householder who otherwise cannot reach heaven. In MDhP 264, the life of gleaning is again praised, because the one who lives by gleaning does not take any life for the practice of sacrificial rites in the forest. Here the concept of gleaning is positively treated in connection with non-violence (*ahiṁsā*). The concept of gleaning fits well with non-violence, because a man practising gleaning does not cook food and, hence, never takes away the vital element of life.

The last ten chapters of the *Mokṣa-dharma* are the story of a snake, named Padma, who attains perfection through an oath to live by gleaning. A Brāhmaṇa, wishing to meet Padma, tries to show that he is an excellent man worthy of meeting him. He describes himself as eating by gleaning (*uñcha-śilâśana*) in order to show that his standard of behaviour is sufficiently high to deserve a

---

[26] MBhBhD, vol. 5, *Śānti-parvan* 430.

[27] There are various terms for gleaning; *uñcha-vṛtti, uñcha-vrata, uñcha-śīla, uñcha-śilâśana*. Although these terms differ slightly in meaning, the meaning or intention will be one and the same.

[28] MBh 12.184.18:

> *uñcha-vṛttir gṛhastho yaḥ sva-dharma-caraṇe rataḥ /*
> *tyakta-kāma-sukhârambhas tasya svargo na durlabhaḥ //*

meeting with Padma.[29] After the meeting with Padma, the Brāhmaṇa enters the forest having decided to practice gleaning. With this description, the whole episode covering ten chapters ends without a concrete description of gleaning.[30]

4. The practice of non-possession in the final two life stages.

In the life stages of forest life (*vāna-prastha*) and of wandering mendicant (*parivrājaka*), the practice of non-possession is required or admired, because in both life stages Brāhmaṇas are not concerned with economic growth as they are when in the life stage of householder.

Although they are required to possess nothing in the forest life stage, they are permitted to store a certain amount of food for guests. In the life stage of wandering mendicant, however, they are not permitted to possess even enough food for the following day.[31] The same idea is seen in the preaching of Hārita in MDhP 269. Hārita teaches the mental attitude which wandering mendicants

---

[29] MBh 12.351.4:

asana-dhīr anākāṅkṣī nityam uñcha-śilâśanaḥ /
sarva-bhūta-hite yukta eṣa vipro bhujaṁ-gama //

'This Brāhmaṇa always has wisdom, is far from desire, always eats by gleaning, and meditates for the welfare of all living beings, o Nāga.'

[30] MBh 12.353.9:

sa ca kila kṛta-niścayo dvijâgryo bhujaga-pati-pratideśitârtha-kṛtyaḥ /
yama-niyama-samāhito vanântaṁ parigaṇitôñcha-śilâśanaḥ praviṣṭaḥ //

'Then the excellent Brāhmaṇa went into the forest with conviction in order to practice the purpose taught by the king of snakes, concentrating with the help of *yama* and *niyama*, and intending to live the life of gleaning.'

One of the commentaries on the MBh, *Vyākhyāna-ratnâvali* by Vidyāsāgara (*ca.* 1350 CE), interprets the term *uñcha-śilâśanaḥ* as follows: *uñcha-śilâśanaḥ, kṣetrād vrīhy-ādiṣu svāmibhir apakṛteṣu luneṣu satsu, daivāt patitāṁ mañjarīm ādāyôtpatanti pakṣiṇaḥ. te yatra vṛkṣâdau majuñjarīṁ nikṣipya sthāpayitvā tad-gatān kaṇān bhakṣayanti tatra patita-dhānyena yātra-mātra-śīlaḥ sa uñcha-śilâśanaḥ.*—'The one who acts as follows deserves to be called *uñcha-śilâśana*. Birds fly up seizing in their mouths flowers which fell from the sky. They throw the flowers to a tree. Fixing them on the tree, they eat the seeds of the flowers there. The one who eats the dropped seeds as the only means of sustaining life, when corns of rice and so on are cut on the ground and carried away by their owners, deserves to be called a man who practises gleaning.'

By the strict definition of gleaning, this interpretation seems to indicate that a life of gleaning is very difficult to practice perfectly. From the idea that the practice of gleaning by itself leads one to become a true Brāhmaṇa capable of rebirth in heaven, the content of the act of gleaning becomes strictly defined and its difficulty of practice is stressed. The difficulty of rebirth in heaven seems to require a corresponding difficulty in its achievement.

[31] MBh 12.237.6:

aśvastana-vidhānaḥ syān munir bhāva-samanvitaḥ /
laghv-āśī niyatâhāraḥ sakṛd anna-nisevitā //

'The sage (i.e. Brāhmaṇa in the life of *parivrājaka*) should live with the rule of having no store for the next day. He must eat a little restricted food once a day.'

Cf. MDhŚ 11.16, MBh 12.8.12.

should have when they go begging. The life of wandering mendicants is described as follows:

> '[A wandering mendicant] should not have the least interest in obtaining the smallest amount of things for the maintenance of life. Do not be disappointed with things not gained. A thing gained should not make one pleased.'[32]

A Brāhmaṇa as a wandering mendicant must be interested only in emancipation, not in the amount of things gained or not gained. As the final and highest goal of this life stage is emancipation, a Brāhmaṇa is required to live in order to realise this goal. A store of food cannot be permitted, because it leads to regard for this world, or a life full of adherence.

5. The other ultimate cause of *mokṣa, tyāga* and *jñāna*.

In the initial chapters of the *Mokṣa-dharma* the ultimate cause of pain is thought to be attachment (*tr̥ṣṇā*) which should be extinguished through disgust (*nirveda*). In some chapters, however, we encounter the idea that *jñāna* ('recognition' or 'wisdom') is the principal method of conquering grief or pain. In MDhP 317, the Sage Nārada teaches Śuka a method to avoid or conquer grief. Nārada stresses the importance of correct knowledge about worldly affairs through which man can conquer grief. Living beings cannot banish death, and the dead never return to this world. Thus it is useless to lament the dead.[33] Then he discusses proper knowledge or wisdom which the wise should have.

> 'Those who see the world through wisdom (*buddhi*) do not cry.
> For those who observe all in the right manner never shed tears.'[34]

The essential characteristic of the wise is in their correct recognition of the world and satisfaction in their present condition. The wise do not make an ef-

[32] MBh 12.269.10:

anuyātrikam arthasya mātrā-lābheṣv anādataḥ /
alābhe na vihanyeta lābhaḥ cânam na harṣayet //

Cf. MDhŚ 6.57.

For the reading of *anuyātrikam arthasya*, Bombay and Kumbhakonam versions of the MBh and MDhŚ read *prāna-yātrika-mātrāḥ*.

[33] MBh 12.317.9:

mr̥taṁ vā yadi vā naṣṭaṁ yo 'tītam anuśocati /
duḥkhena labhate duḥkhaṁ dvāv anarthau prapadyate //

'Those who lament someone passed, whether dead or lost, acquire pain upon pain. They acquire two meaningless things.'

Cf. MBh 11.26.4, 12.16.10.

[34] MBh 12.317.10:

nâśru kurvanti ye buddhyā dr̥ṣṭvā lokeṣu saṁtatim /
saṁyak prapaśyataḥ sarvaṁ nâśru-karmôpapadyate //

fort to attain things generally supposed to bring happiness in the world.[35] The wise are satisfied with the present situation of their wealth without attempting to attain more.[36]

The wise who have correct knowledge about the world and feel satisfied with their condition can avoid grief. According to Nārada, such a wise man is one who is happy (*sukhin*) and becomes Brahman. Nārada does not teach that the right knowledge is the only ultimate principle. He still stresses the importance of abandonment (*tyāga*), which is another central concept of his thought (or the thought ascribed to him). In his thinking, the practice of abandonment and the right recognition of the world co-exist without apparent opposition.

However, there exists a theory which places importance only on the idea of recognition, which is rather negative to the concept of non-possession. In MDhP 308, King Janaka answers Sulabhā, a Yogin who doubts Janaka's reputation. She holds that emancipation has nothing to do with possession or social rank, and that it is recognition that brings about emancipation, not the practice of non-possession.[37] This theory is not concerned with the possession of things so long as the final purpose is not subverted by such possession.[38] King Janaka is of the opinion that he arrived at emancipation while he governed the kingdom as king. His opinion opens the possibility of emancipation to those who have secular works tied to the possession of wealth. In the case of Tulādhara, a

---

[35] MBh 12.317.14:

> *anityaṁ yauvanaṁ rūpaṁ jīvitaṁ dravya-saṁcayaḥ /*
> *ārogyaṁ priya-saṁvāsa gṛdhyet tatra na paṇḍitaḥ //*
>
> 'The wise do not make an effort to attain youth, shape, life, storage of things, sound, and living with a lover.'

[36] MBh 12.317.19:

> *anyām anyāṁ dhanâvasthāṁ prāpya vaiśeṣikīṁ narāḥ /*
> *ataptā yānti vidhvaṁsaṁ santoṣaṁ yānti paṇḍitāḥ //*
>
> 'Even if men attain a certain amount of wealth, they go to ruin because they feel no satisfaction with the wealth they have gained. On the other hand, the wise go to satisfaction.'

Cf. MBh 11.2.20.

[37] MBh 12.308.50:

> *ākiṁcanye na mokṣo 'sti kaiṁcanye nâsti bandhanam /*
> *kaiṁcanye cêtare câiva jantur jñānena mucyate //*

[38] In the same chapter, we find a verse which permits possession as follows, MBh 12.308.43:

> *yena yena hi yasyârthaḥ kāraṇenêha kasyacit /*
> *tat tad ālambate dravyaṁ sarvaḥ sve sve parigrahe //*
>
> 'In the world a person has a purpose according to a certain reason. Everyone gets a thing in any case whenever the thing is related with his own purpose.'

merchant, the same idea is indicated, that is, emancipation is possible for those whose occupation is secular.[39]

6. The denial of attachment by the vision of equality arising from disgust (*nirveda*), a common aspect to the vision of Yogin.

Lastly we shall briefly examine the concept of non-possession in relation to Sāṁkhya and Yoga, the most influential systems of thought in the *Mokṣa-dharma*. We often encounter the expression '*yoga-doṣa*' ('faults of *yoga*') which include desire (*kāma*) or attachment (*rāga*). Even though there exist no direct words meaning 'the practice of non-possession', Yogins are required to be indifferent to the possession of things, and they should not be involved with things of worldly value.[40] Yogins must not be pleased by acquisition, and not be anxious about loss.[41]

As Yogins have abandoned a conventional dwelling place, they are described in the same manner as that of wandering mendicants at the fourth life stage. In connection to the concept of non-possession, both are described as having disgust (*nirveda*) for worldly matters. The concept of disgust for acquisition and loss is again seen in the argument about true Brāhmaṇa as well as in the arguments regarding yoga practice.[42]

This concept of disgust is closely connected with the concept of equality, that is, disgust for things of worldly value leads to the view of equality that all paired emotions such as admiration and censure, good and evil, liking and hate, are not objects of interest. The concept of equality seems to have been

---

[39] Both King Janaka and Sulabhā in MDhP 308 are supposed to be disciples of Pañcaśikha, the third teacher of the Sāṁkhya school. It is uncertain whether or not Janaka's ideas about emancipation have any connection with later Sāṁkhya.

[40] MBh 12.232.27:

> *nâbhiṣvajet paraṁ vācā karmaṇā manasâpi vā /*
> *upekṣako yatâhāro labdhâlabdhe samo bhavet //*
>
> 'A *yogin* should not have affection for others by words, act and mind. He remains indifferent, restricted in food, whatever he gains or loses should be equal.'

[41] MBh 12.232.29:

> *na prahaṣyeta lābheṣu nâlābheṣu ca cintayet /*
> *samaḥ sarveṣu bhūteṣu sadharmā mātariśvanaḥ //*
>
> 'A *yogin* should neither be pleased with anything gained, nor be worried with anything ungained. He should be equal to all existing beings, having the same nature of wind.'

MBhAD interprets the simile of wind thus: touching every existing beings, a *yogin* should be clean and inclined to leave, like wind (*mātariśvano vāyoḥ sadharmā sadṛśaḥ. sarva-spṛśann api śuciḥ gamana-śīlo vā*).

[42] The concept of disgust for acquisition and loss may be found in the preaching of Sage Samaṅga to Sage Nārada in MDhP 275. He teaches the concept of disgust and *yoga* practice to Nārada. But the exact relationship between them in his teaching is not entirely clear.

highly preferable in the days of the *Mokṣa-dharma*.[43] King Janaka, who is said to have arrived at infinity, teaches Śuka the concept of equality by means of the frequently used simile of stone and gold.

> 'You have no adherence to your kinsman, no fear for one whom you may feel fear. I see you as the one who regards mud, stone and gold as equal, o, man of great fortune.'[44]

The merchant Tulādhara teaches equality using the same simile of stone and gold.[45] He expresses his idea of equality using a rather unique or paradoxical interpretation of the simile as follows:

> '[14] The blind, the deaf and the insane are always men of the highest consolation. Those whose sense-organs are closed by gods are equal to me who can see [and leave desire]. [15] As the old, the sick and the poor do not have desire for material objects, so I have no desire for enjoyment of wealth and love.'[46]

When we say that we regard gold and stone as equal, it is the value of gold which must be denied. In this interpretation of the simile by Tulādhara, however, the value of stone should be as highly estimated as that of gold instead of simply denying the value of gold. Tulādhara concludes that such a recognition of the world will lead to accomplishment as a Brāhmaṇa.[47] Although the intention in Tulādhara's unusual interpretation of the simile is open to argument,

---

[43] The same idea is seen in the following verse, for example, MBh 12.216.27:

na hi duḥkheṣu śocanti na prahaṣyanti câddhiṣu /
kṛta-prajñā jñāna-taptāḥ kṣāntāḥ santo manīṣiśaḥ //

'The true wise, being perfect in wisdom, satisfied with knowledge and patient, are not made sorrowful by pain and not pleased by happiness.'

[44] MBh 12.313.49:

na bandhuṣu nibandhas te na bhayeṣv asti te bhayam /
paśyāmi tvāṁ mahā-bhāga tulya-loṣṭâśma-kāñcanam //

[45] MBh 12.254.13:

iti māṁ tvaṁ vijānīhi sarva-lokasya jājale /
samaṁ mati-matāṁ śreṣṭha sama-loṣṭâśma-kāñcanam //

'You should know me as one who sees all in the world equally, o, Jājali. You should know me as one who sees mud, stone and gold equally, o, the best of the wise.'

[46] MBh 12.254.14–15:

yathândha-badhirônmattā ucchvāsa-paramāḥ sadā /
devair apihita-dvārāḥ sôpamā paśyato mama // 14 //
yathā vṛddhâtura-kaṇā niḥspahā viṣayān prati /
tathârtha-kāma-bhogeṣu mamâpi vigatā spṛhā // 15 //

[47] MBh 12.254.16:

yadā câyaṁ na bibheti yadā câsmān na bibhyati /
yadā nêcchati na dveṣṭi tadā sidhyati vai dvijaḥ //

it can be said that his interpretation is a challenge to the value system regularised by the Brāhmaṇas.

7. In connection with the Sāṁkhya, there was found no direct reference to the concept of non-possession in the Sāṁkhyaic chapters of the *Mokṣa-dharma*. The Sāṁkhya discusses the consciousness of possession in an epistemological context. It is said that consciousness of possession is caused by the wrong form of self-recognition, and the Sāṁkhya explains the cause of the world transmigration to be an incorrect consciousness of possession, by which man considers the physical body as his own (*mamâyam iti*; MDhP 293.8). Because of this incorrect recognition of the self, the Sāṁkhya says, there occurs the world of transmigration. Therefore, the Sāṁkhya maintains that this wrong recognition should be abandoned, as it is the origin of world transmigration. For this purpose, the Sāṁkhya says, we must recognise the existence of the ultimate material principle (*prakṛti*), which is responsible for the consciousness of possession and of the self. Through this recognition, the original state of the self (*puruṣa*) should be recovered, which will extinguish the previously mentioned consciousness.[48]

In the process of pursuit of the true self, the Sāṁkhya discussed the consciousness of the self, or the consciousness of something belonging to the self, both of which are seen as the self or the function of the self in daily life. The Sāṁkhya considers these to be caused by a false consciousness of the self, and goes further to state that recognition of the true self, *puruṣa* is beyond the self-consciousness of ordinary life. Here the consciousness of possession and self-consciousness are regarded as causes of the wrong notion of the self. It must have been in this way that the Sāṁkhya employed self consciousness (*ahaṁ-kāra*) in its evolution theory from the ultimate material. Self consciousness seems to be needed by the Sāṁkhya as the principal cause of improper cognition.[49]

---

[48] This recognition is stated as follows, MBh 12.295.35–36:

nirmamasya mamatvena kiṁ kṛtām tāsu tāsu ca /
yonīṣu vartamānena naṣṭa-saṁjñena cetasā // 35 //
na mamâtrânayā kāryam ahaṁ-kāra-kṛtâtmayā /
ātmānaṁ bahudhā kṛtvā yêyaṁ bhūyo yunakti mām /
idānīm eṣa buddho 'smi nirmamo nirahaṁkṛtaḥ // 36 //

'[35] Because of the misbehaviour of material nature, why did I act with egotism in various existences here on earth, I who am [naturally] without egotism, as I dwelt in these various existences with a mind that has lost its wits. [36] I have nothing more to do now with her, whose nature is affected by the I-faculty [by egotism], who is now again trying to inveigle me, making herself manifold. Now I am enlightened, free of selfishness and egotism (*buddho ... nirmamo nirahaṁkṛtaḥ*).'

Translation by EDGERTON (1965: 315).

[49] Van BUITENEN (1957) points out that the original meaning of ego-principle (*ahaṁ-kāra*) is the self-declaration of the creator God when he starts the creation of the world.

8. I would indicate the following as the results of the above examination of the concept of non-possession.

(1) The original usage of the concept of non-possession in the *Mokṣa-dharma* is related to the basic problem of how to avoid or conquer grief caused by the loss of someone or something vitally important. The practice of non-possession is offered as a solution to this problem, presupposing the life of a mendicant or hermit which requires the distancing of oneself from secular life. However, with the development of the system of life stages, the role and meaning of householder became important as the base of the system of life stages. When he experiences the loss of something important, the householder cannot easily quit his social position to devote himself to the practice of non-possession to achieve the main purposes of the Brāhmaṇa. A possible solution is to harmonise both requirements, that is, avoidance of grief and achievement of the duty of a householder, in a successive manner. In this solution, to continue to be a householder and a good Brāhmaṇa, the focus of the practice of non-possession moves from the non-possession itself to the inner consciousness. The practice of non-possession came to be performed afterwards at the fourth life stage of wandering mendicant as one of the paths to emancipation.

(2) The final result of the practice of non-possession is mentioned by several terms which mean emancipation. Emancipation is the attainment of something eternal beyond the world of transmigration, which must be gained by a wandering mendicant or a Yogin, both of whom live apart from secular life. On the other hand, it is mentioned that if a Brāhmaṇa at the life stage of householder practices gleaning, this will lead to rebirth in heaven. Rebirth in heaven is the original purpose of the Brāhmaṇa who performs sacrificial duty as a householder. The purpose of gleaning is not the same as the practice of non-possession for the sake of emancipation. With this difference in mind, we may assume that there existed a thought which, placing the most importance on the life stage of householder, pursues the final accomplishment at the stage of householder, thus ignoring the fourth life stage. This is exactly opposite to the idea of distancing oneself from home, which is the basic feature of the fourth life stage. In so far as accomplishment is attained at the stage of householder, it may be called secularism.[50]

(3) Some tales in the *Mokṣa-dharma* tell us that emancipation is possible for those who have a secular occupation. Janaka, a king, and Tulādhara, a merchant, are told that they have reached emancipation or perfection. Janaka becomes emancipated by the practice of non-possession in MDhP 170.268. But he is said to have become emancipated by right knowledge of the world in MDhP 308, denying the practice of non-possession as the way to emancipa-

---

[50] Parāśara's position seems to be a variety of compromise between both views. He places importance on disgust (*nirveda*). Those who perform penance after reaching disgust can attain heaven, Parāśara says. Parāśara preaches the attainment of heaven through disgust.

tion. Tulādhara, selling goods, describes himself as one who has views of equality, performs non-violence and so on (MBh 12.253–256).

There must be a difference in the background of the tales of Janaka and Tulādhara. Janaka has been well known as a wise and ideal king since the days of the *Bṛhad-āraṇyakôpaniṣad*, as the result of which some episodes about Janaka as a man of perfection have been created. On the other hand, Tulādhara is only a merchant. Perhaps his unique interpretation of the simile of gold and stone shows the manifold nature of thoughts of the day in that a merchant, a lower stratum in the system of *varṇa*, could express an opinion which differed from the authorised view promoted by Brāhmaṇas.

BIBLIOGRAPHY

ARAMAKI 1989 = Aramaki, Noritoshi Aramaki: 'The Formation of the *Mokṣa-dharma* Chapter of the *Śāntiparvan* of the *Mahābhāta*', [in:] Editorial Committee (Board) of Essays in Honour of Dr. Kotatu Fujita on His Sixties Birthday (ed.): *Indian Philosophy and Buddhism. Essays in Honour of Professor Kotatu Fujita on His Sixtieth Birthday*. Heirakuji-Shoten, Kyoto 1989: 89–122.

BDhS = *Baudhāyana-dharma-sūtra*. Olivelle, Patrick: *The Dharma-sūtras: The Law Codes of Āpastamba, Gautama, Baudhāyana, and Vasistha*. Annotated Text and Translation. Motilal Banarsidass, Delhi 2000: 196–345.

BEDEKAR 1961 = Bedekar,V.M.: 'The doctrines of *Svabhāva* and *Kāla* in the *Mahābhārata* and other Old Sanskrit Works', *Journal of the University of Poona, Humanities Section* 13 (1961) 1–16.

BÖHTLINGK 1966 = Böhtlingk, Otto: *Indische Sprüche, Sanskrit und Deutsch*. Reprinted, Otto Zeller Verlag, Osnabrück 1966 [first edition: 3 Bänder, St. Petersburg 1863, 1864, 1865].

van BUITENEN 1957 = van Buitenen, Johannes Adrianus Bernardus: 'Studies in Sāṁkhya (II): *ahaṁkāra*', *Journal of the American Oriental Society* 77,1 (1957) 15–25 [reprinted in: Ludo Rocher (ed.): *Studies in Indian Literature and Philosophy, Collected Articles of J.A.B. van Buitenen*. Motilal Banarsidass, Delhi 1988: 53–73].

DhP = *Dhamma-pada*. Oskar von Hinüber; K.R.Norman (eds.): *Dhammapada. With a complete Word Index compiled by Shoko Tabata and Tetsuya Tabata*. Pali Text Society, Oxford 1994.

EDGERTON 1965 = Edgerton, Franklin: *The Beginnings of Indian Philosophy*. George Allen & Unwin Ltd., London 1965.

FRANKE 1906 = Franke R. Otto: 'Jātaka-Mahābhārata-Parallelen', *Wienner Zeitschrit für die Kunde des Morgenlandes* 20 (1906) 317–72 [reprinted in: R. Otto Franke: *Kleine Schriften*. Teil 1, Franz Steiner Verlag, Wiesbaden 1978: 344–399].

GANGULI 1981–82 = Ganguli, Kisan Mohan (tr.): *The Mahabharata, translated into English Prose from the original Sanskrit Text.* 12 Vols, Reprint Fourth Edition, Munshiram Manoharlal Publishers Pvt. Ltd., Delhi 1981–82 [first edition: Calcutta 1883–96].

HOPKINS 1978 = Hopkins, Edward Washburn: *The Great Epic of India, Its Character and Origin.* Reprinted, Punthi Pustak, Calcutta 1978 [first published: New York 1901].

IRIYAMA 2000 = Iriyama, Junko: 'On the verses of burning *Mithilā*, Ku to Jitsuzai (Śūnya and Existence)', [in:] Editorial Committee of Memorial Volume of Dr. Ekyo Ejima (ed.): *Memorial Volume of Dr. Ekyo Ejima*. Shunju-Sha, Tokyo 2000: 501–521.

IRIYAMA 2001 = Iriyama, Junko: 'On the verses of burning Mithilā (2)', *Bukkyo Bunka Kenkyu Ronshu* (*Studies of Buddhist Culture*) 5 (2001) 99–149.

Jātaka = *Jātaka*. V. Fausbøll (ed.): *The Jātaka together with its commentary being Tales of the anterior births of Gotama Buddha.* Vols. 1–6. Reprinted, Pali Text Society, Oxford 1990–91 [first edition: London 1877–96].

MBh = *Mahā-bhārata*. Vishnu S. Sukthankar; S.K. Belvalkar; et al. (ed.): *The Mahābhārata for the First Time Critically Edited.* 19 Vols., Bhandarkar Oriental Research Institute, Poona 1933–1966.

MBhAD = Arjunamiśra: *(Maya-)Bhāratârtha-(pra)dīpikā*, or *Bhārata-saṁgraha-dīpikā*, referred to as 'Ca.' in the critical footnotes of MBh.

MBhBhD = Nīlakaṇṭha Caturdhara: *[Mahā-]Bhārata-bhāva-dīpa*. Ramchandrashastri Kinjawadekar (ed.): *The Mahābhāratam with the Bharata Bhawadeepa Commentary of Nilkantha.* 6 Vols, second edition, Munshiram Manoharlal Publishers, New Delhi 1979 [first edition: Chitrashala Press, Poona 1929–1933].

MDhP = *Mokṣa-dharma-parvan*. In: MBh: 12.168–353.

MDhŚ = *Mānava-dharma-śāstra* [*Manu-smṛti*]. Vishvanāth Nārāyaṇ Mandlik (ed.): *Mānava-Dharma Śāstra [Institutes of Manu], with the Commentaries of Medhātithi, Sarvajñanārāyaṇa, Kullūka, Rāghavānanda, Nandana, and Rāmachandra.* Munshiram Manoharlal, Delhi 1992 [first edition: Bombay 1886].

MURAKAMI 1979 = Murakami, Shinkan: 'Muyoku to Mushoyu—*Mahābhārata* to Bukkyo (1)' ['Non-desire and Non-possession, the *Mahābhārata* and Buddhism (1)'], *Tohokudaigaku Bungakubu Kenkyu Nenpo* (*Annals of Letters, Tohoku University*), 29 (1979) 140–213.

Uttar = *Uttarajjhayaṇa-sutta* [*Uttarādhyayana-sūtra*]. (1) Jarl Charpentier (ed.): *The Uttarādhyayanasūtra.* An introduction, text, critical notes and a commentary. First Indian Edition, Ajay Book Service, Delhi 1980. [first edition: *Archives d'Etudes Orientales*, Vol. 18:1–2, Uppsala 1921–1922].

Aho kauśalam apūrvam. Hermeneutical wrigglings about the *Īśôpaniṣad*

PAOLO MAGNONE

The *Upaniṣads* are the common repository from which the classical systems of Indian thought (with the exception of the Nyāya-Vaiśeṣika) draw their fundamental tenets, ending up, however, in utmost diversity. To confine ourselves to the Vedānta school, Bādarāyaṇa's attempt to summarise and homogenise their bewildering riches in the *Vedānta-sūtras* failed to succeed because of its ambiguity, which has in turn given rise to the most diverse interpretations by the *bhāṣya-kāras*, ranging from Śaṅkara's absolute monism all the way to Madhva's dualism, through various intermediate degrees of monism-cum-dualism represented by the *Bhāṣyas* of Bhāskara, Rāmānuja, Nimbārka and Vallabha.

But 'What did the *Upaniṣads* really say?' (to mimic the title format of many a popular book). Of course, the question admits of no ultimate solution. T h e meaning of the *Upaniṣads* does not exist as such, but manifold meanings are always there for the manifold interpreters to reach after, always on the run ahead of—or behind—them along the circuitous path of the hermeneutical circle that governs interpretation. Interpretation, as Gadamer made finally clear, can never be a direct and linear process of going and grasping the meaning that was always there, but is the result of a *Horizontverschmelzung*, or an interactive fusion between the horizon of the interpreter's pre-comprehension and the horizon of the *interpretandum*, each with its own historical situatedness. This interaction is a recursive process (the 'hermeneutical circle') which results in ever renewed pre-comprehension enabling more and more subtly attuned comprehension of the *interpretandum*.

Thus, the interpreter's world view is an inescapable precondition to his actual theoretical practice of interpretation; at the same time, it must not straitjacket it, but it is essential to the circularity of the process that it must remain open-ended to what comes from the sphere of the datum.

Along these lines, the commentatorial practice on the *Upaniṣads* provides an excellent example of the splendours and miseries of interpretation in an Indian setting. In particular, the *Īśôpaniṣad*, on account of its extreme pithiness, is singularly suited to demonstrate the fruitful impact of the different world views of the individual masters in fostering the comprehension of specially

World View and Theory in Indian Philosophy
Warsaw Indological Studies 5 (2012) 349–365.

enigmatic passages, and at the same time the length they are willing to go to make an authoritative text square each with his own preconceived philosophico-religious outlook. In the following we are going to review a few instances of the different interpretations produced by the great *bhāṣya-kāra*s of the three conflicting Vedāntic schools: Śaṅkara for the Advaita, Vedāntadeśika for the Viśiṣṭâdvaita and Madhva for the Dvaita. The latter's commentary is typically very succinct, consisting of a literal gloss and a (pseudo)-scriptural quotation from some often untraceable Smṛti,[1] so that we shall usually have to resort to the sub-commentator Jayatīrtha for enlightenment.

For the sake of the subsequent analysis, in order to facilitate the reader with a ready confrontation with the original I will premise in each case the root *mantra*s, with the advertence, however, that the editorial requirement to dispense with the Devanāgari, coupled with the common practice of separating words in transliteration, is liable to introduce a *modicum* of unwarranted interpretation: as we shall see, in fact, even the actual shape of the *interpretandum* cannot be taken for granted, as commentators are apt to differ even in the ways they scan the script to isolate the individual words from the uninterrupted strings of graphemes that make up the original *scriptio continua*.

And first of all the opening stanza (ĪU 1):

> *īśā vāsyam*[2] *idaṁ sarvaṁ yat kiṁ ca jagatyāṁ jagat* /
> *tena tyaktena bhuñjīthā mā gṛdhaḥ kasya svid dhanam* //[3]

---

[1] The problem with Madhva's more often than not untraceable citations is a well-known one. Cf. ROCHER (2008) for a comprehensive retrospect of the question, originating with 'Varadācārya's reference to quotations *kaiścid*, that are *svakapolakalpita* ("word of his own mouth"—P.M.), and [Vedāntadeśika's] dismissal of unnamed quotations invented by *pāpiṣṭhāḥ*' (2008: 603) (possibly but not certainly aimed at the Dvaita master); and especially with Appayadīkṣita's wholesale dismissal of Madhva's 'idiosyncratic' theories on the grounds, among others, of his quoting in support totally unknown (*atyantâprasiddha*) sources, of which he lists 29 from Śruti and 11 from Smṛti. In recent times the debate has been taken up again by MESQUITA, on the side of Madhva's critics, with his 1977 monograph, imputing to him the fabrication of untraceable sources but absolving him of the fraudulent intent, on the grounds that he bona fide believed himself an Avatāra of Viṣṇu (through the mediation of Vāyu), hence empowered, like his fellow Vyāsa, to compose scriptures for the enlightenment of the *kali-yuga* people. On the other side, SHARMA, as a staunch Madhva supporter, has tried to exonerate his master from the allegations in his 1961 monograph (revised ed. 2000), and has taken issue with MESQUITA's criticism in a 2001 paper. Most recently, MESQUITA has published a further monograph (2007) collecting a massive corpus of date in support of his conclusions.

[2] Madhva: *īśâvāsyam*.

[3] E.g. OLIVELLE(1998: 407): 'This whole world is to be dwelt in by the Lord, whatever living being there is in the world. So you should eat what has been abandoned, and do not covet anyone's wealth.'

This stanza elicits at once discordant interpretations when subjected to the pre-emptive force of the distinctive world views of the different commentators. It could not be otherwise, as it condenses the relationship between the three principles—supreme self, world and soul—whose different articulation is paramount to the respective doctrines of the three schools.

To an unbiased look (if such thing exists at all) the *Upaniṣad* would seem to lend itself more to an interpretation positing some sort of real distinction, which would suit better its theistic perspective. According to the tenets of Advaita, however, the three principles are of course but one—the Supreme Ātman–Brahman. Therefore, we may predict that it is particularly Śaṅkara who will have to strain the letter of the text in order to distil his desired meaning.

The very first word, *īśā*, instrumental of *īś* ('the Lord' or 'the divine Person'), is bent by the Advaitin Ācārya to mean the Paramâtman, the impersonal supreme self who rules (*īṣṭe*) the universe from within, as being one with the inner self of every creature (*pratyag-ātmatayā*).

But the next word is again a major stumbling block for the Advaita perspective: given that the Paramâtman is the sole reality, and the world merely illusory appearance, what could possibly be the relationship obtaining between the two, conveyed by the word *vāsyam*[4]? Not a relation of immanence, as the term would naturally seem to suggest: the real cannot abide in the unreal. Rather, according to Śaṅkara's glossing *vāsyam* with *ācchādanīyam*, the supreme self must be made to 'clothe' or 'cover' the unreal world, paradoxically veiling illusion in order to reveal the truth, hiding appearance to make reality reappear. This is in fact the gist of the simile employed by Śaṅkara to exemplify the peculiar nature of the *ācchādana* ('covering'): as a piece of fragrant sandalwood may develop an unpleasant smell owing to dampness—a smell which is not its own, and can be easily 'covered' by its own quintessential fragrance stirred up by rubbing—just in the same way the illusory appearances superimposed on the self by the necessities of empirical intercourse can (and must) be 'covered' by the realisation of his true essence which alone is supremely real.[5] One cannot but remark that this interpretation rests on the bold oxymoron of a cover that uncovers. According to common understanding, deceit is unmasked by uncovering it, i.e. getting rid of the cover-up to pierce through to the underlying truth. But Śaṅkara here invites us not to uncover the Advaitic core of reality but rather to recover it by literally re-covering illusion, as it were, by a

---

[4] *Vāsya* can be derived as a gerundive from at least two homophonic roots (and from their causatives), hence meaning, as the case may be, 'to be indwelt, entered into, worn (as a cloth), clothed or enveloped' etc. The commentators play on this ambiguity to distil each his desired meaning.

[5] Śaṅkara, $\bar{\text{I}}\text{U}_1$ 4.2–5: *yathā candanâgarv-āder udakâdi-saṁbandha-ja-kledâdi-jam aupādhikaṁ daurgandhyaṁ tat-svarūpa-nigharṣaṇenâcchādyate svena pāramārthikena gandhena tadvad eva hi svâtmany adhyastaṁ svābhāvikaṁ kartṛtva-bhoktṛtvâdi-lakṣaṇaṁ jagad-dvaitarūpaṁ ... paramârtha-satyâtma-bhāvanayā tyaktaṁ syāt.*

further coating of reality. On the other hand, covering consists in placing something on top of something else: this, however, is exactly what is precluded by non-dual vision. Furthermore, what is covered is occluded by the covering, which prevents the apparition of the true form of the covered by replacing it with mere semblance. On the contrary, according to the peculiar *ācchādana* postulated by Śaṅkara, covering and covered cease to be two; the covering is the same covered that becomes uncovered or unveiled 're-vealing' itself by itself with its true form, which discloses itself occluding or covering not itself but its mere semblance.

Vedāntadeśika's and Madhva's interpretations of *īśā vāsyam* do not differ significantly[6] in spite of their different wording: according to the former, the world 'must be pervaded' (*vyāpyam*), whereas for the latter it is 'fit to be indwelt' (*vāsa-yogyam*), by the Lord.

The third *pāda* (*tena tyaktena bhuñjīthāḥ*) is interpreted in markedly different ways by the three commentators. The most straightforward reading from a grammatical viewpoint is Vedāntadeśika's: 'by renouncing that [world], enjoy'. In everyday life what is enjoyed is the world itself; but here the Svāmin characterises 'that [world]' as an object of illusory enjoyment, which is therefore fit to be renounced when its manifold shortcomings become apparent. Since the natural object of fruition, the world, has thus been given up, the injunction *bhuñjīthāḥ* must needs be qualified 'according to the [suitability of the] meaning and the subject matter':[7] enjoyment must be limited to that group of permissible objects of fruition which are exclusively instrumental in supporting a body serviceable for *yoga*.

Renouncement of the world is not required by Madhva, who accordingly takes *pāda* C to mean 'enjoy [by] what is given by Him [i.e. the Lord]', interpreting *tyaktena* as 'handed over' or 'devolved' rather than 'renounced', and *tena* as an agentive governing the passive past participle instead of as an instrumental agreeing with its predicate. This requires some twist of the grammar, which the subcommentator Jayatīrtha implicitly acknowledges by observing that Madhva's explanation was indeed necessary, as the passage is awkward (*durgam artham*[8]): the reference of *tena* is indeterminate,[9] and it is not proper to say that something 'renounced' (*tyakta*) could be a means of fruition.[10] Now here goes the explanation: *tena* must logically be construed to refer to *īśā* mentioned in the first *pāda*, in spite of the latter being the subordi-

[6] Except for Madhva's peculiar reading of the phrase as compound of *īśa* and *āvāsyam*.

[7] Vedāntadeśika, p. 4.21: [*artha-*][a]*prakaraṇābhyāṁ sidhyati.* [[a] The word *artha*, missing through some oversight, has been restored from an editorial footnote to the passage as well as from a literal citation in the translation on p. 34.19.]

[8] Jayatīrtha, p. 6.29.

[9] Jayatīrtha, p. 6.28: *tena iti parāmarśasya viṣayo na pratīyate.*

[10] Jayatīrtha, p. 6.28: *tyaktasya ca bhoga-sādhanatvam ayuktam.*

nate member of a compound[11] (which would usually prevent it from being directly referred to by another word). Furthermore, because this world is incapable of activity in itself—and for this very reason must be permeated by the Lord, who alone is *svatantra*, or capable of spontaneous activity—whatever we experience can only be 'devolved' by the Lord, and not secured by our own endeavour: therefore, *tyakta* must mean *datta*, 'given' by the Lord, i.e. spontaneously obtained (*yadṛcchayā labdham*).

For his part, in accordance with the strictly ascetic, world-denying stance of his Kevalâdvaita, Śaṅkara bars any kind of enjoyment whatsoever for him who has the *adhikāra*, or 'qualification', for supreme knowledge, and for whom this first *mantra* is intended. As a consequence, his interpretation of the *pāda* cannot but be highly idiosyncratic: 'by renouncing that [world], protect your Self'. Here his understanding of *tena tyaktena* is similar to Vedāntadeśika's, except that he adds the logical remark that, properly speaking, something 'renounced' or 'abandoned' (as a dead son or servant), being a purely negative entity, cannot entertain any positive relationship; therefore, we should read *tyaktena* ('renounced') to mean *tyāgena* ('renouncement'): for while what is renounced no longer exists, renouncement itself is a positive entity capable of affecting us. But it is what comes next, the injunction: *bhuñjīthāḥ*, 'enjoy', that poses a real difficulty for the Advaita master. Surprisingly enough, especially after all the fastidiousness of the foregoing elucidation, here Śaṅkara does not spend many words to smooth out the problem, just one to gloss *bhuñjīthāḥ* with *pālayethāḥ*, 'protect yourself'; nor does Ānandagiri make up for the concision. Jayatīrtha takes issue with this explanation, remarking that the meaning 'to protect' is not proper for the root √*bhuj* in the middle voice (*ātmane-pāda*; according to Pāṇini I.3.66); but one modern commentator, B.K. IYER (1995: 8), is quick to exonerate Śaṅkara on the grounds that Pāṇinian rules do not apply to Vedic passages.

We now come to the two parallel triads of stanzas ĪU 9–11 and 12–14, whose enigmatic diction has given rise to widely diverging interpretations. The first triad runs as follows:

andhaṁ tamaḥ praviśanti ye 'vidyām upāsate /
tato bhūya iva te tamo ya u vidyāyāṁ ratāḥ // 9 //
anyad evâhur vidyayânyad āhur avidyayā /
iti śuśruma dhīrāṇāṁ ye nas tad vicacakṣire // 10 //
vidyāṁ câvidyāṁ ca yas tad vedôbhayaṁ saha /
avidyayā mṛyuṁ tīrtvā vidyayâmṛtam aśnute // 11 //[12]

[11] Jayatīrtha, p. 29–30: *samāse upasarjanī-bhūtasyâpi īśasya buddhyā vivekenâyaṁ paramārśaḥ*. As noted above (n. 6), Madhva reads the first *pāda* as a *tat-puruṣa* compound (*īśa* + *āvāsyam*).

[12] E.g. OLIVELLE(1998: 407, 409): 'Into blind darkness they enter, people who worship ignorance; and into still blinder darkness, people who delight in learning. It's far different from knowledge, they say, different also from ignorance, we're told—so have we heard

At first sight, the gist of the passage would seem to teach the inadequacy of both *avidyā* ('ignorance', literally 'non-knowledge') and *vidyā* ('knowledge') taken separately, and the ensuing necessity of their association, but the manner of expression is striking, and ascribing a positive agency to ignorance or a deluding power to knowledge are paradoxes that require an explanation.

Like Vedāntadeśika, Śaṅkara overcomes the former difficulty by understanding *avidyā* as 'other than *vidyā*',[13] viz. *karman*, exemplified by ritual works. Even so, in conformity with his strictly monistic stance he cannot accord any positivity whatsoever to the performance of rituals, which in his view do nothing but help perpetuate attachment to the illusory world. Not recognising any value in works, Śaṅkara cannot accept in any way the doctrine of *jñāna-karma-samuccaya* ('cumulative practice of knowledge and works') as a means towards liberation—which doctrine would however seem to be taught by the passage under consideration. How does Śaṅkara acquit himself of his duty of allegiance to the Śruti without renouncing his fundamental tenet, that knowledge of the supreme Reality alone is all that is required to attain liberation? His solution is a radical one: he simply denies that the instruction here promulgated is meant for the *mumukṣu*, or the 'seeker after liberation'; on the contrary, such instruction he takes to be meant for the *jijīviṣu*, the worldly-minded 'life lover', recalling the distinction previously made by *jñāna-niṣṭhā* ('stand on knowledge') and *karma-niṣṭhā* ('stand on works'), or *nivṛtti-mārga* ('path of inactivity') and *pravṛtti-mārga* ('path of activity'). According to Śaṅkara, the *Upaniṣad* under discussion does not present a uniform teaching, but contains two different sets of teachings meant for people with different *adhikāra*s, or 'qualifications'. In his view, for instance, whereas the first *mantra* teaches Advaita and renouncement of actions for those entitled to supreme knowledge, the second *mantra* teaches dutiful performance of rites for those entitled to action; and to a hypothetical objector marvelling at the partition Śaṅkara reminds the opposition 'unshakeable as a mountain'[14] previously established between knowledge and works.

Thus, in harmony with the aforesaid partition, he begs to take this triad (as well as the following one) as teaching *karma-mārga* ('path of works') to the worldly man, which stance has a further consequence on the interpretation of *vidyā*. By definition, the worldly man is not entitled to metaphysical knowledge; hence the *vidyā* here in question cannot possibly be *ātma-jñāna* ('knowledge of Self'), which is a prerogative of the world-renouncer, but only some kind of inferior knowledge open to any and all: namely, *devatā-jñāna*, or 'knowledge of the deities', as Śaṅkara clarifies.

---

from wise men, who have explained it to us. Knowledge and ignorance—a man who knows them both together, passes beyond death by ignorance, and by knowledge attains immortality'.

[13] Śaṅkara, p. ĪU$_1$ 10.6: *vidyāyā anyā 'vidyā*.

[14] Śaṅkara *ad* ĪU$_1$ 2, p. 5.9: *jñāna-karmaṇor virodhaṁ parvatavad akampyaṁ yathôktaṁ na smarasi kim*.

In sum, according to Śaṅkara the purport of the passage is to teach some sort of *jñāna-karma-samuccaya* only for the ordinary man, as the renouncer has no use soever for *karman*. On the other hand, the ordinary man has no right to supreme *vidyā*; the passage, then, must be understood to teach that the worldly man should not indulge the practice of rituals alone for their exclusive sake, lest he should plunge into deep darkness; but he should not even be satisfied with mere theoretical knowledge of the gods gained from study of the scriptures, shunning the actual practice of rites, lest he should enter darkness even deeper. He should, instead, combine both, in order to reap their distinct fruits: by the practice of *karman* he overcomes death, i.e. by ritualised action he sublimates natural desire-impelled action binding to death and *saṁsāra*, and by *devatā-jñāna* he attains immortality, i.e. oneness with the *iṣṭa-devatā* ('deity of one's choice'). This latter goal, of course, in Śaṅkara's perspective can only mean relative immortality, not to be confused with the absolute and definitive immortality of final emancipation in the attainment of oneness with *brahman*.

As anticipated, Vedāntadeśika concurs with Śaṅkara in taking *avidyā* to mean *karman*, but the agreement ends here. The synthetic conception of Viśiṣṭâdvaita views the world as really existing and rooted in *brahman*; accordingly, Vedāntadeśika is willing to grant actions their rightful place in so far as they are performed to fulfil one's duty[15] and without attachment, in conformity with the doctrine of *niṣkāma-karman* ('desireless action') propounded in the *Bhagavad-gītā*. Therefore, unlike Śaṅkara, Vedāntadeśika accepts the doctrine of *jñāna-karma-samuccaya* ('cumulative practice of knowledge and works') in some form, namely, as specified later in the text, as *viṣama-samuccaya* or 'asymmetrical accumulation': that is to say, he accepts Śaṅkara's dictum that in conformity with the scriptures knowledge alone is required for liberation, but admits that such knowledge may be enhanced by the subsidiary practice of good deeds. In this view, thus, works are subservient to liberation, though not on a par with knowledge, and their 'asymmetrical association' may be recommended.[16] Hence, unlike Śaṅkara, Vedāntadeśika finds no inconvenience in the passage in question, which he interprets to the effect that 'worshippers of ignorance plunging into darkness' are performers of actions for the sake of fruits, and 'devotees o knowledge plunging into darkness even deeper' are followers of knowledge alone who neglect their practical

[15] Vedāntadeśika, p. 18.5: *atrâvidyā-śabdâbhihitaṁ varṇâśrama-vihitaṁ karma* (quoting the *bhāṣya-kārāḥ*, which the translator takes to mean 'the Commentator on the *Vedānta Sūtras* (Śrī Rāmānuja)' ($\bar{I}U_2$: 55).

[16] He further specifies the flavour of the doctrine he favours, known as *saṁnipatyôpakāraka*, or of the 'proximate subserviency': works perform their ancillary function indirectly, by proximate synergy in furthering knowledge by removing obstacles to it—in contradistinction to Bhāskara's favoured flavour, known as *ārād-upakāraka*, or of the 'remote subserviency': works bring about their own result directly, as an ingredient of the final global result.

duties and fail to nurture knowledge with *niṣkāma-karman* ('desireless action').

The next stanza (ĪU 10), however, does posit a problem for him. In fact, if literally translated as 'one thing [is obtained] by means of knowledge, another by means of works', it would imply the joint efficiency of both knowledge and works on an equal footing, i.e. the doctrine of *sama-samuccaya*, or 'symmetrical accumulation', which Vedāntadeśika rejects as disproved by the scriptures, which unanimously declare the competence of knowledge alone to grant liberation.[17] So, it is now his turn to exhibit his hermeneutical adroitness: he contends that, according to the grammatical rule allowing transposition, here the instrumental case must be read as a replacement of the ablative, which must be supplied in order to satisfy the regimen of *anya* ('other, different'); in other words, he begs to take the couple *vidyā/avidyā* as governed by *anya*, and accordingly interprets '[the means of liberation] is different from [mere] knowledge, different from [mere] works'. It is, indeed, knowledge furthered by works, where the two, however, stand in *aṅgâṅgi-bhāva*, or in 'a relationship of subordinate and principal'.

This would only seem to postpone the difficulty to the third stanza, which again seems to unambiguously state that *vidyā* and *avidyā* are two independent means to attain two separate goals.[18] But Vedāntadeśika spares no effort to show that the discreteness of the means and goals is only apparent. With respect to the means: in reality, *avidyā* is just *karman* as an *aṅga* ('subordinate') of *vidyā*,[19] hence not separate but included in it; if it is mentioned as independent and equal, this is only because it must be viewed as such from the viewpoint of practice,[20] in so far as both the principal and the subsidiary, though essentially one, must be practised independently and equally. With respect to the goal: 'crossing death' and 'attaining immortality' both amount to the same, i.e. attainment of liberation: however, there is no redundancy in the passage,

[17] According to this view, advocated by Yādavaprakāśa, knowledge and works do not entertain a relationship of principal and subsidiary, with works merely assisting knowledge in reaping the one and only fruit—immortality (i.e. deliverance). Rather, they are considered each as a distinct means in its own right, leading to a distinct goal of its own; see VARADACHARI–THATHACARYA (1975: 36). The doctrine of *sama-samuccaya* is rejected by Vedāntadeśika on scriptural grounds, on the strength of 'the number of Śrutis, Smṛtis and Sūtras clearly declaring the relationship of principal and subsidiary obtaining between knowledge and works, and the crossing of death by knowledge alone' (Vedāntadeśika, p. 18.3: *karma-jñānayor aṅgâṅgi-bhāvaṁ vidyayâiva mṛtyu-taraṇaṁ ca vyaktaṁ pratipādayadbhiḥ śruti-smṛti-sūtra-gaṇaiḥ*). Śaṅkara, as we have seen, does not face such problems, as for him the passage is not meant for the *mumukṣu* ('seeker after liberation') in the first place.

[18] As per a literal reading of the *mantra*, '[he who practices the *samuccaya* ('accumulation')] having crossed death by works, by knowledge attains immortality'.

[19] Vedāntadeśika, p. 16.9: *avidyāṁ tad-aṅga-bhūta-karmâtmakām*.

[20] Vedāntadeśika, p. 16.10: *aṅgâṅginor anuṣṭeyatva-sāmyāt*.

and the apparent duplicity is justified, in so far as the first expression (*mṛtyuṁ tīrtvā*, 'having crossed death') lays stress on the destruction of obstacles[21] in the form of natural action leading to rebirth (and 'redeath'), whereas the second expression (*amṛtam aśnute*, 'attains immortality') lays stress on the final achievement ensuing from such destruction of obstacles.[22]

On the face of it, Madhva would seem the most scrupulous of the three commentators in that he provisionally adheres to the literal meaning of the terms involved, taking both *vidyā* and *avidyā* at their face value, as '[metaphysical] knowledge' and 'ignorance' to start with; but the net result is an even more liberal amount of unwarranted speculation in the overall interpretation of the passage.[23] The keystone is in the instrumentals in the second and third stanzas, seemingly specifying *vidyā* and *avidyā* as different means to different fruits. Now, it is implicit in the instrumental case that the instrumentality thereby expressed should be carried out by way of position (as contrasted to negation) of the relevant term.[24] For example, when we say that 'the house was burnt by fire', we obviously mean 'by kindling a fire' (or something of the sort), and it would be preposterous to suppose that we should mean 'by quenching a fire'; this, however, is exactly how Madhva begs us to understand the instrumental of *avidyā* in the passage being considered. In fact, like his fellows, Madhva is unable to find any value in ignorance as such, let alone the capability of producing positive fruits. Therefore, he boldly proceeds to turn the instrumental of *avidyā* inside out, so to speak, by simply postulating the ellipsis of a negative term: *avidyayā*, according to him, must stand for *avidyā-nindayā*, hence means not 'through ignorance' but 'through the blame of ignorance'! To be precise, Madhva does not produce this amazing piece of sleight of hand in explicit terms, for he confines himself to alleging an untraced Smṛti passage to support his claim, as he is wont to do in similar circumstances. But this is what the commentator Jayatīrtha makes of it.[25] For his part, the subcommentator Vādirāja is well aware of the venturesome nature of such interpretation, and tries his best to defend it with a fourfold argument.[26]

---

[21] Vedāntadeśika, p. 17.8–9: *mṛtyuṁ tīrtvêty asyôpāya*[a]*-virodhi-taraṇa-paratvāt.*

[[a] Sc.: *mokṣôpāya-°.*]

[22] Vedāntadeśika, p. 17.9: *amṛtam aśnuta iti prāpti-virodhi-nivṛtti-lābhôkteḥ.*

[23] As Jayatīrtha (*ad* ĪU$_3$ 9, p. 21.10–12) summarises the argument: *yathāvat paramâtma-jñānaṁ mokṣa-sādhanam ity uktam. na kevalaṁ tat. kiṁ nāma. anyathā-jñāna-nindā-samu<c>citam evêty etad-artha-pratipādakaṁ ādya-mantra-trayam*—'Right knowledge of the supreme self has been said to be the means for deliverance—but not just that. What then, pray? It must be associated with censure of false knowledge: this is the purport of the first triad'.

[24] Of course, this is but a particular case of the general 'positivity' of language.

[25] Jayatīrtha *ad* ĪU$_3$ 10, p. 22.8: *avidyayā anyathā-jñāna-nindayā ca iti yāvat.*

[26] Vādirāja *ad* ĪU$_3$ 10, p. 22.12–16: *avidyayā anyathā-jñāna-nindayā ity atra avidyayā mokṣâika-deśa-prāpter asaṁbhavāt avidyā-nindanasya prāk-prastutatvāc ca yathā-śruta-vidyâvidyayoḥ bhinna-phalatvasya sarva-sammatatvenâvaktavyakatvac*[a] *câvidyayā mṛtyuṁ tīrtvā iti mokṣâika-deśa-rūpa-phalasya vakṣyamānatvac ca nindayā iti padam adhyāhṛtya*

This notion of *avidyā* as something instrumental to liberation not through its application but though its rejection reflects back on the interpretation of the first stanza. Here there is no question for Madhva of the feasibility of *jñāna-karma-samuccaya*, as was the case with Śaṅkara and Vedāntadeśika, since he does not share their interpretation of *avidyā* as works, whether to be cumulated or not with knowledge. In what respect is, then, *vidyā* by itself inadequate, and 'leading to even deeper darkness' than *avidyā*? Because although those who resort to *avidyā*, here in its rightful meaning as 'false knowledge'—or, through the lenses of Madhva's theistic perspective, worship of other (false) gods (*anyathôpāsanā*)—are bound for darkness, they do not fare better who j u s t pay allegiance to *vidyā* or 'true knowledge' (*sc.* knowledge of the true God) w i t h o u t at the same time rebutting *avidyā*.

Indeed, Madhva's peculiarly sectarian and proselytising stance is clearly evinced by the probably made-up Smṛti he adduces by way of running commentary to the three stanzas, to the effect that, although the worshippers of any god but Viṣṇu may plunge into darkness, even deeper darkness awaits those Vaiṣṇava devotees who refrain from denouncing misbelievers. *Vidyā* and *avidyā* (in the aforesaid negative sense) should be practised jointly, because each is capable of producing its distinctive fruit. As Jayatīrtha clarifies, *vidyā* and *avidyā* are *upalakṣaṇa*s ('implicit designations') for 'adherence to God's true essence', and, respectively, 'due condemnation of false knowledge':[27] by the latter one crosses over ignorance and sorrow expressed by the word 'death', while by the former one attains knowledge and happiness conveyed by the word 'immortality'.

Even more difficult for the three commentators proves the interpretation of the second triad, running thus:

> *andhaṁ tamaḥ praviśanti ye 'saṁbhūti m upāsate /*
> *tato bhūya iva te tamo ya u saṁbhūtyāṁ ratāḥ* // 12 //
> *anyad evâhuḥ saṁbhavād anyad āhur asaṁbhavāt /*
> *iti śuśruma dhīrāṇāṁ ye nas tad vicacakṣire* // 13 //
> *saṁbhūtiṁ*[28] *ca vināśaṁ ca yas tad vedôbhayaṁ saha /*

vyākhyātam iti bhāvaḥ.—'By ignorance, i.e. by censuring false knowledge: here the commentator has supplied the word "by censuring" by way of explanation, because [1] ignorance as such cannot possibly be a partial factor for the attainment of deliverance; [2] the blame of ignorance has been mentioned previously [and therefore it cannot be implicitly praised here]; [3] as per the current notion of knowledge and ignorance, it would be pointless to declare their fruits to be different, this being a matter of common agreement; and, finally, because [4] in the next verse ignorance will actually be mentioned as a partial factor of deliverance [which by itself it cannot possibly be, as said previously]'.

[[a] The original incorrectly reads °*âvaktavyaktatvāc* through dittography.]

[27] Jayatīrtha *ad* ĪU$_3$ 11, p. 22.29–30: *vidyā-padaṁ īśvarayâthâtmyasya avidyā-padaṁ ca anyathā-jñāna-nindyatvasya upalakṣaṇam*.

[28] Śaṅkara: (*a*)*saṁbhūtiṁ*.

vināśena mṛtyuṁ tīrtvā saṁbhūtyâmṛtam[29] *aśnute* // 14 //[30]

At first sight, this triad appears to duplicate the structure of the previous one, literally reproducing it word for word but for the substitution of the pair of opposites *vidyā*/*avidyā* with the new pair *saṁbhūti* ('origination') / *asaṁbhūti* ('non-origination'). A couple of discrepancies, however, do exist: apart from the ablatives (*saṁbhavād*/*asaṁbhavād*) in the place of the instrumentals (*vidyayā*/*avidyayā*) in stanza 13, the most conspicuous difference is the looseness in the designation of the new pair of opposites, which are termed in turn *saṁbhūti* ('origination')/*asambhūti* ('non-origination'), *saṁbhava* ('becoming')/*asaṁbhava* ('non-becoming') and (on the face of it) *saṁbhūti* ('origination') / *vināśa* ('destruction').

Vedāntadeśika and Madhva, for their part, do not make much of such discrepancies, assuming an obvious correspondence between the two triads. Such correspondence, however, does not suit Śaṅkara, whose interpretation totally disrupts the parallelism with the help of sophisticated arguments which elicit Jayatīrtha's caustic remark alluded to in the title of this paper.

To start with, there is no agreement among the three commentators on the meaning of *saṁbhūti* and *asaṁbhūti*.[31] Śaṅkara takes *asaṁbhūti* to mean the 'ingenerate' which is the cause of generated effects, i.e. the unmanifest Nature (*prakṛti*); and *saṁbhūti* to mean the 'generated', i.e. the effect-*brahman* (i.e. the creator god Brahmā) in the form of the 'golden germ' of creation (*hiraṇyagarbha*). As was the case with the former triad, Śaṅkara considers this triad also as meant for the worldly man, who is directed to meditate both on Nature and on Brahmā to reap the respective fruits. The fruit ensuing from meditation on Brahmā is the attainment of *siddhi*s or 'supernatural powers'[32], as Śaṅkara

---

[29] Śaṅkara: *tīrtvâsaṁbhūtyâmṛtam*.

[30] E.g. OLIVELLE (1998: 409): 'Into blind darkness they enter, people who worship non-becoming; and into still blinder darkness, people who delight in becoming. It's far different from coming-into-being, they say, different also from not coming-into-being, we're told—so have we heard from wise men, who have explained it all to us. The becoming and the destruction—a man who knows them both together, passes beyond death by the destruction, and by the becoming attains immortality'

[31] Other commentators are also at variance as to the meaning of the terms. According to Uvaṭa (p. 55.4 ff.), *asaṁbhūti* means 'non-(re)birth' after death (*mṛtasya sataḥ punaḥ saṁbhavo nâsti*), and Lokāyatikas (materialists) are targeted as zealots of this doctrine; Mahīdhara (p. 55.16 ff.) concurs, but identifies partisans of *asaṁbhūti* as Bauddhas. On the other hand, both identify *saṁbhūti* as *ātman* and censure its exclusive devotees (Uvaṭa, p. 55.10 ff.; Mahīdhara, p. 55.18 ff.) for their intellectual pride (Uvaṭa, p. 55.11: *sva-buddhim adbhūtāṁ vibhāvayantaḥ*—'fancying their own mind very smart'; Mahīdhara, p. 55.19: *sva-buddhi-lāghavam ajānānāḥ*—'not realising the triviality of their mind') which leads them to regard *jñāna-kāṇḍa* ('[Vedic] department of knowledge') alone, neglecting *karma-kāṇḍa* ('[Vedic] department of ritual works').

[32] *Siddhi*s or *vibhūti*s are traditionally reckoned as eight, but their identification is not uniform. The nine candidates include: *aṇiman* ('parvification'), *mahiman* ('magnification'),

specifies further on. The fruit of meditation on Nature consists in the condition of *prakṛti-laya* ('merged into Nature'), described by the subcommentator Ānandagiri as an unconscious state akin to deep sleep, a sort of mock isolation desirable on account of the absence of pain inherent in *saṁsāra*.[33]

Now, the problem arises how to make this interpretation of *saṁbhūti* ('origination') and *asaṁbhūti* ('non-origination') square with stanza 14, which states the fruits of *saṁbhūti* and *vināśa* ('destruction'). Since *saṁbhūti* is expressly brought up by name, the inference lies near at hand that *vināśa* should be a replacement for *asaṁbhūti*, as indeed understood by the other commentators. The stanza would therefore connect meditation on *asaṁbhūti* with crossing over death, and meditation on *saṁbhūti* with attaining immortality. But this is unacceptable for Śaṅkara, who identifies, as we have seen, *saṁbhūti* with Brahmā: the god cannot grant immortality, but only the *siddhis* ('supernatural powers'), which can but help overcome death consisting in powerlessness and finitude. On the other hand, since *asaṁbhūti* has been identified with Nature, meditation on it can truly be said to grant the sort of immortality consisting in absorption in the unmanifest ground of being. So, according to

---

laghiman ('levitation'), *gariman* ('gravitation'), *prāpti* ('extensibility'), *prākāmya* ('unhindered will'), *īśitva* ('supremacy') *vaśitva* ('subjugation'), *kāmâvasāyitva*/*satya-saṁkalpatva* ('self-realising wish'). They are hinted at in *sūtra* 45 of the *Vibhūti-pāda* of the *Yoga-sūtra* (YS 4), but there are discrepancies among the lists given by different commentators. Vyāsa (YBh 4.45) with Vācaspatimiśra (TVai 4.45), Vijñānabhikṣu (YV 4.45) and Bhāvāgaṇeśa (YSP 4.45) omits *gariman,* Rāmānanda (YSMP 4.45) and Sadāśivendra (YSuK 4.45) reduce *satya-saṁkalpatva*/ *kāmâvasāyitva*) to *prākāmya*, while Nāgojībhaṭṭa (YSVṛ 4.45) apparently reduces it to *vaśitva*. *Bhāgavata-purāṇa* 11.15.4–5 (cit. in YV 4.45) likewise has a list without *gariman*. As for Bhoja (YRM 4.45), according to some editions he actually lists all nine, but since the disagreement with the traditional number of eight is inadmissible, the variant reading of Jīvānanda Vidyāsagara's edition (YS_3) should probably be accepted, omitting *prāpti* but subsuming its content under *prākāmya*. Cf. MAGNONE (1991: 131 f.).

[33] Ānandagiri *ad* $ĪU_1$ 14, p. 13.18–19: *sāṁsāri-duḥkhânubhavâbhāvena ca suṣuptivat prakṛti-layasya puruṣeṇârthyamānatâpy upapadyate*. *Prakṛti-laya*s ('merged into Nature') are mentioned also in YS 1.19 (together with *videha*s, or 'incorporeal') as a class of beings experiencing a sort of spontaneous non-cognitive enstasis (*asaṁprajñāta-samādhi*), which, however, is inferior to the corresponding condition acquired through *yoga* in that it only yields temporary results and not ultimate *mokṣa*. According to Vyāsa, *prakṛti-laya*s are those 'whose mind together with its object has dissolved into Nature, so that they experience a sort of isolation, until they come back by the compulsion of their [still unaccomplished] object' (*prakṛti-layāḥ sādhikare* [= *acaritârthe* (Vācaspatimiśra)] *cetasi prakṛti-līne kaivalya-padam ivânubhavanti yāvan na punar āvarttate 'dhikāra-vaśāc cittam*). Vācaspatimiśra (TVai 1.19) expands explaining that *prakṛti-laya*s, having identified with *prakṛti* or its intermediate evolutes, have their internal organ permeated with the corresponding unconscious habits (*vāsanā*), and dissolve into them after the fall of the body. However, their object (i.e. the attainment of discriminative knowledge) being unfulfilled, they are again differentiated by the force of their unaccomplished task, much in the same way as dried-up frogs metamorphosed into lumps of clay revive again with their former frog body when sprinkled with rain; cf. MAGNONE (1991: 39 f.).

his own preconception, Śaṅkara would rather have the stanza say quite the reverse of what it actually does—and he accordingly proceeds to turn it the other way round: i.e. *saṁbhūti* must be metamorphosed into *asaṁbhūti*, and *vināśa*, contrary to all plausibility, must be the same as *saṁbhūti*. The latter part is not difficult: as *hiraṇya-garbha* ('golden germ' of creation) had previously been termed *saṁbhūti*[34] in so far as generated, just so is he now termed *vināśa*[35] in so far as destructible; he is, in fact, *apara-brahman* ('lower Brahman') or *kārya-brahman* ('effect-Brahman'), hence, as an effect, liable to both generation and destruction. The former part, however, poses more of a problem: how to turn the two occurrences of *saṁbhūti* into *asaṁbhūti*? *Sandhi* comes in handy for the second occurrence: because word boundaries need not be acknowledged in the script, *tīrtvā saṁbhūtyā* can conveniently be read as *tīrtvâsaṁbhūtyā*, i.e. a conflation of *tīrtvā* and *asaṁbhūtyā*. The first occurrence, though, is more resilient to possible manipulations, being the very first word of the stanza; but here Śaṅkara performs a veritable *coup de théâtre*, apparently bringing to bear the *guṇa* vowel of the ending of the previous stanza to postulate an *avagraha* of privative 'a' in the next one.[36] Of course, rules of external *sandhi* do not normally obtain across major metrical boundaries, and so it is not surprising that the *dvaitin* Jayatīrtha should sarcastically applaud the hermeneutical exploit as a specimen of *apūrva-vyākaraṇa-kauśala* ('unprecedented grammatical skill').[37]

---

[34] Śaṅkara *ad* ĪU$_1$ 12, p. 12.3–5: *saṁbhavanaṁ saṁbhūtiḥ sā yasya kāryasya sā saṁbhūtiḥ. ... bahutaram iva tamaḥ praviśanti ya u saṁbhūtyāṁ kārya-brahmaṇi hiraṇya-garbhâkhye ratāḥ.*

[35] Śaṅkara *ad* ĪU$_1$ 14, p. 12.12–13.4: *vinaśena vināśo dharmo yasya kāryasya sa tena dharminâbhedhenôcyate vināśa iti. tena tad-upāsanena ... hiraṇya-garbhôpāsanena hy aṇimâdi-prāptiḥ phalam.*

[36] Śaṅkara *ad* ĪU$_1$ 14, p. 13.5–6: *saṁbhūtiṁ ca vināśaṁ cêty atrâvarṇa-lopena nirdeśo draṣṭavyaḥ. prakṛti-laya-phala-śruty-anurodhāt.*—'[In the chunk] *saṁbhūtiṁ ca vināśaṁ ca* the reference must be understood with the elision of an *a*, in compliance with what has been heard as the fruit of absorption into Nature.' Once again, IYER (1995: 36 f.) goes out of his way to justify Śaṅkara, adducing arguments in support of his explanation from other commentators as well as his own to the effect that: (1) by the rule that *utpattimad vastu vināśi avaśyam* ('what is originated must needs be perishable'), *vināśa* must mean *saṁbhūti*, hence *saṁbhūti* must be read as *asaṁbhūti* to avoid repetition; (2) elision of *a* is permissible according to the rule *pṛṣôdarâdīni yathôpadiṣṭam* (A 6.3.109) allowing the elision and mutation of letters in vedic usage; (3) by Jaimini's rule *saṁdigdhe tu* (*saṁdigdheṣu* is the original reading, which however IYER (1995) quotes as *saṁdigdhe tu*) *vākya-śeṣāt* (MS 1.4.29: 'In case of doubt, the meaning should be gathered from the context.')—in this case, the traditional doctrine about *prakṛtilayas* and their reward. His final verdict is: 'Śrī Śaṅkarâcārya's interpretation of the *mantras* gives the correct purport of the *mantra* and is in perfect agreement with the *śāstras* [!]'.

[37] Jayatīrtha *ad* ĪU$_3$ 14, p. 25.9–10: *akāra-lopena saṁbhūtir avyākṛtam ity apūrvaṁ vyākaraṇa-kauśalam ity āstām.*—'As to [the submission that] the word *saṁbhūti* means the Unevolved [i.e. Nature] through loss of an *a*, here is [a specimen of] unprecedented grammatical skill—and so let it remain'.

Madhva's explanation of the triad, however, is no less idiosyncratic, beginning from his interpretation of the meaning of the couple *saṁbhūti*/*asaṁbhūti*. Actually, even for this triad, as for the foregoing, his gloss consists in one long running quotation from the *Kūrma-purāṇa*, presumably forged, as is so often the case with Madhva's quotes, since the passage cannot be traced in the published text. Jayatīrtha explicates Madhva's intent to the effect that *saṁbhūti* means 'creator' by metonymy (i.e. as the cause of *saṁbhūti* or 'creation') whereas *asaṁbhūti*, as is plain to see, by the same token must mean 'un-creator'[38]! The stanza, therefore, threatens darkness and more darkness for those who do not acknowledge Viṣṇu as creator, or one-sidedly recognise him as creator o n l y , whereas he is both creator and destroyer.[39] The knowledge of Viṣṇu's true nature is not confined to the need of avoiding negative consequences, it also yields positive fruits: by the knowledge of Viṣṇu as destroyer one destroys the bonds to the body (and so crosses death), whereas by the knowledge of him as creator of all good things one attains immortality in the form of sameness and identity with Viṣṇu, which not even the liberated can enjoy.

Vedāntadeśika puts forward still another interpretation of the couple *saṁbhūti*/*asaṁbhūti*. The former he takes to mean 'communion' (i.e., literally, 'being together') with *brahman*, on the strength of scriptural passages. This choice, however, leaves him in an awkward position when it comes to understanding the latter member of the couple. As he remarks himself, it would not be proper to understand *asaṁbhūti* in an obvious way, as either prior or subsequent non-existence of *saṁbhūti* (i.e. as its not yet/no longer being there respectively before/after its achievement), because how could the absence of *saṁbhūti*—a means towards immortality—conceivably represent in itself a means for crossing death (as said in the third strophe of the triad)[40]? Therefore, here is the solution advanced by the Svāmin: the word *asaṁbhūti*, while excluding *saṁbhūti*, must mean something that, although not (yet) communion, is proximate to it as its precondition in the form of removal of obstacles: this is the meaning that is

---

[38] Jayatīrtha *ad* ĪU$_3$ 12, p. 23.20: *asaṁbhūtiṁ jagat-sṛṣṭer akartāraṁ*, with the subcommentator's gloss: *na vidyate saṁbhūtir yasmād* (Vādirāja *ad loc.*).

[39] Madhva *ad* ĪU$_3$ 12, p. 23.12–15:

> (...) *evaṁ sṛṣṭi-kartṛtvaṁ nāṅgī-kurvanti ye hareḥ /*
> *te 'pi yanti tamo ghoraṁ tathā saṁhāra-kartṛtām //*
> *nāṅgī-kurvanti te 'py evaṁ tasmāt sarva-guṇâtmakam /*
> *sarva-kartāram īśêśaṁ sarva-saṁhāra-kārakam //*

Here the root expression *ye 'saṁbhūtim upāsate* is boldly taken as tantamount to *ye* [*harim*] *saṁbhūtim nôpāsate.*

[40] Vedāntadeśika *ad* ĪU$_2$ 12, p. 19.9–10: *na câtrâsaṁbhūti-śabdena saṁbhūter anutpattir vināśo vā pratipādyaḥ. amṛta-prāpti-hetutayôktāyāḥ saṁbhūteḥ prāg-abhāvasya pradhvaṁsasya vā mṛtyu-taraṇa-hetutvena vaktum ayuktatvāt.*

gathered by the subsequent substitution of the word *vināśa* for *asaṁbhūti*[41], as well as for want of a better interpretation.

The foregoing review, albeit cursory, may perhaps suffice to give a fair idea of some of the sophisticated hermeneutical strategies devised by the three commentators—i.e. Śaṅkara, Vedāntadeśika and Madhva—to justify their vastly different interpretations. And so, in the end, 'What did the *Upaniṣad* really say' has proved once again a hopeless question, like the squaring of the (hermeneutical) circle. In any case, whatever it did say, in the original setting of master and disciple, when the sacred power of the Word (*brahman*) was called upon 'to sustain them both, to nourish them both, so that their joint effort might be fruitful, and their study might be bright' (to paraphrase the auspicious invocation that would inaugurate their meetings)[42]—and most of all, when the inordinate quibbling of the commentators was not yet there to spoil the truth of the Word (*mā vidviṣāvahai!*)[43]—alas, is no longer for us to grasp. Which, incidentally, may retrospectively justify the ancient Indian aversion for committing the Word to the written leaf, where it would be helplessly exposed to the vagaries of both haters and (misguided?) well-wishers—the same aversion that was shared by Plato, when he wrote about the *logoi* that once written down 'go about everywhere, among the knowledgeable and the ignorant alike, and if faulted or treated unfairly must appeal to their father for help, because, left to their own devices, they can neither defend nor support themselves…'[44]

BIBLIOGRAPHY

A = Pāṇini: *Aṣṭādhyāyī*. Śrisa Chandra Vasu (tr.): *The Aṣṭādhyāyī of Pāṇini*. Sindhu Charan Bose, Benares 1897.

Ānandagiri = Ānandagiri: *Īśôpaniṣad-bhāṣya-ṭīkā*. See: $\bar{I}U_1$.

ĪU = *Īśôpaniṣad* [*Īśā-vāsyôpaniṣad*]. (1) S. Subrahmanyashastri (ed.): *Śrīśaṅkarâcārya-viracitam upaniṣad-bhāṣyam śrīmad-ānandagiry-ācārya-kṛta-ṭīkayā kaṭha-māṇḍukya-taittirīya-bhāṣyāṇāṁ prasi-*

[41] Vedāntadeśika *ad* $\bar{I}U_2$ 12, p. 19.6–8: *tāṁ* [*saṁbhūtiṁ*] *paryudasyann ayam asaṁbhūti-śabdaḥ tad-āsanna-pratibandha-vināśam abhidhatte. saṁbhūtiṁ ca vināśaṁ ca ity api hy anantaram ucyate.*

[42] *saha nāv avatu. saha nau bhunaktu. saha vīryaṁ karavāvahai. tejasvi nāv adhītam astu*—so prays the *śānti-mantra* of the *Kṛṣṇa Yajur-veda*, which would be recited before every session of study of the *Upaniṣads*.

[43] *Śānti-mantra* of the *Kṛṣṇa Yajur-veda*. Literally 'let us not be hostile to each other', but interpreted by some in the given context as 'let us not entertain conflicting views'.

[44] Plato, *Phaedrus* 275e (somewhat abridged and adapted).

ddhâcāryântara-ṭīkābhiḥ saṭīka-taittirīya-vārtikena ca samālaṁkṛtam. Khaṇḍaḥ 1. Maheśa Anusandhāna Saṁsthānam (Śrīdakṣiṇamūrti Maṭha Prakāśana), Varanasi 2004. (2) K.C. Varadachari; D.T. Thathacarya (eds.): *Īśāvāsyopaniṣadbhāṣyam by Śrī Vedānta Deśika.* Critically edited with introduction, translation and notes by... Vedanta Desika Reasearch Society, Madras 1975. (3) Shrisha Rao (ed.): *Īśā-vāsyôpaniṣad-bhāṣya-ṭīkā-prakāśikā-khaṇḍârthāḥ śaṅkara-bhāṣyaṁ ca.* [With Madhva's *Bhāṣya*, Vādirāja's *Ṭīkā*, Jayatīrtha's *Vivaraṇa* and Raghavendrayati's *Khaṇḍârtha*]. www.dvaita.org [2007]. (4) B.K. Iyer (ed.): *Īśāvāsyopaniṣad.* Including the original verses, *Śaṅkara-bhāṣya* text with a literal word by word English translation, copious notes and introduction. Vrajajivan Indological Studies 2, Chaukhamba Sanskrit Pratisthan, Delhi 1995. (5) Ācārya Śivaprasāda Dvivedi (ed.): *Īśā-vāsyôpaniṣat. Hindy-anuvāda--pariśīlana-saṁvalita-śāṅkara-bhāṣyôpetā.* Caukhambā Surabhāratī Granthamālā 171, Caukhambā Surabhāratī Prakāśana, Vārāṇasī [no date]. (6) Devendranath Pandey (ed.): *Īśā-vāsyôpaniṣad-bhāṣya-saṁgraha. Śaṅkara-bhāṣyam, Uvaṭa-°, Sāyaṇa-°, Mahīdhara-°, Prakāśa-°, Yogapakṣyīyam Prakāśa-°, Svāmidayānanda-°,* R. Madhva. Roy, Griffith *kī ṭīkā sapadârthânvayaḥ hindī vyākhyā sahita.* Jagdish Sanskrit Pustakalaya, Jaipur 2001.

IYER 1995 = See: $\bar{I}U_4$.

Jayatīrtha = Jayatīrtha: *Īśā-vāsyôpaniṣad-vivaraṇa.* See: $\bar{I}U_3$.

Madhva = Madhva: *Īśôpaniṣad-bhāṣya.* See: $\bar{I}U_3$.

MAGNONE 1991 = Magnone, Paolo (ed. & tr.): *Patañjali. Aforismi dello Yoga* (*Yogasūtra*). [With Bhoja's *Rāja-mārtaṇḍa* commentary, introduction and subcommentary by...]. Magnanelli Promolibri, Torino 1991.

Mahīdhara = Mahīdhara: *Īśā-vāsyôpaniṣad-bhāṣya.* See: $\bar{I}U_6$.

MESQUITA 1977 = Mesquita, Roque: *Madhva und seine unbekannten literarischen Quellen. Einige Beobachtungen.* Publications of the De Nobili Research Library 24, Institut für Südasien-, Tibet- und Buddhismuskunde der Universität Wien, Wien 1997.

MESQUITA 2007 = Mesquita, Roque: *Madhvas Zitate aus den Purāṇas und dem Mahābhārata: Eine analytische Zusammenstellung nicht identifizierbarer Quellenzitate in Madhvas Werken nebst Übersetzung und Anmerkungen.* Publications of the De Nobili Research Library 24, Institut für Südasien-, Tibet- und Buddhismuskunde der Universität Wien, Wien 2007

MS = Jaimini: *Mīmāṁsā-sūtra.* B.D. Basu (ed.); Mohan Lal Sandal (transl.): *The Mīmāṁsā Sūtras of Jaiminī.* The Sacred Books of the Hindus 27,1. Sudhindre Nath Basu, Allahabad 1923.

OLIVELLE 1998 = Olivelle, Patrick (ed. & tr.): *The Early Upaniṣads.* Oxford University Press, New York 1998.

Phaedrus = Plato: *Phaedrus.* J. Burnet (ed.): *Platonis Opera. Tomus II tetralogias III–IV continens.* Oxford Classical Texts, Oxford University Press, Oxford 1922.

ROCHER 2008 = Rocher, Ludo: 'Review of *Madhvas Zitate aus den Purāṇas und dem Mahābhārata: Eine analytische Zusammenstellung nicht identifizierbarer Quellenzitate in Madhvas Werken nebst Übersetzung und Anmerkungen.* By Roque Mesquita', Journal of the American Oriental Society 128,3 (2008) 603–606.

SHARMA 1961/2000 = Sharma, B.N.K: *History of the Dvaita School of Vedānta and its Literature.* Motilal Banarsidass, Delhi 2000 [first edition: Bombay 1961].

SHARMA 2001 = Sharma, B.N.K: *My Latest Four Research Papers.* Published by the Author, Mumbai 2001.

Śaṅkara = Śaṅkara: *Īśôpaniṣad-bhāṣya.* See: $ĪU_1$, $ĪU_3$, $ĪU_4$, $ĪU_5$.

TVai = Vācaspatimiśra: *Tattva-vaiśāradī.* See: YS_1.

Uvaṭa = Uvaṭa: *Īśā-vāsyôpaniṣad-bhāṣya.* See: $ĪU_6$.

VARADACHARI–THATHACARYA 1975 = Varadachari, K.C.; Thathacarya, D.T.: 'Introduction' to $ĪU_2$, pp. 1–39.

Vedāntadeśika = Vedāntadeśika-svāmin: *Īśâvāsyôpaniṣad-bhāṣya.* See: $ĪU_2$.

YBh = [Vyāsa (ascribed):] *Yoga-bhāṣya.* See: YS_1.

YRM = Bhoja: *Yoga-rāja-mārtaṇḍa.* See: YS_2.

YS = Patañjali: *Yoga-sūtra.* (1) Gosvāmi Dāmodara Śāstrī (ed.): *Sāṁkhya-yoga-darśanam arthāt pātañjala-yoga-darśanam.* [With the scholium of Vyāsa and the commentaries *Tattva-vaiśāradī, Pātañjala-rāhasya, Yoga-vārttika* and *Bhāsvatī* by Vācaspati Miśra, Rāghavānanda Sarasvatī, Vijñāna Bhikṣu and Hariharānandāraṇya]. Edited with introduction, notes, indices, appendices etc. by … Kashi Sanskrit Series 110, Chaukhambha [sic] Sanskrit Sansthan, Varanasi 1989. (2) Paṇḍit Ḍhuṇḍhirāja Śāstri (ed.): *Maharṣi-patañjali-praṇītaṁ yoga-sūtram.* [With the commentaries *Rāja-mārtaṇḍa, Pradīpikā, Vṛtti, Maṇi-prabhā, Candrikā* and *Yoga-sudhākara* by Bhojarāja, Bhāvāgaṇeśa, Nāgojī Bhaṭṭa, Rāmānanda Yati, Anantadeva and Sadāśivendra Sarasvatī]. Kashi Sanskrit Series 83, Chaukhambha [sic] Sanskrit Sansthan, Varanasi 1982.

YSMP = Rāmānanda Yati: *Yoga-sūtra-maṇi-prabhā.* See: YS_2.

YSP = Bhāvāgaṇeśa: *Yoga-sūtra-pradīpikā.* See: YS_2.

YSuK = Sadāśivendra Sarasvatī: *Yoga-sudhā-kara.* See: YS_2.

YSVṛ = Nāgojībhaṭṭa: *Vṛtti.* See: YS_2.

YV = Vijñānabhikṣu: *Yoga-vārttika.* See: YS_1.

Theory of World View

'World view' as a topic of research in Indian studies

CLAUS OETKE

1. This paper pursues the question of whether and under which conditions investigations concerning a topic that is vaguely demarcated by the expression 'world view' promise to be relevant and fruitful. The account is preliminary because it will be confined to an exploration of some pertinent aspects of Indian traditions of thought. On the other hand, the issue will be assessed against the background of some particular conceptual specification of the notion of 'world view'. It is our intention that the considered conceptual specification or 'implementation' of the term 'world view' should be in accordance with the rather vague notion(s) associated with this expression. Nevertheless, it is not meant to merely reflect existing intuitions connected with that expression, and therefore it must be conceded from the outset that there could be other equally legitimate specifications of the pertinent term. It can be reasonably expected, however, that the existence of legitimate divergent ways of defining the notion will not crucially affect the validity of claims suggested in the subsequent paragraphs.

2. The term 'world view', as it is used in the present context, can be considered as a fairly close correlate of the German expression 'Weltanschauung'. There are in fact dictionaries which explicitly declare that 'world view' is another word for 'Weltanschauung'[1] and the expression 'Weltanschauung' occurs as an entry in both technical and non-technical English lexicons and dictionaries. A current explanation of 'Weltanschauung' reads: 'a comprehensive view (or philosophy) of human life and the universe.'[2] The following characterisation of 'world view' accords quite well with such explanations. It reads:

> 'World' view is a comprehensive view concerning (a) the totality of which human beings are necessarily a part and (b) the ways in which those parts are related to this totality.

[1] See e.g. CED, p. 1770.

[2] E.g. FLEW (1984: 37): 'Any general view of the Universe and man's relationship to it. Usually the term is applied to a philosophy affecting the practical (as opposed to purely theoretical) attitudes and beliefs of its adherents'; CED, p. 1743: 'a comprehensive view or personal philosophy of human life and the universe'.

World View and Theory in Indian Philosophy
Warsaw Indological Studies 5 (2012) 369–380.

It is not difficult to see that the expression 'the totality of which human beings are necessarily a part' represents an attempt of capturing a relevant import which the expression 'world' as a component of 'world view' possesses. 'World' occurs equally as a component in expressions, such as 'the world of literature', 'the world of computers' etc. and sometimes it appears like a synonym of 'the earth'. The purpose of the reformulation is to avert those and other readings that imply a restriction to some more specific area. On the other hand the explicit reference to the relation of being a part-of excludes certain types of objects to which the pertinent view could pertain. It is thereby stipulated that e.g. outlooks concerning language or natural numbers should not or not automatically qualify as specimens of the category of 'world view', given that 'language' and 'natural number' do not specify realms of entities of which humans must be a part. Such views could emerge as ingredients of possible world views, however, given that an outlook pertaining to some comprehensive whole to which human beings belong as a part entails them. A pertinent example could be a theory which explicitly claims that human beings are part of a comprehensive universe to which also types of abstract objects, such as languages and numbers belong. In a similar vein issues pertaining to the existence or non-existence of universals could attain the status of a component of a world view even if they would not represent a world view, or 'Weltanschauung', by themselves.

The second part of the elucidation represented by the words 'the ways in which those parts are related to this totality' is not extractable from a compositional analysis of the term 'world view' or its correlate 'Weltanschauung'. It reflects rather the fact that according to a common way of using those words the pertinent topic is broader than the one which would result if one delimited the realm in accordance with the compositional structure. However, against the background of the above presented elucidation, the extension is not capricious because there is a natural connection between the idea that a view pertains to some realm inasmuch as human beings are related to it in a particular manner on the one hand and the idea that a view pertains to the nature of the relation and to everything entailed by the existence of that relation on the other hand.

3. The explanation given so far is approximate and preliminary. We presume, however, that it suffices for demonstrating that the issue of 'world view' is a fairly complex matter. Showing the complexity of the issue is relevant in the present connection because it enhances the plausibility of the claim that investigations concerning world view as Weltanschauung possess potential importance provided the scope of the topic is adequately delimited. We employ the following diagram to illustrate certain aspects of the complexity of this subject. In this manner the above presented rudimentary explication of the notion is supplemented. A major aim consists in pointing out distinctions which are potentially pertinent for cultural or historical studies whose topic lies in particular aspects of the intuitive notion of world view. This could help to obtain a clearer awareness of the specific nature and the limitations affecting individual investigations and their individual subject-matter. On the other hand one can expect that in this manner the chances for detecting possible novel areas of research are increased. The diagram exhibits a number of varieties which could occur either as diverse types of world view or as different components of a world view. It is presented and explained below.

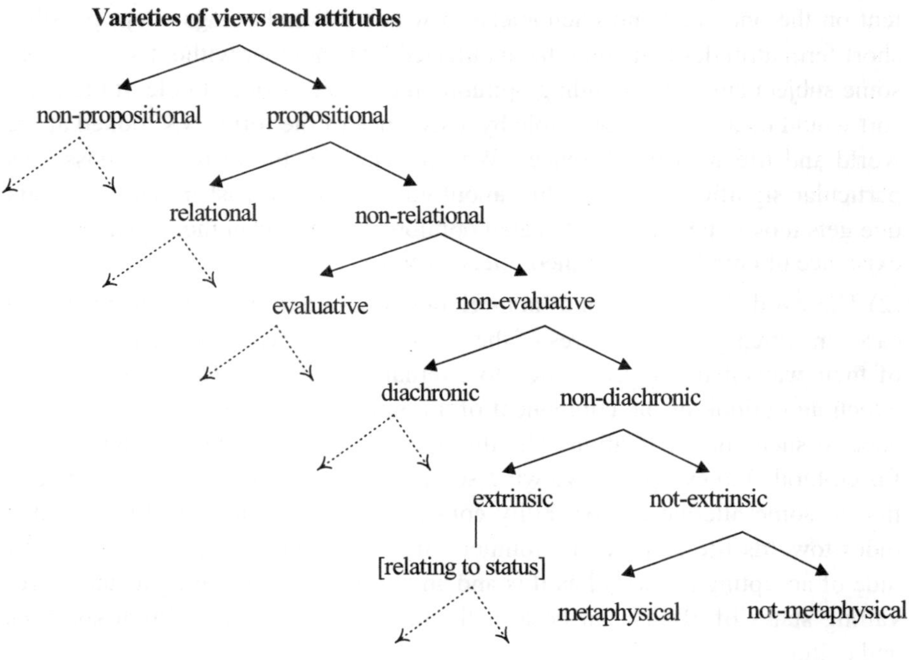

Diagram D

The branches in diagram D embody binary distinctions. If nothing written appears at the lower end of a line, this can be interpreted as a suggestion to the effect that the superordinate item might be sub-classified in the same or similar manner as its counterpart at the right. In this regard the diagram provides only a fragmentary description of the topic.

The above presented diagram is based on the general consideration that the verb 'view' and related expressions occur in constructions which do not necessarily imply the existence of any definite opinion concerning a subject's environment or his existence. Sentences, such as 'NN regards the world as miserable', 'NN viewed/looked at the world with indifference' etc. can be employed for possibly ascribing merely temporary attitudes manifested by behaviour such that a concerned subject is not even disposed to hold a corresponding general belief that something is the case. Since the diagram contains terms which are in need of further explication the following remarks are apposite for providing some pertinent clarifications.

(1) The distinction between 'propositional' and 'non-propositional' relates to the fact that possessing a view does not always entail possession of some belief or opinion with respect to some content expressible by a *that*-clause containing a sentence. The intention of making the distinction here is to differentiate between the occurrence of beliefs or opinions pertaining to some assertible content on the one hand and phenomena in which rational beings adopt possibly short-term attitudes that could be manifested by behaviour without assigning to some subject any corresponding opinion on the other. An example of the latter sort would be a stance expressible by a sentence of the form 'NN looked at the world and life with indifference'. We presume that the distinction possesses particular significance for studies about cultures of the past because the data one gets mostly pertain to advocated opinions leaving open the question of the existence of correlating non-theoretical attitudes.

(2) The words 'relational' and 'non-relational' relate to the difference between cases in which general features of the environment to which humans belong or of their way of living are related to alternative states-of-affairs and cases in which an outlook or the component of an outlook does not involve any reference to such sort of relation. The difference possesses potential significance for cultural studies because viewing something as it is and viewing it in relation to some alternative possibility constitute two significantly different attitudes towards life and the environment of living beings. In particular an attitude of accepting the world as it is and an attitude of questioning actually prevailing states of affairs can be a distinguishing feature of different societies and cultures.

(3) The opposition between 'evaluative' and 'non-evaluative' should signal the difference between stances involving judgements of value and stances which do not. Fatalism arises as a purely non-evaluative stance as long as it entails merely a claim to the effect that courses of events in the world cannot be influenced by human will and human likes or dislikes to some substantial degree. In contrast an evaluative variant of fatalism would occur, if this outlook were combined with a judgement to the effect that the prevailing state of affairs is deplorable —or alternatively that it deserves a positive appraisal.

(4) 'Diachronic' and 'non-diachronic' relate to the divergence between judgements pertaining to the possibility of alterations in time and judgements of which this is not true. The first term in the sense intended here need not refer to views advocating temporal change. A view expressible by the sentence 'All causal laws are invariable in time' belongs to the diachronic variety. Decisive is whether a proposition involves quantifications over different time-segments.

(5) The expression 'extrinsic' represents an attempt to account for a phenomenon that plays a prominent role in a number of teachings of Indian philoso-

phies and maybe elsewhere too. Statements such as 'There are no particulars on the level of ultimate reality' or 'The world of diverse phenomena is illusory' are not appropriately analysed as propositions indicating a property of particulars or the nature of phenomena because they disclaim their very existence, at least on some level of final analysis. One could characterise them as specifying the status of the world of diverse phenomena, provided one keeps in mind that they must not be understood as assignments of some status to a plurality of things considered as existent on the ultimate level of reality. The term 'extrinsic' has been chosen to account for the peculiar feature of statements of the pertinent sort as well as views embodied by them. It should go without saying that not all outlooks which could be classified as a world view or as a component of a world view exhibit this property.

(6) Statements can differ in the respect that they either relate or do not relate phenomena to some level of reality that is not accessible to observation but might be supposed to explain most general features of the observable environment. We have employed the term 'metaphysical' with the intention to refer to the first category without claiming that this usage of the word is the only legitimate one or corresponds to some original or most common way of employment. The distinction itself appears relevant at least against the background of investigations about philosophical or non-philosophical outlooks encountered in different cultures. For the origination of the idea that general features exhibited by the environment to which human beings belong as a part might be due to the existence of objects differing in kind from anything encountered in the phenomenal world is a phenomenon of considerable significance. This marks a difference from traditions where analogous explanatory functions are allocated to the hypothesis of gods and their actions. — It might be appropriate to point out that according to the pertinent sense of the word ontological questions are not *eo ipso* metaphysical issues. In particular views regarding the question of the existence of universals are not classifiable as metaphysical without additional premises.

4. Despite the complexity and breadth of the subject matter partly explicated in the preceding paragraph it would be definitely false to assert that it encompasses everything that matters in Indian religions or philosophies. Presumably the doctrine of Madhyamaka advocated a tenet entailing that the entertainment of any world view is unsuitable and that, strictly speaking, there cannot be any correct world view. The decisive point is that the negation of a world of particulars of which human beings could be a part on the level of final analysis does not exhaust the content of the original teaching of Madhyamaka because philosophical arguments are employed to establish that tenet. In the present connection it does not matter whether the arguments that should support the contention are in fact valid. Decisive is rather the circumstance that if there are such principles or premises not explicitly stated in pertinent textual sources, it follows that Indian philosophy transcends the realm of world views and is essentially more than a systematised 'Weltanschauung'. Ingredients come into play which cannot be plausibly regarded as constituents of a view about any actual or possible world but concern (mostly non-articulated) beliefs about possible ways of obtaining knowledge concerning a world. A similar consequence is equally intimated by the fact that doctrines of means of knowledge (*pramāṇa*) have been explicitly advocated in the context of establishing certain metaphysical or ontological tenets, such as the existence of a soul, the momentariness of all existing particulars etc. One could at most assert that such teachings provide ingredients for a theory of world view inasmuch as they represent methodological principles in whose light the validity of possible world views could be evaluated.

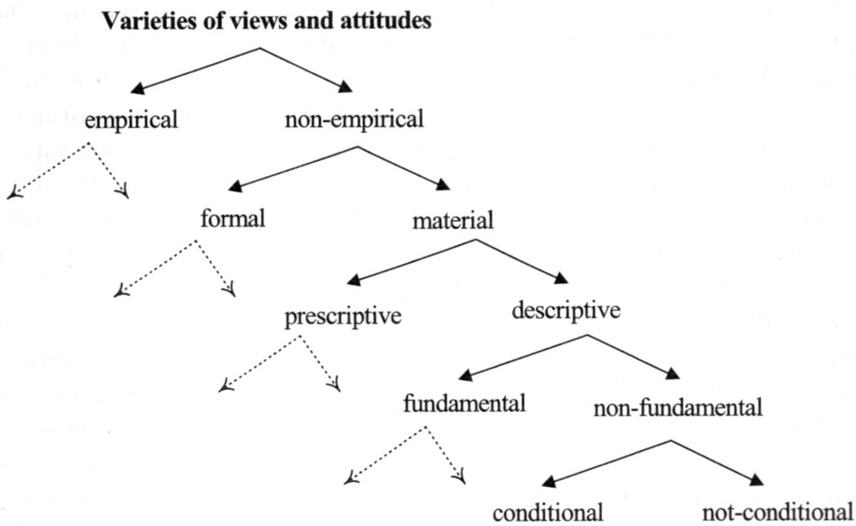

Diagram T

Even if one cannot assert that in the Indian tradition of thought particular schools or teachings were developed which have made the phenomenon of 'Weltanschauung' a topic of enquiry one is able to discern ingredients which at least implicitly concern this issue. Such ingredients could be designated by the term 'theorem of world view', where the possessive construction exemplifies an objective genitive. This label relates in a general way to propositions that concern the phenomenon of world view as an object of attribution of qualities, pertaining to questions such as the correctness of methodological principles establishing particular world views, the status of potential world views, its relevance and other comparable issues on a, so to speak, meta-level. In this regard one can equally differentiate between different conceivable varieties which are illustrated by the diagram T.

The principles of representation are the same as in diagram D. The dichotomy between 'empirical' and 'non-empirical' accounts for the fact that any statement or set of statements pertaining to 'world view' by implying attributions of properties can but need not aim at presenting some description of empirical facts, such as the ascertainment of contingent qualities exhibited by different views about the world that have occurred in the past. On the other hand accounts pertaining to world views can alternatively aspire at an ascertainment of particular qualities exhibited by individual actual or potential specimens of world view or at an elaboration of common features or relational properties pertaining to various actual or possible outlooks concerning a world. This difference is reflected by the dichotomy 'formal' and 'non-formal'. Thus the previous diagram D exemplifies an account of the non-empirical and formal variety. The very idea of a world view has been taken as a starting point and the exposition thereby contrasts with a type of account which analyses, classifies and systematises different varieties of world view that have been found to exist among various people in the world. On the other hand, it is formal in the sense that it neither entails the subsumption of any individual world view or component of a world view under one particular category nor contains propositions implying verdicts about the correctness or the appropriateness to adopt specific views about general features of the environment of human or other rational beings or properties of human life. As far as the dichotomy of prescriptive and descriptive theorems is concerned, one can presume that both components often go together although they can be neatly distinguished. The previously suggested account of Madhyamaka philosophy furnishes a pertinent example in this respect: On the one hand the teaching entails that there cannot be any view presupposing the existence of human beings and their environment on the level of ultimate truth and on the other hand it thereby intimates that it would be inappropriate to entertain views of this sort. In this manner the teaching of Madhyamaka represents a sophistication of the traditional Buddhist criticism of *dṛṣṭi*, a term which represents a notion which sometimes comes pretty close to that of 'Weltanschauung'. Inasmuch as the Madhyamaka-doctrine according to the analysis assumed here puts into question the very possibility of certain views and the appropriateness of adopting them one can characterise those theorems as fundamental. This stands in contrast to the equally possible stance which takes the possibility and adequacy of s o m e sort of view of the pertinent category for granted and merely suspends any definite judgement about the issue as to which particular view is correct and adequate. The difference between conditional and not-conditional theorems should relate to the logical form of pertinent propositions: The intended import is that only those theorems are conditional which, if they were adequately formalised, exhibit a semantic structure in which a (material or non-material) conditional operator has widest scope. Accordingly a theorem, such as 'All world views are inadequate' is not conditional because it can be analysed as a statement in which a conditional is in the scope of a universal quantifier, but not as a statement in which a conditional is the highest operator. In contrast a proposition of the form 'If P, then all world views are inadequate' represents a conditional theorem of world view in the intended sense. A major reason to refer to the distinction between conditional and non-conditional theorems lies in the presumption that their occurrence or non-occurrence can signal a relevant difference regarding level of reflection.

We are inclined to attribute major significance to the consequence that the fact that an account of a tradition of thought can be incomplete and defective as long as it confines its task to an analysis of varieties of 'Weltanschauung' is not a mere theoretical possibility.

5. The above exposition has been given in order to provide some guiding lines for investigations in the areas of non-Western philosophies and cultural traditions. It is presumed that the outlines of a, so to speak, 'logical geography' of a subject matter enhances, among other things, chances to detect phenomena of contingent non-occurrence in traditions of thought. In addition to this they should serve as a foil enabling one to structure observations concerning views held by foreign subjects. The following two examples should illustrate those points.

(1) Perhaps the Indian tradition ignores varieties of comparative world-assessments which are to be found in the Western traditions, such as the idea of a utopian world conceived as something that is possible in principle but never realised. At any rate, conceptions of ideal states-of-affairs representing highest goals of human existence or the occurrence of the view that the world and the universe passes through different stages which are more or less ideal do not vindicate by themselves the existence of relational varieties of world view in the above explicated sense. They merely represent comparative evaluations with respect to different aspects of what is supposed to be an actual world. Nevertheless, the notion of relational tenets of world view helps us to recognise the existence and distinctive nature of comparative assessments which are significantly related to comparative stances where the actual world of experience is seen in contrast to counterfactual utopian alternatives. In H. Glasenapp's introduction into Indian philosophy a passage of a *Brāhmaṇa*-text (*Śata-paṭha-brāhmaṇa* 2.3.1.5) is quoted[3] in which it is declared that the sun would not rise if the priest would not perform the fire-sacrifice in the early morning. Statements like this vindicate that the occurrence of most ordinary features exhibited by the environment is not taken for granted. They presuppose the thought that things could also be fundamentally different from the

[3] GLASENAPP (1958: 32).

way they actually are. Significant is the circumstance that regularities which could be conceived as laws of nature or as manifestations of such laws are here considered as items that are to be sustained by human behaviour. In structural respect the idea is a counterpart of the conception that human action can bring about states of affairs which are approaching some utopian ideal. The main difference is that whereas in the latter case human behaviour might promote the emergence of a better world, in the present example a function of preventing the emergence of an inferior world is allocated to human behaviour. Both varieties comply, however, with the stipulated criteria of a relational variety of 'Weltanschauung'.

(2) In contrast, a number of later religious doctrines tacitly presuppose the existence of invariable causal laws. Buddhism is a most prominent, but not the only, example where, so to speak, a technological conception of religious salvation is based on the fundamental assumption that the relevant causal laws do not and cannot change in the course of time. This assumption is by no means logically mandatory. In the framework of the scheme of diagram D the tenet that causal regularities are invariant through time can be relegated to the category of diachronic metaphysical tenets of world view because its content could be represented by a quantification over time-segments.

6. The observations made in the preceding paragraph do not articulate thoughts which have been asserted somewhere in textual sources; they rather reflect facts which can be ascertained by considering what other subjects thought or did not think. Some of them could be characterised as tacit assumptions. This point possesses some significance against the backdrop of the fact that scholars have intimated that the primary aim of studying Indian philosophy and related matters consists in finding out what other people really thought.

The claim that this postulate is excessively restrictive and inadequate for specifying the nature of the exploration of a world view can be supported by an example which is also suited to reveal an important reason for this inadequateness.

Modern linguistic phonology has developed a method of assessing the phonological systems of different natural languages and linguistic varieties against the background of a restricted inventory of phonological features. It is plain that neither the phonological features nor the descriptions provided in their terms merely reflect something which speakers of a natural language know beforehand. Notwithstanding the circumstance that the idea of assessing phenomena such as philosophical doctrines or systems of belief against the background of some restricted inventory of universally applicable features is highly problematic, some relevant analogies exist. The method of assessing phonological systems of different languages of the world by phonological features entails the assumption that exhibition and non-exhibition of traits are equally significant. One is entitled to presume that in this respect the assessment of cultural phenomena, such as philosophical teachings, is analogous. Therefore a major objective of attempts of outlining 'logical geographies' of some subject matter lies in facilitating the detection of absences. Since 'world view' designates a phenomenon which is hardly less universal than language or the existence of phonological systems it ought be expected that precise accounts of what is present and absent provide comparable insights in both fields. Presumably it holds good in the two realms alike that relevance of facts which investigations reveal does not depend on the circumstance that subjects possess some independent awareness of their existence.

One could doubt that such insights, given that they are possible, are also significant. In this regard some points should be noted.

(1) Characterisations of phonological systems by specifications of occurrence or non-occurrence of features implicitly relate them to other actual or potential alternatives. The situation is analogous in the case of objects, such as ideologies representing some world view.

(2) By virtue of the relation to alternative possibilities such assessments indirectly yield an account of items which an investigator possesses or employs himself. In phonology the analysis of foreign idioms by means of exhibition or absence of phonological features indirectly provides a phonological account of any pertinent meta-language, such as English, Spanish or German. The degree of richness of the implicit account correlates with the richness of the inventory of identifiable phonological features. This in its turn correlates with the universality of its application. Any increase of the number of languages taken into consideration potentially increases the number of parameters in terms of which any arbitrary language can be assessed. Since, however, the supposition of universal ideological features which could play a role comparable to that which phonological features are assumed to play might be illusory, one needs to see the relevant task in detecting and identifying novel and significant features, being aware of the possibility that in the context of assessments of world views of foreign subjects the inventory of potentially novel features is never definitely exhausted.

(3) Exact identifications of unrealised alternative possibilities yield a tool of cultural criticism even if it needs to be handled with appropriate care. In an analogous manner as a phonological system of a language cannot be assessed as imperfect on the basis of the circumstance that it does not possess all phonological units which are possible or exist in s o m e language, one cannot immediately deduce from a mere non-existence of particular ideas the existence of shortcomings. A system's being ideal does not necessarily involve a possession of all elements which it in principle c o u l d have, even if possible extensions might not lead to inconsistencies. Here one needs to consider systematic connections between elements of ideological systems and pay due regard to the aspect of the function a system is apt to play in some actual or

non-actual context. But as soon as those requirements are fulfilled one can be entitled to articulate criticism against ideological systems in view of absences. It seems, for example, that Buddhist thinkers such as Dharmakīrti based momentous philosophical tenets on a particular metaphysical notion of causality which is by no means mandatory. Whereas the possibility of probabilistic regularities had been acknowledged in the form of the tenet that the emergence of particular results from the occurrence of particular causal factors could be thwarted due to the existence of additional factors inhibiting the production of particular results, no room has been provided for the idea that even the most basic causal laws could be probabilistic themselves. It should be justified to consider this as a major shortcoming. To be sure, an acknowledgement of probabilistic causal laws does not only threaten the basis of certain assumptions in the theory of inference (*anumāna*) but is even suited to undermine commonly shared suppositions regarding soteriology both in the Buddhist and in Non-Buddhist traditions. However, at least in the context of philosophy one cannot readily admit the maxim that alternatives deserve to be neglected whenever they challenge some cherished word-view.

(4) Criticism of tenets of world view of foreign subjects against the background of alternatives familiar to us or *vice versa* criticism of our own opinions against the background of alternative possibilities detectable in world views of others is by no means the only dimension in which contrasts between tacit presuppositions and their alternatives can attain significance. Dependencies between different ingredients of actually held world views represent an equally relevant aspect. The following example is apt to illustrate the pertinent point. An analysis of a prominent variety of Dharmakīrti's attempt to prove the momentariness of all physically existent particulars intimates that the argument crucially relies on the supposition of a tenet which might be termed 'an anti-realist view regarding dispositions'. Roughly speaking the pertinent position amounts to a rejection of an alternative 'realist view' of causal dispositions according to which dispositions such as being breakable or being disposed to produce effects of a certain type possess a certain 'categorical basis' in the form of a non-dispositional state, such as a particular molecular structure etc. Here the question as to whether the claims concerning Dharmakīrti's argument are in fact true possesses merely secondary importance. Decisive is the circumstance that a denial of a realist position regarding causal disposition makes it far more difficult to find intelligible the idea of permanent particulars which are able to persist while preserving their individual nature. This result intimates that our common-sense notion of ordinary particulars persisting for a longer or shorter period of time is intimately connected with a tacit, but commonly shared assumption of a realist view of causal dispositions. Hence analyses of doctrines embodying particular views concerning the nature of the world promise to attain specific relevance if they are performed under a contrastive perspective. Their significance derives from their potential contribution for

tasks of self-reflection, such as an exploration of systematic interconnections between different facets of views which people commonly entertain and an identification of tacit underlying principles.

BIBLIOGRAPHY

CED = J. Sinclair (ed.): *Collins English Dictionary*. Third edition, Harper Collins, Glasgow 1991.

FLEW 1984 = Flew, Antony: *A Dictionary of Philosophy*. Revised Second Edition, St. Martin's Griffin, 1984.

GLASENAPP 1958 = Glasenapp, Helmuth von: *Die Philosophie der Inder*. Alfred Kröner Verlag, Stuttgart 1958.

The Correspondence Principle[*]

BRENDAN S. GILLON

1. Introduction

In his book, *Langage et Réalité*, Johannes BRONKHORST (1999) argues that many of the views expressed in early classical Indian philosophy can be understood as obtained from a tacit presupposition he dubs 'the correspondence principle', roughly, the principle that to each expression of language corresponds some part of reality. As BRONKHORST (1999: 12–13) points out, Pāṇini's grammar, the *Aṣṭādhyāyī*, clearly presupposes this principle. The correspondence principle, or some version of it, is not confined to an implicit use by classical Indian thinkers, such a principle is explicitly embraced by many contemporary philosophers and natural language semanticists, who trace the lineage of the principle, not to Pāṇini, but to the German mathematician, logician, and philosopher, Gottlob Frege (1848–1925).

In fact, the correspondence principle has many versions. They vary according to what sort of things are put into correspondence and the mathematical strength of the relation. One version of the principle is what I call a 'semantic' version. It takes the relata to be expressions in a natural language, on the one hand, and set theoretic entities which serve as values for the expressions, on the other. The semantic version does not entail any particular view of the nature of reality, as pointed out by Alfred TARSKI (1901–1983), the Polish logician and philosopher who pioneered the mathematics underlying the semantic version.[1] I shall call a semantic correspondence principle a 'pure' semantic correspondence principle, if it prescinds from any commitment as to whether or not the set theoretic entities used by the principle further correspond to parts of reality. Now, the point of the semantic version is to address the question of how a speaker's understanding of a complex expression in his or her language arises from an understanding of the simpler expressions making it up. It does this by showing how a function can be defined for the expressions of the natu-

[*] This research was supported, in part, by the Social Sciences and Humanities Research Council of Canada (SSHRC 412-2010-1007). I thank Colleen Gillon for several helpful editorial suggestions.

[1] See, for example, TARSKI (1944: 362).

World View and Theory in Indian Philosophy
Warsaw Indological Studies 5 (2012) 381–398.

ral language which assigns values to a complex expression on the basis of values assigned to the simpler expressions making it up.

A special version of the semantic principle, one which seems to have been tacitly presupposed by classical Indian thinkers, foremost among them being Pāṇini, is what I shall call the 'ontico-semantic' version. This version takes the relata to be expressions in a natural language, on the one hand, and parts of reality, on the other. Contemporary philosophers and natural language semanticists also adopt such an ontico-semantic correspondence principle, though, unlike their classical Indian forerunners, their version comprises the purely semantic principle, supplemented by the additional assumption that the set theoretic entities of the purely semantic version give, as it were, the set theoretical structure of real world entities which expressions of natural language are about.

Surely, some form of the ontico-semantic correspondence principle is correct. After all, if there were no systematic correspondence between expressions of a language and parts of reality, how could it be that humans use the expressions of a language to communicate successfully with one another facts about the world in which they live? I shall not, however, delve into this question here.

It is worth noting that there are non-semantic correspondence principles. Perhaps the best known one is Aristotle's correspondence theory of truth, whose relata are mental entities, on the one hand, and parts of reality, on the other.

As I said above, a correspondence principle may also vary by the strength of the relation. For example, in the case of an ontico-semantic correspondence principles, it could be that only some expressions of natural language correspond to some parts of reality. While it seems very plausible to think that corresponding to proper names such as 'Pāṇini' and 'Aristotle' are the actual individuals Pāṇini and Aristotle, it seems very implausible to think that corresponding to such expressions as 'if' and 'or' are parts of reality. It also seems implausible to hold, though some have, that no two expressions correspond to the same part of reality. But this seems far-fetched, since languages often contain synonymous expressions. Consider, for example, such pairs of English nouns such as 'spigot' and 'faucet' or as 'woodchuck' and 'ground hog', or even such proper names as 'Mark Twain' and 'Samuel Clemens' or 'Romain Gary', 'Émile Ajar', 'Fosco Sinibaldi' and 'Shatan Bogat', all names under which Roman Kacew wrote.

Drawing on verses in the *Mūla-madhyamaka-kārikā* (MMK), BRONKHORST (1999) concludes that the verses' author, Nāgārjuna, presupposes an ontico-semantic correspondence principle. I wish to look more carefully into the role which such a principle plays in the arguments contained in these verses. I shall proceed in three steps. I shall first elaborate on the nature of semantic correspondence principles with the help of an artificial, yet simple example. Then, I shall show how certain ontological problems, such as the problem of change, most naturally stated as a problem in ontology, can be restated in semantic terms. The restatement of the problem requires the use of an ontico-semantic correspondence principle. The point will bear on the discussion of the fourth section of the paper. In it, I shall review some of the verses discussed by BRONKHORST and argue that, while some verses are very plausibly construed as asserting claims which depend on a tacit use of an ontico-semantic correspondence principle, others do not. Here, I shall avail myself of important insights and observations found in earlier work by Kamaleswar BHATTACHARYA (1980), (1981), (1985), (1995) and by George CARDONA (1991).

2. Semantic Correspondence Principles

To get a more thorough idea of what a pure semantic correspondence principle is, let us consider a simple example of its application to a set of expressions which are not from a natural language. Consider the set of expressions which result from assembling strings of the first four upper case letters of the Roman alphabet: *A*, *B*, *C* and *D*. Let us call this set ID and let us call IN the set of strings over ID. Examples of members of IN are: *A*, *C*, *BD*, *BCA* etc. Examples of strings which are not in IN are: *E*, *FAC* etc. We can define the set IN inductively on the basis of the set ID as follows:

INDUCTIVE DEFINITION OF IN:

(1.1) If $x \in$ ID, then $x \in$ IN;
(1.2) If $y \in$ ID and $z \in$ IN, then $zy \in$ IN;
(1.3) Nothing else is a member of IN.

The first clause of this definition tells us that all the members of ID are members of IN. In fact, it identifies the simplest expressions in the set IN. The second clause indicates how more complex expression in IN are obtained from one simpler expression in IN and from one expression of ID. Below is a graphic representation of a kind of proof that the expression *BACD* is in the set IN. The expression at the vertex of two converging lines is obtained from the two expressions at the opposite ends of those lines by clause (1.2) of the inductive definition.

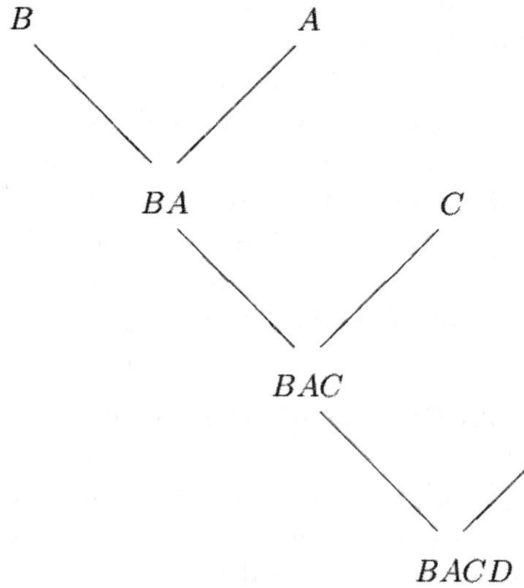

What, one might ask, do these strings of letters express? In other words, what do they correspond to? In fact, they might correspond to all kinds of things: it all depends on what values one assigns to the members of IN. The most obvious systematic way to assign values is to assign them according to the definition of the expressions in IN, since that definition tells us how from the four simple expressions in ID, one can construct all and only the expressions in IN. Thus, it is natural to assign a value to each of the simple expressions in ID. Let us, for example, assign 0 to '*A*', 1 to '*B*', 2 to '*C*' and 3 to '*D*'. Since clause (1.2) tells us how to construct more complex expressions from simpler ones, let us use that construction to assign values to a complex expression on the basis of values assigned to its constituent expressions. Here is one such rule: assign to the complex expression the value which results from adding the value of the right hand constituent expression to four times the value of the left hand constituent expression. Here is a formal version of what was just stated:

SEMANTIC CORRESPONDENCE PRINCIPLE FOR IN:

(2.1) $i(A) = 0$, $i(B) = 1$, $i(C) = 2$, $i(D) = 3$
(2.2) If $y \in$ ID and $z \in$ IN, then $i(zy) = 4 \cdot i(z) + i(y)$

The tree given above can be used to show how the function defined in (2) works.

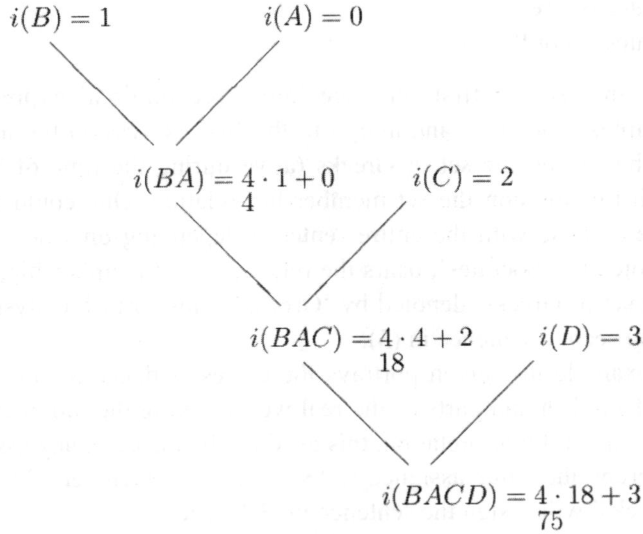

i ensures that to each expression in IN corresponds a natural number, the non-negative integers. Moreover, to each natural number corresponds an expression in IN. Indeed, to each natural number correspond many, many expressions in IN.[2] In fact, as the reader will easily see, the expressions in IN comprise a base four representation of the natural numbers. Notice that providing a complete set of expressions to represent the natural numbers says nothing about the nature of natural numbers. Hence, *i* is a pure semantic correspondence principle.

2.1. Natural language

Contemporary natural language semantics essentially generalises this idea to the expressions of natural language. It assumes, first, that each expression in a natural language can be analysed into minimal expressions; second, that the set of minimal expressions in the language is finite; third, that the set of complex expressions result from a finite set of rules which combine minimal expressions of the language to form the complex ones; fourth, that some value, which is invariant across contexts of use, can be associated with each minimal expression; and fifth, that a value for the complex expressions can be obtained from the values of the less complex expressions making up the complex expression. The last two assumptions, taken together, form a correspondence principle.

[2] If *e* is an expression for a natural number, then so is any expression obtained by prefixing *A* in front of it. Thus, *BC*, *ABC* etc., all denote 6.

As an illustration, consider the two sentences in (3).

(3.1) Socrates is Greek.
(3.2) Socrates is not Persian.

One might analyse the first sentence into three minimal expressions—'Socrates', 'Greek' and 'is'—and assign to the first expression the individual Socrates, to the second the set of Greeks (alive during the time of Socrates) and to the third expression the set membership relation. One could associate the value true or false with the entire sentence depending on whether or not Socrates, denoted by 'Socrates', bears the relation of set membership, denoted by 'is', to the set of Greeks, denoted by 'Greeks'. This sort of analysis can be extended to the second sentence in (3).

While the example just given portrays the correspondence as one between expressions of English and parts of the real world, taking the minimal expressions under the natural interpretation, this need not be the case; any assignment of values whereby the value assigned to 'Socrates' is a member of the set assigned to 'Greeks' will assign the sentence in (3.1) true.

Complications arise even with examples as simple as those in (3). Here is one complication. Consider the sentences in (4). *Prima facie*, one can apply the analysis applied to the sentences in (3) to the sentence in (4.1). Assigning the individual Socrates to the expression 'Socrates' and the set of things which exist to the verb 'exists', the sentence in (4.1) is true just in case Socrates is a member of the set of existent things.

(4.1) Socrates existed.
(4.2) Pegasus did not exist.

Unfortunately, this analysis does not work for the sentence in (4.2), for there is no thing which can be assigned to the expression 'Pegasus'. Something else has to be done to account for the truth of the sentence in (4.2).

The problem illustrated by the sentences in (4) is not confined to proper names which do not have a denotation. Consider the sentences in (5). If the sentence in (5.1) expresses a truth, there is no thesis to which the expression 'her thesis' can refer. And, so long as Bill has not finished writing his novel, there is no novel of Bill's while he is writing it.

(5.1) Alice died before she started to write her thesis.
(5.2) Bill is writing a novel.

The problem here is a purely semantic one: what kind of value, if any, is to be assigned to noun phrases which apparently denote nothing at all so that a suitable truth value can be assigned to the clauses in which they appear. In fact, this problem arises with any verb of creation or of destruction, for these verbs denote a change from a situation in which something has yet to exist to one in which it does exist and from a situation in which something exists to one in which it no longer exists, respectively. This important and unresolved problem in semantic theory accrues to the correspondence principle, which, as noted above, is fundamental to the semantic analysis of meaningful expressions in natural language.

Contemporary semantic theory was anticipated by Pāṇini. In his *Aṣṭādhyāyī*, Pāṇini seeks to pair every Sanskrit sentence with the situation it denotes. He presupposes that each situation can be analysed into an action (*kriyā*), its factors (*kāraka*) and the features they have, and that each sentence can be analysed into the minimal expressions making it up. Here is how in more detail. Pāṇini presupposes that, for a given situation, its action and its factors are paired with minimal expressions denoting them. His grammar appends to each nominal stem the suffixes needed to denote the various features of the thing denoted by its stem and to each verbal stem the suffixes required to denote the various features of the action. This yields an abstract sentence (*alaukikam vākyam*: literally, an extra-ordinary sentence), which is comprised solely of abstract words. Next, the grammar transforms each abstract word into its proper phonologically isolated form. (At this point, the words are given a linear ordering.) And finally, the grammar transforms each word's phonologically isolated form into the correct phonological form as determined by its phonological context, yielding the actual sentence (*laukikam vākyam*: literally, ordinary sentence).[3]

3. Ontology and Semantics

Before turning to some of the arguments found in the *Mūla-madhyamaka-kārikā*, let me take a moment to say something about the connection between semantics and ontology. As noted by Medieval European logicians, some questions can be formulated in two ways: either in the material mode, *modus materialis*, to use their term, or in the formal mode, *modus formalis*. Thus, for example, the ontic question, 'what is a tree', can be recast in ontico-semantic terms as the question, 'what is the denotation of the word «tree»'.

Notice that the first question uses the word «tree», while the second merely mentions it. The word «tree», used in the first question, denotes trees, while the word '«tree»', used in the second question, does not denote trees, but rather denotes instances of the word «tree». In order to use the word '«tree»' to talk about trees, one has to use the semantic word 'denotation'. In this way, the word «tree» and the expression 'denotation of «tree»' denote the same thing, namely, trees. It is easy to see that, in general, any ontic claim or question can be recast in ontico-semantic terms whereby words used in the ontic claim or question are mentioned in its semantic recasting together with an expression for their correspondence with their denotation when they are used.

[3] See GILLON (2007) for further elaboration. For the details of Pāṇini's grammar, see CARDONA (1988).

Bearing in mind that ontic claims can be recast in ontico-semantic terms, let us turn to one central philosophical problem, the problem of change, raised by Greek pre-Socratic philosophers and pursued in great detail by Aristotle. Suppose someone fires a pot in a kiln, thereby changing its colour from red to black. The pot is the same but its colour changes. The colours are accidental properties of the pot; and such a change is said to be an accidental change. The pot also has an essential property, namely, the property of being a pot. An essential property persists through changes in its accidental properties. However, should the pot be smashed, it would no longer exist: after all, a collection of potsherds is not a pot. Such a change is an essential change. An essential change is one in which an essential property is either acquired or lost. Thus, if someone shapes a lump of clay on a potter's wheel into a pot, the lump of clay has undergone an essential change. In general, the creation and destruction of things are essential changes to those things and changes which are not essential are accidental.

Correlated with the difference between essential and accidental change is a difference in identity conditions. Common sense tells us that, even if a pot changes colour from red to black, the pot before the change in colour, the red pot, is identical with the pot after the change in colour, the black pot. However, is the lump of clay from which a pot is made identical with the pot itself? If it were, that would mean that the pot existed before its creation. After all, the lump of clay from which the pot was made existed before the pot existed. But the lump of clay is identical with the pot. Therefore, the pot existed before the pot existed. This is absurd. Therefore, we must conclude that the pot and the clay from which it is made are distinct. The relationship between a physical entity and the material out of which it is made is an important philosophical problem, well debated in classical India and still vigorously debated by philosophers today.

It is possible to recast this problem in ontico-semantic terms. Consider two sentences:

(6.1) Devadatta turned a pot from red to black.
(6.2) Devadatta turned clay into a pot.

The truth of the sentence in (6.1) requires, among other things, that there is something of which 'pot' is true and that there is a time at which 'red' is true of it but 'black' is not and that there is a subsequent time at which 'black' is true of it but 'red' is not. Notice that the thing of which 'red' is true but 'black' is not at one time must be identical with the thing of which 'black' is true but 'red' is not at a subsequent time. Now consider the truth of the sentence in (6.2). It requires, among other things, that there is a time at which the word 'pot' is true of something and there is a subsequent time at which the word 'clay' is true of something. It also requires that some relation be stated between the thing of which 'pot' is true and the thing of which 'clay' is true. If, on the one hand, the relation is identity, then, as a result of plausible ontico-semantic principles, it follows that the sentence

(7) The pot exists

will be true with respect to a situation in which the clay had not yet been made into a pot. If, on the other hand, no relation is specified then the sentence in (6.2) will be true with respect to a situation in which there is clay which will never be turned into a pot and there is a pot.

Even though the ontological problem of change can be recast in ontico-semantic terms, as we have just done, the problem is essentially an ontological one. This is true, because a question in the presentation of the problem as recast in ontico-semantic terms remains an ontic one, namely, the question of the relationship between what 'clay' is true of and what 'pot' is true of. Is it an identity relation or is it some other relation? Thus, just because an ontic problem has been, or even can be, cast in ontico-semantic terms, it does not mean that the problem is a semantic one. Semantic problems are problems which require for their formulation semantic terms and which cannot be recast as problems whose formulation is devoid of semantic terms. The ontological problem of change can be stated without recourse to semantic terms.

4. Nāgārjuna

Let us turn to some of the verses in Nāgārjuna's *Mūla-madhyamaka-kārikā* discussed by BRONKHORST. In some cases, BRONKHORST is, in my view, correct to see in these verses arguments which are most plausibly interpreted as requiring the tacit presupposition of a correspondence principle, in particular, an ontico-semantic correspondence principle; in other cases, though, I think the arguments turn, not on the assumption of an ontico-semantic the correspondence principle, but on purely ontological assumptions. Let me begin with verses of the latter sort.

Consider the two verses at the beginning of chapter 19.[4]

> '[1] If something present and something future indeed depend on something past, then something present and something future would exist in the past.
> [2] If instead something present and something future do not exist in the past, in what way would something present and something future depend on something past?'[5]

[4] See BRONKHORST (1997: 4), (1999: 36–37).

[5] MMK 19.1–2:

pratyutpanno 'nāgataś ca yady atītam apekṣya hi /
pratyutpanno 'nāgataś ca kāle 'tīte bhaviṣyataḥ //
pratyutpanno 'nāgataś ca na staḥ tatra punar yadi /
pratyutpanno 'nāgataś ca syātām katham apekṣya tam //

The principle which is presupposed here is, in my view, not any version of the correspondence principle, but a concurrence principle. The concurrence principle could be formulated as follows: if a relation obtains, then all of its relata obtain simultaneously with it.[6] This is a purely ontological principle. In some cases, this principle is quite plausible. What possible spatial relationship might something which exists have to something which does not? Is Pegasus near or far from Pāṭaliputra? Surely, Pegasus bears no spatial relation to it. Yet, in other cases, contrary to the concurrence principle, it makes perfect sense to speak of a relationship between something which exists and something which does not. Thus, for example, one does not cease to be the child of one's parents, once one, or even both, is dead.

I think that the concurrence principle is also presupposed in the argument in the sixth verse from Chapter 1.[7]

> 'Neither anything existent nor anything inexistent can have a cause. What inexistent thing has a cause? And what use is a cause for something existent?'[8]

The concurrence principle underpins the first rhetorical question: after all, if causation is a relation, then it follows from the principle that a cause and its effect must exist simultaneously. In other words, no inexistent thing has a cause.

The second rhetorical question is based on another principle, namely that a cause and its effect cannot come into existence simultaneously. This too is an ontological principle. It is, of course, inconsistent with the concurrence principle applied to causation. In fact, common sense has often suggested to thinkers that the causation relation satisfies the contrary of the concurrence principle. After all, the arising of a sprout must be preceded by the planting of the seed from which the sprout grows. Such events surely cannot be simultaneous. Indeed, it seems to be precisely this view which sanctions the second rhetorical question. It appears that Nāgārjuna is presupposing the principle that each cause exists before its effect. And while this principle is plausible in the case of seeds and their sprouts, it is absurd in other cases. For surely an upward force applied to a rock, equal to the downward force exerted on it by gravity, is the cause of the rock not falling to the ground. In this case, cause and effect exist simultaneously. Thus, what seems right as a general principle of causa-

---

[6] The need for a principle of this kind to account for several of Nāgārjuna's arguments, including the arguments underlying the verses just cited and the next verse to be cited, has already been pointed out and explained by Claus OETKE (1990) and acknowledged as a possibility by Johannes BRONKHORST (1997: 6).

[7] See BRONKHORST (1997: 5), (1999: 36).

[8] MMK 1.6:

nâivâsato nâiva sataḥ pratyayo 'rthasya yujyate /
asataḥ pratyayaḥ kasya sataś ca pratyayena kim //

tion is that effects do not precede their causes, but whether or not a cause precedes or is simultaneous with its effect depends on the details of the cause and its effect.

Creation, as we saw above, gives rise to the important ontological problem of change. This problem, as we also saw, can be recast in semantic terms. To recast the problem in semantic terms requires an ontico-semantic correspondence principle. But such a semantic recasting, as we saw as well, is completely eliminable. And in this way, the ontico-semantic correspondence principle is incidental to the problem. Now MMK 7.17, discussed by BRONKHORST (1997: 8), (1999: 36), pertains to things coming into existence, or creation.

> 'If something, which has not arisen, comes to exist, it should arise somewhere. If the thing does not exist [there], how does it arise?'[9]

It is useful to think about what the verse says in terms of our earlier example. Suppose a potter places wet clay on a wheel. He spins the wheel and shapes the wet clay into a pot. At some point, the wet clay on the wheel is transformed into a pot. The wet clay from which the pot arises had been, of course, on the wheel before the pot arose, and indeed, up to the moment it arose. Moreover, if the clay had not been on the wheel, the pot which was made from the clay would not have arisen there. The foregoing common sensical view founders only once one assumes that a pot and the clay from which the pot was made are identical. While this identity is expressed by the use of a pronoun which denotes the same thing as its antecedent, no semantic terms are required to formulate the argument. But this identity between the clay and the pot is not stated in semantic terms. Indeed, there is no mention of identity. Rather, identity is presupposed in the use of the pronouns.

Let me now turn to some verses whose arguments are most plausibly interpreted as requiring the tacit presupposition of the ontico-semantic correspondence principle. Here, like others, including BRONKHORST, I adopt Candrakīrti's (PP) delineation of the underlying arguments. I shall confine my attention to the first six verses of the second chapter, which include the two verses BRONKHORST (1997: 6), (1999: 37) discusses, and profit from the excellent elucidation of Candrakīrti's delineation of the arguments by Kamaleswar BHATTACHARYA (1980, 1981, 1985, 1995). As we shall see, Candrakīrti's exposition of the arguments clearly and inescapably requires an ontico-semantic correspondence principle; in fact, as we shall also see, his delineation requires an absurdly strong version of the principle.

---

[9] MMK 7.17:

yadi kaścid anutpanno bhāvaḥ saṁvidyate kvacit /
utpadyeta sa kiṁ tasmin bhāve utpadyate 'sati //

To prepare the way, let us begin with the first verse. It states:

> 'To begin with, what has been travelled is not being travelled; what has not been travelled is not being travelled; what is being travelled, distinct from what has been travelled and what has not been travelled, is not being travelled.'[10]

It makes three claims: first, what has been travelled is not being travelled (*gataṁ na gamyate*); second, what has not been travelled is not being travelled (*agataṁ na gamyate*); and third, what is being travelled is not being travelled (*gamyamānaṁ na gamyate*). Each of these claims, purely ontic, is patently false: the first two contingently false, the last necessarily false.

Surely it is false that what has been travelled is not being travelled. Just because a road has been travelled once does not mean that it will not be travelled again. If Devadatta travelled a road yesterday, he, or someone else, could certainly travel it again today. And surely it is equally false that what has not been travelled is not being travelled. A road which has yet to be travelled might be travelled some day; otherwise, no newly built road would ever be travelled. And finally it is indeed false that what is being travelled is not being travelled, since it is necessarily true that what is being travelled is being travelled.

In his commentary to the first verse, Candrakīrti furnishes an argument for each claim. I start with the first claim, which Candrakīrti immediately recasts in ontico-semantic terms to the effect that the verbal form *gamyate* ('is travelling') is not true of anything in which the action denoted by the verbal root √*gam* ('travel') has ceased (PP 33.8–9). But this ontico-semantic recasting is false for the very same reason its ontic original is false: Just because the action of travelling has ceased in something does not mean that the verbal form *gamyate* ('is travelling') can not be true of it: after all, something which has been travelled once can be travelled again. This is not surprising, since the ontic claim and its ontico-semantic recasting are equivalent.

In spite of the fact that ontico-semantic recasting of the first claim is false, Candrakīrti seems to think that it follows from a clear and plausible application of the ontico-semantic correspondence principle applied to the verbal form *gamyate* ('is being travelled'), the passive voice, present tense form of a verbal root √*gam* ('travel'): he thinks, that is, *gamyate* ('is being travelled') is true of something if, and only if, the action denoted by the root √*gam* ('travel') is connected with it in the present, namely, at the time of utterance of the present tense form of the verbal root √*gam* ('travel'). Moreover, while this principle certainly implies that the verbal root √*gam* ('travel'), in the present tense, passive voice, is not true of anything which does not possess the action at the time

---

[10] MMK 2.1:

gataṁ na gamyate tāvat agataṁ nâiva gamyate /
gatâgata-vinirmuktaṁ gamyamānaṁ na gamyate //

of utterance, even if it did possess the action previous to the time of utterance, it does not imply the semantic recasting of the first ontic claim, contrary to what Candrakīrti suggests.

The second claim, namely that what has not been travelled is not being travelled (*agataṁ na gamyate*), lends itself to the following ontico-semantic recasting: the verbal form *gamyate* ('is being travelled') is not true of anything in which the action denoted by the verbal root √*gam* ('travel') has not arisen. Indeed, Candrakīrti glosses *agatam* ('what has not been travelled') as *anupajāta-gami-kriyaṁ* (PP 33.11: 'that in which the action of the verbal root √*gam* has not arisen'). While this is the natural recasting, it is not the one adopted by Candrakīrti. Rather, he interprets *agatam* ('what has not been travelled') as synonymous with *anāgatam*, literally meaning what has not come but used to mean what is yet to come, that is, the future. In this way, he recasts the original claim as follows: the verbal form *gamyate* ('is being travelled') is not true of anything which will possess the action denoted by the verbal root √*gam* ('travel'). The ontic counterpart to this is that what will be travelled is not being travelled (*anāgataṁ na gamyate*, a claim which is also patently false. Candrakīrti also thinks that the second claim, recast in ontico-semantic terms, follows from the same plausible application of the ontico-semantic correspondence principle used to support the first claim. However, the second claim does not follow from this plausible application of the principle any more than the first claim does.[11]

The question arises: why did Candrakīrti feel compelled to gloss *agata* ('what has not been travelled') as *anāgata* ('what has not come'), that is, as 'the future'? The reason is that Candrakīrti wishes to portray the three claims in this verse as denials of three necessarily exclusive and exhaustive alternatives which must hold for any event (PP 33.3–4). In other words, Candrakīrti thinks that it is necessarily true that precisely one of the following alternatives hold for any event, and in particular, any instance of travelling: namely, that it takes place either in the past, or in the future or in the present. Since, according to Candrakīrti, the verse denies each of these claims, it follows that it is false that there are any instances of travelling. For the verse to fit into this form of argument, Candrakīrti must interpret *agata* ('what has not been travelled') as *anāgata* ('what has not yet come', or the future).

Let us turn to the third claim, namely, that what is being travelled is not being travelled (*gamyamānaṁ na gamyate*). This claim is necessarily false. Yet, two arguments are given to support it. One is a purely ontic argument, which Candrakīrti provides in his commentary to the first verse and set out by Kamaleswar BHATTACHARYA (1985: 9). Another is an argument which Nāgār-

[11] As we learn from CARDONA (1991: section 5.1), the question of whether or not verbs in the present tense, which must be true with respect to the present, are false with respect to the past or the future, had been raised by Patañjali in his *Mahābhāṣya*, in particular, in his commentary to A 3.2.123.

juna gives in the fifth and sixth verses, which is best interpreted in the ontico-semantic way suggested by Candrakīrti.

Here are the verses which contain Nāgārjuna's argument:

> 'When travelling belongs to what is being travelled, it follows that there are two travellings: both that by which there is what is being travelled and that by which there is travelling in it besides.'[12]

It is worth citing Candrakīrti's commentary on this in full, since it is short and clear and brings out the semantic ideas implicit in the verse:

> One travelling is the travelling by dint of a connection with which the path acquires the expression *gamyamāna* ('is being travelled'); the second one, in what is being travelled, being the substratum, is the travelling by which the path is travelled. When there is the travelling of what is being travelled, this pair of travellings follow.[13]

Here, the implicit application of the ontico-semantic correspondence principle is that different occurrences of words correspond to different parts of reality. In particular, in the expression *gamyamānam gamyate* ('what is being travelled is being travelled'), the travelling required for the denotation of *gamyamānam* ('what is being travelled') is distinct from the travelling required for the denotation of *gamyate* ('is being travelled'). This, of course, is inconsistent with there being only one travelling required to make this sentence true. Or, to put the same point in the way Kamaleswar BHATTACHARYA (1980: 86), (1995: 179–180) has, if the word *gamyamānam* ('what is being travelled') in the expression *gamyamānam gamyate* ('what is being travelled is being travelled') attributes travelling to the road, then there is no second travelling to be attributed to the road by *gamyate* ('is being travelled'). Candrakīrti concludes from this contradiction that the sentence *gamyamānam gamyate* ('what is being travelled') is necessarily false. Of course, what is false is the presupposed ontico-semantic correspondence principle which requires that distinct occurrences of words correspond to different parts of reality. In fact, sentences such as *gamyamānam gamyate* ('what is being travelled is being travelled') express necessary truths, not falsehoods. And the reason they express necessary truths is, in part, because the same action is referred to by the two words both with

---

[12] MMK 2.5:

> *gamyamānasya gamane prasaktam gamana-dvayam /*
> *yena tat gamyamānaṁ ca yat câtra gamanaṁ punaḥ //*

[13] PP 34.29 ff.: *yena gamanena yogād gamyamāna-vyapadeśaṁ pratilabhate 'dhvā tad ekaṁ gamanam. tatra gamyamāne 'dhikaraṇa-bhūte dvitīyaṁ gamanaṁ yena so 'dhvā gamyate. etad gamana-dvayam gamyamānasya gamane sati prasaktam.*

suffixes requiring that the actions be in the present, namely, *gamyamānam* ('what is being travelled') and *gamyate* ('is being travelled').[14]

In the next verse, Nāgārjuna seeks to buttress the fallacious conclusion of his previous verse by trying to deduce still further absurdities regarding travelling.

> 'If it follows that there are two travellings, it must follow that there are two travellers, for travelling does not arise without a traveller.'[15]

This argument hinges on two ontic principles: each action has an agent and different actions have different agents. The first principle seems true. But the second is clearly false; after all, the very same person not only can both eat and walk but can do so even at the same time. Though Candrakīrti considers such an obvious counterexample to the second principle, he denies that there is a single agent of eating and walking, even when it is the very same person who is doing both simultaneously. He argues as follows:

> 'Not so, for the factor (*kāraka*) is a capacity (*śakti*), not a substance (*dravya*). And because actions are different, it is surely established that the capacities which bring them about also are established as different. For one cannot be a speaker through the action of standing. If it is supposed that a substance is a single thing, let it be so. But a substance (*dravya*) is not a factor (*kāraka*). What then is? A capacity (*śakti*) is. And it is indeed different (from a substance).'[16]

The argument is, of course, specious, for, as Kamaleswar BHATTACHARYA (1981: 82), (1985: 12) has remarked, it misuses the grammatical concepts. Its semblance of soundness depends on an equivocal use of the term 'factor' (*kāraka*). To see how this is so, let us consider a slight grammatical variant of the sentence used by Candrakīrti, which closely parallels a sentence discussed by Patañjali in his commentary on Pāṇini's *sūtra* A 3.1.126.

(8.1) *Devadattaḥ tiṣṭhan bhāṣate*.
(8.2) Devadatta is speaking while standing.

---

[14] See CARDONA (1991: section 5.3.1) for a presentation of the relevant derivational principles according to Pāṇini's grammar.

[15] MMK 2.6:

dvau gantārau prasajyete prasakte gamana-dvaye /
gantāraṁ hi tiraskṛtya gamanaṁ nôpapadyate //

[16] PP 35.9 ff.: *na evaṁ. śaktir hi kārako na dravyam. kriyā-bhedāc ca tat-sādhanasyâpi śakteḥ siddha eva bhedaḥ. na hi sthiti-kriyayā vaktā syāt. dravyam ekam iti cet. bhavatu evam. na tu dravyam kārakaḥ. kiṁ tarhi? śaktiḥ. sā ca bhidyata eva.* Following Kamaleswar BHATTACHARYA (1980: 88), one could translate the last sentence equally well as follows: 'And they are indeed different [from each other]'.

The Sanskrit sentence in (8.1), like its English translation in (8.2), is true if, and only if, the thing referred to by the proper noun 'Devadatta' is both speaking and standing. If the sentence is said of a situation in which one person is speaking but not standing and another is standing but not speaking, even if both people are named 'Devadatta', the sentences in (8) are false. Grammatically speaking, the thing named by 'Devadatta', a substance, must be the agent (*kartṛ*) both of the action denoted by present participle and by the action denoted by the main verb.

The very same grammatical considerations bear on the sentences below, a slight variant of the sentence Nāgārjuna thinks is false.

(9.1) *adhvā gamyamāno gamyate.*
(9.2) The path being travelled is being travelled.

The only grammatical difference between the sentence in (8.1), where the verbs are in the active voice, and the one in (9.1), where the verbs are in the passive voice, is that, in the former sentence, the agent (*kartṛ*) of each action must be the same, while in the latter sentence, the patient (*karman*) of each verb must be the same.[17]

Now Candrakīrti plausibly supposes the following. First, someone who is both speaking and standing is exercising distinct capacities. Second, while someone is standing and speaking, the capacities which are being exercised to stand and to speak are causal factors (*kāraka*) in bringing about their respective activities. At the same time, however, the person performing the activities is also a causal factor. The question is: which of these factors is the grammatical factor (*kāraka*), or more precisely, the grammatical agent (*kartṛ*), in the sentence in (8.1)? The answer is that it is the substance, Devadatta, and not his capacities. If Candrakīrti's view were correct, the sentences below

(10.1) *Devadattaḥ tiṣṭhati*
'Devadatta is standing'
(10.2) *Devadatto bhāṣate*
'Devadatta is speaking'

would in fact mean: The capacity to stand is standing and the capacity to speak is speaking, respectively. But this is not what these sentences mean. Candrakīrti has conflated the agent of the action with the capacity the agent has by dint of which he or she can perform the action.

5. Conclusion

In sum, we have seen that there are a number of versions of the correspondence principle, some versions relating expressions to the world, dubbed here

[17] See CARDONA (1991: section 5.3.1) for an exposition of the relevant Pāṇinian principles required for the derivations of the sentences.

the ontico-semantic correspondence principles, and some versions relating expressions to set theoretic values and silent regarding how the expressions relate to the world, dubbed the purely semantic correspondence principles. It is the ontico-semantic version which has played a role in Nāgārjuna's arguments, at least as they are spelled out by his commentator Candrakīrti. In some cases, the ontico-semantic correspondence principle plays only an incidental role in recasting essentially ontic claims in semantic terms, as we saw in the case of the arguments adduced by Candrakīrti to support the first two claims in MMK 2.1. In other cases, the ontico-semantic correspondence principle plays an essential role, a point already made by Kamaleswar BHATTACHARYA (1985: 13), but only in so far as it is given an absurdly strong formulation. This is the case with the argument adduced by Candrakīrti to support the third claim in the first verse of Chapter 2. In other cases still, Nāgārjuna's arguments are best interpreted without appeal to any correspondence principle.

BIBLIOGRAPHY

BHATTACHARYA 1980 = Bhattacharya, Kamaleswar: 'Nāgārjuna's Arguments Against Motion: Their Grammatical Basis', in: Arthur Llewellyn Basham (ed.): *A Corpus of Indian Studies: Essays in Honor of Professor Gaurinath Sastri*. Sanskrit Pustak Bhandar, Calcutta 1980: 85–95.

BHATTACHARYA 1981 = Bhattacharya, Kamaleswar: 'The Grammatical Basis for Nāgārjuna's Arguments: Some Further Considerations', *Indologica Taurinensia* 9 (1981) 35–43.

BHATTACHARYA 1985 = Bhattacharya, Kamaleswar: 'Nāgārjuna's arguments against motion', *Journal of the International Association of Buddhist Studies* 8 (1985) 7–15.

BHATTACHARYA 1995 = Bhattacharya, Kamaleswar: 'Back to Nāgārjuna and Grammar', *The Adyar Library Bulletin* 59 (1995) 178–189.

BRONKHORST 1997 = Bronkhorst, Johannes: 'Nāgārjuna's Logic', in: Petra Kieffer-Pülz; Jens-Uwe Hartmann (eds.): *Bauddhavidyāsudhākara. Studies in Honour of Heinz Bechert on the Occasion of his 65 Birthday*. Indica et Tibetica Verlag, Swisttal-Odendorf 1997: 29–37.

BRONKHORST 1999 = Bronkhorst, Johannes: *Langage et Réalité: sur un Episode de la Pensée Indienne*. Bibliothèque de l'École des Hautes Études, Sciences Religieuses 105, Turnhout, Brepols, Lausanne 1999.

BRONKHORST 2010 = Bronkhorst, Johannes: 'Philosophy and Language in India: A Brief Overview', *Antiquorum Philosophica* 4 (2010) 11–21.

CARDONA 1988 = Cardona, George *Pāṇini: his Work and its Traditions*. Motilal Banarsidass, Delhi, 1988.

CARDONA 1991 = Cardona, George: 'A Path Still Taken: Some Early Indian Arguments Concerning Time', *Journal of the American Oriental Society*: 111 (1991) 445–464.

GILLON 2007 = Gillon, Brendan S.: 'Pāṇini's *Aṣṭādhyāyī* and Linguistic Theory', *Journal of Indian Philosophy* 35 (2007) 445–468.

MMK = Nāgārjuna: *Mūla-madhyamaka-kārikā*. (1) Louis de la Vallée Poussin (ed.): *Madhyamakavṛttiḥ Mūlamadhyamaka-kārikās de Nāgārjuna avec la Prasannapadā Commentaire de Candrakīrti*. Bibliotheca Buddhica 4, Pétersbourg 1903–1913 [reprinted: Osnabrück 1970]. (2) P.L. Vaidya (ed): *Madhyamakaśāstra of Nāgārjuna with the commentary Prasannapadā by Candrakīrti*. Buddhist Sanskrit texts 10, The Mithila Institute, Darbhanga 1960. (3) Jacques May (tr.): *Candrakīrti Prasannapadā Madhyamakavṛtti, douze chapîtres traduits du sanscrit et du tibétain, accompagnés d'une introduction, de notes et d'une édition critique de la version tibétaine. Collection Jean Przyluski*: tome 2. Adrien-Maisonneuve, Paris 1959.

OETKE 1990 = Oetke, Claus: 'On Some Non-Formal Aspects of the Proofs of the Madhyamakakārikās', in: David Seyfort Ruegg; Lambert Schmithausen (eds.): *Earliest Buddhism and Madhyamaka*. E.J. Brill, Leiden 1990: 91–109.

PP = Candrakīrti: *Prasanna-padā*. See: MMK.

TARSKI 1944 = Tarski, Alfred: 'The Semantic Conception of Truth and the Foundations of Semantics', *Philosophy and Phenomenological Research* 4, (1944) 341–376.

Cannibalising Nyāya Epistemology

STEPHEN H. PHILLIPS

Like some or even many readers who are specialists in classical Indian philosophies, I live in two worlds within academia, indology and philosophy, and I have noticed that each discipline encourages, systemically, a characteristic *doṣa*, a fault or flaw, an epistemic failing. For indology, the flaw is the historicist fallacy, in particular the tendency to discount—or ignore, purposefully overlook, like Sartrean 'bad faith', which is a failure to acknowledge and engage with—the articulated reasons A that classical philosopher S has for a position P in favour of other reasons U ('U' for 'undercutting') that involve material or other circumstances specified to explain why S holds P. For philosophy, the *doṣa* is similar to what classical philosophers call *apasiddhānta*, advancing a position P that—although true to traditional reasoning about issues surrounding P—cuts off the wider philosophy of a school and its broader tenets, trying to graft P onto an antagonist system. An example of the indological flaw is to try to explain why later Naiyāyikas embrace theism without attending to Nyāya's theistic arguments. This example is transparent, and little explanation is necessary. Furthermore, I have belaboured the historicist flaw in other publications and venues.[1] In this paper, I would like to elaborate a pitfall common to philosophic approaches to classical systems.

A clear example of the philosophic error is not so easy to find as of the indological error. The one on which I will focus will be the lifting of Nyāya positions and arguments to advance in contemporary theory of knowledge, an externalist theory, specifically, the prominent variety of externalism known as reliabilism. Reliabilists hold that a subject S has justification for a belief P just in case P has been produced by a r e l i a b l e method of knowledge. A method of knowledge is understood as a belief-generating process that S can identify and employ to gain knowledge. Reliability is defined as a method's hitting the truth more than 50 per cent of the time. Reliabilists are externalists because they advance a causal theory of knowledge. Naiyāyikas are also externalists in this sense, but they are not reliabilists. An example of the philosophic flaw would be to graft Nyāya arguments for externalism to a modern reliabilism without regard for the broader Nyāya theory. That such borrowing for

[1] PHILLIPS (2008), (2002), (1996) and (1995).

World View and Theory in Indian Philosophy
Warsaw Indological Studies 5 (2012) 399–406.

other purposes is a flaw from a philosophic perspective is rather difficult to see. My aim here is to nail down the nature of the *doṣa*, and not just from an indological but also from a philosophic perspective.

One more general comment before digging in. Taking the indological approach together with the philosophic, I want to say that the two characteristic missteps are not errors just with respect to the other discipline. The historicist flaw in indology is not a flaw only when one assumes the different goals of philosophic study and engagement. For the indological goal of identifying the forces of change cannot be accomplished without taking into account stated reasons A, stated by philosopher S, why he holds P. Surely it is sometimes the case that a philosopher's reason for taking some position P is precisely what he says it is. My contention is that no history of Indian philosophy can ignore such explicitly stated reasons A, since in some cases theory advances on the basis of A. An accurate history cannot ignore A. Similarly, I want to argue that the philosophic flaw of severing a thesis such as Nyāya's externalism in epistemology to advance whatever extraneous agenda is hazardous not only hermeneutically, in its potentiality to skew or misrepresent Nyāya as an historical system, but also from the evaluative perspective of philosophy that has the truth, or justifiably believing the truth, as its goal. This may seem an impossible task. For what could be wrong with using bits and pieces of an ancient system in a fresh attempt to advance knowledge? The worry is not only hermeneutical in character, a likelihood of misrepresenting the classical system. Yes, there is that hermeneutical concern, but also the purely philosophic danger of incoherence, termed classically the fallacy of *apasiddhānta*. In other words, the problem is not just of skewing the system from a historical perspective but of undermining the philosophic goal of believing the truth for good reasons. My point is that, like historicism, *apasiddhānta* is an objective flaw, and so too its correlate, which I shall name 'the borrower's fallacy'. This philosophic fallacy is not dependent upon privileging the *siddhānta* of Nyāya or whatever world view wherefrom the student would carve off a thesis for the consumption of contemporaries, the 'cannibalising' of my title, which has unfortunately a positive connotation in philosophy. This is a bubble that I hope to burst.

The sixteen principal topics of the *Nyāya-sūtra* are listed in the very first *sūtra*, and among these is *siddhānta*, 'facts as known' (to follow Uddyotakara against a position he attributes to Buddhists that the word is synonymous with *pakṣa*, 'theory' or 'point of view'[2]). A stretch of six *sūtra*s in the first chapter (NS 1.1.26–31) is devoted to the *siddhānta*, and both Uddyotakara and Vātsyāyana have much of interest to say. I shall quote the latter on the variety

[2] NV 1.1.31, pp. 267–68: *pakṣa-paryāya eva siddhānta iti ... aho paryāya-śabdeṣu kauśalaṁ bhadantasya.*

of *siddhānta* called 'facts as known by contextual implication' (*adhikaraṇa-siddhānta*). But let us first focus on the *apasiddhānta*.

In the *Nyāya-sūtra*, the last chapter, on debate, lists *apasiddhānta* as a way of losing an argument (*nigraha-sthāna*), a 'point of defeat', not just a kind of inconsistency but 'deep inconsistency', as I'd like to translate. The *sūtra* that defines it, NS 5.2.23, is the next to last *sūtra* of the entire work, suggesting, by way of placement, that this way of losing an argument is a scoundrel's last resort, the opponent surrendering through the force of counter-argument an original thesis at issue: 'Pursuit of a theoretic account that is illicit in not being regulated by what is known' (*siddhāntam abhyupetya aniyamāt kathā-prasaṅgaḥ*). But Vātsyāyana elaborates with an example that leads later Naiyāyikas to group this together with fallacies (*ābhāsa*) of 'rational inquiry' (*vāda*), to make a set of seven or eight, as opposed to a larger group of 'ways of losing an argument' (*nigraha-sthāna*), appropriate to more adversarial controversies. *Vāda* involves no trickery, no mere debating to win, the goal being rather to uncover the truth. It is the best kind of debate and inquiry, and is conducted among those subscribing to the same overall view, despite some disagreements or even factionalism (*eka-deśāḥ*). Vātsyāyana's example has a disputant elaborating a Sāṁkhya position that centres on a common nature or *prakṛti* complete with supporting arguments, who then under the pressure of cross-examination of the thesis that this nature is eternal and unchanging surrenders the view that the existent never goes out of existence. Consideration of the goal-directed character of human action forces the hypothetical Sāṁkhya exponent to admit that some properties do come into existence, endure for awhile, and then do indeed cease to be. According to Vātsyāyana, such admission is no mere minor modification of the world view, but 'gives up the ship', gives up too much of the entire story, too much of the overall view. There is 'deep inconsistency' (*nigraha-sthāna*).

Gaṅgeśa uses the word *apasiddhānta* in several places, and I know of two usages that are particularly telling, one in his treatment of perception, the other in that of inference. Against the Nyāya view that absences are known perceptually, inferentially and by testimony, with no need to admit an additional knowledge source (*pramāṇa*), a Bhāṭṭa opponent (*pūrva-pakṣin*) proposes that absences are known by the special cognitive means of 'non-cognition' (*anupalabdhi*). Then, pushed into a corner by Gaṅgeśa's argument that the result of the Bhāṭṭa's proposed special source of knowledge for absences is itself an absence, an absence of cognition, and would have to be itself cognised in order for its absential object to be known, Gaṅgeśa has his opponent propose that, well, it is cognised. The Naiyāyika retorts that this would be *apasiddhānta*, going beyond the facts as established. The Bhāṭṭa famously holds that any cognition is itself uncognised, a position that Gaṅgeśa endorses. This is the relevant 'fact as known'. I think that, following again Uddyotakara on *Nyāya-sūtra* 1.1.31, the point may be not so much that Kumārila's well-known position on self-knowledge, or cognition of cognition, would have to be given up, though that is true. The point is that the parties to the discussion (here including the Bhāṭṭa) can take it for granted that cognition is not self-luminous, a position that has been laboured out not only within the philosophic inheritance of the two schools but also by Gaṅgeśa himself in earlier sections of the *Tattva-cintā-maṇi*. So the response is not open, involving deep inconsistency.[3]

The second usage of *apasiddhānta* I want to mention, which occurs in a section of the inference chapter, similarly engages possible factionalism, but here, unlike the earlier usage in the mouth of a proponent of the rival school of Mīmāṁsā, through a Nyāya interlocutor. The point is that a proposed way of wriggling out of a difficulty about term introduction in the formulation of a 'negative-only inference' (the example is a definition of earth as that which has earthhood) is no good because, again, it lies in conflict with too much that we take ourselves to know. In other words, the proposal is not an option, albeit on some issues different options are live, competing options championed by what are called factions of Naiyāyikas, none of whom is viewed as giving away the store (on some issues three or even four factions are identified and no *siddhānta*). But here on the issue of the logic of absences, Gaṅgeśa judges that previously detailed views about absences rule out what might otherwise be a promising proposal, helping to solve the problem at hand.[4]

According to the *Nyāya-sūtra*, 'facts as known' (*siddhānta*) may be 'facts as known by context' (*adhikaraṇa-siddhānta*). The example Vātsyāyana gives beautifully makes my overall point. The Nyāya proof (NS 3.1.1) that the knower is different from the senses hinges on our ability to perceive the same object through different sense organs. The proof implicates, Vātsyāyana tells us here, several further theses, including 'the multiplicity of the senses, their being invariably restricted to the same type of object (such as colour or sound), their being known by inferential marks which are a knower's graspings of their characteristic objects, that they help to produce cognitions, that a substance is distinct from a quality such as smell whose locus the substance is, and that conscious beings (i.e. selves) are not restricted to (cognitions of single types of) objects'.[5] In other words, what is proved by the cross-modality argument may seem a small, isolable thesis. But it is not isolated, implicating many other facts, Vātsyāyana clearly sees.

The wide lesson I would like to draw out is that a world view such as Nyāya is conceived by its adherents as, and is in fact, a rather tightly interlocking nexus of propositions, few of which can be separated out to stand on their own

[3] PHILLIPS–TATACHARYA (2004: 424–425).

[4] TCM_1, p. 429; translation: TCM_2, p. 479.

[5] NBh 1.1.30, p. 265: *indriya-nānātvaṁ niyata-viṣayāṇi-indriyāṇi sva-viṣaya-grahaṇa-liṅgāni jñātur jñāna-sādhanāni gandhâdi-guṇa-vyatiriktaṁ dravyaṁ guṇâdhikaraṇam aniyata-viṣayāś cetanā iti.*

or in a different system such that severing can be limited to small digestible chunks. Typically a whole can of wormy ramifications would be let loose. Not appreciating the magnitude of the theory (hidden in the philosopher's version of the subprime mortgage), the student commits what I should like to call the borrower's fallacy, taking on more liability than he can handle. The classical fallacy of *apasiddhānta* is uni-directional, presupposing a coherent body of knowledge that rules out some proposals, so to say, in advance. The borrower's fallacy is also uni-directional, but originates not in Nyāya but in a foreign view and is a problem for the foreign view. For example, Nyāya externalism is a huge piece of theory consisting of dozens of interlocking positions, any one of which trails others and none of which are easily put to use in a foreign agenda, unless the foreigner practically becomes a Naiyāyika herself.

Now I should mention a notion, or principle, in early Nyāya that may seem to run counter to my emphasis on holism and coherence. Vātsyāyana introduces it at the very end of his commentary on *Nyāya-sūtra* 1.1.4, the perception *sūtra*, to answer a question why *manas*, the common or internal sense organ, is not explicitly referred to in the *sūtra*. This is the principle of *tantra-yukti* that says that something learned in the course of studying other schools is to be incorporated into one's own system unless ruled out by *siddhānta*. Thus the *sūtra-kāra* did not have to mention *manas* in the *sūtra* defining perception, we are told, since it is assumed to be a sense organ. But, as Uddyotakara points out, this might lead us to expect very little to be expressly stated by Gautama, since so much is held in common with one or another school (especially, it seems suggested, Vaiśeṣika). My sense is that all this is pretty much mere hermeneutical sophistry and is not taken and is not to be taken very seriously (I know of no Navya Nyāya usage of *tantra-yukti*). Commentators like to see Gautama as flawless and go to great lengths to explain away deficiencies that one suspects are known to be the flaws that they are. Furthermore, as especially Udayana shows in his corpus, it does seem right that one should incorporate what one learns elsewhere, from Praśastapāda for instance, into one's world view so long as there is no discordance. Of course that is a very big qualification. We may be able to take in a lot from Vaiśeṣika and even Mīmāṁsā (though mostly on ontological topics and not much concerning *pramāṇa* where we have very developed views). These two are after all fellow realist philosophies. But how much can be absorbed from Buddhist teachings? There we have to be very careful, because even such a seemingly neutral batch of theory as the nature of inference and of inferential fallacies we find time and again to be perversely explained by the *kutārkika*s ('bad reasoners') who would mislead students, Uddyotakara tells us as elaborated by Vācaspati at the beginning of his *ṭīkā*, explaining why despite the brilliance and thoroughness of Gautama and Vātsyāyana, additional commentarial efforts are called for, such as Uddyotakara's and indeed his own 'Notes'.[6]

The reason why *apasiddhānta* is a fallacy sheds light on the borrower's pitfall. I know I myself am guilty, and I find philosophy graduate students commonly committing it. It is also a fallacy of scholarship, since the ways in which individual bits of *siddhānta* interconnect have usually been drawn out in Nyāya literature. That's what a Nyāya author does, namely, to bring out the connections which permit, in particular, new inferences to be constructed to answer new questions or challenges from within Nyāya or without. One reason why it has been difficult for scholars to differentiate the views of Navya and Prācīna Nyāya is that there are not so many differences. One has to be a rather patient student not to commit the fallacy of *apasiddhānta*, since, we are not Gautama nor the *bhāṣya-kāra* nor the 'teacher', *ācārya*, Udayana. Nyāya covers a lot of ground, both historically and philosophically.

Philosophy is not to be carried out piecemeal, at least not according to Nyāya—a position with which I agree. This attitude runs directly counter to that endorsed by the early analytic philosopher, Bertrand Russell[7] who reacted strongly against the oversystematic methods of German and British idealists. But while the humility of Russell and his analytic followers is admirable, as is too their acquiescence to science and suspicion of brittlely deductive philosophy, still we must recognise that views about self, knowledge, action, and things interlock. I think Nyāya philosophers progressively saw this themselves. Even the Nyāya theology, which is perhaps not so well implicated by Gautama in the *sūtra*s, ties up pretty tightly with, for example, both the realism about objects of cognition and the epistemology of inference (inference is the source of knowledge of God). But not to get side-tracked with what is possibly the exception that proves the rule (I admit that Nyāya theology is practically detachable), let me continue with the more telling example of the epistemology of testimony and the reliabilism I have already mentioned. To look at testimony as a source of knowledge or justification within the context of current theorising, which is dominated by a Western heritage, runs the risk, let me repeat, not just of tearing the holistic fabric of Nyāya but of injuring that to which it is grafted. The Nyāya theory of knowledge is a whole book of theses, some of which run directly counter to reliabilism or to presuppositions of a reliabilist project.

There is in contemporary epistemology overall (not just with the reliabilist), a concern that has deep roots running back to Socrates and more lately Descartes: what is the fundamental basis or bases of epistemic entitlement? The

[6] NV, p. 1; NVTṬ, p. 2: *yady api bhāṣya-kṛtā kṛta-vyutpādanam etat tathâpi dignāga-prabhṛtibhir arvācinaiḥ kuhetu-santamasa-samutthāpanena ācchāditaṁ śāstram na tattva-nirṇaya-paryāptam ity uddyotakareṇa sva-nibandha-uddyotena tad apanīyata iti prayojanavān ārambha iti. …*

[7] RUSSELL (1912), esp. chs. 14 and 15.

reliabilist answers this question by appealing to a track record. A belief-generating method proves itself trustworthy by giving us the truth in most instances and in at least better than half the cases. Thus the reliabilist is prone to see Nyāya's 'perception', for instance, as a method that has survived such scrutiny, that has been shown reliable in action, apparently following the well-known Nyāya inference to veridicality of cognition C from success of effort directed by or based on C, an argument seemingly easily liftable. Thus human perception is indeed reliable but hardly factive, hardly infallible concerning all things perceived. Our best epistemic methods are fallible but on the whole give us the truth. But now notice that in this way what are actually different ways of process identification get conflated. Reliabilism is concerned with determining the reliability of a method of knowledge, whereas Nyāya is concerned with distinguishing between genuine *pramāṇa* and pseudo-*pramāṇa*, between genuine perception which is factive and pseudo-perception which is not. For Nyāya, that genuine perception or indeed testimony produces knowledge is *a priori*. That no false cognition is produced by a genuine knowledge source is a matter of definition. Any false cognition will have been produced by a pseudo-*pramāṇa*.

To be sure, Nyāya endorses a certification procedure that is similar to the standard reliabilist approach, legitimation by appeal to track record. For example, some particular person's authoritativeness may be judged by the truth of her assertions in the past. But by Nyāya's lights, the history of truth-telling would be considered evidence not in support of *pramāṇa* types such as perception, inference, or testimony, whose inerrancy is a conceptual truth. Rather, such review would be undertaken to determine whether the particular person's statements are results of the *pramāṇa* testimony and not pseudo-testimony (*śabdâbhāsa*). It is tempting to see the positions as the same. But note that the reliabilist would land in utter scepticism, no perfect correlation with truth occurring with any method, if the infallibilism of Nyāya's 'knowledge sources' were imported into her theory. The graft would poison the host.

The main lesson is that as much as philosophic interpreters may want to offer up select classical positions and arguments for the consumption of contemporary philosophers who know little or nothing of intricacies, an interpreter should always heed systematic ties and constraints, however unattractive to the uninformed contemporary, before serving up a platter of severed theses. And typically there will be good philosophic reasons for this, not just reasons of sound hermeneutics. Nyāya is a world view, like other classical *darśana*, all not easily emendable or consumable by a larger fish.

BIBLIOGRAPHY

NBh = Vātsyāyana Pakṣilasvāmin: *Nyāya-bhāṣya*. See: NS.

NS = Akṣapāda Gautama: *Nyāya-sūtra*. (1) Taranatha Nyaya-Tarkatirtha; Amarendramohan Tarkatirtha; Hemantakumar Tarkatirtha (eds.): *Nyāyadarśanam. With Vātsyāyana's Bhāṣya, Uddyotakara's Vārttika, Vācaspati Miśra's Tātparyaṭīkā & Viśvanātha's Vṛtti*. 2 Vols., Second edition, Munshiram Manoharlal, New Delhi 1985 [first edition: Calcutta Sanskrit Series 18, 19, Metropolitan Printing & Publishing House, Calcutta 1936, 1944].

NV = Uddyotakara: *Nyāya-[bhāṣya]-vārttika*. See: NS.

NVTṬ = Vācaspatimiśra: *Nyāya-vārttika-tātparya-ṭīkā*. See: NS.

PHILLIPS 1995 = Phillips, Stephen H.: 'Review of Purushottama Bilimoria, *Śabdapramāṇa, Word and Knowledge*', *Philosophy East and West* 45,2 (1995) 273–280 [reprinted as prologue to the Indian republication: Delhi 2008: xix–xxv].

PHILLIPS 1996 = Phillips, Stephen H.: 'Philosophic India Studies Since Mid-century in North America', in: K. Satchidananda Murty; Amit Dasgupta (eds.): *The Perennial Tree*. Indian Council of Philosophical Research, New Delhi 1996: 161–76.

PHILLIPS 2002 = Phillips, Stephen H.: 'The Universal in Classical Indian Philosophy', *Evam* 1.1 (2002) 1–10.

PHILLIPS 2008 = Phillips, Stephen H.: 'Engagement with Sanskrit Philosophic Texts', in: Arvind Sharma, Rita Sherma (eds.): *Hermeneutics and Hindu Thought*. Springer, Berlin 2008: 169–78.

PHILLIPS–TATACHARYA 2004 = Phillips, Stephen H.; Tatacharya, N.S. Ramanuja (tr.): *Epistemology of Perception. The Perception Chapter of Gaṅgeśa's Tattvacintāmaṇi*. American Institute of Buddhist Studies, New York 2004 [Indian edition, Motilal Banarsidass, Delhi 2009].

RUSSELL 1912 Russell, Bertrand: *The Problems of Philosophy*. Oxford University Press, Oxford 1912.

TCM = Gaṅgeśa: *Tattva-cintā-maṇi*. (1) N.S. Ramanuja Tatacharya: *Tattva-cintā-maṇi of Gaṅgeśa*. Vol. 2: *Anumāna-khaṇḍa*, Part One (With the *Prakāśa* commentary by Rucidatta Miśra and a subcommentary by Dharmarājādhvarin). Kendriya Sanskrit Vidyapeetha Series 33, Tirupati 1982. (2) Stephen H. Phillips (tr.): 'From the *Tattva-cintā-maṇi* by Gaṅgeśa: The *kevala-vyatireki-prakaraṇam*: Negative-Only Inference (Annotated Translation and Commentary)', in: Piotr Balcerowicz (ed.): *Logic and Belief in Indian Philosophy*. Motilal Banarsidass, Delhi 2010: 447–517.

The Meaning of a Diversity of Established World Views or Tenets (*siddhānta*) in the Science of Debate: with Special Reference to Jayanta's Interpretation of the *Abhyupagama-siddhānta* (NS 1.1.31) and Its Evaluation in the Development of Nyāya System*

HIROSHI MARUI

1. Introduction.

The sixteen categories (*ṣoḍaśa-padārthāḥ*) of the Nyāya system (*nyāya-śāstra*) may be regarded as 'the headings of chapters of a handbook of logic and dialectics.'[1] The sixth category is the '*siddhānta*', variously translated as 'settled opinion or doctrine, dogma, axiom, received or admitted truth',[2] 'a proved fact, established truth, dogma, settled doctrine',[3] 'accepted conclusions',[4] 'principle or dogma',[5] 'tenet',[6] 'Doctrine (or Theory)',[7] 'proved doctrine'[8] etc.; henceforward referred to as 'established doctrine' or '(established) tenet', or simply '*siddhānta*'. Since it was listed as a subject of the science of dialectics (*nyāya*), the subject of *siddhānta* must have occupied its own place in the science of

* This paper is a part of the present author's research results supported by 2012 Grant-in-Aid for Scientific Research (A) (No. 23242004) from the JSPS. It is a revised version of the original paper read by the present author on 28 April 2008 during the International Conference 'World view and theory in Indian philosophy' held in Barcelona 26–30 April, 2008. The original paper was a part of the present author's research results supported by 2008 Grant-in-Aid for Scientific Research (C) (No. 17520045) from the JSPS.

[1] KEITH (1921: 174).

[2] MONIER-WILLIAMS (1997: 1216). This series of meanings is given immediately after 'demonstrated conclusion of an argument.'

[3] APTE (1965: 1681). These meanings are listed under the third group. Under the second group are: 'the demonstrated conclusion of an argument, established view of any question, the true logical conclusion (following on the refutation of the Pūrvapakṣa).'

[4] DASGUPTA (1975: 294).

[5] KEITH (1921: 175).

[6] POTTER (1977: 208).

[7] JHĀ (1983: 47 ff.).

[8] CHATTOPADHYAYA–GANGOPADHYAYA (1982: 36–39).

World View and Theory in Indian Philosophy
Warsaw Indological Studies 5 (2012) 407–432.

debate. But as far as I know, very little has been done to clarify the dialectical function of *siddhānta* in the discipline of *vāda* or Nyāya system.[9]

In the *Nyāya-bhāṣya* (NBh) Vātsyāyana tries to elucidate why Akṣapāda sets up the *siddhānta* as an independent subject and provides the following description of the specific role that the *siddhānta* is to play in the process of debating:

> '[Though it is an object of valid cognition (*prameya*)], it (the *siddhānta*) is separately mentioned [as a subject of Nyāya system] because discussion (*vāda*), tricky disputation (*jalpa*) and wrangling (or destructive criticism, *vitaṇḍā*) take place only when there is a difference among established doctrines, and not otherwise.'[10]

According to this explanation, the difference of established tenets acts as a starter of any sort of controversy (*kathā*). But, was it the function or the only function that the subject item '*siddhānta*' was supposed to play in the science of dialectics presented in the first and the fifth chapters of the *Nyāya-sūtra* (NS)?

There are a dozen *sūtra*s (see below) that include the term '*siddhānta*' or refer to the subject, but we cannot find any *sūtra* among them that seems to have a direct connection with the above explication by Vātsyāyana.

—Enumeration of the sixteen subjects of Nyāya system:

NS1.1.1: *pramāṇa-prameya-saṁśaya-prayojana-dṛṣṭānta-**siddhāntâ**vayava-tarka-nirṇaya-vāda-jalpa-vitaṇḍā-hetvâbhāsa-cchala-jāti-nigraha-sthānānāṁ tattva-jñānān niḥśreyasâdhigamaḥ.*

—Definition and division of *siddhānta*:

NS 1.1.26: *tantrâdhikaraṇâbhyupagama-saṁsthitiḥ **siddhāntaḥ**.*

NS 1.1.27: ***sa*** *(siddhāntaḥ) catur-vidhaḥ sarva-tantra-pratitantrâdhikaraṇâbhyupagama-saṁsthity-arthântara-bhāvāt.*

NS 1.1.28: *sarva-tantrâviruddhas tantre 'dhikṛto 'rthaḥ **sarva-tantra-siddhāntaḥ**.*

NS 1.1.29: *samāna-tantra-siddhaḥ para-tantrâsiddhaḥ **pratitantra-siddhāntaḥ**.*

NS 1.1.30: *yat-siddhāv anya-prakaraṇa-siddhiḥ so **'dhikaraṇa-siddhāntaḥ**.*

NS 1.1.31: *aparīkṣitâbhyupagamāt tad-viśeṣa-parīkṣaṇam **abhyupagama-siddhāntaḥ**.*

—Definition of *vāda*:

NS 1.2.1: *pramāṇa-tarka-sādhanôpālambaḥ **siddhāntâviruddhaḥ** pañcâvayavôpapannaḥ pakṣa-pratipakṣa-parigraho vādaḥ.*

---

[9] The only noteworthy observation I can presently call attention to in this connection is, KEITH (1921: 175–177).

[10] NBh on NS 1.1.1, p. 46.1–2: *tasya (siddhāntasya) pṛthag-vacanam, satsu siddhānta-bhedeṣu vāda-jalpa-vitaṇḍāḥ pravartante, nâto 'nyathêti.*

—Definition of a pseudo-reason (*hetvâbhāsa*) named *viruddha*:

NS 1.2.6: ***siddhāntam*** *abhyupetya tad-virodhī viruddhaḥ*.

—Enumeration of twenty-two points of defeat:

NS 5.2.1: *pratijñā-hāniḥ pratijñântaraṁ pratijñā-virodhaḥ pratijñā-saṁnyāso hetv-antaraṁ arthântaraṁ nirarthakam avijñātârtham apārthakam aprāpta-kālaṁ nyūnam adhikaṁ punar-uktam ananubhāṣaṇam ajñānam apratibhā vikṣepo matânujñā paryanuyojyôpekṣaṇaṁ niranuyojyânuyogo* ***'pasiddhānto*** *hetvâbhāsāś ca nigraha-sthānāni*.

—Definition of a point of defeat named *apasiddhānta*:

NS 5.2.23: *siddhāntam abhyupetyâniyamāt kathā-prasaṅgo* ***'pasiddhāntaḥ***.

Moreover, we also have to pay attention to the possibility of the historical change of the concept of *siddhānta* in Nyāya. For example, Jayanta explains the meaning of *siddhānta* in the science of dialectics differently from Vātsyāyana. According to him, the *siddhānta* is one of the causes of reasoning or argumentation (*nyāya-pravṛtti-hetu*);[11] specifically it forms the basis of reasoning and argumentation (*siddhantâśrayā nyāya-pravṛttiḥ*)[12] in the sense that it establishes a 'property-possessor' (*dharmi-prāpaṇa*) as the common indisputable subject entity (e.g. *śabda*), with reference to which opposing parties (e.g. Naiyāyikas and Mīmāṁsakas) may conduct a controversy with each other by claiming two contrary properties (*anityatva* and *nityatva*) respectively.[13] Jayanta does not refer to the role of the difference of *siddhānta*s as a dialectical starter,[14] but emphasises the function of the *siddhānta* to prepare the common basis for applying the dialectical method.

Here we cannot afford to enter into a comprehensive study of the meaning(s) and function(s) that were 'originally' attributed to the dialectical category of *siddhānta* in the entire Nyāya system, nor can we commence an exhaustive exploration of the historical change of the meaning(s) of '*siddhānta*' in Nyāya. We would simply like to make the first step to all of these studies by analysing Jayanta's interpretation of NS 1.1.26–31 in the *Nyāya-mañjarī* (NMa). Specifically we will examine his understanding of the *abhyupagama-siddhanta* ('a hypothetical tenet', 'a temporarily accepted tenet') treated in NS 1.1.31.

Before going into the details, however, let me mention a few words about the connection between this article and the main theme of the present volume 'World view and theory in Indian philosophy'. If we may regard an established doctrine or tenet (*siddhānta*) as a component of a certain system of thought or

---

[11] NMa_1 I: 23. 2.

[12] NMa_1 I: 23.8; NMa_1 II: 547.6–7, 547.13.

[13] NMa_1 I: 23.8–13.

[14] When he says that '*siddhānta-bhIdāś catasraḥ*' are the first ground of 'the methodological inquiry of Nyāya' (*nyāya-pravṛtti*; NMa_1 II: 550.6–9), he simply refers to the four kinds of *siddhānta*s, not to the difference of *siddhānta*s.

world view (*darśana*), the inquiry into the meaning of a diversity of world views in the Indian tradition(s) of debate (*vāda*-tradition(s)) entails the examination of the meaning of a difference of tenets (*siddhānta-bheda*) in the same tradition(s). In order to see the significance of the *siddhānta-bheda* in the science of dialectics of Nyāya, we must make a basic study of various possible aspects of the concept of *siddhānta* in the relevant *Nyāya-sūtra*s together with the various corresponding interpretations on each of them in a philological and historical manner. For this purpose the *Nyāya-mañjarī* is undoubtedly one of the most important sources of information. Moreover, the idea of the 'provisionally admitted tenet' (*abhyupagama-siddhānta*) is of special significance in this context because it evidently underwent a considerable change of interpretation[15] after Vātsyāyana and this conceptual change seems to have important implications for the disciplinary development of Nyāya in which more and more emphasis seems to have been put on the static system of the quest for the truth by means of *pramāṇa*s ('the means of valid cognition') rather than the dialectical dynamism.

2. Jayanta's account of the generic definition (*sāmānya-lakṣaṇa*) of the *siddhānta*.

The six *sūtra*s NS 1.1.26–31 are concerned with the *siddhānta*. The NS 1.1.27 classifies it into four kinds: (1) 'a tenet accepted by all systems of philosophy' (*sarva-tantra-siddhānta*), (2) 'a system-specific tenet' (*pratitantra-siddhānta*), (3) 'a tenet implied by the establishment of a topic thesis' (*adhikaraṇa-siddhānta*), and (4) 'a hypothetical tenet', or 'a provisionally admitted tenet' (*abhyupagama-siddhānta*). The subsequent four *sūtra*s NS 1.1.28–31 respectively focus on the explanation of each of the four types of 'tenets'. The definition or explanation of the *abhyupagama-siddhānta* is given at NS 1.1.31:

> 'The "provisionally admitted tenet" is [applied for] the examination of a specific nature of the [object at issue] by admitting it provisionally without proof.'[16]

With regard to NS 1.1.31, Jayanta first presents an explanation of 'some' (*kecid*)[17], then criticises it,[18] and finally gives the interpretation that he regards as proper.[19]

Before we enter into the details, it may be relevant to see how Jayanta understands the definitive character common to all (*sāmānya-lakṣaṇa*) of the four

---

[15] Cf. KEITH (1921: 175–177).

[16] NS 1.1.31: *aparīkṣitâbhyupagamāt tad-viśeṣa-parīkṣaṇam abhyupagama-siddhāntaḥ.* The above is only a provisional English translation. As will be shown below, the interpretation of the *sūtra* differs greatly among Nyāya scholars.

[17] NMa_1 II: 548.5–18: *atra kecid evaṁ vyācakṣate…*

[18] NMa_1 II: 549.1–8: *etat tu vyākhyānaṁ na budhyāmahe…*

[19] NMa_1 II: 549.9–550.5: *tasmād evaṁ vyākhyāyate…*

kinds of *siddhānta* which we find in his explanation of NS 1.1.26 in the *Nyāya-mañjarī*.

> Text 1 (NMa$_1$ II: 544.4–11):
> '[NS 1.1.26:] The tenet is the establishment of the admission of that which has the *tantra* as its substratum.'
> '[NMa *ad loc.*:] The meaning of the word "*tantra*" is etymologically understood as follows: The means by which the establishment of a subject is provided (?, *tantryate*) is the "*tantra*." That is what is called the means of valid cognition (*pramāṇa*). The word "substratum" (*adhikaraṇa*) means the receptacle (*āśraya*). What is meant by the compound "*tantrâdhikaraṇa*" is that which has the "*tantra*" as its substratum, namely that which has a means of valid cognition as its basis. The word "admission" (*abhyupagama*) means "acceptance" (*svī-kāra*), the establishment of which is the determination of the exact character [of an object], namely the specification of its true nature [in the form of] "this has such nature." The word "this" represents something general and the word "such nature" something specific. Accordingly, the tenet is "the establishment of the admission of that which has the *tantra* as its basis", that is to say, what is established as the object of the admission that has the means of valid cognition as its basis and has both general and specific aspects as well. Thus it has turned out that the generic definition of tenet is mentioned [in this *sūtra*.]'[20]

Thus, the term '*tantrādhikaraṇa*' ('that which has the *tantra* as its substratum') in NS 1.1.26, taken as a *bahu-vrīhi* compound, is paraphrased into '*pramāṇa-mūlaka*' ('that which has *tantra*, namely *pramāṇa* ('the means of valid cognition'), as its basis'), the word '*tantra*' being equated with '*pramāṇa*' by means of an etymological analysis (*tantryate 'nena padârtha-sthitir iti tantraṁ pramāṇam ucyate*). Accordingly, the '*tantrâdhikaraṇa-abhyupagama*', taken as a *karma-dhāraya* compound, means 'the admission (*abhyupagama*) that has the means of valid cognition (*pramāṇa*) as its basis'. The *saṁsthiti* is interpreted as 'the determination of the exact character of an object' (*itthaṁ-bhāva-vyavasthā*), namely 'the specification of its true nature [in the form of] this has such and such nature' (*dharma-niyamaḥ idam ittham iti*). For example, according to the Vaiśeṣikas, the doctrine has been established by inference that

[20] NS 1.1.26: *tantrâdhikaraṇâbhyupagama-saṁsthitiḥ siddhāntaḥ*. NMa$_1$ II: 544.4–11: *tantryate 'nena padârtha-sthitir iti tantraṁ pramāṇam ucyate. adhikaraṇam āśrayaḥ. tantram adhikaraṇaṁ yasya sa tantrâdhikaraṇaḥ pramāṇa-mūlaka ity arthaḥ. abhyupagamaḥ svī-kāraḥ, tasya saṁsthitir itthaṁ-bhāva-vyavasthā dharmaniyamaḥ idam ittham iti, idam iti sāmānya-nirdeśaḥ, ittham iti viśeṣa-nirdeśaḥ. evaṁ ca tantrâdhikaraṇâbhyupagama-saṁsthitiḥ pramāṇa-mūlâbhyupagama-viṣayī-kṛtaḥ sāmānya-viśeṣavān arthaḥ siddhānta iti sāmānya-lakṣaṇam uktam bhavati*.

sound is non-eternal (*anityaḥ śabdaḥ*). The definition of 'tenet' (*siddhānta*) applies to the doctrine or rather to the allegedly established fact that sound is non-eternal, because that fact is, for the Vaiśeṣikas, the object of the admission that is based on the inference which is a type of the valid means of valid cognition (*pramāṇa-mūlâbhyupagama-viṣayīkṛtaḥ ... arthaḥ*), and because that fact has a common nature as well as a specific aspect (*sāmānya-viśeṣavān arthaḥ*). It is not exactly clear why the definition requires the attributive qualifier '*sāmānya-viśeṣavat*' ('having both general and specific natures'), but at any rate 'sound' probably corresponds to the common nature and 'being non-eternal' to the specific aspect in the present case. Consequently, the definition of *siddhānta* is formulated above as '*pramāṇa-mūlâbhyupagama-viṣayīkṛtaḥ sāmānya-viśeṣavān arthaḥ siddhāntaḥ*' ('the tenet is the matter or the state of affairs that is admitted on the basis of the means of valid cognition and that has both general and specific aspects'). And almost the same definition is found in the explanatory portion of the *Nyāya-mañjarī* on NS 1.1.1 in which Jayanta tries to give the definition of each of the sixteen *padārtha*s of Nyāya.

> Text 2 (NMa_1 I: 18.5):
>
> 'The tenet is the matter or the state of affairs that is admitted on the basis of the means of valid cognition and that has both general and specific aspects'[21]

3. The *Nyāya-mañjarī* on the *abhyupagama-siddhānta* ('a provisionally admitted tenet').

3.1. The presupposed situation of dispute.

It may be also important to consider what sort of a concrete dialectical situation Jayanta had in mind in his explanation of the *abhyupagama-siddhānta*. It seems reasonable to suppose the following context of debate behind his explanation.

A Naiyāyika disputes with a Mīmāṁsaka over the question whether sound is eternal or non-eternal. The Naiyāyika tries to prove to the Mīmāṁsaka that sound is non-eternal. Opinion differs between the two parties also on the problem whether sound belongs to the ontological category of a substance (*dravya*) or a quality (*guṇa*). But in the present dialectical context the Naiyāyika does not enter into the discussion of this problem. Accordingly, they commence the dispute on the eternality of sound without examining whether sound is a quality or a substance. Additionally, as well as alternatively, for the sake of argument, the Naiyāyika deigns to provisionally accept his opponent's view that sound is a substance, thinking that he will certainly be able to prove the non-eternality of sound and defeat the opponent even though he has made this concession to the opponent Mīmāṁsaka.

[21] NMa_1 I: 18.5: *pramāṇato 'bhyupagamyamānaḥ sāmānya-viśeṣavān arthaḥ siddhāntaḥ*.

3.2. Interpretation by 'some' (*kecid*).

Now we will study the relevant passage in the *Nyāya-mañjarī* on NS 1.1.31. In order to understand fully the meaning of the interpretation of NS 1.1.31 that Jayanta considered to be the proper explanation of *abhyupagama-siddhānta*, it is necessary to compare it with the opposing interpretation which was reported by Jayanta to be offered by 'some [Naiyāyikas]' (*kecid*) and was subsequently rejected by him. The interpretation by 'some' is given as follows.

Text 3 (NMa$_1$ II: 548.3–18):

'[NS 1.1.31:] The "provisionally admitted tenet" is [applied for] the examination of a specific nature of the [object at issue] by admitting it provisionally without proof.'

'[NMa *ad loc.*:] With regard to this [*sūtra*], the following interpretation is given by some [Nyāya scholars] (*kecit*) who adhere to the ablative case-ending of the compound *aparīkṣitâbhyupagamāt* ("by admitting it without proof") and who also follow the generic definition of "tenet" as what is established as the object of the admission that has the means of valid cognition as its basis and what has both general and specific aspects as well. "The tenet is the matter or the state of affairs that is admitted on the basis of the means of valid cognition and that has both general and specific aspects." On the occasion of the dialectical inquiry whether sound is eternal or non-eternal, one should accept the property-possessor or the subject of assertion (*dharmin*) such as sound (*śabda*) without examination, i.e. without examining it with reference to such a property as being a specific quality of ether (*ākāśa*). What will be accomplished by that admission without proof? The answer is given by mentioning *tad-viśeṣa-parīkṣaṇam* ("the examination of a specific nature of the [object at issue]"). Namely, the reason is that it is [only] when the [inferential] property-possessor of the assertion (i.e. sound) is mentioned in its generic form without being examined for the nature of sound such as being a specific quality of ether (*ākāśa*) that the dialectical investigation is possible between two opposing parties (i.e. Nyāya and Mīmāṁsā) as to whether that (i.e. sound) is eternal or non-eternal. If, on the other hand, the sound as qualified by the property of being a specific quality of ether were mentioned as the inferential property-possessor [in the assertion by the proponent, Naiyāyika], then there would follow [a dialectical fallacy in the form of] an assertion that includes a qualifier which has not been established for the opponent [i.e. Mīmāṁsaka, who advocates the theory that sound is not a quality, but a substance].

> In spite of these circumstances, if the opponent proceeds to raise an optional question about the property-possessor, saying “What is the nature of the sound that you assert to be non-eternal—is it a substance or a quality?”, then he will certainly be defeated at the time of raising the optional question in that manner, since he has arrived to the situation of [the point of defeat (*nigraha-sthāna*) named] ‘*arthântara* (irrelevant).
> Even then, in order to make another attempt at defeating [the opponent] who has already been defeated at the second stage above], the proponent (Naiyāyika) will dare to say: “Let sound be admitted to be a substance”, from a desire to display the excellence of his own intellect and from his contempt of the opponent's [poor] understanding.’[22]

According to this interpretation, the ‘*aparīkṣitâbhyupagama*’ in NS 1.1.31 means the acceptance—on the occasion of the dialectical inquiry whether sound is eternal or non-eternal—of the property-possessor (*dharmin*) such as sound (*śabda*) [, with reference to which a property such as the non-eternality (*anityatva*) is to be inferentially predicated,] without being examined, i.e. without examining it with reference to such a property as being a specific quality of ether (*ākāśa*) (*aparīkṣita* = *ākāśa-viśeṣa-guṇatvādi-dharma-parīkṣā-rahita*), about which the proponent Naiyāyika cannot share the same established doctrine with the opponent Mīmāṁsaka (*dharmiṇaḥ śabdâdeḥ nityânityatva-vicāra-carcāyāṁ aparīkṣitasyâiva ākāśa-viśeṣa-guṇatvâdi-dharma-parīkṣā-rahitasyâivâbhyupagamaḥ*). The reason that the Naiyāyika offers this acceptance is that otherwise he could not take up his disputatious investigation against the Mīmāṁsaka as to the specific nature of sound in question ([*tato 'parīkṣitâbhyupagamāt*] *tad-viśeṣa-parīkṣaṇaṁ* [*sidhyati*]). For it is only when the ‘sound’ is mentioned in its generic form (i.e. without any qualification) as the [inferential] property-possessor (in the assertion) without being examined for the nature of sound such as being a specific quality of ether (*ākāśa*) and so

---

[22] NS 1.1.31: *aparīkṣitâbhyupagamāt tad-viśeṣa-parīkṣaṇam abhyupagama-siddhāntaḥ.* NMa_1 II: 548.3–18: *atrâparīkṣitâbhyupagamāt iti yathā-śruta-paṁcamī-nirdeśam anurudhyamānāḥ pramāṇa-mūlâbhyupagama-viṣayī-kṛto 'rthaḥ siddhānta iti ca sāmānya-lakṣaṇam anusarantaḥ kecit evaṁ vyācakṣate—dharmiṇaḥ śabdâdeḥ nityânityatva-vicāra-carcāyāṁ aparīkṣitasyâiva ākāśa-viśeṣa-guṇatvâdi-dharma-parīkṣā-rahitasyâivâbhyupagamaḥ kartavyaḥ. tato 'parīkṣitâbhyupagamāt kiṁ siddhyati. ucyate—tad-viśeṣa-parīkṣaṇam iti. tad-gata-nityânityatva-parīkṣaṇaṁ hi sāmānyena dharmiṇy upādīyamāne vyoma-viśeṣa-guṇatvâdidharma-parīkṣā-rahite saty upapadyate. yadi punar ākāśa-viśeṣa-guṇatva-viśiṣṭaḥ śabdaḥ dharmitvenôpādīyate, paraṁ praty asiddha-viśeṣaṇaḥ pakṣo bhaved iti.*

evam api kṛte yadi paro (recte: *puro*) *dharmiṇaṁ vikalpayet—kīdṛśasya sataḥ śabdasya bhavatânityatvaṁ sādhyate—dravyasya guṇasya vêti, sa evaṁ vikalpayann arthântara-gamanāt tāvat parājita eva bhavati. jitam apy enaṁ punar jetuṁ sva-buddhy-atiśaya-cikhyāpayiṣayā para-buddhy-avajñayā ca vādī bravīti—astu dravyaṁ śabda iti.*

The above is only a provisional English translation.

on that the dialectical investigation is possible against the Mīmāṁsaka as to whether sound is eternal or non-eternal (*tad-gata-nityânityatva-parīkṣaṇaṁ hi sāmānyena dharmiṇy upādīyamāne vyoma-viśeṣa-guṇatvâdi-dharma-parīkṣā-rahite saty upapadyate*). If, on the other hand, the Naiyāyika mentioned a qualified 'sound' as the inferential property-possessor, formulating his assertion into something like 'the sound as a specific quality of ether (*ākāśa*) is non-eternal' (*yadi punar ākāśa-viśeṣa-guṇatva-viśiṣṭaḥ śabdaḥ dharmitvenôpādīyate*), then he would commit a dialectical fallacy, since it would be a pseudo-assertion (*pakṣâbhāsa*) in the sense that the inferential property-possessor would include a qualifier which has not been established for the opponent (*paraṁ praty asiddha-viśeṣaṇaḥ pakṣo bhaved iti*), who advocates the theory that sound is a substance.

This may be called the first stage of the debate context presupposed by 'some'. Namely, a Naiyāyika opens the dispute with a Mīmāṁsaka on the eternality of sound to demonstrate that sound is non-eternal. Though the Naiyāyika holds the established tenet that sound belongs to the category of a quality of the substance ether (*ākāśa*), he does not enter into the issue at this stage, but admits the sound as such so that it may also be accepted as the inferential substrate of the disputed property (*siṣādhayiṣita-dharma-viśiṣṭa-dharmin = pakṣa*) by the Mīmāṁsaka, who adheres to the tenet that sound is a substance.

The interpretation by 'some' does not end here, but it also anticipates the possibility of the second and third stages of the dispute. The second stage is that, in spite of these circumstances (i.e. even when the Naiyāyika mentions unqualified sound as the inferential property-possessor without adhering to his doctrine about the category of sound), if the opponent proceeds to raise an optional question about the property-possessor, saying 'What is the nature of the sound that you assert to be non-eternal—is it a substance or a quality?' (*evam api kṛte yadi paro dharmiṇaṁ vikalpayet—kīdṛśasya sataḥ śabdasya bhavatânityatvaṁ sādhyate—dravyasya guṇasya vêti*), then the opponent will certainly be defeated at this point, since he has arrived to the situation of [the point of defeat (*nigraha-sthāna*) named] '*arthântara* (irrelevant)'[23] (*sa evaṁ vikalpayann arthântara-gamanāt tāvat parājita eva bhavati*).

We can then anticipate the third stage in which, in order to make another attempt at defeating his opponent (even though he has already been defeated at the second stage above), the proponent Naiyāyika will dare to say: 'Let sound be admitted to be a substance [as the established doctrine of your Mīmāṁsā system proclaims]', from a desire to display the excellence of his own intellect and from his contempt of the opponent's [poor] understanding (*jitam apy enaṁ punar jetuṁ sva-buddhy-atiśaya-cikhyāpayiṣayā para-buddhy-avajñayā ca vādī bravīti—astu dravyaṁ śabda iti*).

---

[23] NS 5.2.7: *prakṛtād arthād apratisaṁbaddhārtham arthântaram.*

3.3. Jayanta's criticism.

The problem with the interpretation by *kecid*, in so far as the one presented as such by Jayanta is concerned, is that it is not very clear what is meant by *abhyupagama-siddhānta*. And that was the very point of origin of Jayanta's criticism. He postulated two possible meanings of the term only to refute either.

> Text 4 (NMa_1 II: 549.1–8):
>
> 'We cannot understand this interpretation. Whatever can be established as a tenet of provisional admission (*abhyupagama-siddhānta*) for those who interpret [the *sūtra*] in this manner? First of all, if the provisionally admitted tenet were nothing but the first mention of the property-possessor named sound without being qualified by the property of being a substance or a quality and so on in such a manner as "Sound is non-eternal", then what kind of meaning would be possible for the "provisional admission"? Moreover, what difference could there be between it and the system-specific tenet.
>
> Then if the hypothetical tenet were the mention of sound as qualified by the substantiality (*dravyatva*) which is accepted subsequently [as a property of sound for the sake of argument] by the [proponent] who is proud of his own intelligence, such as "Let sound be admitted to be a substance", then [the part of the *sūtra*] "*aparīkṣitâbhyupagamāt*" would not form a coherent connection [with this meaning of the provisionally admitted tenet]. The meaning of the *sūtra* has been brought by them to a totally different one.'[24]

3.3.1. (Criticism 1) The statement that sound is non-eternal cannot be an *abhyupagama-siddhānta*.

The first possible meaning proposed by Jayanta for *abhyupagama-siddhānta* is the first mention of the inferential property-possessor 'sound' without any (controversial) distinguishing attribute such as the property of being a substance or a quality, in such a manner as 'sound is non-eternal' (*anityaḥ śabda iti dravyatva-guṇatvâdi-viśeṣa-rahita-śabdâkhya-dharmi-nirdeśo yaḥ prathamam upāttaḥ sa evâbhyupagama-siddhāntaḥ*). At first sight it might seem that here

[24] NMa_1 II: 549.1–8: *etat tu vyākhyānaṁ na budhyāmahe. evaṁ vyācakṣāṇānām eṣāṁ abhyupagama-siddhānta iti ko nu vyavasita iti. yadi tāvat anityaḥ śabda iti dravyatva-guṇatvâdi-viśeṣa-rahita-śabdâkhya-rahitaḥ śabdâkhya-*[a]*dharmi-nirdeśo yaḥ prathamam upāttaḥ sa evâbhyupagama-siddhāntaḥ, tatrâbhyupagamârthaḥ kīdṛśaḥ, kaś ca pratitantra-siddhāntād asya viśeṣaḥ.*

athâstu dravyaṁ śabda iti sva-buddhy-atiśayâbhimānena paścād abhyupagamyamāna-dravyatva-viśiṣṭa-śabda-nirdeśaḥ abhyupagama-siddhāntaḥ, tarhi sūtram aparīkṣitâbhyupagamāt iti na yojitam, anyatrâiva tais sūtrârtho nīta iti.

[[a] NMa_2: °*-śabdâkhya-rahitaḥ śabdâkhya-*°.]

Jayanta anticipates the possibility that the *abhyupagama-siddhānta* is the first mention of unqualified 'sound' which forms only the *dharmin*-part of the assertion (*pratijñā*, *pakṣa*), the first step of the five-membered dialectical formula. But it is not the case. It is more likely that the first mention of unqualified 'sound' corresponds merely to the *abhyupagama*-(= *aparīkṣitâbhyupagama*); the *abhyupagama-siddhānta*, in this case, is not the p a r t of the statement, but the w h o l e statement that sound is non-eternal. Otherwise we could not understand Jayanta's second critical comment on this possibility: 'Moreover, what difference could there be between it and the system-specific tenet (*pratitantra-siddhānta*)?' (*kaś ca pratitantra-siddhāntād asya viśeṣaḥ*). What Jayanta intends to say by it must be that, if the statement that sound is non-eternal were meant by the *abhyupagama-siddhānta*, it would be nothing but a system-specific tenet which has already been defined by NS 1.1.29 and therefore there would be no need at all to propound it as a different kind of tenet.

Moreover, if we understand the passage in such a manner, it will fit in quite well with Jayanta's description of the explanation by '*kecid*' mentioned in the Text 3. We should especially note the following two points.

(1) 'Some [Naiyāyikas]' (*kecid*) are reported by Jayanta to adhere to the ablative-case ending of the '*aparīkṣitâbhyapagamāt*' when they interpret NS 1.1.31 (*aparīkṣitâbhyupagamāt iti yathā-śruta-paṁcamī-nirdeśam anurudhyamānāḥ ... kecit evaṁ vyācakṣate*).

From this point it seems clear that according to their explanation, the *aparīkṣitâbhyupagama* is not the *abhyupagama-siddhānta*, since the former, mentioned in the ablative-case ('*aparīkṣitâbhyupagamāt*'), does not stand in appositional relation (*sāmānâdhikaraṇya*) with the latter. On the contrary, we may safely say that they consider the *tad-viśeṣa-parīkṣaṇa* to be such because of the appositional relation between the two in the *sūtra*. Accordingly, we may conclude that in their view what is defined as the *abhyupagama-siddhānta* in the *sūtra* is the *tad-viśesa-parīkṣaṇa* that is accomplished by the *aparīkṣitâbhyupagama* ([*tato 'parīkṣitâbhyupagamāt*] *tad-viśeṣa-parīkṣaṇaṁ* [*sidhyati*]).

What, then, is the *tad-viśeṣa-parīkṣaṇam* (*tad-viśeṣa*-° = *tasya aparīkṣitasya viśeṣa*-° = *dharmiṇaḥ śabdâdeḥ nityânityatva-vicāra-carcāyāṁ aparīkṣitasyâiva ākāśa-viśeṣa-guṇatvâdi-dharma-parīkṣā-rahitasya viśeṣa*-°)? Is it the *tad-gata-nityânityatva-parīkṣaṇam* ('the examination whether the sound as such is eternal or non-eternal') which immediately occurs in the explanatory sentence that follows (*tato 'parīkṣitâbhyupagamāt kiṁ siddhyati. ucyate—tad-viśeṣa-parīkṣaṇam iti. tad-gata-nityânityatva-parīkṣaṇaṁ hi sāmānyena dharmiṇy upādīyamāne vyoma-viśeṣa-guṇatvâdi-dharma-parīkṣā-rahite saty upapadyate*)? But the process of examination or the subject of inquiry itself cannot be termed the tenet. It will also be clear from the next point.

(2) Likewise, those 'some [Naiyāyikas]' follow the general definition of *siddhānta*, according to which 'the tenet (*siddhānta*), i.e. the referent of the

term '*siddhānta*', is the matter or the state of affairs that is allegedly established on the basis of the means of valid cognition [and that has both common and specific characters'] (*pramāṇa-mūlâbhyupagama-viṣayī-kṛto 'rthaḥ siddhānta iti ca sāmānya-lakṣaṇam anusarantaḥ kecit evaṁ vyācakṣate*). From this point it follows that the *tad-viśeṣa-parīkṣaṇa* as the possible candidate for a case of *siddhānta* is the alleged fact established by the examination on the basis of the means of valid cognition.

Consequently, if we read carefully the above description of the explanation by *kecid* in the *Nyāya-mañjarī*, we may safely draw a conclusion that according to those some Naiyāyikas the *abhyupagama-siddhānta* (=*tad-viśeṣa-parīkṣaṇa*), as is exemplified in the above context, is the state of affairs which is expressed by the statement that sound is non-eternal and which is to be established through the process of the five-step inferential schema from the acceptance of sound without being examined for its specific property—that is to say—the (alleged) fact that sound is non-eternal. And this conclusion, too, supports the observation mentioned above: what is posited by Jayanta in his critical comment (NMa_1 II: 549.1–8) as the first possibility for the meaning of *abhyupagama-siddhānta* in the explanation by *kecid* is not the mere reference to the *dharmin*-part of the syllogism, i.e. 'sound', but the whole statement that sound is non-eternal.

At any rate, after presenting this anticipated meaning of *abhyupagama-siddhānta*, Jayanta offered a criticism: *tatra abhyupagamârthaḥ kīdṛśaḥ, kaś ca pratitantra-siddhāntād asya viśeṣaḥ*. The meaning of the first part of his criticism is not very clear, but perhaps he meant by the rhetorical question that there would be no sense of the 'the provisional admission' (*abhyupagama*) in the term *abhyupagama-siddhānta* if the term were to denote, for example, the fact of sound being non-eternal that is to be fully established by inference. The second part of Jayanta's criticism, on the other hand, is easy to understand and has already been explained above (in the first paragraph of 4.3.1). If we adopted this meaning, there would be no difference between the *abhyupama-siddhānta* and the *pratitantra-siddhānta* ('a system-specific tenet'), since the non-eternality of sound is not acceptable for the opposing System of Mīmāṁsā.

3.3.2. (Criticism 2) The temporary admission that sound is a substance cannot be an *abhyupagama-siddhānta*.

The second possible meaning of the *abhyupagama-siddhānta* that Jayanta posited for refutation is the mention of sound as qualified by the substantiality (*dravyatva*) which is accepted subsequently (as a property of sound for the sake of argument) by the [proponent] who is proud of his own intelligence, such as 'let sound be admitted to be a substance' (*astu dravyaṁ śabda iti sva-buddhy-atiśayābhimānena paścād abhyupagamyamāna-dravyatva-viśiṣṭa-śabda-nirdeśaḥ abhyupagama-siddhāntaḥ*). Jayanta rejects this possibility as improper because then (the part of) the *sūtra* '*apekṣitābhyupagamāt*' would not form a coherent connection with this meaning of *abhyupagama-siddhānta* (*sūtram aparīkṣitābhyupagamāt iti na yojitam*). For, since those 'some [Naiyāyikas]' (*kecid*) interpret the *aparīkṣitābhyupagama-* as, for example, the temporary acceptance of unqualified sound without examining whether it is a quality or a substance, there would be no way to build up in NS 1.1.31 a coherent connection between this interpretation and the temporary admission that sound is a substance. If they were to understood the *abhyupagama-siddhānta* in this sense, they would have to interpret the *apekṣitābhyupagamāt* in the *sutra*, not as the temporary acceptance of sound without examining it with reference to such a property as being a specific quality of *ākāśa*, but as the temporary admission that sound is a substance.

This is how Jayanta rejects the interpretation by 'some' (*kecid*).

3.4. The explanation that Jayanta considers to be proper.

Finally he presents the interpretation that he considers to be appropriate.

> Text 5 (NMa$_1$ II: 549.9–550.5):
>
> Therefore, [the *sūtra*] is interpreted [by us] in the following manner. The provisionally admitted tenet (*abhyupagama-siddhāntaḥ*) is nothing but the provisional admission of something without being examined which is made for the sake of argument [by the proponent] (*aparīkṣitâbhyupagama*) by the skilful use of his own intellect, such as "Let sound be admitted to be a substance." [The requirement of the condition] that [every tenet] should be the object of the admission based on valid cognition (*pramāṇa-mūlâbhyupagama-viṣayī-karaṇa*) is to be fitted to the generic definition of tenet merely in the intention of the proud proponent in such a manner as "Let even the substantiality of sound be admitted to be based on the means of valid cognition, and yet [I say] it is non-eternal. Certainly there is no substance at all that has no parts in it which is non-eternal, but even if the sound were such (i.e. a substance), I will prove that sound is non-eternal."
>
> How can you explain the ablative case ending, then?
>
> What is the matter with the ablative case ending? The reality is, indeed, just as it is explained by us. Moreover, the use of ablative case ending can be justified in the following manner. The answer is given with the ablative case ending to the one who asks, "Why is the substantiality (*dravyatva*) provisionally admitted to be in sound, then?" [The answer is] because the examination of the specific property (non-eternity) of that (i.e. sound) is possible because of the provisional admission [of the substantiality of sound]. Therefore, the provisional admission of something without examination, too, may be a kind of tenet called *abyupagama-*

> *siddhānta*. It should not be considered that the provisionally admitted tenet is nothing but the examination of "a specific property of that (subject in question)" because of the appositional expression [between *tad-viśeṣa-parīkṣaṇam* and *abhyupagama-siddhānta*], since an examination constitutes [not a tenet itself, but] the foundation of a tenet. Therefore the meaning of the *sūtra* is that the *abhyupagama-siddhānta* is the provisional admission of what has not been examined [for its controversial specific property] which is done by the proud proponent for the purpose of examining its specific property [in question]. And in many cases this is exactly how philosophers argue with each other.'[25]

According to this interpretation, the *abhyupagama-siddhāntaḥ* is nothing but the *aparīkṣitâbhyupagama*, the provisional admission of something without being examined which is made for the sake of argument [by the proponent] by the skilful use of his own intellect, such as 'let sound be admitted to be a substance' (*aparīkṣitâbhyupagama eva sva-mati-kauśalyena kriyamāṇaḥ abhyupagama-siddhāntaḥ—astu dravyaṁ śabda iti*). Jayanta recognised two problems in this interpretation for him to solve, namely how to satisfy the condition of *pramāṇa-mūlâbhyupagama-viṣayī-kṛtatva* (= *pramāṇa-mūlâbhyupagama-viṣayī-karaṇa*) in the generic definition of *abhyupagama-siddhānta* and how to explain the ablative case-ending of the '*aparīkṣitâbhyupagamāt*' in the *sūtra*.

With regard to the first difficulty, Jayanta tried to clear it away by saying that the requirement of *pramāṇa-mūlâbhyupagama-viṣayī-karaṇa*, i.e. the condition that every tenet (*siddhānta*) should be the object of the admission based on valid cognition, is fulfilled merely in the intention of the proud proponent in the form of 'let the substantiality of sound be admitted to be based on the means of valid cognition, and yet (I say) it is non-eternal. Certainly you would say that there is no substance at all that has no parts in it which is non-eternal, but even if the sound were such (i.e. a substance), I will prove that sound is non-eternal' (*pramāṇa-mūlâbhyupagama-viṣayī-karaṇaṁ tu sāmānya-lakṣaṇe*

[25] NMa$_1$ II: 549.9–550.5: *tasmād evaṁ vyākhyāyate—aparīkṣitâbhyupagama eva sva-mati-kauśalyena kriyamāṇaḥ abhyupagama-siddhāntaḥ—astu dravyaṁ śabda iti. pramāṇa-mūlâbhyupagama-viṣayī-karaṇaṁ tu sāmānya-lakṣaṇe prauḍha-vādy-abhiprāyeṇâiva yojyam. dravyatvam api pramāṇa-mūlaṁ śabdasya bhavatu, tathâpi tasyânityatvam iti. kila niravayavaṁ dravyaṁ anityam iti nâsty eva, śabdasya tu tādṛśasyâpy anityatvam ahaṁ sādhayāmîti.*

kathaṁ tarhi paṁcamī. kiṁ paṁcamyā. vastu tāvad īdṛśaṁ yathā vyākhyātam asmābhiḥ. paṁcamy api cêtthaṁ yojyate. kim-arthaṁ punar ayam aparīkṣita eva śabda-gata-dravyatvâbhyupagamaḥ kriyata iti pṛchate uttaraṁ paṁcamyâbhidhīyate—yasmād aparīkṣitâbhyupagamāt tad-viśeṣânityatva-parīkṣaṇam avakalpate, tasmād aparīkṣitâbhyupagamo 'pi abhyupagama-siddhāntaḥ. na tu tad-viśeṣaṇa-parīkṣaṇam (tad-viśeṣa-parīkṣaṇam?) eva sāmānādhikaraṇya-nirdeśāt abhyupagama-siddhānta iti mantavyaṁ, parīkṣaṇasya siddhāntâśrayatvāt. tasmāt tad-viśeṣa-parīkṣaṇârthaḥ aparīkṣitâbhyupagamaḥ prauḍha-vādinā kriyamāṇaḥ abhyupagama-siddhānta iti sūtrârthaḥ. ittham eva ca tatra tatra pravādukānāṁ vyavahāraḥ.

prauḍha-vādy-abhiprāyeṇâiva yojyam. dravyatvam api pramāṇa-mūlaṁ śabdasya bhavatu, tathâpi tasyânityatvam iti. kila niravayavaṁ dravyaṁ anityam iti nâsty eva, śabdasya tu tādṛśasyâpy anityatvam ahaṁ sādhayāmîti).

Concerning the second point, on the other hand, Jayanta first shows a defiant attitude. When demanded, 'how can you explain the ablative case-ending, then?' he replies, 'What is the matter with the ablative case-ending? The reality is, indeed, just as it is explained by us. (Preference should be given to the reality, in case there is a discrepancy between the reality and the verbal form)' (*kathaṁ tarhi paṁcamī. kiṁ paṁcamyā. vastu tāvad īdṛśaṁ yathā vyākhyātam asmābhiḥ*). He then tries to justify the use of the ablative case-ending in the *sūtra* in the following manner. The ablative case-ending in question is applied to supply an answer to the question of why the proponent provisionally admits without examination that sound is a substance (*kim-arthaṁ punar ayam aparīkṣita eva śabda-gata-dravyatvâbhyupagamaḥ kriyata iti pṛchate uttaraṁ paṁcamyâbhidhīyate*). The answer is that the provisional admission of the substantiality of sound is done because it enables the proponent to make an examination for the specific property of sound in question, i.e. its non-eternality (*tad-viśeṣa-parīkṣaṇam*), against the opponent who advocates the doctrine that sound is a substance; therefore, the provisional admission of something without examination, too, may be a kind of tenet called *abyupagama-siddhānta* (*yasmād aparīkṣitâbhyupagamāt tad-viśeṣânityatva-parīkṣaṇam avakalpate, tasmād aparīkṣitâbhyupagamo 'pi abhyupagama-siddhāntaḥ*).[26]

Then Jayanta tried to reinforce his argument by rejecting the anticipated objection that it is not the *aparīkṣitâbhyupagama*, but the '*tad-viśeṣa-parīkṣana*' ('the examination for the specific property of that', e.g. the examination for the non-eternality of sound) that should be regarded as the *abhyupagama-siddhānta* because of the appositional relation (*na tu tad-viśeṣaṇa-parīkṣaṇam* (*tad-viśeṣa-parīkṣaṇam?*) *eva sāmānâdhikaraṇya-nirdeśāt abhyupagama-siddhānta iti mantavyaṁ*). The reason for his denial of this objection is that an examination (*parīkṣaṇa*) itself cannot constitute a tenet (*siddhānta*), but is founded on it (*parīkṣaṇasya siddhāntâśrayatvāt*). Accordingly he concludes, 'Therefore the meaning of the *sūtra* is that the *abhyupagama-siddhānta* is the provisional admission of what has not been examined (for its controversial specific property) which is done by the proud proponent for the purpose of examining its specific property (in question). And in many cases this is exactly how philosophers argue with each other' (*tasmāt tad-viśeṣa-parīkṣaṇârthaḥ aparīkṣitâbhyupagamaḥ prauḍha-vādinā kriyamāṇaḥ abhyupagama-siddhānta iti sūtrârthaḥ. ittham eva ca tatra tatra pravādukānāṁ vyavahāraḥ*).

[26] Here Jayanta seems to say that one should understand the *sūtra* by completing it with the bold words: *yasmād aparīkṣitâbhyupagamāt tad-viśeṣânityatva-parīkṣaṇam avakalpate, tasmād aparīkṣitâbhyupagamo 'pi abhyupagama-siddhāntaḥ*.

4. The *Nyāya-bhāṣya* and the *Nyāya-vārttika* (NV) on the *abhyupagama-siddhānta*.

Now we will see how the two earlier Nyāya scholars interpreted NS 1.1.31.

The oldest extant commentary *Nyāya-bhāṣya* of Vātsyāyana comments on the *sūtra* as follows:

> Text 6 (NBh on NS 1.1.31):
>
> '[NS 1.1.31:] The "provisionally admitted tenet" is [applied for] the examination of a specific nature of the [object at issue] by admitting it temporarily without proof.' (Translated according to NBh).
>
> '[NBh *ad loc.*:] When a thing of a certain kind (e.g. sound) is provisionally accepted (e.g. as a substance) in such a manner as "Let sound be admitted to be a substance; but still it is eternal or non-eternal", that is to say, when, admitting it to be a substance, its specific character, namely eternity or non-eternity, is examined, it is called the provisionally admitted tenet (*abhyupagama-siddhānta*). It is brought forward from a desire to show off the excellence of [the proponent's] own intellect and out of contempt for the other's (i.e. the opponent's) [inferior] intellect.'[27]

Obviously Vātsyāyana and Jayanta, when they explain what the *abhyupagama-siddhānta* is, refer to the same concrete debate situation in which the proponent admits without critical examination (the opponent's tenet) that sound is a substance in order to explore its specific character in question, investigating, for example, whether sound is eternal or non-eternal. It is not very clear what Vātsyāyana meant by the '*abhyupagama-siddhānta*' in this portion, but in NBh on NS 1.1.26 he undoubtedly understood the *abhyupagama-siddhānta* as 'the provisional admission of what has not been examined (and determined as such by the opponent) (*aparīkṣitâbhyupagama*, *anavadhārita-parigraha*) for the purpose of examining its specific property [in question]' (*tad-viśeṣa-parīkṣaṇāyâbhyupagama-siddhāntaḥ*). Therefore Vātsyāyana, too, does not care about the appositional relation between '*tad-viśeṣa-parīkṣaṇam*' and '*abhyupagama-siddhāntaḥ*'.

[27] NS 1.1.31: *aparīkṣitâbhyupagamāt tad-viśeṣa-parīkṣaṇam abhyupagama-siddhāntaḥ*. NBh on NS 1.1.31: *yatra kiñcid artha-jātam aparīkṣitam abhyupagamyate, astu dravyaṁ śabdaḥ, sa tu nityo 'nitya iti dravyasya sato nityatânityatā vā tad-viśeṣaḥ parīkṣyate, so 'abhyupagama-siddhāntaḥ sva-buddhy-atiśaya-cikhyāpayiṣayā para-buddhy-avajñānāc ca pravartata iti*.

Cf. NMa_1 II: 548.16–18 (in Text 3): *jitam apy enaṁ punar jetuṁ sva-buddhy-atiśaya-cikhyāpayiṣayā para-buddhy-avajñayā ca vādī bravīti—astu dravyaṁ śabda iti*.

Text 7 (NBh on NS 1.1.26):

'[NS 1.1.26:] The tenet is either the establishment (i.e. the established doctrine) in a branch of learning (*tantra-saṁsthiti*) or the establishment [of an object which is consequential to] another tenet that has been established as a certain topic thesis (?, *adhikaraṇa-saṁsthiti*) or the establishment on the basis of a tentative admission (*abhyupagama-saṁsthiti*).' (Translated according to NBh).

[NBh *ad loc.*:] The *tantra-saṁsthiti* is the establishment of an object in a system of learning. A branch of learning (*tantra*) is the instruction of a collection of interconnected units, i.e. a system of knowledge (*śāstra*). The *adhikaraṇa-saṁsthiti* is the establishment of an object which is consequential to another tenet that has been established as a certain headline of argument (?). The *abhyupagama-saṁsthiti* is the acceptance of an object which has not been definitely determined. The provisionally admitted tenet (*abhyupagama-siddhānta*) is for the sake of examining a specific nature of that (object) (*tad-viśeṣa-parīkṣaṇa*).'[28]

Thus Vātsyāyana and Jayanta share basically the same idea of the *abhyupagama-siddhānta*.

Uddyotakara, on the other hand, offers a totally different interpretation of NS 1.1.31.

Text 8 (NV on NS 1.1.31):

'The *sūtra* contains the expression *aparīkṣitâbhyupagamāt*. The portion *aparīkṣita-°* means "not mentioned in the *sūtra*s (*asūtrita-°*)". [Therefore the *sūtra* means that] the matter that is not [explicitly] stated in the *sūtra*s (the basic work of one's own system), but is implicitly accepted in the system is the *abhyupagama-siddhānta* ("assumed tenet"). For instance, it is a case of *abhyupagama-siddhānta* for the followers of the Nyāya system that the internal organ (*manas*) is a sense-organ, and it is so for the followers of the Nyāya system and those of the Vaiśeṣika system as well that an auditory organ is ether (*ākāśa*).

[Objection:] The portion *aparīkṣita-°* should mean something that is not accepted in the system [of one' own school but is temporarily admitted for the sake of argument (*aparīkṣitaḥ śāstrânabhyupagataḥ*)]. It is brought forward from a desire to

[28] NS 1.1.26: *tantrâdhikaraṇâbhyupagama-saṁsthitiḥ siddhāntaḥ*. NBh on NS 1.1.26: *tantrârtha-saṁsthitis tantra-saṁsthitiḥ. tantram itarêtarâbhisaṁbaddhasyârtha-samūhasyôpadeśaḥ śāstram. adhikaraṇânuṣaktârtha-saṁsthitir adhikaraṇa-saṁsthitiḥ. abhyupagama-saṁsthitir anavadhāritârtha-parigrahaḥ. tad-viśeṣa-parīkṣaṇāyâbhyupagama-siddhāntaḥ.*

show off the excellence of one's own intellect and out of contempt for the other's [inferior] intellect.
[Answer:] That is not right. Why so? Because ... Therefore, it is not the meaning of the *sūtra* that the temporal admission of that which is not accepted in the system should be a sort of tenet [called *abhyupagama-siddhānta*].'[29]

Uddyotakara asserts that the '*aparīkṣita*' in the compound '*aparīkṣitâbhyupagama*' stands for the matter which is not (explicitly) stated in the *Sūtra*s (the basic work of one's own school) (*aparīkṣitaḥ* = *asūtritaḥ* = *arthaḥ sūtreṣu nôpanibaddhaḥ*). Accordingly, the *abhyupagama-siddhānta* is interpreted by him as the *aparīkṣitâbhyupagama*, namely, that matter which is not explicitly stated in the *Sūtra*s [of one's own school], but is implicitly accepted in the system [of one's own school] (*yo 'rthaḥ sūtreṣu nôpanibaddhaḥ śāstre câbhyupagataḥ so 'bhyupagama-siddhānta iti*). For instance, it is a case of *abhyupagama-siddhānta* for Naiyāyikas that the *manas* is an *indriya*, and it is so for Vaiśeṣikas and Naiyāyikas that the auditory organ (*śrotra*) is a [delimited] space (*ākāśa*).

Moreover, Uddyotakara evidently refers to Vātsyāyana's interpretation when he critically mentions the assertion that the '*aparīkṣita*' should mean something that is not accepted in the system [of one' own school] which is [temporarily] admitted [for the sake of argument] (*aparīkṣitaḥ śāstrânabhyupagataḥ*).[30] He denies this interpretation because it is not reasonable for the proponent to hold in disdain the [poor] understanding of his opponent.

5. More evidence for the archaic nature of Jayanta's interpretation—the *Caraka-saṁhitā*.

Apart from the impression of a forced explication of NS 1.1.31 in NV, the consideration of the fact that Uddyotakara criticises (what is similar to) the interpretation by Vātsyāyana would naturally lead us to assume that NBh gives an older and perhaps more traditional explanation of NS 1.1.31 than NV. In addition the validity of this assumption will be certainly enhanced by the discovery of a by far closer connection of the *Caraka-saṁhitā* (CarS) with NBh than with NV with regard to the description of *abhyupagama-siddhānta*.

---

[29] NV on NS 1.1.31: *aparīkṣitâbhyupagamād iti sūtram. aparīkṣito 'sūtritaḥ. yo 'rthaḥ sūtreṣu nôpanibaddhaḥ śāstre câbhyupagataḥ so 'bhyupagama-siddhānta iti. yathā naiyāyikānāṁ mana indriyam iti. vaiśeṣikāṇāṁ naiyāyikānāṁ ca śrotram ākāśam iti.*

aparīkṣitaḥ śāstrânabhyupagataḥ. sva-buddhy-atiśaya-cikhyāpayiṣayā para-buddhy-avajñānāc ca pravartate iti.

tan na yuktam. kutaḥ. parâvajñānasyâyuktatvāt. ... tasmāt nâyaṁ sūtrârtho 'śāstritâbhyupagamaḥ siddhānta iti.

[30] See NVTṬ on NV 1.1.31, p. 223.16–17: *evaṁ sva-matena sūtraṁ vyākhyāya bhāṣya-kāra-vyākhānaṁ dūṣayati—śāstrânabhyupagata iti.*

Text 9 (CarS *vi* 8.37, p. 362):

> 'Siddhānta—Siddhānta (theory) is the conclusion which is established by scientists after testifying in several ways and proving it with reason. This is of four types—sarvatantra siddhānta, pratitantra siddhānta, adhikaraṇa siddhānta and abhyupagama siddhānta. ... Abhyupagama siddhānta (hypothetical theory) is that which is held up by physicians temporarily and hypothetically during debate though the idea is unproved, untested, uninstructed and irrational—such as—'I will speak proposing that *dravya* is predominant or properties are predominant or *vīrya* is predominant.'[31]

A glance at Text 9 will show that there is a close correspondence between the *Caraka-saṁhitā* and the *Nyāya-sūtra* concerning the description of *siddhānta*. Among others, the fourfold classification is exactly the same. With regard to the *abhyupagama-siddhānta*, we can clearly see in the above passage the idea of temporary or hypothetical acceptance of a matter for the sake of argument, nearly the same idea as is found in Vātsyāyana's explanation of the *abhyupagama-siddhānta*. On the other hand, it would be very difficult to assign the meaning of 'not being explicitly stated in the *sūtra*s but being implicitly accepted in the *śāstra*' (*sūtreṣu nôpanibaddhaḥ śāstre câbhyupagataḥ*)—the meaning ascribed by Uddyotakara to the '*aparīkṣita*' (see Text 8)—to the four adjectives of the object of acceptance in the *Caraka-saṁhitā*'s definition, i.e. *asiddham aparīkṣitam anupadiṣṭam ahetukaṁ vā*.

6. Conclusion.

The explanation of the *abhyupagama-siddhānta* offered by Jayanta is nearly the same as the description of it by Vātsyāyana. If we take the *Caraka-saṁhitā*'s corresponding account of the *abhyupagama-siddhānta* into consideration, we may safely conclude that Jayanta's view does not deviate from the Nyāya tradition, but is rather commensurate with it.

On the other hand, Uddyotakara's understanding of the *abhyupagama-siddhānta* seems to have exerted a greater influence upon the later development of Nyāya's concept of *siddhānta*. Vācaspatimiśra and Udayana[32] evi-

---

[31] Translation by Priyavrat Sharma (CarS, p. 362). CarS *vi* 8.37, p. 362: *atha siddhāntaḥ. siddhānto nāma sa yaḥ parīkṣakair bahu-vidhaṁ parīkṣya hetubhiś ca sādhayitvā sthāpyate nirṇayaḥ. sa ca catur-vidhaḥ—sarva-tantra-siddhāntaḥ pratitantra-siddhāntaḥ adhikaraṇa-siddhāntaḥ abhyupagama-sidhhāntaś cêti. ... abhyupagama-siddhānto nāma sa yam artham asiddham aparīkṣitam anupadiṣṭam ahetukaṁ vā vāda-kāle 'bhyupagacchanti bhiṣajaḥ, tad yathā dravyaṁ pradhānam iti kṛtvā vakṣyāmaḥ, guṇāḥ pradhānam iti kṛtvā vakṣyāmaḥ, vīryaṁ pradhānam iti kṛtvā vakṣyāmaḥ ity evam-ādiḥ.*

[32] At the end of TRS on TR, v. 61, Varadarāja mentions Udayana's view of the *abhyupagama-siddhānta*: *para-tantrôktaḥ sva-tantre câniṣiddhârtho 'bhyupagama-siddhānta ity ācāryāḥ*. Varadarāja evidently refers to Udayana as '*ācāryāḥ*'; see, for instance, TRS, p. 206.7–9: *atra bhāṣya-vārttika-ṭīkāsu saṅkulāni vacāṁsi prabodha-siddhāv ācāryair asmad-*

dently followed his interpretation in their commentary and sub-commentary on the *Nyāya-vārttika* respectively. Moreover, the compendium of the Nyāya system written by Varadarāja (the middle of the twelfth century), i.e. the *Tārkika-rakṣā* (TR) with his auto-commentary *Sāra-saṁgraha* (TRS), gives quite a similar explanation of the *abhyupagama-siddhānta*.[33]

> Text 10 (TRS on TR, v. 61):
>
> '[The author of TR] explains the *abhyupagama-siddhānta* and adduces an example [of it].
>
> "[TR 61cd–62ab] That which is proved to be exist in another system of learning and is assumed in one's own system is indeed the *abhyupagama-siddhānta* («assumed tenet»). For instance, the admission of the internal organ (*manas*) [is a case of *abhyupagama-siddhānta*] in Nyāya."
>
> The assumption of the internal organ that is proved to be exist in the system of Kaṇāda is a case of *abhyupagama-siddhānta* for the followers of the Nyāya system.'[34]

In the times of Navya-nyāya, too, in his *Nyāya-sūtra-vṛtti* (NSVṛ), Viśvanātha interpreted NS 1.1.31 in the same way as Uddyotakara:

> Text 11 (NSVṛ on NS 1.1.31):
>
> 'Accordingly, that which is not directly mentioned in the *sūtra* is the *abhyupagama-siddhānta* ("assumed tenet").'[35]

Now, what could we say more about this conceptual shift of the *abhyupagama-siddhānta*, not to say about the reason for it?

The idea of *siddhānta-bheda* as a starter of controversy as found in the *Nyāya-bhāṣya* on NS 1.1.1 (*vide supra*, p. 408) must have been positively fostered in the inter-darśanic world of discourse, though we find no reference to the idea at least in the discussed portion of the *Nyāya-mañjarī*. The tradi-

---

ukta evârthe saṅkalitānîti na saṅkaṭaṁ kiñcit. For *Prabodha-siddhi*, see *Vivṛti* on TRS, p. 206.23: *pariśiṣṭâpara-nāma-prabodha-siddhi-granthe.*

[33] It is interesting to note that a much more popular compendium of Nyāya written by Keśavamiśra, i.e. *Tarka-bhāṣā*, retains the traditional view. TBh, p. 40.6–11: *prāmāṇikatvenâbhyupagato 'thaḥ siddhāntaḥ. sa catur-dhā sarva-tantra-pratitantra-adhikaraṇa-abhyupagama-siddhānta-bhedāt. ... caturtho yathā jaiminīyasya nityânitya-vicāro yathā bhavatu tāvac chabdo guṇaḥ iti.*

[34] TRS on TR 61cd–62ab: *abhyupagama-siddhāntam udāharaṇaṁ ca darśayati.*

sādhitaḥ paratantre yaḥ svatantre ca samāśritaḥ // (TR 61cd)
sa hy abhyupagamo nyāye manaso 'numatir yathā / (TR 62ab)

kāṇāda-tantra-sādhitasya manasaḥ samāśrayaṇaṁ naiyāyikānām abhyupagama-siddhānta iti.

[35] NSVṛ on NS 1.1.31: *tathā ca sākṣād asūtritâbhyupagamo 'bhyupagama-siddhāntaḥ yathā manasa indriyatvam iti.*

tional concept of *abhyupagama-siddhānta*, too, is vividly characterised by a dialectical dynamism. Jayanta retained this idea of *abhyupagama-siddhānta*, in spite of Uddyotakara's challenge to the older interpretation of NS 1.1.31, although there is no sign in the *Nyāya-mañjarī* of Jayanta's awareness of Uddyotakara's argument on the *abhyupagama-siddhānta*.

On the other hand the emphasis on the static nature of 'being-proved-ness' of *siddhānta* seems to have started fairly early. Jayanta also accepted this idea when he interpreted NS 1.1.26 (see Text 1), as we have already seen. There, he paraphrased the definitive character of *siddhānta*, i.e. '*tantrâdhikaraṇâbhyupagama-saṁsthitiḥ*' ('the establishment of the admission of that which has the *tantra* as its substratum'), in such a way that the fact of being based on *pramāṇa*s could be counted as a condition for the *siddhānta*. But it is rather a forced interpretation and therefore seems to reflect a later development of the idea of *siddhānta* as the sixth subject of Nyāya. The idea of being based on *pramāṇa*s as a condition for the *siddhānta* did not exist in Vātsyāyana's comment on that *sūtra*. He took the compound as a *tat-puruṣa* which includes a *dvandva* (*tantram* + *adhikaraṇam* + *abhyupamaḥ*) as the first member,[36] which interpretation of his fits in quite well with the subsequent *sūtra*s and also has the advantage of the three instances of '*abhyupagama*' (NS 1.1.26, 27 and 31) retaining the same meaning.

The introduction of the idea of *pramāṇa-mūlatva*, however, gave rise to, at least, two problems for Jayanta. One problem was how to apply this requirement to the retained notion of *abhyupagama-siddhānta*, i.e. a tenet which is not finally, but only provisionally admitted for the sake of argument. And his answer to this problem was that the requirement is not factually, but fictitiously satisfied by the intention of a proud proponent. In other words the proposition at issue, simply for the sake of argument, is provisionally treated by the proponent as a tenet established on the basis of a *pramāṇa*.

The other problem was how to explain the situation in which a pair of system-specific tenets (*pratitantra-siddhānta*s) stands in opposition to each other. To this problem he offered two solutions, the second of which is noteworthy in the present context. Namely, his answer was that the requirement is satisfied in its real sense only for one specific tenet, whereas the other one has the requirement fulfilled only on the level of the intention of the tenet-holder concerned.[37]

---

[36] *tantrâdhikaraṇâbhyupagama-saṁsthitiḥ* = *tantra-saṁsthiti* (= *sarva-tantra-siddhānta* + *pratitantra-siddhānta*) + *adhikaraṇa-saṁsthiti* (= *adhikaraṇa-siddhānta*) + *abhyupagama-saṁsthiti* (= *abhyupagama-siddhānta*).

[37] NMa_1 II: 546.9–13: *asya* (= *pratitantra-siddhāntasya*) *kathaṁ pramāṇa-mūlatā. sthāne praśnaḥ, satyam etat. āsmākīne hi pratitantra-siddhānte* ***pramāṇa-mūlatvaṁ yathârtham*** *eva. sāṁkhya-siddhāntasya tu pramāṇa-mūlatvâbhāve 'pi paratantratva-khyāpanāyôdāhṛtaḥ.* ***tad-abhiprāyeṇa*** *vāsya* ***pramāṇa-mūlatā*** *vaktavyêti.*

Now, the final conclusion of the present paper is that the studied portion of the *Nyāya-mañjarī* seems to represent a certain historical phase of the shifting process within the Nyāya system from the science of dialectics to the *pramāṇa-śāstra* in which more and more emphasis was laid on the dependence of *siddhānta* upon the means of valid cognition (*pramāṇa-mūlatva*), whereas less and less stress was placed on its implications for the dialectical dynamism which presupposes the lively tension of the multi-doctrinal world of debate.

7. Additional remark.

It may be relevant to add the following two points as an appendix.

First, the idea of provisional admission that formed the very core of the traditional concept of *abhyupagama-siddhānta* in the science of debate according to the above conclusion, seems to have been kept alive for ages in actual discussion among Indian philosophers, whether a proposition provisionally admitted may be recognised as a kind of tenet (*siddhānta*) or not. It may suffice here to offer a few instances. Two are taken from the *Nyāya-mañjarī* itself, and the other is from the *Śloka-vārttika* merely to show that this idea of provisional admission is adopted not only in Nyāya, but also in other systems of Indian philosophy.

> 'It is asserted [by opponents such as Cārvākas and Buddhists] that [a Vedic injunction should not be a source of knowledge] because its eternality or the like have not yet been established, or rather, if it is admitted as a concession [to Mīmāṁsakas who insist on the eternality of the *Vedas*] that [they are eternal and so on, a Vedic injunction] is still less a source of knowledge] because [they] lack the property of a speaker's reliability.'[38]

> 'Moreover, the difference of exclusion cannot be caused by the difference of what is excluded. Even if we admit as a concession [to the Buddhists that it is the case], still we argue: if the difference of exclusion were to be caused by the difference of what is excluded, then the sameness of that (i.e. exclusion) would be caused by the sameness of what is excluded.'[39]

---

[38] MŚV *Codanā* 21, p. 38:

nityatvâder asiddhatvād ***abhyupetyô****cyate 'tha vā /*
sutarām apramāṇatvaṁ vaktṛ-prāmāṇya-varjanāt //

[39] NMa$_1$ II: 17.11–18.2: *na câpohya-bhedād bhedo 'py apohasyâvakalpate. ...* ***abhyupagamyâpi brūmaḥ****—yady apohya-bhedād apoha-bhinnatvam, apohyâikyāt tarhi tadâikyenâpi bhavitavyam. ...*

'If you say that a cognition of the smoke will be produced again by the sense-organ immediately after the recollection of the property of being a means of getting delight, it is not so because we have not experienced [such a cognition]. O r l e t that cognition of the smoke b e a d m i t t e d , but even then. ...'[40]

Second, POTTER (1977: 394–395) substitutes 'a short essay written for this volume by Janakivallabha Bhattacharya' for a summary of the *Nyāya-kalikā* (NKal) attributed to Jayanta, a concise digest of the sixteen core topics (*ṣoḍaśa-padârtha-tattva*) of the Nyāya system. The short essay is concerned with the authorship of the *Nyāya-kalikā*. J. BHATTACHARYA (1977) does not reach a conclusion, but simply puts forward some points which, in his view, may be considered to serve for or against the identity of the two authors. One point against the identity of authorship is described by him as follows:

> 'A point may be raised against the said identity of Jayanta[41] with Jayanta Bhaṭṭa. Jayanta Bhaṭṭa is a great critic of the Buddhists. This Jayanta, the author of [the] *Nyāya-kalikā*, departs from the traditional explanation of *abhyupagama siddhānta* (one of the kinds of tenets) and follows the Buddhist interpretation of the term. The explanation of the term is as follows: "Aparīkṣito api kaścid artho buddhyātiśaya-cikhyāparyiṣayā [*sic!*—ed.] prauḍha-vādibhistathetyabhyupagamyamānoabhyupagamasiddhāntaḥ" [*sic!*—ed.] (*Nyāyakalikā*, p. 9). *Translation*: "The uncritical popular tenet is accepted in order to demonstrate the superiority of one's own intellect".'[42]

Here BHATTACHARYA provides the text of the *Nyāya-kalikā*'s definition of the *abhyupagama-siddhānta* along with his free English translation of it. This concept of the *abhyupagama-siddhānta*, in his view, is different from the Nyāya's 'traditional explanation' of the term and agrees with the Buddhist interpretation of it. Then BHATTACHARYA argues that the author of the *Nyāya-kalikā*, who followed the Buddhist view instead of the Nyāya's tradition, cannot be identical with Jayantabhaṭṭa, who criticises the Buddhists harshly here and there in the *Nyāya-mañjarī*.

But the *Nyāya-kalikā*'s definition of *abhyupagama-siddhānta* is substantially identical with the interpretation of NS 1.1.31, which Jayanta considers to be proper in the *Nyāya-mañjarī* (*vide supra* § 3.4). According to both, the

[40] NMa_1 I: 179.8–10: *agnau sukha-sādhanatvânusmaraṇânantaraṁ punaḥ dhūma-jñānam indriyād utpadyata iti cet—mâivam, ananubhāvāt.* ***bhavatu vā*** *dhūma-jñānam, tathâpi ...*

[41] Janakivallabha BHATTACHARYA (1977: 394–395) seems to distinguish two Jayantas. He calls the author of the *Nyāya-kalikā* simply 'Jayanta' and that of the *Nyāya-mañjarī* 'Jayantabhaṭṭa' without stating any reason.

[42] BHATTACHARYA (1977: 394–395).

abhyupagama-siddhānta is the tenet provisionally accepted (as a concession to the opponent) for the sake of argument. Moreover, this seems to be the Nyāya's traditional concept of the term. BHATTACHARYA simply mistook as 'traditional' a newly and rather forcibly imposed interpretation accepted by Uddyotakara, Vācaspati and Varadarāja. It is not certain why he thought that the author of the *Nyāya-kalikā* 'follows the Buddhist traditional interpretation of the term'. Perhaps BHATTACHARYA had the argumentative method of *prasaṅga* in mind, but the *prasaṅga* is quite different from the traditional concept of *abhyupagama-siddhānta*. The aim of *prasaṅga* argument is to prove that a given proposition (of an opponent) is false by showing that an undesirable conclusion necessarily would follow if it were admitted as true. On the other hand, the aim of a provisional acceptance of a proposition X in case of the *abhyupagama-siddhānta* is to show that a proposition Y is true or false, even if the proposition X is provisionally admitted as a concession to the opponent.

From these reasons the above argument of BHATTACHARYA is totally wrong.

In any case the conclusion of the present study provides a piece of evidence for Jayanta's authorship of the *Nyāya-kalikā*. Even if it were admitted as a work written by a different author, it is not likely that it was written long after Jayanta when the traditional interpretation of the *abhyupagama-siddhānta* was out of date.

BIBLIOGRAPHY

APTE 1965 = Apte, Vaman Shivram: *The Practical Sanskrit-English Dictionary*. Fourth Revised & Enlarged Edition. Motilal Banarsidass, Delhi 1965.

BHATTACHARYA 1977 = Bhattacharya, Janakivallabha: 'Nyāyakalikā', in POTTER (1977: 394–395).

CarS = *Caraka-saṁhitā* [*vi* = *Vimāna-sthāna*]. Priyavrat Sharma (ed., tr.): *Caraka-Saṁhitā: Agniveśa's Treatise Refined and Annotated by Caraka and Redacted by Dṛḍhabala (Text with English Translation)*. Vol. I: *Sūtrasthāna* to *Indriyasthāna*. Jaikrashnadas Ayurveda Series 36, Varanasi–Delhi 1981.

CHATTOPADHYAYA –GANGOPADHYAYA 1982 = Gangopadhyaya, Mrinalkanti; Chattopadhyaya, Debiprasad (tr.): *Nyāya Philosophy. Literal Translation of Gautama's Nyāya-sūtra with Vātsyāyana's Bhāṣya. Indian Studies* (*Indian Philosophy in its Sources*). 5 Vols., Indian Studies Past & Present, Calcutta 1982 [reprinted: Indian Studies Past & Present/Firma KLM Private Limited, Calcutta 1975–1992].

DASGUPTA 1922 = Dasgupta, Surendranath: *A History of Indian Philosophy*. Vol. I, Cambridge University Press, Cambridge 1922 [reprinted: Motilal Banarsidass, Delhi 1975].

JHĀ 1983 = Jhā, Gaṅgānātha (tr.): *The Nyāyasūtras of Gautama with Vātsyāyana's Bhāṣya and Uddyotakara's Vārttika, translated into English*. Vol. I, Reprinted, Rinsen Book Co., Kyoto 1983 [first edition: Allahabad 1915].

KEITH 1921 = A.B. Keith: *Indian Logic and Atomism*. Oxford University Press, Oxford 1921 [reprinted: Motilal Banarsidass, Delhi 1977].

MONIER-WILLIAMS 1997 = Monier-Williams, M.: *A Sanskrit-English Dictionary*. Motilal Banarsidas, Delhi 1997 [first edition: Oxford 1899].

MŚV = Kumārilabhaṭṭa: *Śloka-vārttika*. Ramanatha Sastri (ed.): *Śloka-vārttikavyākhyā (Tātparyatīkā) of Bhaṭṭombeka*. 2nd. Edition, Madras Sanskrit Series 13, University of Madras, Madras 1971 [first edition: 1940].

NBh = Vātsyāyana Pakṣilasvāmin: *Nyāya-bhāṣya*. Anantalal Thakur (ed.): *Gautamīyanyāyadarśana with Bhāṣya of Vātsyāyana*. Nyāya-catur-granthikā Vol. I, Indian Council of Philosophical Research, New Delhi 1997.

NKal = Jayantabhaṭṭa: *Nyāya-kalikā*. Ganganatha Jha (ed.): *The Nyāyakalikā of Jayanta*. The Princess of Wales Sarasvati Bhavana Texts, Benares 1925.

NMa = Jayantabhaṭṭa: *Nyāya-mañjarī*. (1) K.S. Varadacharya (ed.): *Nyāya-mañjarī of Jayantabhaṭṭa with Ṭippaṇi—Nyāyasaurabha by the Editor*. 2 Vols. Oriental Research Institute Series 116 & 139, University of Mysore, Mysore 1969, 1983. (2) Pt. Sūrya Nārāyana Śukla (ed.): *Nyāyamañjarī of Jayanta Bhaṭṭa*. Part I, Kashi Sanskrit Series 106, Chowkhamba Sanskrit Series Office, Varanasi 1971.

NS = Akṣapāda Gautama: *Nyāya-sūtra*. Walter Ruben: *Die Nyayasutra's: Text, Übersetzung, Erläuterung und Glossar*. Deutsche Morgenländische Gesellschaft, im Kommission bei F.A. Brockhaus, Leipzig 1928.

NSVṛ = Viśvanātha-[nyāya-pañcānana-bhaṭṭâcārya]: *Nyāya-sūtra-vṛtti*. Taranatha Nyaya-Tarkatirtha; Amarendramohan Tarkatirtha; Hemantakumar Tarkatirtha (eds.): *Nyāyadarśanam. With Vātsyāyana's Bhāṣya, Uddyotakara's Vārttika, Vācaspati Miśra's Tātparyaṭīkā & Viśvanātha's Vṛtti*. With an introduction by Narendra Chandra Vedantatirtha. 2 Vols. 2nd edition, Munshiram Manoharlal Publishers, New Delhi 1985 [first edition: Calcutta Sanskrit Series, 18, 19, Metropolitan Printing & Publishing House, Calcutta 1936, 1944].

NV = Bhāradvāja Uddyotakara: *Nyāya-vārttika*. Anantalal Thakur (ed.): *Nyāyabhāṣyavārttika of Bhāradvāja Uddyotakara*. Nyāya-catur-granthikā Vol. II, Indian Council of Philosophical Research, New Delhi 1997.

NVTṬ = Vācaspatimiśra: *Nyāya-vārttika-tātparya-ṭīkā*. Anantalal Thakur (ed.): *Nyāyavārttikatātparyaṭīkā of Vācaspatimiśra*. Nyāya-caturgranthikā Vol. III, Indian Council of Philosophical Research, New Delhi 1996.

POTTER 1977 = Karl H. Potter: *Encyclopedia of Indian Philosophies*. Vol. 2: *Indian Metaphysics and Epistemology: The Tradition of Nyāya-Vaiśeṣika up to Gaṅgeśa*. Princeton University Press/Motilal Banarsidass, Delhi–Varanasi–Patna–1977.

TBh = Keśavamiśra: *Tarka-bhāṣā*. N.N. Kulkarni (ed.): *Tarkabhāṣā (Exposition of Reasoning) by Keśavamiśra*. Revised second Edition, Poona Oriental Series17, Oriental Book Agency, Poona 1953.

TR = Varadarāja: *Tārkika-rakṣā*. Sampathkumaracharyulu (ed.): *Varadarāja's Tārkikarakṣā-sārasaṁgraha with the Commentary Vivṛti of Hariharadīkṣita*. Haripriyāprakāśanam, Tirupati 2004.

TRS = Varadarāja: *Tārkika-rakṣā-sāra-saṁgraha*. See: TR.

GENERAL INDEX

Please note that the translations in brackets provided for Sanskrit terms in the Index are compiled from respective contributions to the Volume and are those of the authors.

A

C

D

E

L

O

P

U

V

W

X

Y